Telecommunications Technologies Reference

Brad Dunsmore

Toby Skandier

Christian Martin, Joel T. McKelvey, and Tim Woods

Cisco Press

Cisco Press
201 West 103rd Street
Indianapolis, IN 46290 USA

Telecommunications Technologies Reference

Brad Dunsmore

Toby Skandier

Christian Martin, Joel T. McKelvey, and Tim Woods

Copyright© 2003 Cisco Systems, Inc.

Published by:
Cisco Press
201 West 103rd Street
Indianapolis, IN 46290 USA

Printed in the United States of America 1 2 3 4 5 6 7 8 9 0

First Printing September 2002

Library of Congress Cataloging-in-Publication Number: 2001090440

ISBN: 1-58705-036-6

Warning and Disclaimer

This book is designed to provide information about telecommunications technologies. Every effort has been made to make this book as complete and as accurate as possible, but no warranty or fitness is implied.

The information is provided on an "as is" basis. The author, Cisco Press, and Cisco Systems, Inc. shall have neither liability nor responsibility to any person or entity with respect to any loss or damages arising from the information contained in this book or from the use of the discs or programs that may accompany it.

The opinions expressed in this book belong to the author and are not necessarily those of Cisco Systems, Inc.

Trademark Acknowledgments

All terms mentioned in this book that are known to be trademarks or service marks have been appropriately capitalized. Cisco Press or Cisco Systems, Inc., cannot attest to the accuracy of this information. Use of a term in this book should not be regarded as affecting the validity of any trademark or service mark.

Feedback Information

At Cisco Press, our goal is to create in-depth technical books of the highest quality and value. Each book is crafted with care and precision, undergoing rigorous development that involves the unique expertise of members from the professional technical community.

Readers' feedback is a natural continuation of this process. If you have any comments regarding how we could improve the quality of this book, or otherwise alter it to better suit your needs, you can contact us through e-mail at feedback@ciscopress.com. Please make sure to include the book title and ISBN in your message.

We greatly appreciate your assistance.

Publisher	John Wait
Editor-in-Chief	John Kane
Cisco Systems Management	Michael Hakkert
	Tom Geitner
Production Manager	Patrick Kanouse
Acquisitions Editor	Michelle Grandin
Development Editor	Andrew Cupp
Project Editor	Eric T. Schroeder
Copy Editor	Cris Mattison
Technical Editors	Ron Hranac
	Grady Neely
	Laurent Nicolas
	Nancy Roth
	Martin Walshaw
Team Coordinator	Tammi Ross
Book Designer	Gina Rexrode
Cover Designer	Louisa Klucznik
Composition	Mark Shirar
Indexer	Tim Wright

CISCO SYSTEMS

Corporate Headquarters
Cisco Systems, Inc.
170 West Tasman Drive
San Jose, CA 95134-1706
USA
http://www.cisco.com
Tel: 408 526-4000
     800 553-NETS (6387)
Fax: 408 526-4100

European Headquarters
Cisco Systems Europe
11 Rue Camille Desmoulins
92782 Issy-les-Moulineaux
Cedex 9
France
http://www-europe.cisco.com
Tel: 33 1 58 04 60 00
Fax: 33 1 58 04 61 00

Americas Headquarters
Cisco Systems, Inc.
170 West Tasman Drive
San Jose, CA 95134-1706
USA
http://www.cisco.com
Tel: 408 526-7660
Fax: 408 527-0883

Asia Pacific Headquarters
Cisco Systems Australia,
Pty., Ltd
Level 17, 99 Walker Street
North Sydney
NSW 2059 Australia
http://www.cisco.com
Tel: +61 2 8448 7100
Fax: +61 2 9957 4350

Cisco Systems has more than 200 offices in the following countries. Addresses, phone numbers, and fax numbers are listed on the Cisco Web site at www.cisco.com/go/offices

Argentina • Australia • Austria • Belgium • Brazil • Bulgaria • Canada • Chile • China • Colombia • Costa Rica • Croatia • Czech Republic • Denmark • Dubai, UAE • Finland • France • Germany • Greece • Hong Kong • Hungary • India • Indonesia • Ireland Israel • Italy • Japan • Korea • Luxembourg • Malaysia • Mexico • The Netherlands • New Zealand • Norway • Peru • Philippines Poland • Portugal • Puerto Rico • Romania • Russia • Saudi Arabia • Scotland • Singapore • Slovakia • Slovenia • South Africa • Spain Sweden • Switzerland • Taiwan • Thailand • Turkey • Ukraine • United Kingdom • United States • Venezuela • Vietnam • Zimbabwe

About the Authors

Brad Dunsmore is a New Product Instructor with the Advanced Engineering Services—NIM—for Cisco Systems in Research Triangle Park, North Carolina. He develops and deploys network solutions and training for Cisco SEs, CSEs, selected training partners, and customers. He specializes in SS7 offload solutions and WAN communication methods. Prior to his two-year tenure with Cisco, he worked for Adtran Telecommunication as a Technical Trainer, Electronic Systems as a Systems Engineer, and Bell Atlantic as an ISDN Support Specialist. Brad holds certifications from many vendors including Microsoft's MCSE+Internet and MCDBA, CompTIA's i-Net+, A+, and Network+, Apple's Product Professional, and Cisco's CCNA, CCNP, and CCSI designations. Brad was also selected as a technical reviewer for the new A+ certification. His previous publications include *Mission Critical Internet Security*, the *CCNA Study Guide*, the *A+ DVD*, and *CCNA Test Yourself Practice Exams* (all for Syngress Media).

Toby Skandier is an Educational Consultant at Sprint Corporation. Since his first foray into the computing and networking fields in 1985, Toby has started a PC-related consulting company; taught for Sprint Corporation, Cisco Systems, and at community colleges; and developed courses for Sprint and Cisco. A member of the IEEE Computer Society and the ACM, Toby holds CCNP, CCDA, MCSE, CTT+, MCT, A+, Network+, i-Net+, and Server+ certifications.

About the Contributing Authors

Christian Martin (CCIE #4487) is a Network Architecture Consultant for Verizon Internet Services, where he has worked for the past 5 years. Among his responsibilities is the network support and evolution of an SMDS aggregation network composed of over 300 DS3 circuits, 700 T1s, and over 1000 routers. He was also responsible for the deployment of Verizon's current NMS, the design of Verizon's first long-distance IP network, and continues to provide technology oversight on all products and services being deployed in the VIS network. He has 8 years of industry experience, and is currently pursuing a joint BS/MS in Systems Engineering at George Mason University. Christian lives in Leesburg, VA with his lovely wife Maria and his dog Shadow. He wrote Chapter 11, "Switched Multimegabit Data Service."

Joel T. McKelvey is a Senior Technical Marketing Engineer focused on DOCSIS networks at Cisco Systems, Inc. In this position he is responsible for designing, testing, and integrating cable network technologies and architectures. He has spoken on DOCSIS and cable related topics internationally at numerous conferences and events. He has published papers on DOCSIS specifications and cable IP network services including: *QoS on DOCSIS Cable Networks*, *Open Access Technologies and MPLS-VPNs*, and *Security Concerns for Cable IP Networks*. At Cisco he led development teams on several DOCSIS 1.0 products. Mr. McKelvey has 13 years of experience in internetworking with several major companies in the field. He is a Cisco Certified Networking Associate, a Cisco Certified Cable Communications Specialist, and a member of the Society of Cable Telecommunications Engineers (SCTE) and the IEEE. He wrote Chapter 13, "Cable Modem Technology and CATV."

Tim Woods, CCIE #5474, is a Technical Marketing Engineer with Cisco Systems. He started his career in computers and networking while attending Clemson University and working at AT&T Global Information Solutions (formerly NCR). Tim began working at Cisco Systems in 1998 as a Technical Assistance Center (TAC) Engineer and then moved into his current TME role. His day-to-day efforts keep him busy with testing, assisting other teams, and writing documentation. Outside of work Tim enjoys spending time with his family and friends; without their love and support, projects like this would not be possible. He also enjoys mountain biking and ultimate frisbee. He wrote Chapter 12, "DSL."

Manuel A. Irizarry (CCIE #3777) is a Customer Support Engineer in the Cisco Technical Assistance Center, Multiservice Group. He helps troubleshoot and support the Voice over IP products. He graduated from the University of Dayton in 1987 with a BSEE. He has worked at MCI as a Second Level Support for the

HyperStream Frame Relay Network. He lives with is wife, Sandra, daughter, Sabrina, and son, Francisco. Manny contributed to several areas of discussion within the ATM chapter.

Travis Powell has been at Cisco Systems for two years and is currently working as a software engineer for Cisco in Research Triangle Park, NC. He works for the Network Services Integration Test Engineering Internal System (NSITE) (ISET) group, where he is currently testing network management products. Travis has extensive experience with SS7 and the service provider infrastructure. He specialized in SS7 with Lucent for three and a half years, and prior to that worked for two years in a NOC for Bell South located in Charlotte, NC. Travis contributed to the LNP whiteboard found in Chapter 2, "Signaling System 7 Network."

About the Technical Reviewers

Ron Hranac is a Technical Leader for Cisco Systems' Broadband Network Engineering group. Ron's industry activities include the publication of hundreds of articles and papers, and he is past chairman of a National Cable Television Association ad hoc Subcommittee to research 75-ohm traceability at the then National Bureau of Standards. Ron is a Fellow Member of the Society of Cable Telecommunications Engineers and an At-Large Director on its national Board of Directors. In 1987 he became the first person in the cable industry to be certified in SCTE's BCT/E program and went on to complete certification at both its Technician and Engineer levels. Ron reviewed Chapter 13.

Grady Neely is currently employed as a Field Technical Support Engineer of ADTRAN, Inc. He supports Verizon, SBC, MCI, and AT&T in their deployment of ADTRAN high-speed and low-speed products. He has a BSEE from the University of Alabama. He and his wife Kate are currently expecting their first child.

Laurent Nicolas is Technical Leader in the Voice Solutions Architecture Group in San Jose, CA. He worked for the last three years for Cisco Systems on IP telephony solutions involving SS7, ISDN, R2 on the legacy side and MGCP, H.323, and now SIP for control or signaling of Voice over IP. He is involved in the definition and validation of Class 4 and Class 5 architectures based on the above protocols for deployments in various countries: groomer and tandem/transit long distance services and residential and business accesses.

Previously, Laurent worked for 13 years for IBM France, most of the time in the Networking Division. He held positions in Product Assurance/System Test, Management, Architecture, System Design, and Development. He was strongly involved in the Architecture, System Design, and Development of a broadband multiservice network architecture and the associated multiservice switch. His main contribution was the definition and development of ATM support, but he was also active in connection management issues in a multiservice network: transporting several classes of traffic including circuit emulation and voice service, bandwidth reservation, and connection admission control; traffic policing and shaping; and traffic scheduling.

Laurent graduated as an Engineer from Ecole Polytechnique in France in 1984.

Nancy Roth is a Technical Trainer with Cisco Systems. She has a BS in computer science. Her previous work experience includes UNIX, AS400, and Novell Systems Administration; computing center manager for a community college; and computer engineer working with various database and object-oriented programming languages. Her volunteer work includes church and community projects.

Martin Walshaw, CCIE #5629, CCNP, CCDP, is a Systems Engineer working for Cisco Systems in South Africa. His area of specialty, New Technologies, keeps him busy both night and day. During the last 15 years or so, Martin has dabbled in many aspects of the IT Industry, ranging from programming in RPG III and Cobol to PC Sales and Training. Martin eventually decided that his calling was in networking—more specifically, Cisco. When Martin is not working, he likes to spend all his available time with his wife Val and with two young hooligans Joshua and Callum. Without their patience, understanding, support—and most importantly, love—projects such as this would not be possible.

Dedications

I would like to dedicate this book in loving memory of Robert Franklin Caldwell. Father, you will be missed.

—Brad

I would like to dedicate this book to my wife Karen, whose patience and support through this grueling process made it all possible.

—Toby

Acknowledgments

From Brad Dunsmore:

There are so many people that need to be thanked and acknowledged for their contributions to this book, and their commitment to getting this book to press. First, I would like to thank the great folks at Cisco Press for their patience. John Kane, Michelle Grandin, and Drew Cupp have been patient and supportive with the particularly interesting schedule that this book has been on. Your hard work and occasional nudge to get the chapters moving faster helped make this a success.

There are also countless people who have been directly involved with me, and provided insight and assistance when requested. Laurent Nicolas, Grady Neely, Nancy Roth, and Martin Walshaw have all been great technical editors. Your candor, technical ability, and honesty have been appreciated. Gary Pate, Lloyd Jones, Ken Stallings, and Angie Reed all contributed to this book because they taught me a great deal of what I know now. The education received from you guys is immeasurable.

Toby Skandier, good friend, you have helped get this project off the ground with hard work and your willingness to tackle a tough task in a short time. This book could not have been done without your help. Thank you is also extended to Christian, Joel, and Tim for your help in the 11th hour of the writing process. Thank you for making the diving catch.

I would also like to acknowledge the great folks at Cisco, with whom I now work. They are the smartest people that I have ever met, and from them I learn more and more each day. Thank you, Ilona for taking a chance and adding me to your group some two years ago.

Lastly and most importantly, I would like to acknowledge my wife Tammy. It's hard to believe that someone would put up with long hours of seclusion and writing for over a year. Your support during this process made everything possible, even in the most difficult times.

From Toby Skandier:

I would like to acknowledge my co-author of this book, Brad Dunsmore, for his expert guidance and boundless confidence in my capabilities. Brad has always been a great friend and an excellent reference for a variety of technical issues. I would further like to acknowledge my employer, Sprint Corporation, as well as my supervisor, Al Smith, for their commitment to ever-increasing my level of expertise in the field of data and telecommunications. Additionally, my thanks goes out to the Cisco Press team assigned to this work. Inasmuch as I am an expert in certain technical areas, I am a novice in the world of publishing. This group of impressive professionals has been able to draw a level of productivity from me that I was not aware existed. More than that, they made my work presentable. Finally I would like to acknowledge each and every one of the technical editors and contributors on this project for their expertise and invaluable contributions to the final quality of this book.

Contents at a Glance

Contents

Introduction

Over the past several years, markets have opened up around the world that require a broader understanding of service provider networks and telecommunications technologies. In that time, it has become difficult to find a single comprehensive reference guide for both North American and international technology.

This book is designed to serve as a reference guide for a broad range of technology that is found in modern telecommunications networks. The coverage in this book is not limited to the technologies in North America, as it details many of the international communication methods as well. The intention is to be informative of service provider technology regardless of your location.

There are many books on the market that cover specific aspects of telecommunication technologies. Many of them are technology specific or cover only North American methods. This book was created to act as a comprehensive reference guide for individuals whose knowledge must span both international boundaries and various technologies. You will learn about telecommunication methodology as it is deployed around the world, as well as how it operates.

Who Should Read This Book

This book is written for individuals who wish to learn about the technologies used throughout the world for data and voice communication. It is written in such a way that someone with little background in telecommunications can read and understand the material, but it is also technical enough for a field engineer to use as a reference guide.

It is recommended that the reader have the following prerequisite knowledge:

- Fundamental understanding of WAN communication
- CCNA or equivalent experience

Expert Whiteboards

Expert Whiteboards are sections that have been included in most chapters. The purpose of these sections is to discuss an advanced topic of the technology or to detail a specific deployment solution. These sections are written by a variety of engineers to add real-world applications to technologies discussed in each chapter.

Chapter Summaries and Review Questions

The "Summary" and "Review Questions" sections at the end of each chapter are designed to reinforce some of the most important topics that are discussed in that chapter. Use them to assess your understanding of the chapter's subject and then review as necessary. The review questions are in multiple choice, lab-based, and fill in the blank format. The answer for each question is discussed in detail and explained for complete understanding. You can find the answers to the review questions in Appendix A.

This chapter covers the following topics:

- **Analog introduction**—An introduction to the technologies covered in this chapter.
- **Analog signal basics**—A discussion of the fundamentals of the analog signal including amplitude, wavelength, and frequency.
- **Bandwidth and signal distortion**—An overview of bandwidth and distortion, including signal attenuation, noise, and digital-to-analog converters.
- **Analog service deployments**—A discussion of basic deployments, including tip and ring circuits, integrated digital loop carriers (IDLCs), and GR-303-CORE.

CHAPTER 1

An Overview of Analog Communication

Analog Introduction

This chapter introduces terms and concepts commonly associated with analog communication. Topics covered in this chapter include a brief analog signal overview, analog signal composition, and different analog deployment methods. Although most of this book focuses on the different aspects of digital communication methods, an understanding of analog communication is essential to recognizing the fundamental differences between them and to building a strong foundation of knowledge.

An analog signal is described as the creation of a signal that is analogous, or similar, to the original signal stream. Several common household products use analog communication, including televisions, radio, and telephone systems. When I speak to my colleague, Susan, the sound waves travel through the air and into her ear. Her eardrum vibrates, creating the sounds that she interprets as spoken words. The common analog telephone operates in much the same way.

When you speak into the handset of a phone, the sound waves from your mouth vibrate a diaphragm inside the receiver. This process causes a circuit to open and close within the receiver, which creates a flow of electricity. This flow of electricity has a frequency about the same as the original sound wave, and it is transmitted over the carrier network to the destination. The remote subscriber's phone reverses the process and they hear the original spoken words, as shown in Figure 1-1.

Figure 1-1   *Basic Analog Signal Transmission*

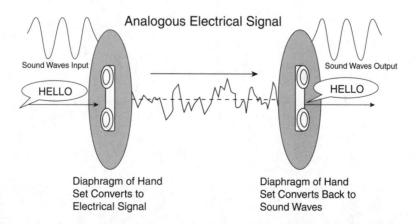

Of course the telephone handset is not all that goes into a subscriber's analog circuit. Many different pieces of equipment, both subscriber and carrier, provide an acceptable quality of service (QoS). Prior to the discussion of some of the standard telecommunication company (telco) deployments, this chapter takes a closer look at the components of an analog signal.

Analog Signal Basics

Telecommunication, as it is currently deployed throughout the world, is based on the flow of electricity from one location to another. Whether you are surfing the Internet or talking to your friend on the phone, electricity is constantly flowing throughout the infrastructure. As you might have guessed, there are different types of signals that can be transmitted. The two main types that this book focuses on are analog and digital signals. One difference is that some mediums, such as fiber optics, transmit light over the carrier network. The digital principles are the same, but lasers and light emitting diodes (LEDs) facilitate the signal transmission.

Analog and digital signals are inherently different from each other and can be thought of as residing at opposite ends of the same spectrum. Because of their differences, you need to use devices such as digital-to-analog converters (DACs) to bridge the gap between the signal types. DACs are covered in the section "Digital-to-Analog Converters" later in this chapter.

The major difference between analog and digital signals is the signal stream itself. Analog signals, also referred to as continuous signal streams, are a continual signal flow of fluctuating frequencies and amplitudes. This means that an analog signal looks similar to a sine wave (sinusoidal wave), as shown in Figure 1-2. You typically find sine wave illustrations depicting the same frequency and amplitude relationship throughout, but a complex wave has been used here to show that these relationships fluctuate depending on the frequency.

Figure 1-2   *Analog Signal Stream*

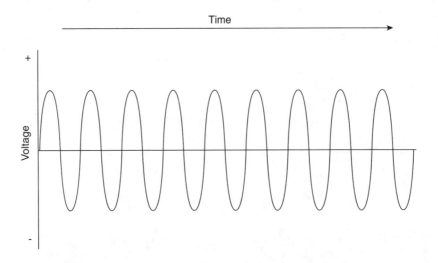

Digital signals are represented as discrete electrical values that are transmitted individually over the given medium. Rather than having an almost endless set of possible values (as is found in analog signals), digital signal values commonly equal one of two to four different values, both positive and negative. Digital signals are transmitted as 1s and 0s, which is commonly referred to as binary. For more information on digital signal flows, refer to Chapter 3, "Analog-to-Digital Conversion."

As with any technology, analog signals are not without their own basic concepts and terminology. Analog signals are composed of three main components:

- Amplitude
- Wavelength
- Frequency

Refer to Figure 1-3 for a graphic representation of all three components.

Figure 1-3   *Amplitude, Wavelength, and Frequency of an Analog Signal Stream*

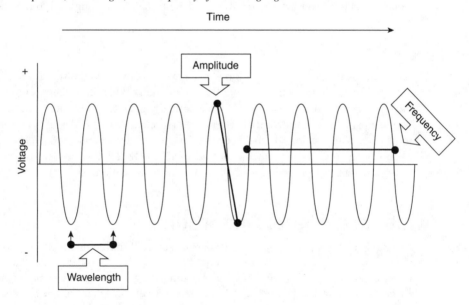

Amplitude

The amplitude of an electrical signal is the distance from the lowest vertical endpoint to the highest vertical endpoint. It's important to remember that with amplitude, the distance above and below 0 is equidistant.

Wavelength

The wavelength is the measurement from one signal wave to another. Whatever point is chosen on the first signal wave must also be selected on the second wave to measure a complete wavelength. A common representation of this is measuring from the crest of one wave to the crest of the next wave. The wavelength is directly related to the frequency of said signal stream. As the frequency of the signal wave increases, the wavelength decreases. The decrease is caused by the increased iterations (frequency) of the signal wave during the same period of time.

Wavelength is measured in segments called meters, and the meter values directly correspond to an associated frequency. The relationship of wavelength to frequency is realized through the following formula:

Wavelength = 300/Frequency

The meter measurement is most often used in radio communication as a band or frequency range. For example, you divide 300 by 2498 kHz to get a value of 0.1200960. Multiply that value by 1000 (to convert it into MHz), and the value equals roughly 120 meters.

Frequency

Frequency is the measurement of how many cycles per second the signal waveform goes through. Typically measured in hertz (Hz) or kilohertz (kHz), this denotes how frequently the signal repeats itself. The human voice normally operates between 50 Hz and 5000 Hz, with the majority of the activity between 300 Hz and 3400 Hz (3.1 kHz). This means that most voice conversations are between 300 cycles per second and 3400 cycles per second. So, if you have ever heard someone talk about a 3.1 kHz call, they are referring to a specific frequency range that is found in analog voice communication.

Bandwidth and Signal Distortion

The basic analog signal structure suffers from several limiting factors. First and foremost, the analog signal is limited by the amount of bandwidth or number of bits that it can transmit during a given period of time. Remember that bandwidth does not equal speed. Electrons are transmitted through the infrastructure at a constant rate, regardless of the medium. Even when fiber optics are in use, the optic medium does not physically transmit light any faster. The key to bandwidth is how many bits you can transmit at a time. If you can transmit 10 bits at a time rather than 5, you have higher bandwidth but the speed isn't any different.

Analog signals are also susceptible to both signal attenuation and line noise which are associated with the copper facilities that they are transported over.

Analog signal streams are simple avenues of communication. Although they provide adequate paths for speech transmission, they simply cannot provide much of the high-speed service required by today's data market.

In the scope of modern technology, analog communication has a limited bandwidth. Even at its highest bandwidth rates, it cannot compare to some of the lowest digital capacities. If you take away bit robbing from digital communication (56 kbps per channel), the most basic denomination is 64 kbps per channel. That still gives you more bandwidth than your analog circuits can provide.

With all of that said, it is also important to point out that the major limiting factor when dealing with analog bandwidth is the service provider. Analog circuits are deployed with filters in place, called low and high pass filters. The purpose of these filters is to ensure that transmission of the analog signal only uses a specific frequency range. The filters remove anything below and above the 3.1 kHz range needed for the analog voice channel. This fact severely limits analog circuits.

Attenuation, noise, and crosstalk are all problems that affect communication mediums. Some mediums are more susceptible to these problems than others, but even so, great care must be taken when planning and deploying your network infrastructure. All of these can destroy the signal and degrade the QoS provided to the subscriber.

Signal Attenuation and Noise

The first problem that you face with electrical current flow is the ability to maintain the signal strength. As a signal is transported down a facility, it gradually weakens with distance, as shown in Figure 1-4. The vector in Figure 1-4 illustrates the area of the signal that is attenuated as the signal travels away from the signal source.

Figure 1-4   *A Vector of Attenuation on an Analog Signal Stream*

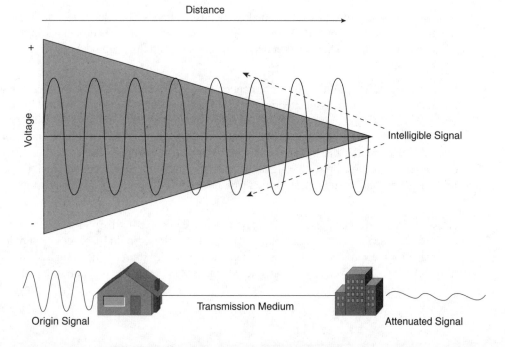

Attenuation affects both analog and digital signal streams. Because the signal degrades over distance, there is a finite value to the distance that a signal can traverse without being strengthened or regenerated. Attenuation increases with either higher frequency ranges or cable length. The type of cable that you use also makes a difference. To put this in perspective, a telco drop cable of 22 gauge has less attenuation than a drop cable of 26 gauge at the same cable length, provided that the signal frequency remains constant. The lower number gauges are sturdier cables.

Attenuation is a loss measurement that is annotated in decibels (dBs). Though it is normally denoted as –dB to identify how much loss has been experienced. Accordingly, –2 dB is a stronger signal than –4 dB. Something else to remember about attenuation is that signal voltage is cut in half with every 6 dB. In other words, a signal with –8 dB has half the line voltage of a –2 dB signal. This is important to remember when comparing readings from multiple drop cables.

If attenuation goes unchecked, the signal degrades to the point that the receiving end cannot process any of the transmitted information. A signal stream with a higher frequency is affected to a greater extent by attenuation. As the frequency increases, the signal rapidly degrades en route to the destination. It is for this reason that the receivers of high-speed equipment have a more difficult time in deciphering the intended signal. Another difference between analog and digital is the way that attenuation can be corrected.

Digital signals are composed of discrete values and are therefore easy to detect and regenerate. The use of a digital repeater allows you to extend the signal distance by completely regenerating the signal. As the weakened signal comes into the repeater, it is regenerated and appears to originate from that repeater rather than the original source.

Analog signals are not regenerated. Analog signal streams, because they are continuously fluctuating, must be amplified. As the signal attenuates, the volume is turned up on the transmission medium. There is a fundamental problem with this method of signal strengthening.

When the signal is amplified, the amplification device turns up the volume on everything, including any line noise associated with it. Think about sitting in your room listening to your radio and the signal is filled with static. You can turn up the volume of the radio in an attempt to hear the music more clearly, but that will also increase the volume of the static. The more you amplify the signal, the louder the line noise becomes. After a while, it is counterproductive to amplify the signal because the line noise makes up too much of the received signal and anything transmitted is unintelligible. This brings up the next topic— noise.

Noise is an additive that degrades signal quality and can make it difficult for equipment to decipher between the actual signal and the noise itself. Noise, in this case, does not hold any value for the signal stream. Noise can come from many sources, including radios, ultraviolet light, and even heavy machinery located too close to the transmission path.

Noise, also referred to as line noise, does not affect all carrier mediums the same way. For example, the effects of noise are more pronounced on mediums such as twisted copper pair, and less pronounced on fiber-optic mediums. If you're in the local area network (LAN) sector, you're probably familiar with not running Ethernet cables too close to lighting fixtures or electrical conduits. Doing so can allow a significant amount of noise into the signal stream.

Because your analog circuit is most likely deployed on a twisted pair, normally 22 Ga to 24 Ga wire, noise is something that you are exposed to. Figure 1-5 shows an analog signal with noise woven into it.

Figure 1-5   *Analog Signal with Noise*

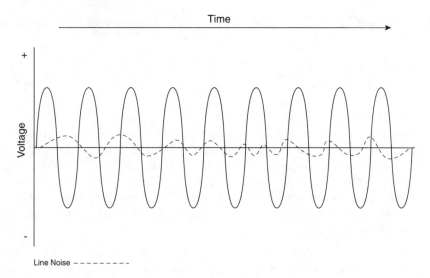

One of the most common forms of noise is crosstalk. An example of crosstalk is picking up a phone and being able to hear someone else's conversation that is being transmitted through an adjacent pair. This can be caused by faulty equipment, connectors, or poor wire shielding.

When electricity flows through a cable, an electromagnetic field is created. The electromagnetic field can cause interference with adjacent wiring, also known as electromagnetic interference (EMI). EMI gains strength as the frequency of the signal increases. Technologies with higher frequencies undoubtedly encounter more problems with crosstalk. Two main types of crosstalk that service providers encounter on a daily basis are

- Near-end crosstalk (NEXT)
- Far-end crosstalk (FEXT)

From the service provider's point of view, NEXT occurs at the subscriber end of the circuit and FEXT occurs at the line termination of the central office (CO), as seen in Figure 1-6.

Figure 1-6   *Identification of NEXT and FEXT on a Local Loop*

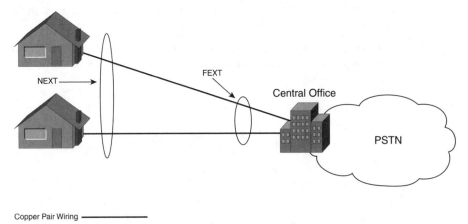

To counter the effects of EMI, the pairs of copper wiring are twisted. The twists not only help disperse EMI but also allow the cable to counter the effects of attenuation. More twists per foot cancel EMI more effectively. For example, CAT3 cable is twisted approximately three times per foot, and CAT5 cable is twisted approximately five times per foot. Hence, CAT5 cable can support higher bandwidth at the same cable length. The twisting of the cable pairs only works for a certain distance, after that point you have to amplify or regenerate the signal.

NEXT can be caused by poorly twisted cables, loose connectors, or bad connectors or wires. If there are nicks in adjacent wires' cladding, exposed copper between wires can also cause crosstalk. Pay attention to how the cable is made, especially if you are making the connectors yourself. If the twists in the cables end too far from the connector, you can experience crosstalk at higher frequencies.

FEXT measurements tend to be less than that of NEXT because of the attenuation of the signal. By the time the signal reaches the destination, it is inherently weaker than when it started. For this reason, FEXT is more common on shorter cables.

Digital-to-Analog Converters

DACs convert between digital and analog signals. Two common implementations of this type of equipment are modulator-demodulators (modems) and the conversion that is applied at the CO for each analog circuit.

A modem converts the unipolar digital signals that are transmitted by your computer into an analog signal stream. A unipolar signal is a signal that has only a single voltage polarity. So, instead of having both positive and negative sides to a signal stream, only a positive or negative side is present. Different forms of compression have been developed to allow for transfer rates as high as 53 kbps over an analog circuit. The bandwidth in these 56 kbps technologies is constrained because of crosstalk concerns at the CO. True 56 kbps causes problems with standard voice transmission channels, so limiting them allows for peaceful coexistence between voice and modem.

These digital-to-analog (D/A) and analog-to-digital (A/D) conversions are necessary because the signal coming from your computer is digital, but the communication path is analog. In the event that the circuit is digital in nature, such as an Integrated Services Digital Network (ISDN) circuit, the A/D and D/A conversions are not necessary. The only thing that the equipment might require is the formatting of the digital signal into an ISDN-compliant stream.

Analog circuits also require an A/D conversion, but at the CO. This conversion is necessary because the service provider infrastructure is composed of many different types of digital mediums. The only portions of the service provider network that are typically analog are the analog service lines and their associated facilities.

From a basic standpoint, the analog signal is converted into a digital signal, multiplexed into a high-bandwidth circuit for transmission through the service provider network, and converted back into an analog signal at the remote CO, as shown in Figure 1-7, for the terminating subscriber connection.

Figure 1-7   *A/D Conversion Example*

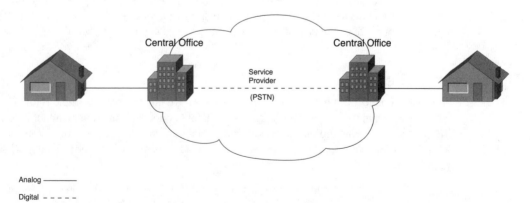

The line termination for each analog circuit at CO must also do a conversion (unless deployed through a Subscriber Line Carrier [SLC], in which case it is done prior to the CO). The primary focus of this book is on digital communication mediums. For an overview of the pulse code modulation process (PCM), refer to Chapter 3.

Analog Service Deployments

Typically when you think about analog service, you imagine huge telecommunication corporations with hundreds of switches and millions of customers. This concept contains several general ideas about what the service provider or the public switched telephone network (PSTN) really is. Even if you are new to the industry, chances are you have been exposed to the infamous cloud. The cloud that encompasses anything and everything related to the service provider.

These companies provide services to just about every home and business in the world. The services that are provided to you are done so on what is called the local loop. The local loop is the length of the cable between your residence or business and the CO. The most common service that comes to mind is probably analog phone service. The phone cable doesn't just go into the wall and disappear into the service provider's cloud. There are several pieces of equipment that your analog circuit interfaces with to provide you with your service.

First and foremost, your telephone is part of a circuit between your residence/office and the service provider's CO. There are two logical sections of this circuit: the subscriber's portion and the service provider's portion. The service provider owns all the equipment leading up to the subscriber's premise. The subscriber's portion and the service provider's portion both terminate at a device called the network interface device (NID). The NID is a defined interface in the United States that separates the telco's equipment from the customer's equipment. This box is used because the United States federal government limited what services and equipment the telephone company can provide in the Divestiture Hearings of 1984. Although you might not recognize the term NID in an international environment, chances are that you use something similar to it.

The local service provider provides a circuit to either a business or a residence. In doing so, the wiring from the CO to your location is the responsibility of the phone company, and the wiring on your side of the NID throughout your premise is your responsibility.

Tip and Ring Circuits

The analog connection that is provided to you is referred to as a tip and ring circuit. The name comes from the tip and ring portions of the old connectors in manual switchboards. Today, the tip and ring are the two wires that compose the analog connection. Typically deployed over a two-wire circuit, the center two pins are the most commonly used in RJ-11 modular plugs.

Basically, the way the phone circuit functions is that while your phone is on hook, or hung up, the physical circuit between your phone and the CO is open. After the phone goes off hook, or is picked up to dial, the circuit is closed and −48 VDC of power is supplied to your line from batteries at the CO. This point can be confusing because the circuit is not completed, and yet you can receive a ringing tone from the CO. That ring tone is accomplished with AC voltage. There is a bridge in the phone that blocks the DC voltage from passing unless the phone is off hook. When the phone goes off hook, the switch flags the circuit as busy, and it doesn't pass any further ring tones to your receiver.

NOTE   This basic service description does not take into account the advanced network services such as call waiting.

The tone that you are accustomed to hearing in your ear (your dial tone) is actually a tone generated from the switch to let you know that your circuit is ready to place a call. After you hear that tone, you begin dialing the proper digits to reach your desired party, as shown in Figure 1-8. If you are using a tone dial phone (non-rotary), you hear specific tones as you press the individual numbers. These are called dual tone multifrequency (DTMF) tones. Each character on the phone handset has its own pitch, which the switch interprets as a dialed digit. Not all technologies supply a tone for you prior to placing a call. This is covered in later chapters in this book.

Figure 1-8   *Analog Telephone Circuit States*

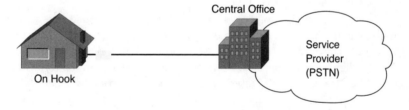

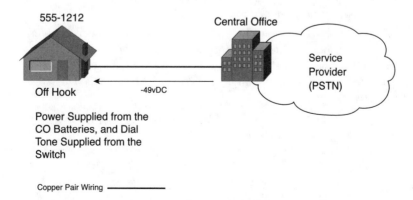

Expert White Board: Analog Signaling Methods

Several different types of basic analog signaling provide an analog circuit with basic on-hook and off-hook functionality:

- Loop start signaling
- Reverse battery signaling
- Ground start signaling
- E&M signaling

The first type of analog signaling is loop start signaling. Loop start was actually just discussed when describing a tip and ring circuit. Loop start signaling is common in analog installations. It functions by closing a two-wire loop (circuit) to seize a circuit. When the phone is on hook the loop is open, or not completed. When the receiver is picked up, the loop is closed, seizing the circuit to the CO. The CO listens for the seizure by placing battery on the ring wire and ground on the tip wire.

Reverse battery signaling for analog lines is simple when compared to the loop start signaling method. Loop start applies battery to the ring lead and ground to the tip lead. Reverse battery signaling reverses this approach by providing battery on the tip lead and ground on the ring lead for circuit seizure.

Ground start signaling is another type of analog signaling. Ground start signaling is most commonly found in switch to switch or private branch exchange (PBX) to switch applications. This form of signaling is accomplished by applying ground to the tip wire at the local switch in the connection. Because the remote switch is monitoring the tip wire for ground, after it is detected, it closes the circuit loop to provide for an active call.

E&M signaling goes by several definitions. You might hear it called Ear and Mouth, Earth and Magnet, or Receive and Transmit. Regardless of how it is defined, they all function in the same way. E&M signaling is typically only found on connections between switches, between PBXs, or between a combination of a switch and PBX. Most people use the Ear and Mouth terminology because it is easier to remember the function of each wire. At either side of the E&M connection, the switch or PBX listens for ground on the E wire and transmit ground locally on the M wire.

E&M signaling can operate in two different ways, standard mode and wink mode. In standard mode, the originating switch goes off hook and waits 210 milliseconds (ms) before sending digits. The originating switch waits between 140 ms and 200 ms because the terminating switch briefly goes off hook (between 140 ms and 200 ms) for a period of time that is called the wink.

In wink mode, the originating switch sends digits after waiting only 150 ms. The decreased wait period allows for a faster call setup process.

COs, also known as end offices (EOs), are centralized locations that include device switches, multiplexers (MUXs) and demultiplexers (DEMUXs), Digital Access and Crossconnect Systems (DACSs), and a wide variety of other equipment that is discussed in detail later in the book.

On a basic scale, look at an image of your analog phone service to your home. In Figure 1-9, the solid line represents the house connected to the CO through a pair of copper wiring. Life would be simple if this was all that was required to provide you with analog service.

Figure 1-9   *Basic Representation of Analog Phone Service*

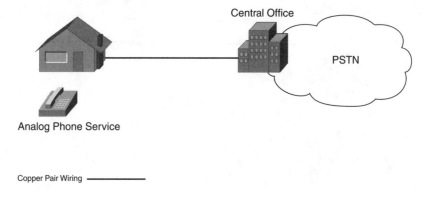

IDLC

In fact, many things have been added to improve your service, as well as save the telco money. In days of old, if the phone company wanted to provide service to 24 houses in a neighborhood, they had to run 24 pairs of copper wiring. This quickly became a great expense for the provider. Figure 1-10 shows the use of an individual line to each house. IDLCs, also known as SLCs, and time-division multiplexing (TDM) circuits were created to help alleviate this issue.

IDLCs deploy service to densely populated residential or business areas as well as saving on the amount of copper wiring. The process of saving or gaining the copper wiring back is known as pair gain. Figure 1-11 shows the deployment of an IDLC in a neighborhood.

Figure 1-10   *Deployment of Multiple Analog Circuits Without the Use of IDLCs*

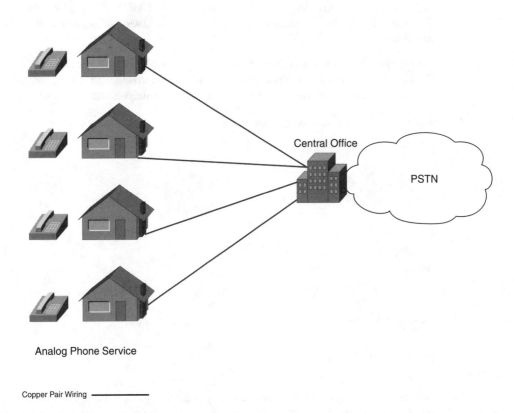

SLCs include various port densities, including SLC-48, SLC-96, SLC-500, and SLC-2000. You can find the larger SLCs in medium to large business areas because they allow for the deployment of a host of analog and digital services. The SLC naming conventions are Lucent coined names for the IDLC product line. Referring to the section on attenuation earlier in this chapter, IDLCs can help to alleviate the amplification issues that are associated with analog circuits. By placing the analog loop closer to the subscriber, multiple amplifications are not necessary in most cases.

Figure 1-11 *Deployment of an IDLC in a Neighborhood*

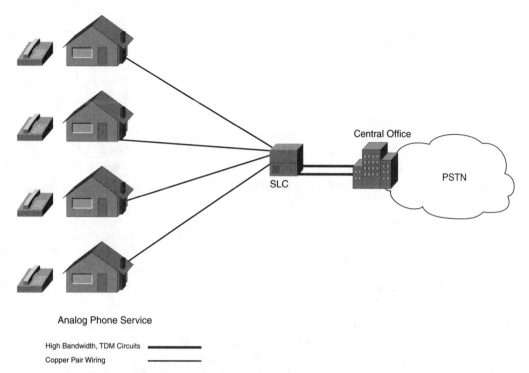

IDLCs use a high-bandwidth digital trunk or set of trunks to communicate back to the CO to provide service from the PSTN to the deployed area. When the loop carriers were first deployed, they typically used a T1 or E1 trunk back to the provider's CO. However, the recent developments in the area of digital technology, most notably synchronous optical network (SONET) and synchronous digital hierarchy (SDH), have enabled service providers to deploy fiber-optic trunks directly to IDLCs from the CO. These fiber links allow the service providers to deploy larger numbers of trunks, and provide more bandwidth-intensive services to their customer base. For more information on these technologies, refer to the following chapters:

- Chapter 5, "T1 Technology"
- Chapter 6, "E1, R2, and Japanese Carrier Technology"
- Chapter 14, "SONET and SDH"

IDLCs are deployed by using a set of standards from Bellcore that is called GR-303-CORE.

GR-303-CORE

The set of standards in GR-303-CORE was developed to specify an outline for future infrastructure deployments in reference to the use of IDLCs. The basis for these standards was to improve upon the limitations of standard IDLC deployments and to facilitate the integration of many digital mediums at the same time. GR-303-CORE is intended for use with digital mediums, but it does provide for the integration of both analog and digital mediums. GR-303-CORE provides for a way to bridge or translate analog circuits into digital trunks for transmission back to the CO.

Some of the new services designed into the framework are Hybrid Fiber Coax (HFC), xDSL, Fiber to the Curb, and the integration of ISDN equipment directly into the SLC. This design set the pace for what is now called Next Generation-IDLC (NG-IDLC). GR-303-CORE also specifies a set of standard deployment methodologies for bridging the gap among vendors and technologies.

Within the GR-303-CORE standard, there is a specification of a Timeslot Management Channel (TMC), which is for the transmission of call messaging for multiple TDM circuits. This signaling channel specifies on-hook and off-hook states with robbed-bit signaling (RBS). Although this streamlines the call setup process, it limits the channels to 56 kbps each. This loss of 8 kbps is because of the RBS stealing the least significant bit for said call states.

The new standard allows for a full digital signal Level 3 (DS-3) worth of T1 traffic (28 T1s), and the ability to provide redundancy on links that carry data traffic. In all, GR-303-CORE adds to the current deployment of the IDLC infrastructure by providing an open framework for technology integration, seamless call management over multiple TDM circuits, and the capacity for many more circuits than its predecessors did.

Internationally, the European Telecommunications Standards Institute (ETSI) has created a set of standards that provides for many of the same features by using slightly different terminology. The ETSI V5 standard set has several specifications, including V5.1 and V5.2. The V5.2 specification describes the communication between the access node (AN) and the local exchange (LE). V5.2 links can use either a single E1 trunk for communication or up to 16 E1 trunks in what is called a V5.2 bundle. One of the main differences between V5.1 and V5.2 is that V5.2 adds the capability to use primary rate access (PRA) circuits. In the case of the V5 standards, the AN is equivalent to the IDLC that GR-303-CORE uses, and the LE is the service provider's switch interface.

Each E1 carrier circuit within the V5.2 bundle is identified by using a link ID during normal operation. A provision is also made for the blocking of a specific link ID, when the AN identifies a need for disallowing traffic to a specific link. Two types of blocking are typically associated with the V5 standards, deferred and non-deferred. In the case of deferred blocking, the AN requests that a specific link ID be blocked from traffic. The LE flags all unassigned DS0s in the link as blocked, and blocks individually assigned DS0s as they become unassigned (because of call disconnect).

Non-deferred blocking operates in a slightly different way. The AN requests that a specific link be blocked to the LE. The LE switches the assigned digital service 0 (DS0s) (active calls) to a standby set of DS0s, and flags the requested link as blocked. The LE might reject the request by sending an unblock message in response to the request from the AN.

The link ID is assigned at both ends of the connection. The link ID identifies the individual links in a bundle so that both ends can agree on the location of calls between them.

The V5 standards support a host of different services between the AN and LE, which include the following

- Analog service support
- ISDN basic access (BA) and PRA Service (V5.2)
- Permanent leased line
- As with GR-303-CORE, the V5 specifications are designed to provide explicit communication instructions for analog communication through an AN, digital ISDN communication, permanent leased line (E1 facility), and the conversion between analog and digital services.

Summary

The telecommunication infrastructure uses two main types of signals: analog and digital. Analog signals are found in products that you use on a daily basis, ranging from TVs and radios to telephones. The fundamental difference between analog and digital signals is that analog signals are continuous waveforms that constantly vary in amplitude and frequency, and digital signals are represented by discrete values that are commonly denoted by 1s and 0s.

Amplitude, wavelength, and frequency are the three major components of a standard sinusoidal waveform. The amplitude measures the total height of the waveform. The wavelength is the distance between the same points on two adjacent waveforms. Frequency is the value that represents the number of cycles that a signal repeats in a second.

Common problems exist for both analog and digital signals. Attenuation is the loss of signal strength on a given medium over distance. This loss causes the signal to weaken as it travels from the source. If the signal is too weak, it is unintelligible to the receiving equipment. Noise is a byproduct that affects the signal. It can significantly degrade the QoS. Bad connectors, poor cable quality, environmental events, and co-located machinery can contribute to noise on a circuit. Crosstalk is a form of noise commonly found in voice and data circuits. In voice circuits, it can cause a subscriber to hear the conversation of an adjacent pair.

Analog circuits are deployed to subscribers by a copper pair of wire from the CO (less common) or by a copper pair from an SLC. The SLC allows the telco to regain copper pairs by placing local loops closer to the subscriber's premise. The SLC, in turn, communicates with the CO through a high-bandwidth trunk that uses a protocol such as GR-303-CORE.

Review Questions

Give or select the best answer or answers to the following questions. The answers to these questions are in Appendix A, "Answers to Review Questions."

1 What is the main difference between analog and digital signal streams?

   a Digital signal streams are immune to line problems such as crosstalk and attenuation.

   b Digital communication is a continuous signal stream that contains a varying range of frequencies and amplitudes.

   c Analog signal streams are composed of discrete values that can be transmitted as 1s or 0s.

   d Analog signals are considered continuous signal streams and digital signals are discrete signals, which are commonly transmitted as 1s or 0s.

2 Define the term frequency as it relates to an analog signal.

3 Given Figure 1-12, what equipment (denoted by **X**) would you use to alleviate the attenuated analog signal?

Figure 1-12 *Analog Signal Regeneration*

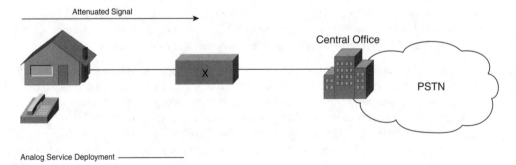

a Subscriber Line Carrier

b Network Interface Device

c Amplifier

d Modulator-demodulator

e Digital repeater

4 Which of the following items causes crosstalk on a circuit?

a Wires in a pair of wires that are untwisted too far from the connector head

b Nicks in wire cladding of adjacent wires

c Loose connections on either end of a suspected cable

d All of the above

5 At which location within the local loop can you find a device that is GR-303-CORE compliant?

a NID

b IDLC

c CO

d ISDN

This chapter covers the following topics:

- **Signaling introduction**—An introduction to signaling.

- **Signaling System 7 (SS7) node types**—Covers network nodes, also referred to as signaling points, which are physical entities on the SS7 network. The links are the signaling communication paths between them.

- **Signaling types**—Discusses channel associated signaling (CAS), as found in traditional time-division multiplexing (TDM)-based circuits, and common channel signaling (CCS).

- **Why SS7 was developed**—Covers the histroy of and reasons for developing SS7.

- **Signaling links and link sets**—Discusses signaling links, which are physical connections between SS7 nodes and are responsible for the reliable transmission of SS7 signaling messages between those nodes.

- **Point codes**—Covers how messages are routed within the SS7 network.

- **Message transfer part**—Covers Message Transfer Part Layer 1, Message Transfer Part Layer 2, and Message Transfer Part Layer 3.

- **SS7 upper-layer protocols**—Within the upper layer of the SS7 stack (Layer 4), there are several protocols that you can use for call messaging functions.

- **Intelligent Network**—The Intelligent Network (IN) infrastructure provides a suite of services that are inherently not provided by the SS7 network. This list also includes services that are provided to the network operator.

- **Expert Whiteboard: Local Number Portability (LNP) Operation in North America**—A whiteboard by Travis Powell about LNP operation in North America.

- **Capability Set 3 (CS-3)**—CS-3 is the next generation of IN functionality that builds upon what is already in place from CS-1 and CS-2 in the service provider network.

CHAPTER 2

The Signaling System 7 Network

Signaling Introduction

Chapter 1, "An Overview of Analog Communication," covers some of the more common aspects of hardware associated with service providers. Chapter 1 looks at what makes up analog service, including hardware from both sides of the network interface device (NID). This chapter builds on what you have learned about the service provider network by discussing the complementing functions of call control and signaling.

Although this chapter focuses on Signaling System 7 (SS7), it is not intended to be an all-inclusive tutorial because there are entire books on this subject. This chapter is designed to give you a good overview of signaling and SS7 operation so that you have a good foundation for some of the technology discussed later in this book.

SS7, also referred to as Common Channel Signaling System 7 (CCS7) or C7 internationally, is the current signaling infrastructure throughout most of the world that allows you to place calls from your work, home, or any other telephone equipped location. SS7 was created to provide a more efficient way of transferring call signaling between network nodes to allow timely delivery of those messages. SS7 also enables call control and network resiliency without impacting the bearer traffic of the call itself. Bearer traffic is the actual call that the signaling is to control, whether it is voice, video, or data.

What Is Signaling?

Signaling can be defined as a series of messages transmitted from one network node to another to allow for all aspects of call control. On a basic level, the signaling is what provides services to the customer, connects calls end to end, disconnects calls, and bills each call to the proper parties. This is not to say that all connections require signaling, as there are permanent connections within the service provider network that do not require signaling. However, most modern telecommunication networks have signaling in one form or another. Whether the signaling is CAS, as found in traditional TDM-based circuits; CCS, as found in Integrated Services Digital Network (ISDN); or SS7, signaling controls and manages circuit functions.

SS7 Node Types

Several devices in this chapter pertain to the SS7 network infrastructure. As a whole, the SS7 network has been built by using links and nodes. The network nodes, also referred to as signaling points, are physical entities on the SS7 network, and the links are the signaling communication paths between them. The three devices you see the most are the *Service Switching Point* (SSP), *Signal Transfer Point* (STP), and the *Service Control Point* (SCP). It is important to note that in most international implementations, the SSP and the STP can be integrated in the same node. Figure 2-1 shows the basic SS7 device icons that appear in the figures throughout this chapter.

Figure 2-1 *Basic SS7 Device Icons*

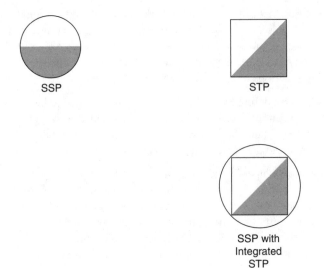

SSP

STP

SCP

SSP with
Integrated
STP

SSP

SSPs are switches that reside at service provider end offices (EOs) or central offices (COs). The SSPs are responsible for call management, call processing, and routing calls through the network to the proper destination.

SSPs are classified as two distinctly different types of switches, national or international, as shown in Figure 2-2. Although two types of SSPs are identified, a third can be argued to exist when both national and international functions are served within the same SSP. The third switch type is known as a *hybrid SSP*. This allows for the numbering plans of both the national and international switches to be independent of each other. A numbering plan is a table that performs digit analysis and aids in the routing of calls to the proper party.

Figure 2-2   *National and International SSPs*

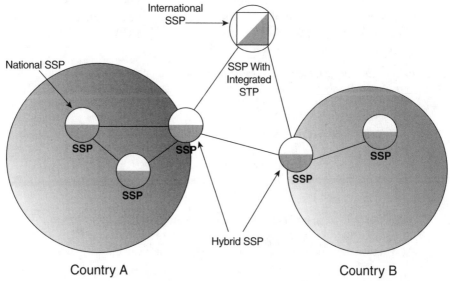

A national SSP is a SSP that is located within a country which only communicates with other switches within that country. An international SSP is a SSP that is responsible for the routing of calls between different countries. There is also a hybrid SSP that functions at both national and international levels. This SSP can be considered an international gateway and has point codes associated with both networks.

Each country should have at least one international gateway SSP to enable the smooth transition between national and international networks and between national and other national networks.

Because the SSP has point codes associated with different types of networks, you might need to differentiate between the national and international point codes. This is resolved with the use of a network indicator. The network indicator identifies what type of switch the point code belongs to. The following values are used for network indicators:

- 0 = International
- 1 = Reserved
- 2 = National
- 3 = National spare (only in countries where carriers can share point codes)

The most important thing to remember is that the network indicator must match on both sides of the link, regardless of what network indicator you use.

In the international signaling network, it is not recommended that there be any more than two STPs between the origination and the destination of the call. During times of failure this can extend to three or four, but it is not intended to remain at that number for long. This limit on STPs is set in place to cut down on the complexity of the international signaling network and the amount of time that is taken for signaling delivery. This is not to say that there aren't cases in which there are more than two STPs between origination and destination. In actuality, it is common in North America but not necessarily recommended.

In North America, there are references to different classes of SSPs, which are not typically used internationally:

- Class 1 = Regional toll office
- Class 2 = Sectional toll office
- Class 3 = Primary toll office
- Class 4 = Tandem switch
- Class 5 = Subscriber (EO) switch

The hierarchy is in reverse order. In other words, the Class 5 switch is at the bottom of the hierarchy. The two switch types that this chapter focuses on are Class 4 and Class 5. Figure 2-3 shows the pyramid scheme for the North American class of switches.

A Class 5 SSP is a switch that has subscribers. The Class 5 SSP provides services to customers such as emergency services, caller ID, three-way calling, call forwarding, voice mail, and connection to long distance and international trunks. When you pick up the phone in your home, you are ultimately connecting to a Class 5 SSP.

A Class 4 SSP is also known as an access tandem (AT) or tandem switch. These switches do not directly connect to subscribers but are in place to help route calls through the service provider network. Without ATs in place, your switch has to connect directly to any other switch to place a call. Refer to Figure 2-4 for a diagram of a Class 4 and Class 5 SSP interconnect.

Figure 2-3   *North American Switch (SSP) Hierarchy*

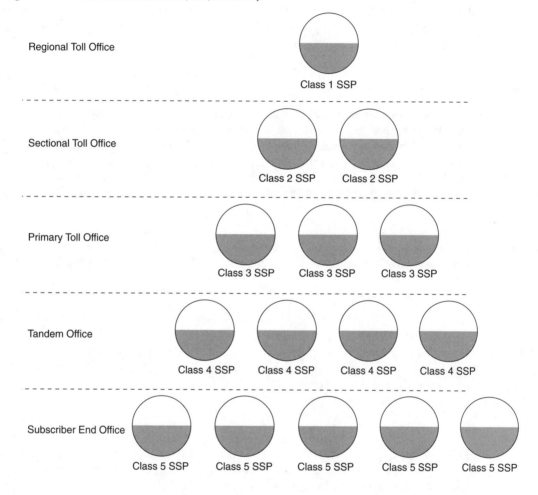

Regional Toll Office — Class 1 SSP

Sectional Toll Office — Class 2 SSP   Class 2 SSP

Primary Toll Office — Class 3 SSP   Class 3 SSP   Class 3 SSP

Tandem Office — Class 4 SSP   Class 4 SSP   Class 4 SSP   Class 4 SSP

Subscriber End Office — Class 5 SSP   Class 5 SSP   Class 5 SSP   Class 5 SSP   Class 5 SSP

Figure 2-4   *Class 4 and Class 5 SSP Interconnect*

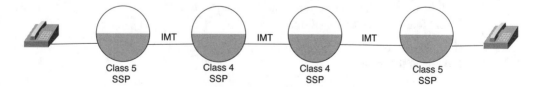

Class 5 SSP — IMT — Class 4 SSP — IMT — Class 4 SSP — IMT — Class 5 SSP

When SSPs do connect to each other, they connect through high-bandwidth links, also known as Inter-Machine Trunks (IMTs). The IMTs manage the transmission of the bearer traffic, and depending on what type of signaling is used, IMTs also manage the signaling traffic.

STP

STPs are devices that route call signaling messages through the SS7 network, which aids the SSPs in getting the messages delivered to the proper network nodes. STPs act as a packet switch, switching calls through the network based on the routing decisions that the SSPs make along the call-signaling path. They are deployed in pairs, known as mated pairs, and they are capable of making intelligent decisions to reroute call signaling in the event of a network failure, therefore adding resiliency to the switching infrastructure.

NOTE   It is important to know that the STPs can reroute the call signaling if needed but not the bearer portion of the call. The bearer traffic takes a different path when external STPs are used.

Until recently, STPs were used almost exclusively in North America. Because most international switches had this feature integrated, they did not require the use of STPs. The past few years have seen an increasing deployment of STPs in Europe and Australia and throughout the international community.

SCP

SCPs provide specific services to the end customers. SCPs are typically deployed off mated pairs of STPs in North America and off SSPs with the integrated STP functionality internationally. Figure 2-5 displays the placement of the SCP.

Some of the services provided by SCPs are toll free number translation and LNP. SCPs are usually software databases that are accessed with upper-layer protocols such as Transaction Capabilities Applications Part (TCAP). SCPs are directly associated with IN and Advanced Intelligent Network (AIN) features, more about IN and AIN is in this chapter in the section titled, "Intelligent Network (IN)".

The next few sections discuss the different types of signaling methods that you will see throughout this book.

Figure 2-5   *Placement of the SCP*

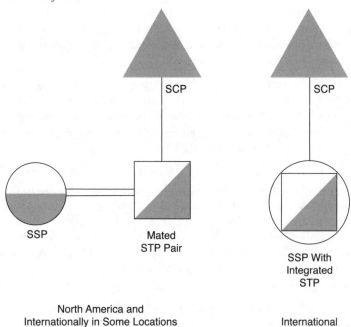

Signaling Types

This chapter covers two main types of signaling: CAS and CCS.

CAS is a common type of signaling in TDM-based technologies such as T1, E1, or J1. CAS is a way of providing signaling in-band or on the same path as the data.

The in-band features are functions such as dual tone multifrequency (DTMF) transmission. These features are interwoven into the data fabric and cannot be separated. Also signaling that accompanies each call for call state control exists and is transported using the least significant bit in the 6th, 12th (Superframe [SF]) and also the 18th and 24th frame if using Extended Superframe (ESF). Because they are taken from the data bits used for the bearer traffic on the circuit, these bits are referred to as robbed-bit signaling (RBS). Therefore, circuits using RBS are limited to 56 kbps per DS0. CAS signaling adds overhead to the total bandwidth of the circuit.

CAS is not the most efficient way of signaling in a network for several reasons. If you think about it, your bearer traffic and signaling take the same path. With that in mind, if you lose your signaling path, your bearer traffic is also lost. CAS does not allow for network resiliency, which means that it cannot reroute signaling traffic through the network in the case of a failure.

Although CAS is an older technology, it is still widely deployed throughout the world. Acknowledging the short-comings of CAS signaling, such as the inability to reroute signaling or provide services, a need was seen to develop a better way of ensuring that signaling gets through the network regardless of failure. The development of communication methods that employed CCS filled that need.

CCS signaling adds several things that CAS signaling does not provide. First, CCS signaling is out-of-band, or unobtrusive to the bearer traffic. This means that the signaling can take a separate physical path than the bearer traffic. It is also possible for CCS to be physically in-band, but logically out-of-band as with ISDN Primary Rate Interface (PRI). CCS signaling also has the capability to provide services to the subscriber base. Billable services such as toll free numbers, LNP, and pre- or post-paid calling card applications contribute to the overall quality of service (QoS) for the subscriber base as well as the revenue of the service providers.

CCS also allows for a more robust management network than commonly associated with CAS. For instance, the facility data link (FDL) that is associated with ESF only provides 12 bits for network management. The FDL is physically in-band, and typically lost if the ESF-based T1 circuit passes through a Digital Access and Crossconnect System (DACS). SS7 provides the ability to manage the network infrastructure out-of-band, therefore putting the management on a different network path.

CCS was developed to allow for inherent service provider network resiliency, services, and network management. Depending on which type of CCS you use, you can provide different levels of redundancy within your network infrastructure. There are three main types of CCS that will be discussed in the next few sections.

Associated Signaling

Associated signaling occurs when your call and signaling take the same path, but the signaling is not obtrusive to the actual bearer traffic. Figure 2-6 shows an associated signaling link between two SS7 SSPs.

Figure 2-6   *Associated Signaling*

Signaling ————————
Bearer – – – – – – – –

Several technologies use this methodology. The TDM-based E1 can use timeslot 16 (TS16) as its signaling channel for CCS signaling, such as ISDN PRI or SS7, and although the signaling is physically in-band, it's logically out-of-band because it does not directly interfere with the data being passed on the line. Thus, it is still referred to as a CCS circuit. The signaling channel is a major distinguishing factor between T1 and E1 circuits. When you use the signaling channel in a CCS application, both circuits reserve a timeslot for signaling traffic.

Another technology that uses CCS is ISDN, which uses a Data channel (D channel) to transmit and receive signaling. Again, this technology is physically in-band, but logically out-of-band. The D channel is separated from the Bearer channels (B channels), which are used for the actual bearer traffic on the circuit.

Quasi-Associated Signaling

Quasi-associated signaling uses a different path than that of the bearer traffic, but the signaling is never more than one hop away from the bearer traffic, as shown in Figure 2-7. Although this functionality is normally handled by communication between STPs and SSPs, quasi-associated signaling can also take place between SSPs if one of the SSPs is designated to have integrated STP functionality.

Because the signaling in a quasi-associated configuration is truly out-of-band, it is more flexible to provide common services to the end user and use the benefits of CCS because it provides access to external devices such as SCPs. Quasi-associated signaling is the preferred method of SS7 communication.

Figure 2-7 *Quasi-Associated Signaling*

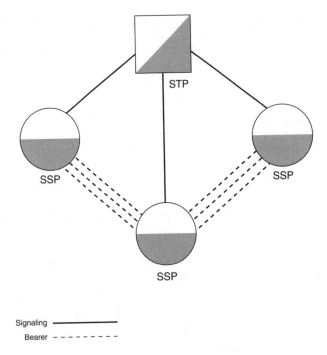

Non-Associated Signaling

Non-associated signaling is similar to quasi-associated signaling but with one major difference. With non-associated signaling, signaling takes place between STPs, as shown in Figure 2-8. In this case, signaling is not necessarily within one hop of the actual call. Every time you add another hop between STPs, you add more and more delay in the signaling network. Significant enough delay can cause problems, including calls being dropped by SSPs and link problems. Non-associated signaling is specified by the International Telecommunication Union (ITU), and the American National Standards Institute (ANSI) refers to non-associated signaling as another type of quasi-associated signaling.

Figure 2-8 *Non-Associated Signaling*

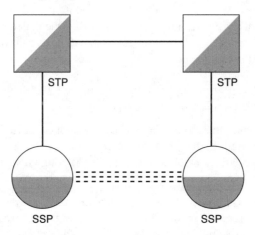

Signaling ———————
Bearer – – – – – – – –

The following excerpt identifies the reasons set forth by the ITU specification as to why you would not want to use only non-associated signaling.

The Message Transfer Part (MTP) does not include features to avoid out-of-sequence arrival of messages or other problems that would typically arise in a fully non-associated mode of signaling with dynamic message routing.

ITU-T Q.700, "Introduction to CCITT Signaling System #7," 3/93

Non-associated signaling is not preferred within the SS7 network infrastructure, although contrary to many books, it can be used. If you do use non-associated signaling, you must pay careful attention to the SS7 network design that is using it.

Why SS7 Was Developed

The introduction of the SSX infrastructure has allowed for the telco to provide a better QoS for its customers. It is intentionally stated as SSX because there are several common channel-signaling systems. From a historical point of view, there was SS4, SS5, SS6, and now SS7. SS4, SS5, and SS6 are legacy systems that are not discussed in detail because they are no longer used and are outside the scope of this book.

Prior to the creation of the SSX infrastructure, call control was inefficient. In the past, if you wanted to place a call from City A to City B, you had to reserve a trunk through all interconnecting switches between the locations to see if the dialed number was available for connection. This seems like normal operation, but if the circuit was busy or unavailable, the trunks reserved through the network were used for no reason. Furthermore, they could have been used for other calls being placed through the network. Why would this be such a big issue? If a call can't be completed, then it can't be billed. Those trunks could have been used for billable calls in the same time period.

In the SS7 infrastructure, the circuits are reserved but not connected through the network until the call is answered. In the event that the call cannot complete, the circuits that have been reserved for the call are released immediately. Although it sounds the same, the circuits in an SS7 network are typically reserved for a shorter period of time.

SS7 helps alleviate this problem because the signaling takes a separate path to get to the remote switch. If the remote circuit is busy, it can return that information out of band and release the circuit at the same time. The SS7 network is also able to reroute signaling traffic based on network congestion or failure. This is referred to as network resiliency.

Another reason that SS7 was developed was due to the slow call setup time. In-band signaling is slower to set up and tear down calls, and although it had been improved, call setup time was still too slow for the fast growing infrastructure. SS7 improved upon the call setup speeds by adding a separate link to the network and by providing a message-based signaling network. The bit states associated with DTMF tones take longer to set up and tear down calls. The purpose of this signaling link was for nothing more than transporting signaling information from node to node in the network.

The ideology behind the creation of SS7 was to create a scalable and flexible network infrastructure that allowed for common signaling messages for call control and also to allow for the integration of newly developed protocols. The various upper-layer protocols, also referred to as user or application parts, allow for everyone to use the same base structure while providing specific services to the end user.

Signaling Links and Link Sets

Signaling links are physical connections between SS7 nodes and are responsible for the reliable transmission of SS7 signaling messages between those nodes, as shown in Figure 2-9. Signaling links can be configured so that they load share traffic over any or all of the links in a designated link set between signaling points. Even distribution of traffic is only achieved if there are several signaling links of the power 2 (2, 4, 8, and so on).

Figure 2-9   *Signaling Links Between SS7 Network Nodes*

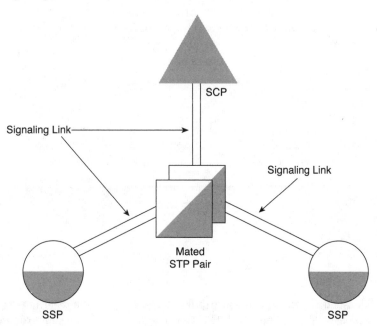

Signaling links are generally deployed over T1s at 56 kbps per digital signal level 0 (DS-0) in North America, and E1s at 64 kbps per DS-0 in the international community. There is a new movement for using an entire digital signal level 1 (DS-1) to transport SS7 signaling traffic. If a DS-1 is used, 1.536 kbps is used for the signaling traffic and 8 kbps is used for framing and maintenance.

Japan specifies the use of a 48-kbps signaling link and a 64-kbps signaling link. The 64-kbps signaling link is left in the Japanese specification because it was the recommended speed set forth by the ITU. A low bandwidth link of 4.8 kbps is also available for signaling transport, but it is not discussed in this book. Signaling links can be deployed on satellite links if SS7 connectivity is required to remote locations.

Some areas of North America offer 64-kbps SS7 links, so it is important that you verify what the speed of your SS7 link is from your provider. When a call setup message is generated by a SSP, a Signaling Link Selection (SLS) occurs. This selection process identifies which signaling link the call is transferred over. Because this operation occurs in each direction, independent of each other, it is possible for the messages in opposite directions to take different paths.

Signaling links are deployed in logical groupings called link sets. Link sets are collections of up to 16 signaling links, and each link is uniquely identified by a Signaling Link Code (SLC) from 0 to 15. Figure 2-10 shows a link set between a SSP and a mated pair of STPs.

SLCs are important identifiers because they notify the SS7 network devices which links are connected to which SS7 network nodes. SLCs are given to you by your provider, and if you don't match what is set in their network (wrong SLC set), you are not able to complete the alignment process.

Figure 2-10 *Links Within a Link Set*

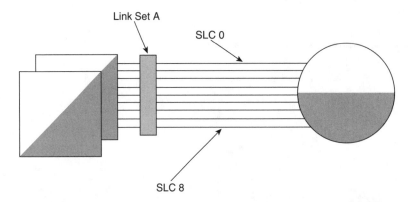

The traffic load of signaling links also differs between the international and North American communities—the ITU and ANSI. ITU signaling links can handle a maximum of 4096 circuits, and ANSI signaling links can handle about 16,384 circuits. Just because the technology supports thousands of Circuit Indentification Codes (CICs) per link does not mean that you ever have that many CICs for any single signaling link. The reason for this is simple: most countries don't allow it.

Hypothetically, if you had 16,384 circuits worth of signaling between SSPs on one link and that link was lost, that would be a disaster for your location. You would lose them all at one time. The number of CICs you are allowed to have per signaling link differs from country to country, so you need to inquire about each country's guidelines when requesting a link.

When loading links, it is generally recommended that you do not design any one link with more than 40 percent traffic capacity, or .40 erlang. The reason for this is simple, if you have a link failure you want to be able to reroute the signaling traffic to a redundant link or a load-shared link. In the case of 40 percent load, even with the traffic reroute you only have 80 percent load on the redundant or load-shared link. Any more than 40 percent causes a link to carry 100 percent capacity or more during a failure, and that certainly can cause problems. This design principle varies from customer to customer, but this is the rule of thumb.

Link Categories

In North America, links are categorized based on what SS7 node types they connect. These categorizations are not used throughout most of the world, but they are helpful in explaining what types of links can be provided. Figure 2-11 shows A-, B-, and C-links, and Figure 2-12 shows D-, E-, and F-links. The following are link types that are commonly associated with ANSI signaling links:

- A-link—Access link
- B-link—Bridge link
- C-link—Cross link
- D-link—Diagonal link
- E-link—Extended link
- F-link—Fully-associated link

A-links provide access into a portion of the SS7 network. They connect SSPs to STPs, SSPs to SCPs, or STPs to SCPs. A-links are common in areas that use STPs, such as the U.S., Australia, and most recently, parts of Europe.

B-links connect non-mated STPs. Because STPs are deployed in mated pairs, at some point they have links to other mated pairs of STPs. The links that connect the two sets together are B-links.

C-links connect mated STP pairs. This link handles communication between the two STPs, and in a failure situation becomes the failover link between them. This link allows call signaling to be rerouted through the network, if necessary.

A-, B-, and C-links are shown in Figure 2-11.

Figure 2-11 *A-, B-, and C-Links*

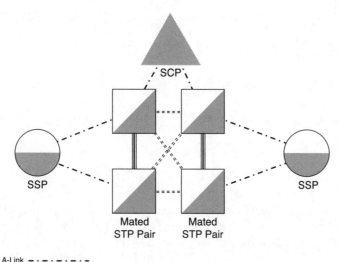

A-Link — · — · — · — · —
B-Link ≈≈≈≈≈≈≈≈≈≈≈≈
C-Link ≡≡≡≡≡≡≡≡

D-links connect devices at different levels of the network hierarchy, such as connecting a local pair of STPs to a regional pair of STPs.

E-links connect SSPs to a mated pair of STPs that are not designated as its home pair.

F-links connect two SSPs together on a direct link. The signaling and the bearer traffic can be on the same T1 or E1 span, but they are on separate logical channels. Because the definition of an F-link is the connection of two SSPs, the signaling and the bearer traffic do not have to be on the same physical span.

D-, E-, and F-links are shown in Figure 2-12.

Figure 2-12 *D-, E-, and F-Links*

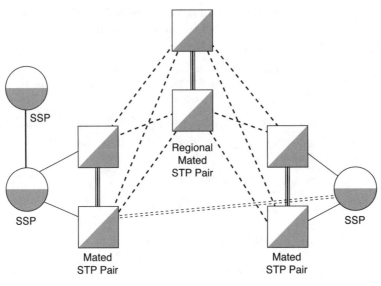

Point Codes

Now that you are familiar with links and link sets, you are ready to begin looking at how messages are routed within the SS7 network. SS7 uses a set of addressing information and call details to route calls from one network node to another. The main addressing scheme is a logical address that identifies each SS7 node, including SSPs, STPs, and SCPs.

The logical addresses are called point codes, and they operate at Layer 3 of the SS7 protocol stack. Layer 3 in the SS7 protocol model is known as Message Transfer Part Level 3

(MTP3). Point codes, along with other identifiers, such as CICs, called numbers, and calling numbers, are used in call processing. Later, this chapter covers how point codes are used in Message Signal Unit (MSU) messages to route calls through the network, but for now this section focuses on their composition.

Originating, Destination, and Adjacent Point Codes

When referring to point codes, four different types illustrate different placements throughout the network. The Originating Point Code (OPC) describes the network device that originates the call. If you are a service provider that is just starting up, you use an OPC to identify your local switch. From your perspective, you are always the originating point for your SS7 traffic, and your point code is the destination point code for bearer traffic that you receive. As an OPC, you are the Destination Point Code (DPC) for other switches and they are the DPCs for you. DPCs identify terminating destinations of calls, and they are always SSPs.

An Adjacent Point Code (APC) is a point code that is adjacent to your point code. The most common representation of an APC is a home STP pair, but another SSP directly interconnected can also be referred to as an APC. The remote SSP is considered the APC for the link set that is received at the OPC.

Figure 2-13 shows a series of SS7 network nodes that are interconnected and their relationship to each other in respect to their point codes.

Figure 2-13 *OPCs, DPCs, and APCs Interconnected*

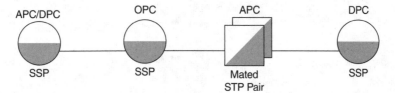

The final type of point code is an Alias Point Code. The Alias Point Code, also referred to as a Capability Point Code, is a point code that exists in software only. The purpose of the Alias Point Code is to group a set of SS7 network nodes together by network function. Alias Point Codes provide the ability to identify which network nodes can provide specific services to customers. Different types of point codes exist, and the point codes themselves differ between the ANSI format used in the U.S. and the ITU format used just about everywhere else.

North American Point Code Format

The ANSI point code format is formulated from three 8-bit octets for a total of 24 bits. Each octet has a range of numbers from 0 to 255, and it is broken down into three subsections (one subsection per octet):

0–255.0–255.0–255
For example: 10.20.30

The first of these sections is the network. The network octet identifies the actual provider that is using the point code. This differentiates between Lucent, WorldCom, and Sprint. The second octet identifies the cluster within the network. Clusters are logical groupings of network nodes, so a network of 20 nodes might have 5 clusters of four nodes each. The last octet identifies the member node of the cluster. In other words, each of the four nodes within the cluster is considered a member. You can almost think of this approach as something like peeling an onion. Figure 2-14 shows these layers. The outer skin is the network, the next few layers are the clusters within the network, and the rest of the layers are the members of those clusters. However, if the customer is a small carrier, it is typically only possible to get a maximum of four point codes from the service provider for the SS7 network. Issuing four point codes at a time to smaller carriers allows the distribution of point codes to be more controlled and efficient.

Figure 2-14   *The Onion-Like Layers of the ANSI Point Code*

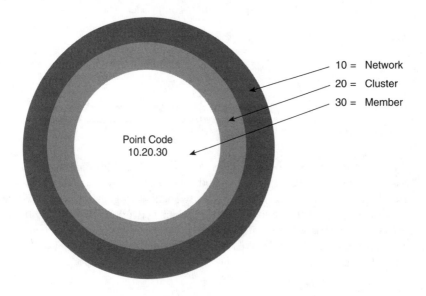

ITU Point Code Format

The ITU point code format is a little different than that of ANSI. The ITU point code is organized into three fields, just as the ANSI point code, but the ITU point code differs in how many bits are in each field. The ITU format calls for a 3-bit field, followed by an 8-bit field, and then by another 3-bit field. This gives the ITU point code a final size of 14 bits.

The first octet indicates the zone identifier (zone ID) of the point code. The zone ID is the geographical zone that the point code is a part of. The zone IDs are listed in Table 2-1.

Table 2-1   *ITU Zone IDs*

Zone ID	Geographical Region
2	Europe
3	Greenland, North America, the Caribbean, and Mexico
4	Middle East and Asia
5	South Asia, Australia, and New Zealand
6	Africa
7	South America

For more information on signaling area network code (SANC) designations, refer to Appendix B "Signaling Area Network Code (SANC) Designations."

The second octet indicates the area or network identifier (network ID). The network ID subdivides each zone ID into smaller areas, such as countries. This can also subdivide large countries into smaller, more manageable sections. Together, the zone ID and the network ID are known as the SANC.

The last octet indicates the signaling point identifier (SPID), not to be confused with the service profile identifier (SPID) used in ISDN. The SPID indicates the node residing in a specific SANC. Figure 2-15 shows the ITU point code format with the SANC highlighted in gray.

Figure 2-15   *ITU Point Code Structure*

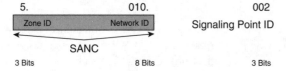

This format fits the international community well because there aren't typically as many network devices requiring point codes as there are in the U.S. Even the U.S. does not use the full range of numbers allotted in each octet.

A couple of locations throughout the world differ from what has been discussed. China uses a 24-bit format that is similar to the ANSI point code structure. Japan has adopted a 16-bit point code format for use in the Japanese national network.

Now that the logical addressing is in place, you are ready to learn about some of the protocols that make SS7 function. Many protocols that are associated with SS7, but this chapter focuses on only a couple of them. These protocols give you a good high-level understanding of how the SS7 network operates and a foundation to work from for the rest of the book. The protocols that this chapter examines are MTP Layers 1, 2, and 3; Telephone User Part (TUP); Data User Part (DUP); and ISDN User Part (ISUP). This chapter also includes a discussion on some of the services that are offered by INs.

MTP

SS7 operates at different defined levels, called layers, and each layer has a specific function. For those of you familiar with the Open System Interconnection (OSI) model, the SS7 protocol stack has a layered model that matches up with the layers displayed for OSI, as seen in Figure 2-16. Technically, the SS7 model is a four-layer stack, with MTP at Layers 1 through 3 and the various user parts at Layer 4. The protocol stacks do not match up 100 percent because the SS7 stack was designed prior to 1984, when the International Organization for Standardization (ISO) developed the OSI model.

Figure 2-16 *The OSI Model and the SS7 Protocol Stack*

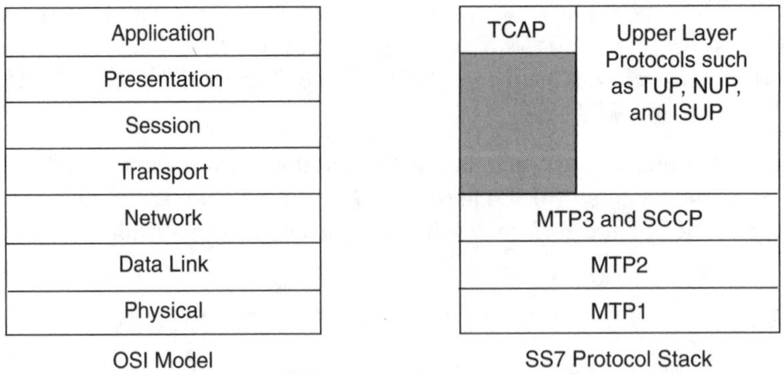

OSI Model	SS7 Protocol Stack
Application	TCAP / Upper Layer Protocols such as TUP, NUP, and ISUP
Presentation	
Session	
Transport	
Network	MTP3 and SCCP
Data Link	MTP2
Physical	MTP1

A couple of exceptions to this rule are the signaling connection control part (SCCP), which operates at Layer 3 of the SS7 protocol stack, and TCAP, which operates at a functional level that is considered Layer 7 (Application) of the OSI model.

SCCP and MTP together form the Network Service Part (NSP). SCCP, which is discussed in a later section, adds both connectionless and connection-oriented functionality to MTP3. These additions to MTP3 allow for the definitive correspondence between the SS7 protocol stack and the OSI model's network layer.

The purpose of MTP is to serve as a set of transport layers for the various user parts and their services. It is also responsible for the detection and correction of network failures and errors in a timely manner. MTP is broken down into three defined layers:

- MTP1—Message Transfer Part Layer 1
- MTP2—Message Transfer Part Layer 2
- MTP3—Message Transfer Part Layer 3

MTP1

MTP1 operates at Layer 1 of the SS7 protocol stack and has equivalent functions to that of OSI's physical layer. It is responsible for the physical and electrical characteristics of the line, which include providing a bearer path for the signaling link. MTP1 can be served on a terrestrial TDM circuit or on a satellite link.

Think about what type of physical medium you're using for the signaling link. Most times, signaling is transferred over a DS0 on a T1 within the U.S. and Japan, over an E1 internationally, or on a DS0 over a V.35 interface. In Japan, remember that 48-kbps signaling links are also available. The requirements for the setup of a signaling data link are as follows:

- The signaling data link must be reserved for SS7 traffic only.
- Echo cancellers, digital pads, and A-Law converters must be removed from the link to ensure a full duplex link between signaling points.
- The standard signaling data link should be 64 kbps, but you can use links as low as 4.8 kbps as long as you adhere to the user part requirements.

The preceding list comes from ITU-T Q.702, "Specification of the Signaling Data Link," 3/93.

On an international note, SS7 signaling data links are required to be 64 kbps and transmitted on TS16 of an E1 circuit. This requirement can be modified if both parties involved agree to a specific timeslot and configure accordingly, but deviation from this timeslot is not likely.

Specifications for a T1-based signaling data link are based on the use of alternate mark inversion (AMI) encoding (for more on T1 or E1 technology, refer to Chapter 5, "T1 Technology" and Chapter 6, "E1, R2, and Japanese Carrier Technology"). Because AMI steals the least significant bit, thus allowing only 56 kbps of data on each timeslot, the standard signaling link speed in the U.S. is 56 kbps. This is the most common speed in the United States, but 64-kbps links do exist. This depends on the provider that you are receiving the signaling link from.

SS7 signaling links can also be deployed over analog facilities, although it is certainly not common. In the case of an analog facility, the link must be at least 4.8 kbps and you must use either V.27 or V.27 bis.

MTP2

MTP2 provides the required Layer 2 functionality in the SS7 network. It is responsible for providing a reliable link for the upper-layer protocols. The explicit device name used at MTP2 is a Signaling Link Terminal (SLT). It is normally built into the signaling point fabric. The functions of MTP2 are as follows:

- **Separation of signal units**—MTP2 provides identification of individual signal units with a flag.

- **Bit stuffing**—The transmission of six consecutive 1s within a signal unit causes it to mimic a flag, which is not allowed. In the case that this occurs, alignment is lost on the link. To ensure that this does not happen, you use bit stuffing.

- **Error detection**—MTP2 uses cyclic redundancy checks (CRCs) in a frame-check sequence (FCS) field to verify the integrity of the transmitted frames. The FCS field is 16 bits in length.

- **Link alignment**—MTP2 is responsible for the initial phases of link alignment and allows the transmission of upper-layer messages.

- **Signal link monitoring**—Signal link monitoring is handled by two error counters; signal unit error rate monitor (SUERM) and alignment error rate monitor (AERM). The AERM is used during the initial link alignment, and the SUERM is used after the link is in service to verify link integrity.

- **Flow control**—Flow control is handled by the different frame types used by MTP2. Busy indicators can be sent, in times of congestion, to back off signaling points to return to a non-congested state.

MTP2 includes two different signal unit types that allow MTP2 to provide the services above. The Fill-In Signal Unit (FISU) and the Link Status Signal Unit (LSSU) are used at different intervals on the SS7 network. A third MTP2 message type, the Message Signal Unit (MSU) assits in routing call signaling through the SS7 network.

FISU

The FISU is the most basic MTP2 signal unit. The purpose of this signal unit is to fill in idle time on the signaling link and provide link synchronization. The FISU acts as a proactive way to detect errors on the signaling link in an attempt to find problems before a call is placed. What we mean by that is while there is no signaling traffic going through the SS7 network, FISUs are sent as a type of heartbeat between signaling points.

Figure 2-17 shows the different fields in a FISU signal unit.

Figure 2-17 *FISU Format*

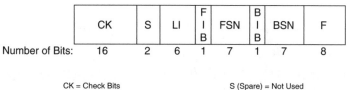

CK = Check Bits   S (Spare) = Not Used

LI = Length Indicator (Not Used)   FIB = Forward Indicator Bit

FSN = Forward Sequence Number   BIB = Backward Indicator Bit

BSN = Backward Sequence Number   F = Flag

The signal units are to be read from right to left, as they are transmitted with the flag bit first. The flag identifies one signal unit from another. There is documentation out there (including ITU Q.703) that identifies the FISU as having an opening and closing flag. The closing flag that is represented is merely the opening flag of the next signal unit. So, if signal unit #3 is the last signal unit transmitted it does not have a closing flag. The Length Indicator (LI) is not used with the FISU, and thus is set to 0.

The backward sequence number (BSN), backward indicator bit (BIB), forward sequence number (FSN), and forward indicator bit (FIB) all work together as part of signal unit identification and the identification of which signal units should be transmitted. The FSN identifies the sequence number of the current signal unit that is being transmitted. The BSN identifies the last good received signal unit and can be used as a way for the receiving end to identify which signal unit is retransmitted. The FIB and BIB indicate which signal units need to be resent.

In normal operation, the FIB and BIB equal the same value (0). If a unit is not received, or it does not pass the FCS, the BIB is set to the opposite value of the FIB. This indicator, with the help of the BSN, identifies which signal unit is retransmitted. The signaling point that originally transmitted the signal unit sees the BIB and uses BSN+1 to identify which signal unit is retransmitted. This function is shown in Figure 2-18.

After the signal unit in question is retransmitted, and it passes the FCS, the BIB is reset to 0. After this point, normal transmission of signal units can resume. A maximum of 127 messages can be marked for retransmission.

Figure 2-18 *Normal Retransmission Procedure*

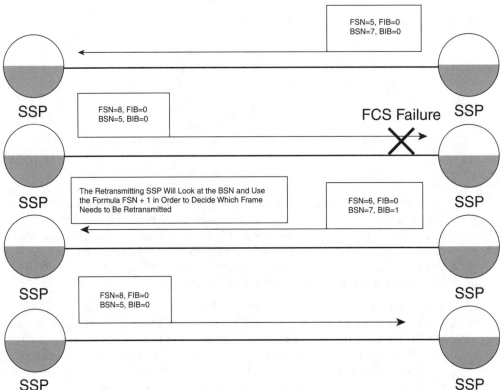

Now that you understand how the fields technically work, it is important to point out that they do not operate in this manner when used in FISU frames. The FSN of a FISU is actually the last known good, received MSU on the signaling link. This FSN does not change until another MSU is received. The next time MSU transmission pauses, the FISU assumes the FSN of that last MSU again. The following example shows that if the last MSU frame number was 5, your FISU frame number will be 5. If the last MSU frame number was 24, the FISU frame number will be 24.

```
MSU FSN = 5       FISU FSN = 5
MSU FSN = 24      FISU FSN = 24
```

In the case of the FISU, it is sent between signaling points during idle time, and it has no significance to the network. For this reason, there is no need to retransmit lost or damaged FISUs.

LSSU

The LSSU is responsible for communicating the current status of the signaling link to the signaling points. In normal operation, the LSSU is not sent between signaling points. It is only sent when an event occurs that affects the link's ability to transmit and receive MSUs. Similar to the FISU, the LSSU is created based on the last MSU that was transmitted on the link. For this reason, the LSSU is not retransmitted on the signaling link. The signal unit format for the LSSU is shown in Figure 2-19.

Figure 2-19 *LSSU Format*

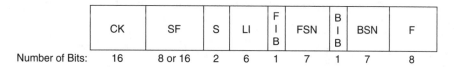

CK	SF	S	LI	F I B	FSN	B I B	BSN	F

Number of Bits: 16   8 or 16   2   6   1   7   1   7   8

CK = Check Bits   S (Spare) = Not Used
LI = Length Indicator (LI=1 or 2)   FIB = Forward Indicator Bit
FSN = Forward Sequence Number   BIB = Backward Indicator Bit
BSN = Backward Sequence Number   F = Flag
SF = Status Field

All fields within the LSSU have the same function that they do for the FISU with the exception of the LI, which is used in LSSUs, and the addition of the Status Field (SF). The LI field indicates in LSSUs whether the SF is 8 or 16 bits. LI=1 causes the SF to be 8 bits and LI=2 causes the SF to be 16 bits. If the receiving SLT cannot process a two-octet SF, the second octet is ignored and only the first octet is processed. The SF indicates what the current status of the signaling link is by using four different values and two other values to transport information about the type of proving that is used during the link alignment process:

- Status Indicator Out of Alignment (SIO)
- Status Indicator Out of Service (SIOS)
- Status Indicator Busy (SIB)
- Status Indicator Processor Outage (SIPO)
- Status Indicator Normal (SIN)
- Status Indicator Emergency (SIE)

The SIO indicates one of two things, either that the link is out of alignment because of a 1s density violation (different than the 1s density violation in T1) or that it is the beginning of the alignment process. In the first case, the SIO is sent if six consecutive 1s are detected. The transmission of six consecutive 1s, as stated earlier in the chapter, mimics a flag, and that is not allowed. You will also see the SIO at the beginning of the link alignment procedure a little later in the chapter.

A SIOS indicates that the signaling point is not able to send or receive MSUs (link down), and it is also seen when a signaling point is turned up. SIOS continues until the initial alignment phase has begun.

A SIB indicates there is congestion at the transmitting signaling point. When congestion is detected, the T5 timer (sending SIB timer) is started and SIBs are sent to the remote signaling point. When the receiving signaling point receives the LSSUs with SIB, it starts the T6 timer (remote congestion guard timer). Every LSSU after that point with SIB resets the T7 timer (excessive delay timer) until a LSSU is received without SIB. After there are no more LSSUs with SIB, the T6 timer is shut off and normal operation resumes. Figure 2-20 displays the congestion timer process by using the T5, T6, and T7 timers.

Figure 2-20   *Congestion Timer Operation*

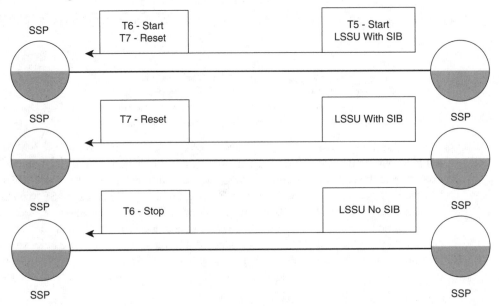

A SIPO indicates that the transmitting signaling point cannot send messages to the functional levels of 3 or 4. SIPO does not mean that all links in the link set are affected, and it is possible for MTP3 to still be functional (just not communicated with). When SIPO is indicated locally, all MSUs received are discarded and LSSUs are sent with SIPO.

NOTE   In the case that SIPO is indicated locally, Local Processor Outage (LPO) is declared on the transmitting side.

After the far end receives the LSSUs with SIPO, it terminates the transmission of MSUs and begins the transmission of FISUs, with the FSN set to the last transmitted MSU. The receiving end is in Remote Processor Outage (RPO).

As the signaling point comes out of a congested state, it notifies MTP3 and returns to an in-service state. After the link has returned to an in-service state, the MTP2 buffers are flushed of old messages. Particularly if the PO was long in duration, old messages can refer to calls that have already been rerouted or released. Furthermore, it is required that both sides of the link synchronize their messages for proper link operation.

Initial Alignment Procedure

For proper link operation to take place, link integrity must be ensured. This process is known as link alignment, and if you can't pass alignment you can't place calls through the SS7 network.

Link alignment provides a procedure for turning up a new link between signaling points and it realigns a link that has lost alignment. In the alignment process, there are two types of alignment: SIN and SIE. The difference between the two types of alignment is the amount of time required at the proving period. Refer to Table 2-2 for a complete listing of the SS7 timers and their values as they pertain to the alignment process.

Table 2-2 *SS7 Alignment Timers and Their Values*

Timer	Value	Link Type
T1	45-50s	64 kbps
Alignment Ready Timer	500-600s	4.8 kbps
T2	5-50s	Low
Not Aligned Timer	70-150s	High
T3	1-2s	N/A
Aligned Timer		
T4	T4(n) 7.5-9.5s	64 kbps
Proving Period Timer	T4(n) 100-120s	4.8 kbps
	T4 400-600ms	64 kbps
	T4 6-8s	4.8 kbps
T5	80-120ms	N/A
Sending SIB Timer		
T6	3-6s	64 kbps
Remote Congestion Guard Timer	8-12s	4.8 kbps
T7	0.5-2s	64 kbps
Excessive Delay Timer	4-6s	4.8 kbps

NOTE   The timers listed in Table 2-2 are based on ITU Q.703 and can vary based on national specifications. For example, the T4 timer can vary between 2 and 9.5 seconds.

After the type of alignment has been selected, the proving period ensures that Layer 2 is able to transmit and receive MTP3 and above traffic reliably. Integrity is verified by checking the error rate involved with the signaling link. If the proving period expires without excessive errors, the link is said to have completed link alignment. SIOS is sent in the case of the SLT being unable to send or receive MSUs for reasons other than SIPO. The following list of bulleted items describes the timers involved with the alignment process and how they are used.

- **T2 Timer**—Link state Is Not Aligned. During this timer, the link is not aligned and SIO is being sent from the transmitting SLT to the remote end. If a link failure occurs during this timer, T2 is restarted. If the timer expires without excessive errors, T2 is stopped and T3 is started.

- **T3 Timer**—Link state Is Aligned. During this timer, the SLT is aligned with the remote end and is sending and receiving SIN or SIE. The signaling link can detect and discriminate between signaling unit frames but it is not ready to send and receive upper-layer messages yet. SINs or SIEs are exchanged by the signaling points to decide which method of proving period is employed. After the exchange of SIE or SIN has occurred, T3 stops. If a link failure occurs during this timer, T3 stops and T2 is restarted.

- **T4 Timer**—Link state Is Proving. The proving period that was selected in T3 is used for the proving process. As far as the proving periods are concerned, SIE can take no more than one error and SIN can take no more than four. If excessive errors occur during T4, SIOS is sent and alignment is not possible. During this timer, if the point codes or SLCs do not match on both ends, the timer also fails and restarts T2.

- **T1 Timer**—Link state Is Aligned Ready. After the alignment procedure completes, the T1 timer (Aligned Ready Timeout) is stopped. The Aligned Ready Timeout is used to provide a window of time in which the total link alignment procedure should take place.

MSU

MTP3 is the OSI model's network layer equivalent. As stated before, the addressing is based on a point code structure, which uniquely identifies each node within the network. The MSU, found in MTP2, contains the MTP3 routing label and routes call state messages from signaling point to signaling point. Because the MSU used is signal message routing, even though it is an MTP2 message, it is discussed in this section. The MSU carries the upper-layer call control and network management messages that are used by upper-layer protocols, such as the ISDN User Part (ISUP). Figure 2-21 details the header composition of the MSU.

Figure 2-21 *MSU Format*

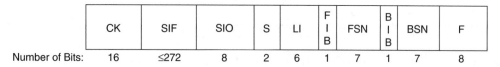

CK	SIF	SIO	S	LI	F I B	FSN	B I B	BSN	F

Number of Bits: 16 ≤272 8 2 6 1 7 1 7 8

CK = Check Bits

LI = Length Indicator

FSN = Forward Sequence Number

BSN = Backward Sequence Number

SIF = Service Information Field

S (Spare) = Not Used

FIB = Forward Indicator Bit

BIB = Backward Indicator Bit

F = Flag

SIO = Service Indicator Octet

There are a couple different fields associated with the MSU: the Service Indicator Octet (SIO) and the Service Information Field (SIF). The SIO indicates which upper-layer protocol is being used on the network. Figure 2-22 details the layout of the SIO sub-field in the MSU, and Table 2-3 details the specific field values. The SIO sub-field has several bits denoted as A, B, C, and D. These bits identify which bits are read first. The A-bit is read first, followed in order until the D-bit. ANSI T1.111 identifies the bit patterns of 1110 and 1101 as reserved for national application use.

Figure 2-22 *SIO Composition*

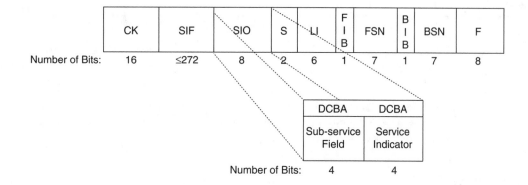

Table 2-3 *SIF Value Identification*

D	C	B	A	Value
0	0	0	0	Signaling Network Management Messages
0	0	0	1	Signaling Network Testing and Maintenance Messages
0	0	1	0	Spare
0	0	1	1	SCCP
0	1	0	0	TUP
0	1	0	1	ISUP
0	1	1	0	DUP—call and circuit related messages
0	1	1	1	DUP—facility registration and cancellation messages
1	0	0	0	Reserved for MTP Testing User Part
1	0	0	1	Broadband ISDN User Part
1	0	1	0	Satellite ISDN User Part
1	0	1	1	Spare
1	1	0	0	Spare
1	1	0	1	Spare
1	1	1	0	Spare
1	1	1	1	Spare

The Sub-service field contains the network indicator bits that identify which type of switch is being used. Although four bits are allocated to this field, only the D and C bits have values, which are shown in Table 2-4.

Table 2-4 *Sub-Service Field Value Identification*

D	C	Value
0	0	International Network
0	1	Spare (for international use)
1	0	National Network
1	1	Reserved (for national use)

You can use the value of 3 (1 and 1) in national applications that can require message priority for flow control. ANSI T1.111 specifies the use of this field for priority values of 0 through 3 only if this field does not discriminate between national and international messages. The priority codes allow for protocol-specific use of the Sub-service fields. You only use this in a closed national signaling network.

The SIF identifies an upper-layer protocol message that is used by the protocol in use, which is specified by the SIO. The format of the SIF depends on the upper-layer protocol. Some of the message types include Emergency Changeover messages, Management Inhibit messages, Traffic Restart Allowed messages, and Signaling Route Set Test messages.

The SIF length is governed by the LI in the MSU frame. Unlike the LSSU messages, the LI can have many different values. The SIF field can be up to 272 octets (272 8-bit fields), as shown in Figure 2-20. There can be up to 268 information octets, or 272, with the last four reserved for the routing label. The LI field can have a value ranging from 1–63. Values of 1–62 identify the exact number of octets that are in the SIF. A value of 63 identifies that the SIF is 63 octets or larger.

Depending on the upper-layer protocol in use, the SIF can include the routing label. The routing label identifies the SLS for the MSU, the OPC, and the DPC. For ITU networks, each point code field is 14 bits and the SLS field is 4 bits for a total of 32 bits. ANSI specifies 24 bits for the OPC and the DPC and another 8 bits for the SLS for a total of 56 bits. The SLS in the ANSI network used to be set to 5 bits but was increased to 8 bits because of scalability concerns. The format of the routing label is shown in Figure 2-23.

Figure 2-23 *MSU Routing Label*

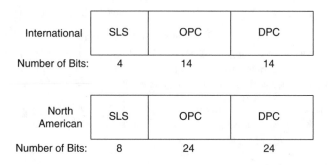

MTP3

MTP3 handles the routing of call-control signaling and network management messages through the SS7 network. MTP3 has two distinct areas of operation: signaling message handling and signaling network management. MTP3 acts as an interface for upper-layer user parts to communicate with each other. That being said, it is the responsibility of MTP3 to ensure that the messages originating from one signaling point are delivered to the same upper-layer user part at the destination signaling point.

The actual routing of the messages can take several different paths through the network. The messages can either be relayed through a mated STP pair or directly from one SSP to another. This ability is enabled by the use of the routing label. The routing label explicitly states the origination and the intended destination of the signal unit. Signaling message handling is broken down into three areas: message routing, message distribution, and message discrimination.

Message routing is the function of the SSP, STP, or SSP with STP functionality to analyze the signal unit to decide where to send the packet and which signaling link to send it out of. The receiving signaling point uses message distribution to deliver locally destined signal units to the proper user part. Message discrimination is the ability of the SSP to identify whether or not the received signal unit is destined for a circuit that is locally installed or not. If the signal unit is identified as not belonging locally, it is handed over to the message routing function.

Within the routing process there is a procedure for sharing the load, also known as load sharing traffic, among several links. Balanced load sharing helps to ensure that one link between signaling points does not get congested with too much signaling traffic. It is recommended that the number of links in a linkset be a power of two. This will allow for balanced load sharing.

Load sharing can be performed one of two ways:

- Load sharing across several links within the same link set
- Load sharing across several links that do not necessarily belong to the same link set

In the case of load sharing across link sets, it is referred to as a combined link set. In international network operation, it is required that both types of load sharing are supported.

The second main function of MTP3 is signaling network management. This accomplishes several things, including network failure recovery (through signaling traffic rerouting) and congestion control. Signaling network management also includes a methodology for rerouting traffic after the network failure has been corrected.

Message routing and network management, similar to every other function of SS7, are accomplished through the use of messages. Several different types of messaging within the network management fabric are identified:

- Signaling traffic management
- Link management
- Route management

Signaling traffic management is responsible for the management of the signaling link in the case of a failure. This means that it handles functions of signaling traffic rerouting in the case of a failure, signaling point restart after the failure is cleared, and signaling traffic back off in the case of congestion. Signaling link management is responsible for signaling link alignment of new links, signaling link restoration on corrected failures, and signaling link deactivation, if necessary. The signaling route management comprises several different functions to facilitate the transfer of network status information. This allows the SS7 network to test and block or unblock specific signaling routes and to define a set of signaling route test procedures.

Now that you have learned about the major components of the SS7 network, there are a couple of things that you need to make sure you obtain from your service provider if you ever need an SS7 link. These items absolutely must match between you and the service provider or you cannot operate properly in the SS7 network:

- Point codes—OPCs, DPCs, and any APCs that are required.
- CIC ranges—If these don't match on both ends, you cannot complete calls properly.
- SLC—Make sure that you are configuring to use the proper signaling link out of the link set.
- Glare—The procedure that will be used in the event that both sides select the same trunk at the same time for separate calls. This is also known as a *dual seizure*.

SS7 Upper-Layer Protocols

To this point, this chapter has covered much of what makes up the infrastructure of the SS7 network. It has detailed the transporting functions that allow for communication between SS7 nodes. Now take a look at what makes your calls work. Within the upper layer of the SS7 stack (Layer 4), there are several protocols that you can use for call messaging functions. DUP, TUP, National User Part (NUP), and ISUP are all used for call messaging.

DUP and TUP are legacy protocols that were used prior to the latest messaging advances created by ISUP. Although this chapter does discuss them, it is important to remember that they are not typically used within the SS7 network. However, some countries, such as China, still employ them to some degree.

DUP

DUP was first created as a standard in 1988 (Q.741) and later revised in 1993 as X.61. The main purpose of this standard is to act as the transmission vehicle for data-centric call messaging. Not intended for voice, its features include call setup, tear down, and facility registration. Because it is an upper-layer protocol in the SS7 stack, it directly interfaces with and requires help from MTP3 to route the messages from signaling point to signaling point.

Several main messages are associated with DUP connections. The messages are found in two basic types: call control and circuit management. They include but are not limited to the following:

- Call control:
  - Address Message
  - Calling Line Identity Message
  - Call Accepted Message
  - Call Rejected Message
  - Clear Message
- Circuit management:
  - Circuit State Message
  - Facility Registration and Cancellation Messages

The Address Message is sent during an initial call setup. This message identifies the originating and terminating point codes and the class of service (CoS) information. The Calling Line Identity Message can be sent as part of the Address Message, but it is normally sent after the Address Message has been received by the terminating signaling point. This message identifies the originating network information for the call that is being processed. The Call Accepted Message notifies the originating signaling point that the call has been accepted, and it can contain the destination network identity. The Call Rejected Message notifies the originating end that the call cannot be processed. This message starts a call termination and returns a cause code back to the originating signaling point. The Clear Message clears a call and releases the resources back into the available for use pool.

The Circuit State Message identifies the state of the circuit and supervises its operation for failure. Facility Registration and Cancellation Messages share information about user facilities and are not associated with any particular data call between points.

Figure 2-24 identifies the basic routing label of the DUP message format.

Figure 2-24 *DUP Routing Label*

HGFEDCBA			
TSC	BIC	OPC	DPC

Number of Bits: 8   12   14   14

The DPC is transmitted first, followed by the OPC, Bearer Identification Code (BIC), and the Time Slot Code (TSC). The BIC identifies the actual DS0 that the call is on. The TSC is used in cases where the circuit is multiplexed, in conjunction with the BIC. The TSC also identifies the speed of the channel (for example: 64 kbps equals 01110000).

TUP

TUP is an upper-layer protocol that completes voice call control. TUP is a legacy protocol and it is no longer widely used throughout the world. Because there are countries around the world that still use TUP, its support is essential. TUP does not specify control for anything other than analog circuits, and therefore, must be used with another protocol such as DUP for digital circuit control.

As the predecessor to ISUP, TUP provided call setup, tear down, and access to service interfaces. TUP also provides support for circuit verification, also called Continuity Tests (COTs). This allows communicating signaling points to validate each circuit between them to ensure that they are capable of carrying a voice call. One main problem was described with TUP—its lack of support for ISDN.

As you can imagine, there are several call setup and tear down messages. This section focuses only on a subset of these message types. A couple of message groups exist within this standard:

- Forward Address Message Group:
    - Initial Address Message (IAM)
    - Subsequent Address Message
- Forward Setup Message Group:
    - General Forward Setup Information Message
    - Continuity Check Messages
- Backward Setup Request Message Group:
    - General Request Message
- Successful Backward Setup Request Message Group:
    - Address Complete Message (ACM)
    - Charging Message
- Unsuccessful Backward Setup Request Message Group:
    - Simple Unsuccessful Backward Setup Information Message

The IAM identifies the information for each call, including the DPC, OPC, and CIC. The IAM can also be sent with additional information that identifies any services that should be charged on the call. Figure 2-25 shows the composition of the TUP routing label.

Figure 2-25 *TUP Routing Label*

CIC	OPC	DPC
12	14	14

Number of Bits:

The CIC identifies where the call is transmitted between SSPs. This is the identification of the bearer path. Looking at Figure 2-26, it is important to realize that CICs do not equal a specific DS0 on a synchronous medium. CIC #15 can possibly equal TS22 on an E1. For this reason, it is imperative that each signaling point agrees on which CIC equals which timeslot. Also, CICs change from one hop to the next, so it is also important to keep track of which call leg is using which CIC. For instance, the second leg of a call can use a different CIC, similar to CIC #3 (TS12). If Figure 2-26 does not make sense, remember that calls are routed through the SS7 network one hop at a time.

Figure 2-26 *Call Leg CIC Assignments*

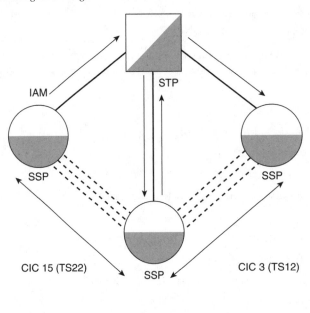

The Subsequent Address Message can send any remaining digits through the network, as either a single message or multiple independent messages. Calls can be routed through the network by using digit analysis prior to the reception of all the dialed digits. This function allows call setup speed to increase. Another function of the Subsequent Address Message also uses the call routing prior to the collection of all the dialed digits. In the instance of variable length dial plans (as found in Germany), Subsequent Address Messages allow the originating switch to route the call as soon as enough digits are received to resolve the next hop. If the destination switch requires more digits to route the call, the destination waits until it receives enough Subsequent Address Messages to route the call.

The General Forward Setup Information Message is sent in response to a General Request Message. It can include several items required for call setup, including the calling party information. COT Messages validate the integrity of the circuit path (speech path). COT tests are necessary because the signaling network takes a separate path than the bearer service. Normally, COT is set to something around 10 percent (1 in every 10 calls gets COT), unless it is a satellite link, in which case it might be necessary for every call setup. COT is a maintenance tone that is transmitted in a loop through the bearer path to make sure that it is received in the same state.

The ACM informs the calling party that the called number has been located and that the resources are being verified and alerted. In typical operation, you can see this as the response to the IAM after the call has been routed to its final destination. The Charging Message sends billing information through the network in reverse direction.

The Simple Unsuccessful Backward Setup Information Message communicates, in a backward direction, the reason for the call failure back to the originating signaling point.

NUP and BT-NUP were created to add to the functionality of TUP, by providing integrated support for ISDN within the call setup procedures. These protocols are similar to TUP, so they are not discussed in detail. A formalized protocol was developed several years later, with ISDN built into the fabric for call setup and tear down. This protocol is ISUP.

ISUP

The ITU's answer to the shortcomings of TUP was the creation of ISUP. ISUP is the most widely used protocol for call setup transport worldwide, and it is designed to provide call management and access to services for both voice and data calls. ISUP has been designed as an extensible protocol suite that can be modified as needed by different country requirements. For example, say that Country A specifically needs a field for a proprietary billing system. The extensible nature of this protocol allows them to create that field so that all switches in Country A can understand it. For these reasons, you can see that just about every country has their own ISUP variant. It is important to know what ISUP variant you are communicating with at your switch and plan accordingly.

ISUP, similar to all other upper-layer protocols, uses the services from MTP (discussed earlier) to exchange messages between signaling points. Routing of ISUP messages is accomplished by using point codes and a SLS at MTP2 with a MSU routing label and point codes and CICs in the ISUP IAM messages. One thing that has not yet been discussed is the use of the E.164 numbers. These E.164 numbers are what you recognize as a phone number, and Figure 2-27 shows the different portions of the number. E.164 numbers assist with the call routing in SSPs as they do a digit analysis to determine the intended destination of the call. Number analysis is outside the scope of this chapter.

Figure 2-27 *E.164 Number Configuration*

E.164 Number

CC = Country Code
NDC = National Destination Code
SN = Subscriber Number

Example: 65-XXXX-XXXX (Singapore)
Example: 81-X-YYYY-ZZZZ (Tokyo)
Example: 1-XXX_YYY_ZZZZ (United States – North American Numbering Plan)

Basically, these numbers are split up into groups that are based on geographic regions, and within these regions each exchange has a specific number of nodes local to it. They are split up in a similar way to that of point codes. Instead of Network.Cluster.Member (U.S.) or SANC.SPID (ITU), it is formatted as a country code, national destination code, and subscriber number. The U.S. uses the North American Numbering Plan (NANP), which is a combination of the numbering plan area (NPA), numbering exchange (NXX), and station code (four digit code). E.164 number composition varies from country to country, dependent on how the numbering scheme has been developed.

Another major difference between ISUP and TUP is the fact that ISUP uses en bloc signaling. En bloc signaling sends all the dialed digits during the initial setup phase, instead of just a few digits followed by one or more subsequent address messages. However, it is important to point out that ISUP can also support overlap signaling, although it is not as common when ISUP is used. TUP uses overlap signaling. Although most switches now use the en bloc signaling method, it is still possible to use overlap signaling if necessary.

There are two signaling methods that you can use with ISUP: link-by-link or end-to-end. Link-by-link signaling is used when the messages need to be processed by each signaling point within the signal path. An example of this type of message is an IAM. Each SSP has to receive the IAM, complete digit analysis to decide if the call is local, and if not, reformat the routing label for the next hop transport. End-to-end signaling is used for a specific type of application request between the originating and destination signaling points. An example of this is SCCP transport for an application request with TCAP.

ISUP provides about 100 messages, and this section only focuses on a small subset of them. The message types are IAM, ACM, Call Progress (CPG), Answer Message (ANM), Release (REL), and Release Complete (RLC). Figure 2-28 shows the ANSI and ITU formats for an IAM.

Figure 2-28 *IAM Composition*

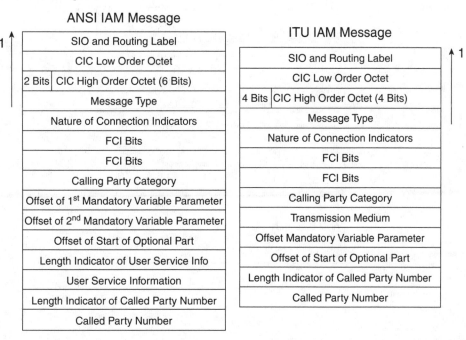

The IAM and the ACM are used in the same manner as with other protocols, such as TUP. The CPG notifies the originating signaling point that the call is being forwarded through the network. Although this can be transmitted as a separate message type, the CPG is typically part of the ACM. The ANM identifies when the called party answers the call that is being sent to them. The CPG, ACM, and ANM are all messages that are sent in the backwards direction. The REL notifies the other end of the call that the call is being torn down. After a REL is sent, the transmitting SSP does not need to wait for a RLC before it releases the circuit because the call has already terminated. On the receiving end, the remote SSP sends a RLC in acknowledgment of the REL message. Refer to Figure 2-29 and Figure 2-30 for an overview of a basic call setup and teardown procedure.

Figure 2-29 *Basic ISUP Call Setup Flow*

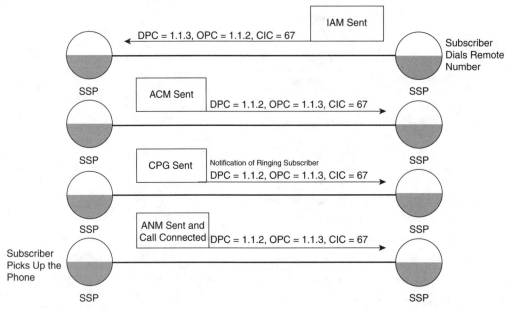

Figure 2-30 *Basic ISUP Call Teardown Flow*

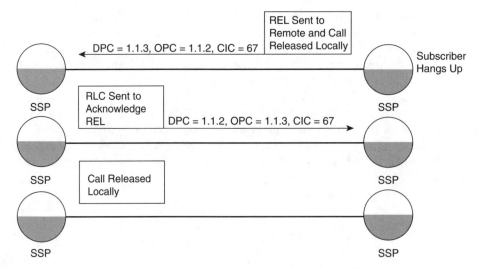

Intelligent Network (IN)

The purpose of the IN infrastructure is to provide a suite of services to subscribers that are inherently not provided by the SS7 network. This list also includes services that are provided to the network operator.

A distributed service architecture allows service providers to support a wider range of services and to deploy them to a larger subscriber base. Without this architecture, subscribers are limited to the services that their SSP was able to provide. These services can be erratic offerings, and the cost of scaling is high. IN created a model that allowed for the delivery of services and call routing assistance in a distributed manner.

The development of an IN infrastructure was a difficult task by itself. A set of standards had to be created that remained vendor independent and that allowed different vendors to interoperate with the same IN equipment. These standards also had to allow changes to the vendor equipment without interrupting the subscriber services.

Finally, these services had to be network infrastructure independent to allow providers flexibility in managing their own network.

The bulk of the requests for network services are made through TCAP queries. The use of TCAP allows network devices to request and receive information such as toll free number lookup, Caller ID Deluxe, and LNP. Caller ID Deluxe transports the calling party's number and the name that it is registered to under normal circumstances.

Several components make up the IN network core. These components consist of Physical Entities (PEs) and Functional Entities (FEs). Each PE can provide one or more FEs.

FEs

FEs are specific tasks that PEs carry out. FEs can be grouped within one PE or distributed across several PEs. In other words, two different FEs can be carried out by the same SSP or they can be distributed across two separate SSPs (one each). However, you can't distribute one FE across multiple SSPs. You can offer redundant FE instances, which are distributed over several PEs throughout the IN network. Some of the more common FEs are the following:

- **Service Switching Function/Call Control Function (SSF/CCF)** — This definition is actually two separate functions, and they are normally used in conjunction with one another. The SSF is the interface in which the CCF communicates with the Service Control Function (SCF). Without this interface, the CCF cannot be controlled by the SCF, and services are not possible. The CCF is the physical call control, as handled by devices such as SSPs.

- **Call Control Agent Function (CCAF)** — The CCAF allows subscriber access into the service network. The CCAF provides the interface in which subscribers can access each service.

- **Service Control Function (SCF)**—The SCF controls the service logic and the internal service processing. The SCF is the actual internal operation of the service.

- **Service Data Function (SDF)**—Each service has its own set of data. The SDF provides access to this data for the SCF. For instance, access into the database that holds the toll free number lookup.

- **Special Resource Function (SRF)**—The SRF handles a set of functions that are required for subscriber interaction with services. Services include DTMF digit collection, voice recognition, and Interactive Voice Response (IVR) services.

- **Service Management Function (SMF)**—SMF provides the control framework for the service creation, deployment, and management. The SMAF and SCEF interface directly with the SMF.

- **Service Management Access Function (SMAF)**—The SMAF provides the logical viewing window to the SMF.

- **Service Creation Environment Function (SCEF)**—The SCEF provides the ability to create, test, and set up services into the SMF. Products of the SCEF are the service logic and data templates.

PEs

Several of the PEs (SCP and SSP) have been discussed earlier in this chapter. PEs are actual devices that carry out the programmed functions to provide the stated service. Although they have different definitions, some of the following PEs can be combined within the same physical unit:

- **SSP**—SSPs are responsible for call management and call processing and for routing calls through the network to the proper destination. In the case of IN, SSPs are responsible for identifying which calls require service interface and providing that interface to the subscriber.

- **SSCP**—The SSCP combines the SSP and SCP functionality into one piece of equipment. Access to the services is faster, but communication protocols and methods with other devices will not change.

- **SCP**—SCPs provide specific services to the end customers. SCPs are typically deployed off a mated pair of STPs in North America and off of SSPs with the integrated STP functionality internationally. Moreover, they contain the Service Logic Programs (SLPs) and the required data to provide the individual services to the subscriber. Multiple SCPs deployed in a region with the same SLPs can be used for load balancing the service traffic.

- **Network Access Point (NAP)**—NAPs provide CCF and CCAF functions within the IN infrastructure. NAPs do not have any direct access to SCPs, but they can identify calls that are destined for services. In such cases, the NAP must route the call to a SSP with SCP access.

- **Adjunct (AD)**—This device functions much the same as a SCP, but it is directly connected to a SSP over a high-speed link. ADs can provide faster communication with SSPs, but the actual messaging remains the same as in SSP to SCP communication.

- **Intelligent Peripheral (IP)**—The IP contains the SRF discussed above. This device is responsible for DTMF digit collection, voice recognition, and IVR services.

- **Service Node (SN)**—SNs control IN service interaction with subscribers and can act as a AD, IP, or SSP at the same time. Usually deployed near several SSPs to provide multiple services at the same time.

- **Service Data Point (SDP)**—The SDP handles the customer data and contains the SDF. When a service is called upon that requires data, the SDP is accessed.

The relation between FEs and PEs can be seen in Figure 2-31.

Figure 2-31 *Relationship Between FEs and PEs in the IN*

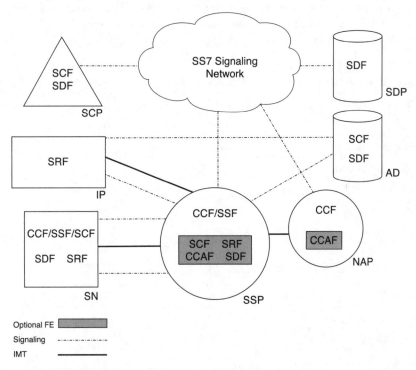

IN has been developed as a set of tiered deployment stages that allow for backward compatibility between legacy technology and the extensibility to create and modify services as needed. It is important that these services are deployed seamlessly to the subscriber. In an effort to ease this difficult procedure, IN was designed as three separate capability sets (CS-1, CS-2, and CS-3). These capability sets have been deployed in succession over the core IN network.

Capability Set 1 (CS-1)

CS-1 is the first capability set that was used with the IN architecture. It was designed to support all developing IN services and to set the framework for compatibility of future service offerings. CS-1 also takes into account that there are proprietary services that do not necessarily go through ITU-T's process for standardization. The CS-1 standard describes two different types of services: Type A and Type B.

Type A service is what is known as a single-ended service. In other words, if the service is started at one end of the connection, the service only affects that end of the connection. The remote end of the connection can also call upon the same service, at the remote end, and it acts upon it independently. All other types of services are referred to as Type B and are not used because of operational and deployment complexity. These types of services are difficult because many of them require shared call control between the switch and external network devices. Table 2-5 lists a subset of the services supported by CS-1.

Table 2-5 *Subset of CS-1 Service Support*

Service Name	Service Code	Fully Supported in CS-1
Abbreviated Dialing	ABD	Yes
Attendant	ATT	Yes
Authentication	AUTC	Yes
Authorization Code	AUTZ	Yes
Automatic Call Back	ACB	No
Call Distribution	CD	Yes
Call Forwarding	CF	Yes
Call Transfer	TRA	No
Call Waiting	CW	No
Customized Recorded Announcement	CRA	Yes
Multiway Calling	MWC	Yes
Originating Call Screening	OCS	Yes
Reverse Charging	REVC	Yes

The CS-1 of IN follows a specific method for call service control and handling. For the most part, these steps remain the same from call to call:

1   A call comes into the network structure with the proper dialed digit pattern or off hook indication. The CCF recognizes CS-1 functions even though it is not aware of how to process the IN functions directly. The call is passed on to the SSF.

2   As shown in Figure 2-31, the CCF and SSF are, in most cases, woven into the same IN device. The SSF function analyzes the incoming call to make a decision based on which service is being requested by the subscriber. After this decision has been made, a TCAP query is formulated to the SCF.

3   The SCF receives the query, makes a decision on which service is being requested, and returns a response to the SSF. This response can include service logic for translations, a prompt for digit collection, or a query to a remote SDF.

4   After the SSF receives this response, it instructs the CCF on how it should route the call to the selected service.

Capability Set 2 (CS-2)

CS-2 expands on the types and complexity of services that CS-1 might not have been able to provide completely. Both CS-1 and CS-2 are subsets of the complete IN architecture. CS-2 provides several types of services, including Telecommunication Services, Service Management Services, and Service Creation Services. Service Management Services and Service Creation Services are new service types with the advent of CS-2. Table 2-6 lists a subset of the additional services added by CS-2.

Table 2-6   *Subset of Additional CS-2 Service Support*

Telecommunication Services		
Service Name	**Service Code**	**Fully Supported in CS-2**
Internetwork Freephone	IFPH	Yes
Internetwork Premium Rate	IPRM	Yes
Conference Calling	CONF	Yes
International Telecommunication Charge Card	ITCC	No
Originating and Terminating Carrier Identification	OCI/OTC	No
Blocking/Unblocking of Incoming Calls	BUIC	No
Emergency Calls in Wireless	ECW	No
Charge Card Validation	CCV	Yes

continues

Table 2-6 *Subset of Additional CS-2 Service Support (Continued)*

User Service Interaction	USI	Yes

Service Management Services

Service Name	Service Code	Fully Supported in CS-2
Telecommunications Service Customization	TSC	Yes
Service Control Customization	SCC	Yes
Subscriber Service Activation Deactivation	SSAD	Yes
Subscriber Profile Management	SPM	Yes
Subscriber Service Limiter	SSL	Yes
Billing Report	BR	Yes
Subscriber Traffic Monitoring	STM	Yes

Service Creation Services

Service Name	Service Code	Fully Supported in CS-2
Feature Interaction Detection	N/A	Yes
Cross-Service Feature Interaction Detection	N/A	Yes
Creation Initiation	N/A	Yes
Editing	N/A	Yes
Data Rule Generation	N/A	Yes
Data Rule Distribution	N/A	Yes

Although the new services in CS-2 add a lot more flexibility and manageability to IN, the call flow is still handled the same way as in CS-1. The lists of services in Table 2-6 by no means are exhaustive, as there are many more services that are currently offered. More are created and modified on a monthly basis to provide better services to the subscriber base. Several of the more commonly used services were mentioned earlier: toll free number lookup, Caller ID Deluxe, and LNP.

Toll free number lookup occurs on a daily basis, and chances are that hardly anyone realizes that there is service interaction involved with it. In fact, most people think that the 800 number they dial is the actual number that they are ringing. This is simply not the case. For all of the 800 numbers, there are sets of databases (usually SCPs) that have records of all the issued 800 numbers and their corresponding telephone numbers. When the proper number is dialed, say 800-555-1212, a TCAP query is issued to find out what the actual number is that the call should terminate to. The number is returned back to the inquiring SSP, and the call is routed through.

This first service is largely deployed in North America, but national specific deployments of it do exist elsewhere. In Australia there are 800 numbers and 13 numbers, both of which require translation. In essence, you don't have to use 800 numbers to provide this type of service (ToS).

Normal caller ID passes the calling party's phone number on to the called party for identification. The user can then decide whether or not to pick up the call. Caller ID Deluxe provides not only the calling party's number, but their directory information. So, instead of 919-555-1212, you receive Brad Dunsmore 919-555-1212.

The last service that this section covers is LNP. LNP makes sure that if you move, your phone number moves with you. So, if I live on the east side of Atlanta, and I move to the west side of Atlanta, LNP ensures that my phone number is ported to the exchange of my new residence.

Expert Whiteboard: LNP Operation in North America

The Telecommunications Act of 1996, which became law on February 8, 1996, was designed in large part to open local exchange markets to competition by removing existing statutory, regulatory, and operational barriers that have thwarted the ability of new entrants to provide competitive, local telecommunications services in the U.S. One of the most significant steps that Congress took to effectuate this goal was to require all local exchange carriers (LECs), both incumbents and new entrants, to provide number portability in accordance with requirements prescribed by the Commission. The 1996 Act defines "number portability" as "the ability of users of telecommunications services to retain, at the same location, existing telecommunications numbers without impairment of quality, reliability, or convenience when switching from one telecommunications carrier to another." Number portability is essential to meaningful, facilities-based competition in the provision of local exchange service because survey data show that customers are reluctant to switch carriers if they must change telephone numbers.[1]

Without number portability, customers ordinarily cannot change their local telephone companies unless they change telephone numbers. If a customer changes local telephone companies and receives service at the same location from a different telephone company that is providing service from a different switch, the customer's new local telephone company typically must assign the customer a new seven-digit number (NXX code plus line number) associated with the new switch and new telephone line.[2]

There are three different categories of number portability:

- Service Provider Portability
- Location Portability
- Services Portability

Service Provider Portability

The FCC First Report and Order (96-286) required all LECs to begin a phased deployment of service provider LNP in the 100 largest Metropolitan Statistical Areas (MSAs) no later than October 1, 1997, and to complete deployment in those MSAs by December 31, 1998. Service provider portability allows subscribers to keep their existing telephone number (for incoming calls, outgoing caller identification, and billing) when changing to a different telephone company. At this time, service provider portability is the only method that has been mandated by the FCC.

By June 30, 1999, all cellular, broadband PCS, and covered SMR providers must provide a long-term database method for number portability in switches for which another carrier has made a specific request (by September 30, 1998) for provision of number portability.[3]

The components that make up an LNP-capable network include the following:

- SSP—Generates LNP queries
- STP—Performs Global Title Translation (GTT) to route the queries
- SCP—Contains the LNP database, where queries are sent
- Service Management System (SMS)—Updates the SCP database with location routing numbers (LRNs)
- Number Portability Administration Center (NPAC) connectivity

Long-term number portability has been implemented through LRN architecture. Under LRN architecture, each switch is assigned a unique 10-digit LRN. The first six digits identify the location of that switch (typically NPA-NXX), followed by four digits that are unique. When a number is ported, each customer's telephone number is matched in a regional database with the LRN for the switch that currently serves that telephone number. Each LNP database serves an area that corresponds to one of the original Regional Bell Operating Company (RBOC) service territories.

LNP administrators (LNPAs), which are neutral third parties, administer the regional LNP databases. The telecommunications carriers within each particular region have formed a limited liability corporation (LLC) to negotiate service contracts with the LNPA for that region, and additional telecommunications carriers can join an LLC at any time. The North American Numbering Commission (NANC) recommended that a NPAC database be established for each of the seven original RBOC regions. The commission also adopted the NANC's recommendation that the administrative functions of the LNPAs include all management tasks required to run the regional databases. The Mid-Atlantic, Mid-West, Northeast, and Southwest LLCs each separately endorsed Lockheed-Martin IMS to administer the LNP databases. The Southeast, Western, and West Coast LLCs each separately endorsed Perot Systems, Inc., The LLCs for the Southeast, Western, and West Coast regions have since reported that performance problems prompted them to terminate their contracts with Perot in favor of Lockheed.

When a customer changes from one LEC to another, the recipient switch ports the customer's number from the donor switch by uploading the customer's telephone number to the administrator of the relevant regional LNP database. This associates the customer's original telephone number with the LRN for the new carrier's switch, which allows the customer to retain the original telephone number. The regional database administrators then electronically transmit (download) LRN updates to carrier-operated local service management systems (LSMSs). Each carrier then distributes this information that the carrier uses for providing number portability. Downloading of LNP/LRNs to the individual companies is accomplished by the NPAC interacting with the local SMS, which updates the appropriate SCPs.

For a carrier to route an interswitch telephone call to a location where number portability is available, the carrier must determine the LRN for the switch that serves the terminating telephone number of the call. After number portability is available for a given NXX, all interswitch calls to that NXX must be queried to determine whether the terminating customer has ported the telephone number. This is accomplished by sending an LNP query to the STPs that are performing GTTs for the dialed digits. This STP pair then passes the query to the appropriate subsystem on the SCP to retrieve the LRN associated with the called telephone number.

The industry has proposed, and the commission has endorsed, an N minus one (N–1) querying protocol. Under this protocol, the N–1 carrier is responsible for the query, "where 'N' is the entity terminating the call to the end user, or a network provider contracted by the entity to provide tandem access." Thus the N–1 carrier (for example, the last carrier before the terminating carrier) for a local call is usually the calling customer's local service provider; the N–1 carrier for an inter-exchange call is usually the calling customer's inter-exchange carrier (IXC). An N–1 carrier can perform its own querying, or it can arrange for other carriers or third parties to provide querying services on its behalf.[2]

To route a local call, the originating local service provider examines the seven-digit number that its customer dialed, for example, 555-2222. If the called telephone number is on the originating switch (for example, an intraswitch call), the originating local service provider simply completes the call. If the call is interswitch, the originating local service provider compares the NXX, 555, with its table of NXXs for which number portability is available. If 555 is not such an NXX, the originating local service provider treats the call the same as it did before the existence of number portability. If it is an NXX for which portability is available, the originating local service provider adds the NPA, for example "708," to the dialed number and query (708) 555-2222 to an SCP containing the LRNs downloaded from the relevant regional database. The SCP returns the LRN for (708) 555-2222 (which is typically (708) 555-0000 or (708) 555-9999) and uses the LRN to route the call to the appropriate switch with an SS7 IAM message that indicates that a query has been performed. The terminating switch then completes the call. To route an inter-exchange call, the originating local service provider hands the call off to the IXC and the IXC undertakes the same procedure. An example of this is shown in Figure 2-32. It represents a typical LRN call flow.

Figure 2-32 *Originating Switch LNP Processing Direct to Recipient Switch*

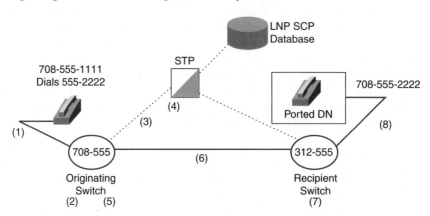

NOTE   For additional call flows see the "Generic Switching and Signaling Requirements for
Number Portability" from the Telcorida document.

Scenario: LNP Call Flow

End user A 708-555-1111) dials end user B (708-555-2222). Assume that end user B
(708-555-2222) ports their number to a different LSP. End user A's local service provider
can be connected through a direct connection to end user B's LSP if this is an intralocal
access and transport area (LATA) call. See the following steps for a detailed description of
LNP LRN.

1 Caller dials 555-2222.

2 The originating switch performs digit analysis on the dialed digits to determine how
to route the call. The originating switch determines that end user B is in a portable
NPA-NXX (708-555) and that end user B does not reside on the originating switch.

3 The originating switch sends an AIN (Info_Analyzed) query based on the dialed digits
to the LNP SCP.

4 The LNP SCP sends an AIN (Analyze_Route) response that contains the LRN (312-
979-XXXX) of the recipient switch.

5 The originating switch receives the LNP SCP response and analyzes the data. The
LRN is translated in the LNP routing tables and an ISUP route from the originating
switch to the recipient switch is determined. The LRN is stored in the Called Party
(CdPN) parameter and the dialed digits are stored in the Generic Address Parameter
(GAP) of the ISUP IAM. The Forward Call Indicator (FCI) is set to indicate a query
has been performed (bit M=1 of the FCI).

6 The call is routed from the originating switch to the recipient switch based on the LRN.

7 The recipient switch receives and processes the contents of the IAM message. The switch determines that an LRN is received and that it is its own LRN. The switch replaces the CdPN parameter's contents with the dialed digits stored in the GAP parameter. The switch does digit analysis on the dialed digits and finds the end user on the switch.

8 The recipient switch completes the call from End user A to End user B.

Location Portability

Location portability is basically geographic portability when a subscriber moves from one LEC's territory to another LEC's territory. With location portability comes the possibility of loss of NPA-NXX geographic recognition. Today an NPA-NXX distinguishes where a call originates. For example, area code 303 is for Denver, Colorado. If location portability was being used and a subscriber moved from Denver, Colorado to Atlanta, Georgia, when the subscriber made calls the receiving customer might think the call was coming from Colorado. This might not seem like a big deal, but it raises rate center and billing concerns. For example, what if your old next-door neighbors in Denver didn't know that you had moved. They pick up the phone and dial your 303-NXX-XXXX and your phone rings at your new house in Atlanta. It is a long distance call, but your neighbors thought they were dialing across the street; who pays for that call? Then add in alternate billing services such as collect calling, third number billing, and so on, and the complexity keeps growing.

Services Portability

The FCC defines the concept of service portability as the ability of a subscriber to change their ToS while retaining their existing telephone number. An example of this is migration from POTS service to ISDN. In this case, the customer is not changing service providers, but rather, changing their CoS or ToS.

References

Following are the references for the whiteboard:

- [1]FCC 2nd Report and Order (97-289) issued 8/14/97

  www.fcc.gov/Bureaus/Common_Carrier/Orders/1997/fcc97289.txt

- [2]FCC 3rd Report and Order (98-082) issued 5/12/98

  www.fcc.gov/Bureaus/Common_Carrier/Orders/1998/fcc98082.txt

- [3]Primer for Local Number Portability

  www.ported.com/midlnp.html

- FCC 1st Report and Order (96-286) issued 7/2/96

  www.fcc.gov/Bureaus/Common_Carrier/Orders/1996/fcc96286.txt

- FCC 1st Reconsideration Order (97-74) issued 3/11/97

  www.fcc.gov/Bureaus/Common_Carrier/Orders/1997/fcc97074.txt

Capability Set 3 (CS-3)

CS-3 is the newest set of features to be added to the IN infrastructure. CS-3 is the next generation of IN functionality that builds upon what is already in place from CS-1 and CS-2 in the service provider network. Some of the services that are added with CS-3 are the following:

- Feature interworking—Features can now interoperate with one another, which allows for multiple simultaneous services to be deployed to the subscriber at one time or over one call.

- Number portability—Number portability is not deployed and active throughout the service provider network in many different countries.

- Enhanced services for Narrowband Mobile Networks.

- Enhanced services for Broadband Mobile Networks.

- Support for IP-Based Network Interworking.

- Support for Broadband ISDN (B-ISDN).

- Support for Technology Transparency.

Summary

Signaling is a function that is required to facilitate call control and management. There are two different types of signaling: CAS and CCS. CAS is the older, less efficient way of call control. Found in technology such as T1, the main identifying characteristic is that the signaling is woven into the data stream. CCS is out-of-band signaling, which means that it is not intrusive to the data. ISDN PRI is physically in-band but logically out-of-band because a separate DS0 is used for signaling. For this reason, ISDN is considered CCS.

SS7 is used in almost every country in the world and is used for the set up and teardown of calls and for the management of the switched network infrastructure. There are three main components in the SS7 infrastructure: the SSP, STP, and SCP. SSPs are switches that are responsible for routing calls through the network, accessing services when required, and managing all phases of call control. SSPs connect into the signaling network and the bearer network. SSPs are interconnected with high-bandwidth links that are known as IMTs. STPs aren't much more than packet switches for signaling, whose purpose is to switch call signaling through the network at a high rate of speed, which is based on their configured routing table. STPs only interface with the signaling network and aren't concerned with the actual call path. SCPs, along with other IN equipment, provide services to subscribers otherwise unavailable in the SS7 network.

There are three main signaling types that are used in CCS environments: fully-associated, quasi-associated, and non-associated. Fully-associated is used when the signaling and data take the same physical path but are separated logically, as with ISDN PRI. Quasi-associated signaling is used in instances of STPs communicating with multiple SSPs; the signaling is never more than one hop away from the bearer traffic. Non-associated signaling is used when there is communication on the signaling path between different mated pairs of STPs. Whenever possible, quasi-associated signaling is desired.

Signaling links are physical links between signaling points within the SS7 network. Up to 16 links can be combined (0 through 15) to form a link set. Load sharing can be accomplished across links within the same link set or of differing link sets. In the case of load sharing across link sets, it is referred to as a combined link set.

Point codes route traffic through the SS7 network from the origination to the destination. There are three main classes of point codes: OPC, DPC, and APC. The OPC is the origination of the call, and the DPC is the destination. An APC is something like a pair of STPs connected to a SSP. Point codes are the IP addresses of the SS7 network, and they differ in format between ANSI, which is used in the U.S., and ITU, which is used everywhere else. The ANSI point code is made up of three 8-bit octets, and the ITU point code is made up of a 3-bit field, an 8-bit field, and a 3-bit field. The first and second fields combine to form what is called the SANC. Remember that there are exceptions to these rules. China uses a 24-bit point code and Japan uses a 16-bit point code.

The SS7 model has four different layers as it relates to the ISO OSI model. The first three layers are the MTP Layers 1, 2, and 3, which roughly correlate to the first three layers of the OSI model. The models do not directly match up because the SS7 model was in place prior to 1984 (the year of the creation of the OSI model). The last layer is actually a combination of all upper layers and all upper-layer protocol operations, such as ISUP, TUP, and TCAP, all of which take place at that layer. MTP1 is responsible for the electrical and physical characteristics of the signaling link. MTP2 is responsible for the reliable transmission of MTP3 traffic, and ensuring link integrity. MTP3 is responsible for routing the proper upper-layer call messages through the network from signaling point to signaling point.

There are many upper-layer protocols, but the one most commonly used today is the ISUP. ISUP builds on some of the shortcomings of TUP by adding support for ISDN, and it efficiently handles call control and circuit management. Some of the messages that are used by ISUP are the IAM, ACM, ANM, REL, and RLC. These messages are used in basic call setup and tear down.

IN is a set of standards that describe the framework for a host of services to be provided to the subscriber. It is designed to offer an infrastructure to support services not available in the common SS7 network and to provide a distributed and extensible way of doing so. The IN is split into three main capability sets: CS-1, CS-2, and CS-3. CS-1 and CS-2 provide a host of services to the user. CS-2 takes it a bit further with management and service creation services. Of these services, several of the more commonly deployed are Caller ID Deluxe, 800 Number Lookup, and LNP. CS-3 adds several functions to the IN infrastructure, including IP-based network interaction, support from B-ISDN, and support for network technology transparency.

Review Questions

Give or select the best answer or answers to the following questions. The answers to these questions can be found in Appendix A, "Answers to Review Questions."

1 What is the main difference between CAS and CCS Signaling?

   a CAS is logically in-band but physically out-of-band.

   b CCS isn't intrusive to the data, and it is considered in-band.

   c CAS is considered in-band signaling, and it is intrusive to the data.

   d There is no difference between them.

2 What are the three main SS7 network nodes that were discussed in this chapter?

   _____

   _____

   _____

3 Which geographic region does the U.S. fall under in the ITU point code structure?

   a 1

   b 4

   c 5

   d 3

   e None of the above. ANSI point codes are used.

4 What is the purpose of a C-link?

   a It connects a SSP to a SSP.

   b It connects mated pairs of STPs.

   c It connects devices in different levels of the hierarchy.

   d It connects a SSP to something similar to a STP.

5 Which of the following timers have to do with congestion?

   a T2

   b T6

   c T3

   d T5

   e T4

6 Which layer in the SS7 stack do point codes operate at?

   a MTP1

   b MTP4

   c MTP2

   d MTP3

7 What does the following icon stand for?

   a SSP and STP

   b STP

   c SRF

   d SSP

   e NAP

8 What is the recommended percentage of traffic that you should configure a signaling link to carry?

_____

_____

_____

9 Identify the device that the following definition is discussing: This device functions much the same as a SCP, but it is directly connected to a SSP over a high-speed link. They can provide faster communication with SSPs, but the actual messaging remains the same as is used with SSP to SCP communication.

a NAP

b AD

c IP

d STP

10 What is one thing you should check if your alignment is failing at the T4 proving timer?

_____

_____

_____

This chapter covers the following topics:

- **Understanding digital communication**—When attempting to delve into the details of how analog signals become digital, it is helpful to understand the history and motivation behind the move to the digital transmission of analog signals. It is also important to be clear on the advantages that digital transmission has over analog transmission.

- **The signal conversion process**—Details on the process of converting an analog signal into a digital bit stream. The four phases of the process are explained in straightforward terms, while the entire flow of events is rendered in explicit detail.

- **Variations on the pulse code modulation (PCM) theme**—After a firm understanding of the basics of PCM is well in hand, this discussion serves to offer alternatives to the standard PCM technique. These additional techniques are presented in terms with which you are already comfortable.

CHAPTER 3

Analog-to-Digital Conversion

Understanding Digital Communication

Digital communication is the transmission of information by discrete pulses of electricity or light impulses. The simplicity in digital communication belies its vast power. Often, you can get away with paying attention only to whether a pulse exists in a particular moment of time. Contrast this with the need to monitor every infinite change in signal strength to correctly duplicate a waveform, as in the case of analog communication.

In digital communication, you need concern yourself only with on or off, yes or no, true or false. Only two states exist, which greatly simplifies the information that needs to be transmitted across a communications medium. This alone greatly improves the quality of what you transmit, by eliminating endless "shades of gray" and concentrating only on "black and white."

Motivation for Digital Communication

Just imagine being tasked with the chore of recognizing every shade of gray possible. This presents, literally, an infinite number of possibilities. Contrast this with having to recognize only black and white (see Figure 3-1). All of a sudden, the job gets a lot easier. Furthermore, the chance of committing an error in recognition diminishes, as does the possibility of, for example, a little dust introducing some form of recognition difficulty. Dingy white is still white, and faded black is still black, as long as black and white are the only two choices. As you will see shortly, this reduction in the possibility of error and this loose tolerance for recognition are also benefits of digital communication.

Figure 3-1   *Shades of Gray Analogy*

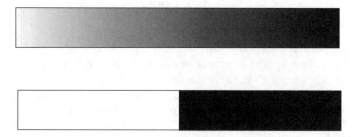

With this analogy in mind, consider that the main impetus for the development of digital communication was the need for a better way to store musical information, with fewer errors and more quality. In the 1920s, for example, music had to be stored as analog waveforms etched in wax, which could then be read only a limited number of times.

Evolution of Digital Communication

The idea was that analog information could be represented as distinct pulses of information, like Morse code, where only a few simple combinations are combined to represent a larger, more complex set of symbols. After conversion, analog information is stored and retrieved with more accuracy and quality than by directly recording analog information. The idea arose early on to use a bi-state mechanism as the combining element for digital communication. This was the dawn of what is now known as binary digital communication, where 1s and 0s are used exclusively in the transmission and storage of information.

This might be a good time to clarify a fact that is sometimes overlooked when talking about binary digital information. It is important to realize that the 1s and 0s referred to in digital communication are simply human interpretations of what is being stored or communicated. For example, a 1 might indicate that a memory location is holding a charge, or that a communications line is electrified at that moment in time, and a 0 might indicate that no such charge or electrification exists. The use of 1s and 0s is just a way to work with large quantities of binary information and to mathematically predict or analyze various trends and situations.

Improvements Over Analog Communication

Recall the earlier analogy of being tasked with recognizing shades of gray, as opposed to just black and white. The point was made that dust could settle on the object, making it more difficult to correctly identify exactly which shade of gray you were looking at, especially if the shades were infinitesimally close to begin with. Quality assurance in this task would be tricky, at best.

However, if you had to identify the objects only as black or white, it would take quite a bit of dust to obscure the underlying blackness or whiteness. This is also the case with digital signals. So much tolerance is built into the receiving mechanism, that common interference does not alter the perceived value of the digital signal. A slightly stronger or weaker pulse is still read as a pulse. A slight to medium disturbance in the signal, where no pulse should be, is still perceived as the lack of a pulse.

In contrast, analog transmission systems accumulate interference and impairments. After being introduced, these anomalies cannot be easily eliminated. Any change to the original signal permanently alters the quality of the signal, sometimes distorting it to an unrecognizable extent. The effect is heightened when you amplify the analog signal to compensate for signal loss. Any interference that the signal has already picked up is amplified, along with the original signal.

If you go back to the black and white analogy, you can see that if you were asked to perform the recognition process in a slightly darkened room, you would have more trouble identifying the shades of gray, but the identification of black or white would still be relatively simple. This is an example of signal loss. Because colors and grayscale are transmitted by relative reflection of light, less light means less signal arrives at your eye. In fact, a complete signal loss (complete darkness) makes even the recognition of black and white lean entirely to the black (which translates as no optical data or "0"). In this case, it doesn't matter if you're being asked to recognize shades of gray or just black and white. You can't see or recognize anything. The point is, perceived as all 0s, a complete loss of signal is as equally catastrophic in digital transmission, as it is in analog.

In the case of analog and digital communication, you are hindered more by the loss and amplification of the analog signal than by the loss and regeneration of the digital signal. It is a simple task to restore a digital pulse to its original strength and shape, as compared to restoring a potentially distorted analog signal to its original form. A distorted pulse is still a pulse. This is because the digital signal is distorted by analog interference, which is easily ignored. This same analog interference hides within an analog signal, which makes it all but impossible to reverse.

The Signal Conversion Process

By way of review, an analog signal is one in which each point on the waveform is meaningful (a continuous waveform). Analog signals are graphically depicted as sinusoidal waves (see Figure 3-2). This is also the motion that a guitar string exhibits when plucked. The string moves through and past the origin (the x-axis showing time, here), which is nearly an equivalent distance toward the guitar as away from the guitar.

Figure 3-2   *Sinusoidal Analog Waveform*

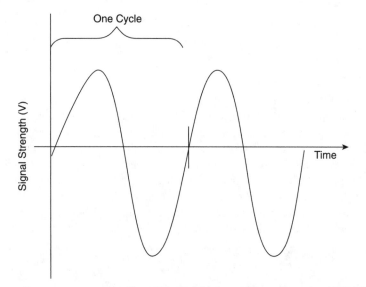

Although the positive amplitude is often illustrated to be the same as the negative amplitude within the same cycle, in reality, because the signal is usually trailing off or attenuating (losing signal strength) as time goes on, these depictions can be slightly inaccurate. The amplitude of a crest in the waveform often is smaller than that of the previous crest. The concept of a cycle, in graphical terms, which might be easier to understand than the technical definition, is the portion of a waveform that begins and ends at the horizontal axis that is heading in the same direction at the beginning and end. This means that one upsweeping and one downsweeping crest makes up a cycle. Figure 3-2 shows a waveform with two cycles.

In contrast, a digital signal contains discrete pulses, in which only the existence or absence of a pulse, and sometimes the rising or falling disposition of one or more edges of the pulse (as in Manchester encoding), is meaningful. Only the amplitude of the pulse, not the voltage levels attained throughout the creation of the pulse, is important. Digital signals are graphically depicted as square waves (see Figure 3-3). Digital waveforms are also discussed as having cycles, although the physics of analog waves do not govern digital waves.

Figure 3-3   *Square Digital Waveform*

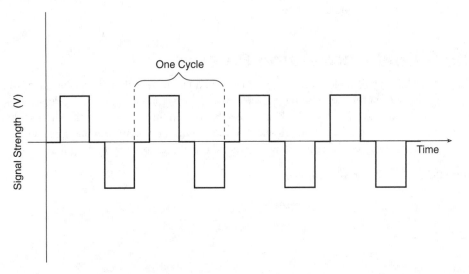

The physical difference between digital waves and analog waves is that unless you employ some form of bipolar line coding scheme (positive and negative representation of the 0s and 1s in a form designed for the transmission medium), such as alternate mark inversion (AMI) or bipolar 8-zero substitution (B8ZS), and transmit all 1s, you might not answer every positive crest with a negative, as in the case of an analog waveform. Line coding schemes such as AMI and B8ZS are covered in more detail later in this book during the discussion of T1. After being coded into digital, the analog source can be represented by a series of bits that have few 1s over various stretches of the bit stream. These 0s are often depicted as no pulse, hence no crest in the wave. Nevertheless, even two consecutive 0s, because of the time slots assigned to the lack of electrical activity, can be considered to make up one cycle in the digital waveform.

Figure 3-3 shows a digital pulse stream that represents some form of bipolar return to zero (BRZ) technology, which is transmitting all 1s in this case. The half-pulse width transmission of zero for each pulse helps keep true to the zero-voltage reference, especially during the transmission of all 1s. This can occur for an extended period during testing or in certain equipment failure conditions to keep the line up. In this case, an extended period without a return to zero might allow the signal to wander, which causes the positive or negative pulses to read as 0s, depending on which way the signal wandered. Digital line coding schemes are covered in detail in Chapter 5, "T1 Technology."

Converting an analog signal into a digital form that adequately represents the original waveform, after its conversion back to analog, is accomplished by a series of four time-tested processes:

- Filtering
- Sampling
- Quantizing
- Encoding

When grouped together, these processes are known collectively as *pulse code modulation* (*PCM*), which is documented in the International Telecommunication Union Telecommunication Standardization Sector (ITU-T, formerly the CCITT) standard G.711. The sections that follow discuss all four processes in greater detail.

Filtering

Filtering can be thought of as the process of isolating only the contiguous frequencies that you are interested in digitizing. One of the simplest examples is that of an analog voice source, which is intended for digitization and subsequent transmission over digital circuits.

In the case of an analog voice source, the contiguous range of frequencies of interest that communicate across a circuit is the 3100 Hz (often expressed 3.1 kHz) range, from 300 Hz to 3400 Hz, inclusive. This is the most common range of spoken voice.

If frequency, which is expressed in hertz (Hz) or cycles per second, is foreign to you, think of it as pitch or tone. A higher frequency produces a higher pitch, which some might consider more treble, whereas a lower frequency produces a lower, more bass pitch.

Filtering, in this example, is the exclusion of any frequencies below 300 Hz and above 3400 Hz. For the purpose of computing sampling frequency (which is discussed next), the maximum frequency is 4 kHz. This provides a more than adequate sampling rate for what is known as voice frequency (VF).

Sampling

While working for AT&T in 1928, a scientist by the name of Harry Nyquist published the paper "Certain Topics in Telegraph Transmission Theory," in which he outlined what is now referred to as the Nyquist Theorem. This paper was many years ahead of its time. Decades passed before the equipment was available to enable this theorem for digitizing voice for storage or transmission.

Before getting into the Nyquist Theorem, you need to understand the term sampling. *Sampling*, in this case, is the measuring of the amplitude of the analog waveform at regular (equal) intervals. These equal intervals are computed by using the Nyquist Theorem.

The Nyquist Theorem states that to adequately represent an analog wave in digital form, you must sample the analog waveform at a rate at least twice that of the highest frequency to be transmitted. As noted earlier, the maximum voice frequency, for the purpose of computing the sampling frequency of the analog waveform, is 4 kHz.

Using the Nyquist Theorem, you can determine that you need to sample the analog signal that is being transmitted at a rate of 8000 times per second. The Nyquist Theorem dictates that you multiply the maximum frequency of 4000 Hz by two, which yields 8000 samples per second. Figure 3-4 illustrates this mathematical relationship, including units of measure. This numeric value is important to consider in the encoding phase of PCM, which is discussed later in this chapter.

Figure 3-4   *Nyquist Theorem Calculations*

4000 Cycles / Second   (Maximum Frequency)

x   2 Samples / Cycle   (Nyquist Multiplier)

8000   Samples / Second

The equipment responsible for capturing these samples 8000 times per second uses two inputs. One of these inputs is the constant stream of analog information from the source. The other input is a clock signal that occurs 8000 times a second. The result is that only the source signal that exists each time the clock pulse arrives at the gate is captured (sampled).

These 8000 samples become the only part of the original analog waveform to remain after the sampling process. If you think of these samples as pulses of varying amplitude, you have what is known as a pulse stream (or pulse train). These pulses are modulated (or varied), based on how the original analog waveform varies. By definition, this is pulse amplitude modulation (PAM). You can consider a PAM signal as the result of the sampling process and the input for the quantizing process.

It's a simple task to compute the equal interval between samples. By splitting a second 8000 ways, you come up with the value 0.000125 seconds (or 125 μs). Therefore, every 125 millionths of a second, regardless of the frequency or amplitude of the analog waveform, a sample is taken. Figure 3-5 illustrates the sampling process.

Figure 3-5   *The Sampling Process*

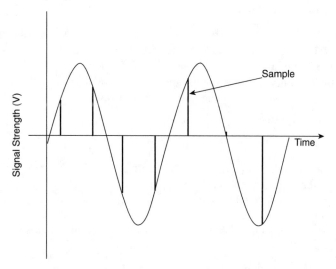

a. Samples at Regular Intervals

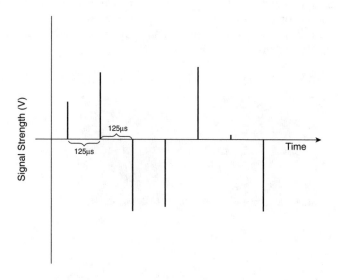

b. The PAM Pulse Train with the Waveform Removed

As shown in Figure 3-5, samples taken at adequate intervals provide a guideline to aid receiving equipment in the reconstruction of the original waveform. The receiving equipment performs a sort of "connect-the-dots" with the pulses in the PAM pulse train.

This, together with specialized circuitry, provides a waveform that is indistinguishable from the original version by the human ear.

Looking at the pulse stream in Part b of Figure 3-5, you might assume that the digital conversion is well in hand, but consider the fact that the amplitude of each pulse in the train is but one in an infinite range of possible amplitudes. By definition, this is still an analog signal. Nevertheless, only one step stands between the PAM signal and being ready to encode a true digital bit stream—quantizing or quantization.

Quantizing

Now that you have a PAM signal in the form of a pulse train, you need to evaluate the voltage levels of the individual pulses, based upon a standard scale. Only by adjusting each pulse's amplitude to match a value from a finite set can you hope to use a finite series of digital bit patterns to turn each sample into a portion of a bit stream that can reconstruct the pulse train at the receiving end. This is the object of the encoding process that is discussed in the next section.

From the preceding discussion, you might have already surmised that the result of the quantizing phase is still not the final digital signal, though the quantized PAM signal can be thought of as digital. Because 256 discrete voltage levels are more difficult to transmit and receive with as few errors as only two or three levels (in the case of bipolar line coding), further refinement of the quantized digital signal occurs next, in the encoding phase. This portion of the conversion process might well have the least distinguishable output. Nevertheless, it is a crucial step towards digitization. Figure 3-6 clarifies the fairly abstract nature of the quantizing phase.

Figure 3-6   *Imperfections in the Quantizing Process*

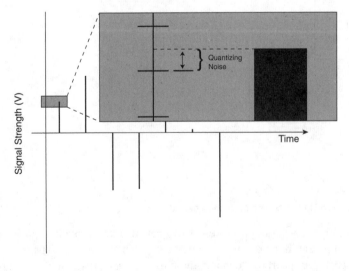

Because the original PAM signal is made up of pulses that can have amplitudes within an infinite range, it is necessary to use a finite scale to prepare the PAM signal for the encoding phase, at which point each pulse in the train is converted to a series of 0s and 1s. You cannot expect each original PAM pulse to fall exactly on one of the finite points of the scale, which means that you end up with some altered pulses, with no accompanying information to guide you back to the original pulse. These discrepancies are referred to as *quantizing errors* or *quantizing noise*. These errors do not produce audible differences to the human ear. In fact, minimizing the effect of quantizing errors is the subject of an upcoming discussion on a process called companding.

The PAM pulse is rounded to the nearest point on the scale, regardless of whether that point is higher or lower than the actual sample. This is the first step toward minimizing quantizing errors. The biggest reduction in quantizing noise comes from the use of a non-linear companding law.

Two algorithms are in use today for error reduction in the quantizing phase:

- **μ-Law (pronounced mu-law—also known as μ-255)** — Used in North America and Japan

- **A-Law** — Used in Europe and the rest of the world

These are known as *companding algorithms* because they effectively compress the PAM signal for error reduction on the transmitting end and expand the signal back to normal on the receiving end.

Analog information that has been quantized by one algorithm becomes incompatible with equipment that uses the other. It is common to convert between the two standards for communication between conflicting equipment. The digital signal level 0 (DS-0) created by North American or Japanese equipment can be converted to the DS-0 that is common in other parts of the world. Then, traffic that might have been multiplexed into a T1 or other T-carrier circuit can be multiplexed into an E1 or other related circuit. The responsibility of conversion usually falls on the party using μ-Law companding; meaning that international communication takes place with A-Law companding. A DS-0 can be defined as the 64-kbps bit stream that has not yet been multiplexed and is the direct product of the PCM process.

Remember that the process of quantizing exists solely to prepare the analog waveform for digitization during the encoding phase. You are limited to 8 bits per sample when encoding. If you take 8000 samples per second, you wind up with 64,000 bits per second (64 kbps) for each original analog waveform. Eight bits can vary 2^8 (256) ways, which means that you are allowed only 256 discrete points on the y-axis during the quantizing phase. If this logic is not apparent to you, consider that the word "bit" comes from a concatenation of the words "binary digit." This implies the use of the binary (or base-2) numbering system. Because there are only two possible values in this numbering system (0 and 1), the total number of possible values able to be represented by eight binary digits is found by raising two (the number of discrete values in the numbering system to which each digit can be set) to the power of eight (the number of digits being considered at one time — eight bits per sample). To further dilute the effect, these 256 points must be divided evenly between positive and negative pulses.

Depending upon whom you ask, you are liable to hear that toll-quality voice needs 4000 or more points on the vertical scale to reproduce the original signal on the other end in an acceptable manner. This assumes a linear relationship between the original PAM signal and the PAM signal that you use for encoding, which is a technical way of saying the two PAM signals are the same. Unfortunately, this approach would require 12 or more bits per sample during the encoding phase, which would result in higher bit rates, which in turn would result in higher circuit frequencies, which would lead to shorter circuit run lengths because of the increased attenuation of higher frequencies. Companding offers a compromise. Remember that companding would not be necessary if you could encode the information with 12 or more bits, instead of just 8.

The principle of companding is based primarily on the idea that lower amplitude PAM pulses are more sensitive to quantizing noise (a higher signal-to-noise ratio) than are higher amplitude pulses and, to a lesser degree, on the statistical probability that analog traffic presents with lower amplitudes (lower volume) most of the time. This simply means that in a linear quantizing arrangement (all intervals between points on the vertical axis are equal), the quantizing noise can represent a larger percentage increase/decrease in lower-amplitude pulses than in higher ones, which greatly affects the reproduced fidelity of low-volume information. As Figure 3-7 illustrates, an equal amount of quantizing noise, in absolute terms, winds up being an appreciably larger increase for the lower-amplitude pulse, in relative terms. This is the same concept as the perception of time to humans. As you get older, a year (although the same as every other year, in absolute terms) seems shorter because it represents a relatively shorter period, compared to the years of life you have stored away in your memory. To the toddler, however, that same absolute year seems like forever because it is a relatively larger portion of their existence.

Figure 3-7 *The Greater Effect on Low-amplitude Pulses*

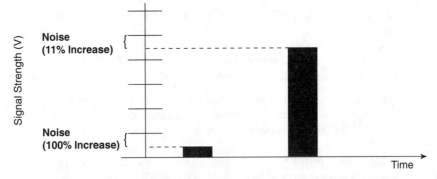

Because the noise is relatively greater at these more popular and vulnerable amplitudes, concentrate on reducing the quantizing error at these amplitudes by placing the points on the vertical axis closer at the lower amplitudes than at the higher ones. This way, you have excellent quality for the majority of the traffic and surprisingly good quality for the rest. For those that would like to follow along mathematically, Figure 3-8 shows the formulas for computing the quantized PAM signal (y) from the original PAM signal (x), for both μ-Law and A-Law. For many of us, it suffices to merely understand that the two technologies are different and that conversion is required between them.

Figure 3-8   *Companding Equations*

μ-Law

$$y = \text{sgn}(x) \ \frac{\ln(1+\mu|x|)}{\ln(1=\mu)}, \ -1 \ <= \ x \ <= \ 1$$

sgn (x) : + or -, based on x
μ = 255 (hence the name μ-255)

A-Law

$$y = \begin{cases} \text{sgn}(x) \ \dfrac{A|x|}{1+\ln A}, \ 0 <= |x| <= 1/A \\[3ex] \text{sgn}(x) \ \dfrac{1+\ln A|x|}{1+\ln A}, \ 1/A \ <= \ x \ <= \ 1 \end{cases}$$

A = 87.6

The ranges for PAM signals (x and y) are normalized to ±1 volt, for the purposes of these equations. Figure 3-9 shows these equations graphed. Pay special attention to the logarithmic S curve.

Figure 3-9   *Graphs Comparing A-Law and μ-Law*

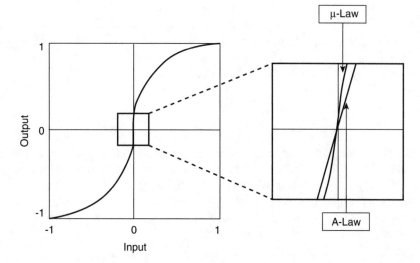

In Figure 3-9, you also see that the A-Law curve is straighter near (0,0) than is the μ-Law curve. In reality, these algorithms approximate logarithmic behavior by specifying segments, within which quantized values are actually linear. Although technically there are 16 segments in these pseudo-logarithmic curves, eight in the positive quadrant and eight in the negative, toward the origin, segments are effectively combined because of the collinear nature of these segments.

The difference in the graphs of the two companding algorithms stems from the fact that A-Law combines more linear segments than does μ-Law. In fact, whereas μ-Law is considered a 15-segment curve (two are combined to form one), A-Law is credited with only 13 segments (four are combined). Although the difference in the equations causes the (x, y) coordinates to plot differently, both algorithms are made up of 16 quantum values (quantized values) in each of 16 linear segments, for the 256 total values represented by an 8-bit code.

The relationship between consecutive linear segments is fairly straightforward. Each segment exhibits half the slope of the preceding segment (it splits the difference between the previous segment and horizontal). Each consecutive segment also doubles the range of amplitudes covered by the previous segment. This also implies that the resolution is cut in half (the quantizing error can as much as double for a sample), because each segment has a fixed 16 quantum values that increasingly must occupy larger ranges of amplitude on the vertical axis.

In practice, both algorithms employ a scheme of 128 positive decimal quantum values (0 to 127) and 128 negative values (–0 to –127) in their quantizing scales, although these values map differently. This difference follows to the encoding phase. In addition, a few mathematical tricks are performed, in the case of encoding A-Law, all of which contribute to the incompatibility between the companding algorithms, and between the resulting PAM signals and encoded bit streams. One-way transmission is a common ramification of mismatched companding algorithms at opposite ends of a circuit.

NOTE   There are 256 discrete values, 0 to 127 and –0 to –127. The actual zero signal level is not represented. The first bit is the sign bit, which allows for a value of 0 with a negative sign bit, basically –0, as the first value below the x-axis.

Encoding

The final phase of the conversion process is one that this chapter has been alluding to for a while. This is what it's all about. After this phase, you have a stream of binary digits that is the digital traffic for transmission across the digital circuit. First, you need to understand that the term *encoding*, as it is used here, does not mean the same thing as encoding when it applies to transforming a bit stream into pulses of electricity. That type of encoding is discussed in chapters relating to digital circuits.

This type of encoding refers to taking the adjusted (quantized) PAM signal and converting each sample into a stream of 8 bits, based on that sample's pulse amplitude. Similar to the quantizing scheme, the encoding method is based on the companding algorithm in use. As you will see, the 8-bit codes that each algorithm generates for the same quantum value are completely different.

Figure 3-10 shows a graphical representation of the segmented approach to encoding μ-Law quantum values. Although the bit patterns are opposite from what you might expect in the seven least significant bits (minimum is all 1s, whereas maximum is all 0s), it is easier to diagram than the A-Law process. Even though the A-Law algorithm equates values in a more logical way (zero basically means zero), the final product is the result of performing an exclusive OR (XOR) function with 0x55 (01010101). This process has its roots in days gone by but remains as an artifact of the original technology. Basically, during the transmission of a low-amplitude (silent) signal, the XOR operation ensures that pulses are still encoded, as opposed to the encoding of mostly 0s, which can jeopardize synchronization.

Figure 3-10 *The Segmented Encoding Process for μ-Law*

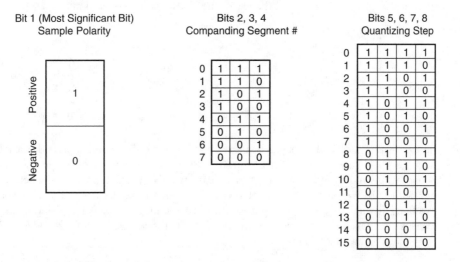

The segmented encoding process follows the same structure for both companding algorithms, but differs in the encoded values for similar sample-pulse amplitudes. The common structure is illustrated in Figure 3-10, but the values for bits two through eight are decidedly not the same. The first, or most significant, bit represents the PAM pulse's polarity. The next 3 bits represent the eight possible segments, based on the polarity already discussed. Yes, there are 16 segments in all, but recall that these are distributed as eight for each of the two polarities. Therefore, you obtain the unique values for the 16 segments when you consider the first 4 bits together (polarity and segment number). The last 4 bits represent the 16 linear steps in the segment indicated.

The conversion of the encoded value into a binary quantum value that ranges between the decimal values 0 and 255 can be accomplished by leaving bit one alone, the polarity, and inverting bits two through eight. For example, referring to Figure 3-10, an encoded value of 11000101 represents a quantized pulse in the fourth positive segment (marked segment 3) that falls closest to the eleventh quantizing step (marked 10 in the diagram). To turn this into a value between 0 and 255 in binary, leave the first bit alone and invert the remaining 7 bits. This results in 10111010, which is a decimal 186. On the positive scale, encode quantum values between 128 and 255, inclusive. The quantum value 186 is near the halfway point on the positive scale, which is where the description of the encoded value 11000101 would have placed the pulse.

What the preceding paragraph is talking about is μ-Law encoding. A-Law, although more difficult to illustrate, is fairly simple to explain. In fact, the quantum value matches the initially encoded value, so that no inversion of bits two through eight is necessary. The trick comes when the initially encoded value is obtained. Before a true A-Law bit stream is realized, you must XOR the initially encoded value with the hexadecimal value 55 (decimal 85), which in binary is 01010101. As you can see, the even bits are inverted in the final product. Figure 3-11 illustrates the use of the XOR Boolean operation.

Figure 3-11 *The XOR Operation*

In English, Figure 3-11 says that a single operand (and only a single operand) must be a 1 to get a yes (1) answer. Otherwise a no (0) is the result, even when both operands are 1s, which would return a yes answer if you were using either the OR or the AND operation, but not with XOR. Whenever a 0 is XORed with the original data, the same value as the original results, but when it is a 1, the opposite value is the solution. This is the phenomenon that causes the XOR of 0x55 to invert only the even bits for samples quantized and encoded by using the A-Law algorithm.

So, for the same quantum value as in the previous example, which was 186, the initial A-Law encoded value is actually decimal 186 or binary 10111010. This is read as the eleventh step in the fourth positive segment. Sound familiar? Remember that just because both μ-Law and A-Law describe a quantum value of 186 the same way, the two algorithms place this step of this segment at slightly different points on the scale. A quantized pulse that maps to 186 in one companding algorithm does not map to 186 in the other.

What this means is that, contrary to what you might think, the conversion process is not a simple numerical replacement. In fact, one of the simpler methods requires two conversions. The μ-Law information must first be converted to a 16-bit code, which provides sufficiently generic information. Then this 16-bit code can be converted into A-Law.

Never mind conversion headaches. You're simply trying to produce an A-Law byte from a sample. However, one more step remains. The 10111010 value must be XORed with 01010101. This produces 11101111, a value that does not directly resemble either the quantum value or the initially encoded byte. The one detail that has remained throughout the manipulation is the sample's polarity. The most significant bit has not been altered. For this reason, the polarity (most significant) bit has the same values in the same situations for both μ-Law and A-Law. The same cannot be said for bits two through eight.

Variations on the PCM Theme

PCM is great when you have an application that requires 56 to 64 kbps of digital bandwidth. Sometimes analog traffic can handle a little more loss of integrity. As long as you go in realizing integrity might be jeopardized, you can do quite a few things to preserve bandwidth and get the most out of your digital circuits. Some modern techniques make it difficult for the average human ear to detect anything different from the quality afforded by good old-fashioned PCM. This section introduces two fairly well established technologies that provide an alternative to standard PCM and allow more devices to communicate over the same medium, with minimal to no loss. Additional standards should not be difficult to grasp, after you understand the two presented here. They are differential pulse code modulation (DPCM) and adaptive differential pulse code modulation (ADPCM).

DPCM

DPCM capitalizes on the fact that the amplitudes of samples of analog information that are captured at the Nyquist rate (twice the limited maximum frequency of the analog source), or higher, tend to be close to one another a high percentage of the time. If this is the case, why not simply look at this difference between the amplitudes of adjacent samples, rather than the amplitudes of the samples themselves? Noting only this differential provides the ability to represent the samples in a way that uses fewer bits than if you were to directly encode the amplitudes of the samples, as in standard PCM. Figure 3-12 illustrates the concept of measuring only the difference between amplitudes of adjacent samples.

An important difference between these differential methods and standard PCM is that quantizing in DPCM and ADPCM is not performed on the actual sample pulses, but instead on the difference between the pulses. If the difference is small, as expected, the quantizing noise can actually be less, especially at higher amplitudes, than in the case of PCM. So with potentially less noise and fewer bits required for transmission (often only 3 or 4 bits per sample, as opposed to 8), it's no wonder these technologies are so popular.

There's no magic to this technology. It's mathematical prediction. Like any prediction, however, the results can be off sometimes, though more so with DPCM than ADPCM. DPCM has a simple prediction mechanism. It starts with a fully described initial value, as PCM does for all samples. It then predicts the next sample will be the same as the last. The fact that it is not the same is not a problem, because it only encodes the error in the prediction. The receiving end predicts by using exactly the same algorithm and circuitry as the transmitting end, so it understands how to reconstruct the actual pulse from the prediction error that is transmitted. The problem arises when there are not enough bits in the scheme to represent the prediction error. In other words, the change between sample amplitudes is off the scale.

Figure 3-12 *DPCM's Focus*

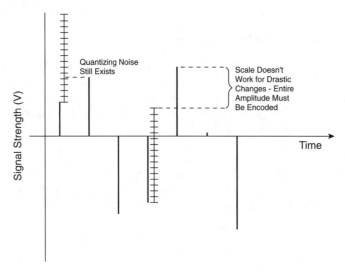

ADPCM

What happens during the less common occurrences when the change between amplitudes of consecutive samples is not close enough to be represented adequately with DPCM? Basically, the quantizing noise can be great. With DPCM, there is no mechanism to circumvent this situation, aside from encoding the actual sample, rather than what might have become an inaccurate prediction. Enter ADPCM. The adaptive part of ADPCM is an enhancement to DPCM. In general, everything works the same, but with ADPCM the range that the 3 or 4 bits represent can change, as necessary (see Figure 3-13).

With this ability for the encoding circuitry to alter the range, when the distance between amplitudes increases beyond what the current range can handle, the range can grow to accommodate the distance, although quantizing noise might increase. But the converse is also true. If the distance decreases, the range can decrease, likely reducing quantizing noise in the process. These alterations in noise occur because regardless of the range, with a fixed number of bits representing the difference in amplitudes, the number of points in the adaptive range remains the same. So the same fact that causes the wider ranges to be more loss-inducing causes the narrower ranges to be less so.

Figure 3-13 *ADPCM's Adjustable Range*

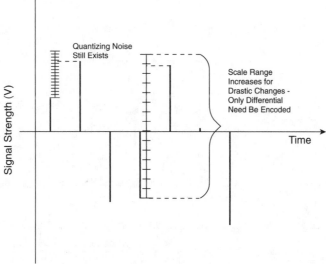

The prediction mechanism that ADPCM uses is a bit more complex than that of DPCM. In general, ADPCM keeps a running average of a set number of previous differences that were encoded. It keeps its prediction current by also incorporating two or more of the most recent predictions, which forms a weighted average. A good example of this is ITU-T standard G.721. In the case of G.721, the adaptive predictor forms an average by using the last six difference values before they are quantized (or more appropriately, dequantized by the embedded decoder circuitry) and the last two predicted values. Proprietary versions of ADPCM can work differently, although the principles are the same. In fact, G.721 (also see more current G.726) specifies only a 32-kbps ADPCM algorithm, although other implementations specify rates such as 40 kbps, 24 kbps, and 16 kbps.

What's this about the encoder containing a decoder? Well, one way to make sure the decoder at the receiving end knows what step size (what range of quantizing steps) the transmitting device is using is if the encoder in the transmitting device is in synchronization with what the decoder at the receiving end is expecting. This way, if the transmitter changes its quantizing range, the receiving end uses the same data to change its dequantizing range. Figure 3-14 shows a block diagram of a sample ADPCM encoder and decoder pair. The encoder contains the decoder's blocks as a subset. The encoder circuitry has updated its predictions and quantizing steps (range) for the next round, by using the same binary code that it is sending to the decoder. This ensures that the identical circuitry of the decoder uses this same information to arrive upon the same results as the encoder's embedded decoder.

Figure 3-14 *Block Diagram of an ADPCM Encoder/Decoder Pair*

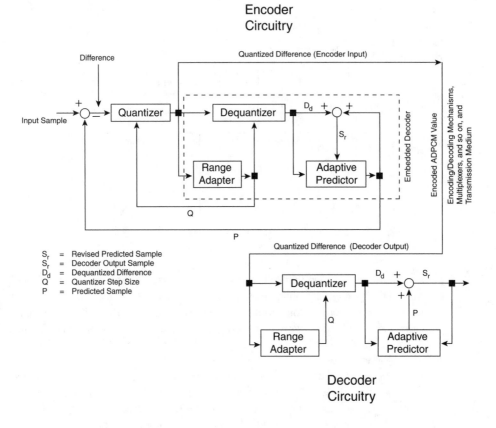

Other Modulation Schemes

Besides the popular versions of ADPCM (G.721 is definitely not the only one), several other encoding methods are in use today for various applications. One of these is Delta Modulation (DM). DM works on the basis that the relative change in the direction of the amplitude from one sample to the next is adequate information to successfully reconstruct the analog waveform at the receiving end. As a result, DM requires only a single bit to represent this directional information. The next sample's amplitude is greater than or less than the current sample's amplitude. It's as simple as that. What's not so simple is the solution for the unfortunate situations when the fixed step size assumed by the decoder on the receiving end becomes unfaithful to the reality of steeper or flatter slopes than the norm. Two forms of distortion error occur in these circumstances, slope overload and granular noise (see Figure 3-15).

Figure 3-15 *Delta Modulation Distortion*

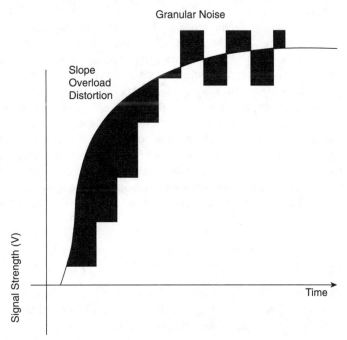

With DM, each bit represents an entire sample. As a result, each one of these samples encoded as a bit is represented in a primitive way, with a relatively small amount of information being transmitted about the sample. This is the main reason that the noise distortion discussed here can be so damaging to fidelity. One way of keeping both types of noise within acceptable limits is to make the step size fairly small, while sampling at a much higher rate than the Nyquist rate. Because there is only one bit per sample, the bit rate matches the sampling rate. Therefore, if you are producing 32 kbps of traffic, you are using a sampling rate of 32,000 samples per second. You must take care not to completely erode the compression benefits, in the form of bandwidth savings, that this technique is designed to offer. Thus, DM alone cannot always effectively overcome these issues, but there is another technique based on DM that can. It's called Continuously Variable Slope DM (CVSD). CVSD allows for the monitoring of a flow-control bit stream, which can come in the form of all 1s to increase the step size to avoid slope overload or all 0s to decrease the step size to allow for a less steep slope, thus curtailing the effects of granular noise.

Other adaptive forms of DM simply watch for trends by remembering previous directions. When the same direction is followed for many samples, the prediction is made that the slope might be fairly flat. So, to decrease the effects of granular noise, the step size is decreased. Conversely, if the direction has been alternating between positive and negative, the indication is that the slope is greater than expected. In this case, the step size is increased to avoid slope overload distortion.

In addition to the time-domain methods discussed in this chapter, frequency-domain approaches also exist, with certain advantages. With Sub-Band ADPCM (SB-ADPCM), the input speech is split into several frequency bands, or sub-bands, and each is coded independently by using ADPCM on the isolated frequencies. At the receiving end, the bits are decoded and the sub-band frequencies are recombined, which yields the reconstructed speech signal. The advantages of doing this come from the fact that the noise in each sub-band is dependent only on the coding in that particular sub-band. As a result, you can use tighter encoding schemes and quantizing steps with sub-bands that are perceived as more important to the human listener. In this way, the noise in these frequency regions is low, whereas in other sub-bands you can allow a higher level of noise, as these frequencies are perceived as less important. Sub-band *codecs* (coder/decoder) produce toll-quality speech by using only 16-32 kbps. Because of the filtering necessary to split the speech into sub-bands, these codecs are more complex than simple DPCM encoders and introduce more coding delay. The complexity and delay are still relatively low, when compared to most hybrid codecs.

Summary

In this chapter, you learned the history and motivation behind the development of digital transmission and storage technology. You also learned why digital formats improve upon the quality offered by comparable analog technologies.

You were presented with each stage of the conversion process for producing a digital bit stream from an analog source. These stages are as follows:

- **Filtering**—Where only the standardized voice frequency is allowed to enter the process

- **Sampling**—Where the analog waveform is observed 8000 times per second, producing another form of analog signal known as the PAM signal

- **Quantizing**—Where each sample's pulse in the PAM signal is adjusted to match one of 256 discrete levels on the vertical axis, at which time the companding process is applied to the PAM signal, an event that must be reversed at the receiving end

- **Encoding**—Where the adjusted PAM signal is converted into a bit stream, by assigning an eight-bit code to each of the 256 quantization levels from the previous stage

Finally, this chapter presented alternate technologies that have their roots based in the analog-to-digital conversion technology outlined in the beginning of this chapter. These technologies include DPCM, ADPCM, DM, CVSD, and SB-ADPCM.

Review Questions

Give or select the best answer or answers to the following questions. The answers to these questions are in Appendix A, "Answers to Review Questions."

1 Which of the following are examples of the difference between analog and digital communication? (choose two)

a The term frequency only applies to digital communication.

b The term bit rate only applies to digital communication.

c The quality of an analog signal is generally better than that of a digital signal.

d The quality of a digital signal is generally better than that of an analog signal.

e Circuits and sending and receiving equipment are identical in analog and digital technologies.

2 Which of the following is *not* a stage in the analog-to-digital conversion process?

a Sampling

b Encoding

c Filtering

d Pulse conversion

e Quantizing

3 What is the earliest stage in the conversion process at which the signal technically can be considered digital?

a Sampling

b Quantizing

c Filtering

d Encoding

e Pulse conversion

4 Which of the following ITU-T recommendations covers PCM in general?

   a   G.711

   b   G.721

   c   G.726

   d   G.729

5 Which of the following advanced processes adapts the quantizing scale to more closely match the wider or narrower variation between adjacent pulses?

   a   PCM

   b   DPCM

   c   ADPCM

   d   DM

   e   CVSD

   f   SB-ADPCM

This chapter covers the following topics:

- **Introduction to digital dataphone service (DDS)**—An overview of DDS.
- **DDS operation**—A discussion of DDS circuit deployment, DDS equipment, and line coding.
- **Switched 56 (SW56)**—An overview of SW56.
- **Circuit testing patterns**—A discussion of how to use testing patterns in DDS to help isolate network problems.
- **Configuring a Cisco router for DDS/SW56**—An explanation of how to configure DDS and SW56 on Cisco routers.

CHAPTER 4

Digital Dataphone Service and Switched 56

Introduction to DDS

This chapter provides an overview of the DDS, how it is deployed, and how it operates. Although it is fast becoming antiquated, it remains an integral part of understanding how digital services are deployed. This chapter also discusses the similarities between DDS and SW56 and details about the differences between these closely related service offerings.

DDS is referred to as a digital signal customer service (DS-CS) and is deployed on a four-wire metallic interface. DDS was originally pioneered by AT&T about 20 years ago as one of the first digital offerings to subscribers. It was designed to offer a circuit at a single digital signal level 0 (DS-0) subrate of a digital signal level 1 (DS-1) signal. At the time of its inception, the lease of a T1 (carrier facilities for a DS-1) was not exactly inexpensive and most WAN connections did not require that much bandwidth.

Years after AT&T pioneered the service, American National Standards Institute (ANSI) standardized the DDS technology with standard ANSI T1.410-1992. By today's hardware standards, DDS is outdated but there are still uses for it. Many of the deployments have to do with local to regional connections for daily transaction uploads, such as banks, restaurants, and stores. However, it is also possible to deploy other services such as Frame Relay on top of DDS.

In some areas, DDS is preferred because it can be deployed relatively easily as compared to a technology such as Integrated Services Digital Network Basic Rate Interface (ISDN BRI). ISDN circuits normally have more equipment associated with them for the service provider to roll them out to customers; not to mention a ton of switch provisioning.

Depending on who you speak with, DDS stands for digital data service, digital dataphone service, dedicated digital service, or a host of other definitions. The key thing to remember is that even though some people define the abbreviation differently, they all refer to the same technology. Although this technology is specific to North America, it is essential to understand it in order to build on it with later technologies.

DDS Operation

This section covers the following topics:

- DDS circuit deployment
- DDS equipment overview
- Line coding

DDS Circuit Deployment

The DDS connection from the service provider uses a four-wire interface. There are two pairs of wires, one for Transmit (Tx) and one for Receive (Rx). Almost all DDS deployments use twisted copper pairs, and the pins within the modular plugs (RJ-48S) are 1, 2, 7, and 8. DDS circuits within the United States are separated into two halves at the network interface (NI), the user side and the network side, as shown in Figure 4-1. This is due to the divestiture of 1984. DDS circuits are commonly deployed to a device called a smart-jack.

Figure 4-1 *DDS Circuit Separation at the Network Interface*

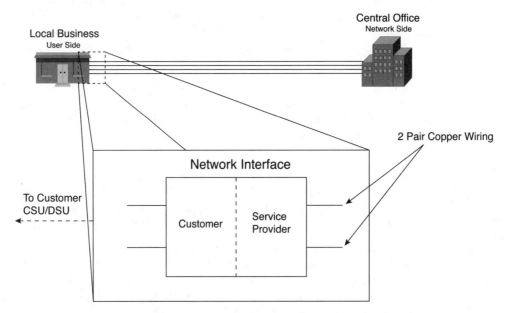

DDS is a synchronous technology, but DDS equipment can support asynchronous rates, depending on the user's data terminal equipment (DTE). The main difference between synchronous and asynchronous has to do with the clocking. With synchronous mediums there is only a single clock, and with asynchronous mediums there are multiple clocks. For example, if you have ever looked in Dial-up Networking on any Windows machine, chances are you've seen asynchronous settings. When you look at the dial-up connections, you see that there is a list of items such as start and stop bits and parity. When you hear someone say "8, none, and 1," they mean 8 bits, no parity, and 1 stop bit.

DDS circuits are commonly deployed with loop bandwidth rates of 2.4 kbps, 4.8 kbps, 9.6 kbps, 19.2 kbps, 56 kbps, or 64 kbps, depending on the application of the circuit. Refer to Table 4-1 for a complete list of loop rates. 56 kbps and 64 kbps are by far the most common rates deployed.

Table 4-1   *DDS Loop Transmission Rates with and Without Secondary Channel*

Loop Rate Without Secondary Channel	Loop Rate with Secondary Channel
2.4 kbps	3.2 kbps
4.8 kbps	6.4 kbps
9.6 kbps	12.8 kbps
19.2 kbps	25.6 kbps
56 kbps	72.0 kbps
64 kbps	-

Within the specified loop rates there is something known as the secondary channel. The secondary channel allows for the transmission of out of band management functions, and the actual channel takes its bandwidth from the overhead associated with the DDS circuit.

The reason that the start and stop bits are required is because there is more than one clock source within asynchronous communications. Without these bits in place, the communicating devices would have no way of distinguishing between intended data and garbage on the line. The bits act exactly as they sound, as a start and stop point for data. Synchronous communications do not require these methods because both sides have specific, agreed upon intervals of time to send data. Therefore, both sides will always know how to identify the intended data.

DDS circuits actually run closer to 72 kbps with overhead, but traffic does not use more than a total of 64 kbps. This is dependent on the loop rate that is to be deployed. In lower loop rates such as 9.6 kbps, the loop rate is specified at 9.6 kbps. 64-kbps loop rates do not use a secondary channel because all 8 bits are set aside for data. This is discussed further in the Framing section later in this chapter.

The length of cable between the central office (CO) and the subscriber's location (without repeater) can be up to 18 kft (18,000 feet) at its peak bandwidth capacity of 64 kbps, but closer to 60 kft when a circuit of 2.4 kbps is used. This length of cable is what is known as the local loop.

Amplitude and pulse shaping requirements are in place, and must be met by the DDS line equipment to avoid interference with other circuits (known as crosstalk) at the CO. One of the ways that this is handled is through the use of a transmit filter. The transmit filter is located at the customer's end of the loop, and filters strong repetitive patterns. Modern DDS customer premises equipment (CPE) normally has a transmit filter built in. These filters do not take into account any possible customer wiring issues. They deal strictly with the signal being sent from the service provider.

DDS Equipment Overview

Before discussing DDS line operation, several devices should be examined:

- Channel service unit (CSU)
- Data service unit (DSU)
- Office channel unit-data port (OCU-DP)
- Multijunction unit (MJU)

You can use a CSU in DDS and numerous other technologies. Typically referred to in tandem with DSUs (CSU/DSU), you can use these devices in DDS, FT1/T1, FE1/E1, and several other technologies. The CSU is the interface that communicates directly with the service provider network (see Figure 4-2). The CSU terminates the DDS circuit, allows for maintenance through loopback and test patterns, and formats the information transferred to it from the DSU for transmission over the installed network.

Figure 4-2   *Identifying the CSU Portion of DDS Equipment*

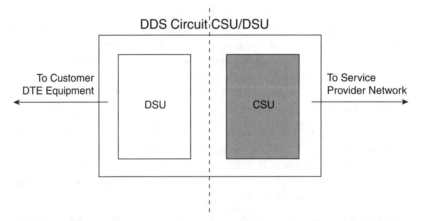

In the United States, the CSU is also responsible for power surge, power cross, and lightning protection. A power cross is something like a power line detaching and landing across pole telephone drops. The protection is two fold because the CSU protects your equipment from a power spike coming from the service provider, and it also protects sensitive service provider equipment from any type of power spikes that may originate from your side of the network. This type of protection was made necessary by the divestiture of the AT&T in 1984.

DSUs are devices that connect to the customer's DTE. For example, it connects to a router that does not have DDS support or to a PC at your desk. The purpose of the DSU is to convert the unipolar signal from something like a computer into a bipolar balanced signal so that it can be transmitted through the service provider's network (see Figure 4-3). The difference between unipolar and bipolar signals is the fact the unipolar signals (uni) only have a single polarity, and bipolar signals have two different polarity states.

Figure 4-3 *Identifying the DSU Portion of DDS Equipment*

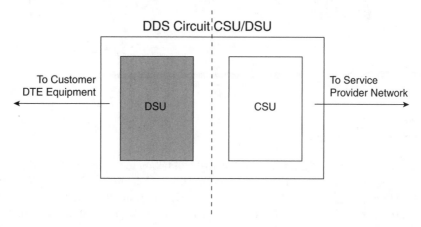

DSUs can connect to your equipment in several different ways, including V.35 and X.21. A V.35 or X.21 connection identifies that the CSU/DSU is a separate piece of equipment that terminates the DDS circuit. A CSU/DSU can also be an expansion card directly configured in the Cisco router in use.

Prior to the divestiture, the CSU and DSU were separate boxes, both owned by the RBOC. Since that time, they have become the responsibility of the customer. You typically see the CSU and DSU within the same unit, such as a router with DDS support. Don't let the terms DSU/CSU and CSU/DSU fool you, they are the same thing. It just depends on who you are talking to. If you are speaking with a service provider representative, chances are they say CSU/DSU because the CSU is from their vantage point. Most customers, on the other hand, refer to DSU/CSU for the exact same reason. Either way is correct.

The OCU-DP provides the four-wire DDS interface to the subscriber and is usually a card located in a T1 channel bank at the CO. If there are multiple DDS circuits with loop rates lower than 56 kbps or 64 kbps, a Subrate Data Multiplexer (SRDM) combines them into a single digital service 0 (DS0) for multiplexing into a digital signal level 1 (DS-1) signal. The channel bank acts as a T1 multiplexer that can provide multiple DDS, ISDN-BRI, and subrate FT1s (fractional). These services are combined, or multiplexed, into a single DS-1 signal. In turn, these DS-1 links are normally multiplexed into a higher bandwidth link such as a DS-3 through a M13 MUX or a Digital Access and Crossconnect System (DACS), as shown in Figure 4-4.

Figure 4-4 *Multiplexing at the Central Office for DDS*

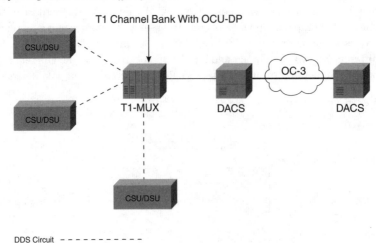

The definition of multiplexing is the action of taking multiple circuits and combining them into a larger circuit with more bandwidth. This is where the term time-division multiplexing (TDM) comes from. TDM and 24 DS0s with 8 kbps of overhead are combined to form a DS-1 signal. Each DS0 is allotted a moment in time to transmit information through the circuit. Refer to Chapter 5, "T1 Technology," for more information on T1 circuits and TDM.

OCU-DP cards can provide variable rates of service up to 64 kbps, depending on the subscriber's needs. Most of the time, DDS is thought of as a point-to-point, nailed architecture. The term nailed refers to a circuit that is always connected and always being paid for. However, some hardware can also provide a point-to-multipoint service for DDS by using a polling mechanism. Figure 4-5 shows a DDS deployment with an MJU.

When a point-to-multipoint configuration is required, the service provider will use an MJU. In communication downstream from the primary CSU/DSU, data can be sent to one or more of the connected CSU/DSUs at the remote ends of the circuit. DDS does not employ any type of mechanism to avoid data corruption from multiple devices transmitting simultaneously or to ensure that one device does not monopolize the circuit bandwidth. These functions are left up to the customer's CPE.

Referencing Figure 4-5, CSU/DSU A acts as the hub for the connection. It can communicate individually with each remote CSU/DSU (B-E) or broadcast to them all at once. Furthermore, communication is between one of the remote devices and the hub. Communication between remote devices such as B and E is not necessarily specified. This topology is common for local stores that are uploading their receipts for the day to a regional sales center.

Figure 4-5   *Point-to-Multipoint DDS Connection*

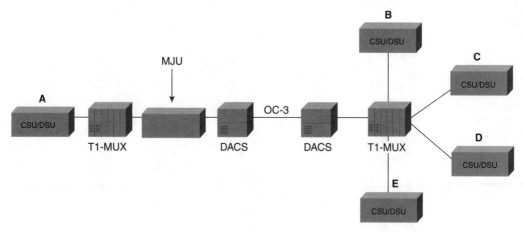

Line Coding

The topics covered in this section include the following:

- Alternate mark inversion (AMI)
- DDS line coding rules
- 64-kbps loop rate

Alternate Mark Inversion

To quickly review Chapter 3, "Analog-to-Digital Conversion," encoding is the last step in the pulse code modulation (PCM) process. Encoding allows the digital equipment to transmit a digital signal through a network by using 1s and 0s. The line coding scheme that you use with DDS is called AMI. AMI is a bipolar return to zero (RZ) type of encoding. To simplify this, bipolar means that there are two different voltage states (positive and negative), and RZ means that before each transition there is a brief RZ so that the signal has a reference point (see Figure 4-6).

Figure 4-6   *AMI Line Coding and AMI Line Coding with BPVs*

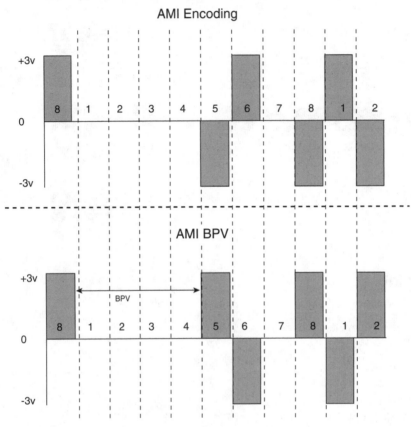

In Figure 4-6, just before each bit position with a binary 1 there is a brief RZ prior to moving to the next bit position. Again, referencing Figure 4-6, look at the bottom half of the image, which introduces the next point of bipolar violations (BPVs). One of the basic premises of AMI is that every other binary 1 must be transmitted as the alternate polarity. So, if your first 1 is positive, the next needs to be negative. The polarity alternates between binary 1s because the average voltage must equal zero to avoid the buildup of DC voltage on the circuit. The buildup of DC voltage, also known as capacitance, blocks the flow of DC current if its level becomes too great. To that point, remnant DC voltage on service provider circuits make it difficult for circuit equipment to be powered properly because the DC voltage is not passed through effectively.

To put this into perspective, think about rolling billiard balls down a hallway. Some of the balls you roll all the way to the other end, and some you roll with less force, which causes them to stop in the middle of the hallway. Eventually, the buildup of billiard balls in the middle of the hallway prevents any of the other balls from reaching the other end.

If you have two consecutive 1s with the same polarity, it creates a BPV. BPVs, such as transmitted 1s, must alternate polarity every time. Excessive BPVs can be the product of faulty equipment and can destroy transmitted data, so it's best to control their frequency. This doesn't, imply that you should never have them.

You can use BPVs in some network types to transmit different circuit states and represent long bit patterns of 0s. As you will see later on in the book, some line coding schemes, such as bipolar 8-zero substitution (B8ZS) and High Density Bipolar of Order 3 (HDB3), intentionally insert BPVs to maintain 1s density regulation.

Because DDS is a synchronous network type, timing is an important issue. DDS equipment needs to derive a reliable timing source from somewhere on the network. The way this is done in DDS, T1, E1, and most other digital network technologies is through a system called Phase Lock Loop (PLL). PLL gives your equipment the ability to derive timing from the transmitted signal, more specifically the 1s transmitted on the circuit. A pseudo-steady stream of 1s allows a device's receiver to lock onto the signal source and derive the required timing.

The problem is that not all bits transmitted are 1s. Remember that a 0 is not transmitted as a discrete voltage state. So, it's conceivable that if you have too many 0s in a row, you can lose timing on the network. This problem is known as a 1s density violation. AMI has no way of combating too many 0s in a signal stream, so it is designed to steal the least significant bit to ensure that at least 1 in every 8 bits is a 1 (see Figure 4-7).

Figure 4-7   *AMI Stealing the Least Significant Bit for 1s Density*

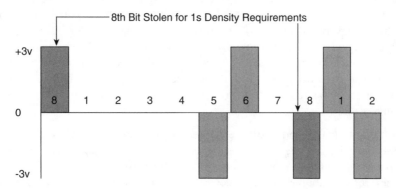

DDS Line Coding Rules

By stealing the least significant bit, AMI limits transmission rates to 56 kbps per DS0. However, AMI functions a bit differently in DDS (no bit robbing).

The AMI line coding differs slightly between DDS circuits with the secondary channel and DDS circuits without the secondary channel. Table 4-2 lists the naming conventions for describing coding patterns throughout the rest of this section.

Table 4-2   *Naming Conventions for Line Coding Schemes*

Symbol	Definition*
0	Indicates that a 0 is transmitted.
B	Indicates +/-A volts with polarity determined by the bipolar rule.
V	Indicates +/-A volts with polarity in violation of the bipolar rule.
X	Indicates 0 or B, depending on the required polarity of a violation; a pulse of correct polarity or a 0 introduced in a reserved time slot preceding a BPV to maintain zero signal average.
N	Indicates that the bit value is disregarded and a 0 or 1 is acceptable.

*   The definitions of naming conventions are from ANSI T1.410-1992.

Although DDS uses AMI, BPVs indicate the circuit states and provide a vehicle for zero substitution. To this end, DDS does not technically use a pure version of AMI line coding. The following section applies to DDS circuits of 2.4 kbps to 56 kbps without secondary channel.

V is the symbol for a BPV on a DDS circuit. It is typically represented as X0V when coding in full stream. The X0 preceding the V is selected in whichever polarity is required to maintain an average 0 signal. BPVs can also identify that there is no data to be transmitted through an idle message. This message is encoded as BBBX0V when using 2.4-kbps, 4.8-kbps, 9.6-kbps, or 19.2-kbps loop rates, and BBBBX0V when using the 56-kbps loop rate. The idle message is momentarily delayed from the last data bit to ensure that the messages are separated and that the equipment on the receiving end does not interpret them as data.

Zero substitution is handled differently between loop rates. In the case that there are six consecutive 0s, the lower loop rates are required to encode them as 000X0V. This allows both ends of the DDS circuit to identify this string as six consecutive 0s. With a 56-kbps circuit, zero substitution is done when seven consecutive 0s are detected. It is encoded as 0000X0V. A zero substitution cannot be sent and received in succession. This can cause an excess of 0s being presented to the equipment and cause it to lose PLL sync.

The line coding when using a secondary channel is handled differently because of the framing that is required. No framing is required with circuits that do not use the secondary channel. All loop rates below 56 kbps use an 8-bit byte that includes 6 D-bits (Data), and the 56-kbps loop rate uses a 9-bit byte that contains 7 D-bits. The last two bits are reserved for framing and secondary channel control, respectively. The F-bit uses a pattern of 101100 for framing, and the OCU-DP strips it off for transport over the network. The remote OCU-DP replaces it before sending it to the remote CSU/DSU (see Figure 4-8).

Figure 4-8 *Tracing Framing Bits Through the DDS Network*

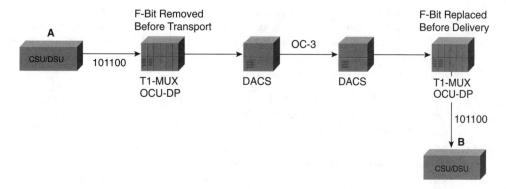

C-bits are used for secondary channel purposes and can have one of two values:

- 0—The CSU is transmitting management messages through the DDS network.
- 1—The CSU is transmitting data through the DDS network.

C-bits should not be set to 0 during the transmission of subscriber data because network functions invoked degrade circuit service. The C-bit is set to 0 in the event that a control code such as a data mode idle (DMI) or control mode idle (CMI) message needs to be sent through the network to identify that no data is present for transmission.

The D-bits transmit data, and at the loop rates of 2.4 kbps, 4.8 kbps, 9.6 kbps, and 19.2 kbps there are no limitations on what can be transmitted. A complete string of six 0s can be transmitted because the data stream can still be recovered at the other end of the connection. On the other hand, 56-kbps circuits cannot transmit all 0s because of 1s density concerns. Specific to 56-kbps circuits, there are two coding rules identified for data transmission.

- A DSU cannot transmit all 7 D-bits in a byte as 0 in a point-to-point or multipoint DDS circuit configuration.
- A DSU cannot transmit all 7 D-bits in a byte as a 0 in the same frame that the C-bit is set to 0. This pertains only to a point-to-point configuration.

These coding rules are described for 56-kbps circuits because DS1 equipment can misinterpret the string of 0s and mark the data stream with an unassigned multiplex code (UMC). If the data is marked with a UMC, it is unrecoverable at the remote end of the DDS circuit.

64-kbps Loop Rate

The last major topic to cover in this section is the use of 64-kbps loop rates. Restating what was discussed earlier, the 64-kbps loop rate does support the secondary channel described in the previous paragraphs. The 64-kbps loop rate uses the exact same framing sequence as the other loop rates, including the removal and replacement of the framing bits at each end of the circuit. 64-kbps DDS circuits also use a 9-bit byte structure, similar to a 56-kbps circuit with secondary channel. The difference is that the 64-kbps circuit sends data in a pattern of DDDDDDDFD, as opposed to the DDDDDDDFC on a 56-kbps circuit with secondary channel. That last bit is for data, not control; therefore, the control channel (secondary channel) is not available.

CSU/DSUs on a 64-kbps loop need to adhere to coding rules to prevent the mimic of network control signals. Because all 8 bits are used with the 64-kbps loop rate, it is possible that normal traffic can be misinterpreted by network equipment as a request for a loopback or even that the circuit is out-of-service (OOS). To avoid this problem, Cisco equipment can be set to scramble the data stream. Because the network equipment looks for specific bit patterns for testing functions, modification of the bit stream does not allow the network equipment to start a maintenance function without a proper request.

SW56

SW56 services evolved from the DDS offering in the United States. From the beginning, it was realized that DDS was an expensive way to communicate for corporations because they were always connected to the network and always paying for the connection, regardless of its use. Remember that DDS is digital end to end, and a point-to-point (or multipoint) offering. Basically, you have to pay for the entire circuit from Miami to New York. Even if you didn't send any data during a month, you had a fairly hefty charge for the lease of the circuit. Enter SW56.

SW56 normally provides service over two pairs of copper wiring, just as DDS, but it can also be deployed by using a single pair in proprietary configurations. SW56 operates exactly as it sounds, by switching calls through the network on a call-by-call basis. Savings with SW56 are two-fold. First, you pay a fraction of the circuit costs by only paying for the local loop on your end of the circuit. Second, you use phone numbers to dial remote locations and you are billed on a call-by-call basis. Figure 4-9 traces a call through the service provider's network between customer sites.

Figure 4-9   *Call Progress Through a SW56 Network*

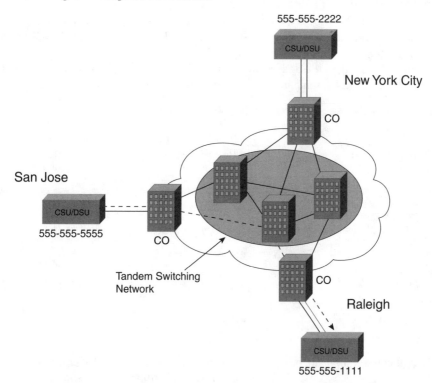

SW56 uses an in-band signaling method. It is interwoven with the data and is not separated for call setup and teardown. This is in contrast to a technology such as ISDN, which uses a logical channel for call control. The dialing mechanism that SW56 service uses is dual tone multifrequency (DTMF). DTMF is a widely deployed method of tone generation that is also used in most analog deployments.

As shown in Figure 4-9, if the corporate headquarters in San Jose wants to connect to a regional office located in Raleigh, NC all it has to do is call 555-555-1111. During this time, it is likely that the customer is paying a premium rate for the long distance call, but it is still less than a standard DDS circuit. After the call is terminated, the billing is stopped and the billing record is generated by the service provider. Because the call likely travels through more than one provider, the service provider has to use a non-biased settlement service to decide who gets how much money out of the call.

Circuit Testing Patterns

In the event of a suspected faulty circuit or equipment, you need to have a way to determine the source of the errors. Circuit testing patterns identify problems with equipment on both the customer's and service provider's end. Modern CSU/DSUs can loop up the circuit, in either direction, to test and isolate problems (see Figure 4-10). If a pattern is sent and it doesn't receive the same pattern back, it is likely an issue with the remote equipment.

Figure 4-10 *Equipment Loopback for Problem Isolation*

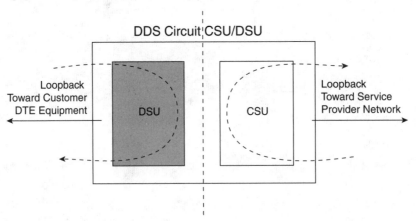

Within the equipment, it is essential to test the CSU and DSU. Bit error rate tester (BERT) tests and stress patterns (SPs) are normally started from the service provider but can also be started manually in most equipment. You can use several BERT tests and SPs for testing digital equipment. Also, while running test patterns you can manually inject errors into the signal stream to make sure that the same error is received.

The following list is a set of basic testing patterns that you can commonly use on DDS circuits. You can also use these test patterns for testing many digital mediums on the market:

- 511 pattern—A Quasi-Random Signal Source (QRSS) signal that is repeated after a total count of 511 bits has been reached. QRSS can also be defined as Quasi Random Signal Sequence.

- 2047 pattern—A QRSS signal that is repeated after a total count of 2047 bits has been reached.

- SP1—A pattern consisting of a low 1s binary series (01000000).

- SP2—A pattern consisting of an average 1s binary series (00110010).

- SP3—A repeated pattern of 100 octets with pattern (01111110). Followed by a repeated pattern of 100 octets with pattern (00000000).

- SP4—A repeated pattern of 100 octets with pattern 11111111. Followed by a repeated pattern of 100 octets of 00000000.

Cisco equipment also supports the following testing patterns:

- Full—Transmits a full-bandwidth line loopback request to a remote device, which you use for testing.

- Payload—Transmits a payload line loopback request to a remote device, which you use for testing the line and remote DSU.

- Smart-Jack—Transmits a loopback request to the remote smart-jack, which some service providers attach on the line before the CPE. You cannot put the local smart-jack into loopback.

- 0in1—Not used in DDS (B8ZS required).

- 1in1—Transmits an all-1s test pattern for signal power measurements.

- 1in2—Transmits an alternating 1s and 0s test pattern for testing bridge taps.

- 1in5—Transmits the industry standard test-pattern loopback request.

- 1in8—Transmits a test pattern for stressing the timing recovery of repeaters.

- 3in24—Transmits a test pattern for testing the 1s density tolerance on AMI lines.

- QRW—Transmits a quasi-random word test pattern, which is a random signal that simulates user data.

Setting a Cisco device up in a test pattern mode is simple. The first thing that you do is access the proper serial interface from global configuration mode:

```
Router(config)#interface serial 0/0
```

After you are in the desired interface, you can select the stress pattern or testing pattern that you want to run:

```
Router(config-if)#loopback remote stress-pattern 1
%LINEPROTO-5-UPDOWN: Line protocol on Interface Serial1, changed state to down
%LINK-3-UPDOWN: Interface Serial1, changed state to down
%SERVICE_MODULE-5-LOOPUPREMOTE: Unit 1 - Remote unit placed in loopback
```

Configuring a Cisco Router for DDS/SW56

This section details how to configure a Cisco router with a WAN interface card (WIC)-1DSU-56K4 for DDS or SW56 operation.

Just as you do with the test patterns, you must enter the proper serial interface that is associated with your WIC for DDS/SW56 configuration:

```
Router(config)#interface serial 0/0
```

From this interface you can begin to configure the DDS circuit. The first command to enter is whether you are using DDS or SW56. If you use **switched**, you also have to specify dialer in-band for the dialing method:

```
Router(config-if)#service-module 56k network-type switched
Router(config-if)#dialer in-band
Router(config-if)#no shutdown
```

With SW56 circuits, it might be necessary to specify the carrier that you are using, in case of a specific carrier echo cancellation tone prior to placing calls. Three settings are available, and when the circuit is set to **sprint**, an echo cancellation tone is sent at connection setup. The other settings are **att** and **other**, and neither sends an echo cancellation tone:

```
Router(config-if)#service-module 56k switched-carrier sprint
```

If you select **dds**, you are required to configure the circuit loop rate (clock rate), the source of the timing, and you might also specify an IP address or encapsulation type. Unless you are configured in a back-to-back DDS circuit, select line as the clock source. The service provider gives you the timing on a live circuit:

```
Router(config-if)#service-module 56k network-type dds
Router(config-if)#service-module 56k clock rate 56
Router(config-if)#service-module 56k clock source line
Router(config-if)#ip address 192.168.1.1 255.255.255.0
Router(config-if)#encapsulation ppp
Router(config-if)#no shutdown
```

If you are using a 64-kbps DDS circuit, you can configure data scrambling to avoid transmitting data that appear to be a network management function:

```
Router(config)#interface serial 0/0
Router(config-if)#service-module 56k clock rate 64
Router(config-if)#service-module 56k data-coding scrambled
Router(config-if)#no shutdown
```

Summary

DDS is a leased-line technology that provides variable loop rates to customers. Loop rates available are 2.4 kbps, 4.8 kbps, 9.6 kbps, 19.2 kbps, 56 kbps, and 64 kbps. DDS service is deployed over a two pair copper service from the service provider's CO to the customer's premise. The circuit interconnection occurs at the NI, which also separates where the responsibility of the service provider ends.

Several functions and devices make up a basic DDS connection: the OCU-DP, CSU, DSU, DTE, and DCE. The OCU-DP is a card that resides in a T1 channel bank that is responsible for providing the four-wire DDS service to the customer. It is multiplexed into a DS-1 signal, and then DACS into a higher bandwidth circuit for transmission through the service provider's network. The CSU is responsible for terminating the DDS circuit, for providing an interface for loopback, and for protecting the customer's and service provider's equipment from power surges and power crosses. The DSU is responsible for converting the unipolar signal of the DTE (normally a computer) into a balanced bipolar signal.

DDS circuits use a version of AMI line coding. AMI is a bipolar coding structure that states that every other transmitted 1 must be of the alternate polarity. If the 1s transmitted are not alternated, a BPV occurs. BPVs can transmit idle codes and management codes, but excessive BPVs caused by faulty equipment destroy the transmitted data.

SW56 is based on DDS, but it has a major difference in the fact that the circuit is not leased from end to end. SW56 circuits are a switched service that allows the customer to lease only the local loop portion of the circuit. When a connection is desired, a call is placed by using a phone number, and a connection between nodes is established. The customer is only charged for the duration of the call.

Testing patterns and SPs help isolate network or equipment problems. The most common patterns are 501, 2047, SP1, SP2, SP3, and SP4. The 501 and 2047 patterns transmit a QRSS pattern until 501 or 2047 bits are reached. After that point, they are repeated. The SPs test different 1s and 0s densities on the circuit equipment to ensure that the equipment at both ends can run the specified patterns.

Review Questions

Give or select the best answer or answers to the following questions. The answers to these questions are in Appendix A, "Answers to Review Questions."

1 How many wires do you use on a DDS circuit?

  a 2

  b 4

  c 6

  d 8

2 Which pins does a DDS circuit use?

  a 4, 5

  b 2, 3

  c 1, 2, 7, 8

  d 5, 6, 7, 8

3 What is the function of an OCU-DP?

  a To terminate the DDS circuit and protect the customer's equipment from power surges

  b To multiplex 24 DS0s into a DS-1 signal

  c To convert the unipolar signal of a computer into a bipolar balanced signal

  d To provide the 4-wire DDS interface to the customer

4 Which line coding do you use on a DDS circuit?

   a CMI

   b B3ZS

   c B8ZS

   d HDB3

   e AMI

5 What is the function of a multi-junction unit (MJU)?

   _____

   _____

   _____

6 Which of the following is not a possible DDS loop rate?

   a 2.4 kbps

   b 57.6 kbps

   c 19.2 kbps

   d 9.6 kbps

   e 4.8 kbps

7 How is an idle code coded on a 19.2-kbps DDS circuit?

   a BBBX0V

   b X0XXBB

   c 00XXBB

   d B0BB0V

8 Which of the following is the maximum loop rate of a DDS circuit, including overhead?

   a 56 kbps

   b 64 kbps

   c 72 kbps

   d 96 kbps

9 What is the main difference between a DDS circuit with a secondary channel and a DDS circuit without a secondary channel (other than the channel itself)?

_____

_____

_____

10 What is the main benefit of SW56 technology over DDS?

_____

_____

_____

This chapter covers the following topics:

- **T1 physical characteristics**—Covers the equipment involved in the production and transmission of the T1 signal, and the line preparation that must be performed to prepare the physical circuit for use as a T1.

- **T1 line-coding schemes**—Details the differences between the two main methods of encoding user traffic into a form transmissible over the T1 circuit.

- **T1 framing and formatting**—Explains the two alternatives for adding control bits to the T1 bit stream, so that frame boundaries can be identified by the receiving equipment.

- **T1 troubleshooting**—Offers practical advice on the test patterns that you can use to discover problems with a T1 installation. You also learn the significance of the three major carrier alarms that test equipment and data terminal equipment (DTE) can indicate.

- **Configuring a T1 controller**—Gives a sample configuration for Cisco equipment, with specific commands that are necessary to synchronize on each device, so that conflicts that can disable service do not occur.

CHAPTER 5

T1 Technology

This chapter introduces you to a specific digital circuit that is known as T1. You will become familiar with the method by which data is transformed into pulses of electricity, light, or some other media-dependent signal. This chapter also details the framing formats that the industry uses to form the T1 signal before it is transmitted. Finally, you will learn some valuable troubleshooting techniques and be presented with a sample configuration for Cisco devices.

By the end of this chapter, you should have no trouble understanding the value of T1 circuits and similar circuits in the family of digital signal transmission. Remember as you read that the development of T1 and related technology has resulted in the reduction of cost, both from a service provider standpoint and from the perspective of the service subscriber. This reduction in cost comes in forms such as the reduction of copper to service the same number of logical connections, which includes the cost of laying and maintaining the outside cable plant. Further savings result from the relative scale of equipment needed to terminate a single circuit, as opposed to each individual circuit that the T1 replaces.

In Chapter 3, "Analog-to-Digital Conversion," you are presented with a formula for calculating the digital rate of a bit stream generated from an analog source signal. What you can do with this digital signal is varied, but one of the most popular implementations for this 64-kbps bit stream is to combine it with others similar to it into a circuit that has, as one of its characteristics, a specific number of grouped channels. The number of channels depends on the circuit in question. Other noteworthy traits of such circuits that are produced by combining these 64-kbps bit streams, which serve to further differentiate them from one another, are as follows:

- Line-coding schemes
- Frame format schemes
- Physical distribution options
- Geographical popularity and support
- Required equipment for implementation

Differences among such multiplexed circuits can also be noted in the technical specification documents that should be consulted to find details of their implementation, although many such documents tend to treat a trait, rather than the circuit. Such specifications usually give details on the same characteristic for each group of circuit rates. This chapter details the primary features of one of these circuits that combines channels to create an autonomous entity, T1 (also written T-1). AT&T developed T1s in the early 1960's as inter-office trunks, but tariffed their use to consumers in 1984, after divestiture of the Regional Bell Operating Companies (RBOCs). You commonly use T1s as private WAN links within organizations and as public circuits that are offered by service providers to interconnect subscriber private branch exchanges (PBXs) and LANs, or as access trunks to the public network.

Table 5-1 compares and contrasts the most identifying features of three of the world's most popular families of digital telecommunications circuits. These are the T-, E-, and J-carriers. As a group, these families compose the plesiochronous digital hierarchy (PDH). Details of both E1 and J1 circuits appear in Chapter 6, "E1, R2, and Japanese Carrier Technology." Table 5-2 depicts the North American Digital Hierarchy (NADH), of which T1 is a member.

Table 5-1 *Plesiochronous Digital Hierarchy*

n	North America (Tn)		Europe (En)		Japan (Jn)	
	Number of DS0s	Rate (Mbps)	Number of DS0s	Rate (Mbps)	Number of DS0s	Rate (Mbps)
1	24	1.544	32	2.048	24	1.544
2	96	6.312	128	8.448	96	6.312
3	672	44.736	512	34.368	480	32.064
4	4032	274.176	2048	139.264	1500	97.728

Table 5-2 *North American Digital Hierarchy*

Digital Signal Level	Number of DS0s	Rate (Mbps)	Equivalent T1s
DS-0	1	0.064	n/a
DS-1	24	1.544	1
DS-1C	48	3.152	2
DS-2	96	6.312	4
DS-3	672	44.736	28
DS-3C	1344	89.472	56
DS-4	4032	274.176	168

In Table 5-2 the signal level known as DS-1C is basically the equivalent of two T1 circuits (48 DS-0s). Although the DS-1C signal is named after the DS-1 signal, the two DS-1s carried by the DS-1C are not easily accessible. You will read shortly about other signal levels that are created by multiplexing smaller signal levels.

The term plesiochronous comes from the Greek and means "nearly the same clock." This refers to the timing of the circuits not being identical. The actual signals they use come from different sources, but approximate each other so closely that communication is highly reliable. In other words, an expected disparity occurs between different links on the same circuit with respect to timing. However, because it is expected, it can be limited to a certain tolerance. Over the long term, the signals from different legs of the same circuit can become out-of-phase with one another. Even though the timing of the bits, and of the bit stream in general, can be said to be at the same rate, the actual times that the same bit event occurs can be completely different (phase difference).

Switching and cross-connect devices can exploit the relative closeness of the timing between the two links but can eventually be required to add or delete bits to compensate for the difference. The practice of intentionally dropping bits in an attempt to regain or maintain circuit timing is referred to as a controlled frame slip. Here, the word frame does not mean the same as it does in local-area networking. This type of frame is discussed in detail later in this chapter in the section "T1 Framing and Formatting."

There is an important issue surrounding the PDH and the general industry push to replace this technology with others that are more efficient and accessible (with regard to the actual information). The issue is that after individual channels are combined (multiplexed) into any one of these transmission media, it is not possible to access the individual channels or component circuits (in the case of the larger circuits) without first demultiplexing the transmission signal.

To clarify, multiplexing is the combining of individual source signals into a composite signal, which is characterized by capacity equal to or greater than (for additional overhead) the sum of the component signals. For example, it is through multiplexing that 24 DS-0s are combined into a single DS-1. However, when you multiply 24 by the individual channel rate of 64 kbps, you arrive at 1536 kbps. Upon closer inspection it can be seen from Table 5-1 that a T1 has a bit rate of 1544 kbps. The additional 8 kbps comes from formatting overhead that will be presented shortly.

The point is, those additional 8 kbps do not relate to any or all of the original traffic that emanated from the individual channels, but rather only from the formatting of the frame structure employed during the multiplexing process. Before these channels are broken back out at the receiving end, this overhead is removed, and the end devices on each receiving channel have no knowledge that the overhead was ever added to the circuit. In other words, the overhead is for the implementation of the larger multiplexed circuit, not for the individual channels.

The multiplexing used with the PDH is known as time-division multiplexing (TDM). TDM is characterized by all sources getting an interleaved slice of time, known as a timeslot, every n timeslots, where n is the number of channels being multiplexed. Concisely, a TDM circuit is one that offers the entire frequency of the multiplexed circuit for a specified fraction of the time that the circuit is in operation. The fraction is usually equal to $1/n$, where n is the number of channels being multiplexed. The timeslots in TDM do not vary with regard to their order of occurrence. For example, timeslot 5 always follows timeslot 4, and timeslot 1 always follows timeslot *n*, where *n* is again the number of channels being multiplexed.

Although TDM is the only multiplexing scheme that standard T1 technology uses, it is far from the only multiplexing scheme in existence or even in common use. Other schemes include, but are not limited to, frequency-division multiplexing (FDM), where a channel is assigned a slice of the overall frequency of the multiplexed circuit for the entire time of its operation (popular in inter-office trunks before TDM took over); and wavelength division multiplexing (WDM) and dense wavelength division multiplexing (DWDM), a set of technologies that increases the transmission capabilities of optical fiber by splitting the medium into multiple channels. Each channel is carried on different wavelengths of light. WDM is similar to FDM, in that these wavelengths represent the inverse of frequencies, each one a subset of the complete circuit. Each channel in WDM and DWDM has access to only its component frequency for the entire duration of the operation of the circuit, as in FDM. Figure 5-1 gives a visual representation of TDM. MUX is short for multiplexer.

Figure 5-1   *TDM*

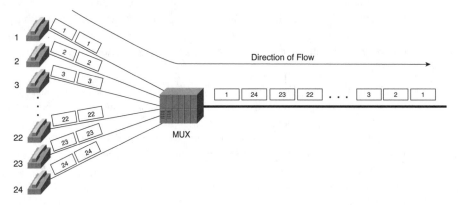

DS-0 is found in all aspects of the PDH. A DS-0 is the 64-kbps output of the analog-to-digital (A/D) conversion process that is detailed in Chapter 3. There is no T-carrier equivalent to the concept of a DS-0. Starting with T1, there is a corresponding DS level that numbers concurrently with the T-carriers. In other words, a T1 circuit carries a signal known as DS-1, and a T3 carries a DS-3 signal. It is the 24 DS-0s, one from each channel, that are multiplexed into a single DS-1. As mentioned earlier, there is no way to access the individual DS-0s that have been multiplexed into a DS-1, without first demultiplexing the DS-1 into the component DS-0s.

T1 Physical Characteristics

Recall from Chapter 3 that signals attenuate, or lose strength, as they travel along the transmission medium. Analog technology combats this loss with the use of amplifiers, which strengthen the level of any analog interference that also might have been picked up. For digital technology, such as T1, repeaters replace amplifiers. Repeaters are devices that regenerate a weakened signal, allowing noise and interference to be filtered out, thereby reconstructing the signal in its original form. The links between repeaters in a T1 network, and the links between end devices or central office (CO) equipment and their respective nearest repeaters are called spans. A T1 span is generally 6000 feet in length. The span between the end device or the CO and their nearest repeater is only 3000 feet, because when the equipment is put into a loopback state the roundtrip distance is 6000 feet.

A typical T1 installation might see customer equipment such as a router with a serial interface connected to a channel service unit/data service unit (CSU/DSU) with a V.35 cable. Figure 5-2 shows the pertinent equipment from the DTE to the service provider's network. The CSU/DSU is connected to a telecommunication company (telco) smart-jack with either a 15-pin D-shell connector or an 8-pin modular connector. The smart-jack is the telco demarcation point (demarc) and is telco property at the customer premises that connects to the telco's CO through two twisted pairs of copper (22–26 gauge), one for the transmit direction and one for the receive direction. T1 communication is full duplex, in that transmission and reception occur simultaneously. Most smart-jacks are addressable by equipment in the CO. This addressability feature allows telco personnel to send a signal to the smart-jack, which places it in loopback. After the smart-jack is placed in loopback mode, testing can be done on the circuit, up to the smart-jack.

Figure 5-2   *T1 Connection Between CPE and Telco*

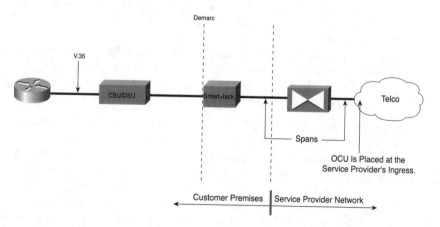

The CSU/DSU is a dual-function device that was once two separate devices before digital circuits were deployed to subscribers. The DSU connects to the CPE, and the CSU interfaces with the telco's network, where it eventually mates with an office channel unit

(OCU), the service-provider equivalent of a CSU. Each half of the CSU/DSU has specific functions that it supplies to the T1 circuit, but the main functions are, collectively, the protection of the telco's equipment from anomalies generated by the CPE, line equalization, and monitoring of the bit stream. In the preceding description of a typical T1 installation, a PBX with built-in multiplexer and CSU/DSU, connecting directly to the smart-jack, can easily replace the router.

As far as physical connectors are concerned, those that you see at the customer premises vary, especially with regard to the connection between the DTE and the data circuit-terminating equipment (DCE), which, in this case, are the router and CSU/DSU, respectively. DTE is a term that generally refers to the equipment that generates the traffic being transmitted across the network. DCE describes the equipment that takes the signal from the DTE and converts it into a format that is compatible with the network. These terms also describe the relationship between a PC and its modem.

The connectors that are fairly standardized are those that connect the CSU/DSU to the smart-jack. Again, these can be either a 15-pin D-shell connector (only on the CSU/DSU or PBX T1 card) or an 8-pin modular connector (on the smart-jack or both devices). On the smart-jack, the modular connector is referred to as an RJ-48X (RJ means registered jack), which has shorting bars that automatically create a loopback to the CO if the cable from the CSU/DSU is unplugged at the smart-jack. In other words, when the connector is removed from the RJ-48X receptacle, pin 1 shorts over to pin 4 and pin 2 shorts over to pin 5, which creates a physical loopback toward the network (service provider). The interface at the CSU/DSU is referred to as just RJ-48 (or specifically RJ-48C), because it has no shorting bars. The connection between these two jacks is a straight-through 8-conductor twisted-pair cable with matching 8-pin modular connectors on each end.

The CSU/DSU and smart-jack form a coupled unit. That is to say the signal is simply passed between them over a straight-through cable, with no change in pin function. For instance, transmitting toward the network is done on the same pins in both devices. Contrast this to the relationship between two devices, where one is considered DTE and the other DCE. In such a case, the transmit and receive pairs swap positions in the interfaces, so that a straight-through cable can be used for interconnection. Compare this with the RJ-48C and RJ-48X jacks that both face the network from the same perspective.

Figure 5-3 shows the corresponding transmit and receive pairs for the DB-15 and modular connectors. The DB-15 connectors are usually marked with respect to pin numbers, but the modular connector requires learned familiarity with pin numbering. Figure 5-3 also shows a graphical representation of pin numbers for the 8-pin modular connector. Pin 1 is found on the left side of the connector as you hold the insertion end up with the keying clip away from you (that is, with the contacts toward you). For testing or demonstration purposes, it is possible to make a T1 crossover cable by connecting pins 1 and 2 on each side to pins 4 and 5, respectively, on the other side. This cable can then connect two CSU/DSUs together, each one responding as if they were actually connected to a T1 network.

Figure 5-3   *T1 Connector Pinouts*

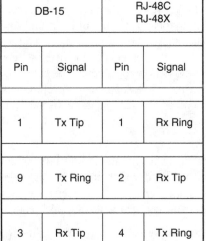

DB-15		RJ-48C RJ-48X	
Pin	Signal	Pin	Signal
1	Tx Tip	1	Rx Ring
9	Tx Ring	2	Rx Tip
3	Rx Tip	4	Tx Ring
11	Rx Ring	5	Tx Tip

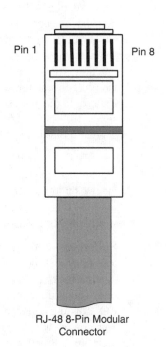

RJ-48 8-Pin Modular
Connector

Another interface that finds its origin in the days when DSUs and CSUs were separate devices is the DSX-1. This was the interface between the CSU and DSU and was considered the demarcation interface, with the CPE on one side and the service provider's equipment on the other. The physical connection was usually 8-pin modular or DB-15. Today, with the CSU and DSU functionality being integrated more often than not in one device, the demarc tends to be the opposite side of the CSU, its DS-1 interface with the provider's network.

Although the DSX-1 signal is the same as the DS-1 signal, the DSX-1 is a shorter-distance interface, which is not able to be deployed to the service provider's network without interfacing locally to a device with CSU functionality. The DSX-1 interface often connects two devices, such as PBXs or a PBX and a multiplexer, to each other locally, which simulates an actual T1-network connection. In COs the DSX-1 signal and interfaces interconnect pieces of equipment within the same office. Based on the distance between devices, line equalization (short-haul build-out) must often be applied to the DSX-1 interface to add gain to the signal, which allows it to be recognized and accepted by the opposing device. Line equalization is usually set in terms of feet, ranging from 0 to 655 feet, in roughly 133-foot increments.

Related to line equalization (inversely), but found on DS-1 connections to the service provider's network, is long-haul line build-out (LBO). LBO serves at least two main purposes. A more antiquated purpose stems from older repeaters requiring at least 7.5 dB of attenuation, with respect to the nominal signal level. If the CPE supplies a stronger signal than the repeater expects, pulses are not interpreted as the 1s they are intended to represent, and an all-0s signal results. More common today is the use of long-haul LBO to equalize signal strength between two or more customers whose circuits meet at a non-repeated line junction. This is a mutual cross-connect point or other such facility, whereby multiple circuits convene for redirection to the customers' respective first repeaters. If one customer is closer to the junction than the other, without LBO applied to the closer customer's DS-1 signal, the potential for crosstalk interference to affect the more distant customer's signal is great. Long-haul LBO is generally configurable ranging from 0 to –22.5 dB, in –7.5 dB increments.

The intent of the parenthetical comment in the first sentence of the last paragraph, regarding the two build-out schemes being inversely related, was to point out that while moving away from the 0 setting with line equalization, the signal level becomes stronger. Conversely, while moving away from 0 in the setting of long-haul LBO, a weaker signal level results.

Bridged taps and loading coils are common, everyday occurrences in the world of analog telephony distribution. Bridged taps are lengths of cable that are spliced into the primary distribution run, at a point as close to the subscriber as the facility can reasonably be tapped into. This is done to provide service without having to run a new pair all the way from the CO. Loading coils are sort of like non-powered analog amplifiers for frequencies in the voice range, which block frequencies outside of this range. Both bridged taps and loading coils are destructive to the quality of the T1 signal and must be removed before placing a T1 circuit into service.

The 6000-foot span between repeaters comes from the specifications for signal loss budget. Although different service providers vary as to where they decide to install a repeater, the customary rule of thumb is to install a repeater where the signal is measured to have a level of –30 dB (30 dB less than the original signal). A dB is a measurement of signal strength, with respect to a known value (relative power level). For audio levels, a dB is measured against a level of sound that is equivalent to the volume threshold of human hearing. For electrical signals, as in the case of a T1 signal, a dB represents the ratio of the observed signal strength, with respect to the initial signal strength from the source.

The mathematics behind dB values employs the science of logarithms. The logarithmic function results in a positive value when based on an argument greater than or equal to 1. For arguments less than 1 (but greater than 0), the logarithm is negative. Therefore, if gain has been introduced, and the resulting signal is stronger than the original signal, the logarithm is computed for a value greater than 1, and the result is positive. Conversely, if the signal experiences loss, in comparison to the original signal level, the ratio is less than 1 and the result of the logarithmic function is negative. It is important to understand that the negative sign in front of the dB level does not imply a negative signal level. In fact, the logarithmic function is undefined for values less than or equal to 0. The following examples illustrate the concept of the logarithmic function as it relates to dB of signal loss or gain.

- Formula for calculating dB loss or gain:
  - 10 log (observed signal level/initial level) = loss or gain in dB
- For an observed signal level equal to the original level:
  - 10 log (1) = 0 dB (neither gain nor loss)
- For an observed signal level 10 times the original level:
  - 10 log (10) = 10 dB (gain)
- For an observed signal level 1,000,000 times the original level:
  - 10 log (1,000,000) = 60 dB (gain)
- For an observed signal level one tenth the original level:
  - 10 log (1/10) = –10 dB (loss)

You now can compute that a loss of 30 dB represents a signal level observed at one thousandth of the initial signal level.

T1 Line-Coding Schemes

After all traffic is in digital form, whether by conversion or naturally, to transmit it across the T1 circuit you need to choose a line-coding scheme that allows the signal to make it across the physical medium without attenuating to the point of becoming unrecognizable. Internal wiring is in a more controlled environment and usually conforms to stricter standards than outside plant with regard to noise, interference, crosstalk, and capacitance. As a result, it is not as important to worry about the line coding for internal wiring, because the cabling often offers enough signal protection.

Outside wiring is a different story. Two metallic conductors that run in close proximity to one another and are separated by some form of dielectric, such as plastic and air, form a capacitor. In practice, if you attempt to send pulses across a circuit and you allow the current to flow in only one direction, as is the case with many inside-wiring encoding techniques, a capacitance builds up on the pair of wires, which causes some level of resistance to the normal flow of electrons. This eventually results in a discharge that can be mistaken for traffic. With today's internal wiring, the twisted pairs counteract the capacitance by creating a mutual inductance between the conductors of the pair.

Because external wiring cannot be counted on to be as homogeneous as internal wiring, and because the run length of the unshielded wiring inside is less than is required outside, line coding is chosen in such a way so as to prevent the situation that leads to a build-up of charge between the pairs. Therefore, if the cause is the flow of electrons in a single direction, the solution is to alternate the direction of flow for the electrons—an alternating current of sorts. Line-coding schemes that alternate polarity of pulses transmitted are considered to be bipolar. Figure 5-4 shows examples of bipolar signals with varying characteristics.

Figure 5-4 *Various Line-Coding Schemes*

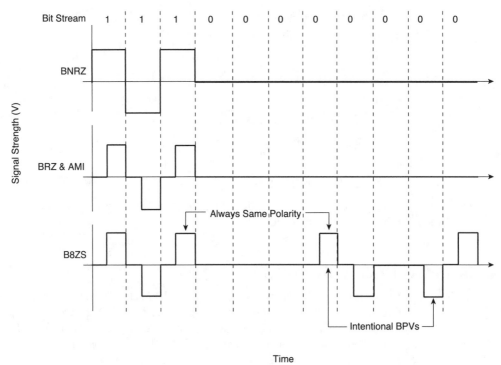

If the pulse simply moves through the zero-voltage reference point, without traveling along the axis at that point, the signal is considered a bipolar non-return to zero (BNRZ) signal. Conversely, if the signal does spend some amount of time at the zero-reference point, regardless of whether a 0 value is being transmitted, the signal is considered a bipolar return to zero (BRZ) signal. BRZ returns the signal to the zero-voltage reference during the transmission of a digital 0 and for half of the bit width of a 1's pulse. This prevents the loss of the center zero-value, during long stretches of consecutive pulse transmissions, which eventually results in misinterpreted pulse readings because the transmitting node is actually using a different scale from the receiver. An example of a BRZ signal is generated by the alternate mark inversion (AMI) line-coding scheme. BRZ and AMI are shown as the same graph in Figure 5-4. Another form of AMI, and hence BRZ, line coding is bipolar 8-zero substitution (B8ZS). Although similar to AMI, B8ZS is better suited for data transmission. B8ZS is covered later in this section.

The reason that the industry bothers with fancy versions of BRZ line coding is that standard BRZ line coding cannot satisfy the requirements of the original T1 equipment, for which the specifications were written. Remember the term plesiochronous. To be timed nearly the same, based on different clock sources, there has to be a third variable tying the two clocks together. That variable is the pulse stream on the T1 circuit. In fact, the two clocks need not actually be in phase with one another, but they are required to be running at the same frequency. This is much easier than remaining locked into the same phase.

If the requirement is to make sure that the clocks on either end are phase-locked with each other, the complexity of the T1 network is unacceptable, due to the delays that are inherent with multiple devices interconnecting and sending synchronous information all around the world. There would be no hope for transcontinental or satellite-based T1 circuits. All that is required is that there be enough pulses in the pulse stream to allow the receiving clock to remember the pulse width the sending node's clock is operating under. Because timing is recovered from the pulse stream, phase shift can be more than a frame's worth, while it would have to be less than the width of a pulse, otherwise.

With the preceding argument in mind, you need to specify exactly how many 0s, or bit times without pulses, can be coded consecutively, before the receiving circuitry loses its bit-width reference and declares a loss-of-signal condition (confusing the string of 0s with no signal at all). There is also a minimum percentage of pulses that must be seen within a bit stream, in addition to the maximum consecutive 0s allowed. The minimum requirements for any T1 pulse stream follow:

- Maximum 15 consecutive 0s
- Minimum 12.5 percent 1s density

To satisfy these requirements, AMI uses a process known as pulse stuffing. AMI forces the least significant bit (LSB) of every channel-byte to be a 1, thus reducing each channel to a 56-kbps conduit, and dropping the data rate of the T1 to only 1.344 Mbps. In doing so, AMI ensures that one out of every eight bits is a 1, thus satisfying the 12.5 percent minimum 1s density requirement. At the same time, if no more than seven 0s are allowed to pass, before a pulse is stuffed into the pulse stream, the requirement of no more than 15 consecutive 0s is in no danger of being violated. AMI also specifies a type of error known as a bipolar violation (BPV). AMI requires that any two consecutive pulses be of opposite polarity, no matter how much zero traffic comes between the two pulses. Although not the best error-detection method known, detecting and counting BPVs is actually a fairly accurate measure of the network's stability. Excessive BPVs can indicate failing equipment or overpowered facilities.

Nevertheless, AMI takes a rather large chunk out of the potential of a T1 circuit. In an effort to capture the stolen bandwidth, which was barely missed by voice applications, but would greatly benefit the data applications that were beginning to appear on the market, B8ZS was developed in the 1980's. B8ZS still watches for BPVs and it is still a BRZ technology. It also still watches out for the 1s density and consecutive 0s requirements of the T1 circuit, but it offers what is known as clear-channel transmission, where the entire DS-0 is available for user data. B8ZS works on the principal that if the transmitting node adds pulses to the bit stream, and the receiving node is able to easily recognize these pulses, and is able to determine the original values of the bits that were substituted, no user bandwidth needs to be sacrificed to satisfy the circuit's requirements.

As Figure 5-4 shows, when B8ZS circuitry detects a series of eight consecutive 0s, regardless of whether the boundary corresponds to a channel-byte, it substitutes a distinctive pulse pattern that has little chance of appearing naturally in normal traffic. In fact, this pattern contains two BPVs, which AMI would never allow, but which B8ZS receiving equipment recognizes and converts back to the eight 0s that were in the original data. As far as the receiving DTE is concerned, the substitution never occurred. The pattern is described in the standards as 000VB0VB. Numbering from left to right, the fourth bit of the eight consecutive 0s is an intentional BPV (V = violation). Because the transmitting circuitry remembers the previous pulse's polarity, it simply uses it to create the violation, instead of to prevent it, as it normally would. Any BPVs occurring outside of this pattern are still errors and are treated as such.

The fifth bit in the series 000VB0VB is bipolar (B), with regard to the previous intentional violation. This serves two purposes. First, it makes the pattern more distinct. Second, it atones for the transgression of the BPV, which is normally avoided to minimize line capacitance. The sixth bit is skipped, and the seventh and eighth bits are always opposite in polarity to the fourth and fifth bits, respectively, which causes another BPV and a correction. The next pulse that occurs naturally (after the eighth natural 0) is the same polarity as it would have been if the substitution had not taken place. The end result is that if at least one out of eight consecutive bits is a 1, the substitution does not take place, but the minimum requirements are still met. If substitution is required, the minimum requirements are more than satisfied. In fact, a pattern of all 0s is transmitted as 50 percent pulses.

T1 Framing and Formatting

You've been introduced to the concept of multiplexing multiple source flows into a single circuit. How the receiving end knows where in the resulting stream of bits each channel's traffic can be found is the result of two processes, known as framing and formatting. Recall from Chapter 3, that each 64-kbps bit stream is created from 8000 samples per second, each sample being represented by a single 8-bit byte of information. A T1 multiplexer does not buffer traffic from the channel sources. As a result, each byte created must be accepted by the T1 multiplexer as it is created. As the multiplexer collects a byte from each channel, it creates a frame. With 24 channels, each contributing a byte to the frame, each frame consists of 192 bits.

If each frame were placed back-to-back, the receiving end would still have no reference to where the channel bytes were located in the bit stream. For this reason, the multiplexer begins each frame with a single framing bit, making each frame a total of 193 bits. Figure 5-5 shows a framing bit inserted between the last byte of one frame and the first byte of the next frame. If you think about it, the aforementioned 8-kbps T1 overhead can be explained by these framing bits. If each channel puts out 8000 bytes per second, and each frame is created with one of these bytes from each channel, there must be 8000 frames created every second. With a single framing bit added to each frame, 8000 framing bits (also referred to as F-bits) per second compose the entire 8 kbps of overhead associated with the T1 circuit.

Figure 5-5   *The Use of F-bits in DS-1 Frames*

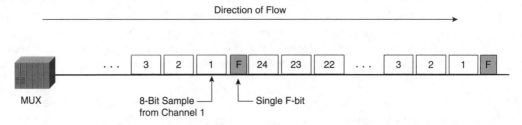

The following framing formats are discussed in the upcoming channel-bank sections:

- D4 Superframe (SF)
- Extended Superframe (ESF)

The value assigned to successive F-bits depends on the framing format chosen for the particular T1 circuit and is fixed for SF, as all SF F-bits are used for the alignment pattern. For ESF, some F-bits are fixed in value, while others vary from superframe to superframe. As with line coding, the framing format must be identical on both ends of each link in the T1 circuit. It is recommended that line coding and formatting be identical throughout the T1 circuit, across all links, but if this is not possible (read feasible), conversion must be performed at the junction of disparate coding and formatting. It is the collection of F-bits, with their controlled values over a series of frames, that allows receiving equipment to recognize frame boundaries by first recognizing superframe boundaries.

Although it is common to attribute the framing format known as D4, or SF, to the D4 channel bank, SF was actually introduced with the D2 channel bank. The term channel bank originally referred to the equipment that terminated the T1 circuit. Channel banks came in different forms, but the most accommodating channel banks afforded channel-by-channel access to the multiplexed T1 signals. Channel banks generally also include the functionality of T1 multiplexing. The various formats for channel banks that the industry regards as standards follow:

- D1 (1962)
- D2 (1969)
- D3 (1972)
- D1C (1973)
- D4 (1976)
- D5 (1982)

D1 Channel Banks

The original channel-bank standard was developed in 1962 by Western Electric and was called D1. D1 was characterized by the use of the LSB of every channel byte for on-hook/off-hook signaling. This left only 56 kbps on each channel for user traffic, a limitation that could not be lifted, even with the use of a line-coding technique designed for clear-channel transmission, such as B8ZS. Fortunately, this practice would change with future implementations. Recall, however, that this initial format was designed for use in voice-only circuits and that 56 kbps of speech quality is not that different from speech transmitted at 64 kbps.

With only seven bits per sample being allowed for each channel, the D1 channel bank was able to use a less complex companding algorithm known as μ-100, as opposed to the μ-255 algorithm discussed in Chapter 3. This allowed the diodes that performed the logarithmic companding process to be less precise and thereby require less cooling. The segmented approximation companding technique would not be introduced until later.

The D1 channel bank operated on two streams of channelized bytes to reduce the speed required of the early multiplexing electronics. Channels 1 through 12 contributed in that order to one stream, and channels 13 through 24 contributed to the other. The D1 channel bank interleaved the two streams into one. So, consecutive channels did not have consecutive timeslots. A byte from channel 1 was followed by a byte from channel 13, which was followed by bytes from channel 2, channel 14, channel 3, and so on.

For alignment to the frame structure, you can use two broad methods. Either a unique code can be sent in front of each frame to identify that a frame is to follow or bits can be inserted between frames, which forms a nearly unique code over the collection of inserted bits. The former method adds excessive overhead to the bit stream, but allows realignment or alignment verification at each frame. High-level data link control (HDLC) is an example of this type of frame alignment. You usually use this method for protocol-based framing.

For framing closer to the physical layer, as in the case of T1 (which can actually carry HDLC information with its own brand of framing), the use of framing bits inserted between frames is generally employed. This technique requires more frames to be analyzed and potentially dropped when alignment is lost, a condition known as out-of-frame (OOF), but it requires less overhead. With the quality of digital transmission pathways, chances are best taken with less overhead, despite the mild threat of more data loss. The receiver is more certain of alignment, the longer the alignment string inserted into the F-bits is. It is also customary for receiving equipment to not declare a state of misalignment solely based on one or two alignment-bit errors.

Because of the less costly F-bit alignment method, this format was chosen for the original DS-1 signal during the time of the D1 channel bank. The alignment pattern was a simple alternating 1s and 0s pattern in the F-bits. The concept of a SF was not considered for D1 channel banks. The alternating pattern succeeded because naturally occurring, long-term, alternating values every 193 bits is neither typical nor probable.

If an OOF condition is declared, the D1 channel bank steps back in the bit stream a set number of bits and begins checking for the alignment pattern every 193 bits. If the current position does not prove to be the F-bit location, the equipment advances bit by bit until the pattern is recognized. OOF is declared over when eight consecutive frames are recognized by the alternating F-bit pattern.

D2 Channel Banks and the SF

D1 channel banks were originally designed to connect a pair of nearby COs, where the analog signals would then be switched locally. When AT&T decided to use T1 to connect offices in tandem, the switches required analog signals for processing, so the digital signal would be converted back and forth from analog to digital and back again. The repetitive re-sampling of the analog signal resulted in increased quantizing noise by the time the signal made it to its final destination. The D2 channel bank was designed to minimize the signal-to-noise ratio that was so problematic with the D1 channel bank.

Additionally, the D2 channel bank saw the introduction of the SF format, which deviated from setting the F-bits to the arbitrary alternating pattern that was used by D1. However, similar to D1, the D2 channel bank used an interleaving scheme, although different from that used by D1, for combining the 24 channels onto the T-carrier. In fact, it used a two-stage scheme that started by taking 96 channels and splitting them into eight groups of 12. Channels are arranged sequentially within their respective group. The eight groups are then byte-interleaved to form a 96-channel signal. This composite signal is then inversely multiplexed onto four distinct DS-1 signals, each of the four being comprised entirely of two out of the eight 12-channel groups. All four DS-1 signals have to be terminated on the same D2 channel bank on the receiving side. Remember that this scheme was developed long before the intention of supplying T1 service to the subscriber.

The SF format groups 12 DS-1 frames (a 24-byte group of channel-bytes with an F-bit) into a data structure that is known as a superframe. Although signaling is carried in every channel-byte of the DS-1 signal used with D1 channel banks, SF formatting places signaling in every sixth byte of each channel, again by robbing the LSB. Because of this use of user data bits to communicate signaling information, the term robbed-bit signaling (RBS) is commonly used, because user data is irretrievably lost.

The justification is that for voice traffic, the LSB of a sample has the least effect on quantizing errors, should the signaling bit be different from the original user bit. Furthermore, only every sixth LSB is robbed. Figure 5-6 depicts the idea behind every sixth byte of each channel having the LSB robbed for signaling. Note that this translates to the 6th and 12th frames of each SF that is carrying signaling information. This fact will be revisited shortly, during the discussion of the F-bit values and their use. The signaling bits can carry different values, which results in four possible settings. The bits are referred to as the A-bit (frame 6) and B-bit (frame 12). Because more bits are freed up for user traffic, it was decided that the D2 channel banks would use μ-255 companding, instead of the μ-100 employed by the D1 channel banks.

Figure 5-6 *The SF Format*

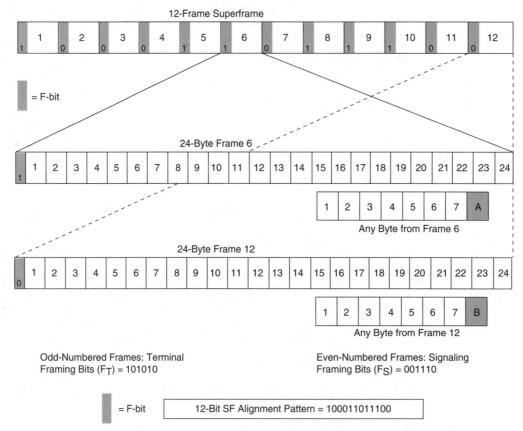

The set 12-bit pattern for the 12 F-bits is 100011011100. When this pattern is placed end-to-end, you cannot find this particular sequence of bits by starting on any F-bit but the first. You should be aware of two additional key points. The first is that the F-bits of the odd frames form what is called the frame alignment signal, or terminal framing bits (F_T), and the F-bits of the even frames in the SF compose what is known as the multiframe alignment signal, or signaling framing bits (F_S). The second is that the F_T bits provide the alignment function that D1 used every F-bit for (the pattern of alternating 1s and 0s remains), while the F_S bits quickly identify the locations of frames 6 and 12, where the signaling (hence the name) bits are located. The receiving equipment is looking for the transition of the F_S bits from 0 to 1 for frame 6 and from 1 to 0 for frame 12. If the six F_S bits are placed end-to-end, these are the only two transitions that occur. To overcome even the modest inconvenience of RBS, D2 channel banks allow common-channel interoffice signaling (CCIS), in which a 64-kbps channel is allocated for signaling, thus making all 8 bits of each channel in every frame available for user data.

D3 and D1D Channel Banks

While AT&T was attempting to produce a cheaper D1 channel bank, they discovered that much of the technology of the D2 channel bank also needed to be included. As a result, the D3 channel bank was suitable for long-haul connections, as was the D2. Similar to the D1, the D3 only operates on 24 channels. Unlike the D1, the D3 does so in a single stream, which precludes the need for interleaving non-consecutive channel-bytes.

Nevertheless, an upgrade was made available to give D1 channel banks D3 functionality. The upgrade could be purchased for less than a new D3 channel bank. The upgraded D1 was referred to as the D1D channel bank. The D1D is identical to the D3 in almost every way. The big difference is that the D1D uses the channel-byte sequencing method of the D1 channel bank, which makes it incompatible with the D3. In other words, both opposing D1s have to be upgraded, while switching one out with a D3 is not an option. Because the SF format and μ-255 companding are used with the D3 channel bank, it is closest in function to the D2, with the only notable differences being the number of channels on which it operates and the sequencing of the channel-bytes.

D4 Channel Banks

The SF format is also referred to as the D4 format, even though the D4 channel bank was not the first to provide SF functionality. The main impetus for the creation of the D4 channel bank was the 48-channel T1C (DS-1C) circuit that AT&T was concurrently designing. Also employing the SF format and μ-255 companding, the D4 channel bank standardized what we consider the channel-byte sequencing in use today, while allowing selectable backward compatibility with the previous models.

The D4 channel bank accepts analog voice, voice-band data (an example of which is a digital source modulated by a modem for transmission over an analog circuit), or digital signals by converting them to the appropriate format for the directly connected T1 or T1C. Two D4 channel banks can be directly connected through their T1C interfaces. Tandem interconnection of D4 channel banks even allows connection to a T2 circuit.

D5 Channel Banks and the ESF

The D5 channel bank is basically a D4 channel bank with the ability to multiplex 72 and 96 channels for direct connection to a T2 line. Additionally, the D5 channel bank introduces the ESF format. Although the D4 SF format was a vast improvement over the framing format of the D1 channel bank, it lacked certain accommodations for management and signaling. Although this was not a huge problem for voice traffic, as signaling could be included through RBS, data traffic could not use RBS and still get the most out of the T1 bandwidth.

Out of fairness to SF, T1-node CPE interfaces can be designed specifically for data applications. Such interfaces do not add RBS bits to the channels that have these non-voice inputs.

As a result, ESF was designed with a larger data structure, thereby allowing more functions to be derived from the F-bits of each SF, which for ESF is twice the length of the SF. This means that 24 F-bits are available with ESF and that not all the bits are required for alignment. Figure 5-7 shows the format of the ESF frame structure and the use of the F-bits with ESF.

Figure 5-7 *The ESF Format*

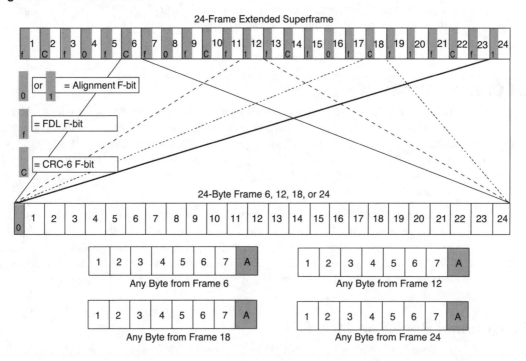

One of the problems the ESF format helped to overcome was the need to first take a D4-formatted circuit out of service before performing any testing procedures on it. This is simply due to the fact that there is no additional overhead, over which the testing signals can travel, without disrupting normal user-data traffic. For this purpose, the ESF format allows use, even proprietary use, of the 12 facility data link (FDL) bits, which are the F-bits for all of the odd-numbered frames in the ESF. Doing the math, you can verify that 4 kbps are available for FDL functions. To clarify, if you use 1 bit per frame, you use 8000 bits per second, as frames are produced at this rate. Because FDL bits come from every other frame, this cuts the 8 kbps in half, which results in the 4-kbps data rate of the FDL channel.

The alignment pattern for the ESF format is always set to 001011 and is installed in the F-bits of frames 4, 8, 12, 16, 20, and 24. The ESF alignment pattern is similar to that for SF in that repeating the pattern end-to-end precludes finding the pattern in these bits by starting in any F-bit but the first (frame 4). Unlike SF, however, the ESF alignment pattern has no component that points to the signaling frames (6, 12, 18, and 24). Such a pointer was never necessary after the SF boundary was defined. It was just an added redundancy defined for SF. The number of signaling bits for voice applications has doubled. They are now referred to as A-, B-, C-, and D-bits and appear in frames 18 and 24, in addition to the familiar frame 6 and frame 12 positions of the SF format. As a result, with ESF, there are 16 signaling states available.

The other six F-bits present in the ESF format are used for a 6-bit cyclic redundancy check (CRC-6), which is an error detection scheme that uses the identical algorithm to compute a 6-bit value that is based on the transmitted bits throughout the SF, not including the F-bits. If the value in these bit positions does not equal the locally computed value, based on the same algorithm and the same data-bit positions, an error is assumed and a counter is incremented. Data is not discarded at this level, but the CRC counter aids in management of the circuit by representing the bit-level health of the T1.

T1 Troubleshooting

There is a variety of testing that can be done to baseline or troubleshoot a T1 circuit, regardless of the frame formatting in use. With ESF formatting, there are even more benefits because testing and messaging can be performed without first taking the circuit out of service, as is necessary in the case of D4 formatting. ESF formatting makes use of the FDL bits to send a special data unit toward the CO equipment. At the CO, a device called a line-monitoring unit (LMU) is non-intrusively bridged across the circuit, where it reads the FDL bits from the signal and generates alarms if necessary.

In the specifications, specific registers are called for in CSUs that support ESF formatting. These registers are designed to maintain a history of problems that occur over a 24-hour period, usually updated in 15-minute increments. During the breakup of AT&T, it was ruled that the service provider has no natural rights to access information or control hardware beyond the demarc on the customer premises. ANSI T1.403 specifies that CSUs should communicate their register contents to the service provider (LMU) every second, instead of waiting for the LMU to poll the CSU for its information. If this information passes through a device known as the Digital Access and Crossconnect System (DACS), the FDL bits are regenerated along with the rest of the framing, and any communication across these bits is lost, regardless of whether the traffic is standards-based or proprietary. Because the FDL is not in constant use, manufacturers include functionality in their equipment, which allows it to communicate to, configure, and manage the remote device. One of the most popular uses of the FDL bits is the bit error rate testing (BERT).

BERT Testing

BERT testing is the sending of a known pattern onto the T1 circuit and monitoring whether the same pattern is received at the testing point. The testing point can be the other end of the circuit. It can be somewhere in the middle (for example, if the service provider is on-site and testing back to their office). It can be the same location from which the pattern was generated. It can even be the same device that generated the pattern. It is possible to send out a code, either in-band with the data or across the FDL bits, to place a device into a loopback state, which means that anything that device receives, it turns around and sends back to the transmitting device. Whether anything is done to the traffic before sending it back depends on what kind of loopback is implemented. Three types of loopback are used for various reasons:

- Network or line
- Payload
- DTE

The network loopback is controlled either by the service provider or at the CSU control panel or terminal interface. The loopback is generated from the network by repeating an unframed binary 10000 pattern, which can be sent in-band with the user data (AT&T) or across the FDL bits (ANSI). The network loop is then taken down with an unframed 100 pattern. The network loopback is invaluable for testing the efficacy of LBO settings configured by the network and on the CSU. This value is derived from the fact that the signal from the network is returned to the network, so that service providers can conduct BERTs, thus verifying the integrity of the portion of the T1 circuit that extends from them to their customer. This loopback is intended to allow bit-by-bit testing of the data stream because the framing is not regenerated but instead is returned as it was originally generated by the testing entity. Network loopbacks allow testing only up to the CSU functionality of the CSU/DSU.

The payload loopback is similar to the network loopback, in that network traffic is returned to the network, and the loop-up signal can be sent from the network. The difference is that testing with the payload loopback turned up tests through the CSU/DSU, up to the DTE interface of the CSU/DSU, in addition to the T1 facility. As such, the entire bit stream is reframed and regenerated before being sent back to the network.

Finally, DTE loopbacks are not actuated from the network, but must be turned up from the CSU/DSU panel, a terminal interface to the CSU/DSU, or by a code sent from the DTE. This loopback is made at the DTE side of the CSU/DSU. It sends the signal from the DTE back to the DTE. The CSU/DSU is also thoroughly tested during the DTE loopback, as it simulates a 4-kft (4000 feet) line before returning the signal to the DTE.

Although there are various patterns that can be transmitted during a BERT test, the following list contains the most popular patterns and their associated uses:

- Mark, or all 1s, simulates a keep-alive signal, which places the maximum bit count on the T1 and tests repeater power integrity.

- Space, or all 0s, discovers improperly configured equipment in the path of the test. This tests a B8ZS-coded circuit. If AMI exists in the path, it converts the intentional BPVs that are generated by B8ZS into legitimate bipolar pulses. Because the verification is performed after B8ZS removes its intentional BPVs, receiving anything but all 0s indicates the presence of AMI in the circuit.

- 1:1 is an alternating pattern of 1s and 0s, which is a one-to-one ratio of 1s to 0s. This pattern offers a signal with an appreciable number of pulses without taxing components. Such a pattern is useful when verifying round-trip connectivity.

- 1:7 is a repeating pattern of one mark, which is followed by seven 0s. This pattern creates a one-out-of-eight, or 12.5 percent, 1s density, which tests the minimum requirements.

- 3-in-24 is a pattern that not only tests the minimum 1s density by having three 1s out of 24 bits (12.5 percent), but also the maximum consecutive 0s limitation. This is because the pattern (100010001000000000000000) finishes with a string of 15 0s that are broken by the beginning mark of the next instance of the pattern. This pattern is occasionally referred to incorrectly as 3:24. This implies that there are three 1s for every 24 0s, when the ratio is actually 3:21.

- 2047, or $2^{11}-1$, is a pseudorandom pattern that consists of a maximum of 10 consecutive 0s and 11 consecutive 1s. A binary number that consists of only 11 1s has a value of 2047. This pattern is effective in testing digital dataphone service (DDS) and Integrated Services Digital Network Basic Rate Interface (ISDN BRI) circuits. Similar patterns, the names of which work out mathematically, as does 2047, are 63, 511, and 4095. Each one has similar applications and uses varying maximum blocks of 1s and 0s.

- $2^{20}-1$ is a pseudorandom pattern that consists of a maximum of 19 consecutive 0s and 20 consecutive 1s, which is a moderate test of the equipment's ability to handle excessive consecutive 0s.

- $2^{23}-1$ is similar to $2^{20}-1$, but it allows a maximum of 22 consecutive 0s and 23 consecutive 1s, thereby creating a more stressful test with excessive consecutive 0s.

- The Quasi-Random Signal Source (QRSS) is a version of the $2^{20}-1$ pattern, with consecutive 0s kept under the maximum of 15. This is the best pattern for simulating live data.

The term mark means a pulse and space refers to the lack of a pulse (1 and 0, respectively). Cisco equipment has a series of **debug** commands that allow BERTs to be conducted.

T1 Errors

The errors on T1 circuits come from two major categories:

- Format (or frame-level) errors
- Logic (or bit-level) errors

Format errors are those that violate the frame structure and its coding and 1s density requirements. Format errors include, but are not limited to, the following situations:

- BPVs
- Loss of signal (LOS)
- Loss of frame (LOF), or OOF
- More than 15 consecutive 0s
- Less than 12.5 percent 1s density
- Malformed pulses (width and height)

Both D4 and ESF are capable of detecting format errors, either directly or through the coding method that is employed.

In contrast to format errors, logic errors on a T1 circuit are basically caused by the insertion or deletion of pulses. It is possible for such an action to result in a format error, provided that the pulse affected represents a framing bit, but this is not a forgone conclusion. For certain even-count insertions or deletions that occur between consecutive pulses, logic errors can go completely undetected by T1 equipment. For example, if D4 formatting is being used, and no F-bits are altered, there is no mechanism to verify the insertion or deletion of pulses, and neither AMI nor B8ZS is capable of recognizing insertions that did not cause BPVs. In the case of B8ZS, this includes events that cause its intentional BPVs to appear illegitimate. ESF is able to detect a preponderance of insertions and deletions by way of the CRC-6 bits, which are computed on all original bits of the frame and compared by the receiving node to the CRC-6 that is computed on the arriving bits.

To clarify some of the terms in the preceding discussion, OOF occurs when the receiving circuitry cannot lock on the alignment pattern for the incoming frames. This condition persists until a configured amount of time passes, during which the alignment pattern is continuously recognized. LOS is usually the result of power loss or complete system failure on one side of the T1 and is characterized by the receipt of continuous unframed 0s. An LOS condition is usually declared after the receipt of 175 consecutive bit times with no pulse. BPVs can be caused by several factors, such as improper signal levels, opens or shorts in the wiring of the circuit, or mismatched line coding. These can result in frame errors if the F-bits are compromised egregiously enough, which tends to indicate the overall degradation of the circuit, possibly due to a failing component.

Because of the variety of components that can go into constructing a T1 circuit, each one potentially having its own clock source (the plesiochronous factor), it is likely that enough delay is introduced into the signal, from time to time, to disrupt the normal flow of traffic.

This delay is called jitter (low levels are referred to as wander), and too much can result in CRC-6 errors or in a phenomenon known as timing or frame slips. T1 components use phase-locked loop circuitry to try to keep the phase shift to a minimum. Controlled frame slips are the intentional discarding of frames, in an attempt to reacquire the alignment pattern before synchronization is lost. Occasionally, uncontrolled frame slips are necessary, whereby the T1 equipment clears its buffers, declares an OOF condition (after two of any four F-bits are in error), and attempts to regain synchronization by searching for the alignment pattern.

Other important terms to be familiar with involve the reporting and tracking of error conditions. For example, an errored second (ES) is one in which one or more format or logic errors occur. When the count gets up to about 320 in a single second, a severely errored second (SES) is counted. Consecutive severely errored seconds (CSES) are generally counted to determine when a failed signal state should be declared. In more specific terms, ten CSESs result in a LOS.

Alarm Conditions

T1 alarm states are commonly referred to based on the colors of the lights that the original T1 equipment used to designate that particular alarm condition. Each of the three alarms discussed in this section are considered major alarms and are not usually declared for events that do not directly result in some form of failed signal state or OOF/LOS condition. In fact, many manufacturers specify a set of minor alarm conditions that serve to alert administrators to the impending risk of a major alarm. If a minor alarm is not warranted, counters are still incremented, so that proactive management can possibly prevent more serious conditions.

The first two alarm conditions presented here are the red and yellow alarms, known collectively as carrier failure alarms (CFAs). When a T1 device receives errors beyond a sometimes-configurable threshold, it declares a red alarm condition. Often two or three seconds of continuous LOS or OOF will trigger a red alarm. In this case, the device immediately attempts to transmit a code that signals the opposite end to declare a yellow alarm condition. Thus, knowing which end is in which condition makes it easier to begin pinpointing the cause of the problem. Generally 10 to 20 seconds of healthy signal ends the CFA condition.

Very often, however, the complete circuit goes down, which places both ends into the red alarm. In this situation, neither end has the ability to transmit the yellow alarm code to the other end. On D4 circuits, the yellow alarm is signaled to the opposite end by setting the second most significant bit in each byte to 0, thus disrupting all traffic that might otherwise be traveling in that direction (any bit affects data, but the second bit also gravely affects voice traffic). This is rarely an issue because transmission in one direction is not usually beneficial. ESF circuits signal the yellow alarm by alternating eight 1s and eight 0s in the 12 FDL bits for at least one second.

The third major alarm, the blue alarm, is also known as the alarm indication signal (AIS) and as a keep-alive signal. It is characterized by a continuous stream of unframed 1s. A T1 node that receives the AIS sends out the yellow alarm signal. This pattern serves at least two primary functions:

- Signify a malfunction in the transmitting node (the CSU is not receiving data from the DTE side)

- Keep repeaters and other equipment supplied with pulses for timing recovery

A T1 repeater can also generate the AIS toward the CSU, which in turn generates the yellow alarm signal, which places the opposite end in the yellow alarm.

To summarize, the red alarm is not a transmitted signal, but rather a condition entered into by equipment that is receiving a signal with problems. The yellow and blue alarm signals are actually transmitted across the circuit. If intelligent DTE or a test set is in place and able to detect these signals, the following summarizes the significance of the yellow and blue signals from the perspective of such equipment:

- The yellow alarm signal indicates problems in the transmit path.

- The blue alarm signal indicates problems in the receive path.

Configuring a T1 Controller

This section gives two examples of how to configure a T1 controller on Cisco networking devices.

To access the T1 controllers for configuration, you have to be in global-configuration mode and then select the appropriate T1 controller.

Example 5-1 shows the simple configuration of a T1 controller for ESF framing and B8ZS line coding. Additionally, the controller is being configured to supply equalization (gain) for cables up to 133 feet.

Example 5-1   *Configuration of a T1 Controller*

```
router#configure terminal
router(config)#controller t1 0/0
router(config-controller)#framing esf
router(config-controller)#linecode b8zs
router(config-controller)#cablelength short 133
router(config-controller)#clock source line primary
router(config-controller)#no shutdown
```

The commands listed in Example 5-1 allow you to configure a basic T1 controller. You need to be aware of your timing requirements. Verify whether you should receive timing from the line (if the circuit is from a service provider, chances are you are to clock to the line). The timing defaults to line, and by adding **primary** to the timing statement, you are identifying the device's primary timing source.

Configuring a T1 Hairpin

Figure 5-8 shows the use of a drop and insert function, which is also referred to as a hairpin connection. This allows you to redirect timeslots and then drop out the remaining timeslots to another device. Here, timing is important to remember because the same circuit's DS-0s travel through multiple devices. In Example 5-2, the **clock source internal** command at the end of the **controller t1 0/1** configuration is necessary if this controller will be providing the timing to the device at the other end of the cable attached to **controller t1 0/1**.

Figure 5-8   *T1 Hairpin Configuration Using Drop and Insert*

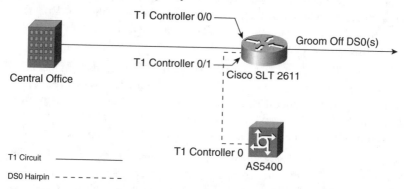

Example 5-2 shows the sample configuration of two T1 controllers within the same Cisco Signaling Link Terminal (SLT) 2611. Figure 5-8 shows the relationship between the SLT and its external neighbors. The **channel-group** command under **controller t1 0/0** identifies channel 1 as the signaling channel that is referenced by commands to pass this signaling on to another device. The **tdm-group** commands establish the numerical identifiers that are used in the final command of the configuration. Using these identifiers, the **connect** command mates the same 23 channels from one controller to the other and specifies an arbitrary connection name (hairpin) that appears in the configuration, but that does not have to reference any other command.

Example 5-2   *Hairpin Configuration of a Cisco SLT 2611*

```
router#configure terminal
router(config)#controller t1 0/0
router(config-controller)#framing esf
router(config-controller)#linecode b8zs
router(config-controller)#cablelength short 133
router(config-controller)#clock source line primary
router(config-controller)#channel-group 0 timeslots 1
router(config-controller)#tdm-group 1 timeslots 2-24
router(config-controller)#exit

router(config)#controller t1 0/1
router(config-controller)#framing esf
router(config-controller)#linecode b8zs
router(config-controller)#cablelength short 133
router(config-controller)#tdm-group 2 timeslots 2-24
router(config-controller)#clock source internal

router(config-controller)#exit
router(config)#connect hairpin t1 0/0 1 t1 0/1 2
```

Summary

In this chapter you were introduced to the PDH, which includes digital carriers from all over the world, each one based on the same 64-kbps DS-0. The NADH takes its place in the PDH and exhibits a couple of additional levels, in comparison to the other hierarchies. T1 fits near the bottom of the NADH and is a component of higher-level circuits.

The T1 circuit extends from the CSU function on the subscriber side to the CO, over two 22- to 26-gauge copper pairs that operate in duplex mode. T1 line repeaters can be placed every 6000 feet between the customer premises and the CO, but only 3000 feet from the customer to the first repeater, and from the last repeater to the CO. A device called a smart-jack is used as the demarcation point. The smart-jack is placed at the customer premises and allows control by the CO.

Line coding is required to transmit a T1 over the physical medium that connects the subscriber to the service provider. T1 circuits require that no more than 15 consecutive 0s be transmitted, and at least 12.5 percent of the traffic must be 1s, on average. AMI and B8ZS are both BRZ line-coding schemes that satisfy these requirements in different ways. AMI limits bandwidth, and B8ZS permits user traffic to run on clear channels.

As the multiplexer collects a byte from each channel, it creates a frame. With 24 channels, each contributing a byte to the frame, each frame consists of 192 bits and a framing bit, which makes each frame a total of 193 bits. 8000 framing bits per second comprise 8 kbps of overhead associated with the T1 circuit. D4 and ESF both use an alignment pattern that comprises some or all of the F-bits. ESF offers additional functionality with its expanded SF size. Formatting methods were introduced with devices called channel banks, which started with D1 in 1962 and extended up to D5 by the 1980's. On-hook and off-hook status is communicated by RBS, in which actual user traffic is overwritten by this status signaling.

Troubleshooting a T1 is made easier by the ability to send loop codes to T1 devices or to place them into loopback mode directly from the console of the device. When in loopback mode, a device returns the traffic it receives on its receive pair. BERT tests can be run while the T1 device is looped up, thus verifying the integrity of various portions of the T1 circuit. Various test patterns can be injected onto the T1 circuit, each one with a different purpose. T1 errors come in two forms, format and logic errors. Both formatting methods (D4 and ESF) can detect format errors because they both have F-bits to be monitored. Only ESF is capable of detecting most instances of logic errors, by way of the CRC-6 bits. An OOF condition results from too many F-bit errors, and a LOS condition stems from a complete lack of pulses being detected on the circuit.

Three major alarms are specified for T1 management. They are denoted by their original lighted colors. Two of them, the red and yellow alarms, are considered CFAs because they are related and both signify that a severe problem exists on the network. The third alarm, the blue alarm, is also known as the AIS. It is characterized by a stream of unframed 1s, which generates a keep-alive signal while the device is attempting to come back up.

Review Questions

Give or select the best answer or answers to the following questions. The answers to these questions can be found in Appendix A, "Answers to Review Questions."

1 How many DS-0s make up a T1 circuit?

   a 16

   b 24

   c 32

   d 30

2 What is the difference between AMI and B8ZS?

   _____

   _____

   _____

3 What is another term for the alarm indication signal?

   a Red alarm

   b Yellow alarm

   c Blue alarm

   d CFA

4 How many bits are in a frame, including the F-bit?

   a 191

   b 192

   c 193

   d 194

5 How many frames are in a D4 superframe? How many in an extended superframe?

   a 1, 2

   b 12, 12

   c 12, 1

   d 192, 384

   e 12, 24

6 What are the FDL bits used for in ESF formatting?

_____

_____

_____

7 What are the CRC-6 bits used for in ESF formatting?

_____

_____

_____

8 In the D4 superframe, what are the two types of F-bits and their uses?

_____

_____

_____

9 What condition is declared when two out of four consecutive F-bits are found to be in error?

   a OOF

   b LOS

   c BERT

   d SES

10 What does a node that is in red alarm or that is receiving the keep-alive signal attempt to do?

_____

_____

_____

This chapter covers the following topics:

- **E1 introduction**—An introduction to E1 including a brief discussion of its history.

- **E1 physical characteristics**—An overview of the physical characteristics of E1.

- **E1 framing**—A discussion of E1 framing including NO-CRC-4 framing and CRC-4 framing.

- **E1 line coding**—Includes coverage on High Density Bipolar of Order 3 (HDB3) line coding.

- **Configuring an E1 controller**—A discussion of basic E1 controller configurations and an Expert White Board on configuring an E1 hairpin.

- **R2 signaling characteristics**—An overview of R2 signaling. Although this is a signaling type, and not a circuit, R2 is included here because it is almost always associated with E1 circuits.

- **R2 configuration on a Cisco E1 controller**—This section builds upon the basic E1 configuration coverage by adding support for R2 signaling.

- **Japanese Digital Hierarchy (JDH)**—An overview of the JDH and how it maps to the North American Digital Hierarchy (NADH) and the international community.

CHAPTER 6

E1, R2, and Japanese Carrier Technology

E1 Introduction

If you work in North America, you may or may not have ever had any exposure to an E1 circuit. E1 is the Level 1 digital signal that is found in the International Digital Hierarchy developed by the International Telecommunication Union Telecommunication Standardization Sector (ITU-T, formerly CCITT). Most countries around the world use E1 circuits, with the exception of North America and Japan. Parts of Korea, Taiwan, and Hong Kong also use T-Carrier interfaces, although this use is decreasing gradually.

NOTE   Japan uses T-Carriers and a national specific format known as J1. J1 will be covered later in this chapter.

The E-Carrier data rates and operation were derived from a set of ITU standards that range from G.703 to G.822. Admittedly, the E-Carrier technology is different than its North American counterpart, but it still uses many of the same pulse code modulation (PCM) principles. Referring back to Chapter 3, "Analog-to-Digital Conversion," remember that the companding method is a major difference between E-Carrier (A-Law) and T-Carrier (μ-Law). The companding algorithm is only important when using the T- or E-Carrier circuits for voice. Extremely poor voice quality can result from a companding mismatch during a voice call. However, if data is to be transported, the companding differences are no longer an issue.

Upon its inception in the late 1950s, one of the main problems with the T1 design was its initial line coding format. As you might recall, alternate mark inversion (AMI) steals the least significant bit to ensure against 1s density violations. Again, this limits the amount of bandwidth available per digital service 0 (DS0) to 56 kbps. Although ANSI wanted everyone to use its set of standards, the ITU decided against T-Carrier and created its own set of standards.

E1 Physical Characteristics

Similar to T1 technology, an E1 refers to the carrier facilities associated with the digital signal. E1 circuits are also dedicated point-to-point synchronous circuits. Similar to T1, E1 circuits are equally susceptible to timing issues associated with multiple clock sources. Don't confuse the synchronous circuit with the plesiochronous network structure. Remember that plesiochronous networks contain multiple synchronous circuits with different clock sources.

An E1 circuit differs in several ways from a T1 circuit. The first, and most noticeable, is the allocation of DS0s. An E1 circuit has 32 DS0s, instead of 24 DS0s, which gives it a total bandwidth of 2.048 Mbps. Out of these 32 DS0s, 30 or 31 of them might be for bearer traffic (depending whether or not you use timeslot #16 [TS16] for signaling or bearer traffic).

An argument can be made as to whether E1 circuits are common channel signaling (CCS) or channel associated signaling (CAS). By definition, CCS states that the signaling is not intrusive to the data, but CAS states that signaling is intrusive, or non-separable from the data. The fact is, you can use E1 circuits in several different ways. Basic E1 circuits are typically found in CAS configurations. When the circuit is set up as CAS, TS16 splits between the circuit timeslots at timed intervals and the bits for one timeslot cannot be shared with another.

However, when you use an E1 circuit in a CCS configuration, all the timeslots use or share TS16 as a common resource. For example, if you use the E1 circuit as a Signaling System 7 (SS7) signaling link or as an Integrated Services Digital Network Primary Rate Interface (ISDN PRI) the circuit can be considered CCS. The reason for the CCS classification is that in both instances, TS16 can provide signaling for any of the other timeslots on the circuit. Although the signaling is physically in-band, the signaling is logically out-of-band because the signaling is carried over a separate timeslot.

You do not have to use TS16 for signaling, particularly in the cases of ISDN PRI and SS7. It is common in both of these instances to have E1 circuits with 31 channels available for bearer traffic. ISDN PRI circuits can be deployed in groups with something called non-facility associated signaling (NFAS). NFAS allows a single ISDN D-channel to provide call control for up to 479 B-channels. So, in a NFAS group with 5 PRIs, the first PRI uses TS16 as the NFAS D-channel. You can use TS16 in PRIs 2–5 for bearer traffic.

SS7 is a similar case to ISDN. A single signaling link can provide call control for thousands of timeslots (trunks). Within the first E1 span, circuits can use TS16 as the SS7 signaling link, and subsequent E1 circuits can use TS16 for bearer traffic.

There might be other instances that allow you to reclaim the 16th timeslot for bearer traffic, particularly if you are using the same vendor's equipment on both ends of the circuit and a proprietary signaling format has been put in place. However, these proprietary signaling formats are not nearly as common as the usage described with NFAS or SS7. Figure 6-1 shows the allocation of the channels for an E1 circuit.

Figure 6-1   *DS0 Allocation on an E1 Circuit*

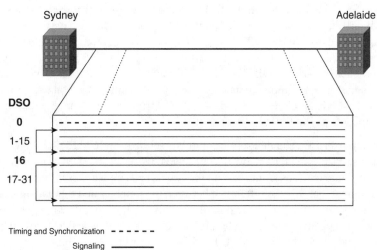

E1 circuits, similar to T1 circuits, are referred to as co-directional interfaces. A co-directional circuit is defined when timing information and the bearer traffic take the same physical path between nodes and in the same direction. Figure 6-2 shows a co-directional circuit deployed as two copper pairs of wiring. Remember that because of time-division multiplexing (TDM), it is possible to carry 32 timeslots over just four wires.

Figure 6-2   *Co-Directional Circuit Between Endpoints*

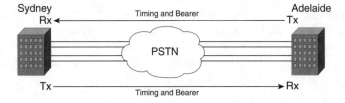

E1 circuits are deployed throughout the international community on one of three types of medium:

- 120 ohms unbalanced twisted copper cable

- 75 ohms balanced coax cable with Bayonet Neil Concelman (BNC) connectors

- DB-15 connector

If using twisted pair, you are using pins 1, 2, 4, and 5 of the modular plug. Pins 1 and 4 are a pair, as are pins 2 and 5. Similar to T1, to make a cross over you cross pins 1 and 4 and cross pins 2 and 5. If using balanced coax cable, you most likely have two BNC connectors: one for Tx and one for Rx. DB-15 connectors are more common with T1 deployments, but you can use them with E1 circuits. A DB-15 connector has 15 pins and is similar to a monitor cable connector. DB-15s are only found inside premises as a short haul connector from a smart-jack or similar connector. The type of medium that you use depends solely on what your service provider can deploy to your location. Cisco makes equipment that can accommodate any of these types of connection.

E1 circuits also use a channel service unit/data service unit (CSU/DSU) for communication with the service provider's network. For review purposes, the DSU function takes a unipolar signal (such as from a computer system) and converts it into a bipolar balanced signal. Remember that the difference between the unipolar and bipolar signals is that the unipolar signal only has a single polarity, positive or negative. The bipolar signal has both positive and negative polarities. The CSU function of the device interfaces directly with the network and terminates the circuit. The CSU also formats the information from the DSU for transmission over the E1 circuit.

A common configuration with E1 circuits on Cisco routers is for the computers to communicate with the router over Ethernet. The router, in turn, is connected to the E1 circuit and it forwards specified traffic out the E1 connection.

When an E1 circuit is deployed, attenuation must be taken into consideration. The general rule of thumb when deploying E1 circuits is that you can deploy regenerators every 4800 feet, or if there is –40 dB or more loss on the circuit. Irrespective of the standard loop length, as the dB loss reaches higher than –40 dB, the signal might be too weak for the receiving equipment to use effectively. –40 dB is only an estimate because the dB loss can vary from –38 dB to –44 dB before a repeater is placed on the circuit. The actual cutoff for the signal depends on the circuit location and the service provider installing the circuit. This amount of loss can be caused by faulty equipment on the line, bad cabling, or extreme environmental conditions in loop lengths less than 4800 feet.

NOTE   Remember that with digital signals, you use regenerators. The regenerator does not just amplify the signal as with analog but completely regenerates the digital signal stream.

E1 rates are not expressly limited to 2.048 Mbps. As with T1, subrate offerings have been specified in ITU specifications. These subrate offerings vary depending on location and what your service provider can provide to you. The two commonly deployed services are the data rates of 64 kbps (a single DS0) and 384 kbps (six DS0s). 384-kbps subrate E1s are most commonly used in video conferencing applications, and can also be deployed in combination with ISDN. The physical and electrical characteristics of these subrate interfaces do not differ from that of a full 2.048-Mbps E1 circuit. This also dictates that these subrate interfaces include TS16 as the signaling timeslot.

Subrate circuits have a set of priorities that define which timeslots you should use first. This allows the service provider to divide single E1 circuits into many subrate circuits through a device such as a Digital Access and Crossconnect System (DACS).

NOTE   There is always a catch with technology. Although it is stated that you use TS16 for signaling, you do not have to use it if an out-of-band or proprietary signaling method is in place. In these cases, you can use TS16 for regular traffic transmission, as any other timeslot.

E1 Framing

E1 frames are larger than their T-Carrier counterparts. The E1 frame has a total of 256 bits (8 bits * 32 timeslots). Instead of grouping frames into segments of 12 Superframe (SF) or 24 Extended Superframe (ESF), E1 circuits group frames into clusters of 16. This is known as a Multiframe 16 (MF16). Each MF16 is 4096 bits long.

Within each MF16, even and odd frames serve different purposes. Even frames control actual frame alignment and odd frames identify circuit alarms. Several different types of bits are used in a standard E1 frame. Not only are there different types of bits in each frame, but you can use these bits differently depending on whether you are using cyclic redundancy check with 4 bits (CRC-4) framing.

Within frame 0 of the MF16, TS16 manages MF alignment by using what is called the Multiframe Alignment Signal (MFAS). This process is detailed over the next few pages. TS16 in the remaining frames within the MF16 is set aside for CAS, ISDN, or QSIG signaling. QSIG is based on Q.931, and is primarily deployed for private branch exchange (PBX) applications.

NO-CRC-4 Framing

The first bit in each frame is a reserved bit that can be used for a CRC if you are using CRC framing. CRC-4 framing is the most common type of CRC framing and is discussed further in the next section. CRC-8 and CRC-16 framing also exist, and the number specifies how many bits are set aside for the CRC. However, CRC-8 and CRC-16 are rarely if ever used. In the event that you are not using CRC, the first bit is flagged as a 1 if the circuit is connected between two different countries. If the circuit is within national borders, the first bit can be used for any user application (and not necessarily flagged as a 1).

On even frames without CRC, the next seven bits are used as the framing alignment signal. This allows the framers in the CSU/DSU on each end of the circuit to synchronize their patterns and align the signal. Figure 6-3 shows the difference between the even and odd frames when there is no CRC framing. Pay attention to the 7-bit framing alignment signal in the even frame.

Figure 6-3 *Framing Alignment Without CRC*

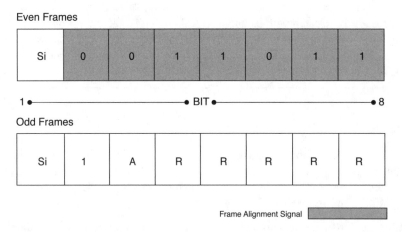

The first bit in each frame (Si) is reserved for international use. The bit is to be flagged as a 1 in the event that the E1 circuit traverses an international border. If it does not, the first bit can be used for a national application, such as providing added error monitoring control. The A-bit is used for alarm transport, and the bits marked as R are reserved bits that can be used for national applications.

In the odd frames without CRC, the second bit is flagged as a 1 intentionally to avoid mimicking the frame alignment signal. The third bit of odd frames is used for alarm transport. During normal operation, the third bit is equal to 0. If a loss of signal (LOS)—Red Alarm—is detected on the line, the circuit equipment attempts to transmit a remote alarm—Yellow Alarm—to the other end of the circuit by toggling the third bit to a 1. Figure 6-4 shows the circuit equipment toggling the third bit in the frame for alarm transport when a LOS is detected.

Still within odd frames, bits 4 to 8 are reserved bits that can be used for link maintenance and monitoring, nationally specific applications, or in some instances even nationally proprietary synchronization messages. If the bits are not being used for a specific function, they are toggled to 1 within the CSU/DSU.

Figure 6-4 *Alarm Detection and Transmission*

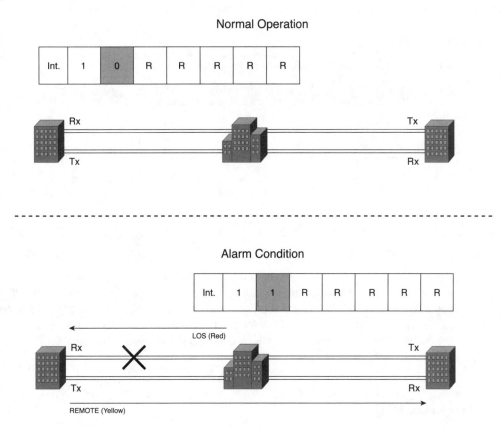

CRC-4 Framing

CRC-4 framing uses a CRC to verify the integrity of the framing sequence. When you use CRC-4 framing, the frames are broken down a bit differently. CRC-4 framing splits each MF16 into two equal segments, often called submultiframes.

The first submultiframe groups frames 0 through 7, and the second submultiframe groups frames 8 through 15. Within each submultiframe, the even frames (0, 2, 4, 6, and so on) place the CRC bits in the first bit position. CRC bits located in 0, 2, 4, and 6 act as a CRC for the first submultiframe. CRC bits located in frames 8, 10, 12, and 14 act as the CRC for the second submultiframe. There are four CRC bits, thus the term CRC-4 framing. Odd frames use the first bit position to denote an error when detected by the CRC bits. The error is flagged with an E-bit. Figure 6-5 shows the locations of the C-bits that you can use for the CRC, and the E-bit that flags detected errors.

Figure 6-5 *CRC Bits and Error Detection Bits in CRC-4 Framing*

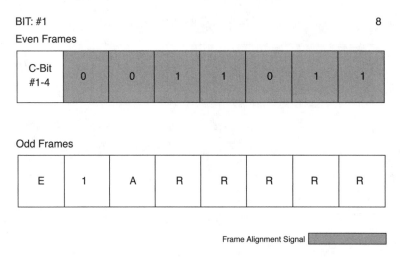

Far-end block errors (FEBEs) are transmitted to a sending device to indicate that an error has occurred at the receiving end. FEBEs are commonly detected if the framing types do not match on both sides of the circuit. For instance, if you have set your CSU/DSU to NO-CRC-4 framing, and the service provider is set to CRC-4 framing, it results in a FEBE on the circuit. The reason for this is that the remote end is expecting to receive the CRC bits in the even frames, but you are not sending them.

E1 Line Coding

Although E1s are different circuits, they still must have a way to encode information onto the circuit path. Two types of line coding can be associated with E1 circuits: AMI and HDB3. Although both are possible, AMI is rarely if ever used on an E1 circuit. For this same reason it is rarely used on T1 circuits; the use of AMI limits your data rate per DS0 to 56 kbps. Nevertheless, it is an option and is included on Cisco E1 controllers for configuration.

HDB3 Line Coding

HDB3 line coding is the ITU answer to the 1s density problems associated with phase locked loop (PLL) circuits. The history of HDB3 is somewhat interesting. Believe it or not, it was actually created by the ITU prior to the development of bipolar 8-zero substitution (B8ZS) by ANSI. So in essence, this was the ITU's answer to the limitations set forth by AMI. When using HDB3, no more than three consecutive 0s are allowed on the circuit. As with B8ZS, HDB3 inserts a unique bipolar violation that both ends of the circuit understand as a string of 0s. The way that this works is that if there is a string of four 0s, the last zero is encoded as the same polarity of the last known pulse. On the receiving end, when two pulses are received as the same polarity, the receiver changes the second pulse back into a 0 because it understands that change to be equivalent to the initial string of 0s. Figure 6-6 shows how HDB3 deals with a string of 0s by encoding it as a unique bipolar violation.

Figure 6-6   *HDB3 Unique Bipolar Violations*

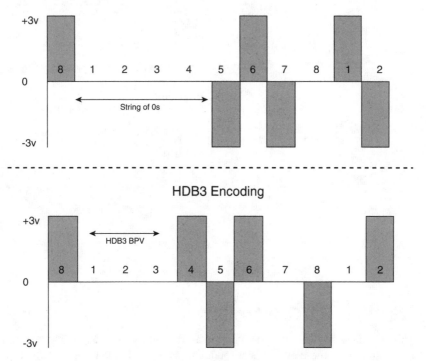

To take this a step further, HDB3 also states that the unique bipolar violations must alternate for the line coding pattern to be kept. However, it is possible that the last known good pulse remains the same polarity. Because HDB3 must ensure that the bipolar violation alternates, HDB3 forces the alternate polarity on the next encoded bit (which at this point is a 0) to the opposite 1 polarity state. In other words, if the standard bit encoding does not allow for the alternating of the bipolar violation, HDB3 manually alternates the bit pattern. The remote device also can decode this group as a string of 0s. Figure 6-7 shows how HDB3 alternates the bit pattern, if needed, when inserting the unique bipolar violations.

Figure 6-7 *Alternating HDB3 Bipolar Violations*

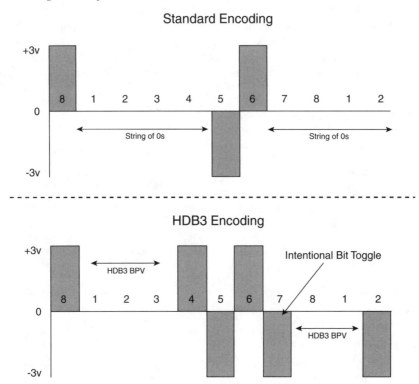

Configuring an E1 Controller

This section shows you how to configure an E1 controller a couple of different ways. The E1 controllers in these exercises are standard dual port E1 controllers with drop and insert (VWIC-2MFT-E1-DI). It is important to remember what IOS version and Cisco equipment you are using. Command syntax can change from box to box.

Basic E1 Controller Configuration

To access any type of controller for configuration, you have to be in global configuration mode. After you are there, select the appropriate E1 controller. Example 6-1 shows the commands required to configure an E1 controller for normal operation.

Example 6-1 *Configuring an E1 Controller for Normal Operation*

```
2600-1(config)#controller e1 0/0
2600-1(config-controller)#framing no-crc4
2600-1(config-controller)#linecode hdb3
2600-1(config-controller)#clock source line primary
2600-1(config-controller)#no shutdown
2600-1(config-controller)#^C
2600-1#wr
```

NOTE   The line coding has been set in the example to show the syntax, but the defaults are CRC-4 for the framing and HDB3 for the line coding.

The commands listed in Example 6-1 allow you to configure a basic E1 configuration. You need to make sure that you are aware of your timing. Verify whether you are receiving timing from the line (if the circuit is from a service provider, chances are you have to clock to the line). The timing defaults to the line, and by adding **primary** to the timing statement you identify the device's primary timing source. The default framing is CRC-4 and the default line code is HDB3.

Expert White Board: Configuring an E1 Hairpin

The second type of configuration for E1 controllers is an advanced and specific configuration known as a hairpin. Figure 6-8 shows the use of a hairpin configuration, also known as a drop and insert, to connect a Cisco network to a traditional TDM-based SS7 infrastructure. This connection allows you to redirect timeslots carrying SS7 signaling out through an Ethernet interface and then drop the remaining timeslots to another device. You typically see this type of configuration in some of Cisco's SS7 Interconnect solutions that use Cisco's signaling link terminal (SLT) and a drop and insert multiflex voice WAN interface card (VWIC) (2MFT-E1-DI). It is important to remember timing because the same circuit's DS0s travel through multiple boxes. Example 6-2 shows how the hairpin configuration from Figure 6-8 is configured on the Cisco SLT.

Figure 6-8 *E1 Hairpin Network Diagram Using Drop and Insert*

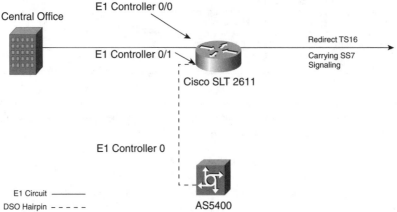

Example 6-2 *Configuration of an E1 Hairpin*

```
2600-1(config)#controller e1 0/0
2600-1(config-controller)#framing no-crc4
2600-1(config-controller)#linecode hdb3
2600-1(config-controller)#clock source line primary
2600-1(config-controller)#channel-group 0 timeslots 16
2600-1(config-controller)#tdm-group 1 timeslots 1-15,17-31
2600-1(config-controller)#no shutdown

2600-1(config-controller)#controller e1 0/1
2600-1(config-controller)#framing no-crc4
2600-1(config-controller)#linecode hdb3
2600-1(config-controller)#clock source internal
2600-1(config-controller)#tdm-group 2 timeslots 1-15,17-31
2600-1(config-controller)#no shutdown
2600-1(config-controller)#end
2600-1(config)#connect Hairpin e1 0/0 1 e1 0/1 2
2600-1(config-connect)#^C
2600-1#wr
```

There are several things of interest about the configuration in Example 6-2.

Within the first controller, the command **channel-group 0 timeslots 16** states, when used, what DS0 SS7 signaling is located on. This is a specific application but it illustrates the grooming of a single DS0 away from the rest of the DS0s.

Still in the first controller, the **tdm-group** statement instructs the E1 controller to combine DS0s 1 through 15 and 17 through 31 into a single group.

E1 controller 0/1 does not have a channel group because the signaling that was coming in from the telecommunication company (telco) has already been groomed off of the circuit. Therefore, it is not necessary here.

E1 controller 0/0 is receiving circuit timing from the service provider's network. The clock source is set to internal from E1 controller 0/1. This is to ensure that timing is passed onto the next device. Because it is a back-to-back E1 connection between the 2611 and the 5400, you need to specify one side as internal because they both default to the line. If they both default to the line, it causes clock slips.

E1 controller 0/1 also has a **tdm-group** statement with the same DS0s listed. This sets up a group of DS0s 1 through 15 and 17 through 31 on controller e1 0/1.

Finally, there is a **connect** statement that is entered in global configuration mode that connects the two TDM groups together and creates the path to drop out the remaining DS0s to the AS5400. Without this command, the two **tdm-group** statements are useless. The syntax for the **connect** statement is as follows:

```
connect name-of-connection e1 controller tdm-group e1 controller tdm-group
```

R2 Signaling Characteristics

R2 signaling is a standard for both analog and digital communication that was put in place for the transmission of call control signals in the mid-1950s. R2, similar to SS7, is a set of international standards that are deployed throughout the world with the exception of North America. A separate set of signaling standards were developed for North America (R1 signaling). Also similar to SS7, many different variants of R2 exist, which are deployed on a country-specific basis. While configuring E1 with R2, it is important to know which variant you are using. Table 6-1 lists a subset of the country variants that are supported by Cisco Systems equipment. Refer to the Cisco Web site (cisco.com) for up-to-date information.

Table 6-1   *R2 Country Variants Supported by Cisco Equipment*

Argentina	Greece	Paraguay
Australia	Guatemala	Peru
Bolivia	Hong Kong (China variant)	Philippines
Brazil	India	Saudi Arabia
Bulgaria	Indonesia	Singapore
China	Israel	South Africa Panaftel
Colombia	ITU	Telmex (Mexico variant)
Costa Rica	Korea	Telnor (Mexico variant)
Croatia	LAOS Network (Thailand variant)	Thailand
East Europe	Malaysia	Uruguay
Ecuador ITU	Malta	Venezuela
Ecuador LME	New Zealand	Vietnam

R2 was designed as a method of transporting signaling information on a channelized E1 circuit between switches. You can use R2 as a tie-line replacement for communication back to a CO or a PBX when configured on an E1 controller. Tie lines can be thought of as circuits that are static through the network rather than the typical switched circuits. In other words, you can access the remote end of the circuit, most times by just picking up the phone. Another similar representation is the private line, automatic ringdown (PLAR) circuit. A colleague I worked with at Adtran Telecommunication, Ken Stallings, describes this as the Bat Phone. Commissioner Gordon just picks up the phone and the red phone at Bruce Wayne's residence starts ringing.

R2 Call Control

Most definitions of R2 signaling state that R2 is a compelled signaling type. However, semi-compelled and non-compelled R2 signaling types also exist. The following definitions of these signaling types come from Cisco's web site:

> **R2-Compelled**—When a tone-pair is sent from the switch (forward signal), the tones stay on until the remote end responds/Acknowledges (ACK) back with a pair of tones that signals the switch to turn off the tones. The tones are compelled to stay on until they are turned off.
>
> **R2-Non-Compelled**—The tone-pairs are sent (forward signal) as pulses so they stay on for a short duration. Responses (backward signals) to the switch (Group B) are sent as pulses. There are no Group A signals in non-compelled interregister signaling.
>
> **R2-Semi-Compelled**—Forward tone-pairs are sent as compelled. Responses (backward signals) to the switch are sent as pulses. It is the same as compelled, except that the backward signals are pulsed instead of continuous. [sic]

Non-compelled is the most common form of interregister signaling, and R2 supports all three types. R1, found in North America, only supports semi-compelled or non-compelled signaling. Fully compelled signaling is not supported by R1.

R2 signaling messages are broken down into several different areas. Two main types of signaling exist, each with its own sub-classes, line signals, and interregister signals. Line signals are supervisory signals that are used for circuit management between carrier circuit endpoints, and the interregister signals are used for the actual call setup and teardown messages. Specific to R2 signaling, registers are actually the endpoints of the call, and the signals that pass between the registers are called interregister signals.

Line Signaling

Line signals apply functions such as seizing a circuit, clearing a circuit in a forward or backward direction, answering signals, and blocking signals, as described in Table 6-2.

Table 6-2   *Forward and Backward Line Signals*

Forward Line Signals	Definition
Seize	At the beginning of a call, reserves a circuit for a call in the forward direction.
Clear-Forward	Terminates a call in the forward direction.
Forward-Transfer	Starts an international assistance operator.
Backward Line Signals	**Definition**
Seize Acknowledgment	Acknowledges receipt of the Seize signal in the backward direction and changes the state at the called party location to be seized.
Answer	Indicates that the called party has answered and begins Billing and Measurement System (BAMS) functions.
Clear-Back	Terminates the call in the backward direction.
Release-Guard	Acknowledges the Clear-Forward signal in the backward direction to notify the calling party that the circuit has been returned to an idle state.
Blocking	Applies an intentional blocking state to a circuit. While this state is applied, no calls can be accepted or placed.

R2 signaling is split into three different standard areas: analog, pulse, and digital. The analog version of R2 line signaling is designed for telco carrier circuits and is specified for one-way use on a four-wire circuit. This type of signaling equates to analog call control by using what is called tone-on-idle signaling. Tone-on-idle stipulates a forward and backward direction. With each direction, the tone can either be on or off. For example, if the tone is on in a forward and backward direction, the circuit is said to be idle. Table 6-3 lists the different states of tone-on-idle signaling.

Table 6-3   *Tone-On-Idle Signaling States*

Registered Signaling State	Forward Direction State of Tone	Backward Direction State of Tone
Idle	On	On
Seized	Off	On
Answered	Off	Off
Clear-Back	Off	On
Release	On	On or Off
Blocked	On	Off

During a basic call setup, a call is placed from calling to called party. The called party is the forward direction, and the calling party is the backward direction. When the call has been placed, a circuit seizure takes place. When the call is answered, the tone is off on both ends, which signifies that the circuit is not idle. When a release occurs, the tone is turned on again, which represents an idle state, and it notifies the equipment that it is again able to make or accept a call. Figure 6-9 shows a typical analog call flow with R2 signaling.

Figure 6-9   *Basic Call Setup and Teardown Using Tone-on-Idle Line Signaling*

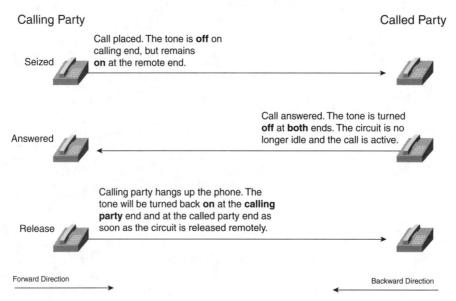

When the call is released, the remote end must either reset the tone to the on state or a timeout occurs, in which case the tone is restored anyway. If for some reason this tone is not set back to the on state, the circuits remain in a blocked state and are unable to place or accept calls. Pulse signaling handles call control in the same way that analog does with the exception of the duration of the tones. Typically deployed with satellite links, pulse signaling only pulses the circuit state changes. In other words, instead of providing a constant tone, the tone only lasts long enough to signal the actual circuit state change and is then removed.

Digital line signals use a different format for conveying circuit states. Instead of tones, digital circuits use a 2-bit binary code. There are four bits allocated (A through D) for CAS signaling in TS16, but generally you only use the A and B bit. Furthermore, the binary codes are not necessarily equal in both directions for the same signal. Table 6-4 lists the line signal states for a digital circuit. The basic line signaling call flow is the same as in Figure 6-9, with the addition of the Seize Acknowledge message.

Table 6-4   *Circuit State Values for Digital Circuits*

Circuit State	Forward Direction	Backward Direction
Idle or Released	1 0	1 0
Seized	0 0	1 0
Seize Acknowledge	0 0	1 1
Answer	0 0	0 1
Clear-Back	0 0	1 1
Clear-Forward	1 0	0 1
	1 0	1 1
Blocked	1 0	1 1

Interregister Signaling

Interregister signaling is considered a multitone (MT) signaling type. Each digit dialed is collected as two discrete tones from a set of six possible tones in both directions, which combine to form the specified MT value. The use of MT signaling identifies single tone signals as faulty. A common form of MT is dual tone multifrequency (DTMF). Although not the same as R2, anytime you pick up a touch-tone phone and dial a number, the tones that you hear in your ear are DTMF tones. MT signaling is much faster than older legacy signaling, such as pulse dialing, because instead of requiring a physical circuit to open and close several times for each digit, MT merely collects tones, which requires no mechanical operation. Therefore, several digits per second are possible.

Interregister signaling consists of the actual call control signaling between the registers (signaling nodes). Interregister signals are split four ways. First, they are segmented between forward and backward signal types and then segmented again with each direction. First, the forward signals are split into Group I and Group II signals. These signals consist of the actual tone values assigned for digit collection.

Group I messages, listed 1 through 15, identify the individual digits dialed (1 through 9 and 0) with messages 1 through 10, respectively, and then other attributes with messages 11 through 15. Refer to Table 6-5 for a complete listing of the Group I and Group II messages for forward signaling types.

Table 6-5   *Forward Signaling Message Groups I and II*

Signal Number	Definition
Group I	
1	Digit 1
2	Digit 2
3	Digit 3
4	Digit 4
5	Digit 5
6	Digit 6
7	Digit 7
8	Digit 8
9	Digit 9
10	Digit 0
11	Country code indicator
12	Country code indicator (no echo canceller required)
13	Test call
14	Country code indicator (half echo canceller inserted)
15	Not used
Group II	
1	Subscriber without priority
2	Subscriber with priority
3	Maintenance equipment
4	Spare
5	Operator
6	Data transmission
7*	Subscriber
8*	Data transmission
9*	Subscriber without priority
10*	Operator with forward transfer facility
11 through 15	Reserved for national use

*Used in international networking
The compilation of this table was based on Tables 6 and 7 from ITU-T Q.441.

Group I also identifies the country code indicator and the end of the dialing sequence (1 through 15). Group II messages, also listed 1 through 15, identify the subscriber priority setting (on or off), whether maintenance is to be set up, and if the call is to be a data transmission. Only the first ten messages are defined. The last five are reserved for national use.

Backward signals are also split into two groups, Group A and Group B. These signals acknowledge received digits and requests for retransmission of a digit. These signals also signify the end of a signaling series. Table 6-6 lists the messages associated with Groups A and B.

Table 6-6   *Backward Signaling Messages Groups A and B*

Multitone	Definition
Group A	
1	Send next digit
2	Send last digit (n-1)
3	Address complete, change to Group B
4	Congestion in the national network
5	Send calling party's category
6	Address complete, charge, setup speech conditions
7	Send last digit (n-2)
8	Send last digit (n-3)
9	Spare
10	Spare
11	Send country code indicator
12	Send language or discrimination digit
13	Send nature of circuit
14	Request for information on the use of an echo suppressor
15	Congestion in an international exchange or at its output
Group B	
1	Spare
2	Send special information tone
3	Subscriber's line busy
4	Congestion (after changeover from A to B)
5	Unallocated number

continued

Table 6-6   *Backward Signaling Messages Groups A and B (Continued)*

Multitone	Definition
6	Subscriber's line free, charge
7	Subscriber's line free, no charge
8	Subscriber's line out of order

The compilation of this table was based on Tables 4 and 5 from ITU-T Q.441.

The compelled interregister signaling works in a logical flow. The following lists the sending and receiving tasks of basic interregister signals as they are transmitted through the network:

- A circuit is seized in the forward position (outgoing).

- The originating network equipment begins sending the first forward interregister signal to the receiving node.

- The receiving node begins transmitting the first backward interregister signal in the backward direction to the originating network node. This signal serves as the acknowledgment to the inbound interregister signal.

- The originating node ceases the forward interregister signal when the acknowledgment is detected.

- The receiving node ceases the backward interregister signal when it detects that the forward interregister signal is no longer being transmitted to it.

- The originating node sends the next forward interregister signal upon detection of the ceased backward direction interregister signal. At this point, the originating node is aware that the receiving node is ready for the next signal.

R2 Configuration on a Cisco E1 Controller

Earlier in this chapter, you looked at how to configure some basic E1 scenarios on a Cisco 2611. This section builds upon the basic configuration by adding support for R2 signaling. One thing to remember about R2 signaling, which is specific to the 2600 or 3600 series, is that you must have a High Density Voice Network Module (NM-HDV) card installed to configure it. This is required because you need digital signal processors (DSPs) to operate properly. DSPs process streams of voice or data traffic that are time sensitive. Without the use of DSPs, voice is typically choppy and of poor quality.

Use the following steps to configure R2 signaling:

```
2600-1(config)#controller e1 0/0
2600-1(config-controller)#framing no-crc4
2600-1(config-controller)#linecode hdb3
2600-1(config-controller)#clock source line primary
```

The first four lines in this configuration are exactly as you configured before, but now you add the necessary information for the R2 signaling. To do this, you need to know what type of line signaling you are using (analog, digital, or pulse) and what type of interregister signaling you are using (R2-compelled, R2-non-compelled, or R2-semi-compelled). The command in this case is as follows:

```
2600-1(config-controller)#ds0-group 1 timeslots 1-15 type r2-digital r2-non-compelled
```

After that has been completed, you can also customize your signaling for any specific variants that are required in your country. The default load is sufficient in most cases, but you can control many different variables associated with the R2 signaling. Great care must be taken in modifying any of the variables. Unless you are sure what the settings should be, modification of the timers and message types is not recommended. The next set of commands show how to set an E1 controller to use the R2 defaults for Australia:

```
2600-1(config-controller)# cas-custom 1
2600-1(config-ctrl-cas)#country australia use-defaults
2600-1(config-ctrl-cas)#^C
2600-1#wr
```

Australia is used in the previous example, but other country specifics might be required. Replace **australia** with the necessary country and, followed by **use-defaults**, the controller sets variables to the default settings for your country.

JDH

Japan uses a digital hierarchy that is similar to both the NADH and ITU Digital Hierarchies. The Telecommunication Technology Commission has specified its own set of standards for use within Japan. Based off of the ITU standards, the Japanese standards preface the ITU specifications with a JT. So ITU G.701 becomes JT-G701. Within these standards, circuit speeds are specified for a 1.544-Mbps link.

JDH is based on 64-kbps DS0s, as with every PCM TDM network. However, subrates at 64 kbps are generally not offered because technologies such as digital dataphone service (DDS) are not deployed. The lowest rate offered in the JDH is 1.544 Mbps and is referred to as a J1 circuit. J1 circuits are widely deployed as trunks between switches and as subscriber end services. J1 is largely based on T1 facility standards with the exception of the line coding.

NOTE   There is information in different publications about a Y1 trunk interface in the JDH that is specifically for PBX-based applications. According to the JT specifications, however, there is no reference to a Y1 interface or a 2.048-Mbps link. Those same JT specifications state that 2.048-Mbps links should be removed from the documentation because they are not used.

The line coding, as specified in G.703, is coded mark inversion (CMI). CMI makes one significant improvement upon AMI line coding, and that is the ability to deal with 1s density issues without stealing the least significant bit. The way this is done is by creating discrete alternating voltages for 1s and 0s, as shown in Figure 6-10.

Figure 6-10 *Coded Mark Inversion Encoding an 8-Bit Word (10110101)*

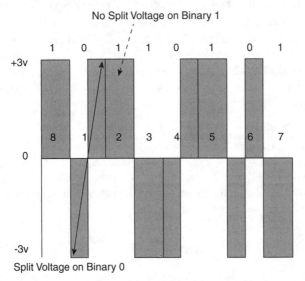

Remember that AMI operation specifies that a 0 is no voltage. Because the CMI codes even 0s, equipment on both ends have something to maintain timing. Y1 framing is similar to that of T1 in the fact that it uses a 193-bit frame (8 * 24 DS0s + 1 framing bit). One major difference in reference to the framing is that you can use only 24-frame ESF. This is because 12-frame SF does not allow for the use of CRC. J1 circuits are commonly deployed with 110-ohm twisted pairs, and balanced cable with male DB-15 connectors. The pin assignments in Table 6-7 are for Y1 DB-15 connectivity.

Table 6-7 *DB-15 Pin Assignments for J1 DB-15 Connectivity*

PIN	Function
2	Transmit Tip
9	Transmit Ring
4	Receive Tip
11	Receive Ring
1	Shield

Following the J1 in the JDH is the J2 circuit. The J2 circuit is composed of four J1 circuits, which you typically use in multiplexing applications for J3 circuits.

JDH actually specifies six levels of digital communication, as does E1 (DS0 through DS5). The first and second levels of the JDH digital signals (DSs) are equivalent to that of the NADH, but beginning with digital signal level 3 (DS-3) the values are different. Refer to Table 6-8 for a comparison of Japanese, international, and North American Digital Hierarchies.

Table 6-8   *A Comparison of International Digital Hierarchies*

Digital Signal Level	North American (T1)	International (E1)	Japanese(J1)*
0	64 Kbps	64 Kbps	64 Kbps
1	1.544 Mbps	2.048 Mbps	1.544 Mbps
2	6.312 Mbps	8.448 Mbps	6.312 Mbps
3	44.736 Mbps	34.368 Mbps	32.064 Mbps
4	274.176 Mbps	139.264 Mbps	97.728 Mbps
5		565.148 Mbps	397.200 Mbps

*The levels specified in the Japanese hierarchy match those specified in JT-G702. Nothing past 1.544 Mbps is specified for J1.

Summary

The ITU developed E-Carrier technology after T-Carrier had been created to attempt to correct some of its shortfalls. The major problem associated with T-Carrier was the initial line coding method, AMI. AMI steals the least significant bit to ensure against 1s density violations. When the E1 circuit was developed, HDB3 ensured that no more than three 0s are transmitted over the circuit at any given time. This is done by inserting a unique bipolar violation to signify that a series of 0s has been transmitted. The remote end of the circuit, also set to HDB3, understands the BPV as a string of 0s and decodes it accordingly.

E1 circuits are made up of 32 64-kbps DS0s, and 30 or 31 of them can be used for bearer traffic. TS0 is used for timing and synchronization and TS16 is used for signaling. In the event that an out-of-band or a proprietary signaling method is put in place, it is possible to reclaim TS16.

E1 framing is different from T1 framing in that it uses MF16. The TS0 in even frames manages actual frame alignment and the odd frames identify circuit alarms. Within frame 0 of the MF16, TS16 manages MF alignment by using the MFAS. The two main types of framing are CRC-4 and NO-CRC-4 framing. The difference between them is that CRC-4 framing ensures the integrity of the frames that are using a CRC. CRC-8 and CRC-16 also exist, and the number refers to how many bits are in the CRC. These bits are not typically used in E1 circuits.

R2 is a method of CAS signaling that allows for call control to take place between registers. Registers are merely the signaling endpoints of the call. The two major types of signaling in R2 are line signaling and interregister signaling. Line signaling manages circuits between registers. It is responsible for seizing, answering, and disconnecting circuits. Interregister signaling is responsible for the actual digit collection between registers and the acknowledgment of those digits. Other features include notification of last digit and request for commencement of billing.

The JDH specifies six different levels of digital signals, and the first three match the NADH. J1 circuits, also based on 64-kbps DS0s, are equivalent to T1 circuits at 1.544 Mbps, except that they use a different line coding standard, CMI. CMI corrects some of the issues with AMI, most notably its inability to deal with a long string of consecutive 0s. CMI allows for a voltage transition on 0 bits, therefore allowing the receiving equipment to maintain PLL during the transmission of 0s through the network.

Review Questions

Give or select the best answer or answers to the following questions. The answers to these questions are inAppendix A, "Answers to Review Questions."

1 How many DS0s are included in an E1 circuit?

   a   16

   b   24

   c   32

   d   30

2 What similar function do B8ZS and HDB3 serve?

   _____

   _____

   _____

3 What is the function of the third bit in odd frames of NO-CRC-4 framing?

_____

_____

_____

4 How does a J1 circuit differ from a T1 circuit?

_____

_____

_____

5 If you use a Multifrequency signaling type, such as R2, and a digit is collected with a single tone instead of two; what happens?

_____

_____

_____

6 Name two signaling formats that allow you to reclaim TS16 for bearer traffic.

_____

_____

_____

7 How does CMI alleviate the 1s density issues that are commonly associated with AMI line coding?

_____

_____

_____

8 What is the maximum cable distance allowed without a digital regenerator on an E1 circuit?

_____

_____

_____

This chapter covers the following topics:

- **T3 technology**—After a brief description of the North American Digital Hierarchy (NADH), which shows digital service 1 (DS1), DS2, DS3, and DS4 levels, focus turns to T3—at how multiplexing is performed, the physical media, the line coding, and the framing types. A configuration is also given.

- **E3 technology**—In this section, the international digital hierarchy is described, along with more details about E3 multiplexing and framing. Unchannelized E3 is also covered.

- **Beyond the X3 barrier**—The purpose of this section is to illustrate how to get more bandwidth in addition to what is offered with T3 and E3.

T3 and E3 Technology

As the technology in telecommunications advanced, so did the requirements for customer circuits. As more and more businesses and users were connected to the infrastructure, it became apparent that even DS1 and E1 circuits would no longer be sufficient. Higher bandwidth circuits were required to allow for growth and to provide more services to subscribers. DS3 carrier systems, just as DS1 carrier systems, allow for a level of pair gain.

NOTE	Remember, pair gain is the function of gaining pairs by deploying multiple circuits over a time-division multiplexing (TDM)-based circuit such as DS1 or E1. Because two pairs can serve 24 or 30 circuits, you are said to be gaining pairs when you are actually just avoiding having to deploy them.

DS2 is an intermediary step that is covered in the "M12 Multiplexing" and "E12 Multiplexing" sections later in this chapter. T2 and E2 were developed as the second digital hierarchy level but were hardly ever used. Particularly in the U.S., T2 saw only developmental and internal service provider deployments. This step is important because although not used, it is included within the T3/E3 framework. Just as you would multiplex DS0s into a T1 or E1, you multiplex a number of T1/E1s and T2/E2s into a T3 or E3, respectively.

This chapter discusses the framing, line coding, and operation of the T3 and E3 carrier systems. Within each section, the deployment of these circuits is analyzed and accompanied by configuration examples. Furthermore, there is a brief discussion of the higher levels within each digital hierarchy.

T3 Technology

T3 (or DS3) was created to aggregate 28 T1s, or 672 DS0s, in a single circuit. In unchannelized mode, it provides around 44 Mbps of usable bandwidth. This section describes how this is achieved.

Evolution of the North American Digital Hierarchy

As explained in Chapter 5, "T1 Technology," DS1 technology was introduced to groom several telephony pairs in a single circuit (24 DS0s), which resulted in savings for telephone companies (telcos) in copper, office space, and other equipment.

In the same way, DS1c (48 DS0s), DS2 (96 DS0s), DS3 (672 DS0s), and DS4 (4032 DS0s) were defined to groom more and more telephony circuits. The DS0, DS1, DS1c, DS2, DS3, and DS4 hierarchy is the NADH, also referred to as the plesiochronous digital hierarchy (PDH). Plesiochronous means almost synchronous, and you will see that the DS1s inside the same DS3 do not need to share the same clock. Europe (International Telecommunication Union [ITU]) and Japan have their own PDH hierarchies, which differ by the speed and the number of DS0s that are supported.

DS3 is a North American standard (American National Standards Institute [ANSI] T1.404, ANSI T1.107).

In parallel, it became apparent that there was a need to offer not only telephony pairs to customers but also digital circuits to enterprises, as shown in the following example.

As a small startup company, you began with a single digital dataphone service (DDS) connection for WAN connectivity. At first, this circuit was more than adequate to provide the bandwidth that your company required. About six months later, you added two new sites and you graduated to Switched 56 (SW56) to cut down on costs.

About a year later, with your company growing rapidly, you decided that it was time to get a combination of T1 and Fractional T1 (FT1) circuits to accommodate the increased demand. Your applications now include Internet Web and FTP services, video conferencing, and telecommuting for your employees. You are adding more and more T1 circuits to keep up with your explosive growth. The costs are adding up quickly, and you need to find a way to eliminate this growing problem. You decide to investigate the costs of a T3 circuit from your service provider.

Simply put, after five to ten T1s, your costs will compare to that of leasing a T3. This of course varies from provider to provider. The point is that if you are to be spending the money, why not spend the same amount on more bandwidth?

Service providers can also offer FT3. An FT3 is a T3 in which only a subset of the 28 T1s are active, and a client is charged only for the T1s that are being used. It also offers the ability to quickly increase the bandwidth offered to the customer by activating more T1s.

For speeds above T3, Synchronous Optical Network (SONET) is now the preferred choice (Chapter 14, "SONET and SDH").

Synchronous or Asynchronous

As you learned in Chapter 5, the T1 circuits are synchronous technology. It would be easy to assume that a T3 is automatically synchronous, but in most cases that is simply not true. In a channelized environment, a single T3 can contain 28 T1 circuits. Each of the T1 circuits is synchronous, but their relation to one another is asynchronous.

Typically, T3 circuits are considered to be asynchronous because they take 28 circuits (each with its own clock source) and modify them so that they can be transmitted as a single data stream. So why does this make T3 asynchronous? To reach the bandwidth rate of 44.736 Mbps, two stages of multiplexing must occur. The first stage involves multiplexing T1 circuits into T2s. To multiplex these circuits completely, bit stuffing must occur on each T1 circuit to remove discrepancies between their clock sources. The second stage involves the multiplexing of T2 circuits to create a T3 circuit. Again, bits must be stuffed to ensure clock synchronization. When you combine the lower level circuits, bit stuffing, and overhead you have an asynchronous T3 circuit.

Not all T3 circuits are asynchronous. Several years ago, a synchronous form of T3 technology was developed, called synchronous transmission (SYNTRAN). SYNTRAN is not widely used as a T3 technology, but it formed the basis for a couple of modern technology giants, SONET and Synchronous Digital Hierarchy (SDH). SONET and SDH are the basis for almost all the world's high bandwidth optical trunks, and they continue to increase in bandwidth capacity.

What differentiates SONET and SDH from something like T3 is that no bit stuffing needs to occur to ensure mutual clocking. Synchronous Transport Signal 1 (STS-1) and Synchronous Transport Module (STM-1) channels can be multiplexed without any further modification to the signal.

As far as T3s and E3s go, asynchronous transmission is by far the most common application that you will find.

Channelized and Unchannelized T3

Asynchronous T3 circuits have two modes that they can be leased in—channelized or unchannelized. The difference between the two of them is rather simple. The channelized T3 is composed of 28 T1s (672 DS0s) and has all the associated overhead and bit stuffing. Unchannelized T3 circuits are composed of a single, non-multiplexed DS3 signal. Because unchannelized T3 has no bit stuffing or overhead, all the bandwidth is available for user transmission.

A T3 is clocked at 44.736 Mbps. A channelized T3 offers 672 DS0s, so the maximum user rate is 43.008 Mbps, the difference being the overhead and bit stuffing.

On an unchannelized T3, the maximum user rate can be from 44.2 Mbps to 44.407 Mbps. The larger of the two rates is available if the C-bits are not needed for any management functions.

Channelized T3 circuits are normally deployed in a point-to-multipoint configuration because of the ease of distribution. Because you have 672 DS0s available to you, as long as your multiplexer supports it, you can groom and redirect any number of DS0s in any number of directions. This is a viable solution for a company that wants to manage all WAN connectivity from a central location. By doing so, the corporate office (CO) can provide more bandwidth to the offices that need it and manage the rest of the bandwidth efficiently. A topology example is given in Figure 7-1.

Figure 7-1 *Channelized T3 in Point-to-Multipoint Configuration*

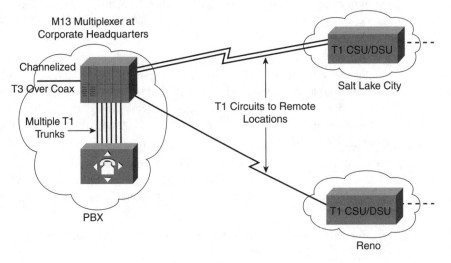

Unchannelized T3 circuits (44.2 Mbps) come in a single pipe of bandwidth. The unchannelized circuits are commonly deployed in a point-to-point configuration because no DS0s or DS1s can be separated from the signal stream. This is useful for applications that require a large amount of bandwidth between two locations such as university distance learning centers. A topology example is given in Figure 7-2.

Figure 7-2   *Unchannelized T3 Link Between University Locations*

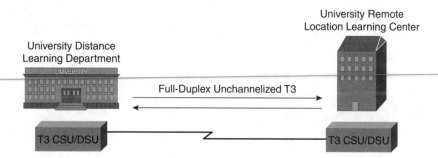

T3 circuits are also used as the physical layer for technologies such as Asynchronous Transfer Mode (ATM) and Frame Relay. In these cases, the T3 circuit is the physical transport layer for the Layer 2 frame or cell switching technology. ATM uses an unchannelized T3 and requires a delineation mechanism to identify ATM cells; two methods are defined, physical layer convergence procedure (PLCP), which is adding a specific frame format (and overhead) and a header error control (HEC)-based delineation method. Although Frame Relay over T1 is more common, a standard for Frame Relay over T3 does exist.

Sorting out the Mess

The NADH is split up into four different levels: DS1 to DS4. The most common of these digital signal levels are DS1 and DS3. For more information on DS1 in a DS1 carrier system, refer to Chapter 5. For the remainder of this chapter, the 3rd digital signal level is referred to as either DS3 or E3 (realizing that those are just the carrier systems).

When you talk to someone about a DS3 circuit or even read about it in a book, you normally find that a DS3 is described as having 28 DS1s in a channelized configuration. To a certain extent that is correct, but not entirely. The total bit rate of a channelized DS3 is 44.736 Mbps. The total bit rate of a DS1 is 1.544 Mbps. Go ahead and do the math (I'll give you a hint: 1.544 Mbps * 28 = 43.232 Mbps). Wait a minute, this doesn't make any sense. I thought all those books said that there were 28 DS1s in a 44.736 Mbps DS3 circuit? The fact of the matter is that there are, but most of those books don't tell you about the overhead and bit stuffing involved in the two-stage multiplexing for channelized DS3s.

NOTE   From here until the end of the chapter, a channelized DS3 is referred to as a DS3, and an unchannelized DS3 is referred to as an unchannelized DS3.

When you take a closer look at DS3 circuits, you realize that there are several different levels of multiplexing going on within the equipment. For every DS3, there are seven DS2s that are multiplexed, and for every DS2 there are four DS1s. As stated before, there are not just 28 DS1s in each DS3. You arrive at a DS3 by adding DS1s + bit-stuffing + overhead to DS2s + bit stuffing + overhead.

NOTE	The DS1 might be channelized (24 DS0s) or unchannelized. The DS0s are not considered when multiplexing the DS1s.

M12 Multiplexing

When you look at DS3 carrier systems, you see a slew of references to M12, M23, and M13 multiplexing. These are merely different stages in the DS3 multiplexing process. Bit stuffing makes sure that all lower level digital signals are transmitting at the same rate through the network. This process is necessary to synchronize several different asynchronous circuits. Bit stuffing is also referred to as justification.

Although a DS1c circuit does exist (two DS1s), it is not used in the M12, M23, or M13 process, as it is in the intermediary step between DS1 and DS2. For review, the DS1c circuit bandwidth rate is 3.152 Mbps.

There are several stages to this multiplexing level. First, four DS1 signals need to be combined. The DS2 frame is built by bit interleaving the four DS1s. Also, the DS1s can have different clocks. For this reason, it is necessary for the multiplex equipment to ensure that the lower frequency levels are synchronized to fit the higher frequency payload rate. This is accomplished by bit stuffing at the individual DS1 level. Each DS1 is stuffed to a total rate of 1.545796 Mbps. After they are combined, the four DS1 signals equal a total bandwidth of 6.183184 Mbps. The second stage is to add the overhead associated with the DS2 circuit that is necessary to manage the four DS1 circuits. The overhead added to this circuit is 128,816 bps. The total bandwidth of a DS2 circuit is 6.312 Mbps:

6.183184 Mbps + 128,816 bps = 6.312 Mbps

This process is shown in Figure 7-3 and the frame format is shown in Figure 7-4.

Figure 7-3   *M12 Multiplexing*

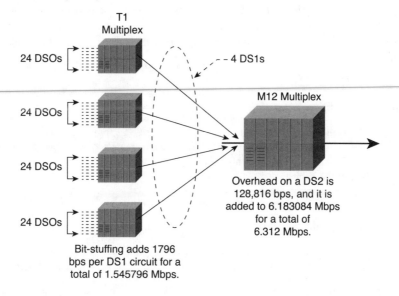

Figure 7-4   *Breaking Down a DS2 M-Frame*

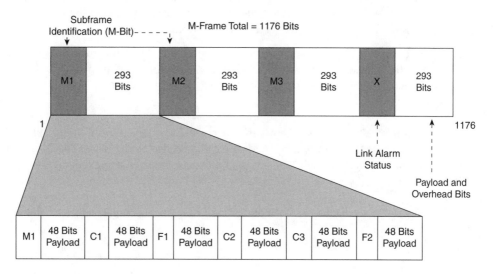

DS2 signal frames are a bit different than the format used with a typical DS1 circuit. DS2 frames more closely resemble a DS3 frame than a DS1 frame because of the nature of the multiplex. A mixture of parity and framing bits keep track of the payload and management information. Refer to Table 7-1 for a description of the various types of bits used in a DS2 frame.

Table 7-1   *Bit Types Found in DS2 Frames*

Bit	Description
M	M-bits identify the different subframes within the DS2 frame. Each DS2 frame is broken down into four subframes, but only three of them are named. In order of occurrence, they are M1, M2, and M3. They also align the subframes of each frame. (The unnamed frame is after the X-bit.)
C	C-bits identify whether or not bit stuffing has occurred on the DS2 multiplex.
F	F-bits identify the position of all overhead bits included in the DS2 frame (to include M, C, and X).
X	X-bits identify the channel that carries the alarm status of the circuit, if necessary.

Taking a closer look at the DS2 frame structure (M-frame), you see that each frame is 1176 bits long and is broken down into four equal 294-bit subframes, each preceded with a M-bit, as shown in Figure 7-4. Within each subframe, you can see that the overhead bits are interleaved with payload. The payload is distributed into equal 48-bit chunks for transmission. Each 48-bit chunk contains 12 bits from each DS1.

Two separate alignment processes happen within the DS2 signal stream. First, each subframe must be aligned, which combines all overhead and payload bits. The two F-bits are used for this process by using the following pattern:

F1=0, F2=1

Second, the four DS2 subframes from each DS2 M-frame must be aligned using the M-bit pattern. The last subframe of an M-frame is preceded by the X-bit. That X-bit carries the alarm state of the circuit. This frame alignment is realized using the following pattern:

M1=0, M2=1, M3=1, X=any

Figure 7-5 shows the values of the F- and M-bits for subframe and frame alignment, respectively.

Figure 7-5   *Frame and Subframe Alignment Signals*

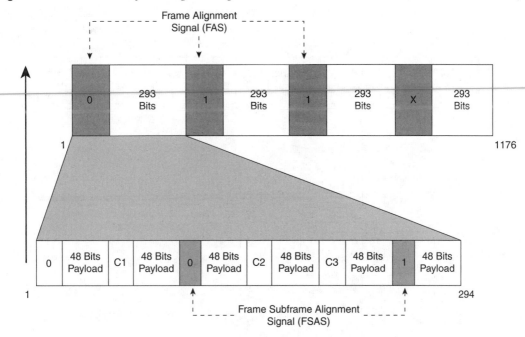

The two alignment processes described above allow the DS2 multiplexer to keep all DS1 signals synched and in order. As you would expect, each subframe has a specific position for each overhead bit. As the frames are repeated, the bit positions and sequence remain the same. However, functions such as alarm transport and bit stuffing toggle the bit values. When bit stuffing is used, you see stuffed bits in the pattern, which are shown in Figure 7-6. When bit stuffing is not in use, the C-bits are set to 0. Of the three 3 C-bits, at least two must be toggled to 1 for there to be active bit stuffing.

NOTE	Maintenance of a DS2 circuit involves the C-bits. If a circuit loopback is required, the loopback takes place at the individual DS1 level. C-bit 3 conveys the loopback status and is displayed opposite to C-bits 1 and 2. This is all right because zero or one C-bit set to 1 indicates no bit stuffing, and two or three C-bits set to 1 indicate bit stuffing.

Figure 7-6 *Bit Stuffing Pattern in the DS2 M-Frame*

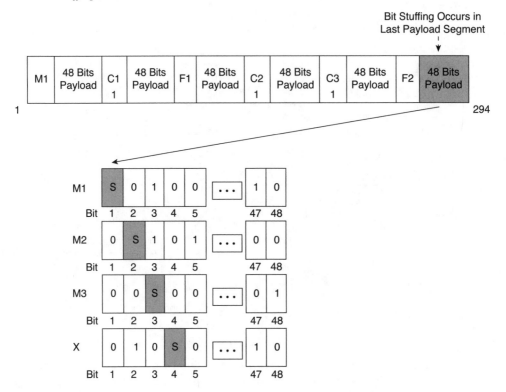

S = Stuffed Bit

M23 Multiplexing

M23 multiplexing involves the combination, using bit interleaving, of seven DS2 signals into a single DS3 signal stream. Hopefully, you are beginning to see a pattern. DS1 to DS2 multiplexing is M12, and DS2 to DS3 multiplexing is M23. The first number in these acronyms stands for the DS level that is multiplexed, and the second number stands for the new DS hierarchy level that is created. Thus, M23 is the function of multiplexing DS2s into a DS3. Figure 7-7 shows the M23 process.

Figure 7-7   *M23 Multiplexing*

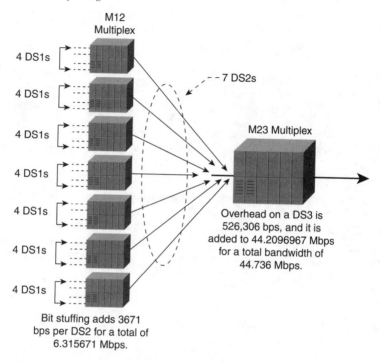

Again in M23, you use bit stuffing to remove clocking variations between the separate DS2 signals. Each DS2 runs at a nominal rate of 6.312 Mbps, and 3761 bps is added to each circuit to bring them to a total bandwidth rate of 6.315671 Mbps. If you combine the total rate of seven DS2s, you get a total bandwidth rate of 44.209697 Mbps. The final addition to the DS3 signal is the remaining overhead of 526,306 bps, which gives you the bandwidth rate that you are accustomed to seeing—44.736003 Mbps. You most commonly see this displayed as either 44.736 Mbps or simply 45 Mbps.

The frame structure of a DS3 is similar to that of a DS2, but it is significantly larger. Within each DS3 frame, there are a total of 4760 bits. Each DS3 frame is also referred to as an M-frame and is further segmented into seven subframes, as shown in Figure 7-8.

NOTE   Multiplexing is achieved by using bit-by-bit interleaving, from DS1 to DS2, and from DS2 to DS3, which makes it difficult to extract a single T1 from a DS3. It requires demultiplexing the entire T3.

Figure 7-8   *Breakdown of a DS3 M-Frame*

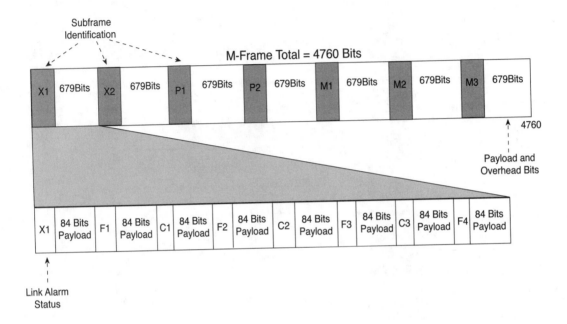

As with DS2, the DS3 M-frame sequence is made up of a series of header bits followed by blocks that are set aside for the actual payload of the circuits. Each of the overhead bits serves a specific function, as noted in Table 7-2.

Table 7-2   *Bit Types Found in DS3 Frames*

Bit	Description
X	The X-bit identifies any significant error detected on the circuit such as an alarm indication signal (AIS). Also called the remote alarm indicator (RAI), X1 and X2 are always set to the same value, either both to 0 during normal operation or both to 1 during the detection of an error.
P	The P-bits function as a way for monitoring the performance of the circuit. The continuous transmission of DS3 frames allots the P-bits for a parity check on the previous frame. In other words, the value that is stated in the current frame is the parity information from the last frame. The values are the same on both bits, either 0 or 1.
M	The M-bit is used much the same way as it is in the DS2 frame structure to align each DS3 M-frame. The difference is that not all subframes contain an M-bit in the DS3 frame structure. The alignment pattern is M1=0, M2=1, M3=0.

Table 7-2   *Bit Types Found in DS3 Frames (Continued)*

Bit	Description
F	The F-bits are used for the subframe alignment sequence. The alignment pattern is F1=1, F2=0, F3=1, F4=0.
C	C-bits are used in M23 framing to identify whether or not bit stuffing has occurred in the M23 multiplex. In the absence of bit stuffing, C-bits can be used for other functions within the signal stream such as network monitoring and management.

DS3 signals also need to use bit-stuffing techniques for synchronization of the DS2 signals. The bit stuffing is a bit more involved because there are seven subframes instead of four and a total of 84 bits per payload block, as shown in Figure 7-9. However, the process is the same. Again, you should pick up on the pattern here; there are seven subframes and each subframe stuffs bits in its own position. In other words, subframe #3 stuffs the third bit in its own subframe.

With modern equipment, the DS2s are handled within the same device and then share the same clock source. In that case, bit stuffing at M23 level is not required (it is still required for M12, because the T1s can have different clock sources), and the C-bits can be used for different purposes.

Figure 7-9   *Bit Stuffing in a DS3 M-Frame*

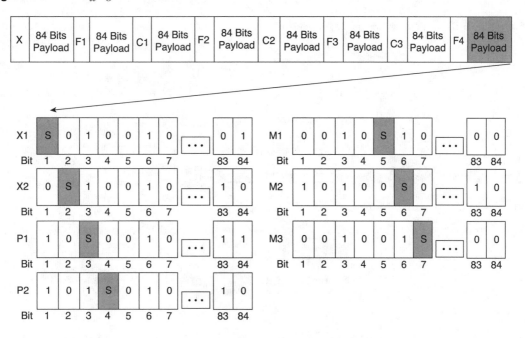

M13 Multiplexing

The last type of multiplexing that you see references for is M13 multiplexing. M13 refers to the complete process of multiplexing DS1s into a DS3. If you were to start looking for T3 multiplexers, the most common feature described is the fact that they are an M13 MUX.

Most T3 equipment does not use the M12 to M23 stage separation because T2s rarely ever take physical form in the service provider network space. The MUX takes care of the transition transparently. The resulting frame is the same as if M12 and M23 were performed.

Deployment Options

Depending on what equipment you use, several different interfaces are commonly found with T3 and E3 circuits. The most likely interface that you are to come across is 75-ohm coaxial cable. The deployment of coaxial cable for T3 generally comes in the form of two separate cables—one for transmit (Tx) and one for receive (Rx). T3 and E3 circuits are high-bandwidth circuits that standard twisted copper pair cannot normally support.

For example, most deployments of T3/E3 circuits today actually start from the CO as a fiber trunk and terminate on your premises at a network interface unit (NIU). From the NIU, the last few feet of cable are coaxial into your T3/E3 device, as shown in Figure 7-10. From there, you can split out the DS1s, E1s, or DS0s in any fashion that your equipment supports.

Figure 7-10 *Typical Deployment of a T3 or E3 Circuit*

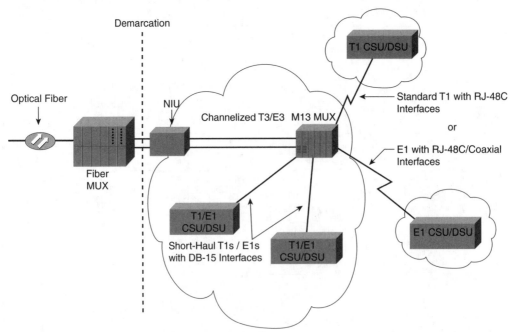

One thing to keep in mind is that by using coaxial cable, you can extend your circuit up to about 450 ft with a –6dB loss. The good thing about fiber trunks to your site is that they allow for much greater distances before signal regeneration is required. Single-mode fiber can allow for distances in excess of 40 km. Some M13 MUX equipment on the market actually allows you to split out T1s or E1s from the same T3 circuit. This is obviously a proprietary function, but it is done at the DS2 level and you can get either four T1s or three E1s out of any of the seven DS2 signals in the circuit.

Another interface that you might come into contact with is a DB-15. This 15-pin interface is not normally an interface for the T3 circuit itself but rather a short-haul T1 interface off of an M13 MUX (refer to Figure 7-10).

Because T3 is typically deployed with fiber in the local loop, it has a much longer distance that it can travel before it needs regenerative repeaters, and EMI is all but eliminated. The only section that you need to worry about is what is connected at your local site.

T3 Line Coding

T3 circuits use one type of line coding, which is similar to bipolar 8-zero substitution (B8ZS) that is used on T1 circuits. Bipolar 3-zero substitution (B3ZS) is used for both T3 circuits and SONET links. Similar to B8ZS, B3ZS inserts a unique bipolar violation (BPV) in the event that a series of three 0s are detected. The insertion of the BPV is to ensure that 1s density requirements are met.

Even though it operates in a similar way to B8ZS, some rules are specific to the way the B3ZS operates. The rules are split into four different categories, which are based on the polarity of the last binary 1 (positive/negative) and the parity of the number of pulses since the last intentional BPV (even/odd). The four categories are as follows:

- If the polarity of the last binary 1 was positive, and the number of pulses from the last BPV is even, the transmission of the BPV is $-1, 0, -1$.

- If the polarity of the last binary 1 was positive, and the number of pulses from the last BPV is odd, the transmission of the BPV is $0, 0, +1$.

- If the polarity of the last binary 1 was negative, and the number of pulses from the last BPV is even, the transmission of the BPV is $+1, 0, +1$.

- If the polarity of the last binary 1 was negative, and the number of pulses from the last BPV is odd, the transmission of the BPV is $0, 0, -1$.

Figure 7-11 shows two of the above cases. The remaining two cases are left as an exercise for the reader.

Figure 7-11 *B3ZS Intentional BPVs*

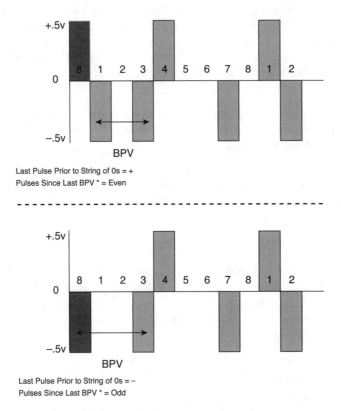

T3 Framing Types

T3 circuits have two main types of framing that can be used. The two types are M23 and C-bit parity framing. The type of framing that you use depends on the service provider that you obtain your circuit from. M23 is more common, but several providers use C-bit. (M23 framing is also referred to as M13 framing.)

M23 and C-Bit Parity

The main difference between M23 and C-bit parity framing has to do with the DS2 multiplexing. In M23 multiplexing, bit stuffing is required to ensure that any differences in the DS2 clock source is removed. Thus, M23 framing uses all the overhead bits that are associated with DS3 signal streams (X, P, M, F, and C). The C-bits identify whether bit stuffing has occurred in a specific DS2 frame. In other words, if you were to have at least two C-bits toggled to 1 in DS2 #5, that identifies DS2 #5 as having bit stuffing turned on.

As stated above, in modern equipment, you expect the DS2 to be handled by the same device and to share the same clock. So there is no longer a requirement to perform bit stuffing at the M23 level. C-bit parity framing is taking advantage of this. With C-bit parity framing, bit stuffing always occurs in all seven available slots, which means that you do not need the C-bits to identify the presence or absence of bit stuffing. The consequence is that the DS2 signals are now set at a constant rate of 6.306272 Mbps, down from the 6.312 Mbps of M23 framing. The 6.306272 Mbps is what is offered to the M12 level, and the speed adaptation is achieved thanks to bit stuffing at the M12 level. After all is said and done, the DS3 bandwidth is still equal to 44.736 Mbps. C-bit framing frees up all 21 of the C-bits for use in network monitoring applications.

DS3 Monitoring with C-Bit Parity Framing

Each of the 21 C-bits can be used for a specific line monitoring function. Refer to Table 7-3 for a complete listing of the bits and their function.

Table 7-3   *C-Bit Functions with C-Bit Framing*

Bit Number	Function
Subframe #1	
C-bit #1	This bit is toggled to a 1 state to identify the use of C-bit parity.
C-bit #2	Reserved.
C-bit #3	Identifies the far-end alarm and control (FEAC). The FEAC identifies remote problems with the circuit and initiates a loopback of the DS3 or individual DS1 circuit.
Subframe #2	
C-bit #1	Reserved.
C-bit #2	Reserved.
C-bit #3	Reserved.
Subframe #3	
C-bit #1 C-bit #2 C-bit #3	Further identify parity traffic through the DS3 network. Designated as CP-bits, these bits are used in congruence with the P-bits that are located at the beginning of subframe 3 and 4. If the P-bits in subframe 3 equal 1, 1, the CP-bits in subframe 4 need to equal the same.

continues

Table 7-3 *C-Bit Functions with C-Bit Framing (Continued)*

Subframe #4	
C-bit #1 C-bit #2 C-bit #3	Transmit far-end block errors (FEBEs). These bits notify the remote end of a specific error that has occurred on the circuit, such as loss of signal (LOS) or out-of-frame (OOF). This is a transport mechanism for yellow alarm-type applications.
Subframe #5	
C-bit #1 C-bit #2 C-bit #3	The C-bits in subframe #5 are used as a facility maintenance link. This link conveys circuit states such as idle codes and specific circuit testing codes. This link is similar to the Facility Data Link (FDL) that is used on DS1 circuits with Extended Superframe format (ESF).
Subframe #6	
C-bit #1	Reserved.
C-bit #2	Reserved.
C-bit #3	Reserved.
Subframe #7	
C-bit #1	Reserved.
C-bit #2	Reserved.
C-bit #3	Reserved.

FEAC (subframe #1, C-bit #3) is a communication channel to carry signal codes. It consists of repeating code words, in the form 0xxxxxx011111111, with two different classes of codes: one for DS1 and one for DS3. The individual DS1 codes do not affect service in such a way that all circuit operation ceases. Most of the DS3 errors cause operations on the link to cease, and they include DS3 LOS, DS3 OOF, DS3 AIS received, and DS3 equipment failure. The only difference is that DS3 equipment failure can be either service affecting or non-service affecting. More details can be found in ANSI T1.107.

Signal codes of LOS and OOF are considered to be red alarms. As discussed earlier in the text, upon receipt of a red alarm the equipment attempts to transmit a yellow alarm to notify the remote end of the problem (also known as RAI). When AIS is received, it is translated as a problem from within the service provider network.

Configuration of a Channelized T3 Interface on a Cisco 10000 ESR

This section focuses on the configuration of a channelized T3 interface for a Cisco 10000 ESR. This expansion card is normally used for channelized applications, but it can be used in an unchannelized mode, if necessary. Each CT3 card has a total of six T3 ports, each denoted by a Tx and Rx pair of 75-ohm female BNC connectors.

This basic configuration gives you an idea of some of the things that you can configure on the card. For more information on the topology, refer to Figure 7-12.

Figure 7-12 *T3 Configuration Topology*

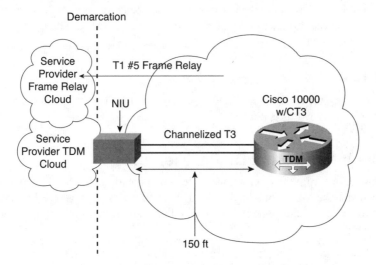

The T3 controller is specified by a 0/0/0 naming convention, and a 4th level (0/0/0/X) specifies the T1 that you want to configure in channelized T3 mode. So 4/0/0/1 is the T3 controller located at 4/0/0, accessing the 1st T1 controller.

The first thing that needs to be done on the channelized T3 interface is to make sure that you have the proper framing, cable length, and timing source set up for the T3 circuit:

```
10K-ESR#config t
10K-ESR(config)#controller t3 4/0/0
10K-ESR(config-controller)#clock source line
10K-ESR(config-controller)#cablelength 150
10K-ESR(config-controller)#framing m23
10K-ESR(config-controller)#no shut
```

After you have made the proper modifications to the T3 controller, you can begin configuring each T1 controller within the T3 circuit. You can remain in T3 controller mode and configure the T1 circuits from there:

```
10K-ESR(config-controller)#t1 5 framing esf    (DEFAULT)
10K-ESR(config-controller)#t1 5 clock source internal    (DEFAULT)
```

Now that you have set up the T1 interface, you can create a channel group. The **channel-group** command groups the DS0s in T1 #5 and creates a virtual serial interface that allows you to finish the Frame Relay configuration on that T1:

```
10K-ESR(config-controller)#t1 5 channel-group 1 timeslots 1-24
10K-ESR(config-controller)#exit
10K-ESR(config)#int s 4/0/0/5:1
10K-ESR(config-if)#encapsulation frame relay
10K-ESR(config-if)#ip address 10.21.13.7 255.255.255.0
10K-ESR(config-if)#encapsulation frame-relay ietf
10K-ESR(config-if)#frame-relay interface-dlci 70
10K-ESR(config-if)#frame-relay lmi-type q933a
10K-ESR(config-if)#no shut
```

This exercise is by no means exhaustive on what can be configured on this box, but it is meant to serve as an introduction to the types of commands that can be used.

E3 Technology

One E3 can transport 16 E1s in a single circuit, or around 34 Mbps of unstructured data. You will now see how this is done.

Evolution of the International Digital Hierarchy

The specifications from the International Telecommunication Union (ITU) on digital hierarchy match the NADH only in theory and the first digital signal level. From there, they deviate in data rates, management capabilities, line coding, framing, and just about everything else.

The first level of the ITU digital hierarchy is the E1 circuit. Running at 2.048 Mbps, this circuit contains 32 DS0s. For more information on E1, refer to Chapter 6, "E1, R2, and Japanese Carrier Technology." The second level is the E2 circuit, and like the NADH T2, it has seen few deployments. E2 is discussed in the multiplexing portions of the next few sections.

In contrast, in Japan, J2 (6.312 Mbps, that is four J1s at 1.544 Mbps) is widely deployed.

The third level of the digital hierarchy for ITU is the E3 circuit. E3 circuits are at a higher bandwidth rate than E2s (34.368 Mbps) but are lower than a T3 circuit. This is because an E3 circuit contains only a total of 16 E1s.

Sorting out the Mess

The international community also had to devise a way to multiplex digital circuits into higher level hierarchies. Multiplexing has some subtle differences in the way that it is done. Interestingly enough, E3 circuits are not used nearly as often any more in the international community since the creation of the SDH hierarchy. In most locations, you are more likely to find optical networks than the continued deployment of E3 circuits.

There are two types of multiplexing that are associated with the international deployments, but the naming of the stages is less formal. For the sake of consistency these two stages are called E12 and E23 multiplexing.

The E-carrier technology is multiplexed in a more standardized approach. When you look at how the technology is multiplexed, you can see that it is always a grouping of four (with the exception of the DS0s):

- 32 DS0s in an E1
- 4 E1s in an E2
- 4 E2s in an E3
- 4 E3s in an E4
- 4 E4s in an E5

E12 Multiplexing

E12 multiplexing is the process of taking four international DS1 circuits (E1) and multiplexing them into a single international DS2 circuit (E2) (Figure 7-13 shows the process). This process is identical to the one described for M12. The multiplexing method is cyclic bit-interleaving with positive justification (ITU G.742), which means that the payload is built by taking one bit from the first E1, one bit from the second E1, and so on. The positive justification is what was described earlier as bit stuffing. To adjust for small clock variations between the E1s, an extra data bit is available for each E1 in each E2 frame. The format of the E2 frame is shown in Figure 7-14. Each E1 can use 205 or 206 bits of data per E2 frame. As for DS2 and DS3, the C-bits indicate whether bit stuffing was performed, that is, whether the extra bit contains user data or is just filler. Each E2 frame contains four sets of three C-bits, one set for each E1. If two or three C-bits are set to 1, it indicates positive justification for this E1. The bit rate of an E1 circuit is 2.048 Mbps, with the justification bit. The available bit rate for one E1 in an E2 frame is around 2.052 Mbps, which, when multiplied by four, gives you a total bit rate of 8.208 Mbps. At this point, the overhead of around 240 kbps per E2 is added to give the nominal rate of 8.448 Mbps.

Figure 7-13 *E12 Multiplexing*

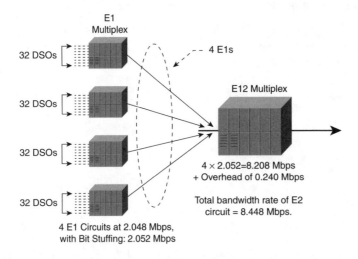

Figure 7-14 *E2 and E3 Frame Format*

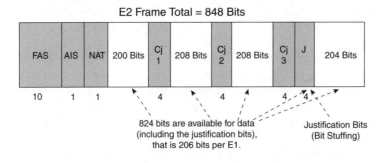

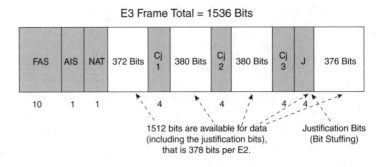

Table 7-4 details the overhead bits in the E2 and E3 frames:

Table 7-4   *E2 and E3 Framing and Overhead Bits (Channelized)*

FAS	Frame alignment signal (1111010000)
AIS	Alarm indication signal
Nat	Bit reserved for national use
CjX	Justification service bits (see explanation above); four sets of three C-bits, one set per tributary

E23 Multiplexing

The next order of multiplexing in the international digital hierarchy is E23. E23 multiplexes four E2s into a single E3 circuit. This process is identical to the one described above for E12. Cyclic bit interleaving is used, as per ITU G.751. This time, the payload is built by taking one bit from each E2 in sequence. The C-bits have the same purpose but at the E2 level now. Figure 7-14 shows the E3 frame format, and Figure 7-15 highlights the bandwidth computation. Each E2 has a total bandwidth of 8.448 Mbps, and with the justification bit, each E2 has an available bandwidth of 8.457750 Mbps. Multiplied by four, it gives you a data rate of 33.831 Mbps. Combined with the overhead of 537 kbps for the E3 framing, the total bandwidth rate is 34.368 Mbps.

NOTE	E3 line coding is not discussed in this chapter because it uses High Density Bipolar of Order 3 (HDB3). For an explanation of HDB3, refer to Chapter 6.

Unchannelized E3 Frame Structure and Operation

For unchannelized transport, E3 frames have two distinct methods of composition: with and without ATM cell interleaving. These two methods are covered in G.804 and G.832. G.832 specifies the framing type that is used when ATM cells are not interleaved into the E3 frame structure. In standard network deployment, G.832 is used. However, E3 circuits that are used in conjunction with ATM networks use the G.804 framing method.

G.832 Framing

Basic E3 framing is specified by the ITU recommendation of G.832. This framing type is most commonly found in network deployments that do not require ATM interworking. The 4296-bit frames are broken down into 8-bit groups called octets, which are then separated between overhead and payload types. Of the 537 total octets, there are seven overhead octets and 530 payload octets, as shown in Figure 7-16.

Figure 7-15 *E23 Multiplexing*

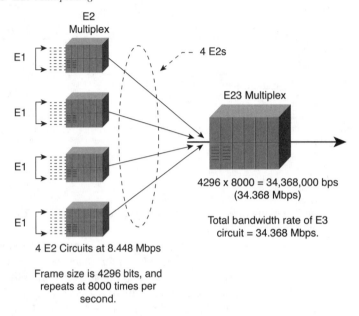

E2
Multiplex

E1

E1

E1

E1

4 E2s

E23 Multiplex

4296 x 8000 = 34,368,000 bps
(34.368 Mbps)

Total bandwidth rate of E3
circuit = 34.368 Mbps.

4 E2 Circuits at 8.448 Mbps

Frame size is 4296 bits, and
repeats at 8000 times per
second.

Figure 7-16 *G.832 Framing Structure*

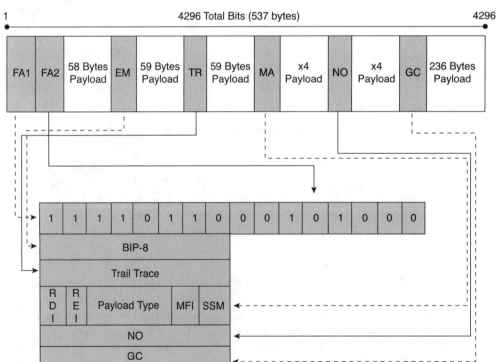

1   4296 Total Bits (537 bytes)   4296

| FA1 | FA2 | 58 Bytes Payload | EM | 59 Bytes Payload | TR | 59 Bytes Payload | MA | x4 Payload | NO | x4 Payload | GC | 236 Bytes Payload |

| 1 | 1 | 1 | 1 | 0 | 1 | 1 | 0 | 0 | 0 | 1 | 0 | 1 | 0 | 0 | 0 |

BIP-8

Trail Trace

| R D I | R E I | Payload Type | MFI | SSM |

NO

GC

The frame alignment (FA) bytes FA1 and FA2 transport the FAS. FA is split into two 8-bit words (11110110, 00101000). The next overhead byte is used for error monitoring (EM).

To provide a parity check on each frame, bit interleaved parity (BIP-8) is used with even parity. The 8 specifies how many bits are used for the parity sequence. The parity computation that is in the current frame is the parity sequence from the last received frame.

The next reserved overhead byte is used for a trail trace (TR). The TR identifies itself to receiving terminal equipment as an active connection in the network. It is transmitted in a repetitive pattern that acts as a heartbeat signal in the network.

The 5th overhead byte is used for maintenance and adaptation (MA). Within this byte, the several bit-level functions are as follows:

- **Bit-1**—Remote defect indication (RDI). Similar in nature to far-end receive failure (FERF), the RDI identifies that an error has occurred at the remote end of the network. The RDI does not identify which circuit the error occurred on. This bit is toggled to 1 when the remote error is detected.

- **Bit-2**—Remote error indication (REI). If errors are detected in the BIP-8 computation, REI is sent to notify the remote end of the circuit that an error has occurred. If the error is active, this bit is toggled to 1.

- **Bit-3 through Bit-5** = These bits identify the payload type in current use. Refer to Table 7-5 for a full listing of the payload types.

Table 7-5   *G.832 Payload Types*

Binary Value	Description
000	Unequipped
001	Equipped, non-specific
010	ATM
011	SDH TU-12s

NOTE   A binary value of all 1s is not used.

- **Bit-6 and Bit-7**—Multiframe indicator.
- **Bit-8**—Timing marker (older implementation) identified whether this circuit was referenced off of a primary reference clock. The newer use of this bit is for multiframe synchronization and is used in conjunction with bits 6 and 7.

The 6th allocated overhead byte is called the network operator (NO). The NO is used for network maintenance and testing.

The last overhead byte is called the general communication channel (GC). The GC is intended for use as a communication channel designated for testing purposes.

G.804 Framing

G.804 specifies the explicit use of ATM with the E3 circuit. This type of framing completely interleaves the ATM cells with the payload octets (bytes). The ATM cells are aligned with the byte structure of the payload octets, but no changes to the G.832 frame type are made. One G.804 frame can then transport 10 ATM cells (530 bytes of payload).

To effectively introduce the ATM cells into the frame structure, they must be scrambled so that they cannot mimic the frame alignment process of the E3 circuit. Each ATM cell is delimited using a process known as HEC. The process calculates a value for the first 4 bytes of the ATM header, and then places the value in the HEC octet.

Configuration of an E3 Interface

The following example is based on Cisco PA-MC-E3 Multichannel E3 port adapter, on a Cisco 7500 router. This adapter provides one channelized E3 high-speed serial interface.

According to information posted on Cisco Systems' web site, the PA-MC-E3 has one channelized E3 high-speed serial interface that provides access to services at E1 (2.048 Mbps) data rates. Also from the same source (www.cisco.com/univercd/cc/td/doc/product/software/ios111/cc111/pamce3.htm#xtocid0), "the PA-MC-E3 complies with CCITT/ITU G.703 physical layer standards and CCITT/ITU G.751 for E3, G.742 for E2, and G.704 and G.706 for E1 fault and alarm detection and response actions."

Please note the references to PDH levels and ITU (formerly known as Consultative Committee for International Telegraph and Telephone [CCITT]) standards.

The configuration of the E3 interface is minimal. There are few options and Cisco IOS provides default values for clocking (line), national reserved bit (1), and idle pattern (0x55). Depending on the hardware, you might have to configure the line length (build-out):

```
router# configure terminal

Enter configuration commands, one per line. End with CNTL/Z.
router(config)# controller e3 4/0/0
router(config-controller)# e1 1 channel-group 0 timeslot 1-31
router(config-controller)# e1 2 channel-group 0 timeslot 1-31
router(config-controller)# e1 3 channel-group 1 timeslot 1-31
...
Each E1 can now be configured, for instance:
router(config)# interface serial 4/0/0/2:0
router(config-if)# ip address 10.10.10.2 255.255.255.0
...
router(config-if)# end
```

Additional configuration commands can specify the clock source (internal or external [line]), and the idle pattern as follows:

```
Router(config-controller)# clock source internal
Router(config-controller)# idle pattern 0xAA
```

The following command can solve some compatibility problems by forcing a value for the national bit that is normally reserved:

```
Router(config-controller)# national bit 0
```

And for troubleshooting, the line can be put in loopback mode:

```
Router(config)# controller e3 4/0/0
Router(config-controller)# loopback local
```

Beyond the X3 Barrier

The big question is, is there anything after T3 and E3? The answer is yes and no. Both the NADH and the ITU hierarchy structures have levels of digital signals that exceed the T3 and E3 bandwidth levels.

The NADH has four levels total in the hierarchy. After DS3, you normally only see documentation on one other bandwidth rate. It is called DS4 (T4), and it runs at a bandwidth rate of 274.176 Mbps. It is composed of 4032 DS0 circuits or six T3s and is by far the most bandwidth offered outside of SONET applications. This type of circuit can be deployed with a fiber to coax crossconnect, just as T3, or (and most probably) you will see it deployed as strictly fiber.

T4s are not circuits that you can call your local service provider and get. This type of bandwidth is reserved exclusively for service provider network connections.

On the international front, there are several levels available after the E3 circuits. The next digital signal in the hierarchy is an E4. The E4 has a nominal bandwidth rate of 139.264 Mbps, and it is comprised of four E3 circuits. The last in line for the international hierarchy is the E5 circuit. An E5 has a huge pipe of bandwidth available to it, weighing in at 565.148 Mbps.

Similar to its little brother, you cannot call your local provider for this type of access. In general, neither of these circuits is deployed in bulk because SDH speeds already significantly outweigh the bandwidth offered in either circuit.

Summary

Moving up the digital hierarchy ladder, you have been introduced to the function and operation of T3 and E3 circuits. Both of these circuits offer a large pipe of bandwidth that can be deployed in either channelized or unchannelized modes.

Channelized applications allow for a much more efficient use of bandwidth, particularly as one group is in charge of routing bandwidth as needed. Channelized DS3s allow for you to redirect DS1s to multiple other locations to facilitate a hub-and-spoke environment. Unchannelized DS3s are not without their own applications though. These types of links are used when it is necessary to provide near real-time video transfer between distances, such as distance learning.

One example of unchannelized T3 is for the transport of ATM cells. Two methods are provided: PLCP, which is adding another level of framing to delineate ATM cells at the cost of additional overhead, and HEC delineation, which identifies ATM cells based on their header.

In North America, a T3 consists of 28 T1s, but adding up 28 T1s won't get you the actual bit rate of 44.736 Mbps. Several levels of bit stuffing are involved, as along with overhead bits that accomplish the total bandwidth rate. Within this bit stuffing structure, there are several different types of multiplexing: M12, M23, and M13.

The nomenclature describes what levels of digital signals are being combined to form the next higher layer. For example, the M12 multiplexing involves combining DS1 into a DS2 signal. The reason for the addition shortfall on DS1 circuits (why they don't add up to 44.736 Mbps) is because both multiplexing stages must take place. Four DS1s + bit stuffing + overhead = DS2. Seven DS2s + bit stuffing + overhead = DS3.

T3 circuits use a form of line coding called B3ZS, which inserts a unique BPV into the signal stream upon the detection of a string of three 0s. This line coding method adequately fulfills the 1s density requirements. Two different types of framing can be used on a T3, either M23 or C-bit. The main difference between the two framing types is how the C-bits are used. In C-bit framing, bit stuffing is always turned on (at the M23 level); therefore, the C-bits are not needed to identify the absence or presence of bit stuffing. Because this is the case, they can be used for other applications on the circuit.

The ITU also has specifications for DS3 level circuits. The E3 is a combination of multiplexing just as the T3 is. The two specified multiplexes that occur are the E12 and E23. A major difference between T3 and E3 (besides all of the physical layer framing and line coding) is the bandwidth rate. The bandwidth on an E3 is significantly smaller than that of a T3 circuit. E3s are based on E1 circuits, true, but there are only 16 total E1s in each E3 circuit. So the total bandwidth is 34.368 Mbps.

E3 circuits use a HDB3 line-coding scheme. HDB3 was created to alleviate the problems that line-coding methods such as alternate mark inversion (AMI) had with 1s density violations. In the event that four consecutive 0s are detected, HDB3 coders insert a unique BPV to represent the string of 0s. With HDB3 set at both ends, all the equipment on the circuit can tell when there is a string of four 0s.

Unchannelized E3 circuits use two primary forms of framing: G.832 or G.804. G.804 is based on G.832 and shares the same frame format. The main difference between the two is that G.832 does not interleave ATM cells directly into the payload octets. In G.804, ATM cell delimitation is taken care of by HEC. HEC creates a calculation that allows the identification of individual cells as they are transmitted.

Beyond the DS3 level, both hierarchies have digital signals of varying bandwidth. In the NADH, the T4 is the largest pipe of non-SONET bandwidth, and it can provide 274.176 Mbps of data, whereas the ITU hierarchy has both an E4 and E5. The E4 has a bandwidth of 139.264 Mbps, and the E5 has a high bandwidth at 565.148 Mbps. All the circuits in this paragraph are not deployed as customer circuits, and if used they are found in service provider backbones. Most of the high bandwidth circuits today are actually SONET- or SDH-based.

Review Questions

Give or select the best answer or answers to the following questions. The answers to these questions can be found in Appendix A, "Answers to Review Questions."

1 How many T1s are found in an unchannelized T3?

_____

_____

_____

2 True or False. T3 circuits are generally considered to be synchronous, similar to T1s.

_____

_____

_____

3 How many 0s must be transmitted in succession before HDB3 transmits a bipolar violation?

  a 4

  b 1

  c 3

  d 5

4 How many E1 circuits are multiplexed into an E2? E3?

_____

_____

_____

5 What was the technology SYNTRAN the basis for?

_____

_____

_____

6 What is the function of a P-bit in a DS3 frame?

_____

_____

_____

7 What is the approximate cable length limit (in feet) of the coaxial cable used for T3 connections?

_____

_____

_____

8 How many bits are in an E3 frame?

_____

_____

_____

This chapter covers the following topics:

- **Integrated Services Digital Network (ISDN) introduction**—The introduction is geared towards explaining the development and progress of ISDN as a digital network structure.

- **ISDN network**—This section introduces you to the physical attributes of the ISDN network and how ISDN circuits are typically deployed. Both Basic Rate Interfaces (BRIs) and Primary Rate Interfaces (PRIs) are detailed and the associated ISDN reference points.

- **ISDN specifications**—This section describes the different ISDN specifications and how they operate in the ISDN network. This section is intended to give you an in-depth view on how ISDN works.

- **BRI**—This section details how BRI circuits operate and how they are deployed in North America, Europe, and Japan. It covers both line-coding schemes and deployments.

- **PRI**—This section describes the operation of primary rate circuits and how they are deployed around the world.

CHAPTER 8

Integrated Services Digital Network

ISDN Introduction

In the days of old, the service providers infrastructure was deployed as a series of analog services. Analog services are acceptable in short distances, but they simply can't provide the quality of service (QoS) and bandwidth over the long haul. Remember that when analog circuits become too attenuated, the signal is merely amplified. This amplification also increases the noise content.

The analog infrastructure was never designed to provide voice, video, and data integration for customers. In today's market, these features have become more and more prevalent, and because of that something had to be designed that could handle these functions.

Modern telecommunication technologies are based on digital principles for reasons of flexibility, efficiency, and feature capability. Although many digital services are available today, ISDN offers some unique features that will solidify its place in telecommunication for years to come.

Originally, ISDN was developed as two separate types of service, N-ISDN (narrowband) and B-ISDN (broadband). The N-ISDN offerings are what this chapter focuses on, and they include BRI and PRI services. BRI and PRI are deployed over what are considered to be narrowband circuits, ranging from 16 kbps of a 64-kbps digital signal 0 (DS0), to a 2.048-Mbps circuit. B-ISDN is directly related to Asynchronous Transfer Mode (ATM) and is discussed in Chapter 10, "ATM and B-ISDN."

ISDN made the first real attempt at bringing services such as voice/video applications to end subscriber premises. If you take a closer look at the abbreviation ISDN, you can begin to understand the basis of the technology. ISDN is meant to integrate services such as voice, video, and data over a digital network. ISDN, because it is digital, offers customers more bandwidth than standard analog service, nominally running at 128 kbps for BRI service (144 kbps if D channel usage is allowed) and 1.544 Mbps for T1 PRI or 2.048 Mbps for E1 PRI.

The ISDN Network

The ISDN network architecture is deployed throughout the world in different ways, but the underlying principles remain the same. Several new pieces of equipment are required to facilitate the digital loop between the service provider and the customer.

The building blocks of ISDN are Bearer channels (B channels) and Data channels (D channels). The B channels are used for the transmission of customer video, voice, and data, and the D channel is used for call-control signaling. There are some cases in which the D channel can be used for data applications. These channel types will be discussed in more detail a bit later.

Circuit Switching

ISDN is referred to as a circuit-switching technology. If you think back to Chapter 2, "The Signaling System 7 Network," you'll remember that Signaling System 7 (SS7) operates by routing calls on a hop-by-hop basis. Don't think about the signaling path, but think about the actual path that the bearer traffic takes. The call moves from switch to switch until it arrives at its final destination. After it is there, a circuit path is opened from one end of the call to the other. That circuit remains open until it is closed by one of the participating sides.

This is exactly how the ISDN network operates. In Figure 8-1, when Keith wants to connect to Chris he must dial a number that is associated with Chris's ISDN circuit. These numbers are commonly referred to as phone numbers, but in the ISDN world they're actually E.164 numbers, or addresses. When Keith calls 555-1212, the call is switched through the network to Chris's location and the call is connected. Remember that as the call transits through the public switched telephone network (PSTN), it's not necessarily ISDN. The circuit path between the two parties is reserved for the duration of the call and released upon disconnect.

One of the problems with network structures such as this is that they can be quite inefficient. The connection might not require all the bandwidth that is allocated and, therefore, can waste what has been given. This is a problem not only with ISDN but also with any traditional time-division multiplexing (TDM)-based technology. To correct this problem, you need to use something similar to statistical multiplexing (stat-muxing). This way, even individual DS0s can be allocated for different applications. For more information on stat-muxing, refer to Chapter 9, "Frame Relay."

Before moving on, an important point to understand about ISDN is that it is a local loop technology. This means that from your local central office (CO) to your premises it is ISDN. However, on the other side of your CO's switch, it can be just about anything, such as ATM or Synchronous Optical Network/Synchronous Digital Hierarchy (SONET/SDH). Figure 8-2 shows the local ISDN loop interconnected to the digital transport network of the service provider.

Figure 8-1   *Circuit Switching*

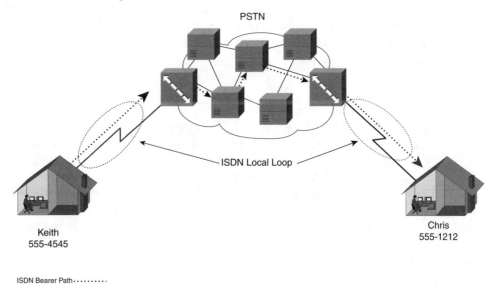

Figure 8-2   *High-Level Overview of an ISDN Local Loopt*

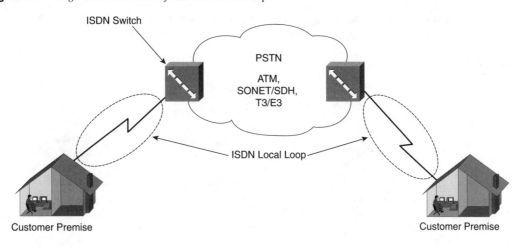

The transit of ISDN can look something similar to ISDN to SONET for transport through the network infrastructure, back into ISDN on the physical plane, and to ISDN Q.931 signaling to SS7 signaling through the network infrastructure, and finally back into ISDN Q.931 signaling on the signaling plane. You will learn more about some of the call flows a little later in the chapter.

The Local Loop

ISDN is deployed between the service provider's CO and the customer's premises. The local loop, deployed over a combination of copper and possibly optical cable, must observe the same stipulations of any digital technology. In other words, the ISDN carrier facilities are equally as susceptible to problems such as cross talk and attenuation as any analog circuit. As far as interference goes, fiber-optic trunks do not need to worry about electromagnetic interference (EMI). Optical trunks can also transport information for much greater distances before the need for signal regeneration. Service providers tend to deploy high bandwidth, fiber trunks to integrated digital loop carrier (IDLC) systems and then provide copper service from there to the customer's premises.

The local loop, if deployed solely over copper facilities, must observe a maximum loop length of about 18 kft (18,000 feet) for BRI and 4800 ft for E1 or 6000 ft for T1 PRI. After 18 kft, the signal has to be regenerated with a device called a digital regenerator. In this chapter, these are referred to as mid-span repeaters. A mid-span repeater functions differently from an analog amplification system in that the signal is completely regenerated upon receipt. Figure 8-3 shows the cable lengths associated with ISDN BRI or PRI circuit deployments in relation to mid-span repeaters.

Figure 8-3   *Mid-Span Repeaters*

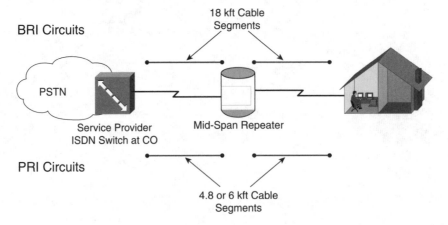

The signal travels from the CO, through the copper pairs, until it reaches the mid-span repeater. At that point, the mid-span repeater dusts off and regenerates the digital signal by locking onto the combination of 1s that are being transmitted from the network. The ISDN loop can travel another 18 kft because the mid-span repeater now looks similar to the origination point of the signal. The mid-span repeater functions the same way in both directions and is not limited to network to user transmission.

There is a grey area with mid-span repeater deployment when circuits fall just to one side or the other of the requirements. A question that a lot of people ask is: when will a mid-span repeater be added to an ISDN circuit? If the loop length is close to 18 kft, sometimes a repeater is added and sometimes it isn't. It depends on who is installing the ISDN circuit and whether they feel that one is necessary. Unfortunately, mid-span repeaters aren't exactly cheap, so these devices aren't deployed unless absolutely necessary.

It is also possible that mid-span repeaters can be installed even if the loop length is well within the allowed limit. The other factor that can dictate the deployment of a mid-span repeater is decibel (dB) loss. Normally, even if the circuit is within 18 kft, a mid-span repeater is deployed if the dB loss on the circuit is between –38 dB and –42 dB or higher. High –dB could mean that there is a problem with some of the facilities or there might be some extreme environmental conditions that cannot be controlled.

Repeaters are normally housed in an environmentally safe casing that shields it from the elements. The cases are normally about five times the size of the actual mid-span repeater card.

Repeaters aren't the only devices that are found on the ISDN local loop. Remember that IDLCs require less copper to customer locations. Connected to a CO through a high-bandwidth trunk, these devices are positioned closer to customer locations to provide more efficient use of available facilities. ISDN services have been integrated into most IDLC equipment by using either three available DS0s for BRI or a full digital signal level 1 (DS-1) circuit for PRI. These functions will be discussed in more detail in the BRI and PRI sections of this chapter.

Echo Cancellation

Echo cancellation is used on BRI circuits because there is only a single pair for both transmitting and receiving information. PRI circuits do not have this problem because they run off of either coaxial cable or two copper twisted pairs, one pair for transmit and one for receive.

Echo cancellation is designed to remove the signal echo from a circuit so that your equipment knows what information is being sent to it. Too much echo without cancellation measures can cause problems with the network equipment. Refer to Figure 8-4 and the description that follows for the basic echo cancellation procedure. Figure 8-4 shows a pair of echo cancellers removing their own signal from the circuit to ascertain the proper signal to be received.

Figure 8-4   *Echo Cancellation*

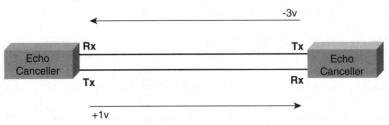

The voltage levels in Figure 8-4 are only examples of possible values.

- The echo canceller on the right sends a signal equivalent to a –3v charge, and the echo canceller on the left sends a signal equivalent to a +1v charge.

- To figure out what is being sent to it, the echo canceller on the right takes the total voltage of the circuit (+1v + –3v = –2v).

- With the total line voltage known, the echo canceller then applies the voltage of what it transmitted, but in the opposite polarity. In other words, –3v becomes +3v.

- The final equation looks something similar to the following: –2v + +3v = +1v. It is now known that a signal of +1v was meant for its receiver.

Network Interface Device (NID)

NID is a common term that describes the interface at which an ISDN BRI circuit connects to the customer's premises in North American implementations. The NID separates the service provider's portion of the ISDN circuit from the customer's ISDN equipment and inside wiring (ISW). This device is a result of the deregulation of the phone company after the divestiture of 1984.

A typical NID is a grey box that sits on the side of the customer's house or office, and it is split into two halves. The customer's side is usually accessible by the customer, but the service provider's side is normally locked with a special type of bolt. A special tool is required to access that side of the NID and service technicians normally carry it with them. If an ISDN technician is ever sent out to your premises, the first thing they will do is try to test from the NID back to the CO. If they test successfully and you can't access the network, chances are there is something wrong with your equipment or ISW.

ISDN Reference Points

ISDN specifies a set of reference points that describe the various network functions associated with an ISDN BRI circuit. These reference points are shown in Figure 8-5. The reference points and equipment include U, S, T, TE1, TE2, and R.

Figure 8-5   *ISDN Reference Pointst*

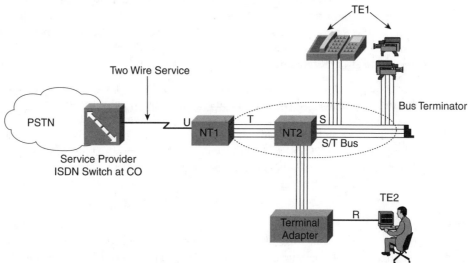

The U interface or reference point, also known as the user interface, describes the access point from the service provider's network into the customer's Network Terminator Type 1 (NT1). Also referred to as the U-loop interface, it is normally represented with a RJ-45 modular plug on the NT1. This interface is used in the United States for customer access, but most of the rest of the world uses an S/T interface.

Next, there are the S and T reference points. You might see these referred to separately as is done here or as a single reference point denoted S/T. The T reference point is located between the NT1 and NT2 devices, and the S reference point is located on the far end of the NT2 device, if the S/T interface is separated. NT1 devices terminate the ISDN circuit. NT2 devices are smart ISDN devices that make multilayer decisions on the ISDN network, such as on routers or private branch exchanges (PBXs). Devices known as NT12s are devices that integrate both functions of the NT1 and NT2 into a single device.

The two pairs of wires on the other side of the NT1 are known as the S/T bus. On this bus you can have up to eight devices, but only two can operate at any one time. The S/T bus can support a maximum length of about 3000 feet, and the bus terminates at the far end to prevent circuit echo, line noise, and distortion. The S/T bus uses pins 3, 4, 5, and 6 for transmission and reception. The S/T interface uses pins 3 and 6 for transmit and pins 4 and 5 for receive if used in a terminal equipment type 1 (TE1) or terminal adapter (TA). If the

S/T interface is used in a NT, the pin assignments are reversed. Pins 3 and 6 receive and pins 4 and 5 transmit.

The next two items are types of equipment rather than actual reference points in the network. TE1 is a device that is ISDN-ready. ISDN-ready means that you can plug it directly into the ISDN network and it functions properly. A common TE1 is an ISDN phone or an ISDN video conferencing device. Terminal equipment type 2 (TE2) is a device that is not directly compatible with the ISDN network. TE2s require a TA to adapt their signal to a proper ISDN network signal. Typically, devices such as personal computers require an ISDN TA to function on the network properly. The link between the TE2 and the TA is referred to as the R reference point.

Most equipment that is sold in the United States integrates the NT1 and TA functionality into the same box. For this reason, there is no S/T bus available to users unless a standalone NT1 is purchased. In that case, the stand-alone product provides the two-pair S/T bus for a device, such as an ISDN video conferencing unit. Most devices also provide plain old telephone service (POTS) interfaces for analog communication through the ISDN circuit. This feature is provided with an analog-to-digital converter.

ISDN Specifications

ISDN has been standardized in a host of different specifications from groups such as the International Telecommunication Union (ITU), Telcordia (formerly Bellcore), and the American National Standards Institute (ANSI). These groups, along with the ISDN forum, are responsible for modeling the ISDN industry. Standards that are in the I group consist of standards set forth for ISDN, both narrow and broadband. The Q group of standards has to do with switching and signaling. The Q standards also include topics such as SS7 and Intelligent Networks (INs). Several standards are associated with ISDN, but the most common standards are as follows:

- I.430—BRI Physical Layer
- I.431—PRI Physical Layer
- Q.921—ISDN Data Link Layer Specification
- Q.931—Call-Control and Signaling Specification

The physical layer specifications for ISDN are I.430 and I.431. They identify the electrical, mechanical, and functional specifications of the circuits. I.430 specifies the basis for a BRI frame as 48 bits. The BRI frame is cycled at 4000 times per second, which gives a total bandwidth of 192,000 bps (48 * 4000). Although 192 kbps is available on the BRI circuit, the subscriber typically only uses a maximum of 128 kbps. 144 kbps is possible if the D channel is also used for data, but D channel use depends on the provider.

I.431 describes the use of either a T1 or E1 circuit for the electrical basis of a PRI circuit. There are specifications for a Japanese PRI (INS-1500), but it is not included in the ITU specification.

ITU Q.921

The ISDN protocol stack consists of three layers: physical, data link, and network. The data link layer function and format is described in ITU Q.921. Q.921 is also referred to as Link Access Procedure on the D channel (LAPD). This part of the protocol stack is largely based on the high-level data link control (HDLC) protocol.

The purpose of Q.921 is to provide for a reliable transport for Layer 3 signaling messages (Q.931), provide identification of frames, and provide flow control mechanisms for data transmission and reception. If you're thinking that these functions look familiar by now, they should. The Layer 2 functionality that you find in ISDN, SS7, Frame Relay, and other technologies are basically the same thing. This is due to the description of what the function of a Layer 2 service should be in functional models such as the Open System Interconnection (OSI) model.

NOTE   Not all technologies implement layer 2 functions in the same way.

Because Q.921 deals with Layer 2 functions, it is important to remember that transmission of frames is involved between ISDN nodes. Q.921 communication takes place only between two immediate points and is not end-to-end. Before you move on, you should understand the Q.921 frame structures and how they are used. Figure 8-6 shows Frame Types A and B for ISDN Q.921.

Figure 8-6   *Q.921 Frame Structure*

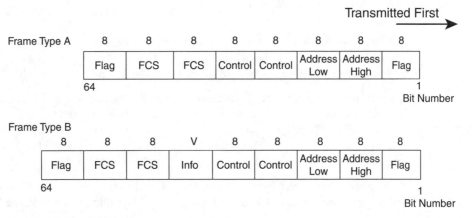

V = Variable Length Field

There are two frame formats that are commonly associated with Q.921, and they are denoted as Type A and Type B. The main difference between the two frame types is the fact the Type B has an information field that is of variable length.

The Flag fields that are on either end of the Q.921 frame identify the beginning and the end of the frame. The flag sequence for both flag types is 01111110, and the closing flag of one frame can count as the opening flag of the next frame. Otherwise, there are back-to-back flag octets in every frame after the first flag octet in the signal stream.

The address octets are set up as a high-order octet and a low-order octet. The high-order octet contains information such as the extended address (EA) bit, command/response (C/R) bit, and the service access point identifier (SAPI). The second octet contains an EA bit and a 7-bit field that is referred to as the terminal endpoint identifier (TEI). Figure 8-7 shows the placement of each of these fields.

Figure 8-7 *Q.921 Address Octets*

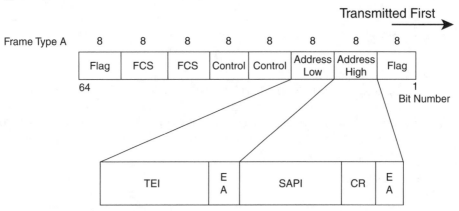

The EA bits identify where the address octets end. Whichever of the two octets are identified by a 1 serves as the last address octet. In normal Q.921 operation you use both address octets, and the bits are set to (read right to left) 0 and 1 respectively.

The C/R bit identifies whether a frame is intended to be either a command or a response. The bit value is determined by the direction of the message and the message type. If the user side of the ISDN connection is sending the message, it uses a 0 value for a command and a 1 value for a response. The network side sends commands with a bit value of 1 and a response with a bit value of 0.

Service access points (SAPs) are the points that Q.921 uses to provide service to Q.931. The access points are denoted with an identifier called a SAPI. In other words, the SAPI is a value that identifies different types of traffic. Table 8-1 lists the different SAPI values and their defined data representations.

Table 8-1   *Q.921 SAPI Values and Data Types*

SAPI	Data Type
0	Call Control
1 to 15	Reserved
16	X.25
17 to 31	Reserved
63	Layer 2 Management

The last field in the address low octet is the TEI. The TEI identifies the terminal equipment on the data link connection. The values range from 0 to 127, and they are split into two different sub-categories: static and dynamic TEI assignment:

- TEI values 0 to 63 are for static assignment, and TEI 0 is most commonly associated with ISDN PRI circuits.

- TEI values 64 to 126 are for dynamic TEI assignment and are commonly found on ISDN BRI circuits.

- TEI 127 is reserved as the broadcast TEI. For instance, when an ISDN device on a BRI circuit comes online and requests a TEI from the network, it uses TEI 127 as the vehicle for the request.

The next several octets in the frame are called control octets, and they can be 16 or 24 bits total (depending on whether or not there is an info octet). The control octets, in conjunction with the C/R bit, identify which type of frame is being sent. Three types of frame groups are used, numbered information (I), unnumbered information (U), and supervisory (S). The main difference between I and U frame types is that U frame types do not guarantee delivery, and they do not require acknowledgments. Table 8-2 lists some of the more common frame types and their functions.

Table 8-2   *Q.921 Control Octet Frame Types*

Frame Type	Definition
Information (I)	I frames identify a sequential order of frames with acknowledgments. Please see the next section for a detailed look at operation. These are standard transmission and reception frames that transport messages such as Q.931 Setup messages.

continues

Table 8-2 *Q.921 Control Octet Frame Types (Continued)*

Unnumbered (U)	U frames are used upon request from Q.931 to facilitate connection management that does not require the receipt of acknowledgments. Particularly, you see these frame types for operations such as TEI assignment requests.
Supervisory (S)	S frames display different layer control states such as RR, RNR, and REJ.
Set Asynchronous Balanced Mode Extended (SABME)	SABME is the first message sent during a Layer 2 connection sequence. Its basic purpose is to reset the link and prepare it for a new connection. SABMEs must be acknowledged by a UA.
Unnumbered Acknowledgment (UA)	UAs are sent in response to a SABME message to acknowledge receipt of the connection request. UAs are also sent to acknowledge the receipt of a DISC message.
Receive Ready (RR)	RR indicates that the ISDN device can begin to receive frames. This is only active after the integrity of the link has been checked. RR messages can also be used in conjunction with N(S) and N(R) to acknowledge previous received frames.
Frame Type	**Definition**
Receive Not Ready (RNR)	RNR specifies that the ISDN device is not ready to receive frames and that transmission should not take place. This can be caused by a link failure, improper network-user settings, or congestion on the circuit.
Reject (REJ)	REJ is sent to request the retransmission of a frame that was corrupted or otherwise not accepted.
Disconnect (DISC)	After multiple frames have been established, the DISC message type can be sent to disconnect the link.
Disconnected Mode (DM)	DM is sent when multiple frame establishment is not possible.
Frame Reject (FRMR)	FRMR reports errors on frames that cannot be recovered by retransmission.
Exchange Identification (XID)	XID is an optional message that allows for the exchange of device information during the synchronization process. Please refer to Figure 8-6 (Frame Type B INFO field) for location within the frame.

Figure 8-8 shows the three main frame categories and their associated bit locations.

Figure 8-8   *Q.921 Control Octets*

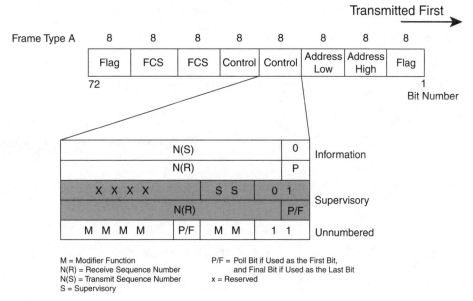

M = Modifier Function
N(R) = Receive Sequence Number
N(S) = Transmit Sequence Number
S = Supervisory

P/F = Poll Bit if Used as the First Bit,
      and Final Bit if Used as the Last Bit
x = Reserved

NOTE   Something to note about Figure 8-8 is the state of the first two bits. The following applies to the Q.921 control octets:

- If the first bit is equal to 0, it is an I frame.

- If the first bit is equal to 1 and the second bit is equal to 0, it is an S frame.

- If the first bit is equal to 1 and the second bit is equal to 1, it is a U frame.

During the data link negotiation process within Q.921, the purpose is to get the link to a Multiple Frame Established (MFE) state. After the link is in MFE, the devices are ready to transmit upper-layer data between them. The negotiation process contains several steps that you need to comprehend to effectively understand and troubleshoot Q.921 operation.

Q.921 Alignment

During the first message transfer in the Q.921 alignment process, a UI frame with a TEI request is sent from the user device to the network using the T202 timer. Remember that the broadcast TEI for this function is 127. Figure 8-9 shows the TEI assignment process between the subscriber equipment and the ISDN switch. Upon receipt of the UI frame, the network responds with the user device's TEI assignment. The operation of the UI frame is the same as defined for U frames in Table 8-2. After the TEI assignment has taken place, the assigned TEI is used. Prior to the assignment of the TEI, the device is in a TEI=Unassigned state, unless a PRI circuit is being used.

Figure 8-9   *Q.921 TEI Request and Confirmation*

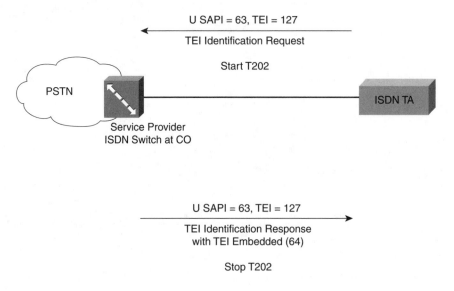

NOTE   Dynamic TEI assignment is only used for point-to-multipoint configurations, as seen with ISDN BRI circuits. Therefore, point-to-point applications, such as T1 or E1 PRI, use a static TEI with the value of 0.

Furthermore, Reference Number (RI) fields differentiate between simultaneous requests from multiple devices so that the ISDN switch can keep track of the different user requests. An Action Indicator (AI) requests that a dynamically assigned TEI be given from Layer 3.

After the TEI has been assigned to a device, there is an audit feature in place that allows for the verification of a TEI called a TEI check. This check allows the network equipment to verify that a specific device has a TEI assigned or to determine if a device has been given a duplicate TEI in error. This check is performed based on the T201 timer.

T201 is started and the check request sent. If multiple responses return with the same TEI, the check is verified by starting the process over. If there are multiple responses a second time, duplicate TEI assignments are known. The network side can request that a TEI be reassigned at this point by sending a TEI identity remove statement to the remote station in question. This same timer finds out which TEIs are no longer being used. If a check request is sent and no response comes back after two consecutive periods, the TEI is released back into the pool as available. The network or user side can start TEI verification.

SABME is sent from the user side to the network side. Remember, the SABME resets the link for a clean connection and it must be acknowledged with a UA frame type. Figure 8-10 shows the start of the Q.921 link. The combination of SAPI and TEI are similar to how a data-link connection identifier (DLCI) works in Frame Relay. They address the Layer 2 portions of the ISDN circuit.

Figure 8-10 *Q.921 SABME and UA Acknowledgment*

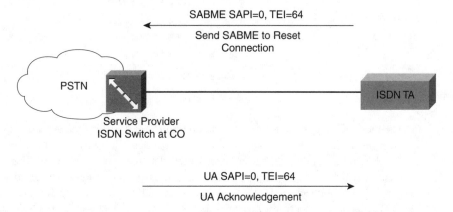

After this point, the data link is said to aligned. Now the two sides are ready to exchange messages and can begin the heartbeat sequence. The heartbeat sequence, or keep-alive, is a series of Receiver Ready poll (RRp) and Receiver Ready final (RRf) messages. These messages basically verify that the link integrity is still acceptable.

During transmission of frames, the N(S) and N(R) frame types indicate which frame number is being sent, and which should be sent next, as shown in Figure 8-11. In other words, if a frame is received with a N(S)=5 and a N(R)=6 this tells you that the number of the frame you are receiving is 5 and the remote receiver expects 6 to be sent to it next.

Figure 8-11 *Q.921 Frame Sequence*

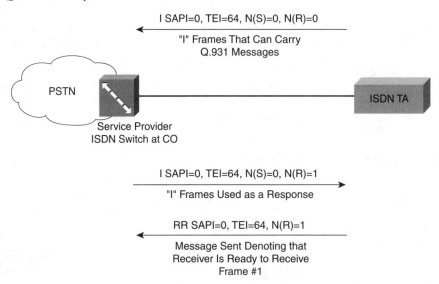

The incrementing of the frames is handled by V(S) and V(R). V(S) is a value that is held by the transmitting station's device. As each frame is sent, the current number is transferred to the N(S) field and the number is incremented. The receiving device uses the N(R) to identify which frame number should be received next. The values are paired as N(S)/V(R) for purposes of checking integrity. At the receiving device, it compares V(R) to N(S) to verify that the correct frame has been sent. After that, a CRC is done to verify that the frame itself is good. When both functions pass, the V(R) is incremented by 1.

Q.921 Timers

Although it does not contain an exhaustive list of ISDN timers, this section discusses the more common timers that you need to understand to troubleshoot ISDN circuits at Layer 2. The timers included are T200 to T203 and N200 to N202 and their default values are shown in Table 8-3.

Table 8-3 *Q.921 Timers and Their Default Values*

Timer Label	Value
T200—Transmission Timer	1 second
T201—TEI Identity Check (Network)	1 second
T202—TEI Assignment (User)	2 seconds
T203—Frame Exchange	10 seconds
N200—Retransmission Attempts	3

Table 8-3   *Q.921 Timers and Their Default Values (Continued)*

Timer Label	Value
N201 — Maximum Number of Octets	260
N202 — Maximum Transmissions of a TEI Identity Request	3

The T200 timer is the indicator for when a frame can be transmitted. This timer must equal more than the time it takes to send a frame and receive its acknowledgment.

The T201 is used during the TEI identity check sequence. See the "Q.921 Alignment" section, earlier in this chapter for a description of T201 operation during the identity check sequence.

T202 works in conjunction with the T201 timer, but from the user side of the network instead of the network side.

T203 is the maximum time that equipment can wait between the exchange of Q.921 frames. Although the default is only 10 seconds, most equipment, including Cisco equipment, can modify this timer as needed. In cases of long distances and delay, this timer should be modified for continued operation.

N200 is the value that identifies the maximum number of transmission attempts. N200 operates by sending X retransmissions of any given frame. If that frame is still not acknowledged after the expiration of the last attempt timer, that frame is dropped.

N201 identifies how many octets are in an information field. The default value of 260 is a static setting that causes an error if frames do not meet these criteria.

N202 equals how many times a TEI identity request is sent. After that point, TEI=unassigned is set.

NOTE   Another timer that you see present on ISDN configurations with Cisco equipment is the ISDN guard timer. This is not specified in Q.921, but it allows for the proper amount of time to authenticate an inbound call on ISDN. If this timer is not used, your ISDN call can time out.

Cisco IOS allows you to troubleshoot Q.921 activity with the **debug isdn q921** command. The most important thing to look for in the output is to make sure that you are sending and receiving traffic. If you are sending but not receiving, you have other problems to look at first. Check to make sure that your physical layer is up. If you are configured in a back-to-back configuration with Cisco equipment, be sure that one side is set to network mode.

Example 8-1 shows sample output from the **debug isdn q921** command for an ISDN PRI circuit on a Cisco AS5300.

Example 8-1 *Sample* **debug isdn q921** *Command Output*

```
AS5300#debug isdn q921
4d22h: ISDN Se0:23: RX <-  RRp sapi = 0  tei = 0 nr = 0
4d22h: ISDN Se0:23: TX ->  RRf sapi = 0  tei = 0  nr = 0
AS5300#
4d22h: ISDN Se0:23: RX <-  RRp sapi = 0  tei = 0 nr = 0
4d22h: ISDN Se0:23: TX ->  RRf sapi = 0  tei = 0  nr = 0
AS5300#
4d22h: ISDN Se0:23: RX <-  RRp sapi = 0  tei = 0 nr = 0
4d22h: ISDN Se0:23: TX ->  RRf sapi = 0  tei = 0  nr = 0
```

When debugging Q.921, it's important to be aware that Q.921 can also be verified in IOS by using the **show isdn status** command. The **show isdn status** command allows verification of the physical layer, Q.921 and Q.931.

ITU Q.931

ISDN's Q.931 is the Layer 3 specification that is responsible for call control and management. These functions include call set up, tear down, and request for services from Layer 2. The purpose of this section is not to go over all of the possible state primitives, but to give you a good understanding of how Q.931 manages ISDN call control.

Q.931 uses a message-based system to control the ingress and egress call functions of an ISDN circuit. Using the D channel as a vehicle for this transport, ISDN Q.931 signaling is referred to as a common channel signaling (CCS) service. As a review, CCS transmits signaling from end-to-end in an out-of-band, non-intrusive way to the bearer traffic. In contrast, channel associated signaling (CAS) is commonly found on T1 circuits and is interwoven into the bearer signal stream.

Some argue that ISDN is not CCS because the signaling and bearer traffic take the same path, but remember that, although it is on the same path, it uses a different logical channel. For that reason, ISDN is physically in-band but logically out-of-band.

To transport the number of messages that are associated with Q.931, it is necessary to have a standardized message format. The beauty of Q.931 is that your equipment doesn't have to process everything that is in the message format. Any information that your equipment doesn't understand is merely ignored. The message format splits values into four subsections:

- Protocol discriminator
- Call reference length indication
- Message type
- Information element

Figure 8-12 shows the basic Q.931 message format with the order of the octets, beginning from top to bottom.

Figure 8-12 *Q.931 Message Format*

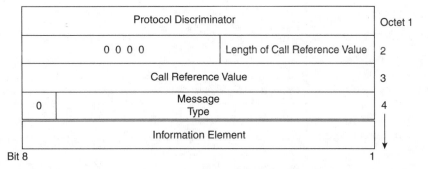

The first field in the Q.931 message is the protocol discriminator. The protocol discriminator identifies user/network call-control message types from other message types that might be found on the network. The protocol discriminator is coded as 00010000 for user/network call-control messages, with the least significant bit (LSB) read first (right to left).

The next octet is the call reference length indication octet. This octet specifies how many octets the call reference value can encompass, and it is considered a portion of the actual call reference. The local end of the ISDN connection uses the call reference to maintain a record of all call requests that are processed. To support BRI access, the call reference must be at least two octets in length and at least three octets in length for PRI access. Figure 8-13 shows the octets involved with keeping track of ISDN call instances.

Figure 8-13 *Q.931 Call Reference Octets*

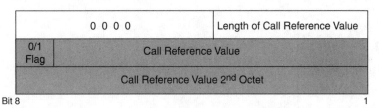

There is a flag in the call reference field that delineates between the originating and terminating side of a connection. If it is set to a 0, the message is being sent from the origination point, and if it is set to a 1, the message is being sent from the terminating side of the connection.

continues

The next portion of the message identifies the actual message type. Refer to Table 8-4 for a listing of the message types and how they are coded in the field. Bits 1 to 5 in the field identify the actual message, and the last 3 bits identify the message class. For example, if the call clearing message class is 010, and the release message type is 01101, they are read together as (bit 1 on right) 01001101.

Table 8-4   *Q.931 Message Types and Binary Values (LSB First)*

Message Class Name	Message Name	Message Value
Call Establishment Message Message Class Value: 000	Alerting	00001
	Call Proceeding	00010
	Connect	00111
	Connect Acknowledge	01111
	Progress	00011
	Setup	00101
	Setup Acknowledge	01101
Call Information Message Message Class Value: 001	Resume	00110
	Resume Acknowledgment	01110
	Resume Reject	00010
	Suspend	00101
	Suspend Acknowledgment	01101
	Suspend Reject	00001
	User Information	00000
Call Clearing Message Message Class Value: 010	Disconnect	00101
	Release	01101
	Release Complete	11010
	Restart	00110
	Restart Acknowledgment	01110
Miscellaneous Message Class Value: 011	Segment	00000
	Congestion Control	11001
	Information	11011
	Notify	01110

Table 8-4   *Q.931 Message Types and Binary Values (LSB First) (Continued)*

Message Class Name	Message Name	Message Value
	Status	11101
	Status Enquiry	10101

ISDN Call Flows

During a basic call flow, the calling party is the origination of the call and the called party is the destination of the call. The calling party sends a Setup message to the called party through the ISDN network. The calling party gets a Setup Acknowledgment and Call Proceeding from the local ISDN switch. The Setup Acknowledge is only used for overlap signaling. If en-bloc signaling is used, Call Proceeding is sent without a Setup Acknowledge. The remote ISDN switch sends a Setup message to the remote ISDN terminal and receives a Call Proceeding and Alerting message in response. The Alerting message travels through the network to the originating ISDN switch, and it sends an Alerting message to the calling party. Also in a backwards direction from the called party, a Connect statement is sent back to the calling party to indicate that the call has been connected and that a voice/data path now exists between them. Refer to Figure 8-14 for an illustration of a basic call setup procedure.

Figure 8-14   *Q.931 Call Setup Procedure*

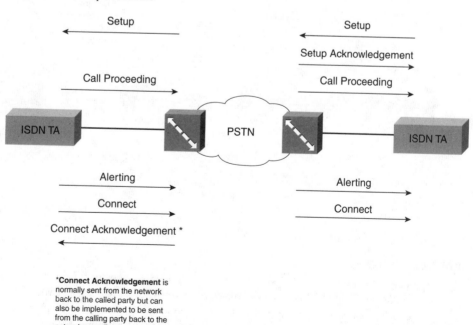

*Connect Acknowledgement is normally sent from the network back to the called party but can also be implemented to be sent from the calling party back to the network as well.

Figure 8-15 shows the call disconnect procedure. A typical call disconnect is rather simple. For instance, say that the calling party hangs up the connection first. In this case, the calling party sends a Disconnect message to the local ISDN switch. The ISDN switch enters a Disconnect Request state and begins clearing the B channels from the call to send them back into the pool of available B channels.

The local ISDN switch requests that the call be disconnected at the called party end and send a Release message to the calling party. The Release message is locally significant and does not mean that the called party has disconnected. Upon receiving the Release message, the calling party releases the B channels and sends a Release Complete to the local ISDN switch. The ISDN switch is then able to allocate the specified B channels for other calls.

The remote ISDN switch for the called party sends a Disconnect message to the called party's customer premises equipment (CPE). The remote call clearing happens in tandem with the local call clearing but is independent of it. The CPE disconnects and sends a Release message back to its local ISDN switch, which in turn, responds with a Release Complete. At this point, the call has been cleared on both sides, and the resources are available for use.

Figure 8-15 *Q.931 Call Disconnect Procedure*

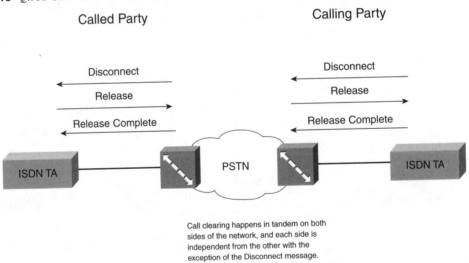

Information Elements

The last field that is included in the Q.931 message format is the information or information element (IE) field. This field can consist of many different IEs that describe the features and capabilities of a given call. For instance, a single Setup message contains more than 15 different IEs including called party number, calling party number, bearer capability, transit network selection, and date and time. IEs are categorized as either single octet or multiple octet IEs. Figure 8-16 shows the format of the IE fields in the Q.931 messages.

The single octet IEs are used for functions, such as requesting more data, identifying that the call reception is complete, and identifying the congestion level. All the important IEs that you need to know to troubleshoot Q.931 are considered multiple octet IEs.

The multiple octet IEs serve most of the useful functions by exchanging the bearer capabilities of the circuits, sending calling and called numbers to the destination, sending called and calling party sub-addresses, sending the requested channel ID, and sending any cause codes if the connection is unsuccessful. Because there are so many of them, this section focuses on some of the more important IEs from a troubleshooting standpoint.

Figure 8-16 *Information Element Formats*

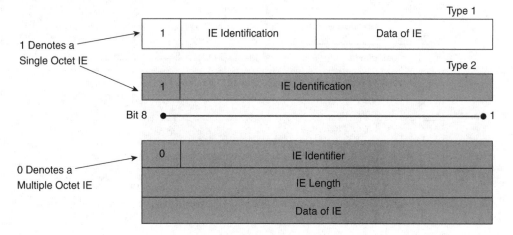

Bearer Capability

The bearer capability IE identifies which capabilities a call is requesting from the network. This IE must be present in the Setup message or the call fails. This can be one of the largest IEs, ranging from 4 to 12 octets, and it contains information such as the type of service (ToS), rate multiplier (if necessary), user information Layer 1 protocol, and asynchronous control information, if needed (start and stop bits/parity). Figure 8-17 shows the fields that are contained in the bearer capability IE.

The bearer capability IE is no small affair because it is responsible for conveying the actual call characteristics to the called device and negotiates between both devices. Within the IE message, the third octet is most important because it specifies the information transfer capability. This identifies the type of traffic that is present on the call. Table 8-5 lists the information transfer capabilities and their coding formats (listed as bit 1 to bit 5 from right to left).

Figure 8-17 *Bearer Capabilities IE Format*

8	7	6	5	4	3	2	1
	Bearer Capability Information Element Identifier
0	0	0	0	0	1	0	0
	Length of the Bearer Capability Contents
Ext. 1	colspan="2" Coding Standard	colspan="5" Information Transfer Capability
Ext. 1	colspan="2" Transfer Mode	colspan="5" Information Transfer Rate
Ext. 1	Rate Multiplier
Ext. 0/1	Layer 1 Ident 0	1	User Information Layer 1 Protocol
Ext. 0/1	Synch/ Asynch	Negot.	User Rate
Ext. 0/1	colspan="2" Intermediate Rate	NIC on Tx	NIC on Rx	Flow Control on Tx	Flow Control on Rx	Spare 0
Ext. 0/1	Hdr/ no Hdr	Multiframe	Mode	LLI Negot.	Assignor/cc	In-band Neg.	Spare 0
Ext. 0/1	colspan="2" Number of Stop Bits	colspan="2" Number of Data Bits	colspan="3" Parity
Ext. 1	Duplex Mode	Modem Type
Ext. 1	Layer 2 Indent. 1	0	User Information Layer 2 Protocol
Ext. 0	Layer 3 Indent. 1	1	User Information Layer 3 Protocol
Ext. 0	colspan="2" Spare 0 0	0	colspan="4" Additional Layer 3 Protocol Information (Most Significant Bits)
Ext. 1	colspan="2" Spare 0 0	0	colspan="4" Additional Layer 3 Protocol Information (Most Significant Bits)

Table 8-5 *Information Transfer Capability Values in Binary*

Information Transfer Capability	Binary Value
Speech	00000
Unrestricted Digital Information	00010
Restricted Digital Information	10010
3.1 kHz Audio	00001
Unrestricted Digital Information with Tones	10001
Video	00011

In Cisco IOS, the bearer capability is listed as a hexadecimal value, as shown in Example 8-2.

Example 8-2 *Q.931 Call Setup Showing the Bearer Capability Value*

```
TX -> SETUP pd = 8 callref = 0x04
 Bearer Capability i = 0x8890
 Channel ID i = 0x83
 Called Party Number i = 0x80, `9195551212'
RX <- CALL_PROC pd = 8 callref = 0x84
 Channel ID i = 0x89
RX <- CONNECT pd = 8 callref = 0x84
TX -> CONNECT_ACK pd = 8 callref = 0x04....
```

In this output, you can see that the bearer capability is 0x8890, which is equal to a 64-kbps data call (unrestricted digital information). Refer to Table 8-6 for a listing of the bearer capability codes and their definitions.

Table 8-6 *Information Transfer Capability Values for IOS*

Bearer Capability	Information Transfer Capability	User Information Layer 1 Protocol
0x8090A2	Speech	G.711 µ-law Speech
0x8090A3	Speech	G.711 A-law
0x9090A2	3.1 kHz Audio	G.711 µ-law Speech
0x9090A3	3.1 kHz Audio	G.711 A-law
0x8890A2	Unrestricted digital information	G.711 µ-law Speech
0x8890A3	Unrestricted digital information	G.711 A-law
0x8890	Unrestricted digital information	64 kbps (64 kbps-data call)

In the next octet, the transfer information rate specifies how many B channels are used on the call. This value is used in tandem with the rate multiplier. However, if only one B channel is to be used on the call, the rate multiplier is not used. The Layer 1 protocol field in octet 5 identifies the voice companding algorithm. This field is useful in troubleshooting, particularly if it is suspected that there is an A-law µ-law mismatch between devices.

Channel ID

The next IE you will see in an output is the channel ID. The channel ID (as with all of the output in a Q.931 debug), is listed in hexadecimal format, as shown in Example 8-3.

Example 8-3 *Q.931 Call Setup Showing the Channel ID Value*

```
TX -> SETUP pd = 8 callref = 0x04
 Bearer Capability i = 0x8890
 Channel ID i = 0x83
 Called Party Number i = 0x80, `9195551212'
RX <- CALL_PROC pd = 8 callref = 0x84
 Channel ID i = 0x89
RX <- CONNECT pd = 8 callref = 0x84
TX -> CONNECT_ACK pd = 8 callref = 0x04....
```

NOTE   Cisco IOS will default to a descending B channel selection order.

Figure 8-18 shows the actual channel ID IE.

Figure 8-18 *Channel ID IE Format*

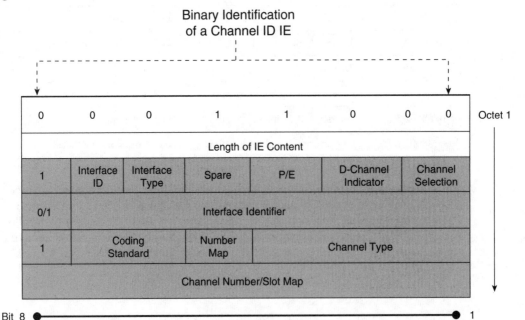

The purpose of this IE is to identify which channel is for bearer services that the signaling is controlling. It is possible to send multiple channels during the call setup phase to provide a selection in the event that a channel is unavailable at the call destination.

Within the message format there are several sections that allow for the channel selection to occur:

- **Octet 1** = This is the binary representation of the Channel ID IE. LSB first, it reads 00011000.

- **Octet 2** = Indicates the actual length of the channel identification.

- **Octet 3** = The last four octets are generally considered to be associated with octet 3:
    - The information channel selection identifies which B-Channel(s) is supposed to be used with an ISDN BRI circuit.
        - 00 = No channel
        - 10 = B channel #1
        - 01 = B channel #2
        - 11 = Any channel
    - The D channel indicator specifies whether the requested channel is actually the D channel. If it is, this field is flagged as a 1.
    - The P/E field states whether the channel specified is preferred or exclusive. If it is exclusive, no other channels can be used.
    - Spare is not used and is always set to 0.
    - The interface specifies whether the circuit is BRI or PRI. BRI is indicated with a 0 and PRI is indicated with a 1.
    - Interface ID is associated with ISDN non-facility associated signaling (NFAS) circuits.
    - The channel type specifies if the channel is a B channel or an H channel (used with B-ISDN).
    - The number/map bit identifies whether the following octet has a channel number (BRI) or a channel map (PRI).
    - The final octet specifies the B channel associated with the PRI circuit. The value identified equals the timeslot on the circuit.

Called and Calling Party IEs

The calling and called number IEs specify the originating and destination numbers associated with the call. The numbers can be a variety of coding structures but are generally seen as ITU E.164 numbers, which mimic telephone numbers. Figure 8-19 shows the formats associated with the calling and called party IEs.

Figure 8-19 *Calling and Called Party IE Format*

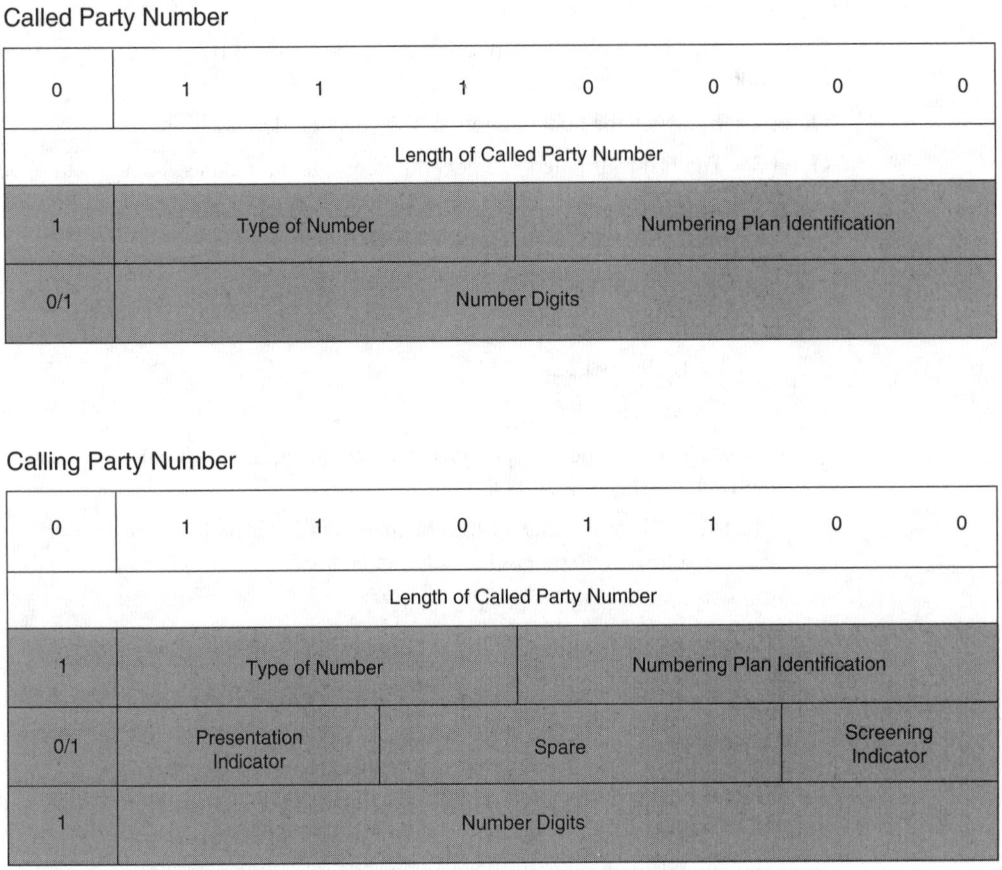

Called Party Number

0	1	1	1	0	0	0	0
Length of Called Party Number							
1	Type of Number			Numbering Plan Identification			
0/1	Number Digits						

Calling Party Number

0	1	1	0	1	1	0	0
Length of Called Party Number							
1	Type of Number			Numbering Plan Identification			
0/1	Presentation Indicator		Spare			Screening Indicator	
1	Number Digits						

The called party IE contains several significant fields. The type of number field describes what kind of number the called party is (LSB first):

- Unknown = 000
- International = 100
- National = 010
- Network Specific Number = 110
- Subscriber Number = 001
- Abbreviated Number = 011
- Reserved = 111

Only unknown, international, national, and subscriber numbers are supported under the numbering plan field. The numbering plan identification field identifies what type of numbering plan is being used for the ISDN number (LSB first):

- Unknown = 0000
- ISDN Numbering Plan E.164 = 1000
- Data Numbering Plan X.121 = 1100
- Telex Numbering Plan F.69 = 0010
- National Numbering Plan = 0001
- Private Numbering Plan = 1001
- Reserved = 1111

The most common numbering plan type you will see is the E.164 numbering plan. The number digits field identifies the actual digits dialed.

The calling party IE has many of the same fields but adds the screening indicator and the presentation indicator. Screening allows the ISDN device to decide on whether the user is allowed to connect. In other words, if the called party has a call screening application in place they can deny calls from specific ISDN numbers.

In the case of an unsuccessful call setup in ISDN, there is a cause code given. The cause code specifies why the call was not able to complete. The cause codes, when given in IOS, are specified in hexadecimal along with a brief description.

SS7 and ISDN

Because ISDN is a local loop technology, it needs to interface to other signaling methods to transport calls all the way through the service provider's network. The call is transported through the network as ISDN, converted to SS7, transported through the service provider's network, and then converted back into ISDN, with protocol conversions taking place at the ingress and egress ISDN switch points within the network. Figure 8-20 shows a general protocol-to-protocol call flow as it is seen in the service provider's network. The IEs associated with ISDN and the IEs associated with SS7 do not map 100 percent. Therefore, it is certainly possible for there to be interworking issues, particularly because there are so many variations of SS7.

Figure 8-20 *ISDN to SS7 Call Flow*

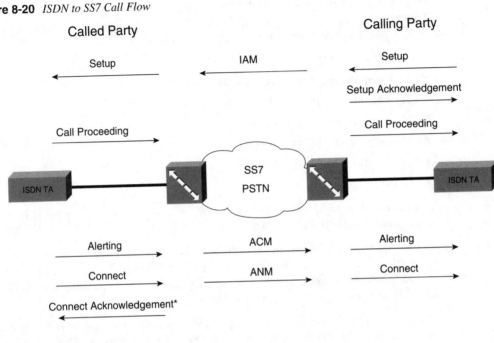

*Connect Acknowledgement is
normally sent from the network
back to the called party but can
also be implemented to be sent
from the calling party back to the
network as well.

BRI

The good thing about the deployment of ISDN BRI is that no one tried to reinvent the wheel. Well, at least for the cabling. Your analog circuits, also known as POTS lines, are deployed over 24-26 gauge copper wiring. ISDN BRI service can be deployed over the same copper wiring to your premises.

Hardware Considerations

When deployed to your premises, they are normally installed in RJ-45 jacks using pins 4 and 5. There is no polarity with the center two pins, you just need to make sure that you have them installed properly at the jack. BRI service doesn't even have to be deployed with RJ-45 interfaces, but most service providers prefer this so as to differentiate that jack from standard analog service.

If you were to plug an ISDN TA into an analog line, there is a pretty good chance that you would short out that equipment if an analog call with –48 vdc came in. Therefore, if the installer deploys a different looking jack, it cuts down on that becoming a possibility. Most ISDN TAs must be powered from an external power source because there isn't any line voltage on a BRI circuit (at least not enough for your equipment).

What this tells you is that if you lose power to your premises, your ISDN goes with it unless you have a significant power backup in place. For this reason, most service providers advise against using the ISDN circuit as the only line at your location. There are two caveats to this issue:

- If you replace analog with ISDN entirely, you lose all phone service in a power outage (no 911 among other problems).

- In most areas, ISDN is not governed by the same tariffs as analog. With analog service, the service provider must repair it within a short time period. As a WAN service, ISDN can take up to a week to repair, leaving you without phone service for that entire length of time.

The service repair window is only a problem in the United States because most European countries are ahead of the U.S. in ISDN deployment and because analog and ISDN circuits are typically treated the same internationally.

BRI Operation

ISDN BRI circuits are always active and use a type of heartbeat to maintain circuit status. On a standard BRI installation, if you plug an analog phone into your ISDN jack you can hear an intermittent click. That click is a good way to see if you are getting an ISDN signal. If you can hear the click, your service is turned on. That doesn't mean that there isn't a problem with the service, just that you have it.

The main selling points for BRI service are that there is increased bandwidth over analog service (128 kbps compared to 56 kbps), you can use multiple devices at the same time, and the dialing time is dramatically decreased. The increased bandwidth comes from the bandwidth provided with the B channels. Even if your BRI circuit only has a single 64-kbps DS0, it still has more bandwidth than a 56-kbps analog device.

However, in some locations only 56-kbps DS0s are available because of service provider equipment restraints. This is becoming less and less common because most service provider infrastructures are now 64 kbps clear (can provide 64 kbps end-to-end). Also, many service providers cannot provide conditioning services to speed up analog connections, stating that analog circuits were never intended for data transmission. Conditioning services include the removal of bridge taps and line loading (where possible) to provide faster analog service.

The typical circuit rate for a BRI service is 160 kbps (with other network overhead, it can be as high as 192 kbps). In this 160 kbps, there are 2 64-kbps B channels, a 16-kbps D channel, and approximately 16 kbps of overhead, as shown in Figure 8-21. BRI combines two B channels to form a larger pipe of bandwidth through a process known as channel bonding. A call is placed on the first B channel, after that a second call is placed on the other B channel. When both B channels are connected, they are bonded together to form the full bandwidth rate.

Figure 8-21 *BRI Circuit Composition*

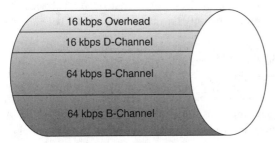

BRI Capabilities and Features

ISDN BRI can support up to eight devices on the S/T bus, but you are limited by the number of B channels that your circuit has. Most service providers don't tell you this, but if you have two B channels with your ISDN service, you can only use two devices at any one given time. After both B channels are in use, you cannot add any other services without disconnecting something. So if your ISDN TA is using both B channels for a data call and you want to place or receive a voice call, you have to drop one of the B channels to facilitate that function.

Most modern ISDN TAs have a feature known as bandwidth allocation control protocol (BACP). BACP allows your device to dynamically drop a B channel to allow you to take an incoming voice or fax call and then reallocate that B channel back to the data call after it is finished. This feature is implemented through the bandwidth allocation protocol (BAP), which works in tandem with BACP. Working in tandem with BAP and BACP, is bandwidth on demand (BOD). Hypothetically, if you only have a limited amount of ISDN usage per month, you do not want to use more than absolutely necessary.

To save money, you want to use your ISDN circuit wisely. BOD allows you to set up your equipment to dial up with a single B channel and then add the second B channel only if necessary. This feature is normally set with a series of thresholds such as 50 kbps for 10 seconds. When using BOD, make sure that your channel addition threshold and subtraction threshold are not too close together. Otherwise, you will constantly add and subtract your secondary channel, which negates the BOD feature.

Increased dialing speed comes from several different things. There is no dial tone generated by the CO on BRI circuits. On an analog circuit, dial tone notifies you that you can place a call. Because the BRI circuit is always active, dial tone is not necessary. If the ISDN TA has POTS ports on the back for analog phones and you can hear dial tone when you pick your phone up, that dial tone is being generated from the equipment.

When you place an ISDN call, you do not hear the handshaking tones (those nasty screeching noises with analog dialup) because ISDN is a synchronous digital network medium. This provides a much faster connection, usually in three to five seconds.

Internationally, BRI service is deployed by using an S/T interface. The U interface belongs to the service provider, and the customer does not need to purchase an NT1 for the circuit. For this reason, most European countries allow you to plug TE1 equipment directly into an ISDN outlet. At that point, you are plugging directly into the S/T bus.

In Japan, Nippon Telephone and Telegraph (NTT) provides two main types of BRI service, INS Net 64 and INS Net 64 Lite. The difference between these two services is that the INS Net 64 service requires a monthly subscription fee. Therefore, most users prefer the INS Net 64 Lite service. The device deployed on these circuits is a data service unit (DSU/TA), which provides the same functions as the NT1/TA devices described above. You can't just buy an ISDN TA in the United States and expect it to work anywhere in the world. For instance, if you purchase an ISDN TA that does not have the Japanese Approvals Institute for Telecommunications Equipment (JATE) approval, there is a good chance that equipment will not work in Japan. Likewise, equipment destined for use in the United States should have the proper Underwriters Laboratories (UL) and FCC Part 65/68 certifications. Certification by these entities does not necessarily mean that the equipment will absolutely not work in other regions, but it is a good idea to make sure your equipment has the necessary hardware approvals for your location. In the field, you are more likely to run into problems with devices that do not support the proper switch protocols for ISDN rather than problems with the hardware certifications.

ISDN BRI Line Coding

ISDN BRI is a digital service that requires a line-coding scheme, similar to any other digital medium. The line coding that exists on BRI circuits is considered to be block line coding rather than linear line coding (such as alternate mark inversion [AMI] and bipolar 8-zero substitution [B8ZS]) because the line-coding schemes use a series of lookup tables for values associated with binary bit combinations. The line-coding type differs in North America. North America uses the 2 Binary 1 Quaternary (2B1Q) line-coding method.

2B1Q Line Coding

2B1Q is composed of four different discrete voltage states, and it transmits two binary digits during each pulse. This is in contrast with most other coding standards such as B8ZS and High Density Bipolar of Order 3 (HDB3), which only transmit one binary digit per pulse. As shown in Table 8-7, each voltage state has a specific value attached to it that does not change.

Table 8-7 *2B1Q Binary Voltage Values*

Binary Representation	Voltage
1 0	+3v
1 1	+1v
0 1	−1v
0 0	−3v

When 2B1Q codes binary digits, it looks a bit different than the other line-coding schemes you have learned about. 2B1Q does not employ the use of the 0 voltage state, and it does not have to adhere to any bipolar violation (BPV) specifications.

Figure 8-22 *2B1Q Line Coding*

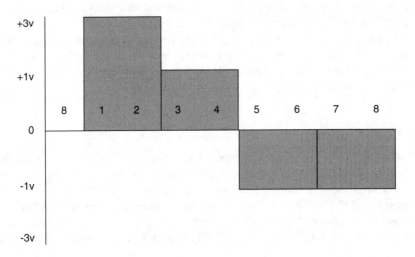

4B3T Line Coding

International BRI circuits, commonly called ISDN-2 or ISDN Basic Access (IBA), use a different type of line coding that is called 4 Binary 3 Ternary (4B3T). This coding scheme is a bit more complicated than most and is also referred to as Modified Monitoring State Block Code 43 (MMS43). The basic premise is to take four binary digits and, using a lookup table, convert them to be used in a strict three voltage state environment of negative, zero, and positive voltage. This function creates an approximately 25 percent reduction in baud rate as transmitted on the BRI circuit. Refer to Table 8-8 for a listing of the binary conversion.

Table 8-8   *Lookup Table for 4B3T Line Coding*

Binary Digits	Bit #	Voltage	Bit #	Voltage	Bit #	Voltage	Bit #	Voltage
0001	1	0-+	2	0-+	3	0-+	4	0-+
0111	1	-0+	2	-0+	3	-0+	4	-0+
0100	1	-+0	2	-+0	3	-+0	4	-+0
0010	1	+-0	2	+-0	3	+-0	4	+-0
1001	1	+0-	2	+0-	3	+0-	4	+0-
1110	1	0+-	2	0+-	3	0+-	4	0+-
1011	2	+-+	3	+-+	4	+-+	1	---
0011	2	00+	3	00+	4	00+	2	--0
1101	2	0+0	3	0+0	4	0+0	2	-0-
1000	2	+00	3	+00	4	+00	2	0--
0110	2	-++	3	-++	2	--+	3	--+
1010	2	++-	3	++-	2	+--	3	+--
1111	3	++0	1	00-	2	00-	3	00-
0000	3	+0+	1	0-0	2	0-0	3	0-0
0101	4	0++	1	-00	2	-00	3	-00
1100	4	+++	1	-+-	2	-+-	3	-+-

Binary representation of 4B3T is shown in Figure 8-23.

Figure 8-23 *4B3T Line Coding*

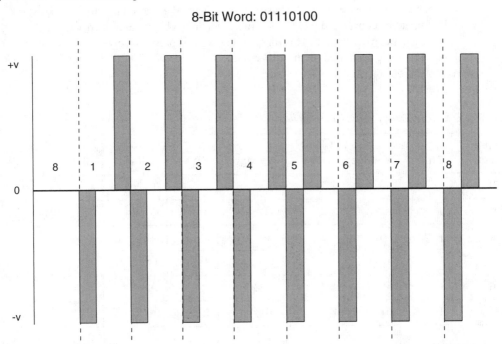

Anatomy of BRI

When configuring an ISDN device for BRI service, you must have the proper information for communication on the service provider's network. First and foremost, you need to know what type of switch you are communicating with. The switch type is important because not all vendors have implemented ISDN in the same way. For this reason, if you tell your equipment that it is communicating with a Lucent 5ESS, but you are actually connected to a Nortel DMS-100, you might not be able to access the ISDN network. Refer to Cisco documentation for all the supported ISDN switch types.

Switch vendors began to diverge on compatibility in the United States in the early to mid-90's, so a set of standards was developed to help alleviate this problem. Contrary to what a lot of people say, NI-1 is not an actual switch, but a set of programming that allows many vendors to communicate with one another over the ISDN network. The National ISDN standards were developed as a three-stage process: NI-1, NI-2, and NI-3 to be deployed over a period of about 10 years. These standards allow customer ISDN equipment to internetwork with a larger number of vendors. Thus, Lucent doesn't have to figure out how to directly communicate with a Nortel switch in all aspects of ISDN. They merely have to program their switches to adhere to the National ISDN standards. The caveat with this is that if you are using a private ISDN configuration, you can use whatever switch type you want.

It is perfectly conceivable to use the primary-ni switch type on E1 circuits as long as they are consistent on both sides of the connection. On back-to-back configurations, it is also necessary to specify one of the two sides as the network. Cisco ISDN devices default to user, and two user devices on the same link do not work. If you have both sides set to user, Layer 2 never comes up.

Service Profile Identifiers (SPIDs) and Telephone Numbers

Possibly the most important single piece of information for a BRI subscriber in the United States is the SPID. SPIDs identify the BRI circuit on the switch along with the circuit ID, and the services that the circuit has assigned to it. For each B channel assigned to the circuit, there is a SPID associated with it, and for each SPID there is an associated telephone number. When you look at the format of a SPID, it looks a lot like a regular telephone number with an added extension. The most common format is 14 digits:

- SPID Format: 91955512120101
- Telephone Number: 9195551212

The last four numbers of the SPID (0101) indicate the sharing terminal ID and the terminal identifier as per the National ISDN Council. When you place a call to another ISDN device, you are placing the call to the telephone number assigned to the circuit rather than directly to the SPID. The SPIDs have local switch significance only.

Depending on how long you have had BRI service, you might not even know that you have SPIDs. By the time the United States reaches a full deployment of NI-3, SPIDs should be automatically downloaded and configured by your device. A lot of equipment already has this function built in, and it depends on the functionality of the switch you are communicating with as to whether or not it will currently work.

With the proper ISDN switch type and the correct SPIDs, your ISDN TA should enter a state that people call synching to the switch. When your ISDN device is synched to the switch, you can place and receive ISDN calls.

BRI Circuit Provisioning

Each BRI circuit is provisioned into the switch framework. The provisioning on the BRI circuits is completed through capability packages. The capability packages, also called ISDN Ordering Codes (IOCs), offer different combinations of bandwidth and service. Not only can the physical characteristics change (1B+D, 2B+D, just D), but the service types also can be modified. That means that a circuit can be provisioned for just voice, just data, or a combination of the two. These capability packages change so often that any direct discussion of them would be outdated by the time you read this.

Although BRI is classically referred to as a 128-kbps circuit, make sure that your capability package supports two B channels. Packages that offer strictly D channel configurations are typically used for applications such as credit card readers or automated gas pumps. In these instances, the D channel manages data transport.

All the services that you generally associate with analog circuits, such as voice mail, call forwarding, Caller ID Deluxe, and conference calling can be programmed for use in ISDN. Unfortunately, this is where most problems associated with ISDN are found. The issue isn't the vendor equipment or the software features, but the combination of the two.

Different vendor equipment reacts in a variety of ways to services offered by service providers. Moreover, not all service providers deploy the same services in the same manner. This combination creates a headache for switch programmers and customers alike. If you have ever been told that ISDN is complex and that It Still Does Nothing, it probably had something to do with a value-added service fiasco. Because of the issues associated with ISDN BRI service for Internet connectivity, it is being gradually replaced with higher bandwidth, and easier to use technologies such as digital subscriber line (DSL) and cable modems. ISDN switch provisioning has classically been a problem because of how many issues arise out of service programming. Not all services work with all the vendor equipment, and different vendor equipment can react differently to the same circuit provisioning. There also have been problems with different service provider switches communicating properly with vendor TAs.

Foreign Exchange (FX)

To deploy BRI circuits to customer sites, the service provider's switch must be able to accommodate the ISDN equipment. This typically includes a fairly large switch such as a Lucent 5ESS or Nortel DMS-100, with adequate port density and a series of line cards both at the CO and IDLCs. When deployed in IDLCs, BRI service typically takes up three full DS0s, so available bandwidth is also a factor. In areas that can't support these requirements, an FX of the circuit might be necessary. At its most basic level, an FX circuit reroutes the local loop through a switch at a CO that does not provide local ISDN service. Figure 8-24 shows a basic depiction of an ISDN circuit that is foreign exchanged to a remote office.

In Figure 8-24, the FX ISDN service is deployed through a switch that does not necessarily provide local exchange service. In some areas, the facilities required are just not available. Rather than upgrade an entire switch for a couple of ISDN customers, the service provider would rather redirect you to a switch or IDLC that is already providing such service.

FX circuits are normally handled by a group called special services. They are typically a separate entity, which means that to test or repair this type of circuit you probably need to go through them directly.

There are cases where FX is not possible due to location or distance from the CO (if you live in the boonies). If this is the case, you might not be able to obtain ISDN service.

Figure 8-24 *Foreign Exchanged BRI Circuits*

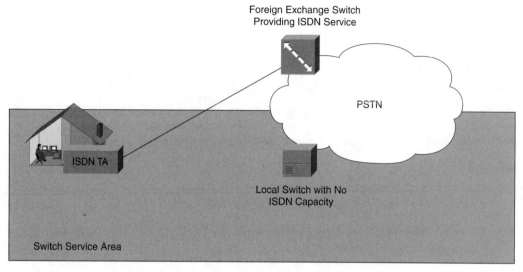

Always On Dynamic ISDN (AO-DI)

AO-DI is a relatively new addition to the ISDN scene. It allows you to maintain a permanent connection to the Internet by using the ISDN D channel. Remember that in BRI service the D channel is 16 kbps and that it is used for call-control and channel management signaling. AO-DI takes approximately 9.6 kbps of the 16 kbps for a link back to the service provider's ISDN switch. With this link, you can download stock tickers, e-mail, and other streaming desktop applications.

One of the main advantages of AO-DI is the fact that you do not need to connect to your service provider and use precious B channel minutes. Not only do you not need to worry about busy signals, but there is no waiting to connect (ISDN connection time only takes a couple of seconds). Instead, you can save your packaged time for use only when absolutely necessary.

Configuring ISDN BRI

The first of two types of ISDN that you will configure is ISDN BRI service. Make sure that before you go to set up your ISDN TA, you have the proper ISDN switch type, your SPIDs, and any telephone numbers that are associated with your circuit. You will be configuring a basic BRI application by using a Cisco router. Figure 8-25 shows a diagram of the network that you will configure in this example.

Figure 8-25 *BRI Configuration Example*

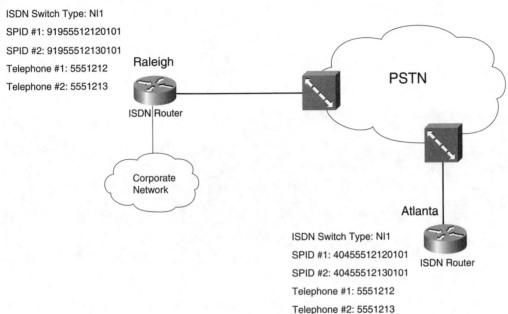

ISDN Switch Type: NI1

SPID #1: 91955512120101

SPID #2: 91955512130101

Telephone #1: 5551212

Telephone #2: 5551213

Raleigh

ISDN Router

PSTN

Corporate
Network

Atlanta

ISDN Router

ISDN Switch Type: NI1

SPID #1: 40455512120101

SPID #2: 40455512130101

Telephone #1: 5551212

Telephone #2: 5551213

The first step for the Raleigh router is to specify the ISDN switch type that you are using. This command has to be configured globally, but you can specify more than one switch type in the router by changing the switch type on the actual interface. The switch types supported are grouped as primary and basic switch types. These names refer to whether or not you are using a BRI or PRI service.

```
Raleigh#conf t
Raleigh(config)#isdn switch-type basic-ni
```

If you want to change the switch type on the BRI interface, you can use the same command with a different switch type.

```
Raleigh(config)#int bri 0
Raleigh(config-if)#isdn switch-type basic-5ess
```

Next, you need to configure any SPIDs that are associated with your ISDN circuit. The number following the SPID is the accompanying telephone number. It is important to remember how many digits are required for dialing. For example, if you are located within a 10-digit dialing area, be sure to enter a 10-digit number.

```
Raleigh(config-if)#isdn spid1 91955512120101 5551212
Raleigh(config-if)#isdn spid2 91955512130101 5551213
```

You have now completed a basic configuration for connectivity back to the ISDN switch. If you want to allow the Atlanta office to call Raleigh, but you also want callback capabilities, you can set up the ISDN callback feature. This ensures a specific level of secure caller identity for inbound ISDN calls.

```
Raleigh(config-if)#dialer caller 4045551212 callback
Raleigh(config-if)#dialer caller 4045551213 callback
```

The previous configuration starts callback for the phone numbers listed if they are detected as inbound ISDN calls. Caller ID is required from the service provider's switch for this option to function properly.

For basic dial out capability on BRI, you can set up the Raleigh router to dial to the Atlanta router if the proper IP address is detected. This can be started as a specific request from a user on the network or as a result of a default route setting on the Raleigh router.

```
Raleigh(config-if)#dialer map ip 10.15.1.1 name Atlanta 4045551212
```

For the dial out to work properly, you need to make sure that the proper username and password is set for authentication and that you enable Point-to-Point Protocol (PPP) and Challenge Handshake Authentication Protocol (CHAP).

After you have configured your BRI service, you can verify the circuit with the **show isdn status** command, as shown in Example 8-4. You are looking specifically for the layer status messages. At Layer 2 you should see MULTIPLE_FRAME_ESTABLISHED.

Example 8-4 *The **show isdn status** Command*

```
Raleigh#show isdn status
Global ISDN Switchtype = basic-ni
ISDN BRI0 interface
        dsl 0, interface ISDN Switchtype = basic-ni
    Layer 1 Status:
        ACTIVE
    Layer 2 Status:
        TEI = 64, Ces = 1, SAPI = 0, State = MULTIPLE_FRAME_ESTABLISHED
    Layer 3 Status:
        0 Active Layer 3 Call(s)
    Activated dsl 0 CCBs = 0
```

Resolving Issues with ISDN BRI

Just as with any technology, there are many things that can go wrong on an ISDN circuit, particularly a BRI circuit that is weighed down with services. This section is intended to serve as a set of pointers for troubleshooting BRI circuits and not just Cisco equipment.

First, make sure that your SPIDs and your switch type are correct. Even some vendor equipment that employs auto-SPID download can malfunction and cause a SPID mismatch. You also want to make sure that the SPIDs given to you by your service provider are actually what the switch programmer put on your circuit. They are as human as you are and can provision wrong SPIDs from time to time.

In the United States, basic-ni gets you by 99 percent of the time and is typically safe as a selection. European and some Oceania countries can usually use the basic-net3 switch type as a similar encompassing switch type. If you know that you are on a Nortel DMS-100, you configured it as such, and your device is still not working, you can try the basic-ni switch type. Sometimes that is the best switch type to use even when yours is known. It might just be a quirk between your vendor equipment and the switch.

Another problem that you can encounter is a cable throw. Cable throws occur when a line technician, needing a pair of wires, takes your set and then reroutes you through a longer pair of cables. For instance, there is a line technician who is looking for a pair of wires for analog service. To find an available pair, he uses his test set to check which of the cables have a dial tone. When he finds a pair with no dial tone, he assumes that the pair is not currently being used and procures them for his analog application.

Remember, ISDN does not provide dial tone, so this can and does happen quite often. When the pair is redirected, your circuit runs the risk of going over the prescribed 18 kft or –dB loss. If the pair is thrown over or close to the loop length requirements, you can have intermittent or complete service loss. This is no easy problem to track down, but there are things that you can do to help figure it out.

Cable length is a funny thing. You would be surprised to find how many problems arise from it. There have been issues with time of day operation, and no, this isn't a new feature. The setting is usually summertime, and the circuit does not function during the day. However, through the midnight hours it appears to work properly.

In cases such as this also try to check the loop length of the circuit. In many cases, the circuit does not operate during the day because it is close to the allowed loop length. When the sun comes out and heats up the cabling, the cable pair expands, which throws the circuit past operational lengths. When the sun goes down the cables cool off, retract, and the circuit can function properly.

As was stated before, –dB can also have an effect on the signal. As the signal travels down the circuit, the signal attenuates. If the signal attenuates too much, the terminal equipment is unable to synch to the digital signal. That being said, somewhere between the range of –38 dB and –42 dB the service provider should be adding a repeater to the circuit. If you are having intermittent problems and all line hardware is testing fine, ask what the –dB on the circuit is. Even if they can't test for you while you wait, they can send a technician to do it manually.

If you are set to have an ISDN BRI circuit installed and you're not sure if it is turned on yet, you can plug an analog phone into the ISDN service jack (only if you are plugging into a U interface). If you listen closely, you can hear a slight clicking noise. That is the heartbeat of the ISDN service, which means that you at least have a signal. The circuit can still have a hardware problem, and you can take it further by calling your local service provider for loop testing. The closer you are to the CO the faster the click is generally.

If you can't get the click in your house, try it again at the NID outside your premises. If you can get a click there, your ISW appears to have a problem. Also, try not to use a cordless phone, as they do not work sometimes even when a signal is present.

When wiring your premises (if you are doing your own wiring), make sure that the jacks that are used for ISDN have what is called a home run. A home run is a length of cable that runs from the NID directly to the jack without any splices. Standard analog lines in houses typically have several splices, but each splice can cause line errors and degraded throughput on an ISDN circuit. For the same reason, ISDN circuits must be devoid of bridge taps on the carrier side. Messy analog ISW can be a headache if upgrading to ISDN.

Also, be aware of how the cable is installed at your premises if you are hiring someone to do it for you. Many analog install technicians will install an analog circuit, and then just coil up any excess wiring before connecting it. These coils can cause what are known as magnetic loops on an ISDN circuit. Magnetic loops can cause performance below even basic analog dialup rates. Any coils should be removed and connected properly.

If there are several locations within your premises that you want to have ISDN at, you can't have an ISDN TA at each location. The problem is that with BRI you can only terminate the circuit once, so additional NT1s cause none of them to work. One thing you can do is purchase a basic NT1, terminate the ISDN line, and then connect your equipment to the S/T bus (they have to be TE1 devices).

This was touched on before, but make sure that you are aware that you are limited to the number of B channels that you have. Eight devices cannot all work at the same time on the ISDN circuit. One data and one voice, two data, two voice, and so on.

Millions of people get their bill every day for ISDN service. A few of them are unpleasantly surprised to find that their bill is about 10 times over what they expected. Most bills come in an envelope, but some come in a box. This is typically indicative of a couple things:

- The subscriber is on a timed package with some sort of pay as you play pricing rate.
- Their Internet service provider (ISP) might not support two B-channel connections.

You might be wondering why this is a problem, but this causes what is affectionately termed thrashing. If your device connects to your ISP on the first channel, but the second is not allowed, the secondary channel is dropped after it connects momentarily. Most equipment attempts to reacquire that connection, and if it isn't configured properly, it continues to attempt to acquire that channel.

This is bad for you if you have a low minute package rate or a strictly pay as you play rate because you end up going way over your allotted time limit in a month. Because most service providers only require about 1/10 of a second to bill you for a call, you can easily rack up charges.

To avoid this problem, be sure that your ISP allows both B channels and that your equipment is configured properly. Most modern equipment can be set to only dial with one B channel or at the very least to discontinue reconnect attempts for the second channel after a couple of tries.

By using a serial device you lose a portion of the BRI bandwidth. A typical 16550 Universal Asynchronous Receiver Transmitter (UART), found in personal computer serial ports, only allows a maximum of 115,200 bps instead of the full 128,000. You can get around this problem by using an Ethernet connection to an ISDN router because you then have at least 10 Mbps.

Last but not least, if your circuit completely quits you can ask to verify that the office equipment (OE) is still assigned to your circuit. The OE is the hardware that is required for ISDN service to operate at the CO and from time to time it can be inadvertently commandeered for other applications, thereby destroying your service.

PRI

PRI is a larger offering of N-ISDN that accommodates more bandwidth and that offers more flexibility. For PBX uses or where SS7 is not readily available, PRI allows for the transmission of voice and data over a single link. In North America and Japan, PRI is deployed over a T1 facility and comprises 23 B channels and a full 64-kbps D channel. In most other international countries, PRI is deployed over E1 facilities using 30 B channels and a 64-kbps D channel. International PRI is also referred to as ISDN-30.

The easiest way to think about PRI is to remember that it is merely ISDN deployed over T- or E-carrier facilities. As a subscriber, this means that you have to configure the T1 or E1 controller first and then add the ISDN functionality. PRI does not use elements such as SPIDs for connectivity to the switch, and the TEI is always set to 0 (because it is a point-to-point connection).

ISDN PRI requires that ISDN facilities are available at the CO. In recent years it has become difficult to keep up with the demand. PRI is still a local loop technology, as is BRI, but it can be expensive depending on the tariff of the associated carrier circuit.

PRI is popular in enterprise voice applications because it does not require any knowledge of SS7 to provide voice service. In many areas, PRI is preferred to SS7 even though SS7 is less expensive. Typically, enterprise customers deploy PRI circuits from their corporate headquarters to remote locations or over dry copper within the same location to facilitate PBX connectivity between all sites. Dry copper is a portion of the circuit that does not go through the service provider's network but is completely contained within the customer's private network.

A more recent application of PRI connectivity is to have ISDN on the local loop and then use a private Voice over Internet Protocol (VoIP) network as the transport system for the long distance haul between sites. At the destination, the call is dumped out of the IP network, back onto PRI facilities, thus saving the customer long distance charges while maintaining the features of ISDN PRI.

Basic PRI deployment is the same as with E1 or T1 circuit deployment, with the addition of the ISDN cards at the CO and the ISDN support at the user end. For this reason, you need to have a channel service unit (CSU)/DSU to terminate the E1 or T1 circuit and then be able to add ISDN support on top of that. The line coding and framing associated with PRI is not discussed in detail because they are the same formats that are used on standard T1 and E1 circuits. For more information on these coding standards, refer to Chapter 5, "T1 Technology," and Chapter 6, "E1, R2, and Japanese Carrier Technology."

The big difference in PRI is how it is deployed in Japan. Japanese PRI, also called INS-Net 1500 by NTT, is normally deployed by using fiber optics to the customer's premises. Figure 8-26 shows the different deployment methods that are supported in Japan with PRI circuits. NTT in Japan offers two main services, one with 23 B+D service and one with 24 B+D service. The 24 B+D service is offered by sending the D channel through a separate trunk to the customer's premises. Therefore, the customer has access to all 24 B channels on the other circuit.

Figure 8-26 *Japanese Deployment of a PRI Circuit*

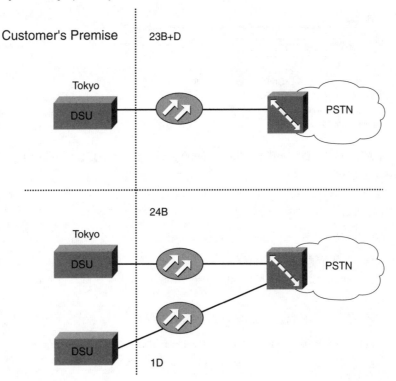

NFAS

NFAS is a function of ISDN that is typically only supported in the U.S. and that allows your equipment to be more efficient with channel use if more than one PRI circuit is in use. The basic premise of NFAS is to take a single D channel and configure it so that it can control multiple PRI circuits (up to 479 B channels). NFAS is limited to 479 B channels because the D channel is only 64 kbps. If you have five PRI circuits coming into the same router, you can use NFAS to reclaim a 64-kbps B channel on four of the circuits. Figure 8-27 shows the use of one ISDN D channel to control multiple PRI circuits to reclaim DS0s for bearer traffic.

The configuration in Example 8-5 shows three T1 controllers, using PRI, that are controlled by the same D channel. The first interface is set up as the primary D channel. For the sake of redundancy, another controller can be set up as the backup D channel, in the case of a loss of signal (LOS) on the primary circuit.

Figure 8-27   *NFAS Configuration with Multiple PRI Circuits*

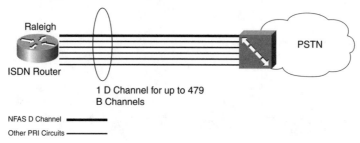

As with any ISDN configuration, you must configure the ISDN switch type in global configuration mode first.

Example 8-5   *Configuration of NFAS on a T1 PRI Circuit Group*

```
isdn switch-type primary-ni
-=snip=-
controller T1 0
  framing esf
  clock source line primary
  linecode b8zs
  pri-group timeslots 1-24 nfas_d primary nfas_int 0 nfas_group 0
!
controller T1 1
  framing esf
  clock source line secondary 1
  linecode b8zs
  pri-group timeslots 1-24 nfas_d backup nfas_int 1 nfas_group 0
!
controller T1 2
  framing esf
  clock source line secondary 2
  linecode b8zs
  pri-group timeslots 1-24 nfas_d none nfas_int 2 nfas_group 0
```

Configuring a T1 and E1 PRI Connection

T1 and E1 PRI configuration is simple. The first thing that you must do is configure the ISDN switch type in global configuration mode and then configure the T1 or E1 controller. Example 8-6 shows a T1 configuration.

Example 8-6   *T1 Configuration*

```
Raleigh#conf t
Raleigh(config)#isdn switch-type primary-ni
Raleigh(config)#controller t1 7/0
Raleigh(config-controller)#framing esf
Raleigh(config-controller)#linecode b8zs
Raleigh(config-controller)#clock source line primary
Raleigh(config-controller)#cablelength short 133
Raleigh(config-controller)#pri-group timeslots 1-24
```

NOTE   In the T1 configuration there is a command for cable length. Remember, this is used in DSX-1 or short-haul applications for T1.

Example 8-7 shows an E1 configuration.

Example 8-7   *E1 Configuration*

```
Raleigh#conf t
Raleigh(config)#isdn switch-type primary-net5
Raleigh(config)#controller e1 7/0
Raleigh(config-controller)#framing no-crc4
Raleigh(config-controller)#linecode hdb3
Raleigh(config-controller)#clock source line primary
Raleigh(config-controller)#pri-group timeslots 1-31
```

NOTE   HDB3 is the default line coding and does not have to be configured if that is what you are using. Although AMI is an option, it is almost never used for E1 circuits. To set up a Japanese PRI, you can use the **primary-ntt** switch type in IOS.

After the controllers have been configured with the **pri-group** command, you can configure the D channel. Any of the group-based commands in IOS create a virtual serial interface. In this case, it is the D channel. Typically, it is referred to as the controller/D channel. T1 PRI can be something along the lines of 7/0:23 and E1 can be 7/0:15. The virtual serial interfaces that are created are zero-based count.

A typical D-channel configuration might look something similar to Example 8-8.

Example 8-8   *Configuration of an ISDN PRI D Channel*

```
interface serial 7/0:23
  no ip address
  isdn switch-type primary-ni
  isdn incoming-voice modem
  isdn protocol-emulate network
  isdn bchan-number-order ascending
```

This configuration is specifically for a back-to-back T1 PRI on an AS5400. You can tell it is back-to-back by the **isdn protocol-emulate network** command. That command sets this router to act as the network side of the ISDN connection.

The command **isdn incoming-voice modem** specifies that incoming calls are treated as inbound analog modem calls and are connected to the proper resources within the device. This same command can map inbound voice calls to the proper voice resources for VoIP when using an AS5300.

The command **isdn bchan-number-order ascending** specifies which direction the B channel selection occurs. The choices are ascending or descending (default).

Resolving Issues with ISDN PRI

Many of the same troubleshooting techniques involved with PRI circuits are standard with T1 and E1 circuits. First and foremost, check to make sure that your controller is up and that no alarms are being detected. As a refresher, a red alarm is if you are receiving a loss of frame (LOF) or LOS. This means that you are unable to receive the proper information from the service provider's network. Next, look for a yellow or blue alarm, also called and alarm indication signal (AIS). If you are receiving a red alarm, your equipment attempts to send a yellow alarm to the remote end to notify them that you are experiencing a problem. The blue alarm is sent from the service provider to both ends of the circuit to notify them that there is a problem within the service provider's network cloud.

After you have verified that there are no alarms detected, check your controller for path code violations and clock slips. Severe clocking slips can cause your circuit to malfunction even if the circuit hardware is operating properly.

The next thing that you should check is the ISDN network status (**show isdn status**). You are looking for Q.921 to be MULTIPLE_FRAME_ESTABLISHED. If that is the case, you should be able to make ISDN calls. If you are in a TEI_UNASSINED or AWAITING_ESTABLISHMENT state, you need to verify your configuration. Remember that if you are in a back-to-back configuration you have to set one of the sides to emulate the network. If you do not, you do not come up on Layer 2.

After you can place calls, the **debug isdn q931** command becomes your greatest asset in troubleshooting ISDN calls. The first thing to monitor is the direction of the disconnect (are you sending or receiving it). You also want to make sure that the bearer capability is correct.

In other words, if you are making a voice call, but it's coming in as data, you have a problem. Receiving a disconnect cause code of "Bearer Capability not Implemented" typically means that a command such as **isdn incoming-voice modem** is missing from the D channel configuration.

Next, take a look at the channel ID, and find out what the status of the attempted channel is with the **show isdn status** command. If the channel the call is being attempted on is B, for some reason it has been busied out. You can manually attempt to reset that B channel or the entire range (although the range isn't recommended in production environments).

Last but not least is certainly the cause code for the release. The **q931 debug** tells you what the cause code is, although it doesn't necessarily spell out the problem for you. They have a tendency to be rather cryptic.

Q.Sig

Q.Sig was developed for private integrated services network exchange (PINX) applications. Based on Q.931, Q.Sig is an evolving technology that allows communication with legacy PBX and key systems. When used with Cisco routers, Q.Sig can connect PBX systems with private IP networks or other service provider network service offerings. Using Q.Sig with private IP transport allows businesses long-haul transport of voice traffic without the need for inter-exchange carrier (IXC) interconnection, which saves on long distance charges.

Summary

ISDN is a network access architecture that offers the ability to integrate voice, video, and data traffic over the same circuit connection. Unlike the analog signaling methods, ISDN employs a CCS signaling type for call setup and channel management. Although ISDN takes the same physical link, it is on a different logical link that is called a D channel and is therefore considered to be CCS.

Two main types of channels are associated with N-ISDN, B channel and D channel. The B channels are used for the transmission of bearer services to include voice, video, and data. The D channel is used as the vehicle for transporting the signaling traffic. A BRI circuit contains two 64-kbps B channels and a 16-kbps D channel, and a PRI circuit contains either 23 or 30 B channels and a full 64-kbps D channel. BRI service is typically deployed as a home user service, and PRI is deployed as an enterprise level service.

ISDN is considered a local loop technology, which means that ISDN is only present between the subscriber and the local ISDN switch. The back end of the switch connected to the PSTN can be any number of communication technologies. The protocols can be converted back into ISDN at either end of the connection.

Three layers are associated with ISDN:

- Layer 1 = I.430 and I.431 (BRI and PRI respectively)
- Layer 2 = Q.921
- Layer 3 = Q.931

I.430 and I.431 specify the physical layer attributes for the ISDN circuit, including electrical and mechanical communication methods. Q.921 specifies the Layer 2 functionality of an ISDN circuit. Q.921 is designed to provide an error free link for the transmission of Q.931 messages and to ensure link integrity. Q.921 provides addressing in the form of TEIs. TEIs identify the end device to the ISDN network switch. BRI circuits have a range of TEIs that can be assigned because they are typically deployed in a point-to-multipoint configuration. PRI circuits always have a TEI=0 because they are deployed over T- and E-carrier facilities in a point-to-point configuration. SAPIs identify the points at which Q.921 can access and communicate with Q.931 messages.

Q.931 handles call control and circuit management within the ISDN network. Q.931 is a message-based signaling format that allows the user or network side to invoke a large number of functions for each call. Addressing on the ISDN network is done through a set of phone numbers (E.164 address) and sub-addresses. The sub-address identifies between two terminals that are using the same phone number. It does not have to be used in the event that there are two different phone numbers allocated.

Review Questions

Give or select the best answer or answers to the following questions. The answers to these questions can be found in Appendix A, "Answers to Review Questions."

1 At which layer of the ISDN stack does Q.931 operate?

_____

_____

_____

2 What type of device is commonly found between the S and T interfaces?

_____

_____

_____

3 How does ISDN BRI service provide both transmit and receive on a single pair of wires?

_____

_____

_____

4 On a Cisco router, what command would give you the following output: 0x8090A2? What does it mean?

_____

_____

_____

5 If your local CO does not have the required facilities to provide you with ISDN service, what might have to be done?

_____

_____

_____

6 If you are not sure that your BRI service has been connected, what can you do as a quick test to verify connectivity?

_____

_____

_____

7 Which of the following messages is not used during the ISDN call setup phase?

a Connect

b Ringing

c Setup

d Call Proceeding

8 If a call needs to traverse the SS7 network, which message type would the Connect message likely be converted into?

a IAM

b ACM

c RLC

d ANM

e REL

9 How many pairs of wires does an ISDN PRI circuit use?

_____

_____

_____

10 Which of the following messages is sent first during a Q.921 negotiation between ISDN devices?

a UA

b SAPI

c RRp

d Setup

e SABME

This chapter covers the following topics:

- **The history of Frame Relay**—The advantages of Frame Relay over traditional time-division multiplexing (TDM). This section also introduces the standards bodies that have been and remain instrumental in the development of Frame Relay, and their individual contributions.

- **Frame Relay specifications**—The specifications that underlie the technology. The specifications are presented from the perspective of four major categories.

- **Frame Relay functionality**—The intricacies behind the way that Frame Relay operates. Detail is given with regard to the format of the actual frames and the signaling that takes place within the network.

- **Frame Relay configuration on Cisco devices**—A sample configuration for a Cisco router, using authentic syntax. This section also offers an explanation of the scenario surrounding the configuration.

CHAPTER 9

Frame Relay

Frame Relay is a packet-switching service that is widely used throughout the world today. Multiple standards bodies have written specifications for Frame Relay; many vendors support each of these specifications in their hardware and software. This chapter covers the history of Frame Relay and the intricacies of its design and usage.

Frame Relay, unlike T1, digital dataphone service (DDS), and plain old telephone service (POTS), is a packet-switching service and not a physical circuit. Frame Relay, as a service, can be deployed on a variety of physical circuits (also referred to as access lines). This, together with the port speed of the ingress switch and the virtual circuit's (VC) bandwidth, are the three main factors that comprise Frame Relay pricing after. Physical access is generally in multiples of 56 kbps or 64 kbps, with the latter incurring higher charges for more expensive encoding (such as bipolar 8-zero substitution [B8ZS] in the U.S.) on the physical trunk. Alternate mark inversion (AMI) is more of a default but only yields 56 kbps per channel. Higher charges are also levied for the obvious increase in subscriber value. Therefore, any physical circuit that can scale in multiples of digital signal level 0 (DS0) is a likely transport for the Frame Relay protocol. This includes, but is not limited to, DDS 56/64, T1/E1, and T3/E3.

The History of Frame Relay

This section chronicles the meteoric rise of Frame Relay as the first digital packet-switched network technology of the telecommunications age. This section also introduces the key players in the development and global acceptance of Frame Relay, from a historical perspective.

The Development of Frame Relay

Frame Relay was developed as public networks matured, thus gradually replacing another packet-switching technology: X.25. Paired with analog transmission media, X.25 became obviated in many markets, because Frame Relay avoids all the inefficiencies that lurk in the shadows of analog technology. Because analog is such a potentially lossy service and because end devices were dumb in the X.25 era, error detection and correction were built into every part of the X.25 infrastructure.

Both X.25 and Frame Relay, but especially Frame Relay, combat the inefficiencies of running data over circuits that employ TDM, as described in Chapter 5, "T1 Technology" and Chapter 6, "E1, R2, and Japanese Carrier Technology." TDM displays characteristics that are particularly optimal for delay-sensitive applications, such as voice. This stems from the fact that the physical circuit is dedicated to the user (subscriber) of that circuit, even when there is no traffic present on the circuit. Because of the bursty nature of data, it is exceedingly more efficient to allow multiple subscribers to use the same physical circuit. Packet switching allows this sharing to occur through a technique known as statistical TDM (STDM). Covered in more detail later in this chapter, virtual-circuit multiplexing is a benefit of Frame Relay, which allows physical circuits to be optimized, from the perspective of the service provider. In simple terms, in TDM circuits any bandwidth that normally goes unused by the subscriber to which the circuit is dedicated can in STDM technologies be borrowed by the service provider on behalf of another subscriber, without constituting a violation of either subscriber's service-level agreement (SLA). STDM also applies to Asynchronous Transfer Mode (ATM), which is presented in Chapter 10, "ATM and B-ISDN."

The flexibility of STDM opens the door for the common service-provider practice of oversubscribing the Frame Relay network. Statistically speaking, odds are in favor of the individual subscribers not all requesting their contractual bandwidth simultaneously. This is analogous to the practice of a bank not keeping 100 percent of its depositors' assets within the confines of the physical building. This is not to say that, barring a repeat of the financial collapse of 1929, the bank cannot honor each and every request for fund withdrawal presented. Indeed, under normal circumstances, the bank uses statistical data to approximate a minimum for the collateral that must be kept on-hand to cover expected activity. The same is true for the service-provider industry. Each provider of Frame Relay network service has a good understanding of the degree to which the network can be oversubscribed, usually with adequate cushioning, before contracts begin to be compromised. Such compromises do occur, on occasion, for which remedies are agreed upon when the contract for service is signed by the subscriber.

Operating over more reliable digital facilities and with more intelligent end devices (such as PCs), Frame Relay has less need for error correction and reliability services within the network. In fact, error correction and reliability, through the use of acknowledgments, are left to the end stations that use the Frame Relay network, perhaps through the Transmission Control Protocol (TCP). Nevertheless, error detection is performed within the Frame Relay network. If errors are detected, the offending frames are removed from the network, so that valuable resources are not expended for the sake of traffic with known errors. End stations are technically not part of the Frame Relay network, at least in the sense that their absence does not affect the network itself.

In 1984, the Consultative Committee for International Telegraph and Telephone (CCITT) established what today are considered preliminary standards for Frame Relay. Since 1992, the CCITT has been known as the International Telecommunication Union

Telecommunication Standardization Sector (ITU-T). The International Telecommunication Union (ITU) itself had been and remains a specialized agency of the UN since 1947, shortly after the UN was created.

These preliminary standards stemmed from AT&T's Digital Multiplex Interface (DMI). DMI was the first to outline a packet-switching service that only specified Layer 2 functionality. X.25, for example, does the brunt of its work at Layer 3. Frame Relay's Layer 2 specifications can be directly related to ISDN standards, as detailed in the next section. In fact, the original intent in its design was to use Frame Relay across ISDN circuits. Today, however, Frame Relay is used across a wide variety of circuits.

Standards Bodies and the Frame Relay Forum (FRF)

In the previous section, you might have noticed a certain amount of credit given to the ITU-T. Although the ITU-T's contribution should not be minimized, there are actually three noteworthy groups in the Frame Relay arena:

- ITU-T
- American National Standards Institute (ANSI)
- FRF

The ITU-T and ANSI are international and U.S. standards bodies, respectively, and "the Frame Relay Forum is an association of vendors, carriers, users and consultants committed to the education, promotion, and implementation of Frame Relay in accordance with international standards," according to the FRF's web site (www.frforum.com). The FRF began in 1990 as a consortium of four companies (which is why it was often referred to as the Gang of Four):

- Cisco Systems
- Digital Equipment Corporation (DEC)
- Northern Telecom (today's Nortel Networks)
- StrataCom

However, the FRF is now composed of hundreds of organizations.

The FRF produces Implementation Agreements (IAs), which are organized documents written from the germane standards of ITU-T, ANSI, and others. Each IA contains references to the official standards relevant to its area of discussion. Although the IAs are not themselves standards, they are completely standards based. An IA's value lies mainly in its ability to demystify the more crucial aspects of what can be more than a dozen separate standards from more than half a dozen separate standards bodies.

This is not to say the FRF does not have its own original recommendations that are considered de facto standards (standards brought into vogue by popular industry/market consent), in their own right. Indeed, the FRF is responsible for many of the innovations that eventually become de jure standards (standards that are standardized by an official committee), because of active lobbying of the standards bodies to include them in official recommendations. Furthermore, both the FRF and the ATM Forum serve to accelerate the development and adoption of standards relevant to their scope. Because the FRF represents such a vast subset of the market's driving force, the standards organizations would be ignoring the voices of the masses were they not to heed the suggestions of the FRF. In the interim, the vendors that compose the FRF and wise vendors that wish to remain compatible and get a jump on the competition implement many of these FRF recommendations. The "Frame Relay Specifications" section in this chapter lists the current FRF IAs.

The market's cry for standardizing Frame Relay resulted in amazingly quick approval within both ITU-T and ANSI, owing largely to the diligence of the FRF and the purpose for which it was created. A major milestone in the development of Frame Relay occurred in 1988, when the ITU-T (still the CCITT) approved recommendation I.122, "Framework for additional packet mode bearer services," in relation to Integrated Services Digital Network (ISDN) standards. Figure 9-1 shows the similarities between the address portions of Frame Relay and ISDN headers, which are both formatted according to the Link Access Procedure on the D Channel (LAPD), as specified in the ITU-T recommendation Q.921.

Figure 9-1   *Similarity Between ISDN and Frame Relay Headers*

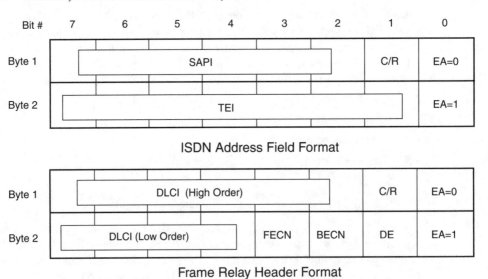

The aforementioned I.122 specifies ways for the useful LAPD frame format to be used in applications other than ISDN, for which it was originally developed. One such application that took advantage of the Layer 2 virtual circuit (VC) multiplexing capabilities of LAPD was Frame Relay. You will soon see that the fields in the LAPD-based Frame Relay header allow multiplexing in the form of multiple VCs (each denoted by a locally significant data-link connection identifier [DLCI], and each unique to the particular user-to-network interface) on a single physical interface.

Chapter 8, "Integrated Services Digital Network," treats the topics of ISDN and its header's address portion in more detail. The fields in the Frame Relay header are detailed later on in this chapter. For now, note that the two data structures in Figure 9-1 are extremely similar in length and in the sharing of the Command/Response (C/R) and Extended Address (EA) fields (with regard to position and function).

Table 9-1 compares the Frame Relay standards, based on functionality and separated by standardizing organization. To emphasize the earlier point that the Frame Relay standards were quickly approved, note that the entire set of ANSI standards were approved during 1990 and 1991. Those that are familiar with the time commonly required to move from draft through approval will be impressed with the expedience of this process. Although ANSI is not affiliated with the ITU-T directly (ANSI is the official U.S. representative to the International Organization for Standardization [ISO] and a few others), the two groups keep their recommendations in close similarity as an effort to provide one standard for global interoperability.

Table 9-1   *Frame Relay Standards*

Description	ANSI Standard	ITU Standard
Service Description	T1.606	I.233
Core Aspects	T1.618 (formerly T1.6ca)	Q.922 Annex A
Access Signaling	T1.617 (formerly T1.6fr)	Q.933

To further stress the fact that Frame Relay is based on standards created for ISDN, ANSI standard T1.606, titled "Frame Relaying Bearer Service Architectural Framework and Service Description," which is the basis for the description of the Frame Relay User-Network Interface (UNI) requirements and general interworking requirements, states that "frame relaying is an ISDN packet-mode bearer service with logically separate C-plane and U-plane information." What this means is that control and user information travel on different channels (out-of-band signaling). This is a clear description of the Bearer channel/Data channel (B-channel/D-channel) nature of ISDN, yet it is a standard upon which Frame Relay is based. Although ISDN is a form of circuit switching and Frame Relay is a form of packet switching, the separation of control and user information is common to both technologies. This point is revisited during the discussion of the Local Management Interface (LMI) and its reserved VC. Now you will take a more in-depth look at the technical specifications that compose Frame Relay.

Frame Relay Specifications

This section details the specific underpinnings of Frame Relay. In particular, you will learn more about the standards, IAs, and header fields introduced in the previous section. There are four broad categories of specification in the case of Frame Relay:

- Framework
- Service description
- Core aspects
- Access signaling

You might recall all but the framework category from Table 9-1 earlier in this chapter. There is also a common congestion-management theme covered by both ANSI and ITU-T. The related standards are T1.606a and I.370, respectively.

Framework Specifications

There is, in fact, only one Frame Relay standard that falls firmly within the framework category—ITU-T recommendation I.122, mentioned previously. Nevertheless, ANSI included coverage of this topic in their recommendation T1.606, also previously mentioned. To reiterate, the purpose of I.122 was and is to provide a general framework for how the LAPD format, originally developed for ISDN, can be ported to other technologies, such as Frame Relay. Refer back to Figure 9-1 to note the similarity between the 16 bits associated with each header.

Service Description Specifications

The applicable Frame Relay specifications in this category are ANSI recommendation T1.606 and ITU-T I.233. From its own abstract, T1.606 establishes an architectural framework within which frame-relaying service is described. It should be interpreted as a guideline to provide more detailed standards on frame relaying. For signaling, T1.606 yields to the common signaling approach for all ISDN D-channel control. In the user plane, this specification provides for a basic bearer service that is the unacknowledged order-preserving transfer of data units from the network side of one UNI to the network side of the other UNI. What this means is that the frame-relaying service is responsible for making sure that information arrives in order but that the service itself does not provide for the sending device to be notified of the success or failure of the information's transmission to the destination. The frame format is based on the definition in ITU-T recommendation Q.921 and the enhancements made to it in ANSI T1.602 (LAPD). The original intention of these standards was for data communication transport capabilities up to 1.544 Mbps (the T1 rate), but specifications now provide for Frame Relay service up to T3 speeds.

Recommendation I.233 is divided into two main parts, each with its separate addenda, which are known as annexes. I.233.1 describes an unreliable frame-relaying bearer service, and I.233.2 standardizes a reliable (in that errors are corrected and frames are acknowledged) frame-switching bearer service. Order preservation for frames is provided for in both sections. I.233 (especially Annex D of I.233.1) also specifies a Layer 2 sub-layer architecture (similar to the Logical Link Control/Media Access Control [LLC/MAC] pair in LAN environments). The upper sub-layer is called the datalink control sub-layer, and the lower sub-layer is referred to as the core sub-layer (DL-CORE in this book and other standards documents). According to I.233.1 Annex D, "The core sub-layer provides only those functions needed to take advantage of the statistical properties of communications. The data link control sub-layer enhances the core sub-layer to support the Open System Interconnection (OSI) data link service."

I.233 is replete with references to ISDN terminology and reference points. Nevertheless, it is ITU-T's recognized Frame Relay service-description specification. In it you can find minimum and maximum limits for frame size, which are based on the application. For example, it is suggested that you use frame sizes of at least 1600 octets in LAN environments to prevent unnecessary fragmentation, and it is mandated that you cannot exceed 260 octets, in the case of interworking with frame switching when using the D channel. As is seen in many of ITU's recommendations, Annex A to I.233.1 provides a helpful definition of the terms of Frame Relay discussions. Annex B, "Support of the OSI network layer service," discusses the use of ITU-T Q.933 or any other capable protocol that can interface down to Q.922 for access signaling in frame-relaying networks. The main intent of this annex is to show how the Frame Relay bearer service supports OSI's Network layer service (Layer 3), as specified in ITU-T X.213. Annexes C and D give effective overviews of the core aspects of the Link Access Procedure, Frame Relay (LAPF). Annexes A and B of I.233.2 are similar in nature to those of I.233.1, described previously.

Core Aspects Specifications

The specifications that deal with the core aspects of Frame Relay are ITU-T Q.922 and ANSI T1.618. Parenthetically, be careful not to get drawn into an office argument over the ANSI specifications. You might be used to higher-level specifications having higher numerical components in their naming, but ANSI throws you a curve with T1.618 and T1.617. Although ITU-T's corresponding specifications are numbered in logical order (Q.933 is higher level than Q.922), ANSI reverses their numbering, making T1.618 the lower-level specification.

The core aspects of Frame Relay treat the description of the frame format and the overall operation of the Frame Relay protocol. The close relationship of Q.922 with Q.921, the aforementioned ISDN standard that defines the LAPD frame format, leads to numerous references to the Q.921 standard from within Q.922. In fact you probably shouldn't frustrate yourself by going through Q.922 without having Q.921 close by.

With regard to the Frame Relay header, Q.922 specifies that a two-octet header is default, with three- and four-octet headers illustrated. These header formats are illustrated and explained as part of the DLCI discussion in the functionality section that follows in this chapter. Annex A to Q.922, at first, seems similar to the main text of the recommendation, but closer scrutiny (and the introductory language of the annex) makes it clear that this annex identifies differences between the main text and the functionality that is required to fully support a frame-relaying service. Annex A provides the means to bring the descriptions contained in I.122 and I.233 to bear. However, LAPF, as defined in I.233, is not necessary in the implementation of Q.922 Annex A.

Access Signaling Specifications

ITU-T Q.933 and ANSI T1.617 deal with access signaling for Frame Relay. In this sense, these specifications represent a third layer to the Frame Relay infrastructure, much as Q.931, which is referenced heavily by Q.933, represents a third layer for ISDN. Nevertheless, the functionality of the Frame Relay network encompasses only the first two layers, as was previously stated. As with Q.931 for ISDN, Q.933 is involved with the specification of the procedures for the establishing, maintaining, and clearing of Frame Relay connections at the UNI. This speaks to the issue of how to implement switched VCs (SVCs). It is, perhaps, Annex A to Q.933 and Annex D to T1.617 that get the most attention from the Frame Relay community. This is because these addenda specify mechanisms for VC status management. This is known generically as LMI and is discussed further in this chapter. In particular, these addenda describe procedures for the following:

- Notification of the addition of a permanent VC (PVC)
- Detection of the deletion of a PVC
- Notification of the availability (active) or unavailability (inactive) state of a configured PVC:
    - Inactive means that the PVC is configured but is not available for use
    - Active means that the PVC is available for use
- Link integrity verification

FRF Implementation Agreements

The IAs of the FRF are listed here for completeness. The full text of these documents is available free-of-charge from various locations on the World Wide Web, including the FRF's own web site at www.frforum.com. IAs with more than one number appearing in the document number have been revised from their original draft.

- **FRF.1.2**, "UNI Implementation Agreement," April 2000
- **FRF.2.1**, "Frame Relay Network-to-Network Interface (NNI) Implementation Agreement," July 1995
- **FRF.3.2**, "Multiprotocol Encapsulation Implementation Agreement (MEI)," April 2000
- **FRF.4.1**, "SVC UNI Implementation Agreement," January 2000
- **FRF.5**, "Frame Relay/Asynchronous Transfer Mode (ATM) Network Interworking Implementation," December 1994
- **FRF.6**, "Frame Relay Service Customer Network Management Implementation Agreement (MIB)," March 1994
- **FRF.7**, "Frame Relay PVC Multicast Service and Protocol Description," October 1994
- **FRF.8.1**, "Frame Relay/ATM PVC Service Interworking Implementation Agreement," February 2000
- **FRF.9**, "Data Compression Over Frame Relay Implementation Agreement," January 1996
- **FRF.10.1**, "Frame Relay Network-to-Network SVC Implementation Agreement," September 1996
- **FRF.11.1**, "Voice Over Frame Relay Implementation Agreement," May 1997, "Annex J added March 1999
- **FRF.12**, "Frame Relay Fragmentation Implementation Agreement," December 1997
- **FRF.13**, "Service Level Definitions Implementation Agreement," August 1998
- **FRF.14**, "Physical Layer Interface Implementation Agreement," December 1998
- **FRF.15**, "End-to-End Multilink Frame Relay Implementation Agreement," August 1999
- **FRF.16**, "Multilink Frame Relay UNI/NNI Implementation Agreement," August 1999
- **FRF.17**, "Frame Relay Privacy Implementation Agreement," January 2000
- **FRF.18**, "Network-to-Network FR/ATM SVC Service Interworking Implementation Agreement," April 2000
- **FRF.19**, "Frame Relay Operations, Administration and Maintenance Implementation Agreement," March 2001
- **FRF.20**, "Frame Relay IP Header Compression Implementation Agreement," June 2001

Frame Relay Functionality

This section describes the practical aspects of Frame Relay. It details the data structures and protocol specifics that make Frame Relay perform the way it does. The discussions that follow present the topics of the previous section in a more pragmatic light, both for PVCs and SVCs. The main topics treated here are as follows:

- VCs (PVCs and SVCs)
- DLCIs
    - Inverse Address Resolution Protocol (Inverse ARP)
    - EA, C/R, and D/C bits
- Contractual values
- Frame discards and recovery
- Signaling

VCs

Similar to X.25 and ATM, Frame Relay is designed around the concept of VCs. A VC is the end-to-end collection of software mappings between ports on two interconnected Frame Relay devices, be they switches or end devices, regardless of how many switches may separate them. Each of the associated VC mappings is identified by a DLCI, which is the next topic in this section. Each VC permits two-way transmission between end devices. In other words, a VC is constructed of one or more (usually more) links between Frame Relay devices, and each link is identified by a DLCI number. Again, the collection of all links between two end devices comprises the VC.

There are three types of VCs: PVCs, soft PVCs (SPVCs), and SVCs. PVCs were the original Frame Relay offering and are still the most prevalent, but SVCs are making inroads within the industry. The easiest way to differentiate PVCs from SVCs is to point out that PVCs must be manually provisioned, or set up, at the time of service subscription. After a PVC is established, its existence is permanent, as its name implies, until the subscriber or provider cancels the contract associated with that VC. SVCs are based upon the contract between the subscriber and provider but are automatically provisioned and torn down (switched or dialed), based on subscriber demand. As you might infer, an SVC can be less expensive than a PVC, as long as usage is not constant. As VC demand approaches a constant level, the cost-efficiency of SVCs diminishes. This is analogous to a circuit-switched product being used constantly. In such a case, a dedicated offering might be a better choice. SVC establishment, maintenance, and teardown are governed by ITU-T recommendation Q.933, using UNI signaling at the network's edge and NNI signaling within the network.

Although for a PVC, the actual path taken through the network (excluding the access circuit) can vary over time, such as in the case of a SPVC, when automatic rerouting changes physical circuits to circumvent outages or other problems, the beginning and end of the circuit does not change. This established end connectivity is the source of the term permanent. The term virtual stems from the fact that statistical TDM (STDM) is being performed and network facilities are not actually dedicated to the subscriber on an ongoing basis, as in the case of TDM technology, such as T1. SVCs are designed to allow the other end of the circuit to change at will, which allows more control and flexibility on the part of the subscriber. Although transparent to end users, SVC establishment through the network is somewhat more complex and only recently gaining in popularity because of applications that drive the use of SVCs. Aside from the need for a signaling protocol, such as Q.933, each provider throughout the end-to-end connection must agree upon the method of signaling to establish, maintain, and tear down the switched circuit. Another subtle requirement that sets SVCs apart from PVCs is that of accounting, whereby connections must be monitored and billed, according to subscriber usage. With a PVC, all this is ironed out in the original contract, and there is no opportunity for change during the normal life of the contract, as there is in the case of an SVC. The next section goes into detail on SVC applications.

An SPVC is characterized as a PVC with set endpoint connections but with connections through the network that can be revised, in the event of failure. Unlike SVCs, SPVCs cannot be torn down at the request of either endpoint. Neither PVCs nor SVCs are generally regarded as resistant to network outages, as are SPVCs. In essence, an SPVC is every bit a PVC, with the exception that an SPVC requires a Private NNI (PNNI) specification for vendor interoperability within the network, and a PVC must be manually provisioned through the network, without the use of a signaling protocol. Vendor interoperability was the hurdle that had to be overcome for SPVCs to become a reality.

DLCI

The DLCI is a 10-bit (1024 possible values—larger DLCIs are allowed by the standards, but not common) numerical value carried in each Frame Relay header. The DLCI signifies the VC to which the frame belongs and helps determine the physical path to be taken out of a device to allow the frame to continue along the same VC. Similarly, the originating device uses the DLCI to inform the ingress switch of the VC over which the customer intends or requires the frame to be transmitted. Refer to Figure 9-2 to see where the DLCI appears in the Frame Relay header.

In any case, the DLCI is nothing more than a locally significant numerical value that represents the entire VC from the standpoint of the current device. Each switching device uses the DLCI to help decide which physical egress port to use, based upon from which physical ingress port the frame originally arrived to the switch. Figure 9-3 illustrates the concept of port/DLCI pairing in switching frames through a Frame Relay switch. In any one switching decision, the switch looks at the incoming DLCI and port pair and makes a predictable outgoing DLCI and port determination to allow the frame to continue its journey on the same VC on which it started.

Figure 9-2   *The Frame Relay Header*

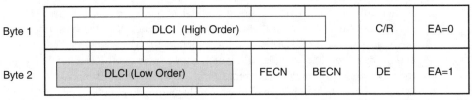

Frame Relay Header Format

DLCI = Data Link Control Identifier
FECN/BECN = Forward/Backward Explicit
                        Congestion Notification
C/R = Command/Response
EA = Extended Address
DE = Discard Eligibility

Figure 9-3   *Port/DLCI Pairing During the Switching Process*

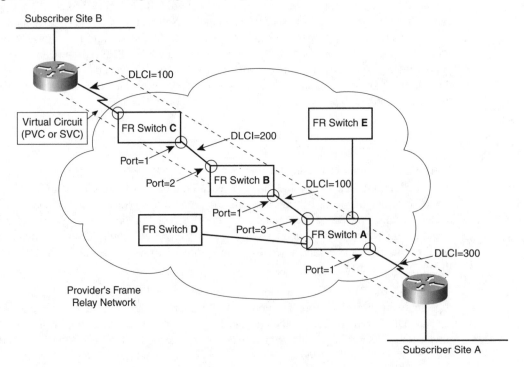

The term locally significant introduces the concept that the DLCI does not have to remain the same throughout the VC. Each numerical value must be unique only between two Frame Relay devices that are connected between the same two ports. In other words, if two devices are connected with multiple ports, the same numerical DLCI value does not represent the same VC because the port number is different. In this way, a port/DLCI pair is similar to an IP address in the sense that the same IP host ID can refer to different hosts, as long as the network ID is different between the two hosts. By the same token, the same network ID can refer to two different hosts, as long as their host IDs are unique. As long as you consider the port number and DLCI as a linked pair, which makes them a unit, you can consider that each pair must be unique in its entirety, within a given switch for a given direction of flow. Each pair can be duplicated and be part of an entirely different VC within another switch, or in the opposite direction within the same switch. This is the nature of a locally significant identifier.

For example, in Figure 9-3, a frame traveling from Subscriber Site A to Subscriber Site B is sent out by the router at Site A. The Frame Relay header notes that the DLCI number for the VC is 300. Switch A receives this frame on port 1. By looking up in its switching table what to do with a frame received on port 1 with a DLCI of 300, the switch discovers that it must send the frame out on port 3 with a DLCI of 100, for the frame to continue on the appropriate physical path within the logical VC. Switch B then receives this frame on port 1 and determines that a frame received on port 1 with a DLCI of 100 should be sent out on port 2 with a DLCI of 200. The incoming and outgoing DLCIs at any stage along the transmission can be identical, as long as the port numbers are different. Similarly, the existence of a DLCI of 100 at two different points in Figure 9-3 is entirely legal, due to the concept of local significance. This process continues through each switch in the network until the frame is delivered to its final destination. Switches D and E are shown only as examples of switches that are not part of the VC in question. Although in this diagram the end devices are routers, which are commonly implemented, they can also be bridges, front-end processors (FEPs), Frame Relay access devices (FRADs), or any other device with a Frame Relay interface. Likewise, the switches can, just as well, be network routers or T1/E1 multiplexers.

Inverse ARP

Although this book is not an IP-centric work, nor does it dwell on any particular Layer 3 protocol unless it is part of the protocol stack featured by a particular chapter, we would be remiss if we did not discuss Frame Relay's interesting method of tying in with the Layer 3 address (often referred to in literature as the protocol address). Although in Ethernet environments, for example, an ARP cache table is constructed to map already-known Layer 3 addresses to learned MAC addresses for local devices (devices on the same IP subnet), Frame Relay has a quite opposite requirement. Although Frame Relay learns about new DLCIs through LMI signaling, there is no mechanism built into the network to also supply the Layer 3 address of the opposing device. Of course, this is necessary if Frame Relay is to appear to be a useable WAN pathway for the LAN.

If static mapping is not desirable, the solution is Inverse ARP (RFC 2390, "InARP"; also known as Frame Relay ARP). Because DLCIs can be thought of as the Frame Relay equivalent to a hardware address, a table mapping this address to a protocol address is required. Realize that although the DLCI is actually a local identifier (meaningful only to the end device and its ingress switch), it serves as the local identifier for the entire VC, and as a result, for the other end device (in fact, all devices throughout the VC). It's this subtle point that allows a table similar to the LAN ARP cache to be a useful, indeed requisite, data structure in Frame Relay.

The difference is, while with ARP in the LAN environment, the device knows the protocol address and needs the hardware address to complete frame formation, Frame Relay hands the end device a hardware address (DLCI) that leads through the VC, directly to the other end device. Although DLCI configuration is often more manual on the customer equipment than it might sound here, it is possible to sneak a peek at the configured DLCIs for a particular access line because of LMI updates by the ingress switch. It's the protocol address that is lacking. This is acceptable due to the fact that this is a WAN environment. The missing protocol address is not, for example, an IP address that might be returned someday during a Domain Name System (DNS) query for a Web server. It is the address of the other end's first Frame Relay device, its router, for example.

The foregoing discussion becomes clearer when you bear in mind that Frame Relay is known as a nonbroadcast multiaccess (NBMA) environment, although Cisco, for one, has implemented proprietary enhancements to mask this characteristic. (Cisco's Building Scalable Cisco Internetworks (BSCI) course is an excellent resource for more information on this subject.) In light of this default functionality, you can say that Frame Relay is similar to a WAN variety of Ethernet without the broadcast capability. The other difference is that, in the case of Frame Relay, you don't commonly need to talk to everyone that shares the network with you. What's more, you already have the hardware address for those with whom you can communicate. The point continued from the previous paragraph is that the device for which the protocol address is needed is not a true end device, but instead the first Frame Relay aware device at the other end. Again, this is often the router at the other end.

There is a common confusion between Inverse ARP and another protocol known as Reverse ARP (RARP). The similarity is that each protocol knows what the hardware address is and needs a protocol address to go along with it. The difference is that RARP finds the local device's hardware/protocol address pairing, and Inverse ARP finds another device's pairing. Their names make them sound interchangeable, but they are quite different in ultimate purpose.

Here's how Inverse ARP works. When an end device is informed of an activated DLCI by an LMI status notification, the end device issues an Inverse ARP request on the new DLCI. The request is handled, as any traffic sent through the DLCI. As a result, the opposing end device receives the request and formulates a reply, which consists of its protocol address.

After it is in possession of the reply, the originator of the request maps the newly learned protocol address to the previously learned DLCI. The foregoing process minimizes the error because of human intervention brought about by manual mapping of protocol addresses to DLCIs.

EA, C/R, and D/C Bits

Now that you have a better handle on the function of the DLCI field in the Frame Relay header, turn your attention to the subtle, yet necessary, fields of the header that define the length of the header and the function of the extended DLCI fields. ITU-T Q.922 defines possible Frame Relay header formats, as shown in Figure 9-4. Figure 9-4 also has a key that defines the fields and bits. Also noted in Annex A of Q.922, the C/R is not currently defined, so the bit is passed transparently by the DL-CORE protocol. The interpretation of this statement is that end systems can feel free to use this bit, knowing that no network function is impacted. In this way, a potentially meaningful proprietary bit is guaranteed to pass from one end device to the other, unhindered by the Frame Relay infrastructure. The EA bit has one simple function—to indicate the end of the header. If this bit is a 0, at least one octet follows before the end of the header is reached. If an octet has EA set to 1, that octet is the last in the header. The next bit begins the Frame Relay information field, which contains such data structures as higher-layer headers and user data.

Figure 9-4 (a) shows the default Frame Relay header format, with the common 10-bit DLCI. (Refer to Figure 9-5 for listings of DLCI categories for each frame-header format.) Figure 9-4 (b) and (c) show the optional three- and four-octet headers with a selectable 10-, 16-, 17-, or 23-bit DLCI. A closer look at this selectable DLCI might be in order. The DLCI/DL-CORE control indicator (D/C) bit is set (equals 1) when the high-order six bits in the last octet of the header (for both three- and four-octet headers) represent DL-CORE control information. The presence of DL-CORE control information means that the DLCI ends in the previous octet (giving 10- and 17-bit DLCI possibilities for three- and four-octet headers, respectively). D/C is reset (equals 0) when the same six bits are the low-order DLCI bits (giving 16- and 23-bit DLCIs for three- and four-octet headers, respectively).

Recall that the three- and four-octet headers are not widely supported, nor are they necessary, due to the local significance of DLCI values. Combine this with the fact that the DL-CORE control function is not currently being implemented (which would technically be the only application pushing the larger formats, aside from an explosive growth in network-device port bandwidth or end-user application instances) but is specified for possible future expansion.

Figure 9-4 *Default and Optional Header Formats*

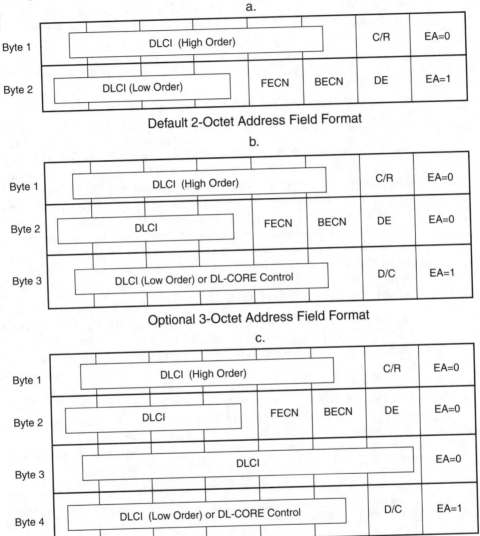

a.

Byte 1	DLCI (High Order)	C/R	EA=0
Byte 2	DLCI (Low Order) / FECN / BECN	DE	EA=1

Default 2-Octet Address Field Format

b.

Byte 1 — DLCI (High Order) / C/R / EA=0
Byte 2 — DLCI / FECN / BECN / DE / EA=0
Byte 3 — DLCI (Low Order) or DL-CORE Control / D/C / EA=1

Optional 3-Octet Address Field Format

c.

Byte 1 — DLCI (High Order) / C/R / EA=0
Byte 2 — DLCI / FECN / BECN / DE / EA=0
Byte 3 — DLCI / EA=0
Byte 4 — DLCI (Low Order) or DL-CORE Control / D/C / EA=1

Optional 4-Octet Address Field Format

DLCI = Data Link Control Identifier
FECN/BECN = Forward/Backward Explicit
Congestion Notification
C/R = Command/Response
EA = Extended Address
DE = Discard Eligibility
D/C = DLCI or DL-CORE Control Indicator

Figure 9-5 (a) lists the categories of 10-bit DLCI. It makes no difference whether the 10 bits come from the default two-octet format or from the three-octet format with a D/C of 1, meaning the high-order bits of the third octet represent the DL-CORE control information, not additional DLCI bits. User frames are assigned DLCIs in the range 16 through 991, based on the VC over which they are transmitted. Figure 9-5(b) presents the situation in which the three-octet header has a D/C value of 0, thereby creating a 16-bit DLCI, with a total of 65,536 possible combinations. In this case, user data travels over VCs with DLCIs in the range 1024 through 63487.

Finally, Figure 9-5 (c) and (d) list the categories of DLCI, when using the four-octet version of the header. First, when the D/C bit is 1, the DLCI is limited to the first three octets and is comprised of 17 bits, creating 131,072 possible combinations. User traffic passes across VCs with DLCIs in the range 2048 through 126975. Second, when the D/C bit is 0, all possible bits (23, to be exact) represent the DLCI. This yields 8,388,608 possible combinations, with DLCIs of user VCs in the range 131072 through 8126463.

Contractual Values in Frame Relay

There are several key values that are agreed upon during the negotiation of the contract and SLA, entered into by the service provider and the subscriber. Those presented here are as follows:

- Committed information rate (CIR)
- Maximum burst rate (MBR)
- Committed burst size (Bc)
- Excess burst size (Be)
- Committed rate measurement interval (Tc)

These values (except MBR), and a few more, are defined in ITU-T I.233.1 Annex A. The primary value recognized and agreed upon contractually when subscribing to Frame Relay service is CIR. The CIR is the average transmission rate for the PVC. It is this value that many companies track to be sure that they are getting at least what they are paying for. Of course, it's the MBR that allows them to get more than what they pay for, although the service provider is still liable for even one incident of frames being discarded at a point below the CIR.

Here's how the numbers interrelate. The CIR is computed from two values. These values are Bc and Tc. The CIR is computed as Bc/Tc. For example, a 64 kbps CIR can stem from a Bc of 64,000 bits and a Tc of 1 second, or from a Bc of 384,000 bits and a Tc of 6 seconds. The MBR is the combination of the CIR with any excess burst rate (Be/Tc). Thus, MBR = (Bc/Tc) + (Be/Tc) or (Bc + Be) / Tc. Assuming that MBR is less than the access-line rate, which is the nominal rate of the physical circuit or logical channel that the PVC rides on, there is a third zone in which no frames are allowed for that PVC, unless a practice known as graceful discarding is observed by the service provider. Figure 9-6 illustrates the three zones that can develop from the values discussed here. The following paragraphs use these zones to discuss discarding frames.

Figure 9-5 *DLCI Categories*

a.

DLCI Range	Function
	10-bit DLCI
DLCI Range	Function
0	In Channel Signaling, if Required
1-15	Reserved
16-511	Network Option: on Non-D-Channels, Available for Support of User Information
512-991	Logical Link Identification for Support of User Information
992-1007	Layer 2 Management of Frame Mode Bearer Service
1008-1022	Reserved
1023	In Channel Layer 2 Management, if Required

b.

DLCI Range	Function
	16-bit DLCI
DLCI Range	Function
0	In Channel Signaling, if Required
1-1023	Reserved
1024-32767	Network Option: on Non-D-Channels, Available for Support of User Information
32768-63487	Logical Link Identification for Support of User Information
63488-64511	Layer 2 Management of Frame Mode Bearer Service
64512-65534	Reserved
65535	In Channel Layer 2 Management, if Required

c.

DLCI Range	Function
	17-bit DLCI
DLCI Range	Function
0	In Channel Signaling, if Required
1-2047	Reserved
2048-65535	Network Option: on Non-D-Channels, Available for Support of User Information
65536-126975	Logical Link Identification for Support of User Information
126976-129023	Layer 2 Management of Frame Mode Bearer Service
129024-131070	Reserved
131071	In Channel Layer 2 Management, if Required

d.

DLCI Range	Function
	23-bit DLCI
DLCI Range	Function
0	In Channel Signaling, if Required
1-131071	Reserved
131072-4194303	Network Option: on Non-D-Channels, Available for Support of User Information
4194304-8126463	Logical Link Identification for Support of User Information
8126464-8257535	Layer 2 Management of Frame Mode Bearer Service
8257536-8338606	Reserved
8388607	In Channel Layer 2 Management, if Required

Figure 9-6   *A Graphical View of CIR and MBR*

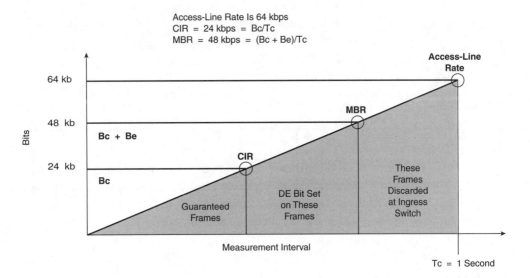

Access-Line Rate Is 64 kbps
CIR = 24 kbps = Bc/Tc
MBR = 48 kbps = (Bc + Be)/Tc

Frame Discards and Recovery

There is a simple rule that makes Frame Relay so elegant in its simplicity—if there is a problem, discard the data. The two main causes for data being discarded are as follows:

- Detection of data errors
- Network congestion

Figure 9-7 shows the Frame Relay header in the context of an entire frame. The flag field at the beginning and end of the frame is the high-level data link control (HDLC) flag (0x7E). This is 01111110 in binary. As in the case of all protocols that rely on the HDLC flag to herald the beginning and end of a frame, Frame Relay transmitting end-devices insert a 0 bit after every string of five 1s. At the receiving end, every 0 that follows five consecutive 1s is stripped off, leaving the original information to be passed on to the receiving hardware and software. This practice ensures that the 0x7E opening/closing flag never is duplicated within the interior of the frame. Q.922 suggests that all applications should support separate opening and closing flags, but that an optional combined flag that is simultaneously the closing flag for the preceding frame and the opening flag for the current frame can be implemented without being considered a violation of the protocol. The recommendation also suggests that the flag fill in space between frames on non-D channels.

Figure 9-7 *A Frame Relay Frame*

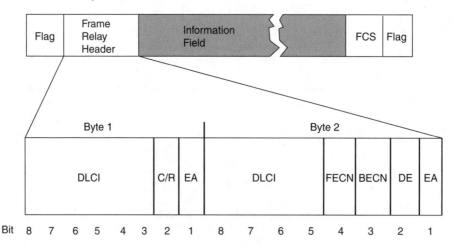

Detection of Data Errors

The frame-check sequence (FCS) field is an error detection mechanism that determines if the data in the frame in question has been compromised during its most recent leg of transmission (such as from switch to switch). The FCS is a computed value that is inserted into this position in the frame. The receiving device computes a value by using the same algorithm, the result of which should be identical to the inserted value. If there is a discrepancy, it is assumed that the frame was damaged during the most recent transmission. The frame is then discarded, without further processing, because there is no way to determine what the original data was. Even if a single bit in the FCS itself is in error, the frame is still discarded because there is no way to determine exactly which bit or bits are to blame for the discrepancy. It is universally held that this is a method of error detection only, and that error correction is left to the end device and to higher-layer protocols that the switches or network devices have no access to.

Another problem with the data comes in the form of an incorrect DLCI in the header. This problem is treated the same as if the FCS did not compute properly. The frame is discarded, because there is no way to determine which DLCI should have been installed in the header. As you can see, Frame Relay takes no chances and makes no assumptions. This attitude preserves network bandwidth and performance, distributing the tasks that an individual end device can perform to the applicable end device. The only problem with this comes from those end-device protocols that are less efficient in their error recovery. Even those protocols that are somewhat efficient can be made inefficient by automatic flow-control adjustments being made because of worsening network conditions or by manual configurations that create constant inefficiency. Therefore, it is important that Frame Relay employ mechanisms that avoid loss of integrity and prevent a major cause of this loss— network congestion.

Network Congestion

Network congestion is a common occurrence within well-used networks. The only true way to avoid congestion is to over-engineer your network, which results in more expense than necessary for the preponderance of operating conditions. Different network implementations might employ equally distinct methods of dealing with congestion. For example, in the case of Ethernet, network congestion results in the expected collision of frames, thus destroying the actual information that is being transmitted by all parties involved. This is an example of a decidedly reactive congestion treatment mechanism. The method used, in the case of Frame Relay and ATM, can be equally reactive, but tends to be more proactive, to the extent that all service providers and subscribers use the associated mechanisms.

Network congestion occurs in two main ways. First, a device receives more input than its buffers can accommodate. This is known as receiver congestion. Second, line congestion occurs when a device tries to transmit more data than the circuit is designed to transport. Because Frame Relay depends on intelligent end devices that handle error recovery in different ways, all of which are beyond the control of the Frame Relay network, Frame Relay must have a method of protecting the network against complete failure, because of inefficient error-recovery methods. It is therefore important that the congestion-management mechanisms of Frame Relay minimize congestion and, if it comes to it, minimize the effects of discards. Congestion signaling bits perform this function and are discussed next.

Signaling

If you follow the standards, you are not required to implement any signaling mechanisms. These are left as optional, according to the standards, but their use improves throughput and performance of the network. Signaling mechanisms are split into three broad categories:

- Control bits for congestion
- Connection status
- Call control (regarding SVCs)

Congestion signaling bits occur directly in the data frames of normal user traffic, and the other two signaling mechanisms have their own special frame types, as dictated by the specification that is adhered to for that particular implementation. The most common of these specifications is discussed here.

Control Bits for Congestion

Occasionally, network congestion can run so completely out of control that the only solution is for the end devices to throttle back on their transmission of frames into the network. An often less agreeable solution is for the network devices to randomly discard frames in an attempt to restore order. Unfortunately, end devices only attempt retransmission, possibly making the situation even worse. Refer back to Figure 9-7, noting the single-bit fields labeled forward explicit congestion notification (FECN), backward explicit congestion notification (BECN), and discard eligible (DE). FECN and BECN are two examples of, as their names imply, explicit congestion notification. FECN and BECN are covered in ITU-T Q.922, Appendix I, "Responses to Network Congestion."

In contrast, TCP employs a form of implicit congestion notification. In other words, TCP deduces but is not told that congestion is occurring when acknowledgments take longer than expected to return or when packets are lost. In the case of FECN and BECN, a device can explicitly notify other devices of network congestion from an upstream or downstream perspective. Figure 9-8 illustrates the concept of explicit congestion notification.

Figure 9-8 *Explicit Congestion Notification*

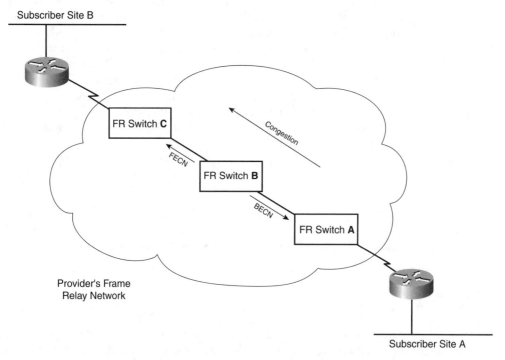

In this example, Switch B becomes aware, through internal processes, that it or the circuit (either virtual or physical) is nearing congestion. At this point, Switch B can begin to set the FECN bit (set means to make it a 1) for all frames headed in the same direction as the traffic causing the congestion. This serves to notify downstream recipients that they might expect problems to arise from the impending situation. The FECN bit can be used by end devices that are capable of notifying opposing transmitting devices that their transmissions might meet with congestion. This affects a state of awareness that is not directly spawned by the Frame Relay network. This awareness can then be acted upon by the transmitting device throttling back, to avoid data loss. This indirect notification can also be affected by the receiving device's use of the Internet Control Message Protocol's (ICMP) source quench function for flow control. A steady flow of such messages signals to the transmitting device that it should pause until the source quench messages cease.

Sometimes more valuable is the ability of the Frame Relay network to notify upstream devices directly that they are causing or contributing to the congestion at hand. To do this, the network device sets the BECN bit of frames that are headed back toward the devices causing the congestion. If these devices are capable of responding to the BECN bit, they can throttle back on their transmission, thereby reducing the frames being fed into the congestion and, thus, reducing the congestion itself. BECN usage affects further traffic reduction by the fact that end devices do not have to notify each other of congestion, as in the case of FECN-bit response.

Because the header of every frame contains not only the FECN and BECN bits, but also the DLCI bits, notification can be limited to one DLCI, notification can span all DLCIs for a particular physical circuit (that is, a particular port on the network device), or congestion notification can affect every DLCI of every port in both directions for a particular device. The strategy taken all depends on the ability of the network device to pinpoint the cause of its growing congestion, whether to the circuit or all the way down to a particular DLCI.

What if setting FECN and BECN bits doesn't seem to mitigate the congestion? The network devices can simply, as noted earlier, discard frames at random. Although this might seem a viable solution, every end device is punished for what might be the sins of a few. Instead, the network device requiring relief can observe the DE bit. Most administrators prefer that precious delay-sensitive traffic, such as voice, not be discarded before data that can be easily retransmitted with no perceptible loss of meaning. For this reason, end devices (those ingress subscriber devices with the greatest stake in identifying frames this way) can tag their less sensitive frames as eligible for discarding (DE bit is set), should the need arise during congestion. The distressed network device can then, less randomly, choose to first discard those frames with DE bits set. If the situation requires further action, all remaining frames are indiscriminately targeted for discarding, until the congestion subsides.

If the end devices are not capable of, or not configured to, set their own DE bits, the ingress network switch (the switch that connects the subscriber to the network) can set DE bits, based on the CIR. Referring back to Figure 9-6, you are now ready to discuss the relationship of the VC's CIR and the setting of the DE bit. The first area in Figure 9-6 indicates that the service provider guarantees contractually to deliver all frames. The SLA prescribes remedies, if this guarantee is broken. This area represents traffic up to the CIR rate.

The next area in Figure 9-6 shows that the DE bit is set for frames that burst past the CIR, but remain within the MBR. If a network device needs to discard frames because of network congestion, these frames are the first to go from this VC. The final area is the bandwidth between the MBR and the access-line rate (referred to in I.233.1 Annex A as access rate). If graceful discarding is in effect, these frames are allowed to pass. However, the DE bits are set, and these frames are susceptible to early deletion, in the case of network congestion.

If the service provider is not practicing graceful discarding, these frames are automatically discarded by the provider's first switch (the subscriber's ingress switch).

It is possible, depending on the service provider, for a customer to subscribe to Frame Relay with a CIR of 0 and a non-zero MBR (and even an MBR of 0, in the case of graceful discarding). The subscriber can then inexpensively burst up to the MBR (or even the access-line rate, in the case of graceful discarding), as long as the subscriber understands that all frames have the potential to be discarded, as they are all marked as DE by the ingress switch.

From the preceding discussion, you can see that it is in the best interest of each subscriber to use equipment that can respond to congestion notifications and to be sure that such equipment is configured with proper thresholds, so as to best make use of the congestion signaling received from the network. To the extent that every subscriber follows this practice, the network is optimized, such that inconveniences are minimized.

Connection Status

Connection status is only one of four extensions to the Frame Relay standards, known collectively as the LMI specification. The following list is from Cisco's Univercd web site "Troubleshooting Frame Relay Connections" (www.cisco.com/univercd/cc/td/doc/cisintwk/itg_v1/tr1918.htm) and presents these four extensions and a brief description of each. The remainder of this discussion is mainly about status messages. The term *common* means that a standards-based implementation of Frame Relay has this feature. The term *optional* indicates that this feature is available, at the discretion of the vendor:

- **Virtual circuit status messages (common)**—Provide communication and synchronization between the network and the user device, periodically report the existence of new PVCs and the deletion of already existing PVCs, and generally provide information about PVC integrity. VC status messages prevent the sending of data into black holes—that is, over PVCs that no longer exist.

- **Multicasting (optional)**—Allows a sender to transmit a single frame but have it delivered by the network to multiple recipients. Multicasting supports the efficient conveyance of routing protocol messages and address resolution procedures that typically must be sent to many destinations simultaneously. DLCIs 1019 through 1022 are reserved for this function.

- **Global addressing (optional)**—Gives connection identifiers global rather than local significance, which allows them to identify a specific interface to the Frame Relay network. Global addressing makes the Frame Relay network resemble a LAN in terms of addressing; ARPs, therefore, perform over Frame Relay exactly as they do over a LAN.

- **Simple flow control (optional)** — Provides for an XON/XOFF flow control mechanism that applies to the entire Frame Relay interface. It is intended for devices whose higher layers cannot use the congestion notification bits and that need some level of flow control.

Recommendation Q.933 Annex A states that status and status enquiry message types can be sent using the dummy call reference, as defined in Q.931, to allow communication of PVC status. It also defines the various timers that each device uses to implement periodic polling. These messages can be sent as a form of keep-alive or to actually request the status of any or all PVCs on the port. This arrangement prevents the tendency to transmit blindly to PVCs that no longer exist.

The mechanism to accomplish this user-to-network status check was originally designed by the FRF and referred to as LMI. Since this original definition, the concept of an optional signaling mechanism to report on link and PVC status has been adopted by the ITU-T and ANSI. LMI is now the generic term that refers to each of these three agencies' separate specifications. Each of the three implementations uses a dedicated PVC, with a reserved DLCI, to transmit signaling frames. As mentioned much earlier in the chapter, this logical-only separation of signaling traffic from user traffic is reminiscent of ISDN technology, which, as you might recall, uses a separate multiplexed D channel (which is sometimes on a completely separate physical circuit, in the case of Primary Rate Interfaces (PRIs)) to transmit signaling information out-of-band from the user traffic on the B channels. Table 9-2 lists the agencies and their associated DLCIs for signaling on the UNI.

Table 9-2   *Reserved DLCIs for LMI*

Protocol	DLCI	Specification
LMI (also known as **cisco**)	1023	FRF.1.1
Annex D	0	ANSI T1.617 Annex D
Annex A	0	ITU-T Q.933 Annex A

In order of vendor support, LMI leads Annex D, with Annex A not enjoying as much vendor participation. Nevertheless, the FRF.1.1 IA calls for adherence to the mandatory procedures of Q.933 Annex A. The tenets of Q.922 are highly regarded in this IA. Whether the market responds to this support remains to be seen. Both ANSI's Annex D and ITU-T's Q.933 Annex A specify a bi-directional symmetry, which makes them acceptable for NNI — an interface between switches of different service providers — with each pair of devices behaving both as data circuit-terminating equipment (DCE) and data terminal equipment (DTE) for one another. Earlier specifications were suited only for UNI implementation, because they provided that only the subscriber equipment issues a status enquiry, and only the service provider's equipment issues a status message. Regardless of the choice, the devices at both ends must be configured to use the exact same specification or signaling cannot occur.

Automatic detection of LMI type is an option on many DTE offerings. When connecting DTE to a service provider's switch, this might not be a problem, but care should be taken to manually set LMI types in a private Frame Relay installation, especially when the same type of equipment is both the switch and DTE. The result of automatic detection of LMI type by all equipment can be unpredictable. Figure 9-9 shows the customary exchange over the UNI.

Figure 9-9 *UNI Status Reporting*

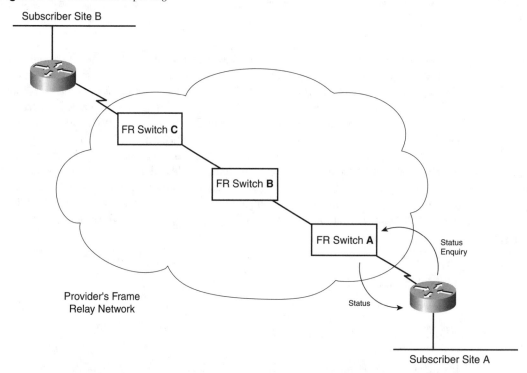

The LMI frame is different from the standard Frame Relay data frame. The LMI frame format is shown in Figure 9-10.

Figure 9-10 *LMI Frame Format*

Field Length, in Bytes :

1	2	1	1	1	1	Variable	2	1
Flag	LMI DLCI	Unnumbered Information Indicator	Protocol Discriminator	Call Reference	Message Type	Information Elements	FCS	Flag

The LMI DLCI is either 0 or 1023, depending on the LMI type. The unnumbered information (UI) indicator is based on the format of the X.25 Link Access Procedure, Balanced (LAPB) UI indicator. The poll/final bit is set to 0 here. The protocol discriminator always indicates LMI. Call reference is always set to all 0s. The message type field indicates whether the LMI frame is a status enquiry or a status message. These are the only two types defined. An information element (IE) consists of a one-octet identifier, a length field, and one or more bytes of actual data. There can be multiple IEs in the LMI frame.

Call Control

In the case of SVCs, the VC is established only when the demand presents itself. As soon as the need for the VC subsides, the circuit is cleared. The very nature of SVCs mandates that the subscriber be allowed to place a call to establish a transient VC for the duration of the demand. ITU-T Q.933 and ANSI T1.617 are the pertinent specifications that describe the mechanism for establishing SVCs. Add to these specifications the FRF's FR.4 IA and you round out the collection of specifications that are designed to allow an end device to contact another end device through the network devices in between and, pending an agreement to communicate, to trigger the allocation of network resources that are provisioned automatically and on the fly, without human intervention in the network.

It is important to distinguish between this type of higher-layer signaling and the signaling presented in the previous paragraphs. Although status signaling includes information about the health of the circuit, call-control signaling includes information about the call, such as measuring data sent, acceptance by the called party, addresses, and bandwidth parameters.

Frame Relay Configuration on Cisco Devices

Now that you have learned the Frame Relay basics, this section details how to configure Cisco devices for use with a Frame Relay network. As a quick review, it is essential to know what kind of circuit you are using for the Frame Relay connection. Many Cisco devices that have channel service unit/data service unit (CSU/DSU) functionality already have Frame Relay capability built into the IOS. Verify that your IOS supports what you need in Frame Relay.

It is also important to know what your CIR and LMI are for your Frame Relay connection(s). If you are setting up multiple sites, you need to have this information available for each site. You also need to have the DLCIs for each site so that you can set up the proper PVCs between sites. After you have all that information, you are ready to begin.

The Frame Relay design you are working with is rather simple, but it gives you an idea of what types of things to configure and look out for. Figure 9-11 shows the Frame Relay network that you are configuring in this example. This is a public Frame Relay configuration.

Figure 9-11 *Example Frame Relay Network for Configuration*

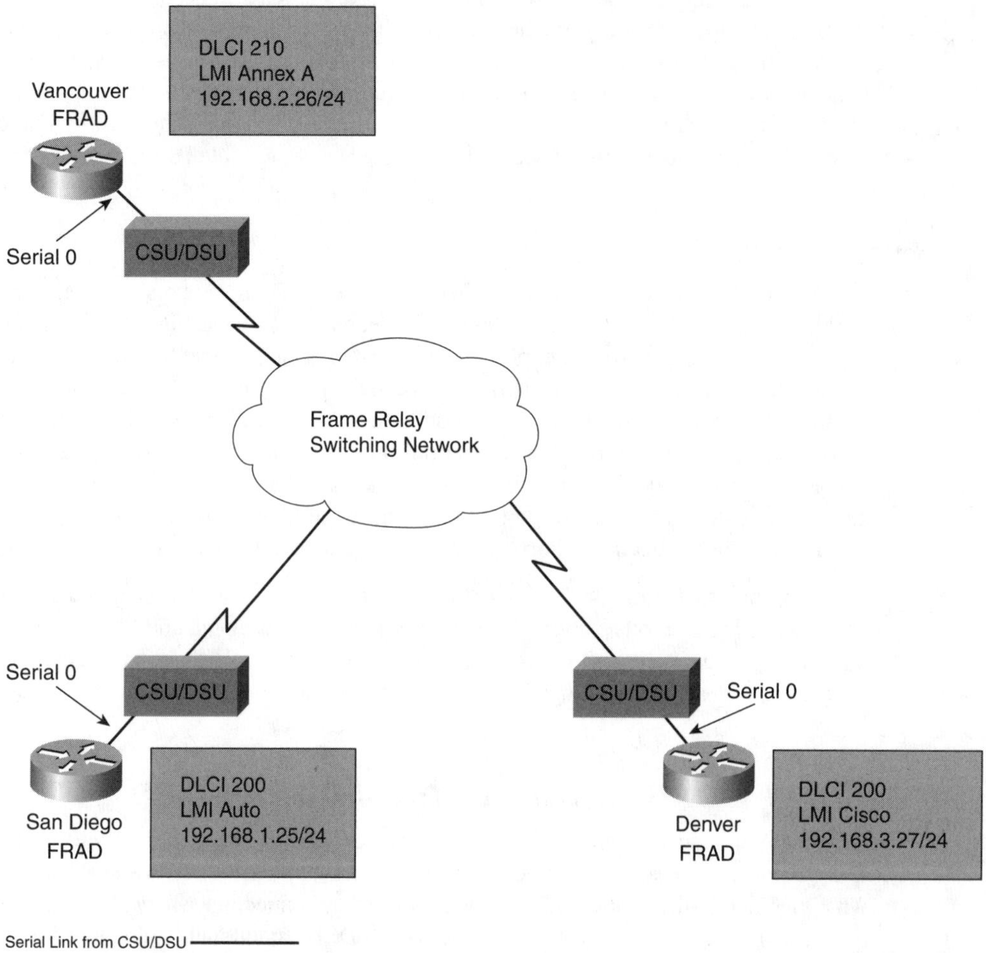

Three different locations exist within the Frame Relay network topology in Figure 9-11. All three locations need to be configured to communicate with the Frame Relay switching fabric but do not need to be configured to communicate with all the other devices. Because this is a public configuration, it is up to the service provider's Frame Relay switches to determine the paths between nodes.

Example 9-1 shows the Vancouver FRAD configuration.

Example 9-1 *Vancouver FRAD*

```
Vancouver>enable
Vancouver#configure terminal
Vancouver(config)#interface serial 0
Vancouver(config-if)#ip address 192.168.2.26 255.255.255.0
Vancouver(config-if)#encapsulation frame-relay ietf
Vancouver(config-if)#frame-relay interface-dlci 210
Vancouver(config-if)#frame-relay lmi-type q933a
Vancouver(config-if)#no shutdown
```

The FRAD located in Vancouver is configured with an IP address of 192.168.2.26 with a 24-bit mask. The Frame Relay encapsulation type is set to **ietf**. You can leave it at the default of **cisco** if you are certain that you are communicating only with Cisco devices. If you are unsure or you know that you are communicating with other vendor equipment, it is required that you use **ietf**. The DLCI is set for 210 and the LMI type has been explicitly set up for Annex A operation (**q933a**). The frame type of **ietf** specifies the format of the header of each Frame Relay frame and is not related to the signaling between the customer premises equipment (CPE) and the ingress switch. This is the job of the **lmi-type** command (**q933a**).

Example 9-2 shows the San Diego FRAD configuration.

Example 9-2 *San Diego FRAD*

```
SD>enable
SD#configure terminal
SD(config)#interface serial 0
SD(config-if)#ip address 192.168.1.25 255.255.255.0
SD(config-if)#encapsulation frame-relay ietf
SD(config-if)#frame-relay interface-dlci 200
SD(config-if)#no shutdown
```

The FRAD located in San Diego has been configured with an IP address of 192.168.1.25 with a 24-bit mask. Again, the Frame Relay encapsulation type has been set to **ietf**. The DLCI has been configured for 200. No LMI type is set because auto LMI was specified in the topology. Auto LMI is the default configuration. It detects the LMI type if LMI is not explicitly set.

Example 9-3 shows the Denver FRAD configuration.

Example 9-3 *Denver FRAD*

```
Denver>enable
Denver#configure terminal
Denver(config)#interface serial 0
Denver(config-if)#ip address 192.168.3.27 255.255.255.0
Denver(config-if)#encapsulation frame-relay ietf
Denver(config-if)#frame-relay interface-dlci 200
Denver(config-if)#frame-relay lmi-type cisco
Denver(config-if)#no shutdown
```

The FRAD located in Denver has been configured with an IP address of 192.168.3.27 with a 24-bit mask. The encapsulation type has been set as **ietf**, and the DLCI has been configured for 200. Remember, DLCIs are only locally significant and can be the same value at multiple locations. After the traffic leaves the FRAD and gets to the Frame Relay switch, the DLCI can change on the next hop. Also remember that after the Frame Relay switch, the network can convert into a completely different technology such as ATM. The LMI type has been set to **cisco** on the Denver FRAD, which means that you are using the original Gang of Four LMI type.

These configuration examples show three endpoints that are not related to one another. This separation is evidenced by the fact that each serial interface is in a different IP subnet. Although DLCIs are locally significant between directly connected interfaces and do not need to be numerically equivalent, those DLCIs that face each other on an end-to-end basis must be in the same subnet.

Furthermore, one of these sites can be made into a hub and logically connect, through IP routing, the remaining two sites (referred to as the spokes of the hub). As such, the hub location can be configured with sub-interfaces of the same physical serial interface. A sub-interface is characterized by multiple streams of data. Each stream is destined for a different endpoint, and all of them are multiplexed into a single stream that emanates from the same physical interface.

In the case of a hub-and-spoke arrangement, the sub-interfaces of the same physical interface need to be placed in separate IP subnets, with each subnet matching that of the remote Frame Relay interface to which it is virtually connected. The primary serial interface has its IP address removed, as all of the IP activity occurs on the sub-interfaces. On the remote devices at the end of the hub's spokes, the VCs related to those of the sub-interfaces on the hub can be established on the primary serial interfaces of the spoke routers. In other words, a sub-interface can, but is not required to, face another sub-interface.

This example is not necessarily how every service provider sets up their network, and there is no guarantee that you will use the same service provider throughout your network topology. Nevertheless, this example should give you a good understanding of some of the basic configuration steps required for Frame Relay.

Summary

This chapter began with a brief history of Frame Relay, which included the details of its development, and an introduction to the standards bodies that played the largest roles in its development. The specifications that govern the implementation of Frame Relay and ensure a large measure of interoperability were then presented in the structure of the following four categories of the protocol:

- Framework
- Service description
- Core aspects
- Access signaling

A listing of the current FRF IAs finished the section on specifications. The next section presented a detailed description of the overall functionality of Frame Relay as a packet-switching service. The following main topics were treated in some detail:

- VCs (PVCs and SVCs)
- DLCIs
- Inverse ARP
- EA, C/R, and D/C bits
- Contractual values
- Frame discards and recovery
- Signaling

These points expanded to include in-depth discussions of the Frame Relay header and the use of special fields within the header, including how some of these fields relate to the optional feature of network congestion control.

The signaling portion of this section was further expanded to include details on the following points:

- Signaling bits for congestion
- Connection status
- Call control (SVCs)

Finally, you were shown a sample configuration for a public Frame Relay implementation.

Review Questions

1 On what technology is Frame Relay largely based?

_____

_____

_____

2 Which of the following companies was not a part of the original Gang of Four?

a Cisco Systems

b Digital Equipment Corporation

c Nortel Networks

d IBM

e StrataCom

3 What is the CIR used for on Frame Relay circuits?

_____

_____

_____

4 What type of circuit is Frame Relay?

_____

_____

_____

5 What is the main difference between a PVC and an SVC?

_____

_____

_____

6 What are the three bits in the Frame Relay header that manage congestion control?

_____

_____

_____

7 What do you use LMI for and what are the three standards in use today?

_____

_____

_____

8 What do you call the numerical value that identifies the virtual circuit between two devices? What is the term that refers to this number, which means it only makes sense between two devices?

_____

_____

_____

9 What is the purpose of Inverse ARP?

_____

_____

_____

10 What does the Frame Relay Forum call its documents that are similar to standards?

_____

_____

_____

This chapter covers the following topics:

- **The development of Asynchronous Transfer Mode (ATM) and Broadband ISDN (B-ISDN)** — A summary of the relationship between these two technologies and the relationship among ATM and competing standards. The prospect of ATM as a future choice for packet switching is also presented. This section also introduces the standards bodies that play roles of varying importance in the development and acceptance of ATM.

- **ATM functionality** — A brief discourse into the workings of ATM, including the reference points where ATM devices meet throughout the network.

- **ATM header components** — A detail of the fields within the ATM header, with regard to purpose and functionality.

- **The B-ISDN reference model and ATM** — A presentation of the standard model for ATM-protocol interfacing. Concentrates on the purpose of each layer and their interdependencies with neighboring layers.

- **Quality of service (QoS)** — An in-depth study of the parameters, both negotiated and non-negotiated, behind the expectations of both the ATM subscriber and the service provider.

- **Traffic parameters** — A detail of the descriptors used in ATM to characterize traffic entering the network. Introduces terms that are essential to defining service classes.

- **ATM service classes** — A deep look into the classes of service found in ATM networks, in preparation for the discussion of the mechanisms that cater to the varying classes of source traffic that must be adapted to ATM standards.

- **Traffic management** — A discussion of the practices of traffic shaping and policing and the algorithms that ATM nodes use to determine if traffic is conforming to contractual agreements.

- **ATM adaptation layer (AAL) types** — A survey of the standard procedures that convert various forms of source traffic into a single type of ATM data structure: the cell.

CHAPTER 10

ATM and B-ISDN

ATM is a cell-switching (actually packet-switching, such as X.25 and Frame Relay) technology that quickly switches fixed-length frames through a network infrastructure that is finely tuned to QoS parameters. ATM allows every manner of digitized traffic to be transmitted with attention to priority, based on delay sensitivity and other special requirements. ATM can be thought of as a more refined version of Frame Relay. Frame Relay allows frames, with almost any length up to 1600 octets, and ATM fixes each cell to 53 octets, which includes a standard 5-octet header.

ATM has its roots firmly planted in the technology known as B-ISDN. The term *broadband* is widely held to mean exceeding T1 rates. This implies everything in the ISDN arena with capacity greater than the Primary Rate Interface (PRI). The International Telecommunication Union Telecommunication Standardization Sector (ITU-T) has written more specifications than space permits on B-ISDN, some specifying aspects of ATM right in the title, but the reader is encouraged to investigate the various topics specified in these recommendations. Just as in the case of the Frame Relay Forum (FRF), there is also an ATM Forum (AF), which functions in much the same way. In other words, although the AF does not produce specifications, per se, it does produce Implementation Agreements (IAs) that carry a great deal of influence with the standards bodies.

Considering the depth of the entire collection of ATM topics, this chapter serves to scratch the surface on most of what is presented and dig deeper on key themes. Entire works more voluminous than this and courses spanning weeks could be and have been created to provide mastery over just a subset of this technology. This chapter begins with an historical overview of ATM and the specifications that contribute to the technology. It then presents the main functionality of ATM, including popular and instrumental facets of ATM network design.

The Development of ATM and B-ISDN

The initial spawning of the basic groundwork for ATM was truly an international effort, featuring unlikely, yet welcome, collaborations and political compromises. For example, pundits often wax technical over issues such as, "From where did we get the 48-octet payload for which ATM is known?" In reality, North America and Japan were leaning toward a fixed 64-octet payload, whereas the rest of the world fancied a 32-octet version. Well, when you average the two, 48 octets just sort of falls out of the equation. That was about the extent of the technical nature behind the 48-octet choice. At least everyone agreed to a fixed-length cell. The rationale behind this decision is rather simple—if you can count on the size of each data unit and if you can count on the access rates for all subscribers (at least the committed maximum), you can predict delays and round-trip delivery times with an amazing level of accuracy. This is crucial if you are going to develop a technology that can provide guarantees and QoS promises that can be kept—for even the most high-speed, delay-sensitive traffic, such as uncompressed video.

This single point, practically by itself, sets ATM out in front of competing packet-switching technologies. In fact, ATM has been positioned as a full-service LAN/WAN protocol that is capable of performing better than existing protocol suites that have the current market share. Of course, quality isn't everything. Just try replacing a technology such as TCP/IP with a better one. The world's vendors, programmers, customers (practically everyone) will laugh at the prospect of retooling the world's hardware and software implementations, including applications, to replace what we already have. ATM is not without its faults, however. Even the most efficient cell production mechanism (see the "AAL5" section later in this chapter) is guaranteed to rob five of every 53 octets for overhead. That's well on its way to being 10 percent overhead, and that's the best case! It only gets worse for the other adaptation types. Luckily with ATM, you can throw all the bandwidth you need at this problem. Many agree that the benefits of ATM far outweigh its penalties. Today, technologies such as Packet over Synchronous Optical Network (SONET) are emerging as standards that might usher ATM out in the coming years. Because data communications technology becomes increasingly more capable, as time goes on, of handling more complex processes entirely in hardware, it is no longer so impressive to implement ATM to perform its predictable method of switching entirely in hardware.

The result of having a more capable standard in existence, alongside more popular ones, is that interworking (a term coined to mean the interfacing of disparate WAN technologies, similar to the use of translational gateways for simple protocol conversion) and encapsulation techniques become common. Frame Relay-to-ATM interworking and multiprotocol over ATM (MPOA) are two such technologies that are beyond the scope of this book.

Although B-ISDN and ATM sound like different technologies, ATM is completely based on the concept of B-ISDN. Nevertheless, the progeny has outshined the parent, in this case. All attention, most notably from the AF, seems to be leaning toward ATM as a separately developing technology. With that, let's take a closer look at the organizations that are responsible for the success of these standards.

Standards Bodies and the ATM Forum

The standards bodies that have the greatest influence over how ATM is accepted and implemented throughout the world and that ensure multivendor interoperability are as follows:

- ITU-T (well over 100 specifications)
- American National Standards Institute (ANSI) T1S1 Committee (more than 20 specifications)
- Internet Engineering Task Force (IETF) (more than 40 specifications)

Even the FRF has about four IAs that treat ATM, especially its interworking with Frame Relay. The largest body of work seems to have come from the AF and its almost 200 IAs, which govern the private use of ATM technology. Much of the latest public-network recommendations that make their way into international specifications owe their existence to the AF. Just to give you an appreciation for the sheer magnitude of ITU-T coverage, both in breadth and volume, for ATM and B-ISDN, specifications appear in the following series:

- **E-series**—Overall network operation, telephone service, service operation and human factors
- **F-series**—Non-telephone telecommunication services
- **G-series**—Transmission systems and media, digital systems and networks
- **H-series**—Audiovisual and multimedia systems
- **I-series**—Integrated services digital network
- **J-Series**—Transmission of television, sound programme and other multimedia signals
- **M-series**—Maintenance: transmission systems, telephone circuits, telegraphy, facsimile, leased circuits
- **Q-series**—Switching and signalling
- **Y-series**—Global information infrastructure and internet protocol aspects

---

NOTE   The preceding series definitions are exactly as they appear at www.itu.int/rec/ recommendation.asp.

Specific recommendations and implementation agreements are cited throughout this chapter, as the topics to which they pertain are presented.

To reiterate, the ITU-T originally developed ATM to answer a need for a technology that would handle the public high-speed transfer of voice, video, and data on behalf of B-ISDN. What wound up happening was that the ITU-T and the market saw other directions for this technology that had the same basic goals in mind but that could also be used for LAN applications and private implementations. The market, in 1991, was comprised of four intrigued vendors that formed a consortium, now known as the ATM Forum. The four corporations were Cisco Systems, Sprint Corporation, Northern Telecom (Nortel Networks), and NET/ADAPTIVE.

Today, however, similar to the FRF, the AF is comprised of many hundreds of corporations. End users are even allowed to join. ATM, similar to Frame Relay, is not an access circuit itself, but rather a protocol that describes the relaying of fixed-size frames, called cells, across physical access links. Besides other recommendations, the AF, in its User-Network Interface (UNI) IAs, specifies the physical links for which ATM is standardized. Some of the more common links follow:

- Digital signal level 1 (DS-1), DS-3

- E1, E3, E4

- SONET/Synchronous Digital Hierarchy (SDH) Synchronous Transport Signal 1 (STS-1), STS-3c/ Synchronous Transport Module 1 (STM-1), STS-12c/STM-4 (most common)

- Fiber Distributed Data Interface (FDDI) 4B/5B

- Fiber channel 8B/10B (private UNI, STS-3 speed)

- Plesiochronous digital hierarchy (PDH) bit rates 6.312 and 97.728 Mbps (Japan)

ATM Functionality

This section details the technical foundation for ATM. In subsequent sections, you will see the five-octet header formats used with ATM. You will then see ATM as a layered model, much as any other layered approach to comprehending a protocol by classifying and ordering its core components, after which you will be presented with a discussion on topics that deal with how user information is adapted for cell production and how different traffic is classified for QoS treatment.

Generally speaking, ATM differs from STM, in that STM technologies, such as T1, have dedicated timeslots for each transmission source. In the case of T1, channel 3, for example, always contributes a byte to a frame immediately after channel 2 does so. Channel 1 always comes right after channel 24, and so on. A source's turn to transmit is synchronized with every other source. A product of STM is the concept of multiple sources supplying traffic to help build a frame. With ATM, no frame is built. What's more, each source has no synchronized timeslot. The capability for bursting beyond expectation is present in ATM, just as it was in Frame Relay. A minor overlap exists between the STM/ATM discussion and that of time-division multiplexing (TDM)/statistical TDM (STDM). Recall that in STDM switching equipment can borrow from underused channels to satisfy bursting data flows from other sources, but timeslots still exist. The discussions overlap only slightly. None of these terms are interchangeable. Figure 10-1 shows a standard ATM network, which introduces key ATM terms that appear throughout the chapter.

Figure 10-1   *Sample ATM Network*

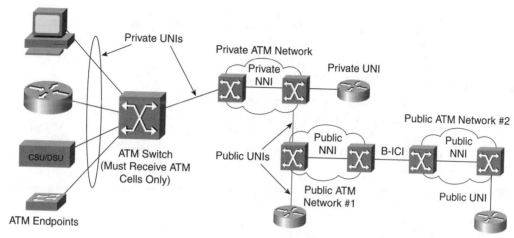

An ATM network consists of a set of ATM switches that are interconnected by point-to-point links. ATM switches support three primary types of interfaces: the aforementioned UNI, the Network-to-Network Interface (NNI), and the Broadband Inter-Carrier Interface (B-ICI). The UNI connects ATM endpoints (such as hosts, routers, and LAN switches) to an ATM switch. The NNI connects two ATM switches within the same organization.

Depending on whether the switch is owned and located at the customer's premises or is publicly owned and operated by a service provider, UNI and NNI can be classified further as private or public, respectively. A private UNI is the reference point between an ATM endpoint and a private ATM switch. Its public counterpart lies between an ATM endpoint or private switch and a public switch. Don't let this one catch you. (An NNI is a reference point only between switches in the same organization, and a B-ICI does not involve a private organization, leaving UNI to describe the interface between a private switch and its ingress/egress public switch). A Private NNI (PNNI) describes the reference point between two ATM switches within the same private organization. A public one describes the reference point between two ATM switches within the same public organization. The B-ICI lies between two public switches from different service providers (public organizations).

The standards for signaling across these interfaces are delineated by the same criteria as the reference points just presented, although there is not a great difference between the basis for UNI and NNI. In fact, the NNI specifications are largely compliant with the corresponding UNI specifications. The specification for private UNI is AF UNI 3.x/4.0. AF PNNI (P-NNI) 1.0 covers PNNI. The ITU-T writes the specifications for the public versions. Q.2931 (for point-to-point—Q.2971 for point-to-multipoint) and Q.2764 specify public UNI and NNI signaling, respectively, and the I.4XX series specifies the physical-layer characteristics of the UNI, including header format and header error control (HEC) creation. The AF, uncharacteristically for a public specification, keeps the B-ICI 2.0

implementation agreement. However, the IA states that it is basically the ITU-T NNI specification, with added layers above the ATM layer, such as AAL and other inter-carrier service-specific layers, that the NNI does not have (NNI stops at the ATM layer).

ATM Header Components

It is imperative to understand the functions of the fields in the ATM header to fully understand how ATM operates. Figure 10-2 shows formats of the headers for the UNI and NNI interfaces explained earlier in the ATM Functionality section. It is not uncommon to see the UNI specification used throughout a virtual circuit, but the NNI format is never seen between an endpoint and switch. The entire list of fields in both headers follows:

- Generic flow control (GFC) (4 bits on UNI/absent on NNI)
- Virtual path identifier (VPI) (8 bits on UNI/12 bits on NNI)
- Virtual channel identifier (VCI) (16 bits)
- Payload type identifier (PTI) (3 bits)
- Cell loss priority (CLP) (1 bit)
- HEC (8 bits)

The following six sections detail the purpose of these fields.

Figure 10-2 *ATM UNI and NNI Header Formats*

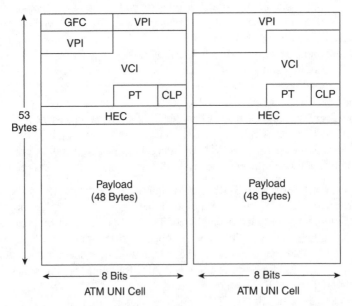

GFC

GFC exists only in the UNI header format. The next field, the VPI, suffers the loss of four bits by the presence of the GFC field. Its function is not widely supported and ranges from a flow-control mechanism, as its name implies, to a discriminator between multiple endpoints on the interface (reminiscent of the terminal endpoint identifier [TEI], which is assigned manually or by the switch in ISDN), to a priority indicator for traffic on that interface. Generally, the GFC is set to four binary 0s but can be used in proprietary implementations, which usually means that equipment on each end of the link must agree to its use (and probably be of the same brand). If a non-zero value is sent out, that value is echoed by a participant and set to all 0s in returning cells for a non-participant.

VPI

The VPI is one of two parts of the data structure that functions in much the same manner as Frame Relay's data-link connection identifier (DLCI) that you learned about in Chapter 9, "Frame Relay." Together with the VCI, the VPI creates a locally significant pair of values that are taken as a unit within a particular cell. Just as with a DLCI, the VPI/VCI pair is a logical representation of the entire virtual circuit (VC), sort of a way to point all the way to the opposing endpoint.

The VPI is larger in the NNI header format, because of the absence of the GFC field. This was originally omitted because developers of the standards imagined that a greater number of virtual paths (VPs) might be necessary in the network, as opposed to in the local subscriber loop. Regardless of whether the NNI format is used within the network, the ingress switch always terminates the UNI and, as a result, sets the GFC field to all 0s. This makes the GFC a locally significant tool, if it is used at all. Doing the math, the UNI segment of an ATM network can reference $2^8 = 256$ unique VPs, and the NNI interface can make reference to $2^{12} = 4096$ unique paths. This increase, although only 16-fold, multiplies through the possible VCI values that are discussed next.

VCI

The VCI makes up the second of two parts of the locally significant identifier pair that was explained in the previous section, VPI. Figure 10-3 shows a graphical representation of virtual path and virtual channel connections (VPCs and VCCs). VPC and VCC describe possibly multiple VPIs and VCIs, respectively, along the path from endpoint to endpoint.

Figure 10-3   *VPC and VCC*

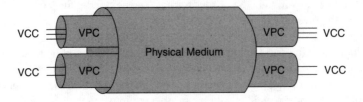

VPC = Virtual Path Connection (Identified by VPCI or Multiple VPIs)
VCC = Virtual Channel Connection (Identified by VCCI or Multiple VCIs)

Theoretically, each interface between endpoint and switch or between switch and switch can reference $2^{16} = 65,536$ possible virtual connections per VP. When this is distributed through the possible VPs, as presented in the VPI section, a grand total of 16,777,216 UNI and 268,435,456 NNI VCs can be created, theoretically. No VCI between 0 and 31, inclusive, should ever be used for user traffic, especially on VPI 0. Table 10-1 lists commonly observed special VCI values, which are based on recommendations in ITU-T I.361. The term *metasignaling* literally means information about signaling. This is a rarely used feature, as VCI 5 has proven to be adequate for signaling, even in large networks.

Table 10-1   *Reserved VCI Values*

VCI	Function
0	Idle (Unassigned) cells
1	Metasignaling (allows set up of signaling channels themselves)
2	General broadcast signaling (not used in practice)
3	VP segment Operation, Administration, and Maintenance (OAM)
4	VP end-to-end OAM
5	Signaling from an edge device to its ingress switch (UNI)
6	VP resource management (RM)
15	FORE's Simple Protocol for ATM Network Signaling (SPANS)
16	Interim Local Management Interface (ILMI) for link-parameter exchanges
17	LAN emulation (LANE)
18	PNNI for ATM routing in private networks

ATM switches are capable of switching cells from one physical port to another, according to how VCs are configured, regardless of the permanent or switched nature of the VC. If the switch terminates VPs and pays attention to both VPI and VCI values in each cell, it is said that the switch is performing virtual channel switching. In this situation, incoming VPIs and VCIs could be altered in the outgoing cell to match the expectation of the next-hop switch or endpoint. If, instead, the switch only pays attention to the VPI, it is said to be performing VP switching. Figure 10-4 shows a graphical representation of VP and virtual channel switching. In the case of VP switching, the complete set of virtual channels present in the incoming VP must switch in their entirety, without any VCI changes, to an outgoing VP, with no additions or omissions of VCIs during switching.

This explains what is occurring at switch C in Figure 10-4. This switch only pays attention to the physical port and VP on which the cell arrived. This switch's translation table does not even contain a field for the VCI. Although only VCI 100 is shown, every cell on every virtual channel with a VPI of 50 and coming in on physical port 8 retains the VCI in its cell header, even though the VPI is subject to change and does in this example. Another subtle point—the VPI did not change from the input to the output of switch B. This is perfectly fine, as the physical port number differentiates the two seemingly identical VPIs. In other words, VPI 50 on port 6 is a different entity from VPI 50 on port 3 on the same switch. In fact, in the same situation, the VCI also could have remained unchanged, at 300, on the output of switch B. What this really says is that the port/VPI/VCI triplet must be unique, but as long as it is, any two of the three values can be the same for input and output, and the triplet can still reference a completely different virtual link.

Although a subtle distinction, efficiency increases with VP switching over virtual channel switching because the switch neither examines nor changes the VCI, but rather keeps that part of the cell header the same, thus leaving the cell on the same virtual channel, even though VP identification can change. Another advantage is that the switch need only keep VPI information in its translation table, thus saving memory and expediting lookups. VP switching can be thought of as an entire VP crossconnection. As a practical example, end ATM switches can manage VCs, although these same VCs are transparently tunneled through the ATM backbone by using VP switching.

Figure 10-4 *VP and Virtual Channel Switching*

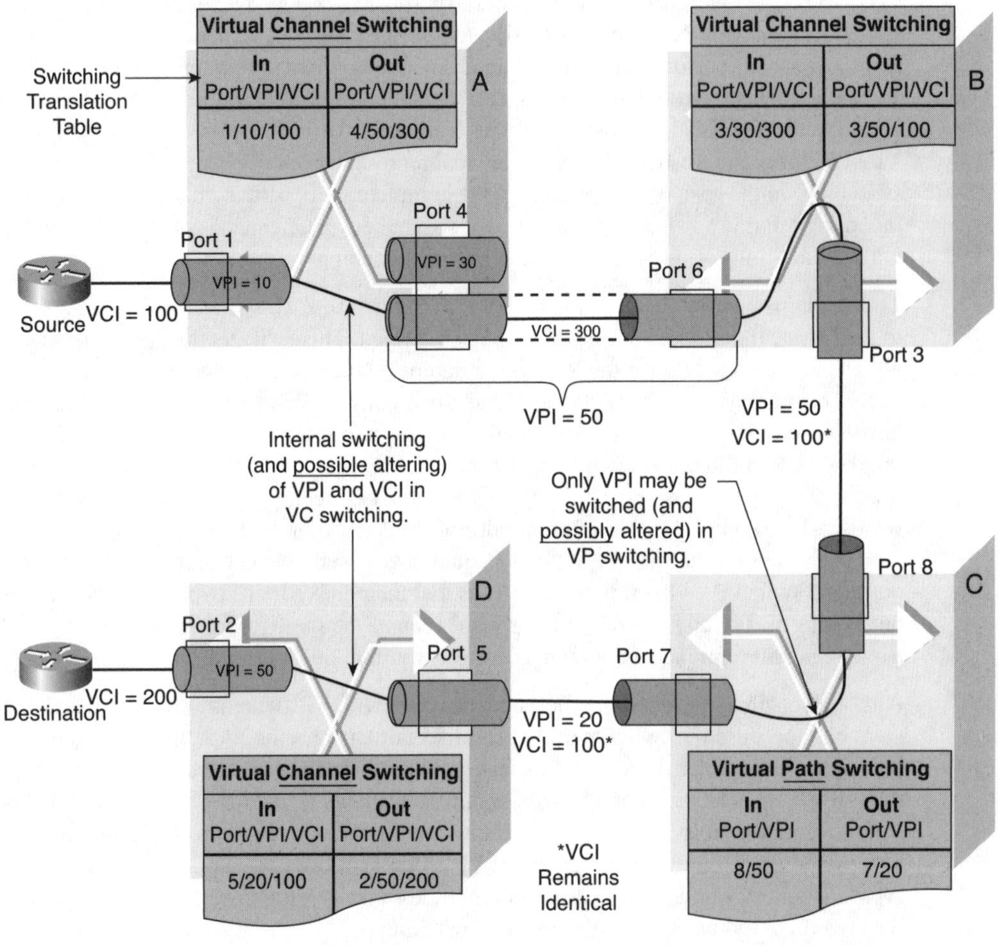

Payload Type (PT) and OAM Cells

The PT field is comprised of three bits that act as individual signals. This field can also be referred to as the PT identifier (PTI). Table 10-2 lists the basic aggregate meaning of the eight possible three-bit values.

Table 10-2 *PT Values*

PT	Meaning
000	User cell, no explicit forward congestion information (EFCI), AAL-indicate = false
001	User cell, no EFCI, AAL-indicate = true
010	User cell, EFCI, AAL-indicate = false
011	User cell, EFCI, AAL-indicate = true
100	OAM cell: Segment
101	OAM cell: End-to-end
110	RM-cell: Available bit rate (ABR) congestion control
111	Reserved for future use

In English, Table 10-2 says that if the most significant bit (MSB) is 0, the cell payload is user data (usually, but wait until the discussion of Table 10-3). If it's a 1, the cell either contains OAM or RM information. The middle bit signifies network congestion along the path from which it arrived (EFCI), but only if it is a user-data cell, not OAM (the MSB must be 0). Otherwise, it becomes an RM-cell (as long as the least significant bit [LSB] is a 0, because all 1s is reserved), which assists in dynamic rate adjustment for congestion avoidance on VCs configured with the ABR class of service (CoS). The final permutation is for the MSB to indicate user payload, and the LSB becomes an end-of-frame indicator for AAL5, which is explained shortly. Suffice it to say that for AAL5, user traffic has simply been chopped up into cells and sent on its way. You expect to see a 1 in the LSB, known as the AAL-indicate bit, if there is only one cell in the frame or if that cell is the last segment of the frame. A 0 in the LSB simply indicates to AAL5 that more cells are to come in the related frame. Other AAL types, or the ATM application itself, can apply their own uses to this bit.

For more information on OAM, consult ITU-T recommendation I.610. RM is discussed in more detail in the section, "ABR" later in this chapter. Figure 10-5 shows the OAM cell format and the values for the specific fields you will see within the payload of this type of cell.

Figure 10-5   *OAM Cell Format and Usage*

Cell Header	OAM Type	Function Type	Function-Specific Field	Reserved for Future Applications	Error Detection Code (CRC - 10)
5 Bytes	4 Bits	4 Bits	45 Bytes	6 Bits	10 Bits

OAM Cell Type	Value	Function Type	Meaning	Value
Fault Management	0001	AIS	Indicate Defects in Forward Direction	0000
		RDI	Indicate Defects in Backward Direction	0001
		Continuity Check	Continuous Monitoring of Connections	0100
		Cell Loopback	Check Connection/ Continuity Localize Errors Test Connections Before Putting into Service	1000
Performance Management	0010	Forward Monitoring	Online Quality Assessment	0000
		Backward Monitoring	Indicate Performance Assessment in the Backward Direction	0001
		Monitoring & Reporting		0010
Activation/ Deactivation	1000	Performance Monitoring	Activate and Deactivate Performance Monitoring and Continuity Check	0000
		Continuity Check		0001

The OAM cell type and function type fields are listed in the matrix in Figure 10-5. Together, these fields pinpoint the function of the OAM cell and dictate the function of the cell's payload, called the function-specific field. The error detection code field, as seen in the diagram, is a 10-bit cyclic redundancy check (CRC-10) just for the payload (the header has its own, in the HEC field, discussed shortly). As you can surmise, OAM cells allow the central configuration of performance management and the determination of connection quality. OAM cells use the same pathways as user data cells. It is through the PT field in the header that these cells are recognized as OAM cells. As Table 10-3 shows, with certain VCI values, the meaning of the PT field changes slightly.

Table 10-3 *VPI/VCI Effects on PT*

Meaning	VPI	VCI	PTI
Segment OAM F4 flow cell	Any VPI value	Decimal 3	0X0
End-to-end OAM F4 flow cell	Any VPI value	Decimal 4	0X0
VP RM-cell	Any VPI value	Decimal 6	110
Segment OAM F5 flow cell	Any VPI value	Any VCI value other than decimal 0, 3, 4, 6, and 7	100
End-to-end OAM flow cell	Any VPI value	Any VCI value other than decimal 0, 3, 4, 6, and 7	101
Virtual channel RM-cell	Any VPI value	Any VCI value other than decimal 0, 3, 4, 6, and 7	110
Reserved for future virtual channel functions	Any VPI value	Any VCI value other than decimal 0, 3, 4, 6, and 7	111

Some of these values should look familiar from Table 10-2, namely those with the MSB of PT set to 1. These are management (not necessarily OAM) cells, by definition. The new stuff should be the concept of having management cells with the MSB of PT set to 0, as in user data. The catch is that these cells ride on reserved VCIs: 3 and 4, regardless of what value VPI has. You should expect to see user data on VCIs with values no less than 32 (see ITU-T I.610). After a VCI value of 3 or 4 is observed, the receiving station understands the PT field is meaningless.

Regarding F4 and F5, there exist five network management levels: F1 through F5. As defined by I.610, F1 through F3 refer to OAM flows transferred through the network by the means of a dedicated channel, which is supported by specific octets of the transmission systems (for example, section overhead [SOH] and path overhead [POH] octets in SDH—see Chapter 14, "SONET and SDH"), for the physical layer (that is, not through the use of ATM cells). Specifically, F1 refers to flows on the regenerator section level; F2 refers to flows on the digital section level; and F3 refers to flows on the transmission path level, which extends between systems that assemble/disassemble the payload of the physical transmission system. These are the same systems that recognize cell boundaries and perform HEC verification (network switching devices, for example).

F4 and F5 are at the ATM layer and are transmitted by specific ATM cells that are referred to as OAM cells. F4 refers to VPCs, and F5 is for VCCs. The distinction between segment and end-to-end OAM flows is that end-to-end flows are terminated by the extreme endpoints of the VPC or VCC, which includes customer premises equipment (CPE). Segment flows only extend from one connection point to the next one in line for the VPC or VCC in question. The subtlety is that the endpoints can be involved in both flows, just not in communication with the same opposing device, assuming more than two connection points exist in the ATM network, which is likely because this is only two endpoints.

Therefore, as long as the VCI is 3 or 4, you can expect the cell to be an OAM cell for whichever VP is referenced by the VPI. RM exists at the VPC level and the VCC level. It might make sense to mention that Table 10-2 was strictly VCC in accuracy. As you can tell from Table 10-3, a VCI of 6 indicates RM at the VPC level. In this case, the PT is the same as for RM at the VCC level. Again, more on RM is coming up later in this chapter in the "ABR" section.

CLP

The CLP field serves the same function as the discard eligibility (DE) bit served in Frame Relay. If a network device determines that cell loss must occur to prevent a catastrophic event because of congestion, the cell with the CLP set to a value of 1 is targeted for deletion before those with a CLP of 0. The term tagging refers to the practice of setting the CLP bit to 1 to indicate cells that are more expendable than those with a CLP of 0. The AAL on the transmitting endpoint can perform the tagging function (known as pre-tagging), which is preferable because the endpoint should have the best idea about which cells are more important. Tagging can also be left to any and all switches in the network, based on contractual values that are discussed later. For now, this should remind you of Frame Relay's handling of the DE bit, based on the committed information rate (CIR). It is common to see ATM tagging performed by the ingress public switch on contractually excessive burst traffic. This is less desirable, but not as bad as in the case of Frame Relay. Although switches look only at ATM headers, and QoS evidence (in the form of AAL types) is carried in the payload of the cells, ATM permanent virtual circuits (PVCs) and switched virtual circuits (SVCs) are created with service classes associated with them, which means that any QoS information that is being implied by the payload of the cell can be mirrored on the VC, so that the ATM switches in the network can be aware of the more delay-sensitive cells.

HEC

The HEC field is a multipurpose data structure. It has the job of detecting and possibly correcting header bit errors and providing a landmark for cell-boundary detection and cell synchronization for those media that do not have their own synchronization methods. The following discussion presumes the use of HEC-based cell delineation and synchronization. Examples of media that do not use the HEC for these purposes are Fiber Distributed Data Interface (FDDI) and DS3 using physical layer convergence procedure (PLCP) framing. The HEC is a CRC that is computed in a similar fashion to the frame check sequence (FCS) of Frame Relay and just about every other checksum used in telecommunications and data networking. The HEC is only computed on the other four octets of the cell's header, not on any portion of the 48-octet payload. It is this massive coverage that allows the HEC to go so far as to correct single bit errors in the header. The HEC is computed in such a way as to ensure that a cell header containing all 0s (an empty cell) does not result in a HEC of all 0s. This feature aids in the synchronization process, which is discussed shortly.

Also, similar to other implementations of checksums and CRCs, the HEC is recomputed at each ATM device and compared to the installed value. Every ATM device knows the algorithm used for producing the HEC value (one good source for the algorithm begins on page 32 of the ATM Forum B-ICI 2.0 IA—af-bici-0013.003). Mismatches can be corrected (if supported and if only one bit is in error), or else the cell is discarded. Another reason each device must compute the HEC is that switches alter the VPI/VCI combination as standard operating procedure. Because these fields are part of the header, the HEC must change each time the VPI or VCI change. Each ATM device that follows the standard has two modes of operation for error control:

- Correction
- Detection

Most devices are capable of using the HEC field to detect multiple errors, but in general, only one is correctable. Normal operating mode finds the receiving device in the correction state. The device remains in the correction state indefinitely unless an error is found. If the header contains only one error, it is corrected. If more than one error is present, the cell is discarded. In any event, the presence of any number of errors places the device in the detection state. After it is in the detection state, the first error-free header places the receiver back in the correction state. Until that time, headers with errors result in the immediate discarding of each damaged cell, even if only one error exists. While in the detection state, no errors are corrected. This stems from the fact that cells with errors are rare enough that if one arrives, there is likely a problem that will continue to damage cells, and one or two fixable cells are not worth the effort if every cell requires scrutiny by an already busy device. Furthermore, in the case where a train of bit errors occurs, it is possible to mistake an uncorrectable series of errors as a single correctable error. Allowing such a mistake to result in a doomed attempt to correct the error compromises the validity of the bits, which would be falsely regarded as correct. Thus, remaining in the detection state ensures that the first good header, which likely heralds the end of the error train, will be the only thing that will result in a return to normal operation.

Figure 10-6 shows a graphical representation of how the synchronization process is carried out by using the HEC field. The three states through which a receiver passes are as follows:

- Hunt state
- Presync state
- Sync state

Figure 10-6   *The HEC Field and Synchronization*

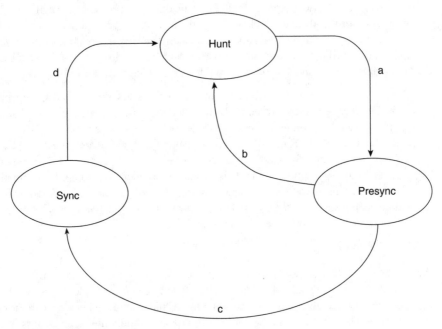

State Transitions

(a) First Detection of Cell Boundary
(b) One Incorrect HEC
(c) Delta (Consecutive) Correct HECs
(d) Alpha (Consecutive) Incorrect HECs

The receiving device (any ATM device, including endpoints and switches) attempts to locate the HEC of the cell header by checking the data stream, one bit at a time. The hunt state is characterized by shifting the bitstream, bit-by-bit, until a group of eight bits matches the computed CRC for the preceding four octets. The receiver enters the presync state after a single match is discovered. The reason for the presync state is that it is possible, although somewhat of a fluke, to have a match somewhere other than in the boundary of the ATM cell header. To prove that the header has been found, the data stream is now checked one cell's worth of bits at a time to see if delta consecutive HECs are correct. The standard suggests a value of 6 for delta. If just one incorrect HEC is computed during the presync state, the process returns to the hunt state.

The sync state is entered after the delta quantity of consecutively correct HECs has been observed in the presync state. If, at any time after entering the sync state, the receiver detects alpha consecutive incorrect HEC values, it again enters the hunt state, and the process continues as described here. The standard recommends that alpha be set to 7. The value of delta affects how susceptible the receiver is to incorrect synchronization, and the value of alpha affects how susceptible the receiver is to mistakenly entering the hunt state because of simple bit errors that cause HEC mismatches.

The B-ISDN Reference Model and ATM

Figure 10-7 shows the ATM/B-ISDN reference model. This model actually represents the functions of ATM that are inserted into the B-ISDN model, as presented in ITU-T recommendation I.121. The model is three dimensional in nature, as opposed to the two dimensions you might be used to with the Open System Interconnection (OSI) reference model. You might want to refer to Figure 10-7 as you read through the paragraphs in the remainder of this section.

Figure 10-7   *The ATM/B-ISDN Reference Model*

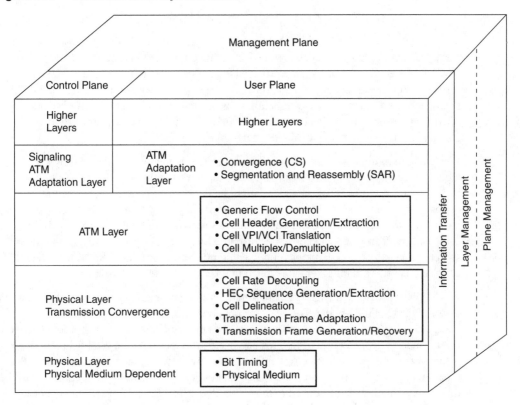

The model is also divided into three planes:

- User plane (U-plane)
- Control plane (C-plane)
- Management plane (M-plane)

The U-plane provides the transfer of user data. The U-plane contains all the standard ATM layers:

- Physical Layer
    - Physical medium dependent (PMD) sublayer
    - Transmission convergence (TC) sublayer
- ATM layer
- AAL
    - Segmentation and reassembly (SAR) sublayer
    - Convergence sublayer (CS)

The ATM layers and AALs are collectively roughly equivalent in function to Layer 2 of the OSI reference model. The C-plane provides the control functions necessary for switched services, such as call connection and release. The C-plane shares the physical and ATM layers with the U-plane because signaling cells must also conform to the rigid standards of ATM, as far as length and header/payload proportion are concerned, but the C-plane contains AAL functions that deal with signaling (SAAL).

It might help to think of the AAL in general terms. It is the layer that takes any sort of higher-layer traffic, including signaling, and adapts it for suitability to the ATM network, including any additional overhead that might be necessary to communicate with the opposite endpoint. The switching process performed by ATM switches in the network does not involve this layer because only endpoints or interworking boundaries reassemble ATM cells. Not requiring the switches to perform this function allows them to concentrate on switching, usually through application-specific integrated circuits (ASICs) that allow hardware-based switching, which is much quicker than software-based switching.

The M-plane provides the management functions and the capability to transfer information between the C- and U-plane. The M-plane contains two sections: layer management and plane management. Layer management performs management functions for and between layers, such as the detection of failures and protocol issues, and the establishment of QoS parameters and layer-specific OAM information flows. Plane management oversees the functionality of the entire system across all planes. The following three sections detail the functions of the layers introduced in the last bulleted list in this section. The higher layers generically refer to those protocols whose protocol data units (PDUs) act as input to the ATM adaptation process that is performed by the AAL. These are usually either Layer 3 protocols that use ATM as a Layer 2 transport directly, or Layer 2 protocols that are interworking with ATM, as an extension to their own functionality.

Physical Layer

The physical layer provides the same reference to functionality as the first layer of the OSI reference model. For example and in general, this layer specifies features such as connector types, pin configurations, voltage levels/optical properties, cable characteristics, encoding techniques, timing constraints, and so on. Specifically, the ATM/B-ISDN reference model highlights two main functions of this layer. The PMD sublayer is where the access line is maintained. PMD is responsible for providing a bitstream that is compatible with the physical circuit that ATM is running across (e.g., SONET/SDH, T3/E3, coupled with the physical medium/encoding scheme that is being used). The TC sublayer is responsible for four main functions:

- **HEC sequence generation and verification**—Similar to the Frame Relay FCS, which verifies data and establishes cell-boundary synchronization (for some media).

- **Cell delineation**—Allows devices to identify cells within a bitstream (based on HEC or PLCP, for example).

- **Cell-rate decoupling**—Maintains synchronization and inserts or suppresses (transmit or receive, respectively) idle (unassigned) ATM cells to adapt the rate of cell flow to the payload capacity of the transmission system.

- **Transmission frame adaptation**—Packages ATM cells into frames that are acceptable to the particular physical-layer implementation (e.g., SONET/SDH, T3/E3—also referred to as cell mapping).

Recall the discussion in the "ATM Functionality" section earlier in this chapter about ATM being an asynchronous technology. Timing alone cannot identify cell boundaries, nor can alignment bits be used across multiple cells, as in the case of superframing or multiframing. Because the HEC value is computed on a relatively small set of bits, it is possible, during initial cell-boundary detection, to quickly verify where in the cell the HEC is for multiple cells. Because the HEC appears in the same location in every cell, regardless of cell type, the entire cell boundary is resolved. This level of certainty, regarding cell boundary detection, obviates the need for STM-type alignment mechanisms and their additional associated overhead. However, it is possible to employ a synchronous physical layer that does use timing and pointers to establish cell boundaries. For example, PLCP framing on DS3 circuits might have alignment bits spread across the payload of multiple cells. See the "HEC" section earlier in this chapter for a more in-depth discussion of synchronization using this field.

A fifth TC sublayer function, presented in the AF UNI 3.1 IA, refers to ITU-T I.432 and the synchronizing scrambler polynomial for SONET/SDH links and DS3 links. If cell formats that were naturally difficult to synchronize on were allowed to repeat, synchronization might be severely delayed. By reversibly scrambling the bits within cells, quasi-random bit arrangement assures that such repeating anomalies are all but eliminated, along with their effects. This also prevents non-varying patterns that can affect the physical circuit itself (for example, 01010101... or 00000000...).

Cell-rate decoupling is performed at each interface, where cells from different sources come together and must be made to fill an entire access line. Idle cells (referred to in the standards as unassigned cells—VPI and VCI both equal 0) do not traverse the network; rather they are created each time it is discovered that legitimate outgoing cells are not plentiful enough to fill the access line. In fact, unassigned cells are treated the same way as invalid cells. The earlier HEC discussion details how invalid cells are handled. ATM source endpoints also add idle cells to satisfy access-line requirements. Finally, transmission frame adaptation goes one step beyond making sure there is enough traffic to satisfy access lines, by actually forming access line-based frames from the cells.

ATM Layer

On an outgoing basis, the ATM layer accepts already-segmented 48-octet data units from the pertinent AAL and places the five-octet headers on them. The process is reversed for incoming cells. As a result, VPI/VCI awareness is a function of the ATM layer. In fact, the ATM switch uses this layer's functionality to perform VPI/VCI translation, as the cell traverses the switching fabric. It is this layer that performs the switching (or cell relaying) within the network and that provides the final verification that an endpoint has received the correct cells (that the cells have not been misinserted). Cell multiplexing, or the simultaneous sharing of physical bandwidth for multiple VCs, is a property of the ATM layer.

AAL

The AAL is the layer that buffers the higher-layer protocols from the specifics of ATM. This layer accepts the specific user traffic from the higher layers and begins the conversion process (adaptation) of this information into 48-octet segments. It is the AAL that passes these 48-octet segments to the ATM layer for header attachment and further processing. Depending on the AAL type, this layer can attach additional overhead to each packet, further increasing the ratio of overhead to total cell size. The specific types of AAL are presented later in this chapter in the section "AAL Types."

The AAL is further divided into two sublayers, with one sublayer possibly being divided further. In order from low-level to high-level of the ATM/B-ISDN Reference Model presented in Figure 10-7, these sublayers and subdivisions are as follows:

- SAR sublayer
- Convergence sublayer (CS)
    - Common part convergence sublayer (CPCS)
    - Service specific convergence sublayer (SSCS)

The CS is responsible for directly interfacing with the higher layers. With this in mind, the general function of the CS is to transfer the data units from the ATM user interface to the

SAR and back. Specific functions of the CS can be derived from the characteristics of the SSCS and CPCS sublayers. Some applications do not use an SSCS, in which case the SSCS is considered null, and the CPCS comprises the entire CS. Although the CPCS is, as its name implies, common to all higher-layer entities (making it the true anchor of the CS and what the SAR sublayer always interfaces with from below), the SSCS takes on a variety of names that are based on the higher-layer entities with which it must interface.

For example, the Frame Relay SSCS (FR-SSCS) is used at the B-ISDN terminal equipment to emulate the Frame Relaying Bearer Service (FRBS) in B-ISDN. It is also used for interworking between an ATM and a Frame Relay network. ITU-T I.365.1 specifies the FR-SSCS. At precisely the same point in the reference model (the higher-level, service specific, subdivision of the CS), when it comes to signaling (as in establishing SVCs by using a special protocol to allow the endpoint to request, from its ingress switch, a connection to another endpoint), the SAAL (Q.2100, a form of AAL5) actually has two standards that perform the SSCS functionality. These are the service specific coordination function (SSCF) specification (ITU-T Q.2130 and Q.2140 for UNI and NNI, respectively), which performs the function you would expect from a basic SSCS; and the Service Specific Connection Oriented Protocol (SSCOP, Q.2110), which provides specific guarantees of cell delivery that ATM, on its own, does not deliver. The point to key on is that the CPCS will not come and go with the higher-layer protocols and applications. The SSCS, however, does just that.

Finally, at the base of the AAL lies the SAR. Compared to that of the CS, the SAR's job is simple. Accept all CS data units and divide them into 48-octet chunks to be handed down to the ATM layer, where the ATM headers are applied. Of course, nothing can be that simple in the world of data communications. Depending on the AAL type in use, the news ranges from not much worse than just described to bad enough to make you wonder why anyone would do such a thing. Rest assured, each AAL type has its place in the infrastructure, and as you will see, those that don't get combined. Nevertheless, one thing can be said about the SAR sublayer—it sends 48-octet PDUs, which are a protocol's output to an adjacent layer (including header and payload), to the ATM layer and it accepts these 48-octet PDUs from the ATM layer, with no exceptions. Ancillary to the user data stream, the SAR must communicate to the ATM layer if more SAR PDUs are to come for the same AAL5 frame (so that the ATM layer can set the PTI field appropriately) and if the ATM layer should set the CLP bit for the associated cell.

QoS

Before discussing the actual AAL types, it's important to understand some of the main characteristics of network traffic and traffic management that make different AAL types so appropriate. In this section, you are introduced to QoS parameters, which are pivotal in the definition of traffic contracts, besides being the basis for some of the derived traffic parameters discussed in the next section, "Traffic Parameters." In the section "ATM Service

Classes," QoS and traffic parameters define the ATM service classes that group these parameters into easy-to-discuss categories. These, along with the definitions of what constitutes cell conformance and what makes a connection compliant, go into the traffic contract for a connection, which is the agreement between subscriber and service provider that defines what the subscriber's obligations are, as far as traffic rates and bursts, for the service provider to guarantee QoS.

It is difficult to discuss QoS without being aware of the existence of connection admission control (CAC), which is a set of bandwidth-reservation mechanisms that serve to control congestion. CAC can determine whether to accept or reject an ATM connection, based on requested QoS parameters and network resources. If the network determines it cannot feasibly stand behind this impending contractual obligation and no alternative can be negotiated that does allow a comfortable margin of satisfying the caller's request, the call is rejected by the network. The more aggressive a CAC algorithm is, the more connections tend to be established. The term overbooking refers to CAC's aggressive assumption that full network resources are not called upon by all endpoints simultaneously, and full booking refers to the less aggressive approach, whereby after network resources appear to be fully allocated, whether currently in use or not, further network access is restricted. The CAC algorithm can fundamentally be thought of as a statistical multiplexing scheme. A summary of the key issues that go into the traffic contract entered into between the subscriber and the service provider follows:

- QoS requirements
- Traffic parameters and descriptors
- Service class
- Cell conformance definition
- Connection compliance definition

For more information on QoS parameters, and on the topics that comprise the preceding list and the upcoming Traffic Parameters and ATM Service Classes sections, consult the ATM Forum's Traffic Management Specification 4.1 (TMS 4.1—af-tm-0121.000) or ITU-T I.356 (QoS only). The primary QoS parameters that are negotiated for an ATM traffic contract follow:

- Dependability parameters
  - Cell loss ratio (CLR)
- Delay parameters
  - Maximum cell transfer delay (maxCTD)
  - Peak-to-peak CDV

Those that are not negotiated, but that are measurable and provide insight into the performance of the network and associated switches, include the following delay parameters:

- Cell error ratio (CER)
- Severely errored cell block ratio (SECBR)
- Cell misinsertion rate (CMR)

TMS 4.1 cautions that QoS parameters are not envisioned to offer instantaneous measurements of network commitment, but rather probabilistic performance over the life of the connection, which is not limited in duration. Also, the network agrees to meet or exceed the negotiated QoS, as long as the endpoint complies with the negotiated traffic contract. In other words, the service provider is released from any contractual obligation for the performance of the network that is compromised by traffic in excess of or out of the classification agreed to through subscriber contractual obligations. See the section "Peak Cell Rate" later in the chapter for a practical example.

Furthermore, the level of precision with which the QoS parameters can be coded (meaning they can get quite precise) should not be confused with a commitment that the network will perform at that level of precision. UNI and PNNI specifications and implementation agreements provide the mechanisms by which QoS parameters can be negotiated between end systems and the network devices in quantitative numeric units. Figure 10-8 shows the relationships between the various parameters that are presented in the following six sections.

Figure 10-8   *QoS Parameters and Equations*

$CTD = T_{MP_2} - T_{MP_1}$ (Elapsed Time from Measurement Point 1 to Measurement Point 2)

maxCTD: $(1-\alpha)$ Quantile of CTD

Peak-to-Peak CDV = maxCTD - CTD $_{fixed}$

$$CLR = \frac{\text{Lost Cells}}{\text{Total Transmitted Cells}}$$

$$FLR = \frac{\text{Lost Frames + Corrupted Frames}}{\text{Total Transmitted Frames}}$$

$$CER = \frac{\text{Errored Cells}}{\text{Successfully Transferred Cells + Errored Cells}}$$

$$SECBR = \frac{\text{Severely Errored Cell Blocks}}{\text{Total Transmitted Cell Blocks}}$$

$$CMR = \frac{\text{Misinserted Cells}}{\text{Time Interval}}$$

CLR

The CLR is defined as the ratio of lost cells to the total number of cells transmitted. For the computation of the CLR, the counts for lost cells and transmitted cells should not include those cells that were counted as members of severely errored cell blocks (to be discussed shortly). The CLR parameter is the value of CLR that the network agrees to offer as an objective over the lifetime of the connection, not an instantaneous or short-term measurement. It allows network devices to decide whether to accept or reject a connection, based on the CLR that is being requested for the new connection, as compared with the capabilities of the network device. This is called CLR signaling and is part of the UNI signaling specification.

For service classes, such as guaranteed frame rate (GFR), also discussed shortly, where the network guarantees made are based on groups of cells (frames), the CLR is not an effective measure of service performance. For this situation CLR is replaced by frame loss ratio (FLR), which is the ratio between the sum of lost and corrupted frames and total frames transmitted. Lost frames are those frames that have been dropped in their entirety, and corrupted frames are those frames that have had a partial set of their cells dropped. FLR, unlike CLR, is not a negotiated QoS parameter. In fact, CLR is not negotiated for the GFR service class, nor is it negotiated for the ABR service class, even though ABR is not based on frames. See the discussion on these service classes later in the chapter in the section "ATM Service Classes."

The following is a quote from the AF's TMS 4.1, which describes in-service measurement techniques for CLR:

The transmitter inserts OAM cells into a transmitted user information cell stream at suitable intervals. Each OAM cell contains a count of the number of user information cells transmitted since the last OAM cell. The receiver keeps a running count of the number of user information cells transmitted (Nt) and received (Nr). Cell loss ratio can then be calculated as (Nt - Nr) / Nt if Nt - Nr is positive. This method under-counts cell loss events if misinsertion occurs during the measurement period. It over counts loss if SECB events are not excluded.

maxCTD

To fully understand maxCTD, you first need to define cell transfer delay (CTD). CTD is the total elapsed time it takes a cell to leave one reference point in the network and arrive at another, which includes the cumulative transmission delay between ATM nodes and the total processing delay experienced between the two reference points. The choice of reference points is not fixed and can be anywhere along the VC but is commonly from one UNI to the other.

It is important to understand the concept of entry and exit events, as defined in ITU-T I.356. An entry event is described as the arrival of the last bit in the cell into an endpoint or network device from an adjacent one, across the measurement point. An exit event is defined as the transmission of the first bit of the cell from an endpoint or network device to another across a measurement point. Figure 10-9 shows a representation of entry and exit events, with regard to CTD. In the figure, MP stands for measurement point.

Figure 10-9   *CTD and Exit/Entry Events*

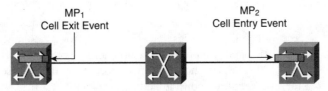

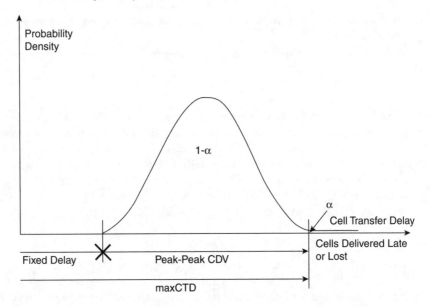

Therefore, CTD is defined as the total elapsed time from when the first bit of the cell leaves MP_1 until the same bit passes through (exits) MP_2 on its way into the associated switch. Both of these events are exit events. Figure 10-9 shows not two exit events, but rather an exit event and an entry event. An exit event need not occur during the exit from a device but is defined to occur during the exit of the first bit from an interface, even if it is actually entering a device.

Figure 10-10 gives a graphical representation of the following maxCTD definition. This definition and the associated diagram apply only to real-time service classes. This caveat, along with Figure 10-10, also applies to the definition of peak-to-peak CDV.

Figure 10-10   *CTD Probability Density Model*

The maxCTD measurement has a complex definition that places maxCTD at an implicitly negotiable point on a probability curve for CTD (represented by the upper boundary of

1-α, where α is based on the CLR negotiated at connection-request time, with 1-α being much larger than a, in practice). The probability density α represents the statistical likelihood that the network will lose cells or will deliver them late. It is the point that separates these probability densities that is negotiated for the contract and referred to as maxCTD. The term quantile represents the probability bounded by such a point as this. When there are 100 quantiles, they are called percentiles. In this case, the maxCTD value negotiated for a connection is considered the 1-α quantile for the CTD probability curve. This means the probability that the CTD will be higher than the maxCTD is no greater than α (where α, again, is based on the negotiated CLR).

Peak-to-Peak CDV

Peak-to-peak CDV represents the difference between the best (fixed CTD) and worst (maxCTD) cases for CTD. In Figure 10-10, fixed delay is the CTD that can be experienced by any delivered cell on the connection during the entire connection holding time. This fixed CTD value can be thought of as being indirectly negotiated because its value is subtracted from the directly negotiated maxCTD to provide the directly negotiated peak-to-peak CDV. As networks have a limited ability to control peak-to-peak CDV, subscribers should not expect to arbitrarily choose small values for this measurement during contract negotiation as a sole means of controlling delay variation.

NOTE   TMS 4.1 Appendix VII, section VII.1.4, discusses measurement methods for CTD and peak-to-peak CDV.

CER

The CER, along with the following two parameters, although not contractually negotiated, provides an indication of intrinsic network performance. Specifically, CER represents the ratio between the number of cells that are delivered with at least one error to the total number of cells delivered (both successfully and errored). The catch is not to count any component cells that were part of blocks that were severely errored, regardless of the disposition of the cells themselves (don't count them, whether good or bad). Such cells are collectively implicated by the following non-negotiated measurement.

NOTE   To measure the CER, Annex C of ITU-T recommendation I.356 describes an Out-of-Service (OOS) method that involves transferring a known data stream into the network at the source measurement point and comparing the received data stream with the known data stream at the destination measurement point. For a more desirable in-service measurement, Annex C of I.356 suggests a bit interleaved parity 16 (BIP-16) indicator to estimate the CER over a block of N cells.

SECBR

The SECBR is defined as the ratio of severely errored cell blocks to the total number of cell blocks transmitted. ITU-T I.610 states that the size of a cell block (N) can be 2^x cells, where $8 <= x <= 15$ and x is an integer. I.610 explains that the 45-octet function-specific field in the OAM cell, when the OAM type is activation/deactivation and the function type is performance monitoring (see Figure 10-5), contains two four-bit fields that express the block size, one field for each direction. I.610 gives the four-bit values that represent the possible block sizes defined earlier in this paragraph.

Whatever the number of cells that comprise a block, each of these cells is transmitted consecutively for a given connection. A severely errored cell block is one in which more than a configurable number (M) of cells are lost, misinserted, or errored. For measurement purposes, a cell block often corresponds to the number of user-data cells transmitted between OAM cells. As a result, you should attempt to coordinate the values of N and M with the frame size on connections for which frame discarding has been enabled (see the section GFR later in this chapter).

NOTE   The SECBR can be estimated in-service for a set of S consecutive or non-consecutive cell blocks by computing the number of lost or misinserted cells in each cell block, identifying cell blocks with more than M lost cell or misinserted cell outcomes as severely errored cell blocks. The total number of such severely errored cell blocks are then divided by S. Because this in-service measurement method does not include delivered errored cells in the estimation of M, it might tend to under count severely errored cell blocks to some degree. A more accurate estimate of SECBR can be obtained by comparing transmitted and received data in an OOS measurement.

CMR

The CMR is simply the number of misinserted cells over a given unit of time. Cell misinsertion most often arises from an error in a cell header that goes unnoticed, allowing a cell intended for one connection to be inserted onto another. By definition, a misinserted cell is one that is received for which there is no corresponding inserted cell. This measurement should not include those cells that comprise severely errored cell blocks. This measurement is a rate, rather than a ratio. The reason for this is that the number of misinserted cells on a particular connection generally has nothing to do with the other cells on that connection. The other measurements have worked well as ratios, because they are all focused solely on traffic in the confines of a particular connection.

NOTE	Annex C of ITU-T recommendation I.356 describes a method using OAM cells for in-service measurement of CMR. Counts, N_R and N_T, of the received and transmitted cells, excluding cells in severely errored cell blocks, are obtained during a measurement period T_M. The CMR is subsequently calculated by dividing the difference (N_R-N_T), which should be positive, by T_M. If cell loss events occur, (N_R-N_T) can be negative, in which case the CMR cannot be computed, nor can the CMR be considered accurate any time cell loss events occur. An OOS measurement method also is described in Annex C. By maintaining a VPC or VCC for a known period of time, with no cells transmitted on it, any cells received on this VPC or VCC have been misinserted.

Traffic Parameters

In this section, you learn about the variable traffic parameters that describe the inherent traffic characteristics of a source device. The three hierarchical categories of parameters and descriptors that are discussed in upcoming paragraphs follow:

- Traffic parameters
- Source-traffic descriptors
- Connection-traffic descriptors

Not all parameters are applicable to every VC. The requirements of the traffic on each VC influence which parameters are considered pertinent. The traffic parameters that can be attributed to the characteristics of a source device follow:

- Peak cell rate
- Sustained cell rate
- Maximum burst size/burst tolerance
- Minimum cell rate
- Maximum frame size

These parameters are instrumental in describing the characteristics of service classes in the section "ATM Service Classes," later in this chapter. Besides QoS parameters, traffic contracts also rely on connection-traffic descriptors, which include source-traffic descriptors, to ensure firm definitions of what is expected, both by the subscriber and the network. Source-traffic descriptors are merely the collection of traffic parameters that apply to a specific ATM source, as the source's negotiable requirements during establishment of a connection. Connection-traffic descriptors are composed of the aforementioned source-traffic descriptors, and a measurement known as the cell delay variation tolerance (CDVT), which is not to be confused with the QoS measurement CDV (discussed in the earlier section "Peak-to-Peak CDV"), besides the conformance definition that is designed to remove any doubt as to what constitutes a valid cell for the connection (that is, one that is accepted by the network devices on that connection). To summarize, here are the components of the connection-traffic descriptor:

- Source-traffic descriptor
- CDVT
- Conformance definition

Traffic parameter values are requested by the calling party, through the call setup message in the establishment of an SVC, and are open for negotiation. If both parties cannot arrive upon a mutually acceptable value for each parameter, the connection is rejected. The following six sections, beginning with Peak Cell Rate (PCR), offer brief descriptions for each of the five traffic parameters and for the CDVT. Different traffic parameters can be negotiated in each direction of a bi-directional connection. This feature comes in handy when there is an asymmetrical flow of information, skewed in one direction versus another.

Peak Cell Rate (PCR)

The PCR can be defined as a throughput-limit parameter. Specifically, it is the maximum cell rate that the source requests, negotiates, and is ultimately restricted to. The inverse of PCR (1/PCR) is the minimum cell inter-arrival time (T) between two consecutive basic events, also known as the peak emission interval of the ATM connection, below which the source is not allowed to space cells. PCR applies to both constant bit rate (CBR) and variable bit rate (VBR) service classes and is the upper bound of the connection's cell rate.

To reiterate a point made in the "QoS" section earlier in the chapter, consider a connection with a PCR of 10 Mbps. As mentioned in that section, if measuring performance instantaneously, TMS 4.1 implies that if the subscriber were to attempt the transmission of 11 Mbps, the network does not guarantee to transmit even at the 10 Mbps PCR. In fact, when measured instantaneously, the subscriber might see a rate substantially below the PCR. To reiterate, the PCR represents a probabilistic performance over the life of the connection.

Sustained Cell Rate (SCR)

The SCR is the upper bound of the average cell rate over some extended period of time. Average refers to the total number of cells transmitted divided by the time it took to transmit those cells, usually the duration of the connection. Used in conjunction with the maximum burst size (discussed next), SCR can be used for policing (how the conformance of cells is determined—to be discussed later in this chapter in the "Traffic Management" section). It is not uncommon to see SCR used as the contractual figure in selling service, with a PCR greater than the SCR being used to configure equipment, so that network resources are reserved adequately and guarantees are conceivable.

Maximum Burst Size (MBS) and Burst Tolerance (BT)

MBS is defined as either the maximum duration that cells can be transmitted by the source at the PCR or the maximum number of consecutive cells that can be transmitted by the source at the PCR. MBS is related proportionately to a measure known as the burst tolerance, which is used in conformance checking of the SCR. The BT, together with SCR and the configured policing option (see the section "Traffic Management" later in this chapter) determine the MBS. It can also be said that the policing option defines the relationship between BT and SCR. From these cyclical definitions, it is apparent that these measurements are completely interdependent on one another. Consult TMS 4.1 if you want a more detailed discussion of the interrelationship between these variables. The specification during call setup of measurements such as SCR and BT allows a greater prediction of what characteristics the connection will exhibit than does the PCR alone, which allows switches and other network devices to allocate resources more adequately.

Minimum Cell Rate (MCR)

If you have been considering the PCR as a counterpart to Frame Relay's CIR, consider the relationship between PCR and MCR. Although the network allows the user to burst up to the PCR when such bandwidth is available, network connections that are based on service classes that specify an MCR (see the "ABR" and "GFR" sections later in this chapter) commit that although available bandwidth can vary, it should never drop below the MCR. Translate this as meaning that it is not a breach of contract by the network if the user does not constantly have the PCR available for transmission. The PCR is the maximum bandwidth that the user is expected to require, and the MCR is the minimum bandwidth that the user considers usable. Likewise, SCR is closely related in function to Frame Relay's CIR. Therefore, service classes that specify an SCR also tend to resemble Frame Relay.

Maximum Frame Size (MFS)

MFS specifies the number of cells that comprise the largest allowable frame in the GFR service class, discussed in the "GFR" section later in this chapter. GFR is the only current service class that specifies groups of cells called frames. Additionally, MFS is a mandatory parameter in any source-traffic descriptor of a connection established using the GFR service class.

CDVT

During the normal operation of the ATM layer, which is where the multiplexing of cells from different sources occurs within network switching devices, switches can change the characteristics of the traffic in comparison to the expectations associated with its original connection. In particular, CDV can be introduced, which affects the peak emission interval (recall, 1/PCR), and the sustained emission interval (1/SCR). See the "Traffic Management" section later in the chapter for a detailed discussion of the relationship between PCR and CDVT and the relationship between SCR and CDVT. While the switch is performing the multiplexing function, cells from one connection can be delayed, whereas cells of another connection are queued and output over the same physical connection. Physical layer overhead and OAM cells can also contribute to the delay of user cells in this way. Even the most time-bound applications can endure some amount of delay, as long as the variation is minimized. Other applications are not affected by variation in delay. It's these differences that are described by varying values for the CDVT variable.

CDVT can be thought of, in simple terms, as the measure of how much jitter (remember, that's jargon for delay variation) generated by an ingress switch between its own ingress and egress interfaces is tolerable by a connection. This value tends to be directly proportional to the intended burstiness of the endpoint's traffic. As a result, for negotiated connections the CAC can refuse the connection if it determines that the CDVT specified by the requesting endpoint implies a level of burstiness that might jeopardize the QoS of existing connections. Indeed, most networks do not admit connections with a high CDVT value. CDVT does not have to be uniform throughout the connection. Different values can apply at each interface along the path of the connection (UNI, NNI, or B-ICI). However, CDVT does not accumulate as traffic crosses these boundaries.

TMS 4.1 dictates that UNI Signaling 4.0 does not support the signaling of this value (although this would be desirable from a traffic-management viewpoint), which means that it is agreed upon before call setup, specifically at subscription time, for each interface individually. In fact, TMS 4.1 requires that an end system choose a value for CDVT at the public UNI from a set of values supported by the network but leaves the decision, as to whether the set of values is to be standardized or to be determined by each service provider, for the future. The AF does recommend that all CDVT values be upper-bounded, because of this parameter's potential effect on network resources.

The value of CDVT can be thought of as a measure of the amount of cell clumping that can be expected to occur from an ATM endpoint. Picture clumps as traffic bursts separated by periods of inactivity, the nature of data traffic. Some endpoints might require a higher CDVT value to improve performance, which indicates that they intend to send data in a bursty manner. Although this burstiness, or higher degree of clumping, is acceptable for traffic that is not time-bound, a much lower value (as close to 0 as possible) is required for real-time applications. See the "Traffic Management" section later in the chapter for a discussion on traffic shaping. Traffic shaping is instrumental in reducing cell clumping; thereby, allowing the CDVT value to remain lower than if no traffic shaping is implemented. If you happen to see the notation CDVT(0+1) in documentation, this means, as it does for other ATM parameters, that all traffic is taken into consideration, regardless of whether it has been tagged for discard (CLP=0 and CLP=1). Think of the plus sign as an ampersand (&). This notation is also used in conjunction with various other traffic parameters, such as PCR and SCR.

In an effort to bring the terms of the preceding sections together, ITU-T recommendation I.371 provides a definition of the granularity of PCR, SCR, CDVT, and BT, as they pertain to the conformance definition for CBR and VBR connections.

ATM Service Classes

Although it would be ideal to have one AAL in its entirety for all applications of ATM networking, the one AAL chosen would be a watered-down version of what is required by all applications. The restriction might be so limiting that certain applications, no matter how you tried to fit them in, would never work out. At the very least, certain features that optimize the performance of an application might interfere with the performance of another. By omitting these features, all applications work, but at least one works not as well. ATM service classes give insight into the broad, yet finite, range of traffic that ATM can support, each with slightly different needs.

The two ends of an ATM physical link can be configured with different service classes, with respect to the same VC. The problem that arises is that because the service class is not communicated within the ATM cell header, the only way switching devices, which look only at the cell header, know what kind of traffic the cell represents is if the switch's configuration for the VC, over which the cell is traveling, conforms to a certain service class (i.e., a certain connection-traffic descriptor).

For example, a PVC carrying voice traffic, which is highly sensitive to delay and jitter (delay variation), would not handle data traffic with the efficiency of a PVC that is configured for such traffic. Conversely, the switch would not know that traffic on a data PVC was actually high-priority uncompressed voice traffic that needed to be sent through the switching fabric and out onto the next link as quickly as possible. Therefore, even the concept of effective queuing depends on service-class configuration. Again, for maximum effectiveness, settings for the same VC should be identical at both ends of the physical link (although not required) and appropriate for the traffic.

The two broad categories of service class are real-time and non-real-time. The following list shows the standard ATM service classes, grouped by these categories:

- Real-time service classes
    - CBR
    - Real-time (rt-VBR)
- Non-real-time service classes
    - Non-real-time nrt-VBR
    - ABR
    - Unspecified bit rate (UBR)
    - GFR (VCC only)

Figure 10-11 shows a matrix of both traffic and QoS parameters that apply to each of the service classes discussed here. The following descriptions for each service class reference these parameters in varying degrees. In deciphering Figure 10-11, understand that "n/a" is used with traffic parameters to mean that the particular source-traffic descriptor (remember, a collection of traffic parameters) does not apply to that service class. For QoS parameters, the term unspecified indicates that that particular parameter is not negotiated for that service class. The reason that unspecified is not used for the traffic parameters is because some of the traffic parameters might be specified, but not as part of that particular source-traffic descriptor grouping. Although subtle, the difference exists.

Figure 10-11 *Service Classes by Parameter*

	ATM Layer Service Category					
Attribute	CBR	rt-VBR	nrt-VBR	UBR	ABR	GFR
End-to-End Timing	Required		Not Required			
Bit Rate	Constant	Variable				
Traffic Parameters$_4$:						
PCR and CDVT$_5$	Specified			Specified $_2$	Specified $_3$	Specified
SCR, MBS, CDVT$_5$	n/a	Specified		n/a		
MCR	n/a				Specified	n/a
MCR, MBS, MFS, CDVT$_5$	n/a					Specified
QoS Parameters$_4$:						
Peak-to-Peak CDV	Specified		Unspecified			
maxCTD	Specified		Unspecified			
CLR	Specified		Unspecified	See Note 1		See Note 6

Notes:
1. CLR is low for sources that adjust cell flow in response to control information, whether a quantitative value for CLR is specified is network specific.
2. Might not be subject to CAC and UPC procedures.
3. Represents the maximum rate at which the ABR source can send. The actual rate is subject to the control information.
4. These parameters are either explicitly or implicitly specified for PVCs or SVCs.
5. CDVT refers to the Cell Delay Variation Tolerance (see Section 4.4.1). CDVT is not signaled. In general, CDVT need not have a unique value for a connection. Different values can apply at each interface along the path of a connection.
6. CLR is low for frames that are eligible for the service guarantee, whether a quantitative value for CLR is specified is network specific.

CBR

An AF term, CBR is known as the deterministic bit rate (DBR) service class in ITU-T recommendation I.371. CBR connections are requested by sources that require a static amount of bandwidth that will be unwaveringly available during the lifetime of the connection. The amount of bandwidth required is communicated through the PCR value during call setup. The network guarantees the negotiated QoS to each and every cell that conforms to the pertinent conformance tests. This commitment is applicable for the source to transmit cells any time and for any duration at the PCR, even if the source transmits cells at the PCR constantly.

Although CBR is designed to service real-time applications such as voice, video, and circuit emulation, which all require tight constraints strictly placed on delay variation, CBR is not restricted to these applications. However, efficiencies might be compromised if inappropriate traffic is sent with CBR connection capability, not only for the source, but also for other sources that share the same network devices and resources. For example, CBR allocation of buffers and bandwidth is likely to be unnecessary for data applications. Furthermore, new connections might be rejected that would otherwise be accepted because of dubious resource availability projections. One point should be clarified. The source is not committed to the constant emission of cells at the PCR. The rate can be at or below the PCR, even with periods of complete silence (lack of transmission). If such activity is common, it might be advisable, from an economic perspective, to change service from CBR to rt-VBR, which is covered in the self-titled section later in the chapter.

Nevertheless, meaningful real-time traffic that arrives with delays beyond the specified maximum CDV tends to be of significantly less value to the application. For example, if receiving buffers are allocated to account for a maximum CDV, exceeding this maximum delay variation often enough would clearly compromise quality, as buffers empty and traffic is perceived to stop momentarily. Of course, at the root of the preceding example is the issue of an accumulated delay variation. Delay variation must be strictly regulated for real-time traffic. Only by the specification and adherence to a maximum CDV can the elastic buffers that are required at the terminating end be allocated appropriately. A good rule-of-thumb is to design the receiving CDV play-out buffers (de-jitter buffers) to handle the theoretical case of a connection crossing three networks, each having three switches working in conjunction, one behind the other.

NOTE   For conformance definitions, consult Section 4.5 of TMS 4.1. Conformance applies to cells crossing the UNI and is based upon one of a variety of algorithms. The selected algorithm is started with the first cell of the connection and is subsequently applied to each passing cell, with every one classifiable as conforming or non-conforming. Even under the best conditions, non-conforming cells can still be observed. As a result, QoS objectives cannot be applied only to those connections for which all cells pass the conformance tests. It is important to draw a distinction between connection compliance and cell conformance. It is possible to have a compliant connection, for which not all cells conform.

Conformance for a CBR connection is characterized by the PCR and the corresponding CDVT for all traffic (CLP=0+1). The source-traffic descriptor for any CBR connection must include the PCR and CDVT traffic parameters (refer back to Figure 10-11). The PCR must be explicitly specified, and the CDVT can be either explicitly specified at the time of subscription or implicitly specified through computed means. For SVCs, the PCR must be specified in the initial connection establishment message. Congestion control is performed by using a technique known as the single leaky bucket method. The idea is that the so-called bucket leaks at the PCR. If the bucket is filled faster than the conforming traffic can leak out, the bucket overflows, and any cells that are lost over the edge (discarded) are irretrievable. Because of the type of traffic associated with CBR, in retransmitting the discarded cells carries little to no value.

The following list specifies possible applications that would be best suited to a CBR connection:

- Interactive video (e.g., videoconferencing)
- Interactive audio (e.g., telephone)
- Video distribution (e.g., television, distributed classroom)
- Audio distribution (e.g., radio, audio feed)
- Video retrieval (e.g., video on demand)
- Audio retrieval (e.g., audio library)
- Circuit emulation services (CESs)
- Alternatively, any data-transfer application that emits traffic smoothly enough or for which the endpoint's response-time requirements justify occupying a fully reserved CBR channel

A graphical representation of CBR is shown in Figure 10-12.

rt-VBR

For real-time traffic, there exist two service classes, the aforementioned CBR and rt-VBR. For CBR, the source-traffic descriptor contains the PCR, as discussed in the CBR section, and for rt-VBR it also contains the SCR and MBS parameters. The practical difference that this alludes to is that rt-VBR, unlike CBR, allows bursty sources to take advantage of statistical multiplexing, thus allowing for a more efficient use of the network's resources, and making room for additional connections that might otherwise be rejected. As with CBR, for rt-VBR connections, meaningful real-time traffic that arrives with delays beyond the specified maxCTD tends to be of significantly less value to the application. ITU-T recommendation I.371 refers to VBR as the statistical bit rate (SBR) service class.

Figure 10-12 *Visual Representations of CBR, VBR, and ABR*

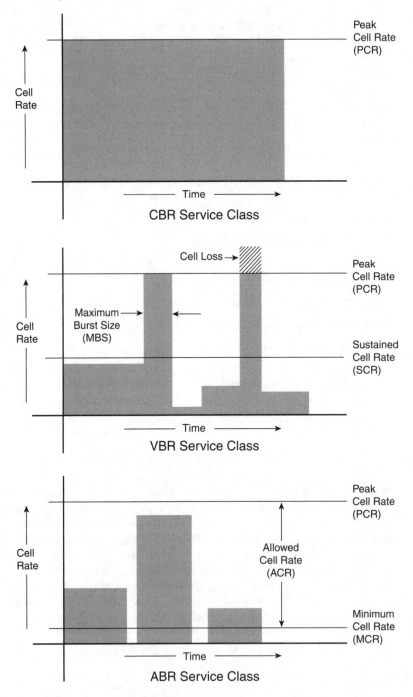

A bit more complex than the simple single leaky bucket algorithm of CBR, the algorithm used by VBR service classes is known as the dual leaky bucket congestion control method. It takes the more numerous parameters into consideration when deciding whether to discard cells. The main rule still applies—no cells transmitted at a rate higher than the PCR. However, there is a new twist. Over the long term, the average rate of cell transmission should be at or below the SCR. This represents the second opportunity for cells to be discarded, should the SCR be exceeded when tested. Recall that SCR is an average, not an instantaneous measure, as is PCR. The MBS dictates the duration of bursts, but the number of these bursts must not allow the average cell rate to exceed the SCR, or bursting will have to cease until the SCR comes back in line. The throttle-back is also required so that the network can carry ABR and UBR traffic. Both are discussed shortly.

Conformance for a rt-VBR connection is characterized by an SCR parameter and corresponding MBS parameter for one or more traffic flows, besides a PCR parameter and corresponding CDVT for at least the all-traffic flow. PCR and CDVT are mandatory traffic parameters in any source-traffic descriptor for a rt-VBR. For rt-VBR switched virtual circuits (SVCs), the PCR for CLP=0+1 must be explicitly specified for each direction in the initial establishment message, and CDVT can be explicit at subscription time or implicit. See the discussion of the dual leaky bucket algorithm in the "Traffic Management" section later in this chapter.

The following list specifies possible applications that would be best suited to a rt-VBR connection:

- A real-time application (including those listed previously for CBR) for which the endpoint can benefit from statistical multiplexing, by sending at a variable rate, and can tolerate or recover from a small, non-zero CLR

- A real-time application for which variable rate transmission allows more efficient use of network resources

- Voice with bandwidth compression and silence suppression

- Compressed video (encoding exploits redundancies and irrelevancies in the video image)

Refer to Figure 10-12 for a visual representation of VBR and its applicable traffic parameters.

nrt-VBR

rt-VBR and nrt-VBR are typically distinguished by their QoS parameters (only CLR is specified for nrt-VBR), but also by the magnitude of the MBSs supported. As traffic from nrt-VBR sources naturally clump more than that from rt-VBS sources, larger MBSs are more typical for nrt-VBR connections. As a result, nrt-VBR sources can burst to the PCR for longer periods of time, with a higher quantity of cells per burst. Some degree of isolation is assumed with nrt-VBR. In other words, connections that exceed their traffic contract are expected not to cause the negotiated CLR to be exceeded on connections that do not exceed their traffic contract.

Conformance for an nrt-VBR connection is characterized by the same factors as an rt-VBR connection. Unlike CBR and rt-VBR, for nrt-VBR connections, there are no associated delay issues related to maxCTD, which, along with CDV, is not specified for nrt-VBR. Furthermore, jitter tolerance, denoted by the value of CDVT, is higher for nrt-VBR than for its real-time counterpart. CLR should be low for cells conforming to the policing algorithm.

The following list specifies possible applications that would be best suited to an nrt-VBR connection:

- Response time-critical transaction processing with minimal delay-variation sensitivity (e.g., airline reservations, banking transactions, process monitoring)
- Frame Relay interworking
- LAN interconnection

ABR

The ABR service class is intended for non-real-time applications that have the capability of reducing and increasing their cell rate, based on network conditions, and that do not have strict delay requirements. ABR uses the bandwidth left over after connections using CBR and VBR service classes have registered for the bandwidth they need. Nevertheless, ABR does provide a minimum bandwidth guarantee, as the network will not establish the connection (CAC) if it cannot guarantee at least the bandwidth designated by the MCR parameter. Although the actual cell rate is related to a form of congestion control known as closed-loop flow control, to be discussed shortly, PCR and CDVT are still specified, as they were with the previously mentioned service classes. Defaults exist for the cell-rate parameters. For PCR the default is the access-line rate, and for MCR the default is 0 cells per second (cps).

Jitter and burst tolerance (CDV and MBS/BT) have no significance and are not specified for ABR connections because cells are emitted as the source detects resources available for successful transmission to the destination. The CLR parameter has meaning for ABR connections, but as long as such connections adjust their cell rate in response to reports of network congestion (obey a specified reference behavior), the CLR should remain fairly low and inconsequential. Furthermore, compliant connections lead to an air of fairness among ABR connections that can be lost if the specified reference behavior is not obeyed.

As a result of the characteristics of the ABR service class, induced by its implementation of closed-loop flow control, it proves to be the best service class for non-real-time bursty traffic. In the cases when bursts are somewhat extended and would otherwise be subject to having some or all of their cells discarded, ABR can implement this form of congestion control, thus avoiding negative policing action. The same requirements, regarding the connection isolation that was discussed, in the case of nrt-VBR, also apply to ABR connections.

The following discussion clarifies the aspects of the closed-loop flow control model of ABR. The term closed-loop is used, because the flow control (sometimes referred to as congestion control, because its implementation serves to reduce network congestion) is conducted through communication between end devices. In contrast, other forms of congestion control discussed so far are isolated to the source of the traffic or left to the network to implement, without the knowledge or consent of either endpoint (referred to as open-loop flow control).

It is only ABR that reliably uses the RM functionality in management cells (recall the introduction of the RM cell in the "Payload Type (PT) and OAM Cells" section earlier in this chapter). RM cells are emitted after a set number of user-data cells. The basis for this model is that each source sends cells at a specific, yet variable, rate. The current assigned rate is known as the allowed cell rate (ACR) and is communicated within an RM cell to the destination in the current cell rate (CCR) field. Table 10-4 shows the format for the 53 octets of the RM cell. The ACR is adjusted no lower than the MCR and no higher than the PCR, in response to network congestion or the lack thereof. The ACR is a computed value, based on another field in the RM cell, the explicit cell rate (ECR). The initial RM cell's CCR field is considered the initial allowed cell rate (IACR), the rate at which the source originally transmits, waiting for the first ECR value to arrive in the returned cell, thus setting the ACR/CCR for subsequent cells until the next RM cell. Depending on the implementation, the CCR can optionally be taken into consideration when a network element or destination decides to reduce the ECR, so that a rate lower than the source is currently using can be avoided, if possible.

Table 10-4   *Field Locations for the RM Cell*

Field	Octet(s)	Bit(s)
Header (standard ATM header)	1 to 5	All
Protocol ID	6	All
Message type: Direction	7	8
Message type: Backward explicit congestion notification (BECN) indication	7	7
Message type: Congestion indication	7	6
Message type: No-increase	7	5
Message type: Reserved	7	1 to 4
ECR	8 to 9	All
CCR	10 to 11	All
MCR	12 to 13	All

continues

Table 10-4　*Field Locations for the RM Cell (Continued)*

Field	Octet(s)	Bit(s)
Queue length	14 to 17	All
Sequence number	18 to 21	All
Reserved	22 to 51	All
Reserved	52	3 to 8
CRC-10 (high-order 2 bits)	52	1 to 2
CRC-10 (low-order 8 bits)	53	All

The values of the ACR, CCR, IACR, and ECR all fall somewhere between, and inclusive of, those of the PCR and the MCR. The ECR is set by the source to be the cell rate the source would like to be authorized to use as its ACR. Similar to the ACR, the ECR must be between the PCR and MCR. The ECR has a floating-point value, the components of which are transmitted in the 16-bit ECR field as a 14-bit pair of values that insert into the formula given in Section 6.7.4.1 of ITU-T recommendation I.371, which gives the ECR an upper limit of 4,290,772,992 cps.

As the RM cell containing the ECR value, which represents the source's desired cell rate, makes its way to the destination, network devices along the way can adjust the ECR downward to reflect their current network capabilities. If the ECR is adjusted below the MCR, the source is not obligated to reduce its cell rate beyond the MCR. A logical loopback for RM cells at the destination returns the cell to the source, where the source learns of the greatest common cell rate that the connection can support along the path to the destination. This information goes into adjusting the ACR perceived by the source that subsequently becomes the CCR that the source includes in the next RM cell. Even lost RM cells can be useful, in that network congestion is the likely cause for the loss, a signal that the ACR/CCR values should be lowered.

The foregoing discussion is only part of what is known as the enhanced proportional rate control algorithm (EPRCA). EPRCA includes various flow-control mechanisms, the functionality of which accumulates, with a basis in the optional, but common, use of the EFCI bit in the PT field of user-cell headers. In the basic form, older (or less capable) network switches that cannot manipulate passing RM cells can set the EFCI bit in the cell header to signal congestion or impending congestion on the connection over which the cell travels. The destination then modifies the next RM cell that it receives from the source.

The RM cell that the destination cell returns is known as the backward RM cell and is characterized by the direction bit being set to 1 (0 indicates a forward RM cell). Depending upon the particular implementation employed by the destination, it can either reduce the ECR or set the congestion indication (CI) bit in the RM cell (see Table 10-4). A CI of 1 means that congestion has been signaled on the connection. If the actual destination needs to declare itself congested, it can reduce the ECR to whatever rate it can support, set the CI or the no-increase (NI) bit (a value of 1 indicates the source should not increase its ACR), or increase the value of the queue length field, which is set to 0 by the source and set to the number of cells queued only by each network element that can change it to a number higher than its current setting. Thus, the end result is that the source is aware of the worst-case queue congestion in the network for that connection. The destination also has the option of generating a backward RM cell without having received a forward RM cell. A familiar term, BECN, catches up to ATM from Frame Relay. These are considered BECN cells and are characterized by CLP values of 0, and the BECN bit in the RM cell set to 1. Additionally, the direction bit should be set to 1 for backward, and either the CI or NI bit must be set to 1.

The next step in the cumulative function of the EPRCA method is known as explicit rate marking (ERM). With ERM functionality, switches along the path can manipulate the RM cell directly, so that even before the cell arrives at the destination and again before arrival back at the source, the switches throughout the connection can modify the ECR, in response to congestion they know about first-hand. Figure 10-13 shows the concept of the next phase of EPRCA, which is known as the segmented virtual source (VS)/virtual destination (VD) method.

Figure 10-13   *Segmented VS/VD Flow-Control Method*

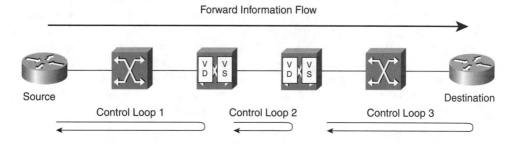

VS = Virtual Source
VD = Virtual Destination

In larger networks, it can be beneficial for a network element to act as a destination and more quickly turn the forward RM cell into a backward one or to create its own backward RM cell before the actual destination has to, which expedites its return to the source and its subsequent rate reduction. This method has a ripple effect, in that earlier throttling back by the source allows the network to remain less congested, thereby protecting the rest of the network from potential cell loss. A specialized form of the segmented VS/VD method, in which not every switch along the connection path is capable of performing the VS or VD function, is called hop-by-hop VS/VD, in which case every network element along the path is capable of performing the VS/VD function.

For a conformance definition for an ABR connection, refer to Section 4.5.4 of TMS 4.1. The following list specifies possible applications that would be best suited to an ABR connection:

- LAN internetworking services (typically run over protocol stacks such as TCP/IP)
- LAN emulation (LANE)
- Computer process swapping/paging
- Any UBR application (discussed next) that can take advantage of the ABR flow-control protocol to achieve a low CLR
- Critical data transfer (for example, defense information)
- Supercomputer applications
- Data communications applications requiring better delay behavior, such as remote procedure call and distributed file service

Refer to Figure 10-12 for a visual representation of ABR and its applicable traffic parameters.

UBR

The AF's UBR service class has no equivalent ATM transfer capability in ITU-T recommendation I.371. UBR is intended for non-real-time applications, which again do not require tightly constrained delay and delay variation. At connection time, no maximum jitter value (CDV) is specified. Traditional computer communications applications, such as file transfer and e-mail, are examples of such applications. The UBR service does not specify traffic-related service guarantees, nor does the network make guarantees with respect to the CLR or CTD. Because the network offers no guarantee of whether or when the data will arrive at the destination, the user application can do this, if necessary.

For UBR, a PCR value can be specified (TMS 4.1 requires PCR and CDVT in any source-traffic descriptor for UBR), but a network may or may not apply PCR to the CAC and UPC functions, which means a connection can be accepted by the network, even when resources are not available to accommodate the PCR, and cells that burst past the PCR might still be allowed to maintain CLP=0. As you will see, this is acceptable for the network because these cells are some of the first to be discarded in times of congestion, just by virtue of their UBR status. When PCR is not enforced, it is still useful to have PCR negotiated. Doing so can allow the source to discover the smallest bandwidth limitation along the path of the connection. The endpoint indicates implementation of the UBR service class by use of the best effort indicator in the ATM user cell rate information element (see UNI 4.0 and ITU-T recommendations Q.2931 and Q.2961.1).

Because no common reference behavior is defined for UBR, in contrast to ABR, fairness among UBR connections cannot be assumed. If necessary, fairness can be achieved through the proper configuration of network elements, with regard to local policy. UBR is not subject to a specific traffic contract but might be subject to a local policy in individual switches and endpoints. Because the UBR service category is inherently open loop, and no flow control exists between endpoints on a connection (in contrast to ABR), applications keep transmitting when network congestion occurs, unless endpoint higher layers are performing flow-control functions. After switch buffers overflow, the network begins to discard cells. In practice, network switches show no mercy on UBR cells, which are some of the first to go during times of network congestion, which is the ramification of there being no traffic contract for UBR.

Because the wanton discarding of UBR cells can randomly affect larger data structures, such as IP packets (e.g., classical IP over ATM), a technique known as early packet discard (EPD) is often implemented in conjunction with UBR. If a single cell of an IP packet is discarded, the packet is in error and is not acknowledged by the destination. The source's timer expires and the entire packet is transmitted again. Subsequent discarding of cells within the retransmitted packet is likely, owing to the nature of UBR connections. Without a mechanism such as EPD, cells of these damaged packets would accumulate in switch and endpoint buffers, thus affecting the performance of the network. EPD can also increase efficiency for VBR and ABR connections.

EPD is designed to recognize when a component cell (part of an AAL5 cell stream) of a packet has been discarded, thus invalidating the cells that make up the remainder of the packet, causing their continued transmission to be wasteful of network resources. Recall from the discussion, earlier in this chapter in the "Payload Type (PT) and OAM Cells" section, of the function of the third bit of the PT field in the ATM header. A value of 0 in this bit indicates that this is not the last cell in an AAL5 PDU, and a 1 in this bit location signifies that it is the last cell. EPD uses this fact to look through the passing cells, discarding each one in the doomed packet, until it arrives at the last cell in the packet. This cell is allowed to pass because the receipt of the cell with the AAL-indicate bit set in the PT field alerts the remaining devices in the connection, especially the destination, that the next cell, which will likely have a 0 in this bit location, is actually the first cell of a new packet. Otherwise, without the receipt of the final cell in the previous packet, the first cell of the next packet would look like a continuation of the previous packet, which was partially discarded by the network.

Selective Discard (SD) is another method, similar to EPD, that is designed to intelligently target cells for discard, so as to prevent unchecked growth of network congestion. SD separates cells into prioritized groups, placing cells of the same priority into a common buffer slot. Discarding of cells can occur in one of various ways. All methods use a buffer policy and a push-out policy. The buffer policy governs which buffer slot the cell qualifies for. The push-out policy decides which low-priority cell is discarded to make room for a cell of higher priority. It is the actual policy in each of these categories that varies from implementation to implementation.

The following list specifies possible applications that would be best suited to a UBR connection:

- Interactive text/data/image transfer (e.g., banking transaction, credit-card verification)
- Text/data/image messaging (e.g., e-mail, telex, fax)
- Text/data/image distribution (e.g., news feed, weather satellite pictures)
- Text/data/image retrieval (e.g., file transfer, library browsing)
- Aggregate LAN (e.g., LAN interconnection or emulation)
- Remote terminal (e.g., telecommuting, telnet)

GFR

The GFR service class is the last of those discussed in this chapter to support non-real-time applications, which are applications that might require a minimum rate guarantee and that can benefit from accessing leftover bandwidth in the network. It does not require adherence to a flow control protocol. Similar to EPD functions for UBR (in fact, GFR is sometimes referred to as UBR+), the GFR service guarantee is based on AAL5 PDUs (frames that can be delineated at the ATM layer) and, under congestion conditions, the network attempts to discard complete PDUs instead of discarding cells without reference to frame boundaries. If subscribers cannot comply with the reference behavior required by ABR but are in need of service guarantees, which UBR cannot provide, GFR is their likely choice.

On the establishment of a GFR connection, the endpoint specifies a PCR, an MCR, an MBS, and an MFS. CDVT is also a mandatory parameter in a GFC connection-traffic descriptor. Although the endpoint can always send cells at a rate up to PCR, the network only commits to carry cells in complete frames at MCR, which can be zero. Traffic beyond MCR is delivered within the limits of available resources. Delay is not specified in the traffic contract for GFR. As long as the endpoint sends conforming frames, the cells of which do not cause the MBS to be exceeded, traffic should be delivered with minimal cell loss. GFR is one of those service classes that specify that excess traffic from each endpoint should have fair-share access to available resources. This is not left to the local policy of network elements, as is the case with UBR.

The user can send frames either unmarked or marked. In contrast to the term tagged, which always means that the network sets the cell's CLP to a value of 1 (as in tagged for discard), the terms unmarked and marked refer to CLP values of 0 and 1, respectively, set by the source. An unmarked frame, therefore, is one in which all cells in the frame have CLPs set to 0. The CLP must be the same for all cells in a frame for it to be considered marked or unmarked. In fact, there are three tests that a cell must pass simultaneously to be considered conforming:

- It must make it through the leaky-bucket algorithm.
- This cell's CLP bit must match that of the first cell in the frame.
- This cell must either be the last cell in the frame or not cause the number of cells in the frame thus far to equal the MFS (because even if the next cell were the last, it would be one too many).

The meaning of a marked frame is identical to that of a marked cell. The endpoint indicates to the network that such a frame is of lesser importance than an unmarked frame. The MCR guarantee only applies to unmarked frames. The network is only allowed to tag cells in unmarked frames if the user has requested the tagging option, through signaling (SVC) or subscription (PVC). Otherwise, the network does not perform tagging. The endpoint is not notified of network congestion for GFR connections. Because frame delineation is not generally visible in a VPC, the GFR service category only applies to VCCs.

The following list specifies possible applications that would be best suited to a GFR connection:

- Frame Relay interworking
- Any UBR application listed above that has data organized into frames that can be delineated at the ATM layer

Traffic Management

Traffic management takes into account the five items outlined as part of the traffic contract, besides those practices that assist in the meeting of these requirements. Two related practices that commonly maintain contractual agreements are traffic shaping and traffic policing. The relationship is that they both occur at the UNI. The difference is that, from the perspective of the originating subscriber, traffic shaping occurs on the subscriber side, and the service provider performs policing. Alternatively, it can be said that shaping is performed on the egress link of the UNI, and policing is performed on the ingress link of the UNI. The intent is the same, in that both practices are designed to keep traffic within the agreed-upon boundaries of the traffic contract. Doing so ensures that one rogue connection does not jeopardize the quality of other connections. The implication is that if a cell passes policing by the ingress switch, the cell is expected to reach the destination. However, policing offers no protection for the cell from network devices in cases of discards related to congestion. Even those cells that make it through policing with a CLP of 0 can still be discarded within the network, should drastic congestion mitigation prove necessary. To keep the equipment cost lower for the subscriber, the service provider can opt to implement an ingress switch that performs both functions.

Proper pairing of policing and shaping ensures the continued successful operation of applications, even as source traffic increases. Additionally, traffic shaping serves to create a more predictable traffic profile for the service provider. Without traffic shaping, which results in a more even flow of cells from the ATM endpoint by delaying transmission of cells that would be in excess of the PCR, traffic policing by the network's ingress switch tends to discard component cells of source packets that exceed the PCR. Because network devices rarely report back to endpoints that cells have been discarded, continued retransmission of packets and their component cells would only serve to exacerbate the situation, further eroding the performance of subscriber applications. TMS 4.1 gives additional detail on the topics of traffic management.

Policing by the network element is also known as usage parameter control (UPC). To be effective and successfully implemented, UPC must be each of the following:

- Capable of detecting illegal traffic situations
- Able to produce rapid response to parameter violations
- Simple to implement

There is no set UPC method to which the specifications require adherence. In fact, the network can use any UPC method that supports the QoS objectives of a compliant connection. UPC involves checking such characteristics as the traffic's burst size and rate. Policing prevents congestion by not admitting excess traffic onto the network when all resources are in use. The method it uses to accomplish this is that it discards cells or it sets the CLP bit of cells that exceed traffic parameters so that they are preferentially discarded over cells that conform to the traffic contract. UPC can be done at both the VP and virtual channel levels. The generic cell rate algorithm (GCRA), which is standardized in ITU-T recommendation I.371, defines cell conformance, based on the traffic contract. The GCRA performs a cell-by-cell determination of whether each cell conforms to the connection's traffic contract. Policing can use the PCR and SCR values to tag or discard cells. For example, cells in excess of the PCR(0+1) flow can be discarded, and those that were not discarded that are in excess of the SCR(0) flow can be tagged or discarded. Together, these two policing actions produce the dual leaky-bucket algorithm.

The GCRA can be thought of as the following:

- Virtual scheduling algorithm

  Or

- Continuous state leaky-bucket algorithm

The standard specifies both algorithms with equivalent results. The GCRA defines the following operationally:

- The relationship between PCR and the CDVT
- The relationship between SCR and the BT

The GCRA specifies the conformance definition of the declared values of CDVT and BT, and the declared values of the traffic parameters PCR, SCR, and MBS. The GCRA is defined with an increment (I) and a limit (L) parameter (both measures of time), using the notation GCRA (I,L). I and L are not restricted to integer values. The interpretation of this notation is that if a cell arrives sometime after the time represented by a starting time, that the incremental measure of time, I, has been added (pushing it into the future), or if it at least conforms to the tolerance specified and arrives earlier than that time, but no earlier than a unit of time, which is equivalent to the limiting time, L, before the original time already described, it is considered to be a conforming cell.

The Virtual Scheduling Algorithm

The virtual scheduling algorithm assumes that the source sends equally spaced cells and, based on this assumption, updates a theoretical or nominal arrival time (T_N). If the actual arrival time of a cell (T_A) is not early, relative to the theoretical time tempered by L (T_A is after $T_N - L$), the cell is conforming; otherwise, the cell is non-conforming. Here's how all of the variables fit together. The theoretical arrival time, T_N, is initially set equal to the actual arrival time of the first cell, $T_A(1)$. As traffic flows, and you join in the algorithm at some arbitrary point in time, if the arrival time of the next cell (call it cell x), $T_A(x)$, is after the current value of T_N (the expected arrival time of the next cell), the cell is said to be conforming, and the theoretical arrival time of the next cell (call it cell x+1), $T_N(x+1)$, is updated to the sum of the time of cell x's arrival, $T_A(x)$, plus the increment, I ($T_N(x+1)=$ $T_A(x) + I$), just to make sure the next expected arrival time is in the future (the time ($T_N(x)$ + I) might have already passed), for the next round of the algorithm that will be applied to the next cell that will arrive (cell x+1). Alternatively, if the arrival time of the next cell, x, is before T_N (i.e., the earliest expected arrival time of that next cell—later is fine), as long as cell x arrives at or after ($T_N - L$), which is the expected arrival time with a grace period equal to the limit value for the GCRA (call ($T_N - L$) the earliest allowed arrival time), during which early arrival is acceptable, then again the cell is considered to be conforming to the traffic contract.

NOTE   You will see shortly that the limit value, L, is often some form of delay-variation parameter, which means that if delay varies beyond the limit, L, the tolerance has been violated with respect to the traffic contract.

Therefore, as before, the expected time of arrival of the next cell (cell x+1), $T_N(x+1)$, is increased by the increment, I, over the early cell's expected time of arrival, $T_N(x)$. This process avoids rewarding increasingly early cells. If the formula for an on-time or late cell is used, the system tends to accumulate a sort of time credit. For example, consider the case where I is set to 20 ms and L is set to 10 ms. What this means is that cells are expected to arrive every 20 ms, but are not penalized for arriving 10 ms before the expected time. If I was added to the actual arrival time, instead of the original expected arrival time, it would be possible for cells to arrive, on average, every 10 ms without penalty. Instead, by incrementing the current expected arrival time by I, the average is kept to the value of I, with cells arriving every 10 ms being penalized after the second such arrival in a row. In fact, subsequent cells that consistently arrive the full tolerance of 10 ms early will still arrive exactly 20 ms apart. This is because the next expected time of arrival is consistently 30 ms in the future. 30 ms comes from the value of I being added to the 10 ms that remain until the next cell's expected time of arrival. There is no penalty for cells arriving in 20 ms (the expected time less the value of L), which is, not coincidentally, the original expectation from the connection. Only after a cell is exactly on time or late will the next cell be allowed to cheat the system by arriving 10 ms after the current cell. The next time a cell is on time this credit will have been repaid.

The only remaining case is if the arrival time of the next cell, x, is even before the more liberal theoretical arrival time, $(T_N(x) - L)$ (i.e., if $T_N(x)$ is after $(T_A(x) + L)$), then the cell is non-conforming and T_N remains unchanged, which should serve to improve the chances for the conformance of the next cell (cell x+1), as $T_N(x)$ possibly will have passed by the time cell x+1 arrives ($T_A(x+1)$ should be after $T_N(x)$, which means conformance, by definition). Nevertheless, the smaller the PCR, the more likely a burst of cells will result in some not conforming.

The Continuous State Leaky-Bucket Algorithm

The continuous state leaky-bucket algorithm can be viewed as a bucket of limited capacity, the content of which drains out at a continuous rate of one unit of content per unit of time. Additionally, the bucket's content is increased by the increment, I, for each conforming cell that arrives. In practice, this limited bucket is a bounded counter that is capable of holding floating-point values. If the content of the bucket is less than or equal to the limit value, L, when a cell arrives, the cell is considered to be conforming to the traffic contract; otherwise, the cell is non-conforming and is discarded. The bucket's capacity (the upper bound on the counter) is fixed at $(L + I)$. Remember that this bucket holds time, not cells or anything else nearly as tangible. Therefore, the incrementing of the limit just pushes the expected arrival time of the next cell into the future, just as the virtual scheduling algorithm did. Thus, the bucket is not growing, because as the top of the bucket extends into time, so does the bottom, which represents the current time.

Theoretically, to establish a beginning to the algorithm, you could say that prior to the arrival time of the first cell $T_A(1)$, the content of the bucket, X, is set to zero (now), or emptied, and the last conformance time (LCT) (the base to compute how much content or time has leaked out of the bucket) is set to $T_A(1)$. This is analogous, in the virtual scheduling algorithm, to setting T_N to the current time. The bucket is empty, and the first cell that arrives cannot possibly be non-conforming. Looking into the future, at the arrival time of cell n, $T_A(n)$, the first step in the algorithm is to compute a test value, X', by taking the current content of the bucket, X (the tolerance is the emptiness still left), and subtracting (increasing the tolerance, or emptiness, of the bucket) the amount the bucket has leaked since the arrival of the last conforming cell (the amount of time that has elapsed between LCT and $T_A(n)$), where this test value, which might become the next value representing the contents of the bucket, X, is constrained to be non-negative. In other words, the bucket can be empty (X' = 0), but is not allowed to have a deficit of content (X' < 0). The second step in the algorithm is to see if X' is less than or equal to the limit value L (the bucket was not caused to overflow). If so, the cell is conforming, and the bucket content X is set to X' plus the increment, I (pushing the expected time for the next cell into the future), and the LCT, is set to the current time, $T_A(n)$. However, if X' is greater than the limit value, L, the cell is non-conforming, and the values of X and LCT are unchanged.

Other GCRA Issues

Multiple, but generally no more than two, instances of the GCRA with independent I and L parameters can be applied to the same flow (similar CLP settings) or to multiple flows (CLP=0 and CLP=0+1) of the same connection. Technically, a cell can be considered to be conforming only if it conforms to all instances of the GCRA that apply to cells with a matching CLP state. In other words, if one instance of the GCRA tests the CLP=0 flow and another instance tests the CLP=0+1 flow, a cell with CLP=0 can be considered to be conforming only if it conforms to both instances of the GCRA. In this same configuration, a CLP=1 cell is conforming only if it conforms to the instance of the GCRA that tests the CLP=0+1 flow. The instance that tests the CLP=0 flow does not apply to such a cell. Furthermore, only the cells that conform, as part of a flow tested by an instance of the GCRA, update the state of that particular instance of the GCRA (refer to the foregoing discussions on GCRA algorithms). For example, a conforming tagged cell (CLP=1) will not update the state of an instance of the GCRA that tests the CLP=0 flow because the tagged cell conforms as a CLP=1 cell or as a CLP=0+1 flow. Non-conformance can result in tagging instead of the assumed discarding of the cell.

A practical implementation of the foregoing concept is the dual leaky-bucket algorithm. Generally, the first bucket screens incoming cells, based on GCRA(1/PCR(0+1), CDVT(0+1)), which is the original single leaky-bucket policy. Those cells found to be non-conforming (in excess of the PCR, regardless of CLP setting) are discarded. All cells that make it through this first policing action are screened based on one of the following policies:

1 GCRA(1/PCR(0)/CDVT(0)) with tagging

2 GCRA(1/PCR(0)/CDVT(0)) without tagging

3 GCRA(1/SCR(0+1)/MBS(0+1))

4 GCRA(1/SCR(0)/MBS(0)) with tagging

5 GCRA(1/SCR(0)/MBS(0)) without tagging

Policies 1 and 2 place cells from the first bucket into a second bucket only if their CLP values are set to 0. Those cells admitted by the first bucket with a CLP already set to 1 are allowed into the network but are the first discarded, should congestion requiring such action be encountered within the network. Again, the congestion-triggered discarding of cells is independent of the policing algorithm employed by the ingress switch. Policies 1 and 2 use the inter-arrival time defined by the inverse of the PCR as the I value for the GCRA. Applicable cells that arrive sooner than the interval computed $(I - L)$, where L is the limit or tolerance, as defined by the CDVT for the connection, are subject to the tagging option in effect.

Policies 4 and 5 are similar to 1 and 2, except that they use the inter-arrival time defined by the inverse of the SCR as the I value for the GCRA. Again, cells with a CLP set to 1 are allowed into the network without first being placed into the second bucket. This is in contrast to policy 3, which uses the same value for I, but considers all flows, regardless of the value of the CLP field. Policy 3 performs no tagging function but instead immediately discards all non-conforming cells.

Policies 1 and 4 simply tag non-conforming cells by changing the CLP from 0 to 1. The cells are still sent into the network but are among the first discarded, should the need arise. Alternatively, policies 2 and 5 immediately discard non-conforming cells. These policies combine the following two functions:

- The stricter action of discarding, as opposed to tagging, cells having a CLP of 0 (similar to policy 3)

- Reducing flow through the algorithm by excluding all cells having a CLP of 1 (in contrast to policy 3)

These excluded cells are still among the first discarded by the network during times of congestion.

The policing algorithms that a network implements is often based on tariffs. It is possible that one or more of these algorithms is not implemented on an ingress switch by the service provider. From the discussion earlier in this section, remember that not only are the CLP=1 cells not tested against policies 1, 2, 4, and 5 (not placed into the bucket), but they do not update the state of the GCRA algorithm.

Recall that the GFR service guarantee provides a low CLR for several cells (in complete CLP=0 frames) at least equal to the number of cells in eligible frames. A frame is eligible if and only if it meets both the following conditions:

- It is conforming; recall for each cell in the frame:
  - The cell conforms to GCRA(1/PCR,CDVT), where PCR is defined for the CLP=0+1 cell stream.
  - The CLP bit of the cell has the same value as the CLP bit of the first cell of the frame.
  - The cell is the last cell of the frame, or the number of cells in the frame up to and including this cell is less than MFS.
- It passes the Frame-GCRA (F-GCRA)(1/MCR,BT + CDVT) test.

The F-GCRA algorithm applies especially for frame-based classes of service, such as GFR.

PCR Algorithm

Recall that the PCR traffic parameter specifies an upper bound on the rate at which traffic can be submitted on a connection. Enforcement of this bound by the UPC allows the network to allocate sufficient resources to ensure that the network performance objectives, based on QoS parameters, can be achieved. With the PCR algorithm form of the GCRA, which has the format GCRA(1/PCR,CDVT), a cell flow is compliant if the cell transmission rate does not exceed the negotiated PCR, with instantaneous measurements subject to the CDVT.

SCR Algorithm

Recall that the SCR is an upper bound on the average rate of the conforming cells of an ATM connection. The measurement duration is long, compared to that over which the PCR is defined. Enforcement of this measurement by the UPC could allow the network to allocate fewer resources than it would be required to reserve, based on the PCR, while still ensuring that the performance objectives, based on QoS parameters, can be achieved. The CDVT is defined in relation to the SCR, according to the format GCRA(1/SCR,BT + CDVT). Relative to the PCR algorithm, the time interval specified by 1/SCR is greater than that specified by 1/PCR. As mentioned earlier, the SCR and BT traffic parameters enable the endpoint to describe the future cell flow of an ATM connection in greater detail than does the PCR alone. With this greater detail, the network can more efficiently use the network resources.

AAL Types

The AAL is the two-way interface between ATM and the rest of the world, which is located in the endpoints, not in the switches. If the concept of application programming interfaces (APIs) is familiar to you, maybe an analogy will put things in perspective. If not, hopefully hearing the same concept in other terms will reinforce the idea. An API in Microsoft Windows is a helper program, of sorts. APIs allow application programmers to write their program in a more generic sense, without needing to know much about the inner workings of the operating system, which today is complex, indeed.

The AAL works even more seamlessly. The higher layers running on equipment in advance of the first ATM-aware device in the network need not know anything about the AAL to use ATM, but the programmer still has to be familiar with the calls supported by the API. As long as the correct AAL type (or SSCS) has been selected, traffic can arrive as input without the need to have been prepared in any way. In this way, the AAL acts on behalf of the higher layers, so that special non-ATM protocols and applications are not required to interface with the ATM network. This also keeps the complexity of the ATM layer and its switching functionality to a minimum, thus further improving the performance of this technology. Because the world wants only one ATM, but because the world has more than one type of input for the ATM network, multiple AAL types have proven necessary. The AAL types presented here and their associated ITU-T recommendations are as follows:

- AAL0
- AAL1 (I.363.1)
- AAL2 (I.363.2)

- AAL3/4 (I.363.3)
- AAL5 (I.363.5)

Figure 10-14 presents these AAL types, referenced against selected characteristics and the aforementioned service classes.

Figure 10-14 *AAL Types, Characteristics, and Service Classes*

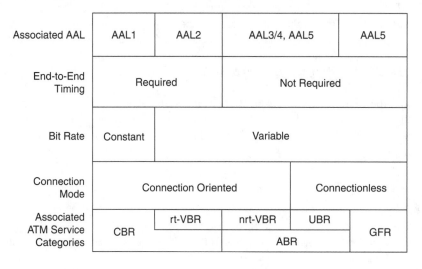

AAL0

AAL0 is not based on specifications or implementation agreements. It is simply a term to denote the input to the AAL of raw cells. AAL0 requires that user equipment provide its own proprietary or standards-based AAL functionality, resulting in fully compliant ATM cells from the higher layers. The main use of this AAL type is for equipment and applications that require an AAL type that is not compliant with the specifications, thus offering as input to the ATM process data structures that do not need to be adapted to the ATM network.

AAL1

AAL1 adapts CBR traffic, such as uncompressed voice and video, into ATM cells and is used for applications that are sensitive to cell loss, delay, and delay variation. In other words, AAL1 would be selected to transfer traffic with a constant source bit rate that must be delivered at the same rate. Because AAL1 must have timing synchronization between the source and destination, it must be implemented across a physical layer service that provides timing, such as SONET, or the timing must be provided outside the ATM network. AAL1 also emulates conventional leased lines. It requires an additional octet of SAR sublayer header information for sequence numbering and indication of the existence of a CS function, leaving 47 octets for SAR PDU payload, as this is the only portion from which an additional octet could come. In other words, the transmitting SAR sublayer accepts the 47-octet SAR-PDU payload from its CS, adds the one-octet SAR-PDU header to create the SAR PDU, and hands these 48 octets to its ATM layer for cell-header attachment. The receiving SAR accepts the 48-octet SAR PDU from its ATM layer, detaches the SAR-PDU header, and passes the 47-octet SAR-PDU payload to its CS. Figure 10-15 shows the format of the SAR PDU generated by AAL1 with traffic from the higher layers.

Figure 10-15 *AAL1 SAR-PDU Structure*

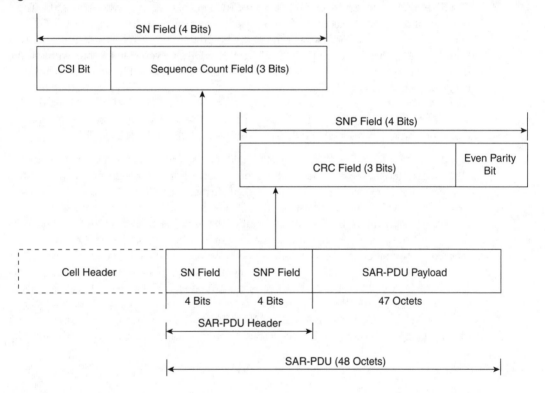

Again, the SAR PDU payload is 47 octets, not all of which is necessarily user traffic. Some of the 47-octet payload can be CS overhead. The structured data transfer (SDT) technology, which is used in circuit emulation over AAL1 connections, uses one octet in even-sequenced cells, thus limiting user payload to 46 octets. These are just examples. The missing octet in the SAR PDU carries the sequence number (SN) and sequence number protection (SNP) fields. The SN field is composed of the convergence sublayer indication (CSI) bit and 3 bits for the sequence count field. The use of sequence count values and CS indications are specified on a service-specific basis.

The CSI indicates to the receiving end if a CS function exists and is conveyed from the transmitting CS to the receiving CS. It can also be used, over four alternating SAR PDUs, to transmit the 4-bit residual time stamp (RTS) value for source clock frequency recovery. The sequence count field is incremented from zero to seven on a rotating basis, based on a count passed down from the CS, and is communicated to the receiving CS. This value is used as a basic tool to detect lost or misinserted SAR-PDU payloads (cells). This realization by the receiving CS can lead to further sequence-count processing, possibly resulting in locating the lost cell in the incoming cell stream, the identification of the number of cells lost, or the identification of the actual misinserted cell without further processing.

The SNP field is further divided into a 3-bit CRC field and a 1-bit even-parity field. The function of the entire 4 bits of the SNP is error protection, in some form. The CRC is computed on the 4-bit SN field, and the parity bit establishes even parity over the entire 8-bit SAR-PDU header. Even parity is characterized by an even count of bits with a value of one. Both of these values are checked by the receiving SAR sublayer, and besides the actual sequence count and CS indication, the result (valid or invalid) is passed up to the receiving CS through a value known as the SN check status. The CRC value is capable of 1-bit correction and multiple-bit detection of errors. The SAR sublayer has a correction and detection phase that works much the same way as with the cell's HEC field.

As ATM is a packet rather than circuit-oriented transmission technology, it must emulate circuit characteristics to provide good support for CBR traffic coming from endpoints such as private branch exchanges (PBXs). A critical attribute of a CES is that the performance realized over ATM should be comparable to that experienced with the emulated TDM technology. Basically, CES is designed to offer the same appearance to the endpoint as a nailed-up T1 circuit. CES implementations are simple, but expensive. CES requires fully meshed configurations and bandwidth is never available to other applications (even when no traffic is being sent). CES is specified in the ATM Forum IA af-vtoa-0078.000, "Circuit Emulation Service Interoperability Specification Version 2.0." The ATM Forum has also come up with what is called voice trunking (af-vtoa-0089.000, "Voice and Telephony Over ATM——ATM Trunking using AAL1 for Narrowband Services Version 1.0"), as a method to allow partial mesh designs that allow sharing of resources that are not currently in use by endpoints.

AAL2

AAL2 provides for the bandwidth-efficient transmission of low-rate, short, and variable-length packets in delay-sensitive applications. More than one AAL2 user-information stream can be supported on a single ATM connection (multiplexing). Short-length packets can be packed into one or more ATM cells with AAL2. Used with time-sensitive rt-VBR traffic, such as compressed voice and video, AAL2 allows ATM cells to be transmitted before the payload is full to accommodate an application's timing requirements. AAL2 does not currently specify a SAR sublayer, but instead implements SSCS and common part sublayer (CPS) functionality. Figure 10-16 shows the structure of the CPS packet and the CPS PDU.

Figure 10-16 *AAL2 CPS Packet and PDU Structures*

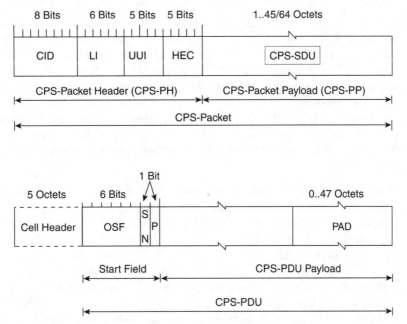

The CPS-service data unit (SDU) (a protocol's input from an adjacent layer, which is often the payload to which it attaches its header/trailer, creating its own PDU) field represents an integrally variable number of octets from either an SSCS or a layer-management entity and is referred to as the CPS-packet payload (CPS-PP). By default, the CPS-PP has a limit of 45 octets, but it can be configured by signaling or management procedures to have an upper limit of 64 octets. It is the 8-bit channel identifier (CID) field that allows multiple sources to share a single AAL2 connection. This channel is bi-directional, in that the same CID is used in both directions. A value of zero, where the CID should be, indicates that the octet is part of padded octets. Values of one through seven for the CID are reserved (one and two are for layer management and signaling, respectively). Values from 8 to 255 represent an individual AAL2 CPS user entity, which means that 248 user processes could be using a single AAL2 connection simultaneously.

The length indicator (LI) field contains the value that is one less than the number of octets in the CPS-PP. This ties in with the maximum configurable payload size of 64 because the largest value that 6 bits can represent is 63. However, when the maximum CPS-payload size is configured at 45 octets, the values 45 through 63 are not allowed. All CPS packets that belong to the same channel (having the same CID) must have the same LI value specified, but other channels on the same AAL-2 connection can have different LI values.

The SSCS and layer-management entities can pass an entity-specific identifier down to the CPS. This identifier is passed to the destination CPS for delivery to the corresponding receiving entity. The CPS-packet header (CPS-PH) contains a field called the user-to-user indication (UUI). The UUI serves to tie the source and receiving SSCS or layer-management entities together, but the possible values of the UUI field have significance. Only SSCS entities have access to UUI values from 0 to 27 (often used to convey the compression type being used or the silence information descriptor for silence suppression), and layer-management entities use values 30 and 31 only. UUI values of 28 and 29 are reserved for future use. Thus, the mere value in the UUI field identifies whether SSCS or layer management is communicating by using this CPS packet. The HEC field calculates a CRC on the first 19 bits of the CPS-PH. This HEC field is also used for error detection, but only on the CPS-PH.

Fractional to multiple CPS packets are packed into the CPS PDU, also shown in Figure 10-16, which contains the 48 octets that serve as the ATM-layer SDU. The first of these 48 octets, the CPS-PDU header, is called the start field (STF). Within the STF are three separate fields. The first is the offset field (OSF). The OSF is the number of octets between the end of the STF and the start of the first CPS packet. If no CPS packet starts in this CPS PDU, the OSF represents the number of octets to the start of the padding. If no CPS packet or padding start anywhere in the CPS PDU, the OSF has a value of 47, the maximum value allowed in this field. The 1-bit SN field numbers the stream of CPS PDUs. The receiver expects to see the SN alternate for consecutive CPS PDUs. This attempts to ensure that the original user traffic arrives in the order that it was transmitted. The 1-bit parity (P) bit works based on odd parity, with respect to the STF.

AAL2 can be used for ATM trunking of narrowband services (af-vtoa-0113.000) for voice, voice-band data, circuit-mode data, frame-mode data, and fax traffic. Voice can be compressed or uncompressed and can include silence suppression. The ATM Forum also produces an IA for AAL2 to provide loop emulation service for narrowband services (af-vmoa-0145.000), which offers an efficient transport mechanism for the services listed for trunking (except circuit-mode data), besides B-ISDN and D-channel traffic over broadband subscriber-line connections, such as xDSL, between customer premises and a service provider's service node.

AAL3/4

AAL3/4 handles bursty connection-oriented traffic (AAL3), such as error messages, or variable-rate connectionless traffic (AAL4), such as LAN file transfers and Switched Multimegabit Data Service (SMDS) traffic. It is intended for traffic that can tolerate delay but not cell loss. To ensure that the latter is kept to a minimum, AAL3/4 performs error detection on each cell and uses a sophisticated error-checking mechanism that, together with 22 additional bits of overhead, consumes 4 octets of each 48-octet payload. AAL3/4 allows ATM cells to be multiplexed, as will be discussed shortly, and accommodates point-to-point and point-to-multipoint traffic. As you can see in Figure 10-17, the AAL3/4-layer structure is somewhat more complex than the preceding two specified AAL types. AAL3/4 has a distinct SAR sublayer, as does AAL1. The portion of the layer described in Figure 10-17 as Common Part (CPCS + SAR) is roughly equivalent to the CPS in AAL2, yet the functional properties of the two sublayers are distinguished from each other in this AAL type.

NOTE   SMDS is a connectionless public data-only (no voice or video) network specification that works sort of like a LAN in a metropolitan-area network (MAN) or WAN. Although SMDS uses addressing similar to ATM (E.164), SMDS only requires one address for each location that connects to the network, not one for each endpoint as ATM does. By virtue of this simplified addressing scheme and its connectionless nature, SMDS does not have the complexities associated with designing, defining, and configuring QoS parameters. As a result, SMDS fails to gain market-share because of its inability to offer guarantees, or even predictability, to applications that are sensitive to time and delay constraints, such as voice and video. Limited coverage for SMDS also makes it less popular for enterprise data networking solutions.

The common part is capable of transmitting user traffic in message or streaming mode. Message mode is characterized by the input from the SSCS or higher layers (the SSCS could be null) to the CPCS (the CPCS SDU) having a tight correspondence to the output (the CPCS PDU) down to the SAR sublayer. Streaming mode also places a single CPCS SDU into one CPCS PDU. Unlike message mode, streaming mode can employ an internal pipelining service that allows the SDU to begin filling the PDU and for the source CPCS entity to begin transmitting the PDU to the destination CPCS entity before the entire SDU has been received by the CPCS. An abort function can be used by the streaming mode service to end the CPCS SDU early, thereby signaling the cancellation of the transfer for the remainder of the CPCS SDU. Both the SAR sublayer and the CPCS can generate the abort function against their respective SDUs.

The AAL3/4 SAR-PDU payload consists of only 44 octets. Figure 10-18 shows the SAR PDU and its related header and trailer fields. The segment type (ST) field indicates whether the SAR PDU is carrying some form of partial message or the complete message. This is based upon how many SAR PDUs the CPCS PDU (i.e., the SAR SDU) requires. The CPCS PDU payload (user data) can be anywhere from one to 65,535 octets in length, with extended lengths as the subject of further study by the ITU-T. Figure 10-18 also shows the binary values for the two bits that comprise the segment type. Thus, with these four values for the ST field, a SAR PDU (i.e., a cell) can be labeled as the beginning of a message (BOM), the continuation of a message (COM), the end of a message (EOM), or the only segment of the message (i.e., single-segment message [SSM]).

Figure 10-17 *AAL3/4 Sublayer Structure*

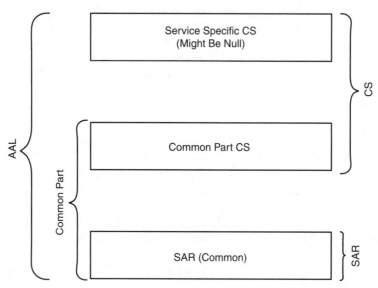

The 4-bit SN field allows the ordered identification of SAR PDUs that make up a single SAR SDU. The source can begin with any of the 16 possible values, because the destination does not compare the sequence number of the last PDU of a SAR SDU with that of the first PDU of the next SAR SDU. Simply stated, this means that endpoints only want to see segments of a message sequenced properly, with no interest in keeping sequencing flowing across successive message boundaries.

The 10-bit multiplexing identification (MID) field can multiplex multiple SAR flows onto a single ATM connection. The value of the MID is zero when no multiplexing is taking place. This multiplexing occurs from one endpoint to another. It is not designed to allow traffic from multiple sources to combine into a single stream for one endpoint. Furthermore, each ATM connection that contains multiplexed traffic appears to be a single entity for the purpose of management and administration. Regardless of the connection orientation of the application, all SAR PDUs of the same SAR SDU have identical MID values. This identical value ties each of the PDUs in with their mutual SAR SDU. This field is the basis behind AAL3/4's ability to interleave PDUs from different SAR SDUs and to identify them at the destination for reassembly into the original SDUs.

The SAR-PDU payload is always 44 octets, but can be padded to the right with zeros for octets that have no user information. These zero-value octets are ignored by the destination because the LI field carries the number of octets of SAR-SDU information that the payload actually contains. If the PDU represents the beginning or continuation of a message, it is implied that this is neither the only nor the last PDU in the SDU. Thus, the entire PDU must be dedicated entirely to the SDU. Therefore, the LI is always be 44 for these segment types.

Figure 10-18 *AAL3/4 SAR PDU Fields with ST and LI Values*

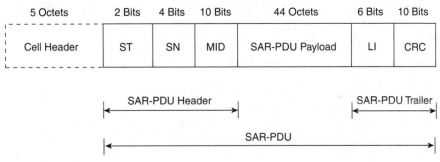

Segment Type	ST Encoding	LI Permissible Value
BOM	10	44
COM	00	44
EOM	01	4..44, 63
SSM	11	8..44

Coding of the ST Field and LI Field, by Segment Type

If the PDU represents the end of a message, the minimum content allowed corresponds to the 4-octet CPCS-PDU trailer, which will be discussed in detail shortly. As a result, the minimum value for the LI of an EOM segment is four, and the CPCS trailer could be preceded by up to 40 octets of SAR SDU content, which allows the maximum value of LI to be a predictable 44. However, for EOM segments, this value is allowed to equal the maximum the field allows, which is 63 for 6 bits. This special case corresponds to the aforementioned abort feature of the streaming mode service. When the destination detects an LI of 63, it realizes that the SAR SDU was aborted mid-stream and that this is not the normal end of the source traffic.

Finally, in the case of a SAR PDU representing an SSM, the maximum value for LI is, again, 44. However, the minimum for an SSM segment is eight, because a SAR SDU (remember this is also the CPCS PDU) that fits within a single SAR PDU must, as a minimum, contain the 4-octet CPCS-PDU header and the aforementioned 4-octet trailer, for a total of 8 octets. The LI value of 63 is not allowed for SSMs because the entire message is transferred with the single PDU, and the abort function has no meaning. The

SAR-PDU trailer's CRC is a standard 10-bit checksum computed on the SAR-PDU header, payload, and LI field. The value installed in this field is compared to the value computed at the destination by using the same algorithm.

As a review for the abort-SAR-PDU format, remember that the format for the PDU is identical to the standard SAR PDU, but three characteristics stand out, concerning the abort-SAR-PDU:

- ST field is coded for EOM.
- Payload can be all zeros and is ignored by destination.
- LI field is set to 63.

The SSCS, if not null, is specified by separate specifications from that of AAL3/4. The SSCS can have its own header and trailer structure, depending on the exact implementation. This header, trailer, and payload form the CPCS SDU. The functions of the AAL3/4 SSCS are beyond the scope of this chapter, as no specific function list could encompass all possible (or even the majority of) SSCS implementations. The CPCS, however, is standard in all implementations, and as such, a list of CPCS functions follows:

- **Preservation of CPCS SDU**—The CPCS preserves the original boundaries of the CPCS SDU that it receives from the SSCS or higher layers, transparently transmitting this structure down through the stack, where it can be recognized in its original form by the destination.

- **Error detection and handling**—The CPCS detects and handles corrupted CPCS PDUs. The resulting corrupted CPCS SDUs are either discarded or are optionally delivered to the SSCS, the procedures for which are not yet specified. For example, the CPCS sublayer can detect Btag/Etag mismatches (discussed shortly). It can discover that the received length and the value installed in the CPCS-PDU length field do not match. The CPCS can also detect and handle obvious problems, such as buffer overflows and improperly formatted CPCS PDUs. The SAR sublayer can also indicate errors to the CPCS.

- **Buffer allocation size**—The source CPCS can communicate to the destination CPCS the maximum buffer size that should be necessary to receive the CPCS PDU.

- **Abort**—The CPCS can notify the SAR that it wants to abort a partially transmitted CPCS SDU. The SAR sublayer's implementation of this request was discussed previously.

- **CPCS-SDU sequence integrity**—The CPCS can ensure that the sequence of CPCS SDUs received from the SSCS or higher layers is maintained within one CPCS connection.

- **Mapping between CPCS connections and SAR connections**—The one-to-one mapping between CPCS connections and SAR connections means that neither multiplexing nor splitting is provided for or among CPCS connections.

- **Handling of congestion information**—Although not yet specified, in the future the CPCS might provide for the bi-directional passing of congestion information between the layers above the AAL3/4 common part.

- **Handling of loss priority information**—Also not yet included in the specification, the CPCS might one day be able to pass CLP information between the layers above the AAL3/4 common part, in both directions, as a means of allowing the application to control its device's contribution to network congestion.

Figure 10-19 shows the format of the CPCS PDU, including its header and trailer fields.

Figure 10-19 *AAL3/4 CPCS PDU Fields*

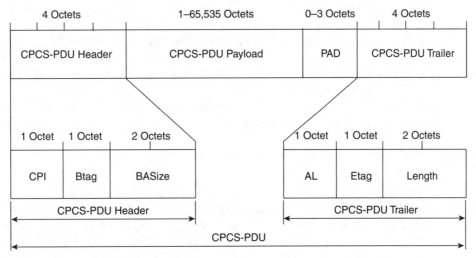

The common part indicator (CPI) field is set to all zeros, in practice, but in the future could represent such things as the units of measure for the other header and trailer fields, with additional uses being considered by the ITU-T. Whatever future functions are developed for the CPI field will be restricted to the common part (CPCS + SAR) of AAL3/4.

The beginning tag (Btag) field is the first of two fields to allow the header and trailer of the CPCS PDU to be matched to one another. The same value in this field will also appear in the end tag (Etag) field, which appears in the CPCS-PDU trailer. Successive CPCS PDUs do not have any mutual association between these fields. Although the tag fields of different PDUs require no relationship across PDU boundaries, it is a common implementation to increment the Btag/Etag pair for successive PDUs using the same MID value.

The buffer allocation size (BASize) indication field carries a relative reference to the size that the destination should use in configuring its buffer to handle receipt of the CPCS SDU. When message mode is implemented, the BAsize equals the number of counting units (the size of which is specified in the CPI field) in the CPCS-PDU payload, also denoted by the length field. Therefore, the BAsize field and the length field are equal for message mode.

For streaming mode, BAsize is at least equal to the CPCS-PDU payload size, but can be greater. In other words, in streaming mode, the BAsize field is greater than or equal to the length field. The fact that the BAsize and length fields rely on the CPI field for their unit of measure means that the length of the CPCS-PDU payload is limited to the product of the largest value that the BAsize field allows and the value of the counting unit indicated in the CPI field. Until further specifications are drafted, this is the largest value 16 bits can represent (i.e., 65,535) multiplied by the default meaning of the CPI field (i.e., 1 octet), for a total of 65,535 octets, with the minimum working out to be 1 octet.

The padding (PAD) field is situated between the end of the CPCS-PDU payload and the beginning of the CPCS-PDU trailer. The sole purpose of the PAD field is to ensure that the overall length of the CPCS PDU is an integral multiple of four. There might be 0, 1, 2, or 3 octets of PAD required to fulfill this purpose. If one or more octets are required, values of zero are commonly used, as these octets are ignored by the destination, based on the number of CPI-defined counting units that the length field indicates are present in the CPCS-PDU payload portion. The last field to discuss appears at the beginning of the trailer—the alignment (AL) field, which is another unused field that exists only to fill the trailer out to 4 octets, matching the header. The AL field must be set to zero and does not convey any information to the destination.

AAL5

AAL5 accommodates bursty data traffic without regard for connection orientation, which includes most non-SMDS traffic (e.g., classical IP over ATM and LANE), using less overhead than AAL3/4. As you will see, no overhead at all comes from the SAR sublayer, which was the principle source of wasted payload for AAL3/4, even to the point of adding a 1-octet field to even the trailer up. AAL5 is also referred to as the simple and efficient AAL (SEAL) because the SAR sublayer simply separates the SAR SDU into 48-octet SAR PDUs, with no header or trailer octets of its own. As a result, AAL5 does not support SAR-PDU multiplexing (the optional SSCS would have to supply this functionality), nor does it support many of the other features that some AAL3/4 applications depend upon, such as sequencing and error protection at the cell-payload level. Nevertheless, with proper application design, AAL5 would be one of the last AAL types to disappear because of its overwhelming savings in overhead. Similar to AAL3/4, AAL5 supports point-to-point and point-to-multipoint, connections.

The AAL sublayer structure depicted earlier in Figure 10-17 also applies to AAL5. Similar to AAL3/4, AAL5 provides message- and streaming-mode services within the common part (CPCS + SAR), and a 65,535-octet limit to the CPCS-PDU payload. Although the specification for AAL5 lists similar functions for the CPCS as AAL3/4, the SAR functionality is notably pared down for AAL5, listing only three functions, compared with eight for AAL3/4. As shown in Figure 10-20, the LSB in the PT field of the ATM cell denotes the continuation status of that cell, which is the SAR PDU, with respect to the SAR SDU.

Figure 10-20 *AAL5's Simple SAR PDU*

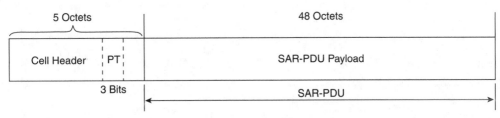

The SAR sublayer communicates to the ATM layer (by use of a primitive) whether each PDU it hands to the ATM layer comprises the beginning/continuation or the end of a SAR SDU. The ATM layer, in the construction of the cell's header, sets the LSB of the PT field to a zero if the cell payload is composed of beginning/continuing SAR SDU content and to a one if the cell payload contains the last of the SAR SDU. This functionality was discussed earlier in this chapter, during the introduction of Table 10-2 in the "Payload Type (PT) and OAM Cells" section. In Figure 10-20, nothing is missing regarding the format of the SAR PDU. It literally consists of 48 octets of SAR SDU material. In other words, the entire SAR PDU is payload, for AAL5. Contrast this with the four octets of overhead in the AAL3/4 SAR PDU, which leaves only 44 octets of payload.

Figure 10-21 shows the AAL5 CPCS PDU, along with the fields that comprise it. The CPCS PDU is made up of the 65,535-octet (or smaller) CPCS-PDU payload (i.e., the CPCS SDU), an 8-octet trailer, discussed shortly, and a padding field of 0 to 47 unused octets, which makes sure the CPCS-PDU trailer is located in the last 8 octets of the CPCS PDU, and the last SAR PDU (these octets can hold any value and are ignored). As a result of this goal, the PAD must come before the CPCS-PDU trailer, if it is needed at all. Remember, the SAR PDU is only 48 octets, so any CPCS SDU larger than 40 octets results in a CPCS PDU (i.e., SAR SDU) that contributed to multiple SAR PDUs, because for a CPCS SDU of 40 octets or less, either padding to complement the payload and trailer to a total of 48 octets or no padding at all is required, which results in a single SAR PDU.

This brings up another point. Any SAR SDU that does not contribute exactly 40 octets to the last (or only) SAR-PDU payload caused some non-zero amount of padding to be implemented. Fourty octets do not require padding because the final PDU contains the 8-octet trailer, which makes a total of 48 octets in the PDU, just what the ATM layer needs.

Figure 10-21 *AAL5 CPCS PDU and Fields*

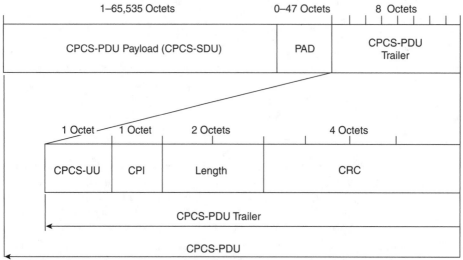

This means that the CPCS PDU is always an integral multiple of 48. This is another function of the PAD. Because the AAL5 SAR sublayer does not have the mechanism to track its own addition of padding, as in the case of the AAL3/4 SAR sublayer (the LI field), the AAL5 SAR sublayer must be handed a SAR SDU that has been padded already, if necessary. In any event, the AAL5 SAR sublayer requires an SDU that is already an exact multiple of 48 octets in length, so that it can concentrate on dividing the SAR SDU into 48-octet PDU payloads and not concern itself with finding extra octets at the end, not to mention some method of keeping track of how many octets it had to pad, which would only lead to more overhead.

Consider the mildly special case of having less than 8 octets left over with which to add the CPCS-PDU trailer to the payload and optional PAD. This is how you would get a total of 47 octets of padding. Obviously, you can't have 47 octets of padding and 8 octets of trailer in the same SAR PDU. To reach 47 octets of padding pad up to 7 (a frustratingly worthless number for the 8-octet trailer) octets in the next to the last SAR PDU and 40 octets (for a total of 47 octets) in the last PDU, right before the 8 octets of the trailer. Remember, the padding is occurring at the CPCS, not at the SAR sublayer. It only becomes visible across future cell boundaries at the SAR sublayer.

The 8-octet CPCS-PDU trailer that you see in Figure 10-21 is composed of 4 fields. The rightmost one is the familiar CRC calculation, this time a whopping 32 bits of CRC. This CRC, despite its prominent coverage, only provides error detection, not correction, over the entire preceding remainder of the CPCS PDU. The CPCS user-to-user (CPCS-UU) indication field is simply used to transfer CPCS user information transparently across the network. The CPI is used much like the AL field of the AAL3/4 CPCS-PDU trailer. The CPI is currently only set to all zeros, which serves to align the trailer to 64 bits. The 2-octet length field is set to zero for the abort function but, otherwise, carries the number of octets in the CPCS-PDU payload. The length field also serves to help the destination detect lost or inserted information errors.

Expert White Board: ATM QoS

In recent years, private businesses and governments have invested greatly in information technology to improve turnaround time in services, to facilitate access to their service anytime of the day from the comfort of there customer's home, and to cut costs by automating the office environment and combining networks. In the past, business and government had at least two networks:

- A data network to provide connectivity among the mainframe, servers, and personal computers
- TDM/switch network to provide voice and video support

Supporting these two networks was costly because of the need to maintain two sets of equipment. This usually meant maintaining two separate groups of technical staff, which require training and support equipment. In this framework, ATM became the solution to consolidate both networks into one network that can transport data, voice, and video. One of the most important characteristics of ATM is the inherent QoS features that were included on ATM from its design.

QoS is important in a network to protect business critical applications, to protect voice and video from congestion and latency, and to guarantee bandwidth to achieve network performance objectives. QoS has the following objectives:

- Controlled latency
- Dedicated bandwidth
- Improved loss characteristics under congestion

ATM accomplishes these objectives by classifying traffic in five service categories or classes. For each service category a set of parameters are defined to characterize the QoS for that service category. These service categories are divided further into real-time and non-real-time classes. The real-time classes are as follows:

- CBR
- rt-VBR

The non-real-time classes are as follows:

- nrt-VBR
- ABR
- UBR

The AF Traffic Management Specification describes these service categories as follows.

CBR Service Category Definition

The CBR service category is used by connections that request a static amount of bandwidth that is continuously available during the connection lifetime. This amount of bandwidth is characterized by a PCR value. CBR service is intended to support real-time applications that require tightly constrained delay variation (e.g., voice, video, and circuit emulation), but it is not restricted to these applications. In the CBR capability, the source can emit cells at or below the negotiated PCR (and can also be silent) for periods of time. Cells that are delayed beyond the value specified by the maxCTD are assumed to be of significantly reduced value to the application.

rt-VBR Service Category Definition

The rt-VBR service category is intended for real-time applications (i.e., those requiring tightly constrained delay and delay variation, as would be appropriate for voice and video applications). rt-VBR connections are characterized in terms of a PCR, SCR, and MBS. Sources are expected to transmit at a rate that varies with time. Equivalently the source can be described as bursty. Cells that are delayed beyond the value specified by maxCTD are assumed to be of significantly reduced value to the application. rt-VBR service can support statistical multiplexing of real-time sources.

nrt-VBR Service Category Definition

The nrt-VBR service category is intended for non-real-time applications that have bursty traffic characteristics and that are characterized in terms of a PCR, SCR, and MBS. For those cells that are transferred within the traffic contract, the application expects a low CLR. nrt-VBR service can support statistical multiplexing of connections. No delay bounds are associated with this service category.

UBR Service Category Definition

The UBR service category is intended for non-real-time applications (i.e., those not requiring tightly constrained delay and delay variation). Examples of such applications are traditional computer communications applications such as file transfer and e-mail. UBR service does not specify traffic-related service guarantees. Congestion control for UBR can be performed at a higher layer on an end-to-end basis. The UBR service is indicated by use of the best effort indicator in the ATM User Cell Rate Information Element (IE).

ABR Service Category Definition

ABR is an ATM layer service category for which the limiting ATM layer transfer characteristics, which are provided by the network, can change subsequent to connection establishment. A flow-control mechanism is specified that supports several types of feedback to control the source rate in response to changing ATM layer transfer characteristics. This feedback is conveyed to the source through specific control cells called resource management cells (RM-cells). It is expected that an end system that adapts its traffic in accordance with the feedback will experience a low CLR and obtain a fair share of the available bandwidth according to a network-specific allocation policy. The ABR service does not require bounding the delay or the delay variation experienced by a given connection. ABR service is not intended to support real-time applications. On the establishment of an ABR connection, the end system specifies to the network both a maximum required bandwidth and a minimum usable bandwidth. These are designated as PCR and MCR. The MCR can be specified as zero. The bandwidth available from the network can vary, but it won't become less than MCR.

Parameters that Define the QoS of the Service Categories

Six parameters define the QoS of the service categories. Three of these can be negotiated between the end user and the service provider. The parameters that are negotiable are as follows:

- Peak-to-peak CDV
- maxCTD
- CLR

The following QoS parameters are not negotiated:

- CER
- SECBR
- CMR

As you can see, ATM provides a variety of service categories that fix any user QoS needs by providing great flexibility. Depending on the end user's application needs, it can choose from a service category and then customize it by defining the parameters to meet the particular networks needs.

Expert White Board Reference

ATM Forum, ATM Forum Traffic Management Specification, Version 4.1, af-tm-0121.000, March 1999.

Summary

ATM, originally a transport method for B-ISDN, is designed to switch cells through a network at high bandwidth rates. You can think of ATM as originating out of ISDN, just as other technologies, such as Frame Relay and Signaling System 7 have. Using a static cell size of 53 octets (48-octet payload and 5-octet header), ATM can switch cells quickly through the network. The fixed cell size allows for the accurate prediction of delay through the network. This paves the way for QoS and allows service providers to offer highly reliable network transmission offerings.

ATM, as a technology, is normally found on service provider backbones rather than as a local loop service to customer sites. Although most customers never tap into the actual ATM infrastructure, its presence greatly enhances the customer network experience. For the most part, ATM is used in service provider networks, but it was also designed for operation in office environments using LANE. LANE, however, has never taken hold because of the cost and complexity of some implementations.

Different service classes provide different levels and types of service for different applications. There is a logical split between real-time traffic classes and non-real-time traffic classes. CBR, commonly associated with real-time traffic, supports time-sensitive communication, such as uncompressed voice. If your traffic needs no specific guarantees for transport through the network, you can use service classes such as ABR and UBR for non-real-time services. ABR allows equipment to use whatever bandwidth is available at the time of transmission. It doesn't give you the absolute highest amount of bandwidth available, but when deployed correctly it is efficient in ensuring that all applications get their fair share.

ATM currently specifies five different AAL types. AAL1 is a specification for CBR traffic and is required for CES, which is used in connecting PBXs or other devices across an ATM network. In essence, CES emulates a nailed-up T1 circuit. AAL2 accommodates connection-oriented VBR traffic, such as compressed voice, that is time sensitive but more tolerant than CBR of delay and delay variation. AAL3 and AAL4 (AAL3/4) provide service for nrt-VBR, ABR, and UBR traffic that can handle a higher amount of delay with error detection, such as Frame Relay. Together they support both connection-oriented and connectionless traffic. AAL5 is similar to AAL3/4, but as its nickname SEAL implies, is simpler and more efficient, which also means it is not as feature-rich.

ATM connections are identified in much the same way as those of Frame Relay, but instead of DLCIs, ATM uses VPIs and VCIs. They are used as VPI/VCI pairs to identify specific connections between ATM nodes and are locally significant to the two connected nodes. A total of 256 VPIs can be used across the UNI or up to 4096 with NNI. However, when you consider the possible number of VCIs per VPI, the possible connection identifiers explode into the millions.

The CLP determines which of the cells can be sacrificed during times of congestion in the network, in preference to cells not marked in such a way. This function serves to lessen the network load during times that ATM equipment cannot keep up with the demand being placed on it. Not all cells are marked as CLP=1, and it is normally something that would go into the network design, regarding traffic shaping and policing. Traffic shaping works on the premise that you might want to make sure that your time-sensitive, irreplaceable voice traffic does not get discarded, but maybe some of your data traffic would be more expendable because of higher-layer safeguards. Policing is based on the need for the network to make sure that one misbehaving endpoint does not jeopardize the QoS that others can exact from the network.

Review Questions

Give or select the best answer or answers to the following questions. The answers to these questions can be found in Appendix A, "Answers to Review Questions."

1 What is the difference between UNI and NNI?

2 Why are there more available VPIs in an NNI header?

3 What do you call a cell that is destined for one connection but because of an error has been delivered to a different connection?

4 For what technology was ATM originally designed to be the transport system?

    a Broadband ISDN

    b Frame relay

    c SONET

    d T3

5 How large is an ATM cell?

   a 53 bytes

   b 24 bits

   c 53 octets

   d 48 octets

6 Which of the following ranges of VCI cannot be used for standard addressing when the VPI is 0?

   a 0 – 32

   b 32 – 63

   c 0 – 31

   d 5 – 36

   e 20 – 35

7 What is the function of the SAR sublayer?

_____

_____

_____

8 What would be the best AAL type to handle compressed video-conferencing traffic?

   a AAL0

   b AAL1

   c AAL2

   d AAL3/4

   e AAL5

9 What is the difference between traffic shaping and traffic policing?

_____

_____

_____

10 What are the two uses of the HEC field on the ATM cell header?

_____

_____

_____

This chapter covers the following topics:

- **History of Switched Multimegabit Data Service (SMDS)**—A brief history of SMDS.

- **Introduction to SMDS**—An introduction including a brief discussion of the SMDS architecture.

- **SMDS features**—Coverage of SMDS features including addressing, multiple access speeds, and seamless internetworking of network layer protocols.

- **SMDS Interface Protocol (SIP)**—Includes a Distributed Queue Dual Bus (DQDB) overview, information on segmentation and reassembly (SAR) of Initial Media Access Control protocol data units (IMPDUs), and details on SIP Levels 3, 2, and 1.

- **Data Exchange Interface (DXI)**-An overview of DXI including information on DXI framing.

- **Internetworking LAN protocols over SMDS**—A brief note about carrying LAN-to-LAN data across metropolitan-area networks (MANs) and WANs using Logical Link Control (LLC) encapsulation.

- **Configuring SMDS**—SMDS configuration information and an example.

- **Resolving SMDS problems**—Information on SMDS troubleshooting including DXI problems, Subscriber Network Interface (SNI) problems, multiple interfaces in the same group, and the pseudo-LAN serial problem.

- **The demise of SMDS**—A section about why SMDS has fallen out of favor.

CHAPTER 11

Switched Multimegabit Data Service

The SMDS is composed of a set of technologies that allow for high-speed, connectionless, LAN-to-LAN networking in MANs and WANs. Connectivity to the SMDS network is provided over digital dataphone service (DDS), T1/E1, or T3/E3 facilities. As a LAN-interconnect service, native support exists for all major networking protocols, such as Transmission Control Protocol/Internet Protocol (TCP/IP), Internetwork Packet Exchange (IPX), and Appletalk. Furthermore, SMDS frames are sized large enough to support seamless transport of IEEE 802.3, 802.5, and Fiber Distributed Data Interface (FDDI) frames without fragmentation. As a switched service, SMDS is economically attractive. It is generally a distance-insensitive transport technology, which means that the price for service is based on speed and the number of sites alone, not the distance between sites, which is the case with private-line services. Network management is performed using the standards-based Simple Network Management Protocol (SNMP), thus making off-the-shelf network management systems a viable option, rather than having to build proprietary systems. Finally, it is designed to provide a seamless integration with and eventual transition to Asynchronous Transfer Mode (ATM). In essence, the name of the service summarizes the overall features:

- **Switched**—SMDS PDUs are switched through a public data network (PDN) rather than directed over point-to-point lines between customer sites.

- **Multimegabit**—SMDS was the first public broadband service deployed.

- **Data**—Designed for data services that exhibit bursty, asynchronous traffic patterns.

- **Service**—Not a technology!

History of SMDS

During the early to mid 1980s, the U.S. Regional Bell Operating Companies (RBOCs) were looking at ways to transform the public switched telephone network (PSTN) into a digital network capable of supporting a vast array of services that allowed for high-speed connectivity, limited error rates, rapid provisioning, and better performance monitoring. As an additional goal, these providers were seeking ways to increase revenues in the data services arena, where, at the time, LAN-to-LAN interconnection was beginning to become a business-critical telecommunications requirement. A vision began to form of a Broadband Integrated Services Digital Network (B-ISDN) capable of meeting all these needs and more. However, the B-ISDN standards process was slow moving. There were too many goals to be accomplished for the service to be fully realized in a rapid way.

At about the same time, members of the Institute of Electrical and Electronics Engineers (IEEE) 802 working group were close to standardizing a technology that would allow for LAN-to-LAN connectivity in MANs. This technology, Distributed Queue Dial Bus (DQDB), was designed to support high-speed, connectionless LAN-to-LAN networking through a cell-switched network. Although this technology was rigorously specified, the 802.6 working group did not describe a service offering that could be leveraged by the RBOCs to offer LAN-to-LAN connectivity over the new digital carrier network being deployed.

Recognizing this deficiency and being acutely aware of the slow-moving B-ISDN standardization process, a technical team at Bell Communications Research (Bellcore) began developing a service that would realize the goals of the 802.6 working group, while at the same time meet some important challenges facing the RBOCs. In particular, Bellcore focused on the following goals:

- **To develop a market-driven service**—The RBOCs were betting heavily on a new, digital network. Digital signal level 1 (DS-1) technology was beginning to replace analog service to connect LANs, and the RBOCs felt that by the time the service was deployable, it would be difficult to incent a migration to a public switched data network. Taking this into consideration, and remembering the original aim of DQDB, Bellcore standardized the initial service description based on customer connectivity to the service at digital service 3 (DS3) rates. In 1989 DS1 access was added and in 1993, low-speed 56 k access was incorporated into the service.

- **To ensure that customers' existing data networking investment was not wasted**— Rather than force customers to redeploy new, expensive hardware and software, Bellcore focused on enabling the new service in a way that would allow existing equipment to be used.

- **To place emphasis on a service, rather than a technology**—The RBOCs previous efforts had always been focused around what would be best suited for implementation in the telephone network, rather than what would best suit the customer's network. ISDN is an example of a service that was ideal for the RBOCs but a poor option for extending customer LANs. In the case of SMDS, Bellcore focused on the service and ignored (for the most part) the network implementation details.

- **To minimize innovation**—Rather than try and build a perfect service that met all possible needs, Bellcore focused on the minimum requirements to deploy a reliable, working data service. Innovation was happening in B-ISDN, and it was taking too long. Market impetus would not allow a slow-moving, consensus-based innovation cycle to dictate the time-to-deploy schedule.

- **To ensure timely delivery**—Because data networking was becoming mission-critical——to both businesses and the RBOCs themselves——it was of paramount importance that Bellcore delivered a service that vendors could implement by the end of 1991.

In 1988, Bellcore produced a Technical Advisory that detailed the requirements necessary to facilitate a service based on DQDB that would allow for MAN/WAN datagram services over existing telecommunications facilities. The specification defined the Switched Multimegabit Data Service, which allowed the DQDB mechanisms to be realized in a telecommunications context without changing the existing transport technology that was becoming prevalent at the time. Within the next two years additional specifications were defined that detailed the requirements for various customer access mechanisms, switch architectures, inter-office and inter-switch interface details, and Operations Support Systems (OSS) facilities. Thus, SMDS was born.

Although the Bellcore specifications defined the service from a telecommunications provider perspective, customer premises equipment (CPE) vendors were still at a loss. For example, there were no internetworking specifications available that would define how to encapsulate TCP/IP packets over SMDS frames. As a result of this additional missing element, in 1990, the SMDS Interest Group (SIG) was formed. The charter of the SIG was to extend the SMDS specifications in a way that allowed customers and CPE vendors to build interoperable internetworking solutions over an SMDS network. In March of 1991, the Internet Engineering Task Force (IETF) published RFC 1209, "The Transmission of IP Datagrams over SMDS," and shortly thereafter both Novell and Apple published specifications describing how IPX and AppleTalk would work over SMDS. With these specifications in place, vendors began shipping products that supported SMDS, and customers began buying into the technology. By 1995, SMDS was widely deployed by nearly every major US and international telco.

As you will see later in the chapter in the "The Demise of SMDS" section, the meteoric rise of SMDS deployment was followed shortly thereafter by an equally rapid decline. Today, only a handful of SMDS customers exist, and those that do are being encouraged to migrate away from the technology as soon as possible. This short claim to fame was not a result of a technological deficiency, but rather, a consequence of the huge amount of momentum behind ATM, which was ultimately too much for the networking industry—in particular the service providers—to resist. In any case, SMDS is a wonderful technology that, even if not of particular relevance today, has a plethora of interesting and useful features to warrant more discussion.

Introduction to SMDS

SMDS is a service more than a technology. In fact, multiple technologies are required to implement an SMDS network. An overview of the SMDS architecture is shown in Figure 11-1.

Figure 11-1 *SMDS Architecture*

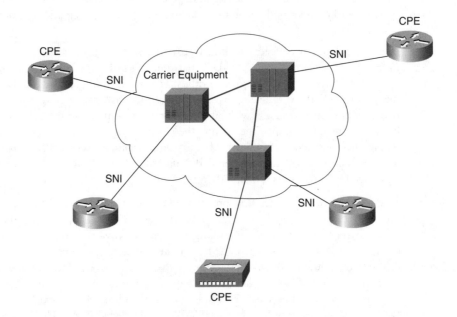

Figure 11-1 shows that there are essentially two major elements to an SMDS network—
CPE and carrier equipment (CE). Between the CPE and the carrier network is the
Subscriber Network Interface (SNI), which is the boundary between the customer and the
provider. The CPE is equipment that accesses the SMDS network—in most cases routers,
bridges, channel service unit/data service units (CSU/DSUs) and terminals. CE is
composed of high-speed switches, intra-office and inter-office facilities (add/drop
multiplexers [ADMs], Digital Access and Crossconnect Systems [DACSs], channel banks,
and the digital lines connecting them), and the OSS systems required to support the
network; for example, network surveillance and billing systems. To provide seamless
connectivity across the SNI, a protocol is required that both the CPE and CE understand
and agree upon. The SMDS Interface Protocol (SIP), which is derived from IEEE 802.6
DQDB, provides the required primitives, data structures, and elements needed to connect
various CPE to the network. SIP is covered in detail in the "SIP" section later in this chapter.
The Data Exchange Interface (DXI) protocol, defined by the SIG, provides a high-level data
link control (HDLC)-like access mechanism to an SMDS network, thereby minimizing the
complexity required for a vendor to develop SMDS CPE. DXI is covered in the "DXI"
section later in this chapter.

SMDS Features

SMDS is a feature rich service—even by today's standards. One of the goals of SMDS was to make it look similar to a LAN—thus making the underlying provider network as transparent as possible to the LAN technology it was interconnecting. Some of the major features are summarized in the following sections.

Addressing

SMDS provides an addressing mechanism based on ITU E.164 formatting, which essentially makes SMDS addresses look exactly like phone numbers. Each CPE can have multiple SMDS addresses (up to 16), which are used for unicast datagram delivery. Broadcast and multicast delivery is also provided through one or more group addresses that are associated with CPE. For security, address screening (AS) and source address verification (SAV) are available. Using AS and SAV, the SMDS network provider can build communities of interest, or more appropriately, Virtual Private Networks (VPNs) within the SMDS cloud.

Multiple Access Speeds

Customers looking to access an SMDS network have many choices when selecting appropriate access speeds. As mentioned earlier, the original focus was on transparent LAN-interconnection, and the RBOCs could best realize this goal using DS3 facilities. However, DS3 speeds are far too high for connecting two 4-Mbps Token Ring LANs. To make the service both economically attractive for the customer and scalable for the provider, five access-classes were defined. Each access-class maps directly to the prevalent LAN speeds of the time. The five access-classes and the corresponding LAN technologies are shown in Table 11-1.

Table 11-1   *SMDS Access-Classes and Corresponding LAN Technologies*

Access-Class	Payload Rate	LAN Technology
1	4 Mbps	4-Mbps Token Ring
2	10 Mbps	Ethernet
3	16 Mbps	16-Mbps Token Ring
4	25 Mbps	25-Mbps ATM LAN
5	34 Mbps	FDDI, Fast Ethernet

Seamless Internetworking of Network Layer Protocols

SMDS accommodates all major Layer-3 protocols. TCP/IP, IPX, Appletalk, Connectionless Network Service (CLNS), Digital Equipment Corporation (DECnet), Xerox Network Systems (XNS) and Virtual Integrated Network Service (VINES) are all supported. SMDS can also be used in bridged networks, can take part in the Spanning Tree Protocol (STP) through extensions defined in IEEE 802.1g, and can support connection-oriented services such as Network Basic Input/Output System (NetBIOS) over 802.2 LLC2. Again, the goal was to make SMDS look like a LAN. For example, address resolution in TCP/IP over SMDS uses Address Resolution Protocol (ARP), just like on Ethernet! Example 11-1 shows an IP-enabled High-Speed Serial Interface (HSSI) that is connected to an SMDS cloud, and the corresponding ARP entries that associate IP addresses to various SMDS addresses.

Example 11-1 *IP over SMDS Address Resolution*

```
SMDS-Router#show ip arp Hssi8/0/0.1
Protocol  Address           Age (min)  Hardware Addr    Type    Interface
Internet  192.168.197.246         223  c155.5555.4630   SMDS    Hssi8/0/0.1
Internet  192.168.197.244         222  c155.5555.1533   SMDS    Hssi8/0/0.1
Internet  192.168.197.242         222  c255.5555.4329   SMDS    Hssi8/0/0.1
```

SIP

The SIP (not to be confused with the Session Initiation Protocol used in Voice over IP [VoIP] networks) is a three-layer protocol stack that maps to the first two layers of the Open System Interconnection (OSI) protocol model. The primary role of SIP is to provide for the features offered by SMDS, as discussed in the previous section. It is one of the access protocols that connects to the SMDS network. SIP is based on, but is not a replacement for, the DQDB protocol specified in IEEE 802.6. SIP does implement many of the functions of the access portion of DQDB, such as bus arbitration in multi-CPE arrangements. Furthermore, SIP is only defined across the SNI, whereas DQDB provides a generic architecture for a shared, counter-directional, dual bus that supports multiple interfaces, access arbitration, numerous bus maintenance functions, and so on. Before continuing the discussion on SIP, a short overview of the DQDB protocol is warranted to place SIP in the correct frame of reference when compared to DQDB.

DQDB Overview

The DQDB protocol was discussed earlier as a precursor to the SMDS service developed by Bellcore. To be clear, this was not the intention of the IEEE when defining DQDB. The IEEE 802 working group is responsible for defining physical and data-link layer standards for use in intraLAN and interLAN networks. Thus, DQDB is part of a larger group of technologies such as Ethernet (802.3), Token Ring (802.5), bridges and switches (802.1), wireless LANs (802.11), and so on. The primary purpose of DQDB is to provide a connectionless Media Access Control (MAC)-sublayer that supports a LLC-sublayer consistent with other IEEE 802 network technologies. So, similar to 802.2, LLC rides over the 802.3 MAC layer, which rides over the physical layer in the 802.3 architecture. 802.2 rides across the 802.6 MAC-sublayer, which rides across the physical layer of the 802.6 subnetwork (see Figure 11-2).

Figure 11-2   *IEEE 802 Network Layers*

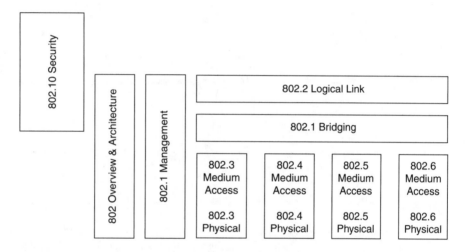

Figure 11-3 shows the generic DQDB access unit (AU) functional architecture. As is seen in Figure 11-3, the DQDB uses a layered model. Each layer is responsible for performing its function, and supporting the layer above it. The multiplexing and physical layer functions provide the framing, line coding, error checking, and bus maintenance functions. The queue-arbitrated functions perform the distributed queuing algorithm that grants access to the bus in an orderly fashion, and prepares the DQDB cells for transmission on the physical media using the physical layer convergence procedure (PLCP). The MAC convergence functions segment the DQDB Initial MAC Protocol Data Units (IMPDUs) into 53-byte Derived MAC PDUs (DMPDUs) that are then available for transmission onto the DQDB.

Figure 11-3   *DQDB Access Unit Functional Architecture*

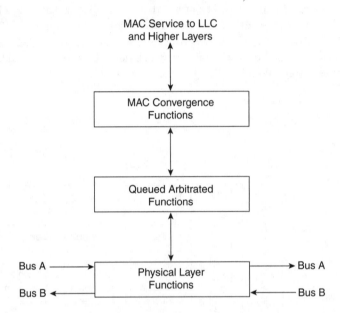

Physically, a DQDB network consists of dual, simplex, counter-directional buses in either an open-ended or closed arrangement. Figure 11-4 shows an open topology and Figure 11-5 shows a closed topology. Each bus has a special AU that performs the Head of Bus (HoB) function. The HoB is responsible for generating empty slots onto the bus when no DMPDUs are queued for transmission anywhere on the bus. It is also responsible for Message Identification (MID) page allocation, which is the means by which each AU always generates a unique MID for each IMPDU. MIDs are essentially a uniqueness mechanism that ensures that, during reassembly, only the original DMPDUs that make up the sent IMPDU are used to rebuild the IMPDU at the receiver. This concept is discussed later in the "SIP Level 2" section. In the event that the current AU serving as the HoB should fail, any station can assume the HoB function.

Figure 11-4   *Open DQDB Network Topology*

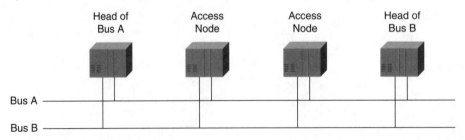

Figure 11-5 *Closed DQDB Network Topology*

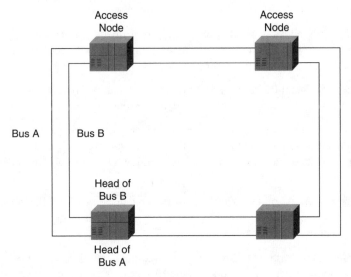

One of the interesting features of the DQDB is the MAC function. As implied by the name, a DQDB network uses a distributed queuing mechanism to control when a station can send data on the bus. As in all shared-access topologies, a mechanism is required to arbitrate access to the medium, or collisions occur. Because collisions render the bitstreams of the two colliding frames unusable, the frames must be discarded and resent. In an 802.3 environment, the MAC layer uses the carrier sense multiple access collision detect (CSMA/CD) mechanism to determine when a station might send data on the wire. However, because DQDB is designed to work over arbitrary distances, the 802.3 MAC layer is insufficient for ensuring orderly access to the media.

Without the ability to bound the physical diameter of the DQDB network, another technique was required to allow for orderly transmission on the media. Two new approaches were devised to accomplish this goal—fixed-length slots and a queue-arbitration algorithm.

A DQDB slot is composed of a 1-byte Access Control (AC) field and a 52-byte segment. The AC field is used by each station to determine the free/busy state of each bus in the network. Figure 11-6 shows the format of the AC field.

Figure 11-6 *DQDB Slot AC Field*

Access Control	Segment					
Busy	SL_Type	PSR	Reserved	REQ_2	REQ_1	REQ_0
1 Bit	1 Bit	1 Bit	2 Bits	1 Bit	1 Bit	1 Bit

The busy bit indicates whether or not the slot can transmit a DMPDU. If set to 0, it is free; if set to 1, it is in use.

The SL_Type bit indicates whether or not the slot is queued-arbitrated (QA) or pre-arbitrated (PA). PA slots are used when isochronous services are required. Because SMDS is used for data, PA slots aren't needed.

The Previous Segment Released (PSR) bit indicates that the contents of a busy slot have been read from the bus and the slot is available for reuse by downstream nodes.

A node uses the REQ_2, REQ_1, and REQ_0 bits to request access to the downstream bus to upstream nodes. Each bit indicates a different priority level, which allows a DQDB node to perform priority queuing. For the sake of simplicity, only one priority is discussed.

Using information carried in the AC field of each slot sent on each bus, and by maintaining two counters, each AU on the DQDB network can determine when they have exclusive access to each bus. The mechanism by which they derive this information is performed by the QA algorithm.

The QA algorithm works as follows. Assume that the network has three nodes in an open topology (Figure 11-7). The first node is the HoB, and is generating empty slots on the network at every opportunity. This means that if no data is being sent by any station, every slot on the network is empty. The number of slots being generated during any time interval is determined by the speed of the bus (because each slot is fixed in length). For simplicity, assume that the bus operates at 53 bytes/sec. Thus, one slot is sent on each bus every second.

Figure 11-7 *A Three-Node DQDB Network*

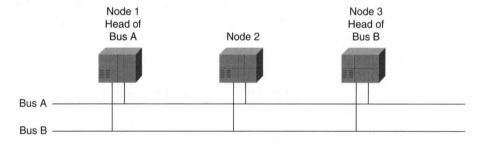

Each node maintains two counters for each bus, the request counter and the countdown counter. Whenever a node has no slot to send, it increments the request counter every time a slot passes on bus B with the REQ_0 bit set. For every slot that is received by the node on bus A that has the busy bit set to 0, the node decrements the request counter (to a minimum value of 0). Thus, the value of the request counter represents the total number of slots that are waiting to be sent by all nodes downstream of this node. This is because each slot with the busy bit set to 0 is seized by one of the downstream nodes that had requested a slot. Because the buses operate at the same speed, the HoB always generates slots at a rate greater than or equal to the number of requested slots on the opposite bus.

Whenever a station has a slot to send on bus A, it copies the current request counter value to the countdown counter and sets the REQ_0 bit in the first available slot on bus B that has the REQ_0 bit set to 0. For every slot on Bus B with REQ_0 set to 1, it increments the request counter and for every slot on bus A with the busy bit set to 0, it decrements the countdown counter. When the countdown counter reaches 0 the station seizes the slot and copies the DMPDU into the segment field of the slot. If there is another slot to send, it starts the process over using the current value in the request counter. Figure 11-8 shows this process.

To transmit LLC data across a DQDB subnetwork, each IMPDU must be segmented into 48-byte DMPDUs that can be placed into the DQDB slot segment. Each DQDB segment contains 4 bytes of overhead that describe the type of information being sent. Because an SMDS network is always sending data, this 4-byte field is always set to 0xFFFFF022 (see Figure 11-9).

Figure 11-8 *The Process*

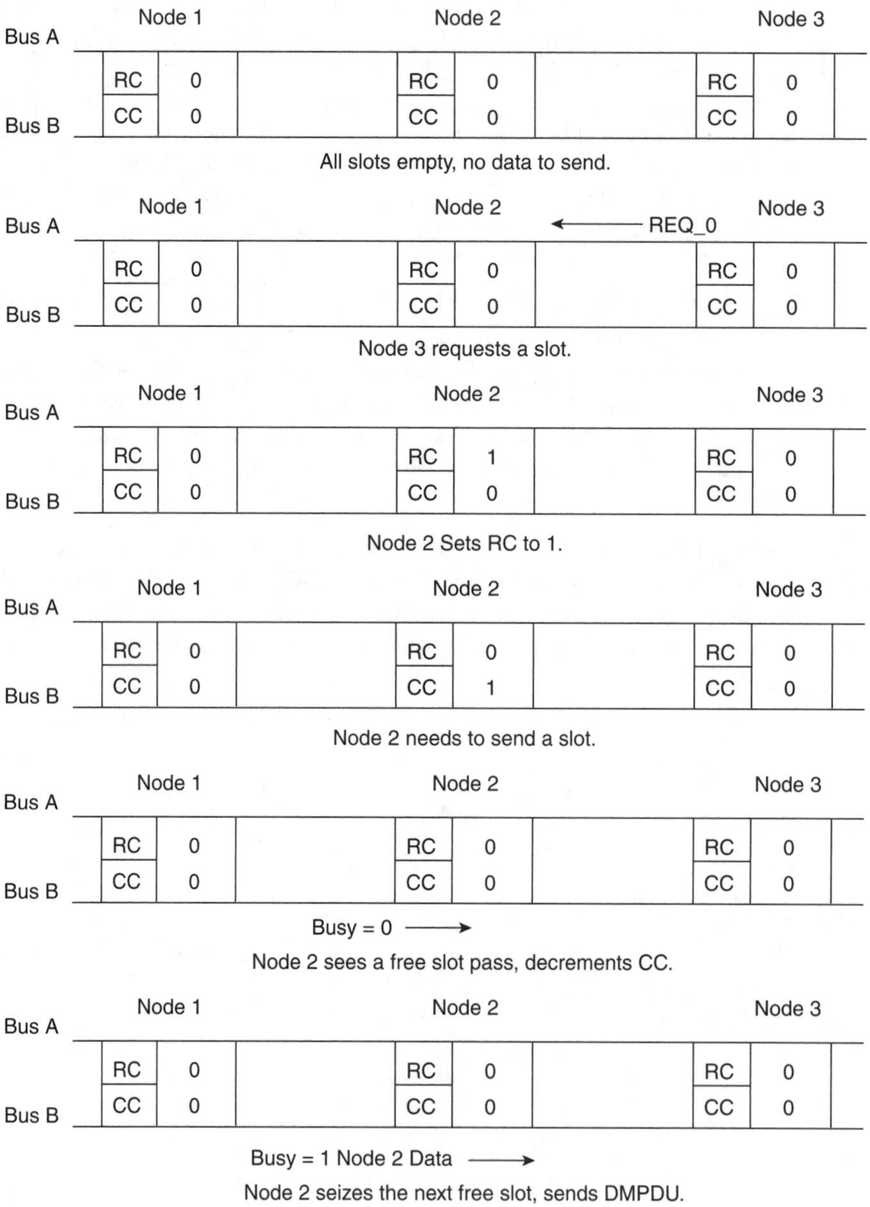

	Node 1		Node 2		Node 3	
Bus A						
	RC	0	RC	0	RC	0
Bus B	CC	0	CC	0	CC	0

All slots empty, no data to send.

	Node 1		Node 2	← REQ_0	Node 3	
Bus A						
	RC	0	RC	0	RC	0
Bus B	CC	0	CC	0	CC	0

Node 3 requests a slot.

	Node 1		Node 2		Node 3	
Bus A						
	RC	0	RC	1	RC	0
Bus B	CC	0	CC	0	CC	0

Node 2 Sets RC to 1.

	Node 1		Node 2		Node 3	
Bus A						
	RC	0	RC	0	RC	0
Bus B	CC	0	CC	1	CC	0

Node 2 needs to send a slot.

	Node 1		Node 2		Node 3	
Bus A						
	RC	0	RC	0	RC	0
Bus B	CC	0	CC	0	CC	0

Busy = 0 ⟶
Node 2 sees a free slot pass, decrements CC.

	Node 1		Node 2		Node 3	
Bus A						
	RC	0	RC	0	RC	0
Bus B	CC	0	CC	0	CC	0

Busy = 1 Node 2 Data ⟶
Node 2 seizes the next free slot, sends DMPDU.

Figure 11-9 *DQDB Segment Format for Data DMPDUs*

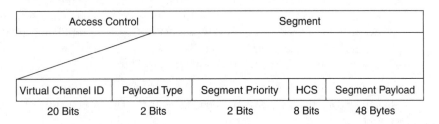

The 4-byte field is composed of three subfields, the virtual channel identifier (VCI), the payload type, and the segment priority fields. Both the segment priority and payload type fields are always set to 0, with the remaining values reserved. The VCI was proposed for connection-oriented data transfer, but never made its way into SMDS. The header check sequence (HCS) field performs a cyclic redundancy check (CRC) calculation on the segment header.

The DMPDU format is shown in Figure 11-10. The segment type indicates whether the segment is the beginning of message (BOM), end of message (EOM), or any of the continuation of message (COM) segments in between. If only one segment is representing the IMPDU, it is a single segment message (SSM). The sequence mumber is a value incremented for each consecutive DMPDU that makes up an IMPDU. This determines if, for example, a COM segment has been lost. The MID field uniquely identifies the IMPDU. The DQDB MAC allows DMPDU interleaving; that is, a receiving station can receive DMPDUs from multiple IMPDUs in an arbitrary sequence.

Figure 11-10 *DMPDU Format*

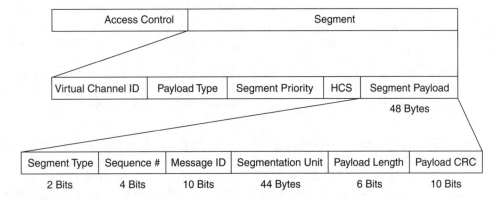

For example, say node 1 sends a segment from an IMPDU to node 3 during one slot time. Based on the current state of the QA algorithm, node 2 can seize the next slot and begin transmitting a segment from a different IMPDU that is destined to node 3. Node 3, then, receives two slots in a row, back-to-back, with DMPDUs from different IMPDUs. By checking the MID in each segment, node 3 can separate the two segments and store them while awaiting the remaining DMPDUs for each IMPDU.

The segmentation unit is a 44-byte chunk of the IMPDU. If the IMPDU does not fall on a 44-byte boundary, the last DMPDU is padded with 0s. The IMPDU format is shown in Figure 11-11.

Figure 11-11 *IMPDU Format*

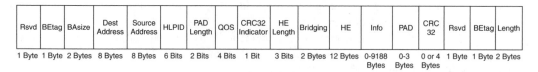

As is seen in Figure 11-11, the IMPDU contains many fields. Of particular importance are the Source Address (SA), Destination Address (DA), and info fields, which determine where an IMPDU is destined, where it came from, and the payload it is carrying. Perhaps of even more interest is the fact that the IMPDU format is exactly the same as the SIP Level 3 PDU. Furthermore, the DMPDU format is essentially the same as the SIP Level 2 PDU. If they are the same, why create SIP?

Recall from the introduction that SMDS was derived from 802.6, but it is not 802.6 in disguise. SMDS is a service offering, and the role of SIP was to allow for the service features. However, in the networking and particularly the telecommunications industries, standards bodies, equipment vendors, and network and service providers generally do not like technologies that are myopic in scope and proprietary or arcane in implementation. If the technologies are, they are risky investments all around. To garner industry acceptance for SMDS, Bellcore chose to align SMDS with 802.6. By aligning with 802.6, Bellcore also ensured a migration path to B-ISDN, while positioning the service providers to use existing equipment and facilities. There was also the belief that customers would like the option of attaching multiple CPE to the SMDS network—although this was a shortsighted assumption.

There are some disadvantages for aligning with 802.6. As anyone with a good familiarity with 802.6 can attest, it is complex technology. For SIP to satisfy its primary function— allowing for all the SMDS features—it need not have a lot of complexity. In fact, with the advent of the DXI protocol, only SIP Level 3 is needed to access the network. Frame Relay and ATM access mechanisms are also available.

There was also the risk of time-to-market delay. IEEE standards take time to develop and have a large contingent of interested parties, many of which don't agree on things. IEEE standardization requires balloting, usually by a few hundred members. Then, the standard must be accepted by the standards board. This process takes time and is prone to delay. By aligning with 802.6, which wasn't published until 1990, Bellcore was taking a risk that SMDS would not be deployed by the target date.

In the end, it is difficult to say whether or not SIP needed to be so closely aligned with 802.6. Cisco did not implement SIP Level 2 and 1 (although the ATM interface processor runs SMDS over AAL3/4 in cell mode). Therefore, it was up to the CSU/DSU vendors to provide some of the SIP functionality. In the early 1990s, Kentrox developed a T1/E1 SMDSU that connected to a Cisco router over an RS-449 serial cable. Shortly afterward, Cisco and Kentrox teamed to provide an SMDS solution over a HSSI connected to a Kentrox SMDSU that attached to the SMDS network at T3/E3 rates. Because these SMDSUs have the additional SIP requirements, they are somewhat more expensive than traditional CSU/DSUs.

SIP Level 3

SIP Level 3 is responsible for addressing and routing SMDS PDUs. It also has error checking functions that allow SMDS network elements (NEs) to detect and isolate problems. Most importantly, it is responsible for carrying the data payload, which is in most cases an LLC-encapsulated network layer protocol, such as TCP/IP or IPX. The format of the SIP Level 3 PDU is shown in Figure 11-12.

Figure 11-12 *SIP Level-3 PDU Format*

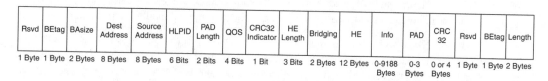

By comparing Figure 11-11 to 11-12, it is clear that these formats are identical. Each field and the function it serves are detailed in the following sections.

Reserved Field

This one-octet field has no current use in SMDS and is always set to 0x00.

Beginning-End Tags (BETags)

The BETag fields prevent two SIP L3 PDUs from becoming merged if both the last L2_PDU of one L3_PDU and the first L2_PDU of the next L3_PDU are lost. If the BETag fields don't match, both the SMDS switching system (SS) and the CPE are required to discard the entire L3_PDU. When transmitting, the BETag is incremented by 1 for every new L3_PDU. The BETag value can range from 0 to 255.

Buffer Allocation Size (BASize) and Length Fields

The BASize and length fields contain the length of the entire L3_PDU, from the DA up to and including the CRC32. If these values don't match, or the number of bytes received doesn't equal both values, the L3_PDU is discarded. This happens if one or more L2_PDUs are lost.

DA/SA

Now comes the interesting part—addressing. The DA and SA fields are used in the same way that a postal address is used on a letter, or that a MAC address is used on a LAN. Both the DA and SA fields are 64 bits long, with 4 bits of address type and 60 bits of address.

The address type field denotes whether or not the L3_PDU is individually or group addressed. If the address type = 1110, the address is a group address. If it equals 1100, it is an individual address. An L3_PDU received with any other value is invalid and is to be discarded. In hexadecimal, these values are C for individual addresses, also called singlecast addresses, and the group address, or multicast address is E.

The address field is constructed in different ways, depending on the numbering authority in the area of the world that the service is being offered. In North America, the DA must conform to the North American Numbering Plan (NANP), and everywhere else it must conform to the International Telecommunication Union Telecommunication Standard-ization Sector (ITU-T) E.164 format. In both cases the address looks like a telephone number. The NANP is a subset of ITU E.164, whereby the address is coded using E.164 format. The purpose of the NANP is to provide allocations for telephone and other telecommunications numbers such as, area codes and local exchange prefixes.

The NANP specifies that the first 4 bits of the DA be set to 0001 for all addresses that are not carried between local access and transport areas (LATAs) by an IXC. If the address is destined for another LATA, the first 4 bits indicate the E.164 country code, the next 40 bits the SMDS address, and the last 16 bits are set to all 1s.

The remaining 56 bits identify the end user SNI. If the destination is in the same LATA as the source, 40 bits of the DA field identify a CPE and 16 bits of the DA are set to all 1s (0xFFFF). The encoding scheme is binary coded decimal (BCD). In the BCD coding scheme, the values 0000 through 1001 are available for use. The remaining values are not used. Thus, every 4 bits (or, every nibble) represents a decimal value from 0 to 9. Because 40 bits are available for addressing, the resulting BCD-coded address can be formatted to look similar to a telephone number (see Figure 11-13). If the traffic is destined for another LATA, the carrier selection field must be inspected to determine the IXC to which the traffic must be routed. The carrier selection field is covered later in the chapter.

Figure 11-13 *NANP Format for SMDS Addresses*

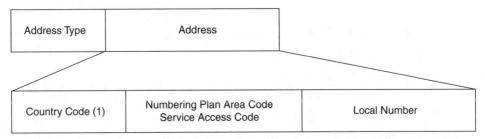

From Figure 11-13, you can see that the E.164 address is separated into three fields, the country code (CC), the mumbering plan area code or service access code (SAC), and the local number fields. In the US, the CC field is always 1. The SAC field contains a numbering plan area-numbering exchange (NPA-NXX) value and the local number contains a local exchange extension. In the US, the North American Numbering Plan Administration (NANPA) is responsible for assigning NPA-NXX information to carriers. The local exchange extension is assigned by the local exchange carrier (LEC). The following are SMDS addresses that are assigned by Verizon.

> Singlecast address: C.120.1201.9999.FFFF
> Multicast address: E.120.1201.8888.FFFF

The addresses appear as telephone numbers in the northern part of New Jersey. In northern NJ, the area code is 201. The NXX value equals the NPA value. In telephone number format the address is the following:

> Singlecast address: 1-201-201-9999
> Multicast address: 1-201-201-8888

Address Subscription

Even though SMDS addresses appear as phone numbers, they behave more like MAC addresses on LANs. Recall that SMDS was derived from DQDB as a mechanism for data exchange across MANs or WANs. Also recall that SMDS had unicast and multicast routing, address screening, and source address verification as design goals. For the SMDS service to provide these features, a mechanism is needed to allow for address subscription, so that customers can build SMDS networks that are flexible, easy to administer, and secure.

When a customer orders SMDS service from a carrier, they need to determine what their addressing requirements are for the service provider to correctly implement the service. For example, assume that the XYZ corporation has six offices that need LAN interconnection. The six offices are broken out as follows:

- **Office 1:** Central datacenter; Corporate headquarters
- **Office 2:** Backup datacenter; Human resources (HR)
- **Office 3:** Marketing, engineering, and finance office
- **Office 4:** Sales office 1
- **Office 5:** Sales office 2
- **Office 6:** Sales office 3

XYZ corp decides that they want to order SMDS service to connect the LANs over DS3 facilities. They also want to create three Closed User Groups (CUGs), such that all the sales offices can connect to each other, the HR office can connect to the finance office, and all offices can connect to both datacenters. SMDS has all the necessary features to meet these goals.

The carrier, armed with XYZ corporation's requirements, allocates three group addresses and one address per circuit per group to which the circuit belongs. The network diagram, with the corresponding address assignments, is shown in Figure 11-14.

Figure 11-14 *XYZ Corp SMDS Network*

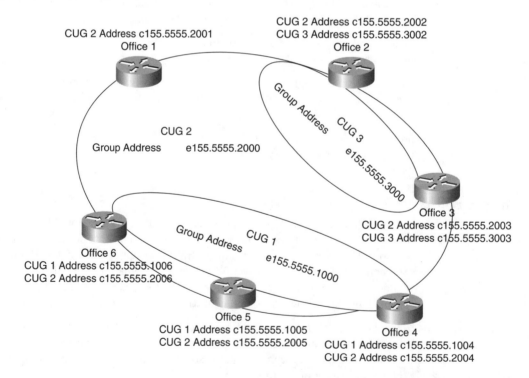

From Figure 11-14, you can see that the service provider has created three CUGs, each with a corresponding group address, and that each site has one singlecast address assigned per

CUG. Because all six DS3 circuits connect to the same SMDS service provider, the SS must prevent address leakage between groups, and also ensure that other SMDS customers do not have access to these CUGs. This is done by the service provider by using address screening.

Address screening works by creating tables that indicate which addresses can communicate with other addresses in the CUG. The SS inspects each source-destination pair and compares it to the values in the table. It also verifies that the SA in every PDU is verified to be configured for the SNI that the PDU is received on. This is known as source address validation (SAV), and acts as an anti-spoofing mechanism. Furthermore, any group addressed PDUs are only delivered to the SNI(s) that are subscribed to that group.

The SMDS specifications dictate the maximum values for address subscription parameters that are presented in Table 11-2.

Table 11-2   *Address Subscription Parameters*

Access Method	Individual Addresses per SNI	Group Addresses per Individual Address
High Speed Access (> DS1)	<=16	<=32
Low Speed Access (56/64k)	<=2	<=3

In Europe and the Pacific Rim, the European/Pacific Rim SMDS Interest Group (ESIG and PRSIG) mandate that all addresses must conform to E.164. Any SMDS PDU that does not conform to E.164 is discarded by the SS upon entry into the network. In all cases, the SS is responsible for address format verification, screening, and SAV. CPE are not required to implement this feature, although many SMDSU vendors provide configuration mechanisms to perform these features on the SMDSU.

Higher Layer Protocol Identifier Field (HLPID)

The HLPID field is responsible for identifying to the CPE which type of data is being carried in the info field of the L3_PDU. The SS does not inspect or act upon this field. Because SMDS supports LAN interconnect and is derived from 802.6, the only supported HLPID value that a CPE can use is 1, which indicates 802.2 LLC encapsulation. Values 48 to 63 are available for local administration and the values 0 and 2 to 47 are reserved for standardization by the IEEE 802.6 team. For our purposes, this value is always set to 1.

Packet Assembler/Disassembler (PAD) and Pad Length

The PAD and PAD length fields ensure that the total length of an L3_PDU is 32-bit aligned. This allows for efficient processing by SMDS NEs, both CPE and SS equipment. The PAD field contains all 0s when used. SMDS NEs use the PAD length field to determine where the info field ends, and can be calculated by the following formula:

PAD Length = 3 − ((Info field bytes + 3) mod 4)

Quality of Service (QoS) Field

The QoS field is not used by SMDS, but was added to align with 802.6. No value is specified for this field in the SMDS specifications; however, most vendors implement this field as 0x00.

CRC-32 and CRC-32 Indication Bit Fields

The CRC-32 field was originally specified in early 802.6 drafts; however, its use was later deprecated when it was decided that the 10-bit CRC carried in each DMPDU segment was sufficient for detecting errors. Today, it is required that an SMDS CPE generate a 32-bit CRC using the formula specified in 802.6; however, a receiving station need only recognize that the field is present.

CRC calculations are performed by passing the bitstream through a circular shift register, which acts as a binary division machine. The dividend is created by using a generator polynomial that is of the degree of the CRC bit length. Thus, a generator polynomial for a CRC-32 machine is $x^{32}+x^{27}+\ldots+x^{1}$. Using binary division, the bitstream is divided by the generator polynomial. The remainder, or modulus, is placed in the CRC field. The receiving side subtracts the CRC value from the received bit stream and performs the CRC calculation on the result. If the quotient of this calculation is non-zero, the PDU is discarded.

Header Extension (HE) and HE Length Fields

SMDS uses the HE and HE length fields to allow for carrier selection and to identify the SIP version number. In SMDS, the HE field is always 12 bytes, or three 32-bit words long. Thus, the HE length field is always set to 011_B. If a PDU is received with any other value, the SS discards it.

The format of the HE field is shown in Figure 11-15.

Figure 11-15 *Header Extension Field Format*

Element Length	Element Type	Element Value	. . . . .	Element Length	Element Type	Element Value	HE PAD
1 Byte	1 Byte	Variable		1 Byte	1 Byte	Variable	Variable

From Figure 11-15, you can see that the basic format of the HE field allows for extensibility. The field is made up of a variable number of length-type-value (LTV) tuples. Because the element length field is variable, the HE PAD aligns the HE field on a 12-octet boundary.

Each tuple corresponds to an HE element, where the possible values and their descriptions are shown in Table 11-3.

Table 11-3   *HE Element Types*

Element Type	Description
0	Version
1	Carrier selection
2-127	Reserved by Bellcore
128-255	For use by other entities

The version element identifies the SIP version in use. As of this writing, only one version of SIP has been specified, and this is represented by a value of 1 in the version element value field. The carrier selection field identifies the IXC to be used when interLATA transport is required. In North America, the carrier is identified using a Carrier Identification Code (CIC), which is assigned to carriers by the NANPA.

If no carriers are selected, the default value for the HE field is as shown in Figure 11-16.

Figure 11-16   *Default Value for the HE Field*

0x03	0x00	0x01	0x00	0x48	0x69	0x20	0x43	0x68	0x72	0x69	0x73
Version			HE PAD								

The first LTV indicates the version of SIP, which is a three-octet field of type 0 and value 1. The second field is a tribute to Chris Hemrick, who is considered to be the mother of SMDS. Ms. Hemrick was responsible for pushing SMDS to the RBOCs and technical management at Bellcore, and for seeing it through to its launch in 1991. For the hexadecimally challenged, the tribute is an ASCII string that reads, "Hi Chris."

Bellcore does not specify HE processing rules for CPE devices. Therefore, the receiving CPE should ignore this field. Sadly, Cisco IOS sets this field to all 0s, so the tribute has been lost in practice.

Information Field

The information field contains LLC-encapsulated data. The field length can be anywhere between 0 and 9188 bytes. The 9188 value was chosen to align the 802.6 IMPDU to exactly 9 kilobytes. This was based on the original assumption that the IMPDU overhead would be 28 bytes; however, the later addition of the HE field made the IMPDU overhead 40 bytes. Thus, the 9188 value has nothing but historical significance.

SIP Level 2

SIP Level 2 is responsible for the segmentation and reassembly (SAR) of SIP L3 PDUs into 53-byte SIP Level 2 PDUs, MID generation and verification, cell ordering maintenance, and the insertion of idle cells into the SMDS network. Also, because the CRC-32 field is not processed by the SS, the SIP_L2 PDU carries a CRC-10 value that detects errors in transmission.

SAR

SAR is handled by SMDS CPE devices, and in the case of DXI-mode access to the network, by the SS's themselves. The purpose of SAR is to break up SIP L3_PDUs into 53-byte L2_PDUs that can be efficiently transported across the network (see Figure 11-17). It is also required so that DQDB-based nodes can access SMDS. Again, part of the reason that SIP was aligned with DQDB was to allow for SIP-DQDB interworking.

In Figure 11-17, you can see that the LLC data is prepended with the SIP L3_PDU header and appended with the L3_PDU trailer. Then, the SAR function begins segmenting the L3_PDU into 53-byte L2_PDUs.

Figure 11-17 *SAR of SIP L3_PDUs*

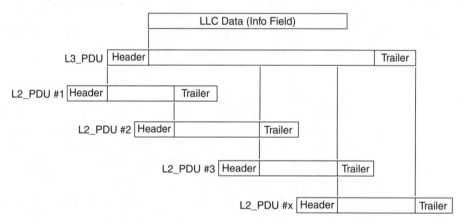

The SIP L2_PDU fields are shown in Figure 11-18.

Figure 11-18 *SIP L2_PDU Field Formats*

Access Control	Network Control	Segment Type	Sequence #	Message ID	Segmentation Unit	Payload Length	Payload CRC
1 Byte	4 Bytes	2 Bits	4 Bits	10 Bits	44 Bytes	6 Bits	10 Bits

Access Control Field

SMDS uses the access control field similarly to the way it is used in DQDB. In a single-CPE configuration, the CPE sets the busy bit to 1 when data is being sent and 0 otherwise. Because there is no upstream from the CPE (there is only one), the REQ fields are always set to 0. The four do not care bits are reserved for use in isochronous transmission, and are not part of the current SMDS implementations.

In the multi-CPE configuration, the REQ bits now come into play. If the SS receives an L2_PDU with any of the REQ bits set, it generates an empty slot on the bus——or transmit circuit——in the opposite direction from which it was received. This allows the CPE that made the request to send data locally without going through the SS. Because the majority of SMDS SNI interfaces deployed are of the single CPE variety you can ignore the multi-CPE scenarios.

Network Control Information (NCI) Field

The NCI field is derived from several fields that are defined in 802.6. In DQDB the NCI field specifies a VCI for use in connection-oriented services, such as voice. Because SMDS is specified to carry data only, this field has a default value of 0xFFFFF022. Both the SS and the CPE discard L2_PDUs with any other value in this field.

Segment Type Field

The segment type field is used in the same way as in DQDB. This field indicates the relative position of an L2_PDU in the sequence of L2_PDUs that make up an L3_PDU. This field has four possible values, as shown in Table 11-4.

Table 11-4   *Segment Type Values*

Segment Type Value	Description
00_B	COM
01_B	EOM
10_B	BOM
11_B	SSM

As expected, the beginning of message (BOM) is the first L2_PDU after segmentation. Each subsequent L2_PDU is a COM, except the last L2_PDU, which is of segment type end of message (EOM). In the highly unlikely event that there is only one L2_PDU after segmentation of an L3_PDU, the segment type field is set as a single segment message (SSM).

Sequence Number (SN) Field

The SN field detects lost L2_PDUs when reassembling the L2_PDUs into an L3_PDU. The BOM contains an arbitrary initial value for the SN which is incremented for every subsequent L2_PDU that makes up the L3_PDU. Because the SN is a 16-bit field, this number is incremented in modulo-16 fashion, such that the value after 65,535 is 0. If there is a gap in the sequence number space upon reception, any L2_PDUs in the reassembly buffer and all subsequent L2_PDUs with matching MID are discarded.

Message Identification (MID) Field

The MID field identifies the L2_PDUs that make up an L3_PDU. This is done by allocating the same MID value for each BOM, COM, and EOM that is built from an individual L3_PDU. In the single-CPE case, the range of MID values can be anywhere from 0 to 2^{10}-1. For SSM L2_PDUs, the MID value must be set to 0.

Segmentation Unit Field

The segmentation unit field contains a 44-octet portion of the L3_PDU. Because the 36-byte L3_PDU header fits cleanly into the BOM segment, the SS can use a switching mechanism called pipelining, whereby the SS begins switching the L2_PDUs without reassembling the L3_PDU upon ingress into the network. This has considerable performance advantages over the store and forward mechanism; however, at a cost. In the event that a L2_PDU is lost on the ingress link, the L2_PDUs that are sent before the lost L2_PDU are needlessly transmitted to the destination CPE, which must start a reassembly process.

The reassembly process sets aside buffer space for an entire L3_PDU (9232 bytes) and starts a timer that is based on the message retrieve interval (MRI) for the access speed of the link that is connected to the CPE. The MRI values are specified as 200 ms for DS1 access speeds and 100 ms for DS3 access speeds. The ESIG uses the same values for E1 and E3, respectively. Because the remaining L2_PDUs are discarded by the CPE, the reassembly process terminates at the expiration of the MRI. As such, memory is needlessly allocated and deallocated, and bandwidth is wasted on the access and inter-switch facilities.

Payload Length Field

The payload length field indicates the total number of data octets in the segmentation unit of an L2_PDU. Because the L3_PDU is aligned on a 32-bit boundary, this field has a set number of possible values. For BOM and COM segments, the value must be 44. For the EOM, the value can be any multiple of 4 between 4 and 44 (4, 8, 12, 16,…, 44). SSM segments can have values between 28 and 44 (in multiples of 4). Using the payload length field, the receiving CPE can determine where the data ends and the padding begins, thus allowing for efficient reassembly.

Payload CRC Field

The CRC mechanism detects single or multiple bit errors during transmission. Because the L3_PDU 32-bit CRC is not required, the 10-bit payload CRC is the only mechanism available in SMDS to accomplish this. The payload CRC uses a 10-bit generator polynomial $(x^{10} + x^9 + x^5 + x^4 + x^1 + 1)$ as the divisor and the entire L2_PDU as the dividend. The remainder is placed in the payload CRC field.

SIP Level 1

SIP Level 1 is broken into two major functions: physical medium dependent (PMD) functions and physical layer convergence procedure (PLCP) functions (see Figure 11-19).

Figure 11-19 *SIP Level-1 Functions*

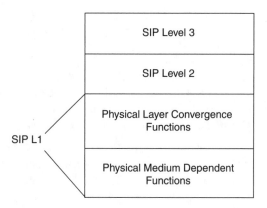

The PMD functions are responsible for orderly bit transmission across telecommunications media, such as DS1 and E3 links. Because SMDS is designed to work over existing telecommunications facilities, the PMD functions are not intended as a replacement for the existing framing and line coding mechanism used by the T-carrier system in the U.S. and the E-carrier system in Europe and Asia. Thus, the PMD used by SMDS is the same as used by other protocols that employ these facilities. The PMD functions describe the framing and line coding used on an access facility. The SMDS specification defines the required PMD parameters for use in North America, as shown in Table 11-5.

Table 11-5 *PMD Parameters*

Facility	Framing	Line Coding
DS1	Extended Superframe (ESF)	Bipolar 8-zero substitution (B8ZS) (recommended)
DS3	C-Bit or M13 (C-Bit recommended)	B3ZS

The European PMD parameters used on E1 and E3 links are a bit more complex. The E1 frame format used for SMDS, as specified in European SMDS Interest Group Specification 002, is shown in Figure 11-20. Figure 11-21 shows the E3 frame format used by SMDS. The physical and electrical specifications for E1/E3 links are defined in ITU-T G.703 and the E1/E3 frame format is defined in G.704.

Figure 11-20 *E1 PMD Frame Format for SMDS*

Frame Overhead	E1 Payload	HDLC Flag (0x7E)	E1 Payload
1 Octet	15 Octets	1 Octect	15 Octets

Figure 11-21 *E3 PMD Frame Format for SMDS*

1111010000$_B$	RAI	National Use	1100$_B$	E3 Payload
10 Bits	1 Bit	1 Bit	4 Bits	1520 Bits

Because SMDS is based on a slotted bus access mechanism, a means for presenting the L2_PDU to the SMDS NEs is required. PLCP is designed to allow efficient delimiting of L2_PDUs, such that an SMDS NE can easily detect the beginning and end of each L2_PDU. PLCP also allows for error detection and remote performance monitoring, which is critical in WANs that are composed of various elements and facilities.

Cisco routers do not implement the full SIP stack—only SIP L3 (over DXI) is supported. Therefore, an SMDSU is needed to provide the SIP L2 and L1 functions that are required to access the network. It is on the SMDSU that PLCP is implemented.

PLCP for DS1 Media

The DS1 PLCP is carried in the DS1 ESF payload, such that the PLCP frame begins immediately following an F-bit anywhere in the ESF payload. The format of the DS1 PLCP frame is shown in Figure 11-22.

Figure 11-22   *PLCP Frame Format for DS1 Media*

2 Bytes	1 Byte	1 Byte	53 Bytes	6 Bytes
1111011000101000	00100101	00000000	L2 PDU	
1111011000101000	00100000	00000000	L2 PDU	
1111011000101000	00011100	00000000	L2 PDU	
1111011000101000	00011001	00000000	L2 PDU	
1111011000101000	00010101	00000000	L2 PDU	
1111011000101000	00010000	B1	L2 PDU	
1111011000101000	00001101	G1	L2 PDU	
1111011000101000	00001000	M2	L2 PDU	
1111011000101000	00000100	M1	L2 PDU	
1111011000101000	00000001	C1	L2 PDU	Trailer

In Figure 11-22, the PLCP frame is made up of ten rows, all of which have four columns except the last row which has a fifth trailer column. The first column is made up of PLCP framing bits, which act as an L2_PDU delimiting mechanism. The second column identifies the row number of the L2_PDU. The row numbers are not sequential, although they do decrease for each row. If the rows are received such that the proper row number sequence is maintained, the PLCP frame is designated as in-frame. If any discrepancies exist in the row number sequence, the PLCP frame is considered out-of-frame (OOF). A loss of frame (LOF) condition occurs if the OOF condition lasts for 24 ± 1 ms.

The B1 byte is the bit interleaved parity 8 (BIP-8) calculation result over the previous PLCP frame. The G1 byte is the PLCP status byte, which conveys far end status information to the transmitter. The G1 byte format is shown in Figure 11-23.

Figure 11-23   *DS1 PLCP G1 Byte Format*

FEBE	Yellow Signal	Link Status Signal
4 Bits	1 Bit	3 Bits

The far-end block error (FEBE) field contains the number of BIP-8 errors that were detected by the receiver in the last PLCP frame. Because a BIP-8 calculation can detect up to 8 bit errors, this value can range from 0 to 8, thus, 4 bits are required. The yellow signal field is set to 1 in every PLCP frame while the receiver is in a LOF condition for 2.5 ± 5 msec. It is cleared (set to 0) after 15 seconds of in-frame PLCP frames are received. The link status signal is used in DQDB networks to allow for reconfiguration in the event of a failure, but they have no use in SMDS.

SMDS does not use the M1 and M2 bytes The C1 byte is the cycle/stuff counter, which is not used on DS1 media. It *is* used on DS3 media, thus, it was added to the DS1 PLCP only for parity with the DS3 PLCP. The C1 byte is covered in the next section.

The PLCP frame is 4608 bytes long, which is exactly the size of the ESF payload. Because an ESF frame contains 24 rows, each transmitted every 125 usec, the total duration of a PLCP frame is 3 ms. The payload efficiency, e, which is the amount of L3_PDU data that can be sent in one PLCP frame divided by the nominal DS1 bit rate, is derived from the following calculation:

$$e = \frac{\left(\dfrac{10L2\_PDUs}{0.003sec}\right) \times \left(44 \dfrac{bytes}{L2\_PDU}\right) \times \left(8 \dfrac{bits}{byte}\right)}{1.544Mbps} = \frac{1.1733Mbps}{1.544Mbps} \times 100 = 75.9\%$$

PLCP for DS3 Media

The DS3 PLCP frame is shown in Figure 11-24. The alignment of the DS%3 PLCP frame within the DS3 M-frame is constantly changing. This is because each DS3 M-frame has a duration that is 106.4 usec (see Chapter 7, "T3 and E3 Technology"), and each PLCP frame averages 125 usec in duration (see the C1 byte description that follows). The PLCP frame can begin anywhere in the DS3 M-frame, as long as the first bit of a PLCP frame nibble (4 bits) immediately follows a DS3 framing bit.

The PLCP format and field functions are the same as the DS1 PLCP, with the exception of the number of rows (12 instead of 10) and the use of the C1 byte. The C1 byte ensures that the PLCP frame averages 125 usec in duration. The DS3 PLCP trailer can vary either 52 or 56 bits. Because the PLCP frame is larger (5524 or 5528 bits) than a DS3 M-frame (4704 bits), it lasts slightly longer than an M-frame. Furthermore, the PLCP frame is nibble-aligned, which means that there might be up to 4 bits of unusable M-frame payload between PLCP frames (this is because the PMD functions must wait for the next framing bit to pass before writing the PLCP bit stream to the M-frame payload). Rather than wait, the PLCP trailer field is stuffed with 4 bits in such a way that the PLCP frame duration averages 125 usec.

Figure 11-24 *DS3 PLCP Frame Format*

2 Bytes	1 Byte	1 Byte	53 Bytes	52 or 56 Bytes
1111011000101000	00101101	00000000	L2 PDU	
1111011000101000	00101001	00000000	L2 PDU	
1111011000101000	00100101	00000000	L2 PDU	
1111011000101000	00100000	00000000	L2 PDU	
1111011000101000	00011100	00000000	L2 PDU	
1111011000101000	00011001	00000000	L2 PDU	
1111011000101000	00010101	00000000	L2 PDU	
1111011000101000	00010000	B1	L2 PDU	
1111011000101000	00001101	G1	L2 PDU	
1111011000101000	00001000	M2	L2 PDU	
1111011000101000	00000100	M1	L2 PDU	
1111011000101000	00000001	C1	L2 PDU	Trailer

Calculating the optimal length of the DS3 PLCP frame is straightforward. Because a DS3 M-Frame is made up of 4704 bits, and each M-Frame is sent every 106.4 usec, you can determine that 1 bit is sent every 0.0226190476 usecs. Thus, every 125 usecs you send the following:

125/0.0226190476 ˜ 5526 bits

Each row of a PLCP frame contains 57 bytes or 456 bits. Thus, a DS3 PLCP frame that is ˜ 5526 bits should have the following:

5526/456 ~ 12

But there are some additional bits left over:

5526 mod 456 = 54

Because the PLCP frame can float in the M-frame by as many as 4 bits (because of nibble alignment), this value is actually a range between 52 and 56 (54 ± 2). Thus, the DS3 PLCP trailer can be either 52 or 56 bits in length to maintain an average PLCP frame duration of 125 usec.

802.6 specifies that the stuffing is done in three-frame cycles, and only by the HoB. The first PLCP frame trailer contains 13 nibbles (52 bits), the second contains 14 nibbles (56 bits) and the third frame contains one of the two values. The mechanism that determines whether or not the third trailer is stuffed depends on the clock source. SMDS SS elements can be equipped with highly accurate, Stratum 1 clock sources through an external building integrated timing supply (BITS) clock. Or they can use less accurate, Stratum 3 internal clock sources. When you use an external source, trailer stuffing is only performed if a timing drift is detected. This is possible because telecommunications links are phase aligned. If you use an internal clock, the HoB trailer stuffs at every other opportunity (every 6th trailer). In the case of SMDS, the CPE (SMDSU) performs trailer stuffing based on the configured clock source (external or internal).

Given that the DS3 PLCP frame contains 12 L2_PDUs that are transmitted every 125 usec, the DS3 PLCP payload efficiency e can be calculated as follows:

$$e = \frac{\left(\dfrac{12L2\_PDUs}{0.00125sec}\right) \times \left(44 \dfrac{bytes}{L2\_PDU}\right) \times \left(8 \dfrac{bits}{byte}\right)}{44.736Mbps} = \frac{33.792Mbps}{44.736Mbps} \times 100 = 75.5\%$$

PLCP for E1 Media

The PLCP frame format for E1 media is shown in Figure 11-25. The E1 format is nearly identical to the DS1 format, with the exception of the F1 byte, which is reserved for growth by the ETSI, and the missing trailer, which is not required for frame alignment.

Figure 11-25 *E1 PLCP Frame Format*

2 Bytes	1 Byte	1 Byte	53 Bytes
1111011000101000	00100101	00000000	L2 PDU
1111011000101000	00100000	00000000	L2 PDU
1111011000101000	00011100	00000000	L2 PDU
1111011000101000	00011001	00000000	L2 PDU
1111011000101000	00010101	F1	L2 PDU
1111011000101000	00010000	B1	L2 PDU
1111011000101000	00001101	G1	L2 PDU
1111011000101000	00001000	M2	L2 PDU
1111011000101000	00000100	M1	L2 PDU
1111011000101000	00000001	C1	L2 PDU

The trailer is not needed because the E1 payload is 30 bytes (240 bits), which divides evenly into the E1 PLCP frame. Because the E1 frame is 4560 bits long, an E1 PLCP frame is sent every 19 E1 frames. Furthermore, because the E1 frame is sent every 125 usec, the E1 PLCP payload efficiency e is calculated as follows:

$$e = \frac{\left(\dfrac{12L2\_PDUs}{0.00125sec}\right) \times \left(44 \dfrac{bytes}{L2\_PDU}\right) \times \left(8 \dfrac{bits}{byte}\right)}{1.920Mbps} = \frac{1.4821Mbps}{1.920Mbps} \times 100 = 77.2\%$$

DXI **402**

PLCP for E3 Media

Figure 11-26 shows the E3 PLCP frame format. As expected, the E3 PLCP frame is nearly identical to the DS3 PLCP frame, with the exception being the number of rows (9 instead of 12) and the size range for the trailer field. The derivation of the E3 PLCP trailer size and the payload efficiency are left as exercises to the reader.

Figure 11-26   *E3 PLCP Frame Format*

1111011000101000	00100000	00000000	L2 PDU	
1111011000101000	00011100	00000000	L2 PDU	
1111011000101000	00011001	00000000	L2 PDU	
1111011000101000	00010101	F1	L2 PDU	
1111011000101000	00010000	B1	L2 PDU	
1111011000101000	00001101	G1	L2 PDU	
1111011000101000	00001000	M2	L2 PDU	
1111011000101000	00000100	M1	L2 PDU	
1111011000101000	00000001	C1	L2 PDU	Trailer
2 Bytes	1 Byte	1 Byte	53 Bytes	17 to 21 Bytes

DXI

Recall from earlier in the chapter that most CPE vendors were not interested in developing the full SIP stack. This was partly because the vendors were concerned about forcing their customers to upgrade to the new hardware that would be required to implement the full SIP, which could result in stranded investment. On the other hand, the CSU/DSU vendors saw this vendor disinterest as an opportunity to expand their product lines. The fact that these opposing sentiments created an opportunity for vendor partnership was underscored by an agreement made between Cisco and Kentrox in early 1992 to work together in bringing a comprehensive SMDS access solution to the market.

The first implementation of the Kentrox SMDSU (or alternatively, SDSU) had an RJ-48X T1 interface to connect to the network, and an EIA 449 serial interface to connect to a Cisco router. With the advent of the EIA 530/V.35 interface, a new model was released that could connect to a Cisco router equipped with a DB-60 serial interface. However, this didn't meet the T3 requirements that customers were clamoring for.

Prior to the development of SMDS, Cisco, in conjunction with T3Plus Networking, worked together to develop a serial interface that was capable of operating at speeds higher than 2 Mbps. Using technology already developed for use in SCSI cables, Cisco and T3Plus released a specification for a HSSI in 1989. The HSSI interface is specified to operate at up to 52 Mbps, which is suitable for DS3 and even the rarely seen Optical Carrier-1 (OC-1) interface. It uses SCSI-1 connectors and a heavily shielded, twisted 25-pair cable that is limited to 50 ft. With this technology available, the CSU/DSU vendors could provide HDLC-based T3 networking solutions to customers with high-speed data requirements. Kentrox took it a step further and developed a T3/E3 SMDSU, which has two BNC connectors (one Tx and one Rx) for DS3 connectivity to the network, and a HSSI interface for connectivity to a router.

Now that the SIP L2/L1 functions can be handled externally through an SMDSU, the router vendors need only implement SIP L3 functions. However, recall that SIP L3 does not have any error checking functionality. It also has no mechanism for detecting far-end problems, such as remote defects and the availability of a remote device. To carry SIP L3 between a router and an SMDSU, while still having the required error checking and monitoring functionality, a carrier protocol was needed. Fortunately, such a protocol has existed for nearly 30 years—HDLC.

The SIG specified the DXI as the HDLC-like link layer for use between CPE and SMDSUs. Similar to the SNI, the DXI isn't a frame format as much as an interface. Figure 11-27 shows this distinction. For simplicity, DXI frame is used instead of HDLC frame throughout the remainder of this chapter.

Figure 11-27 *The DXI and the SNI Functions*

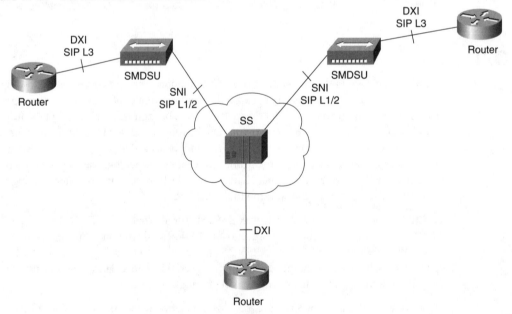

Similar to many other serial-link layer protocols, DXI is HDLC with minor modifications. The purpose of the DXI specification is essentially to standardize the physical media for which DXI runs upon, based on the circuit speed and type attached to the network. This way, vendors can build interoperable, standards-based solutions.

DXI Framing

The DXI uses HDLC framing to transport L3_PDUs to an SMDSU for processing, or in the case of direct DXI access (covered later in the section), directly to the SMDS SS. The format of the DXI frame is shown in Figure 11-28.

Figure 11-28 *DXI Frame Format*

Flag	Address	Control	DXI Header	DXI Info	FCS	Flag
	1 Byte	1 Byte	2 Bytes	0 - 9232 Bytes	2 or 4 Bytes	

Flag Field

The flag field is used as a frame delimiting mechanism, as is standard in all HDLC-like protocols. The DXI flags are always set to 01111110_B. As with other HDLC-like protocols, the sending device employs bit stuffing to distinguish between the HDLC payload and the flags. This is accomplished by inserting a 0 after any sequence of five consecutive 1s. The receiver removes the stuffed bits and passes on the HDLC to the necessary HDLC payload handling functions.

Address Field

The address field indicates the station to which the frame is being sent. This field has two values, 0 is the router and 1 is the SMDSU (or SS in direct DXI mode).

Control Field

DXI employs two types of frames, unnumbered information (UI) frames and test frames. UI frames carry SMDS L3_PDUs, and test frames determine link status by using the poll/final bit. The remaining fields are set to 1.

Information Field

The information field contains a 2-byte DXI header and 0 to 9232 bytes of SMDS L3_PDU data. The DXI header has no current use in DXI, but the fields are reserved for future use.

Frame Check Sequence (FCS) Field

The FCS field is either a 16 or 32-bit CRC that is calculated over the entire DXI frame except the flags. The CRC calculation is performed using one of the following two-generator polynomials:

16-bit:

$$G(x) = x^{16} + x^{12} + x^5 + 1$$

32-bit:

$$G(x) = x^{32} + x^{26} + x^{23} + x^{22} + x^{16} + x^{12} + x^{11} + x^8 + x^7 + x^5 + x^4 + x^2 + x^1 + 1$$

A 32-bit CRC value is more accurate in detecting bit errors than a 16-bit CRC. However, because no negotiation mechanism for detecting the CRC value is present, it must be preconfigured to match between the SMDSU and router interface. Direct DXI mode sets the CRC to 16 by default. The author has never seen an SS use a 32-bit CRC, so for direct DXI over serial digital dataphone service (DDS)/T1/E1 links, this value need not be changed. On HSSI interfaces, this value can be changed with the command **crc** {**16** | **32**}.

Heartbeat Polling

The FCS field provides the error detection mechanism across the DXI. To provide for remote monitoring of the DXI between router and SMDSU or SS, you use a heartbeat poll. The heartbeat poll is a rudimentary hello mechanism employed over the DXI. It works by sending DXI test frames with the Poll/Final (P/F) and address bits set based on the direction of the poll. If three or more consecutive polls are sent without a response, the sending host deems the remote end down. In Cisco IOS, the heartbeat poll mechanism is controlled by the **keepalive** interface subcommand. If a Cisco router interface deems the far end down, it declares line protocol down. A mismatch of the CRC bit between the router and SMDSU renders the heartbeat polls unreadable; thus, the line protocol is declared as down. This is usually the most common error encountered when initially configuring HSSI and SMDSU parameters.

Internetworking LAN Protocols over SMDS

As discussed previously, SMDS was designed to carry LAN-to-LAN data across MANs and WANs using LLC encapsulation. Because most Layer-3 network protocols are encapsulated in LLC while on the LAN, the encapsulation mechanisms for these protocols over SMDS are essentially the same.

Configuring SMDS

Similar to other Layer-2 WAN protocols, SMDS runs over serial or HSSI interfaces. Enabling SMDS on these types of interfaces is straightforward:

```
Router#config t
Router(config)#interface Hssi 1/0
Router(config-if)#encapsulation smds
Router(config-if)#^Z
Router#
```

After enabling SMDS on an interface, you can begin configuring Layer-3 protocol families and the associated address subscription parameters required. Although the details of each of the specific protocol suites and how they work over SMDS are beyond the scope of this book, a sample multiprotocol configuration is shown in Example 11-2 for your reference.

Example 11-2 *Sample Multiprotocol over SMDS Configuration*

```
interface Hssi4/0
!
! enable L3 protocols and assign addresses
!
 ip address 1.1.1.2 255.0.0.0
 decnet cost 4
 appletalk address 92.1
 appletalk zone smds
 clns router igrp FOO
 ipx net 1a
 xns net 17
!
! enable SMDS encapsulation
!
 encapsulation SMDS
!
! set the SMDS address
!
 smds address c120.1580.4721
!
! create static address resolution mappings
!
 smds static-map APPLETALK 92.2 c120.1580.4592
 smds static-map APPLETALK 92.3 c120.1580.4593
 smds static-map APPLETALK 92.4 c120.1580.4594
 smds static-map NOVELL 1a.0c00.0102.23ca c120.1580.4792
 smds static-map XNS 17.0c00.0102.23ca c120.1580.4792
 smds static-map NOVELL 1a.0c00.0102.23dd c120.1580.4728
 smds static-map XNS 17.0c00.0102.23aa c120.1580.4727
!
! Assign an SMDS Group Address for multicast/broadcast
!
 smds multicast NOVELL e180.0999.9999
 smds multicast XNS e180.0999.9999
 smds multicast ARP e180.0999.9999
 smds multicast IP e180.0999.9999
 smds multicast APPLETALK e180.0999.9999
 smds multicast AARP e180.0999.9999
 smds multicast CLNS_IS e180.0999.9990
 smds multicast CLNS_ES e180.0999.9990
 smds multicast DECNET_ROUTER e180.0999.9992
 smds multicast DECNET_NODE e180.0999.9992
 smds multicast DECNET e180.0999.9992
!
! Enable dynamic IP Address Resolution
!
 smds enable-arp
!
end
```

Resolving SMDS Problems

SMDS problems generally fall into four categories:

- Address subscription problems (where resolution is not an answer to the problem)
- DXI problems (CRC, keepalives, and CSU/DSU on T1)
- SNI problems (link down [SMDSU], HSSI problems, line versus line protocol, MTU mismatches)
- Multiple interfaces in the same multicast Group and the pseudo-LAN serial issue

Depending on the configuration, various techniques are used in troubleshooting issues that fall under these categories. Some of the most common problems and resolutions for the latter three of these categories are covered in the following sections. Address subscription and resolution problems depend on the Layer-3 protocol in question, which is beyond the scope of this book. Suffice it to say that regardless of the protocol, the router and the carrier must agree to the addressing parameters on each link, and to any screening requirements—multicast and group expectations, and so on.

DXI Problems

Earlier you learned that the DXI was designed to encapsulate L3_PDUs over a serial interface that is connected to an SMDSU. DXI can also run directly between a CPE and SS across a T1, E1, or DDS facility. In both cases, Cisco IOS treats DXI as the line protocol on the interface. If the line is up and DXI heartbeat polling (interface keepalives) are enabled, the following situations can cause the line protocol to go down:

- **A mismatched CRC length between DXI endpoints**—The CRC value must match on the SMDSU and the router. In most cases, the default CRC-16 is sufficient.
- **A physical (software or hardware) loop toward the router interface (or toward the SMDSU)**—Unlike Point-to-Point Protocol (PPP) and HDLC, which detect and report looped interfaces, SMDS interfaces do not detect loops. Interestingly, the capability exists—the address field in the DXI header is set based on the direction of transmission. Thus, if a router sends a DXI heartbeat poll with the address bit set to 1 in the DXI header and gets a response with the same address, it can assume that the interface is looped back. In any case, after three heartbeat polls are sent without a response, the line protocol is declared down.
- **A bad serial cable**—Cables become crimped and cut, pins get bent on the connectors, and so on. Always check your connectors!
- **A bad SMDSU or bad interface card in the router**—This is a tough one to diagnose. If you have gotten this far in your troubleshooting to no avail, it might be a good idea to get your hardware vendors involved.

In all cases, the DXI heartbeat poll mechanism determines line protocol status (as long as the link is up). If you need to disable DXI heartbeat polls, you can do so by issuing the interface command **no keepalive**. This is often done when connecting routers back-to-back without using SMDSUs. Alternatively, you can disable DXI altogether by issuing the command **no smds dxi-mode**, or in later revisions of IOS (12.0 or greater), **no smds dxi**. By disabling DXI, you must also disable DXI on the SMDSU (or router in back-to-back configurations). Otherwise, the router won't recognize the received DXI frames from the remote device.

SNI Problems

When looking into problems on the SNI, the most common place to focus is on the physical circuit from the SMDSU to the provider. In most cases, SNI problems are related to circuit failures, such as fiber cuts or card failures in ADMs or DACSs. The SMDSU informs the router that the WAN circuit is down by deasserting Carrier Detect (CD) and Clear To Send (CTS) on EIA/TIA serial interfaces, and by dropping communications equipment available on HSSI interfaces. The status of these signals can be checked by performing a **show interface** *interface name* command. If this happens, the router declares *line down, line protocol down*.

There is the possibility that the physical circuit is in good shape, but PLCP is getting errors. This is generally caused by one of two things:

- **Incorrect circuit mapping**—The service provider has provisioned the wrong circuit to your location such that the remote end does not connect to a PLCP-aware device.

- **Framing mismatch**—The service provider has one or more elements optioned with the wrong framing (C-bit or M13). Usually, this type of configuration causes the circuit to drop because of parity errors (on C-bit circuits) and framing errors (on M13 circuits).

In some rare cases a circuit might be provisioned correctly and not be showing many framing or parity errors, yet PLCP still shows problems. This is usually an electrical problem on the circuit, such as a bad repeater or an overextended DS3 cable. It can also be the result of a misbehaving PLCP engine in one of the endpoints.

Another common problem is a mismatch in the serial interface maximum transmission unit (MTU) when both DS1 and DS3 interfaces are in the same CUG. On Cisco routers, HSSI interfaces have a default MTU of 4470, and T1 interfaces have an MTU of 1500. This can cause problems if the HSSI interface is trying to send frames across the SMDS cloud that are in excess of 1500 bytes. This often happens when tunneling is used, or if Intermediate System-to-Intermediate System (IS-IS) is attempting to form an adjacency across the cloud. Where possible, it is always a good idea to synchronize all interfaces to use the same MTU.

Multiple Interfaces in the Same Group and the Pseudo-LAN Serial Problem

One of the unique features of Cisco's SMDS implementation is that it allows you to create multiple interfaces in the same multicast group. It also allows you to address two or more SMDS-encapsulated interfaces in the same logical Layer-3 subnetwork. This is an artifact of an early Cisco feature that allowed multiple serial interfaces to be placed in the same subnetwork for load-balancing purposes. The problem is that SMDS is essentially a LAN interface implemented over a WAN, and LAN subnetworks cannot span multiple interfaces in routers!

The Demise of SMDS

Now that you have learned about SMDS, you might be wondering why you never hear about it. I mean, here you have the only technology until recently that was designed purely for the purpose of seamless LAN-interconnect across a service provider network. Frame Relay and ATM provide nonbroadcast multi-access (NBMA) features, but these features do not provide a LAN look and feel to the WAN. ATM LAN emulation (LANE) is complex and was never adopted by service providers as a PDN service because it doesn't scale well. The recent explosion in Gigabit Ethernet MANs has been impressive, but there is still no intercarrier, wide-area Gigabit Ethernet solution. So what happened to SMDS?

It is hard to say precisely, but SMDS likely fell out of favor because, 1) it wasn't multi-service capable and ATM is and, 2) it wasn't designed for LAN *intra*connect and ATM was. The carriers were looking to build converged networks, and the enterprise market was looking for ways to build high-speed LANs and MANs. Furthermore, SMDS was always seen as a bridge to B-ISDN, not a replacement. Therefore, the B-ISDN standards process trudged forward and began gaining momentum when Fast Ethernet hit the scene. It was clear to the standards bodies (who are made up largely of vendor-employed technologists) that a high-speed (>OC-3c), LAN deployable, multiservice technology was needed, and fast. In essence, ATM would bring a financial windfall to the vendors. SMDS did not fit any of these needs, and thus went into an early retirement.

Summary

SMDS is a service offering from the RBOCs, IXCs and Posts, Telephones, and Telegraphs (PTTs) that is designed to provide LAN-to-LAN connectivity across MANs and WANs. It is based on the IEEE DQDB technology specified in IEEE 802.6, which defines a cell-based, queued-arbitrated MAC sublayer over a shared physical transport. SMDS was developed by Bellcore for use by the baby Bells, and was later enhanced by the SIG, ESIG, and PRSIG groups. It runs over existing time-division multiplexing (TDM)-based digital hierarchies in North America, Europe, and the Asia-Pacific countries. Although highly successful with strong technical and economic merit, it was a short-lived run. Ultimately, ATM usurped SMDS's position as the high-speed WAN/MAN technology of choice.

Review Questions

Give the best answer to the following questions. The answers to these questions can be found in Appendix A, "Answers to Review Questions."

1 What were some of the major motivating factors for the development of SMDS?

_____

_____

_____

2 What are some common Layer-3 protocols that are supported over SMDS?

_____

_____

_____

3 At what layer of the SMDS protocol stack does addressing occur? Segmentation and reassembly?

_____

_____

_____

4 What are the five SMDS access classes? Why does E3 technology only support four?

_____

_____

_____

5 For what is the BETag used?

_____

_____

_____

6 What is a message ID? What purpose does it serve?

_____

_____

_____

7 Why are SMDS L3_PDUs so large?

_____

_____

_____

8 What is the purpose of DXI?

_____

_____

_____

9 What are some common problems encountered on SMDS interfaces?
How can you tell if the problem is DXI related or circuit related?

_____

_____

_____

This chapter covers the following topics:

- **History of digital subscriber line (DSL)**—A brief background on DSL. Discusses the need for high-bandwidth data connectivity and how DSL fulfils the requirements.

- **DSL encoding technologies**—An introduction into the basic mathmatical and engineering principals that make DSL possible. Also covers how different flavors of DSL use different encoding methods.

- **Asymmetric DSL (ADSL) components**—A look at the different physical components used in DSL. Understanding the terminology and each of the components is vital to understanding the technology.

- **DSL circuit attributes**—A look at the different DSL parameters that can be set and tweaked. This information helps the reader understand the overhead involved in DSL, and how to customize each DSL line.

- **DSL modem train-up and framing**—Certain train-up and framing parameters are necessary for proper DSL operation. This section covers some of these parameters.

- **Power levels in DSL services**—Insight into DSL power levels is necessary to understand certain behaviors.

- **DSL technologies**—DSL exists in several flavors. These different flavors have different characteristics and technologies associated with them. This section provides some insight into the different flavors to help you decide which is best for your requirments.

- **DSL circuit concerns**—A brief explanation of the different factors that can affect DSL performace. This section looks at several physical characteristics that contribute to the physical well-being of the DSL line.

- **DSL network architectures**—Several different DSL deployment models are in practice today. This section discusses the basic architectures from which other deployments are built.

CHAPTER 12

DSL

Today's high-tech marketplace challenges you to provide low-cost, high-bandwidth access to data networks. The physical infrastructure of millions of copper circuits already exists. This infrastructure currently provides low-cost, low-speed dialup connectivity, and high-cost, high-bandwidth leased-line connectivity to data networks. Ideally, this challenge can be solved using new technology over the existing physical connections. DSL is one solution to this problem. DSL is a technology that allows for high bandwidth over existing copper circuits. This chapter provides an introduction to the different DSL encoding techniques, and the different DSL flavors. This chapter covers the different DSL components, circuit characteristics, and architectures. Because ADSL is by far the most widely deployed flavor of DSL, the chapter focuses on that for the sake of brevity.

History of DSL

In the 1980s, Bellcore developed high-data-rate DSL (HDSL) technology. HDSL was developed to enhance the capabilities of T1 technology by replacing alternate mark inversion (AMI) encoding with 2 binary 1 quaternary (2B1Q) encoding. HDSL reduces the need for repeaters, and it causes less electromagnetic interference (EMI) in cable bundles. In the 1990s, technology vendors began to see an explosion in the use of the Internet. This Internet revolution increased the demand for pure data, as opposed to voice and data, access to the Internet. The increase of high-bandwidth Internet services, such as video-on-demand, audio-on-demand, e-shopping, e-learning, and telecommuting, has resulted in the demand for higher bandwidth data connections. Studies showed that the majority of the traffic that was sourced from the Internet was destined for the end user (downstream), and that only a small percentage of the traffic was actually sourced by the user (upstream). This conclusion lead to the development of ADSL. ADSL technology, and other DSL technologies, reduce the usage of the public switched telephone network (PSTN) for data services. It provides a method by which the same copper loop can be used for voice and data at the same time, while not increasing the requirements for PSTN switching equipment. The only thing missing was a way to separate the voice and the data. Frequency-division multiplexing (FDM) was added to reserve a separate 4-kHz plain old telephone service (POTS) channel for the voice traffic, and the data band was required to stay above 4 kHz.

As of September 2001, there were 4.7 million DSL lines in North America with a projected 13.9 million lines by 2004. DSL technologies other than ADSL are being implemented because of the need for greater distance coverage and higher bandwidth. As the distance limitations of DSL decrease and the available bandwidth increases, the desire for DSL will grow dramatically. The services offered through the Internet are continuing to grow and demand higher-bandwidth connectivity. This chapter focuses mainly on ADSL because it is the most widely deployed; however, it briefly discusses other DSL technologies.

DSL Encoding Technologies

DSL uses three basic encoding technologies:

- Quadrature amplitude modulation (QAM)
- Carrierless amplitude and phase modulation (CAP)
- Discrete multi-tone modulation (DMT)

The following is a brief introduction to each of the encoding technologies.

QAM

Three attributes characterize all analog carrier signals: amplitude, frequency, and phase. Any combination of these three can represent the digital content. With QAM, the amplitude and phase shift represent multiple bits. The term quadrature comes from the signal being 90 degrees out of phase—four (coming from quad) of these phases, which represents a total of 360 degrees or one complete cycle. A graphical representation of QAM, is called a *constellation*. In Figure 12-1, you can see that the states are present at different amplitudes and phases. Points located at 0, 90, 180, and 270 degrees all have two possible amplitudes, which results in eight different states. With eight unique states, three bits can be transmitted in every state. For example, if the modulated signal is of amplitude 1 at 0 degrees, three zeros (000) are transmitted.

Figure 12-1   *Three Bit per Baud QAM*

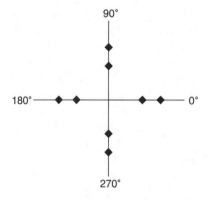

Table 12-1 shows an example of the possible values for QAM8. QAM8 is characterized by a possible eight unique bit patterns.

Table 12-1   *Possible States and the Resulting Bitstream for QAM8*

Amplitude	Phase	Bit Pattern
1	0	000
2	0	001
1	90	010
2	90	011
1	180	100
2	180	101
1	270	110
2	270	111

As more different phase shifts and magnitude levels are used, the more bits of information can be incorporated into each point or symbol. The problem arises when the constellation points are so close together that it is impossible for the receiving end to distinguish from one point to the next because of noise on the line.

CAP

CAP is an *adaptive* form of QAM —that is, it adjusts its symbol values to take into account line conditions (such as noise) at the beginning of a connection. The reason for the carrierless part of the name is that CAP generation involves the removal of the carrier frequency from the output waveform. CAP supports the three channels—POTS, downstream data, and upstream data—by splitting the frequency spectrum (FDM). Voice occupies the standard 0-4 kHz frequency band, followed by the upstream channel and the high-speed downstream channel. CAP performs rate adapting that is based on line conditions by modifying #bits/cycle (constellation size + carrier baud rate). The different carrier frequency pairs (such as 17 kHz and 136 kHz) denote this.

Figure 12-2 shows the frequency spectrum for CAP modulation. Data access is supported in two frequency bands: 25-160 kHz for upstream data and 240 kHz and above (up to approximately 1.5 MHz) for downstream data. The downstream data channel is much wider than the upstream channel, thereby offering much rawer bandwidth.

Figure 12-2 *CAP Frequency Spectrum for ADSL*

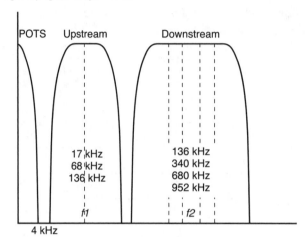

DMT

DMT is a signaling technique that divides the entire bandwidth into 255 subcarriers or subchannels. Each subcarrier is 4-kHz wide. The first subcarrier channel is used for traditional voice and POTS. The upstream data typically runs in channels 7-32 (26–128 kHz) and the downstream date in channels 33-250 (138 kHz–1.1 MHz). DMT is actually a form of FDM. The input data stream is divided into N channels, which have the same bandwidth but a different center frequency. Using many channels with a narrow bandwidth results in the following advantages:

- All channels become independent regardless of line characteristics, so channels can be individually decoded.

- DMT rate adapts in such a way that each of the channels can act independently in the presence of noise; it modifies the bits per subchannel, or tone. This results in less of an overall impact if there is a noise spike at a constant frequency.

Characteristics of DMT

The following are the characteristics of DMT:

- Employs FDM, closely related to orthogonal frequency-division multiplexing (OFDM).

- Defined by American National Standards Institute (ANSI) standard T1.413.

- 256 subchannels defined.

- Each subchannel has a bandwidth of 4.3125 kHz.

- Each subchannel is independently modulated through digital QAM methods.

- Each subchannel gain is as much as 16 bits/sec/Hz for a theoretical data capacity of 64 kbps.

- Transmitted over DC to 1.104 MHz pass bandwidth.

- Theoretical data load capacity of 1.104 MHz is 16.384 Mbps.

- ITU 992.1 (G.dmt), ITU 992.2 (G.lite), and ANSI T1.413 Issue 2 are all standards that define different variations and implementations of DMT-based ADSL.

- The ANSI T1 committee has standardized DMT as the line code to be used in the ADSL transmission system.

Figure 12-3 shows the frequency spectrum for DMT modulation.

Figure 12-3   *DMT Frequency Spectrum for ADSL*

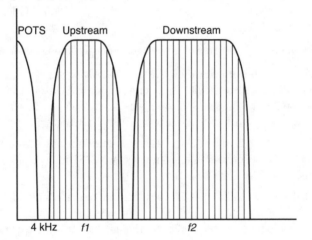

ADSL Components

The physical ADSL infrastructure is made up of several components (see Figure 12-4). Each component plays a role in some aspect of the DSL connection.

Figure 12-4 *DSL Components*

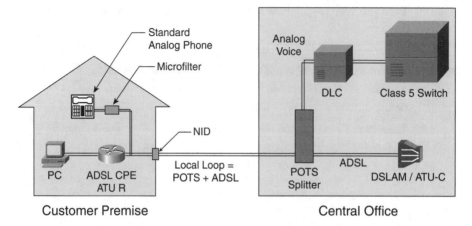

The following is a list of some of the most common components in a DSL environment:

- **DSL access multiplexer (DSLAM)**—DSLAM is the device that aggregates and terminates the DSL circuits. It contains multiple ADSL transmission unit—central offices (COs) (ATU-Cs), and some type of network interface to uplink to the network access point (NAP). (See the section "DSL Network Architectures.")

- **ATU-C**—ATU-C is the device, usually a card in a DSLAM that actually receives the local loop (copper pair) and terminates the ADSL signal. This device is responsible for de-modulating the DSL signal.

- **ATU-Remote (ATU-R)**—ATU-R is the device that resides at the customer premises. The ATU-R is usually integrated into the customer premises equipment (CPE), and is responsible for terminating the ADSL signal at the remote site.

- **Network interface device (NID)**—NID is the device that is the ingress point into the customer premises. This is the point at which the local loop splits into the premises wiring.

- **POTS splitter**—The POTS splitter is a device that resides at the CO and possibly at the customer premises. It filters, or splits, the voice frequencies from the local loop. The splitter is a low-pass filter (LPF) that allows only the voice spectrum to pass to devices that are connected to specific ports. POTS splitters can filter the voice frequencies (0-4 kHz) at the ingress point into the customer premises, or in-line microfilters can be used on the devices that are connected to the premises wiring. Microfilters are basically low-pass filters that allow the POTS frequencies to pass and block all others. The CO must use POTS splitters to provide voice and DSL on the same circuit. Several of today's CPEs have built-in POTS splitters and thus allow for the connection of a normal telephone.

Figures 12-5 and 12-6 represent two different physical wiring deployments at the customer premises. In Figure 12-5, the CPE has an integrated POTS splitter, and Figure 12-6 shows the line being split at the NID. In the latter case, the signal to the POTS phones is passed through a low-pass filter and the data portion of the split is passed through a high-pass filter (HPF). This is done to ensure that the appropriate signals are received in both cases. These two topologies are used depending on where the line is being split and the physical wiring deployment.

Figure 12-5   *Integrated POTS Splitter*

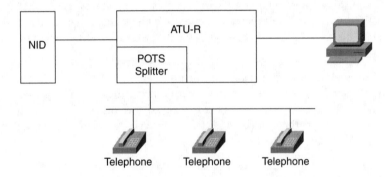

Figure 12-6   *Single In-Line Micro-Filter/Low-Pass Filter*

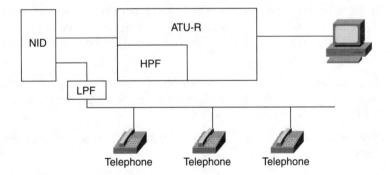

DSL Circuit Attributes

Many attributes characterize the quality of the DSL connection. Some of these parameters are negotiated during the training process of DSL, and others change during the life of the connection. The training process is described in detail in the ANSI T1.413 specification for

DMT. The introduction of the dynamic characteristics requires that the DSL modems be capable of some type of adaptation.

Noise Margin and Attenuation

In many data transmission technologies, you need to establish a noise margin or additional buffer zone between the signal and noise levels present on the physical transmission medium.

Establishing a minimum noise margin is done to maintain a 10^{-7} or better bit error rate (BER), and noise levels increase slightly or while signal levels decrease slightly. When the signal-to-noise ratio (SNR) becomes too low, excessive errors begin to occur in the data stream.

The actual noise margin at any specific time can be determined by starting with the present SNR, then increasing the noise level until a 10^{-7} BER can no longer be maintained. The amount that the noise increases before excessive errors occur is the actual noise margin. This test is sometimes done by setting the provisioned margin at 0 dB, then increasing the noise level until the BER degrades below 10^{-7}.

Noise levels can increase for a variety of reasons, and the signal level can decrease for a variety of reasons. When the signal level decreases, or when the noise level increases, the result is a lower SNR and a lower signal-noise-margin. As signals are attenuated, the SNR (and noise margin) degrades.

Higher DSL rates result in lower SNRs, and lower DSL rates result in higher SNRs. Therefore, the noise margin becomes lower at longer cable lengths or at higher DSL rates. When a BER of 10^{-7} can no longer be maintained, an automatic reduction in DSL rate (retrain) normally occurs.

Rate adaptive DSL (RADSL) is a technique that automatically adjusts the DSL transmission speed to a rate where the appropriate noise margin can be maintained, and allows a 10^{-7} BER to be maintained.

Research has shown that the optimum margins for DMT service are 6 dB downstream and 6 dB upstream.

You must avoid configuring DSL service with more noise margin than appropriate because the system will train to an unnecessarily low DSL rate to provide the specified margin. You must also avoid specifying an exceptionally low margin, such as 1 dB downstream and 1 dB upstream, because a small increase in noise level on the transmission line will probably result in excessive errors and a subsequent retrain to a lower DSL rate.

If a DSL line is at maximum reach (maximum cable length), and the modems will not train, the margins can be set to 0 for troubleshooting purposes only. For example, if a DSL line trains with the margins set to 0, but does not train when the margins are set to 6 dB, the line length is probably at maximum reach (typically 18 kft of 24-gauge wire, 5.5 km of 0.5 mm wire), or a high noise level is present on the line. If providing service at any cost is necessary, a compromise margin (between 0 and 6 dB) can be temporarily selected. In such cases, it is important to determine whether the source of the problem is in the downstream spectrum or in the upstream spectrum, and to make adjustments accordingly. For example, a margin setting of 3 dB in the downstream spectrum might be necessary to provide a preferred DSL rate at 18 kft of wire.

Increasing the transmit power levels also improves the noise margin, but at the cost of interfering with other services in the same cable.

Most DSLAMs and CPE report both the provisioned and actual noise margins for each DSL line. If the actual margin is higher than the provisioned margin, the line should provide an acceptable error rate at the present DSL line rate. If the actual margin drops below the provisioned margin after train-up, there is a high probability of an excessive error rate and subsequent retrain to a lower DSL rate.

The general indicator of acceptable DSL performance is when the actual margin is better than an appropriately configured margin, and the DSL line is running at the desired data rate.

Forward Error Correction

Forward error correction (FEC) refers to the process of correcting errors mathematically at the receiving end of a transmission path, rather than calling for a retransmit of the errored data. Retransmitting data to correct errors uses the available bandwidth to repeatedly send the same information, and the user perceives extremely slow throughput. FEC results in greater effective throughput of user data because valuable bandwidth is not being used to retransmit errored data. However, in the event that the transmission does not contain any errors, FEC does take away some bandwidth by adding unnecessary overhead.

When errors can be corrected without retransmitting the data, the errors are reported as corrected errors. When the algorithm cannot correct errors, they are reported as uncorrected errors. The ratio of corrected to uncorrected errors shows the relative effectiveness of the error correction algorithm, or the relative intensity of the errors.

Two main functions are related to FEC: FEC bytes and interleaving.

FEC Bytes

FEC bytes are also called check bytes or redundancy bytes. FEC bytes are added to the user data stream to produce a means of calculating the presence of errored data and generating a corrected frame without having to retransmit the data. The appropriate number of provisioned FEC bytes generally depends on the type of errors being detected and corrected. The more FEC bytes that are added to the data stream, the more bandwidth the users' data shares with the FEC bytes. In normal DSL operation, this is not usually a problem, but in this instance, the modems are training at a slightly higher line rate to provide the same user bandwidth (throughput), including the additional FEC bytes.

The tradeoff of adding FEC overhead is being able to correct errors without retransmission versus the displacement of user data, but it is generally observed that much better throughput is achieved by increased efficiency in FEC rather than by retransmitting errored data.

In many systems, the selectable number of FEC bytes is 0 (none), 2, 4, 8, 12, or 16. As a basic and general rule, more FEC bytes means more effective error correction. But, in error-free transmission paths, an unnecessarily high number of FEC bytes serves only to occupy additional bandwidth. Sixteen FEC bytes per frame use a higher percentage of bandwidth at a transmission rate of 256 kbps than the same number of FEC bytes at a transmission rate of 8 Mbps. Theoretically, the presence and number of FEC bytes at 256 kbps is more apparent to the user (as reduced bandwidth) than the same number of FEC bytes at 8 Mbps. But again, most systems simply train at a slightly higher line rate to accommodate the additional check bytes, and the net result is that the users' available bandwidth (and throughput) is the same. Most systems calculate and subtract the FEC overhead before reporting the DSL rate, so that the reported DSL rate is actually the users' available bandwidth. Of course, if ATM and IP are transmitted on the DSL line, the ATM and IP overhead must be manually subtracted from the available (and reported) DSL rate.

Some chipsets optimize the number of FEC bytes versus the requested ATM transmission rate. For example, if a downstream rate of 8.032 Mbps and 16 FEC bytes is specified in the line configuration, but the error rate is within the 10^{-7} limit, the chipset might set the number of FEC bytes to a lower number to create the requested user bandwidth. When DMT performance stats are reviewed, the chipset reports the actual number of FEC bytes rather than what was specified in the configuration.

Before specifying the most efficient number of FEC bytes (and the most efficient interleave delay), you must determine the pattern of errors occurring on the transmission path.

Interleaving

Interleaving is the process of scrambling user data in a precise sequence. The purpose of interleaving is to avoid having consecutive errors delivered to the Reed-Solomon (RS) FEC algorithm at the receiving end of the circuit. RS is more effective on single errors or errors that are more spaced in time (not consecutive).

If a noise burst occurs on the copper transmission line, several consecutive data bits can be affected, which results in consecutive bit errors. Because the data is interleaved at the transmitter, de-interleaving the data at the receiver produces not only the original bit sequence, but separates the errored bits over time. (The errored bits appear in separate bytes.) Therefore, the errored bits are no longer consecutive and the RS FEC process is more effective.

Latency

In many systems, interleaving can be set to 0 (off, none), 1, 2, 4, 8, or 16 milliseconds of interleave delay or depth. The more time allocated to interleaving, the more data can be interleaved. But increasing interleaving delay causes additional latency or delay in the time that the data is transmitted and the time that it is available to the receiving user.

As a general rule, the more interleaving delay that is used, the better the RS algorithm can correct consecutive errors. The increased latency normally causes no problem for general data transmission, but digitized voice over a high-latency path results in an extremely unpleasant echo. For this reason, a minimum interleave delay (or no interleaving) is always used on data channels that carry voice traffic. As delay is added to voice transmissions, the problem of echo increases radically and requires additional treatment. Two-way video conferencing can also experience some undesirable effects from excessive latency in the data stream.

A relatively high error rate can usually be tolerated during voice conversations because the human ear might not even detect the errors. Additional consideration of minimized latency versus error correction might be required when analog data or fax is also running on the voice channel. Conversely, greater latency (delay) is not particularly detrimental to data transmission. Increasing latency does not usually reduce the transmission speed (throughput), but it can incur some additional processor overhead. Again, effective FEC (partially resulting from increased interleaving) can contribute significantly to achieving maximum throughput in a noisy environment, which produces higher throughput than when no interleaving is used.

During competitive testing of DSLAMs in a noise-free environment, some vendors set the interleaving delay to 0 to reduce latency in the transmission path, even though this is not normally done for data services over DSL lines.

Bursty Errors

Bursty errors are multiple errors that occur in short timeframes. For example, in a 1-minute timeframe, there might have been a total of 100 errors, but the 100 errors occurred in bursts of 10 errors at a time, spaced several seconds apart.

To determine if errors are bursty, inspect the total DSL trained-up time and errored-seconds counters. If a unit has been trained for 1 hour, has reported 100 errors, and 1 errored second, the errors are bursty. If the unit has been trained for 1 hour, has reported 1000 errors, and 1000 errored seconds, the errors are dribbling.

Look at the ratio of corrected errors to uncorrected errors. If all reported errors are corrected (no uncorrected errors), no further action is required and FEC can correct the errors.

To treat uncorrected bursty errors, increase the interleave delay (interleave depth). In most systems, interleave delay can be set as low as 1000 microseconds (1 millisecond), and as high as 16,000 microseconds (16 milliseconds). If few errored seconds are detected over a period of several hours, additional corrective measures might not be necessary.

Dribbling Errors

Dribbling errors occur usually one at a time (spaced by milliseconds to seconds), and continue to occur over any given timeframe.

To determine if errors are dribbling, inspect the total DSL trained-up time and errored-seconds counters. If a unit has been trained for 1 hour, has reported 1000 errors, and 1000 errored seconds, the errors are dribbling. If the unit has been trained for 1 hour, has reported 100 errors, and 1 errored second, the errors are bursty.

To treat a steady stream of uncorrected dribbling errors, increase the number of FEC bytes. Increasing the number of FEC bytes adds baggage to the data stream, so there could be a tradeoff between correcting errors and possibly reducing the bandwidth available to the user. The effect of increasing FEC bytes depends on the data rate, with slower data rates yielding more bandwidth to the additional FEC bytes. As a general guideline, nothing is gained by adding more FEC bytes than what is required to correct the errors.

Coding Gain

When using FEC, typically RS encoding, errors can be corrected at the receiver without having to use Transmission Control Protocol (TCP) for block retransmits. When errors are corrected in this way, it has the same effect as using higher noise margins without the related reduction in DSL trained rates. This effect is called *coding gain*, and is expressed in dB (the equivalent dB of margin).

Without coding gain, you need a specific SNR to achieve and maintain an Asynchronous Transfer Mode (ATM) data error rate of 10^{-7} or better. With coding gain, you can achieve and maintain a 10^{-7} error rate with a lower SNR and lower noise margins. Errors might still be occurring on the transmission line, but they are being corrected by the RS algorithm. The resulting error-free (corrected) data rate is the same as if a higher noise margin was used.

Fastpath

The Fastpath channel in DMT systems refers to an optional transmission mode with no interleaving. This is conceptually similar to setting the interleave delay to 0, although not exactly the same. Fastpath offers the least latency possible in the DMT chipset (minimum buffering), and is used primarily for voice services. Fastpath offers reduced FEC. Most DMT systems support Fastpath mode.

DSL Modem Train-Up and Framing

The start sequence conducted between two modems is referred to as training or *train-up*.

During train-up, DSL modems start with no data interleaving and no line coding. (Interleaving and line coding must be negotiated between the two modems.) The signal-to-noise level is calculated across the DSL spectrum, and a DSL line rate is established based on three essential factors:

- **Provisioning**—DSL modems will not establish a faster DSL rate than what is specified (provisioned) in the DSLAM. The DSL trained rate is usually specified in terms of available user bandwidth or data rate rather than the actual DSL spectrum used. That is, the reported DSL rate is the actual user-available bandwidth. Most systems subtract the DSL overhead before reporting the trained rate, and the actual line rate is slightly higher than the reported trained rate.

- **Inappropriate DMT options**—An unnecessarily high noise-margin setting results in an unnecessarily low DSL trained rate. The recommended noise margin settings for DMT are 6 dB downstream and 6 dB upstream. (The recommendation for CAP systems is traditionally 3 dB downstream and 6 dB upstream.)

- **Line conditions**—This includes several factors, but primarily two: attenuation and noise levels. More than one noise source can contribute to the total noise spectrum on the line, thus producing multiple noise frequencies with related noise (power) levels. Some noise sources are more detrimental to DSL performance than others, again depending on the spectrum and power level of the noise induced into the DSL circuit.

Training Mode Options

DSLAMs sometimes have options for specifying the training procedure. For example, in the Cisco systems, you might encounter the options standard train and quick train, or standard train and fast train. Standard train relates to a training procedure specified in ANSI standards document T1.413, which is considered the standards reference for DMT ADSL. (Any manufacturer offering the option standard train should ensure that the option is T1.413 compliant.) Quick train, fast train, and so on can be more proprietary and perform best when used with the same manufacturer's modems (and usually the same DSL chipset) on both ends of the telephone line. Further, quick train might not always result in a faster train-up by the modems.

Framing Modes

Framing modes are also referred to as framing structure and framing overhead. Overhead refers to signaling and synchronization between two modems. There are two main standards-based framing modes: full overhead and reduced overhead. Each of these two main modes has two subsets. The resulting four modes are usually referred to as modes 0, 1, 2, and 3. In basic terms, the four modes refer to how data is allocated to an Embedded Operations Channel (EOC), to an ADSL Overhead Control (AOC) channel, and to cyclic redundancy check (CRC) functions.

Data can be transmitted in dual-latency or single-latency mode. *Dual-latency* implies that data is transmitted in both the interleaved and non-interleaved (fast) buffers. In *single-latency* mode, data is allocated either to the fast (non-interleaved) buffer or to the interleaved buffer. In framing mode 3, if data is transmitted only in the fast buffer, only a fast byte carries overhead (EOC, AOC, or CRC) information. If data is transmitted only in the interleaved buffer, only a sync byte carries overhead information. The resulting reduction in administrative overhead allows more bandwidth to be allocated to user traffic.

The terms fast byte and sync byte are generally accepted jargon for fast synchronization byte and interleaved synchronization byte, further referring to the non-interleaved and interleaved channels. The synchronization symbol permits recovery of the frame boundary after micro-interruptions that might otherwise force retraining.

These channels are known as the bearer channels. ADSL uses two types of bearer channels. AS bearer channels are simplex and used for downstream traffic. LS bearer channels are full duplex, and thus used for both upstream and downstream. Up to four (AS0-AS3) downstream simplex channels and up to three (LS0-LS2) duplex channels are synchronized to the 4-kHz ADSL data frame rate, then multiplexed into two separate data buffers (fast and interleaved). These bearer channels are not to be confused with the subchannels or tones in DMT; these are used for framing, not Layer-1 transmission.

Framing mode 0 is sometimes called full async (full overhead with asynchronous timing). This mode has an administrative overhead of 128 kbps, and is usually the required mode when training up to CPE that is only ANSI issue 1 compliant. Async refers to a mode where the timing of the bearer channels is not synchronized to the ADSL modem timing base. In asynchronous mode, additional synchronization functions are performed to synchronize the bearer channels with the modem's timing base.

Framing mode 1 is sometimes called full sync (full overhead with synchronous timing). This mode also has an administrative overhead of 128 kbps. Sync refers to a mode where the timing of the bearer channels is synchronized with the ADSL modem timing base. In sync mode, additional synchronization functions are not necessary and are not performed.

Framing mode 2 is sometimes called reduced separate (reduced overhead with separate fast and sync bytes in the fast and interleaved buffers). This mode incurs 64 kbps of overhead, with 32 kbps allocated to the fast byte and 32 kbps added to the sync byte.

Framing mode 3 is sometimes called reduced merged (reduced overhead with merged fast and sync bytes in either the fast or interleaved buffer). This mode incurs only 32 kbps of overhead, and is now the most commonly used by systems that are DMT issue 2 compliant.

Cisco ATU-C and ATU-R modems support all framing modes, with mode 3 preferred. If in doubt about which framing mode to select in a DSLAM, select reduced merged (mode 3).

Reduced overhead modes, especially mode 3, can significantly increase a user's data throughput by using less of the available bandwidth for administrative functions. The difference between 128 kbps of overhead and 32 kbps of overhead is much more apparent at slower DSL data rates than at higher DSL data rates.

For a complete description of the ADSL DMT framing modes and processes, refer to ANSI specification T1.413.

Power Levels in DSL Services

DSL power levels are much higher than those levels used in voice, fax, or analog data services. This is simply because of the much greater attenuation of signals at DSL frequencies that are caused by the electrical characteristics of telephone lines.

Because the attenuation of a phone line is much greater at ADSL frequencies than at voice frequencies, the phone line is much more attenuative to DSL than to voice, fax, or analog modems. To recover a usable signal at the end of 18 kft of cable, ADSL is usually transmitted at +15 to +20 dBm. This is an exceptionally high power to be transmitted on a telephone line, but it is necessary to attain DSL rates at maximum reach.

The standard unit of measure for telephone system power levels is dBm, which is dB relative to 1 milliwatt of power dissipated across 600 Ohms. 0 dBm is often called milliwatt. 3 dBm refers to a level 3 dB higher than milliwatt, and −3 dBm refers to a level 3 dB less than milliwatt.

Broad spectrum power levels are usually measured in dBm per Hertz (dBm/Hz) rather than dBm. This is often referred to as power spectral density (PSD). Most ADSL DMT is transmitted at −39 to −41 dBm/Hz, and this falls in the range of +15 to +20 dBm.

The following is a simple formula to estimate dBm/Hz when dBm is specified:

PdBm/Hz = PdBm - 60, where PdBm = power in dBm.
(60 is derived from 10 x log 1e6.)
Example:
For an ADSL transmit power level of 20 dBm: P = 20 - 60 = -40 dBm/Hz.

To estimate dBm when dBm/Hz is specified:

PdBm + 60 = PdBm/Hz
Example:
For an ADSL power of -41 dBm/Hz: P = -41 + 60 = 19 dBm

NOTE   This shortcut formula is for the full ADSL spectrum only, and is an approximation for demonstration purposes. This shortcut factor of 60 must not be used for G.Lite, SDSL, G.SHDSL, and so on.

Power Cutback and Power Boost

Power can be reduced during the train-up sequence when DSL modems calculate and exchange information regarding attenuation. This is part of Cisco's RADSL train-up process. And although you can increase power above a nominal level, this is not commonly done because of the interference imposed on other services in the same cable. This is often referred to as *crosstalk* between cable pairs, and results in a degraded SNR.

The ability to change the default transmit power level becomes important when comparing different DSL vendors, or when comparing different DSL chipsets. If a system is set to transmit at an abnormally high DSL power level, it might offer exceptionally good reach and noise margin while inducing excessive noise in adjacent cable pairs. During competitive evaluations, some equipment manufacturers increase power to improve reach and noise (bit error) performance. The same transmit levels cannot be deployed in a production telephone company (telco) environment.

Trellis Coding

Trellis coding is the process of altering the QAM constellation to provide better performance in a noisy environment. Trellis uses a coding algorithm that allows modems to compensate for minor phase or amplitude variations that are caused by noise on the transmission path. The combination of modulation technique and code allows operation at a higher data rate for a given SNR than could be accomplished without the Trellis code. The net coding gain (equivalent improvement in noise margin) from Trellis encoding is usually estimated to be about 3 dB, although theoretically it could be slightly higher.

Trellis coding is less effective when noise is random, such as erratic impulse spikes, or when a high level of white noise (random noise) is present. Trellis coding can differentiate between correct and incorrect symbols by establishing a pattern or history of the effects of an interfering noise source. Therefore, Trellis coding is more effective when noise has recurring, predictable patterns.

A significant advantage of Trellis coding is that it does not expand bandwidth requirements or increase transmit power requirements to maintain acceptable error rates. Trellis coding does require more complex transceivers and Trellis-capable chipsets might have a slightly higher internal power requirement.

It is often debated whether Trellis adds a significant amount of latency to the transmission path. The general view is that although a small amount of data buffering is required for the coding/decoding process, the newer hardware designs have fast processing speeds that minimize latency. The added latency, although theoretically present, is considered negligible in present designs.

The end result of using Trellis coding/decoding is that you transmit at faster line rates with lower error rates, thus providing faster overall throughput in a moderately noisy environment. Trellis coding offers no advantage in a noise-free environment. The benefit or liability of turning on Trellis coding has to be compared to the achieved coding gain, and whether improved transmission quality is needed in a particular situation. DSL transmission on longer telco loops is generally improved by using Trellis coding.

When RS FEC and Trellis coding are both used at the same time, the coding gain is not simply additive. That is, if 3 dB is gained by using RS alone, and 3 dB is gained by using Trellis alone, the combined coding gain is not 6 dB. Using both systems is ultimately more effective than using only RS or Trellis, so it is generally recommended that both be used in DSL service when supported by the system hardware and software.

A variation of Trellis coding, Overlapped pulse amplitude modulation (PAM) Transmission with Interlocking Spectrum (OPTIS), was recently developed for HDSL version 2 (HDSL2). This transmission technology creates a more noise friendly power spectral density for both the upstream and downstream frequencies. It also reduces crosstalk onto other services through the use of the interlocking upstream and downstream frequencies. It uses Trellis-coded PAM(TC-PAM) to create a flexible PSD that boosts the upstream power in the 200-300 kHz range, at the same time notching the downstream power at the same point. This is done so that the transmit PSD is highest in the region where the receiver has the best SNR.

DSL Technologies

Several different DSL technologies exist in the world today. These vary dramatically in their reach capability and bandwidth capacity. The *reach capability* is the maximum distance that the signal can traverse while still maintaining a connection. In Table 12-2, it is listed as maximum distance. The *bandwidth capacity* varies based on a couple of factors. First, some DSL technologies use symmetric bandwidths for the upstream and downstream data. Others use asymmetric. The symmetric is primarily used for commercial and small- to medium-sized businesses, where leased-line replacement is the objective.

Table 12-2 shows a comparison of the different DSL flavors and some of their respective attributes.

Table 12-2   *DSL Technology Comparison*

Technology	Maximum Upstream Speed	Maximum Downstream Speed	Wire Gauge Distance	Maximum Distance (Feet)	Encoding	Standards
ADSL	800 kbps	8 Mbps	Multi	17,000	CAP or DMT	ANSI T1.413 and ITU G.992.1
EtherLoop	6 Mbps	6 Mbps	Multi	21,000	QPSK, 16QAM, 64QAM	Proprietary Technology of Elastic Networks
G.Lite	512 kbps	1.5 Mbps	Multi	22,000	DMT	ITU G.992.2
G.SHDSL	2.304 Mbps	2.304 Mbps	Multi	20,000 +	TC PAM	ITU G.992.1
HDSL	1.544 Mbps T1 2.0 Mbps E1	1.544 Mbps T1 2.0 Mbps E1	26 AWG 24 AWG	9000 12,000	2B1Q	ITU G.991.1
HDSL2	1.544 Mbps T1 2.0 Mbps E1	1.544 Mbps T1 2.0 Mbps E1	26 AWG 24 AWG	9000 12,000	TC PAM	ITU G.991.1
IDSL	144 kbps	144 kbps	Multi	19,000	2B1Q	ANSI T1.601 and TR-393
RADSL	1.088 Mbps	7.168 Mbps	Multi	18,000	CAP or DMT	ANSI T1.413 and ITU G.992.1
SDSL	768 kbps	768 kbps	Multi	10,000	2B1Q	ITU G.991.1
VDSL	20 Mbps	52 Mbps	Multi	3000	CAP/DMT/ DWMT/ SLC	TBD

The following is a brief summary of various DSL technologies (refer to Table 12-2 for specifications):

- **ADSL**—ADSL is one of the more common DSL technologies because it is asymmetric, which means that download speeds are greater than upload speeds. This addresses the requirement for bandwidth of Internet users for web browsing and client server applications. ADSL uses CAP or DMT to encode data on the DSL circuit. CAP is not a standardized method of encoding data for DSL, and DMT has been standardized by ANSI (ANSI T1.413) and ITU (ITU G.992.1). By using a method that has been standardized, it is more likely that an ADSL connection between different vendors will operate properly.

- **EtherLoop**—A proprietary technology from Elastic Networks (formerly a part of Nortel); EtherLoop is short for Ethernet local loop. EtherLoop uses the advanced signal modulation techniques of DSL and combines them with the half-duplex burst packet nature of Ethernet. EtherLoop modems only generate hi-frequency signals when something is present to send. The rest of the time, they use only a low-frequency (ISDN-speed) management signal. EtherLoop can measure the ambient noise between packets. This allows the ability to avoid interference on a packet-by-packet basis by shifting frequencies as necessary. Because EtherLoop is half-duplex, it is capable of generating the same bandwidth rate in either the upstream or downstream direction, but not simultaneously. Nortel is initially planning for speeds ranging between 1.5 Mbps and 10 Mbps, depending on line quality and distance limitations.

- **G.Lite**—A lower data rate version of ADSL was proposed as an extension to ANSI standard T1.413 by the Universal ADSL Working Group (UAWG) led by Microsoft, Intel, and Compaq. This is known as G.992.2 in the ITU standards committee. It uses the same modulation scheme as ADSL (DMT), but eliminates the POTS splitter at the customer premises. As a result, the ADSL signal is carried over the entire house wiring, which results in lower available bandwidth because of greater noise impairments. Often a misnomer, this technology is not splitterless per se. Instead of requiring a splitter at the customer premises, the splitting of the signal is done at the local CO.

- **G.SHDSL**—Defined by ITU standard G991.2 as a single-pair, high-speed digital subscriber line. G.SHDSL is a symmetric technology that allows the upstream and downstream to operate at the same data rate. This is important because this technology is targeted to replace some older communication technologies, such as T1, E1, HDSL, HDSL2, single-line DSL (SDSL), ISDN, and ISDN-based DSL (IDSL). It also has the advantage of needing less power per chipset. G.SHDSL does differ from some other DSL technologies in that it uses TC-PAM. (TC-PAM is often called spectral friendly because it causes less interference to other services within the same cable.) G.SHDSL was developed to be compatible with other technologies and to increase the service distance (reach) while lowering the interference to other services.

- **HDSL**—Operates at 1.54 Mbps and has a reach of 9 kft on 26 American Wire Gauge (AWG) wire. Two twisted pairs can provide T1 service to a customer. HDSL uses 2B1Q line code modulation and both twisted pairs need to be full duplex and cannot coexist on the same twisted pair with POTS. Refer to Chapter 8, "Integrated Service Digital Network," for details of the 2B1Q line code modulation.

- **HDSL version 2 (HDSL2)**—Designed to accommodate the transport of T1 over a single pair over wire. This technology uses OPTIS and is designed for 1.544 Mbps. It can accommodate all services that were offered by the HDSL technology.

- **IDSL**—ISDN-based DSL service uses 2B1Q line coding and typically supports data transfer rates of 128 kbps. IDSL runs on one pair of wires and extends up to 19 kft. The extended distance of IDSL is because it can be repeated. Some versions of IDSL allows for the full use of 144 kbps (2B+D).

- **RADSL**—Any RADSL modem, but it can specifically refer to a proprietary modulation standard designed by Globespan Semiconductor. It uses CAP. T1.413 standard DMT modems, which are also technically RADSL, but generally not referred to as such. The uplink rate depends on the downlink rate, which is a function of line conditions and SNR.

- **SDSL**—Originally developed by Conexant Semiconductors (previously Rockwell). Conexant used the single-rate European SDSL standard TR-90 and implemented Autobaud to autonegotiate the line rate. Because no standard exists for this technology, interoperability is not possible between vendors who use different silicon on either end of the loop. Without a standard, this technology will be short lived. G.shdsl does everything SDSL does plus it provides a path for multi-vendor interoperability, standards-based auto-negotiation of service type and data rate, and achieves 30 to 50 percent better reach at all data rates.

- **Very-high-data-rate DSL (VDSL)**—VDSL is an emerging technology that is designed to provide higher data rates (up to 52 Mbps) to customers. This technology is currently being worked on by numerous standards organizations to develop standards for VDSL. VDSL takes advantage of fiber-optic communications by placing the termination equipment closer to the customer. By deploying the termination equipment in office buildings and multi-dwelling units, decreases in the length of the local loop allow for increased speeds. VDSL is proposed to run in both asymmetric and symmetric modes.

DSL Circuit Concerns

Several factors can affect the performance of the DSL circuit—most notably, the length and wire gauge of the actual copper loop that is installed. However, there are characteristics of the local loop that can cause problems and increase signal attenuation.

Bridge Taps

Bridge taps are unterminated extensions of the telephone line or loop. They can alter the impedance of the local loop, especially at DSL frequencies. Because wavelength and frequency have an inverse relationship, short bridge taps have the greatest impact on wideband services, and long bridge taps have a greater impact on narrowband services. With DC voltage, the bridge tap behaves as an open circuit, but with high frequencies, the loop becomes a transmission line stub. This impedance mismatch can cause a wide variety of problems, but typically it causes a reflection of data bits from the tap-point back to the point of transmission. This results in bit errors. This characteristic degrades the DSL connection. Most loops contain at least one bridge tap, and the effect of multiple bridge taps is cumulative. Premises wiring typically contains additional short bridge taps, which creates additional signal loss. For optimum performance, the DSL should have as few as possible bridge taps in the loop.

Loading Coils

Loading coils are inductors that are added in series with the phone line to compensate for the parallel capacitance of the line. They extend the range of a local loop for voice grade communications. They benefit the frequencies in the high end of the voice spectrum at the expense of the frequencies above 3.6 kHz. At the DSL frequencies, a loading coil acts as an open circuit, preventing those frequencies from passing. Loading coils on DSL circuits prevent DSL connections.

Interfering Signals

AM radio stations have been known to cause issues with DSL loops because of their overlap in the frequency range (AM radio = 550 kHz – 1.7 MHz). Also, different DSL technologies interfere with each other within the same binder.

Radio Frequency Interference

Radio Frequency Interference (RFI) filters are installed in many areas where AM radio stations can be heard during telephone conversations. The most basic RFI filters are simple capacitors that are placed across the local loop (tip-to-ring, tip-to-ground, and ring-to-ground). They have no effect at voice frequencies, but appear as a short circuit at radio and DSL frequencies. RFI filters cause degradation of DSL performance on shorter cable lengths, and can prevent DSL modems from training on longer lengths.

Crosstalk

The electrical energy transmitted across the copper wire line as a modulated signal also radiates energy onto adjacent copper wire loops that are located in the same cable bundle.

In the telephone network, multiple insulated copper pairs are bundled together into a cable that is called a cable binder. Adjacent systems within a cable binder that transmit or receive information in the same range of frequencies can create significant crosstalk interference. This is because crosstalk-induced signals combine with the signals that were originally intended for transmission over the copper wire loop. The result is a waveform that is shaped differently than the one originally transmitted.

Crosstalk can be categorized in one of two forms. Near-end crosstalk (NEXT) is the most significant because the high-energy signal from an adjacent system can induce relatively significant crosstalk into the primary signal. The other form is far-end crosstalk (FEXT), which is typically less of an issue because the far-end interfering signal is attenuated as it traverses the loop.

Cable Length

When everything in the cable system is working perfectly, the most significant factor related to DSL service is *cable length*. As cable length increases, the gauge (diameter) of the wire becomes increasingly significant, and interference from other services in the same cable become more apparent.

Longer cable lengths attenuate all signal frequencies, although more attenuation occurs at higher frequencies than at lower frequencies. This is due primarily to the distributed capacitance along a two-wire transmission line. Two parallel conductors form a capacitor (also called a condenser). As the frequency increases, the reactance (AC resistance) of the line goes down, and at high frequencies, the line can appear to be almost a short circuit. This causes extreme attenuation of ADSL frequencies.

Wire Gauge and Resistance

Most telephone cable installed since 1980 is either 24 AWG or 26 AWG. 26-gauge wire has a slightly smaller diameter than 24-gauge, and many more pairs can be placed in the same space required by 24-gauge wire. (The international equivalent diameters are 0.5 and 0.4 mm.) Before 1970, and especially before 1960, 22-gauge wire was often used. In the 1950s, 19-gauge wire was occasionally installed. The difference between DC loop resistance on an 18,000-foot pair of 19-gauge wire and 26-gauge wire is radical. Smaller wire gauges became popular as lower loop currents were required to obtain acceptable telephone performance, and as the need for many more wire pairs in the cables and conduits developed.

A quick comparison of DC resistance further illustrates the difference between 24- and 26-gauge wire: 24-gauge wire has a resistance of 26 Ohms per 1000 feet, and 26-gauge wire has a resistance of 41 Ohms per 1000 feet, measured at a temperature of 25C/75F. A telephone line is a DC loop, so 18,000 feet of cable is actually a loop of 36,000 feet of copper wire. A significant change in resistance occurs from cool to hot ambient temperature, especially when using aerial cable that is exposed to the sun. Therefore, DSL performance can change between midnight and noon in some climates, simply because of increased resistance that causes increased attenuation as the cable heats between midnight and noon. Recall that as resistance (and correlative attenuation) increases, SNRs degrade.

DSL Network Architectures

The DSL network architecture is made up of three segments: the CPE, the NAP, and the network service provide (NSP). This section contains a brief explanation of the three components. Figure 12-7 shows these three components in a generic DSL network architecture. Figure 12-7 does not show a POTS splitter because it is not a requirement. However, if one were present, it would be placed between the CPE and the DSLAM.

Figure 12-7   *General DSL Network Architecture*

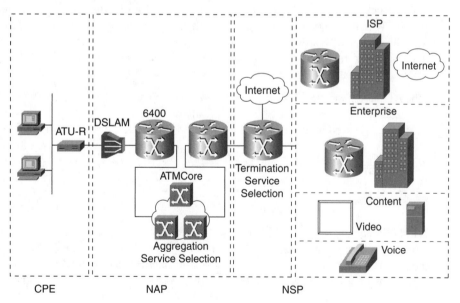

CPE

The CPE segment is made up of the equipment at the customer or remote site. This equipment consists of ATU-R and possibly a POTS splitter, and it provides the DSL uplink to the NAP. The ATU-R is a self-contained unit that is deployed at the customer premises or the remote site. The ATU-R is a standalone unit that consists of an ADSL modem, an Ethernet or USB interface, and an AC power supply. The ATU-R can function logically as a router or a bridge, depending on its make and model. It can also function as a Point-to-Point Protocol over ATM (PPPoA) or Point-to-Point Protocol over Ethernet (PPPoE) client. (These are discussed later in this section.)

NAP

The NAP segment is where the customer premises DSL circuits are terminated and aggregated together to provide connectivity to service providers. The NAP is typically the organization that owns or provides the copper loop for the DSL circuit. This can be the Regional Bell Operating Company (RBOC) or a competitive local exchange carrier (CLEC).

At the NAP, the DSL circuits are terminated on a DSLAM. The DSLAM consists of an ATU-C and a gateway to the NSP. The DSLAM is capable of terminating circuits other than ADSL. With the appropriate card installed, the DSLAM can terminate other types of DSL circuits. The NAP's basic function is to terminate the DSL signal and provide Layer-1/ Layer-2 (refer to Open System Interconnection (OSI) 7 Layer Network Model) connectivity to the NSP.

The ATU-Cs in the DSLAM are aggregated together and handed off to the NSPs. The connection to the service providers is typically done by using ATM. By using ATM, the DSL date is placed into ATM cells and switched over virtual circuits to the service providers. ATM allows for support of quality of service (QoS), which allows for differentiated levels of service to be offered.

NSP

The NSP segment is responsible for providing services over the DSL network. The NSP can be the same organization as the NAP or a totally separate organization. The services provided by the NSP can be Internet access with Internet service provider (ISP) services such as mail, web hosting, and network security. As the technology matures, other services, such as telephony and video, might become prevalent.

Figure 12-8 shows the protocol stack in a DSL network.

Figure 12-8   *Protocol Stack*

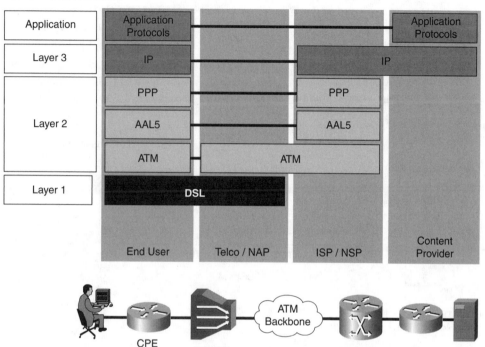

The transport of the DSL customer's data to the NSP can be in the form of many different technologies. Some of the transport methods include PPP and others do not. Figure 12-8 shows where PPP enters into the protocol stack. However, if no PPP is present, such as in the case of RFC 1483 routing, there is no PPP in the protocol stack. The following is a list of some of the most common technologies:

- **RFC 1483 bridging**—With RFC 1483 bridging, IP packets from the end user's workstation are encapsulated in IEEE 802.3 (Ethernet) and enter the CPE ATU-R. In the CPE equipment, the packet is encapsulated with a Logical Link Control/ Subnetwork Access Protocol (LLC/SNAP) header, encapsulated again in ATM Adaptation Layer5 (AAL5), and delivered to the ATM network. The packets are bridged to an Ethernet segment, or they are bridged to a virtual interface within the Broadband Aggregator (BBA) and terminated there.

- **RFC 1483 bridging with routing bridge encapsulation (RBE)**—With RBE, the user's data is still bridged through the CPE; however, the BBA now routes the packets using the Layer-3 header instead of bridging them. This allows for much better performance and security than the traditional bridging deployment. It also allows you to use one IP subnet for a large number of CPEs.

- **RFC 1483 routing**—With 1483 routing the PDU's are routed instead of bridged. This requires that the CPE function as a router instead of a bridge, which allows for a private network between the CPE and the PCs. This does require a separate IP subnet for each BBA interface/CPE pair. Not all CPEs support RFC 1483 routing.

  Figure 12-9 shows the basic topology for an RFC 1483 DSL deployment. The gateway interface is analogous to a default gateway on a PC. It is the default exit point for any address that is not on the device's IP subnet.

Figure 12-9   *RFC 1483 DSL Deployment*

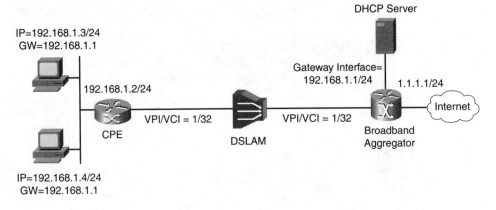

NOTE   The configuration on some, or all, of the devices in Figure 12-9 differs slightly depending on which RFC 1483 architecture is deployed. However, the topology and addressing schemes remain the same. In some instances, RFC 1483 routing can be run from CPE to the BBA.

- **PPPoA**—PPPoA uses PPP (RFC 1331) to encapsulate the higher-layer protocols, such as IP and Internetwork Packet Exchange (IPX). The PPP packet is then encapsulated in AAL5 and transported to the aggregation equipment to be forwarded to the NSP (RFC 2364). An application of using PPP is to have a service provider's infrastructure provide authentication services (Password Authentication Protocol [PAP] and Challenge Handshake Authentication Protocol [CHAP]), IP address management, and billing services. These are the same systems that are used for traditional dialup access. With PPPoA, only a single session per virtual circuit is allowed. It is possible to have multiple VCs and to establish multiple PPP sessions.

- **PPPoE**—Another method to transport higher-layer protocols over DSL is to use PPPoE (RFC 2516). With this method, client software is installed on the PC hosts at the customer site. The client software encapsulates the IP packets in PPP and then encapsulates the PPP packet in Ethernet. The packets are then transported over the DSL network through RFC 1483 bridging to the NSP. PPPoE allows each PC to access a different service, and allows the NSP to track users' information for billing purposes.

NOTE   Some newer CPEs now have the PPPoE client function built-in. This allows them to act as a router for a LAN, while still providing the necessary PPPoE connection.

Figure 12-10 shows the basic topology for a PPPoA or PPPoE DSL deployment.

Figure 12-10   *PPPoA and PPPoE*

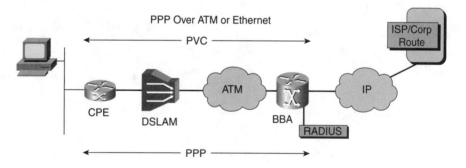

NOTE   In both the PPPoA and PPPoE, the PPP session can be generated on the PC or on the CPE. This is dependent on the feature capability of the CPE and the ISP's requirements.

Sample configurations for all the preceding topologies can be found at www.cisco.com. A simple search will reveal several pages relevant to these topics, or you can visit the technical tips page for direct access to sample configurations:

www.cisco.com/public/technotes/serv_tips.shtml

Expert White Board: Wholesale DSL

In many cases, a local ISP provides DSL connectivity for a larger ISP. In these cases, the DSL provider only wants to terminate the DSL signal and off-load the rest of the services, specifically PPP termination, to the ISP. In this type of a deployment, it is common to tunnel the user's PPP sessions through the Layer 2 Tunnel Protocol (L2TP) back to the appropriate ISP. (For more information on L2TP, see RFC 2661.) L2TP allows the ISP to determine all the Layer-3 attributes of the user while not having to provide the DSL connection. It offers the DSL provider the benefit of not having to provide Layer-3 service. The provider simply provides the Layer-1 and Layer-2 transport for the user's traffic.

In Figure 12-11, the DSL provider is providing the DSL connection and Layer-1 and Layer-2 transport back to the ISP.

Figure 12-11   *PPPoX (PPPoA or PPPoE) with L2TP*

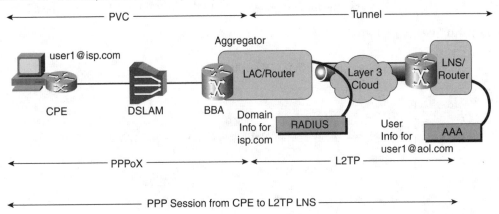

The following is a brief description of the sequence of events that transpires when the user enables the DSL connection:

1   The DSL CPE opens a connection to the DSLAM to enable the DSL connection.

2   After the DSL line is established, the CPE begins to send its initial PPP parameters (LCP). This contains some of the link attributes (e.g., MRU) and the authentication data (e.g., PAP or CHAP).

3   At this point, the aggregator/ L2TP Access Concentrator (LAC) identifies the incoming user as user1@isp.com. The domain extension on the username signals the LAC to start a L2TP tunnel to the ISP's L2TP Network Server (LNS).

4 The user's PPP data is buffered on the LAC until the L2TP tunnel is established; at which point, it is forwarded on the LNS.

5 The user negotiates all stages of PPP, both Link Control Protocol (LCP) and Network Control Protocol (NCP), with the LNS. After completion, the user has the necessary Layer-3 information and can proceed with the desired network services.

6 From this point, forward all the user's traffic is tunneled through the LAC to the LNS. The user/CPE has no knowledge of the DSL provider, including the LAC. It only knows that its IP gateway, also known as the default gateway, is the LNS.

Summary

DSL technology presents a solution to a growing need for increased bandwidth to the home and elsewhere. Various flavors can be used in different scenarios, depending primarily on distance and bandwidth requirements. Many factors govern how good a connection is, and many parameters can be tweaked to improve DSL data rates and SNR margins. The key is to understand the technology and what factors play what roles.

DSL network topologies can vary greatly from one ISP to another, so assuming that a DSL CPE that worked on one carrier will work on another is not recommended. The different topologies have their own advantages and disadvantages, but all the topologies are widely deployed.

References and Standards

The following references were used in the writing of this chapter. They can also be used to further your knowledge of DSL and its deployments:

- www.dslforum.org or www.adsl.com
- www.ietf.org
- www.atmforum.com
- www.itu.int
- www.cisco.com and www.dsl.cisco.com
- www.developer.intel.com

Review Questions

Give the best answer to the following questions. The answers to these questions can be found in Appendix A, "Answers to Review Questions."

1 What are the encoding methods used for DSL?

2 What are the three items that characterize analog carrier signals?

3 What frequency range does voice use in POTS?

4 Into how many subchannels does DMT divide the bandwidth?

5 What is a bridged tap?

6 What is a loading coil and why are they used?

7 What is a POTS splitter?

_____

_____

_____

8 What is NEXT?

_____

_____

_____

9 What are the five methods of transport encapsulation for DSL?

_____

_____

_____

10 What is an NSP?

_____

_____

_____

This chapter covers the following topics:

- **The cable plant**—Covers the cable television (CATV) distribution network.

- **Data-over-Cable Service Interface Specifications (DOCSIS): the cable modem standard**—Discusses the fundamentals of DOCSIS.

- **DOCSIS cable modem initialization sequence**—A thorough coverage of the steps in the cable modem initialization sequence.

- **Binary DOCSIS configuration files**—Detailed coverage of the DOCSIS 1.0 configuration file and DOCSIS 1.1 configuration file.

- **Security and baseline privacy**—Discusses baseline privacy initialization, pre-provisioned certificates, the baseline privacy interface (BPI)+, and other security concerns and features.

- **Fiber node combining**—Covers the process of determining which fiber nodes to associate with which DOCSIS ports.

- **Cable IP network topologies**—Includes Ethernet aggregation architectures, optical carrier (OC)x aggregation architectures, Dynamic Packet Transport/Resilient Packet Ring (DPT/RPR) architectures, and high-speed optical (dense wavelength division multiplexing [DWDM]) core architectures.

- **The future of cable IP networks**—Ideas on the future of cable IP networks.

CHAPTER 13

Cable Modem Technology and CATV

CATV networks originated in the U.S. in the late 1940s as a way of distributing broadcast television channels to locations with poor reception. Antennas were placed on the top of tall hills or other high points and a cable connected homes to the antennas. Using cabled connections, individual homes received strong clear CATV reception. In the 1950s an estimated 14,000 individual homes were connected to a CATV network. Since that time, subscriber penetration has grown to an average of around 70 percent of all U.S. households with even higher penetrations in some locations. The U.S. CATV network passes nearly 97 percent of U.S. households. Outside of the U.S., CATV has also become an extremely popular mechanism for distributing television content. Recent improvements in CATV-based services such as pay-per-view, digital CATV, and cable modems have only served to prove the strength and flexibility of worldwide CATV networks.

Since its inception, CATV has become a large-scale business and a wave of consolidation has occurred in the industry. What began as several small local CATV distribution companies has become an industry dominated by a few large cable operators serving multiple geographic locations. A single large CATV operator, called a multiple service operator (MSO), can control CATV distribution networks in numerous widely dispersed geographic locations. As a result of consolidation, cable operators today range from small cable networks with 200 subscribers to huge MSOs serving tens of millions of homes.

With CATV service penetration at near saturation levels, cable operators realized that continued revenue growth required new services. Cable modem systems were tested as potential new revenue sources as early as the 1970s. By 1996 home computers and cable modems became a major interest for MSOs. Since 1997, cable modem subscriptions have increased exponentially. However, cable modem technology remained challenging while deployments, planned initially for penetration rates of 3 to 8 percent of households, shot into the 20 to 35 percent range. Although cable plants constantly deliver huge amounts of information to the subscriber in the form of television channels, sending information upstream (from the subscriber to the cable operator) was and remains a serious technological and engineering challenge. Early interactive services such as pay-per-view and cable modems required unrealistically demanding CATV network design. Subsequent systems overcame upstream transmission limitations by relying on the telephone system and a telephony modem to transmit information. The reliance on the telephone system is still found in some systems with older cable modems, in cable networks with no available upstream transmission path, and in set-top boxes for such features as ordering pay-per-view.

As cable modem service became increasingly popular, several vendors entered the marketplace with competing proprietary systems. Each early cable modem system offered its own benefits, and its own problems. Certainly these proprietary systems were revolutionary in their ability to transmit home computer data upstream and downstream by using the same cable infrastructure that delivers television signals to the home. However, it quickly became clear to MSOs that the lack of a widely adopted cable modem standard was contributing to inflated equipment prices and causing operators to become constrained by a single vendor's products. Once invested in a single vendor's product, MSOs found it difficult or impossible to change to a different vendor. The Institute of Electrical and Electronics Engineers (IEEE) began development of a cable modem standard, designated 802.14, in 1994, with the goal of establishing a single interoperable cable modem specification. In 1996, four cable multiple system operators (Cox Communications, Comcast Cable Communications, Tele-Communications, and Time Warner Cable) formed a consortium called the Multimedia Cable Network System Partners (MCNS) to evaluate technologies and create a modem technology standard more directly aligned with industry requirements. The first MCNS specification that was released in 1987 eventually became DOCSIS. The International Telecommunication Union (ITU) adopted the DOCSIS specifications in 1998 as an international standard and consequently the IEEE 802.14 efforts were abandoned. Cable Television Laboratories (CableLabs) in the U.S. and tComLabs in Europe were given responsibility for the certification and qualification of DOCSIS-based equipment and the supervision of new aspects of cable modem technology.

This chapter specifically addresses cable modem systems that are based on DOCSIS standards. These standards include DOCSIS and Euro-DOCSIS versions 1.0, 1.1, and 2.0.

The Cable Plant

CATV was initially deployed to bring nearby broadcast television stations to areas where reception was poor or non-existent. In this manner it served subscribers as a unidirectional (one-way) video distribution mechanism, wherein television broadcasts were transmitted downstream from the CATV video distribution point (known as the headend) to the subscriber. This CATV distribution network, often referred to as a cable plant, traditionally consists of branched metallic (aluminum and copper) cabling with amplifiers spaced throughout the network to improve signal strength. Larger coaxial cable, called trunk cable, transmits the signal long distances where it is later branched out onto thinner cables that are sometimes called express cables. Amplifiers exist on both trunk and express cables. At the subscriber premises, a strand of thin cable, called feeder or drop cable, connects the trunk cable to the customer premises equipment (CPE). Figure 13-1 shows a traditional branched coaxial network architecture with drop, express, and feeder cables.

For subscribers distant from the cable headend, a branched all-metallic design can mean many amplifiers between the subscriber and the headend. Amplifiers of older designs were often manufactured as unidirectional devices because of the then unidirectional design of the CATV network.

Although purely metallic coaxial-based networks can still be found in some areas, the constraints of coaxial networks and the huge advances in analog fiber optics have lead to significant improvements in overall cable network design.

Figure 13-1 *Traditional Branched Coaxial Cable Network*

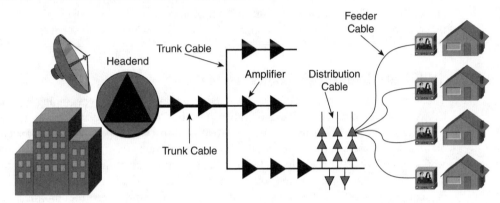

One limitation of all-coaxial cable networks is signal attenuation. Signals that travel along a metallic cable need relatively frequent amplification, particularly signals at higher frequencies. Cable modem technologies, by definition, involve the modulation and demodulation of an analog signal, and when the analog signal has been amplified sequentially several times, issues with signal quality often arise. The frequent amplification of an analog signal not only amplifies transmitted signals, but also amplifies any associated noise and interference, which reduces signal quality. A signal can only be amplified a finite number of times before signal quality becomes unacceptable. Modern CATV networks limit the number of sequential amplifiers (called amplifier cascades). Although older network designs had 20 or even 80 amplifiers in a cascade, newer designs typically have only five to seven amplifiers to optimize signal quality and increase reliability. These amplification constraints that are inherent in metallic coaxial-based CATV networks limit the distance that a subscriber can be from the cable headend and the overall size of the cable plant.

Additional amplification concerns in the cable network relate to the fundamental ways in which frequencies are differentially attenuated when traversing the network. Higher frequencies attenuate more rapidly than lower frequencies. This results in what is often called a slope or tilt effect in signal strength. To mitigate the effects of differential attenuation, amplifiers are often installed in conjunction with equalizers. Equalizers are engineered with a frequency response, which mirrors the cable span that precedes the amplifier and, when used in conjunction with an amplifier, produces a level signal to compensate for differential attenuation. Although with equalizers and amplifiers signal levels can be maintained for all frequencies, one result of differential attenuation is that high frequencies require greater or more frequent amplification than others. This results in compounding noise, distortion, and interference issues on higher frequencies.

A modern CATV network today includes network segments of both optical fiber and coaxial cabling and can serve millions of subscribers in numerous geographic locations. Television content is transmitted to MSOs through cables, broadcast transmissions, and satellite transmissions. Old unidirectional amplifiers have been replaced with two-way amplifiers to allow for both downstream and upstream signals, and the overall numbers of amplifiers in cascades are being reduced. Optical fiber is combined with coaxial in the modern cable plant to provide the connectivity of copper with the benefits of fiber.

The Hybrid Fiber-Coaxial (HFC) Network

The first networks to include a fiber node-type technology were built beginning in 1990. CATV networks today are built exclusively using HFC design and older networks are being retrofitted to receive the benefits of HFC. As a result, most CATV networks today are based on fiber node-based architecture, but they also include elements of the older coaxial networks. The HFC network design helps reduce many of the amplification and attenuation issues and other issues associated with all coaxial cable plants. HFC cable networks can be extended significantly further than coaxial networks without the need for amplification. Because the signal travels over optical fiber, the physical distances between headend and subscriber can extend to more than 100 kilometers—much further than in a coaxial-based plant.

With the advent of HFC topologies, the old trunk cable was renamed express cable. Figure 13-2 shows a typical HFC network design with a remote fiber node attached to express cable, distribution cables, and feeder cables. Express cable typically runs between amplifier cascades and does not have subscriber households directly attached.

Figure 13-2 *Example HFC Network*

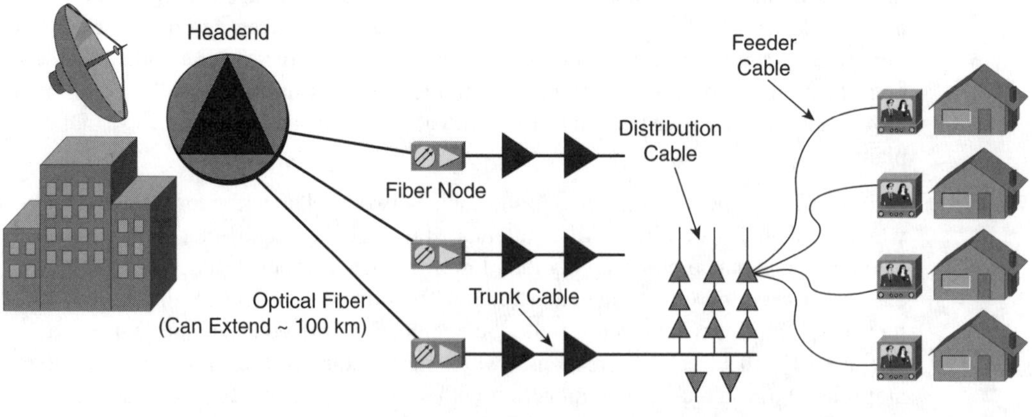

HFC is a hierarchical network design. Each headend includes fiber receiver/transmitter pairs that are connected through long strands of fiber to a remote fiber node. A remote fiber node converts received downstream optical signals to electrical signals and puts them onto the attached coaxial cable. Likewise, when the remote fiber node receives upstream electrical signals on the coaxial cable, it converts them to optical signals and places them on the attached optical fiber. The remote fiber node is connected to the headend transmit and receive lasers through attached fiber and to the subscriber premises through the attached coaxial cable. Fiber nodes also perform important tasks such as filtering frequencies in the upstream outside of a set range (typically frequencies between 5 and 45 MHz are not filtered, although this varies based on the type of cable network).

A fiber node serves a set number of homes or potential subscribers. Because the number of potential subscribers in a specific geographic location does not change frequently, fiber node deployments can usually be designed with a specific number of potential subscribers (known as households passed [HHP]) in mind. In 1990, during initial HFC rollouts, each fiber node was designed to serve 10,000 HHP. By 1995, this number had decreased to 2000 HHP. As optical equipment prices continue to decrease and demands for plant segmentation increase, node size decreases. In 2001, nodes with as few as 250 HHP became common. The number of homes served by a fiber node has significant impact on the deployment of two-way IP cable technologies on that physical section of cable plant.

Cable operators are gradually upgrading their cable plants and reducing the number of subscribers per fiber node in a process called plant segmentation. Because the cable plant is fundamentally a shared transmission medium, plant segmentation allows the cable operator to more closely target subscribers with specific services. Each fiber node can be considered its own small cable plant because upstream and downstream signals are isolated on a per-node basis. Specifically, this implies that the cable operator can make different television channels or other separate services available to separate nodes. Plant segmentation is one of the most important techniques used to control the number of cable modems that are transmitting on a single shared section of the cable plant. The cable operator can also use additional frequencies, called frequency-division multiplexing (FDM), to segment traffic. An operator weighs the costs of additional frequency spectrums versus the capital costs of further segmenting the network, and typically chooses the lower cost alternative.

Headends and Hubs

Simple cable plants that serve a single geographic area can be represented as having a single source for video signal, often a satellite, antenna, or other type of receiver. This source, called the headend, transmits data through a set of fiber nodes throughout the geographic region. Each fiber node then connects to a coaxial distribution network that delivers video to individual subscriber premises. Each fiber node is often analogous to a group of subscribers such as an apartment complex, city block, office building, or neighborhood.

Many MSOs, formed by the consolidation of several geographically disparate cable plants, face challenges when distributing information between local cable networks. To help solve the issues of distance without reducing the economies of scale present in large MSOs, a hierarchical network of distribution points is typically deployed, as shown in Figure 13-3. In a large MSO there usually exists a set of redundant headends where video signals are received. Satellite receivers, decoders, and other expensive equipment can serve many subscriber regions. These large headends are often called super headends and transmit data to several smaller headends for final delivery. Some distribution points, called hubs, are smaller than headends but serve as points at which the core video distribution network is connected through fiber transmitter/receivers to individual fiber nodes. Super headends, headends, and hubs together allow for a small set of signal sources to be used to serve a large number of subscribers in many areas, while maintaining a high level of television service availability.

Figure 13-3 *Hierarchical Headend Architecture*

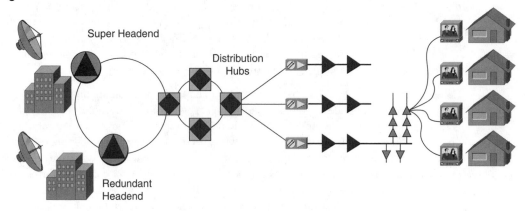

International Television Standards

Three primary color standards exist for broadcast television signals. The U.S. and Japan, for example, use the National Television Systems Committee (NTSC) system (standard created in 1941), which is based on a 6-MHz channel width. Most other countries use the 8-MHz channel width Phase Alternating Line (PAL) standard, and France and several Eastern European countries use another 8-MHz based standard known as Systeme Electronique Couleur Avec Memoire (SECAM). In some countries and regions a 7-MHz variant of PAL is used. Still other locations use a mixture of more than one channel format on a single cable network.

Frequency Allocation

Broadcast channel allocation is different in every region and country. In the U.S., frequency allocation is the responsibility of the Federal Communications Commission (FCC). The FCC decides which entities are authorized to broadcast at specific frequencies. Most regions and countries have authorities responsible for frequency allocation. Types of broadcast signals are usually restricted to specific frequencies by law. Figure 13-4 shows U.S. over-the-air frequency allocation for those frequencies used by cable modems for communication.

Because cable companies distribute information on cables shielded from over-the-air, or on-air broadcast frequencies, a cable operator can broadcast on any frequency that the cable plant can carry. However, a large cable plant can act like a massive antenna and interference with over-the-air broadcasts or other over-the-air signals is common. Specific areas of contention vary from region to region but can include both licensed and unlicensed radio frequencies.

Figure 13-4 *U.S. Broadcast Frequency Allocation 5 to 150 MHz*

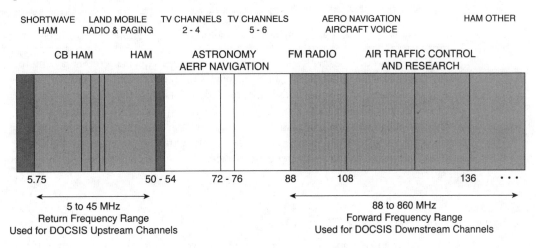

Cable modem standards limit modem transmission (upstream) to frequencies compatible with the return path designs and frequency allocation of the cable network. Downstream transmission is likewise limited to ranges associated with downstream path designs of the cable network. In the U.S. cable modems transmit upstream between 5 and 40 MHz and receive downstream between 88 and 860 MHz, although downstream video signals begin around 52 MHz. The term *split plan* refers to a location in the spectrum where the upstream frequencies and downstream frequencies meet. For locations with different split plans, cable modem communication upstream and downstream is separated at a different point in the spectrum. In all regions the two frequency ranges are actually separated by a slight gap in the spectrum. This gap ranges in size from 12 MHz to 20 MHz as defined in the local region. Location of the split, the ranges available for DOCSIS upstream transmission, and those frequencies used for downstream transmission of DOCSIS and video signals are detailed in Table 13-1.

Table 13-1 *International Split Plans*

Region or Country	Split Plan (High Upstream Frequency/ Low Downstream Frequency in MHz)
North, Central, and South America	40/52
China, Korea, Philippines, Thailand, Singapore, Australia	65/85
Japan, New Zealand	55/70
India, Malta, Eastern Europe	30/48
Western Europe, Ireland, United Kingdom	65/85

Those regions or countries with splits that occur at higher frequencies often have more upstream frequencies available. Because upstream modem transmission is limited to upstream frequencies, more bandwidth is theoretically available in the upstream path in regions with split plans, which occur higher at higher frequencies. In particular, regions such as Japan have experienced a strong demand for cable modem equipment capable of transmitting upstream at frequencies around 50 MHz. Often higher upstream frequencies have less interference than lower frequencies, which results in more reliable cable modem operation.

Requirements for Cable Plant Quality

Because noise and distortion can severely impact the operation of two-way cable IP networks, a set of cable plant quality requirements has been published as part of the DOCSIS cable specification. These requirements set stringent guidelines for plant quality in the upstream and downstream directions.

Cable plant quality is measured in several ways depending on the noise or distortion type. Because of the variable noise tolerances of standardized modulation types (discussed later in this chapter in the section "Modulation Types"), plant and signal quality requirements vary between modulations. In Table 13-2, operational settings are detailed. These operational settings should be considered the absolute minimum. Operation of DOCSIS equipment outside of these ranges is not recommended. The frequencies used for upstream transmission are typically noisier than those used for downstream transmission, and thus more noise tolerant modulation types are incorporated into the standard for upstream transmission.

Table 13-2   *DOCSIS Requirements for Cable Plant Quality*

System/Channel	DOCSIS Specification
Carrier to noise (upstream)	25 dB
Carrier to ingress (upstream)	25 dB
Carrier to interference (upstream)	25 dB
Carrier to noise (downstream)	35 dB
Carrier hum modulation (downstream)	–26 dBc (5 percent)
Carrier hum modulation (upstream)	–23 dBc (7 percent)
Carrier to composite second order and composite third order distortions (downstream)	–50 dBc
Amplitude ripple (downstream)	0.5 dB in 6 MHz
Amplitude ripple (upstream)	0.5 dB/MHz
Group delay (downstream)	75 ns in 6 MHz
Group delay (upstream)	200 ns/MHz

Operating near minimal DOCSIS settings can provide satisfactory service to data-only subscribers; other service and technologies might be less tolerant. Voice services, because of their extensive availability and quality of service (QoS) requirements, require the cable operator to design to superior standards. Specifically, when deploying voice services the cable plant should meet full DOCSIS specifications as listed in Table 13-2. In many cases, the operator might want to design to even better plant quality to add a safety margin or buffer in case of partial plant failure.

Common Cable Plant Issues

As a CATV or cable modem signal is transmitted downstream through the branched cable topology, the signal becomes attenuated and weaker at each branching and with cable distance. What is initially a strong signal requires amplification to adequately reach the subscriber. Noise or interference in downstream frequencies that enters the cable system at some distance from the headend only affects customers past that point. It does not affect all subscribers, as it does not originate at the headend. However, when noise is present it is amplified along with the desired signals. Additionally, each amplifier adds its own noise and distortion to the signals. Noise and interference in the downstream are typically viewed as ghosting or static on video signals. If a cable plant is designed to adequately transmit video signals, it is likely to be of high enough quality to transmit DOCSIS signals. Thus, although noise in the downstream is an issue on the cable plant, it is upstream noise that is the primary concern for DOCSIS deployment.

In the upstream path the additive nature of noise and interference has an increased impact. As noise and interference occur at one or more subscriber sites and travel upstream they are gradually combined with other noise through a process sometimes called noise funneling. What might be an insignificant electronic hum at one subscriber site can be combined with hum from hundreds or thousands of other subscriber sites to become destructive by the time it reaches the headend. In particular, unterminated cables at the subscriber premises can inadvertently receive radio frequency (RF) signals and funnel those into the network. Although each non-terminated cable might only receive a whisper of undesirable RF signal, the cumulative signal after the effect of noise funneling is massive. HFC plant segmentation can help reduce the effect of noise funneling by reducing the number of combined signals traveling on a given upstream path. Because it is impossible to eliminate noise funneling it is vital that the cable IP network upstream noise and that interference levels be characterized and constantly monitored or network outages can occur.

Some common upstream impairments on the cable plant and their mitigation strategies include the following:

- **Ingress noise**—Inadvertently present signals, often from broadcast sources such as amateur, short wave, and citizens' band (CB) radio users. Often a result of bad grounding and poor connections littered through the cable plant. Can be mitigated by the identification of problem frequencies and avoidance of them for upstream transmission. Also mitigated by the use of intelligent cable modem termination system (CMTS) devices that can identify ingress locations and use frequency changes to dynamically avoid this type of noise as it occurs. Most often, a technician must visit the worst ingress locations, and physical changes must be made to the network. Often these locations are also sources of signal leakage and can be located by looking for small (or large) signal leakage (a process known as Cumulative Leakage Index [CLI] testing). Leaks on the order of five microvolts per meter can be sufficient to allow disruptive ingress if there are strong signal sources nearby.

- **Impulse noise**—Caused by bad grounding and loose connections in the cable plant. A classic source is power line arcing. Impulse can be partially mitigated by the use of forward error correction (FEC) and interleaving error correction algorithms. Again, a technician might need to visit the worst locations and make physical changes to the network. In some cases, defective CATV network components such as power supplies must be serviced or replaced.

- **Reflections**—The result of unterminated cable drops, usually at the customer premises. Caused by signals literally bouncing off the end of poorly terminated or unterminated cables. Can be mitigated through equalization coefficients. Technicians can also make changes to the network to reduce severe reflections. Reducing re-flections is important to cable operators as reflections typically result in disturbances in analog video quality, as quickly noticed by subscribers.

- **Laser clipping**—Caused by laser nodes receiving a signal at power levels beyond their supported range. Mitigated by appropriate amplifier alignment and levels in the upstream path. Can also occur in the downstream path and cause modem instability. Most easily monitored with quadrature amplitude modulation (QAM) analyzers.

- **Common path distortion**—Often caused by corroded connections and other cabling issues. Best resolved by physical repair to the damaged cable network infrastructure. Can most easily be located and repaired by starting at the subscriber premises and sampling sequentially along the network towards the headend in a process called divide and conquer.

Other common types of upstream impairments include the following:

- Unwanted signal
- Interference from electrical and magnetic sources (electromagnetic interference [EMI])
- Thermal noise/RF amplifier noise (unless severe, usually no impact on DOCSIS networks)
- Co-channel ingress
- Composite second order distortion (generally a downstream impairment but can impact the upstream)
- Discrete second order distortion
- Composite triple beat distortion (generally a downstream impairment)
- Cross modulation
- Hum
- Intermittent or poor connections
- Poor in-channel frequency response

DOCSIS: The Cable Modem Standard

A bi-directional cable modem technology must take into account existing CATV networks and CATV network quality and requirements for supporting IP networks. Although several proprietary cable modem network technologies exist, the internationally accepted (and by far the most popular) standard for cable IP networking is DOCSIS. Created by the MCNS to drive superior cable IP technology and to encourage competition between equipment vendors, DOCSIS and the analogous European standard Euro-DOCSIS detail the communication between a cable modem and the device to which it connects, the CMTS. Other aspects of a cable IP network are also addressed by the standard such as provisioning, security specifications, and network management. The fundamental value of DOCSIS allows the cable operator to reliably bill for service and use equipment from more than one vendor in an essentially interchangeable fashion.

The DOCSIS 1.0 specification describes the mechanisms by which cable devices such as cable modems can connect to the cable IP network, become provisioned, and actively transmit. DOCSIS also specifies requirements for the cable plant as shown in Table 13-2. Although DOCSIS 1.0 compliant cable modems have been widely deployed, limitations of the DOCSIS 1.0 specification, particularly in the area of QoS and upstream signaling have prompted the release of subsequent standards. The DOCSIS 1.1 specification includes more detailed provisions for QoS, the differentiation of traffic streams, sophisticated multicast transmission, and other important components. The recent DOCSIS 2.0 specification primarily addresses the physical layer aspects of the DOCSIS networks and includes specifications for advanced physical layer communications, which can improve network throughput under certain conditions, and with new CMTS and cable modem hardware. Figure 13-5 depicts connecting the CMTS to the cable modem through the HFC.

Figure 13-5 *Connecting the CMTS to the Cable Modem Through the HFC*

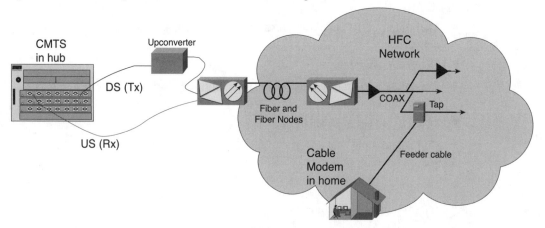

Despite the apparent superiority of more recent DOCSIS specifications, at the time of this writing the vast majority of DOCSIS cable modems deployed are capable of DOCSIS 1.0 communication only. This is in part because of the large installed base of modems that existed prior to the finalization of more recent specifications. However, DOCSIS 1.1 cable modems are being deployed in increasing numbers and eventually the bulk of deployed modems will be based on newer specifications.

DOCSIS and Euro-DOCSIS

DOCSIS and Euro-DOCSIS differ primarily in that the DOCSIS standard specifies a 6-MHz NTSC-type channel width (also known as Annex B, an ITU-T J.83 designation), and Euro-DOCSIS specifies an 8-MHz PAL- or SECAM-type channel width (also known as Annex A). DOCSIS and Euro-DOCSIS device testing, certification, and standards qualification are handled by different organizations.

Modulation Types

Both DOCSIS and Euro-DOCSIS dictate that digital information be modulated and demodulated between modem devices on the cable network using QAM, which is a type of phase-amplitude modulation. The phase and amplitude of the signal are modulated to encode 0s and 1s. QAM modulation encodes symbols on RF waveforms. The number of symbols per second is represented by a modulated signal that is proportional to the bandwidth of the transmission frequency. For example, an 8-MHz wide channel can carry more symbols per second than a 6-MHz wide channel. Each symbol that is modulated onto the waveform represents several bits and thus data. The number of bits that can be represented by a symbol is dependent on the type of modulation used. Modulation types used in DOCSIS networks can encode from 2 bits per symbol up to 8 bits per symbol. However, the number of bits that can be successfully encoded and decoded per symbol is extremely reliant on signal quality. In cable environments where noise and interference are prevalent, modulation formats that supply greater data throughput are more easily corrupted, resulting in either high bit error rates (BERs) or loss of the entire communication channel. Modulation types that encode fewer bits per symbol are more noise tolerant and are often used to mitigate the issues caused by noise and interference.

In the downstream direction on the cable plant the DOCSIS specification includes two types of QAM modulation: 64 QAM and 256 QAM. Upstream transmission occurs in frequency ranges with higher noise levels and interference and DOCSIS dictates the use of more robust modulation types—16 QAM and quadrature phase shift keying (QPSK). DOCSIS 2.0 provides provisions for clean upstream systems (often found where fiber nodes have small numbers of households passed) and allows for 32 and 64 QAM upstream.

Bandwidth for downstream transmission varies from region to region with the CATV standard used locally. For NTSC systems, transmission downstream is on a band 6-MHz wide. On other cable systems the band is 8-MHz wide. Overall throughput on the cable network is directly proportional to the number of symbols that can be transmitted per second. For DOCSIS networks, the frequency range for downstream signals is from 55 to 870 MHz.

Both DOCSIS and Euro-DOCSIS specifications detail upstream frequencies and bandwidth that is not fixed but instead can be one of several widths—200 kHz, 400 kHz, 800 kHz, 1.6 MHz, and 3.2 MHz. DOCSIS 2.0 allows for the use of an upstream channel width of 6.4 MHz, although this is only useful in networks with unusually small amounts of noise and interference. These frequencies can be located anywhere between 4 and 45 MHz but typically are above 20 MHz because of noise limitations. Euro-DOCSIS allows for a frequency range of 5 to 65 MHz. The range of upstream bandwidths allows cable operators to mitigate concerns of noise and interference by placing appropriately sized upstream DOCSIS bands between known noisy frequencies in the upstream spectrum. Multiple upstream frequencies can be used on a single fiber node or group of nodes to supply additional throughput. Certain cable modem and CMTS vendors offer features that allow automatic changes in modulation, bandwidth, and frequency based on the appearance of noise or interference on an active channel.

Determining Modulation Type

Although some CMTS vendors have configured a default downstream modulation of 256 QAM, most vendors have chosen the more common 64 QAM as a default modulation profile. This is because 256 QAM offers less tolerance for network operating and alignment errors and requires better carrier-to-noise ratio performance. Only exceptionally clean cable plants are of high enough quality to run 256 QAM in every home with appropriately low error rates. Often some form of plant repair or in-house wiring repair is required before 256 QAM is reliable in the home. Sometimes connectors and other passive devices inside the home must be replaced. Other solutions include amplitude correction or even complete coaxial cable replacement. 64 QAM is more frequently deployed than 256 QAM as a result of these challenges.

Likewise, most CMTS vendors default to the noise-tolerant QPSK in the upstream. Example 13-1 shows sample output from a Cisco uBR7246 detailing the modulation profile for a particular CMTS upstream channel. The output notes channel width, modulation profile (in this case 16 QAM) and symbol rate for the channel.

Example 13-1 *Example Output of* **show controller** *Command on a Cable Interface*

```
uBR7246#show controller cable 5/0 upstream 0

Cable5/0 Upstream 0 is up
Frequency 19.984 MHz, Channel Width 1.600 MHz, 16-QAM Symbol Rate 1.280 Msps
Spectrum Group 1
SNR 27.6040 dB
Nominal Input Power Level 2 dBmV, Tx Timing Offset 2293
Ranging Backoff Start 0, Ranging Backoff End 4
Ranging Insertion Interval automatic (50 ms)
Tx Backoff Start 0, Tx Backoff End 4
part_id=0x3137, rev_id=0x03, rev2_id=0xFF
nb_agc_thr=0x0000, nb_agc_nom=0x0000
Range Load Reg Size=0x2C
Request Load Reg Size=0x07
Minislot Size in number of Timebase Ticks is = 8
Minislot Size in Symbols =64
Bandwidth Requests = 0x52B
Piggyback Requests = 0x1AA
Invalid BW Requests= 0x1AA
Minislots Requested= 0x2C1A
Minislots Granted = 0x2570
Minislot Size in Bytes = 32
UCD Count = 3250
DES Ctrl Reg#0 = C000C043, Reg#1 = 0
```

Error Mitigation Through FEC

Noise and interference levels fluctuate on cable networks and as a result even the most noise tolerant modulation scheme that is deployed on a cable plant with standard specifications will experience losses. FEC is one mechanism by which errors in transmission can be repaired upon receipt by the receiving device. The DOCSIS specifications include Reed-Solomon (RS) FEC as a mechanism for loss mitigation.

FEC works by placing binary information into a two-dimensional array and then determining parity for each row and each column in the array. After the parity is determined, each row is transmitted in serial with the corresponding parity bit transmitted as an addition to the end of each row. After all rows are transmitted, the parity bits for each column are transmitted in serial.

When delivered to the receiving station, the matrix is reconstructed and the parity bits are recalculated. In the event of a bit error during transmission, the sent parity and the recalculated parity are not in agreement. However, by using the parity information transmitted with the data bits, a damaged transmission can actually be rebuilt if the errors aren't too great. Essentially, several bit errors per transmitted matrix can be mitigated by using FEC. Using FEC, therefore, allows for data to be transmitted on a relatively noisy plant without ill effects.

Although FEC can significantly improve operational BERs, it introduces complexity. It decreases overall bandwidth efficiency because additional information must be included in each packet. However, when FEC is effective, it prevents the loss and subsequent retransmission of entire packets and can reduce overall packet loss characteristics. Extensive analysis concludes that the overhead associated with FEC is lower than that associated with packet loss and therefore FEC can provide significant value. Also important is that stated requirements for plant quality include FEC considerations and FEC should not be expected to compensate for cable networks which fall outside of the specified requirements.

Error Mitigation Through Interleaving

In conjunction with FEC, interleaving of data for transmission can reduce packet loss characteristics on the DOCSIS network. FEC cannot compensate for multiple bit errors occurring in sequence. Such sequential bit errors are typical in an HFC network. Sequential errors are significantly worsened in HFC networks where downstream transmission lasers are overloaded or near overload (input signal strength is too great) and signal is inadvertently dampened (a problem known as clipping).

Interleaving is the process of breaking a sequential data stream into short pieces, and reordering those pieces according to a known pattern. In DOCSIS, data is broken into several rows and columns and then re-sequenced. To better understand the benefits of interleaving, consider three blocks of data upon which FEC parity calculations have been performed. If the three blocks are transmitted in serial fashion, a bit error that impacted six sequential bits of traffic irreparably damages the effected data set, resulting in the need for a packet retransmission. However, if bits from the matrices are interleaved 1-2-3, 1-2-3, 1-2-3, an error of 6 bits only destroys 2 bits per matrix. FEC can likely recover from this failure, rebuild the packets, and retransmission is unnecessary. The interleaving of data complements the functionality of FEC by limiting the number of bit errors in individual data units over time.

Interleaving, such as FEC, adds complexity and latency to the system. Data that is interleaved must be re-created into discrete units, by using hardware resources and buffer space. Interleave depth, the number of data units being simultaneously transmitted, is configurable on the CMTS. Greater depth gives greater error mitigation but increases latency. However, whatever the interleave depth, interleaving can supply greatly needed improvements in bit error performance on networks with multi-bit periodic loss characteristics.

Moving Picture Experts Group (MPEG) Framing

In 1994, an international body of telecommunications companies, equipment manufacturers, and other interested parties agreed upon the (MPEG) standard as the preferred method to compress and distribute digital television and other video signals.

DOCSIS and Euro-DOCSIS specify the transmission of IP packets over the cable plant by using this standard MPEG framing—MPEG frames 188 bytes in size with a 4-byte header. MPEG framing was chosen for the specification in part because of the prevalence of MPEG in the CATV industry and the large existing base of MPEG knowledge therein. Although MPEG framing adds overhead to the system, the ability to leverage existing MPEG knowledge and compatible equipment is compelling. In a DOCSIS cable IP network, IP packets are encapsulated in MPEG frames for transmission and reassembled into more common formats when received.

Because the transmission of RF signals across the cable plant involves physical distances, which are often fairly large, DOCSIS takes into account the time for frame transmission and specifies no more than 0.800 milliseconds of transit delay for frames that are traversing the network.

Throughput for DOCSIS and Euro-DOCSIS

Although it is easy to determine the theoretical maximum throughput for a DOCSIS channel based upon raw data rates, it is not simple to compute the real maximum throughput. DOCSIS control messages, error correction, MPEG headers, and other types of overhead on the cable IP network limit the total available throughput for DOCSIS devices. To determine more realistic throughput numbers, you must calculate the overhead per DOCSIS channel and subtract it from the total theoretical throughput. Although Table 13-3 gives rough estimates for DOCSIS downstream overhead and Table 13-4 gives nominal throughput rates for the upstream, of course IP packet size and other factors, including

CMTS and cable modem capabilities, impact actual performance in any true subscriber deployment.

Table 13-3   *Derivation of Nominal Downstream Data Rates*

Region	U.S./Japan		Europe/Other	
Constellation size (QAM)	64	256	64	256
Bandwidth (MHz)	6	6	8	8
Symbol rate Msym/sec	5.057	5.361	6.952	6.952
Alpha	0.19	0.12	0.15	0.15
Bits/symbol	6	8	6	8
FEC frame sync	0.08 percent	0.05 percent	0.00 percent	0.00 percent
FEC parity bytes	4.69 percent	4.69 percent	7.84 percent	7.84 percent
Trellis coding overhead	6.67 percent	5.00 percent	0.00 percent	0.00 percent
MPEG header	2.13 percent	2.13 percent	2.13 percent	2.13 percent
MPEG pointer byte	0.54 percent	0.53 percent	0.53 percent	0.53 percent
Physical layer throughput (Mbps)	30.34	42.88	41.71	55.62
Physical overhead	13.5 percent	12.4 percent	10.5 percent	10.5 percent
Nominal data rate (Mbps)	26.25	37.57	37.33	49.77

It is commonly observed with the mix of IP packet sizes in currently deployed cable IP networks that, between brands of CMTS, the throughput difference per DOCSIS channel is minimal. This is because of the highly configurable options within the DOCSIS protocol, and the optimizations that can be performed within the CMTS. Some optimizations provide exceptional performance for a few modems and others work exceptionally well only in lab environments. To obtain a stable production network, many compromises must be made to ensure balanced performance with hundreds of modems per upstream port and sufficient protection from normal RF impairments. Overall throughput is a combination of CMTS optimizations for deployment environments and the physical limitations of the DOCSIS inherent in the DOCSIS specifications.

Table 13-4   *Nominal Upstream Data Rates*

Bandwidth (kHz)	QPSK		16 QAM	
	Msym/sec	Nominal Rate Mbps*	Msym/sec	Nominal Rate Mbps*
200	0.16	0.3	0.16	0.6
400	0.32	0.6	0.32	1.2
800	0.64	1.2	0.64	2.3
1600	1.28	2.3	1.28	4.5
3200	2.56	4.6	2.56	9.0

*FEC, signaling, and control messages reduce overall effective throughput. The number of insertion intervals per unit of time and the percentage of contention slots consume 3 to 25 percent of upstream capacity.

DOCSIS Media Access Control (MAC) Domains

Figure 13-6 compares the seven-layer Open System Interconnection (OSI) network reference model with that of a DOCSIS network. The reference design for a DOCSIS network differs from the classic OSI model as a result of the branched nature of the cable network and other elements of DOCSIS design. DOCSIS and Euro-DOCSIS specifications define a MAC domain as having a single transmission source in the downstream and multiple transmission sources in the upstream. Individual cable modem devices within a MAC domain are identified by a 13-bit service ID (SID) that is used as a Layer 2 identifier. This value abbreviates the 48-bit globally unique MAC address for the cable modem.

A total of 8192 total SIDs can be associated with a DOCSIS MAC domain. Several are reserved for special uses including multicast and initial registration, thus a total of only 8171 cable modem SIDs are available. Nevertheless, far fewer than 8171 cable modems should be in each MAC domain for a successful deployment. Because the channel is shared by all subscribers in the MAC domain, throughput limitations and the signaling overhead associated with hundreds or thousands of cable modems tend to limit the number of cable modems to a few hundred per upstream. Management considerations also play a major role in limiting the number of cable modems per MAC domain.

Figure 13-6 *OSI and DOCSIS Layered Network Reference Design*

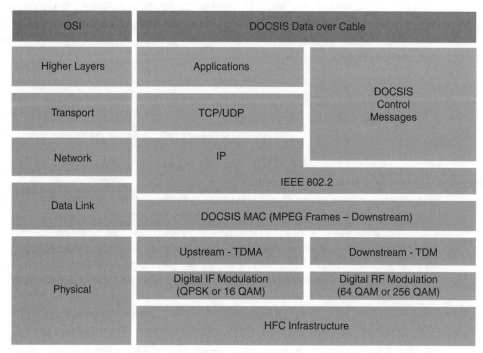

SID and Service Flow Identifier (SFID)

DOCSIS and Euro-DOCSIS 1.0 identify individual cable modems and other cable devices (such as set-top boxes) by a unique SID. This 13-bit Layer 2 identifier value allows traffic to be directed to specific cable modems. Each SID is subsequently allocated specific class of service (CoS) parameters. The DOCSIS 1.0 SID mechanism is efficient in environments where a single traffic stream is associated with each cable device.

However, cable modem users often use their transmission ability to send and receive traffic of several different sorts. Some types of IP traffic, specifically interactive traffic such as voice or video, require a QoS level greater than non-real-time traffic, such as web browsing or file transfers. Also, aggressive traffic streams can unnecessarily dominate transmission capacity and negatively impact other traffic from behind the same cable modem. The limitation of a single SID per cable modem and the resultant single CoS profile per cable modem reduces the service integrity of multiple traffic types traversing a single cable modem.

The DOCSIS 1.1 and Euro-DOCSIS 1.1 specifications significantly increase the differential traffic stream handling capability of the DOCSIS system. When DOCSIS 1.1 traffic is classified into specific streams, each stream is allocated a SFID rather than a SID, and each SFID is associated with a CoS profile. The SFID classification, marking, and rate management features of DOCSIS 1.1 enable the seamless transmission of high and low priority traffic together through a single cable modem. When properly configured, several service flows that share a single cable modem can be given different throughput, latency, jitter, and other characteristics.

DOCSIS and Euro-DOCSIS 1.1 SFID enhancements are specifically targeted toward Voice over IP (VoIP) service delivery. Unlike most access technologies, cable IP networks that use DOCSIS 1.1 devices are inherently capable of supplying all the necessary QoS parameters for VoIP.

Downstream Signaling and Transmission

Transmission of data in the downstream from the single downstream source (the CMTS) is through time-division multiplexing (TDM), wherein traffic bound for each cable modem is transmitted in a particular time slot that is determined by the CMTS at the time of transmission. Transmission capacity downstream is shared adaptively by traffic streams depending on demand. Downstream transmission is therefore dependent on QoS parameters, other parameters such as queuing algorithms, and vendor-specific implementations. Downstream transmission signaling is limited to the identification of traffic by SID/SFID (essentially by a Layer 2 modem identifier). The modem with the appropriate SID listens for and receives data destined for its SID.

DOCSIS 1.0 deliberately defined only a few parameters for the downstream, so as not to constrain CMTS vendors in how they might implement value added CoS or QoS features. However, DOCSIS 1.1 specifies in great detail requirements for classification, marking, and rate management characteristics in the downstream as it does on the upstream.

Upstream Signaling and Transmission with DOCSIS 1.0

Transmission of upstream data is more complex than that of downstream data. DOCSIS accepted substantial complexity to enable high theoretical upstream performance when there are many upstream transmission sources. To obtain high efficiency, traffic must be transmitted in such a way as to minimize collisions. To minimize collisions a combination of contention-based and reservation-based transmission windows are used in a method called time-division multiple access (TDMA). The CMTS controls all traffic transmission in the upstream and sends control messages to all cable modems detailing the allocation of transmission slots. The MAC management messages used to allocate transmission opportunities to the cable modem are called bandwidth allocation map messages. These messages contain reserved bandwidth slots and slots that are allocated to contention-based transmission. To transmit an IP packet upstream, an individual cable modem must first send a request for a timeslot (called an upstream transmission request) to the CMTS during the contention-based timeslot. The CMTS then responds to the requesting cable modem with a granted timeslot for data transmission.

The DOCSIS 1.0 specification deliberately does not define any mechanism by which a CMTS schedules grants, it only provides the format and type of communication messages. This was to enable substantial advancement and product differentiation within the DOCSIS 1.0 CMTS.

Upstream timeslots are allocated to cable modems in units known as minislots. Each minislot consists of 8 ticks. Each tick is defined as 6.25 ms. Upstream granted transmission timeslots consist of multiple minislots.

DOCSIS and Euro-DOCSIS 1.0 TDMA signaling does significantly reduce the incidents of collision on the upstream path. The signaling system was optimized to ensure that a large number of modems would gain relatively fair access to the upstream, remembering that it was nearly impossible to grant more than 30 percent of any single upstream port capacity to a single modem. For traffic streams that include large numbers of small packets, this creates a throughput bottleneck. Optional features within the DOCSIS 1.0 protocol, such as concatenation, enabled substantial reduction of this bottleneck, but not every DOCSIS 1.0 modem is designed to effectively use these features.

Upstream Signaling Enhancements with DOCSIS 1.1

Because of the static provisioning architecture in DOCSIS and Euro-DOCSIS 1.0, the DOCSIS 1.1 specification includes several new signaling mechanisms to help improve upstream throughput and latency characteristics—especially for real-time services such as voice. These features are the following: Unsolicited Grant Service (UGS), UGS with Activity Detection (UGS-AD), and real-time polling. The DOCSIS 1.0 optional features of fragmentation and concatenation were made mandatory in DOCSIS 1.1.

Upstream scheduling features in the DOCSIS 1.1 specification include UGS, which is a process that allows the CMTS to allocate fixed-size regularly occurring grants to a specific traffic stream over a set time. This allows a modem transmitting regularly occurring packets upstream to reserve the capacity by using only a single request for transmission. The modem thus contracts with the CMTS for a specific service, and there is no concern about the modem being denied that capacity by the CMTS. Traffic identified as low-latency and jitter sensitive can be configured for UGS through several mechanisms including the CMTS itself and a DOCSIS 1.1 binary cable modem configuration file.

A concern with UGS is that regularly occurring pre-granted upstream transmission timeslots might be unused if the transmitting host fails or otherwise terminates the upstream connection before the unsolicited grant is complete. In this scenario, UGS-AD improves upon UGS by incorporating Activity Detection—the ability to determine if upstream bandwidth is being used and, if no activity is detected, terminate the unsolicited grant process. UGS-AD can significantly reduce throughput lost to unused UGS requests. In the event of a modem losing its UGS-granted regularly occurring transmission timeslots, it must then request a new set of grants.

Another method for improving latency in the request-and-grant process of upstream transmission is real-time polling. When using real-time polling, the CMTS schedules periodic non-contention-based request polls for the corresponding modem and reserves periodic time slots that are usable by the modem when it has traffic to send upstream. This feature enables higher bandwidth efficiency for flows that have variable bandwidth needs but high packet rates. For example, a VoIP session that supports silence suppression (a VoIP feature) sends traffic only when one of the participants in the phone call is speaking, not during periods of silence.

Fragmentation is the separation of large packets into smaller packets during upstream transmission and the reassembly of fragmented packets upon receipt at the CMTS. Fragmentation is important in scenarios where flows of large packets share upstream transmission with latency-sensitive traffic. Using fragmentation, individual large packets can be split into smaller packets, allowing for the interleaving of delay-sensitive packets. Without fragmentation, the time required to transmit large packets upstream can add significant latency to the transmission of other traffic streams sharing the upstream channel. Fragmentation is important when the upstream bandwidth is low, and the latency of sending a maximum-sized IP packet (1500 bytes) interrupts the regular flow of small packets. This interruption is called jitter.

Fragmentation, although a part of the DOCSIS 1.1 specification, is not a requirement for a DOCSIS 1.1 CMTS. It is possible for a CMTS to become DOCSIS 1.1 qualified without supporting this feature. Nevertheless, it is extremely important when transmitting delay-sensitive traffic on slower upstream DOCSIS channels (those channels with bandwidth lower than 1.6 MHz using QPSK modulation).

Concatenation is another feature designed to improve upstream signaling efficiency. Concatenation allows the transmitting device to transmit several packets as one combined larger transmission during a single grant interval. A cable modem, for example, might have several small packets to transmit to the CMTS. Rather than request grants for transmission of each packet, the cable modem can concatenate the packets into one larger unit and send a single request for upstream transmission. The CMTS subsequently receives the large concatenated unit and separates it into its component packets.

Example 13-2 shows a sample configuration of a line card on a Cisco uBR7246vxr with both concatenation and fragmentation enabled. It also shows spectrum-group information for reference purposes.

Example 13-2 *Sample DOCSIS CMTS Configuration*

```
interface Cable5/0
 ip address 10.1.72.1 255.255.255.0
 secondary ip address 10.1.71.1 255.255.255.0
 no ip directed-broadcast
 no ip route-cache
 no ip mroute-cache
```

Example 13-2 *Sample DOCSIS CMTS Configuration (Continued)*

```
no keepalive
no cable proxy-arp
cable helper-address 10.1.70.30
cable downstream annex B
cable downstream modulation 64qam
cable downstream interleave-depth 32
cable upstream 0 spectrum-group 1
cable upstream 0 concatenation
cable upstream 0 fragmentation
no cable upstream 0 shutdown
cable upstream 1 shutdown
cable upstream 2 shutdown
cable upstream 3 shutdown
cable upstream 4 shutdown
cable upstream 5 shutdown
```

DOCSIS Cable Modem Initialization Sequence

When a DOCSIS cable modem is connected to a cable IP network and powered on, it has no information regarding the network on which it is placed. As part of the overall design for cable modem portability between networks, cable modems must come online with no prior knowledge of specific network conditions. Most specifically, the cable modem has no knowledge of the channels and frequencies on which DOCSIS or Euro-DOCSIS communication is occurring. The DOCSIS modem initialization process is designed to have modems quickly identify, transmit and receive frequencies, negotiate operational parameters with the CMTS, and register fully as a part of the cable IP network, as shown in Figure 13-7. It also must enable the operator to disable service for a non-paying customer.

Frequency Scanning

After a cable modem has powered on and has loaded operating system files from memory it begins to scan known frequencies for a downstream DOCSIS signal. Because of the differences in frequency splits and channel plans among regions and countries, a cable modem might need to scan hundreds of frequencies before finding an appropriate signal. Frequency-scanning algorithms are specific to the vendor who created the cable modem and have a direct impact on the speed with which a cable modem identifies a receive frequency. Laboratory tests quickly find major differences between modem vendors in this regard. When a modem fails to find a downstream channel, it continues scanning indefinitely. In the event of an accidental cable disconnect or other issue, it is important for a modem to continue scanning until a frequency is found.

Figure 13-7 *Cable Modem Initialization Sequence*

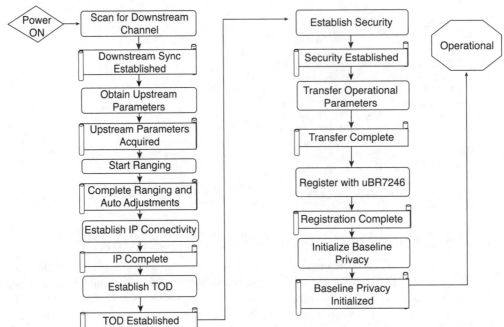

Modems typically begin scanning frequencies at around 450 MHz because most DOCSIS downstream channels occur at relatively high frequencies (lower frequencies that are usually in use by television channels). Initial frequencies that are scanned are vendor specific and depend on modem brand and model. Several channel plans can be scanned. After a scanning cable modem encounters a digital signal that contains the appropriate DOCSIS control messages (a type of DOCSIS message called a clock sync message sent downstream 100 times a second) it identifies that frequency as a receive frequency. From the discovered downstream frequency the cable modem listens to DOCSIS control messages and ultimately learns all the upstream and downstream transmission information it requires to communicate with the CMTS.

UCD Receipt

Included in the DOCSIS control messages sent downstream are messages that contain information on upstream channel frequencies. These messages, called upstream channel descriptors (UCDs), are sent downstream approximately every two milliseconds and allow cable modems in the process of initialization to determine what frequencies are used by the CMTS for the receipt of upstream transmissions. After a UCD has been received and an upstream channel identified, the cable modem waits for another DOCSIS control message, called a MAP message, that indicates a timeslot during which unidentified modems coming online can communicate upstream.

Power Ranging

Modems in the process of initialization must determine a signal strength at which to transmit upstream. Determining the signal strength needed for the CMTS to reach the cable modem is relatively simple because DOCSIS was designed to be compatible with typical signal levels found in the residential environment of a cable network. However, the upstream path of the cable network has substantial variation in signal level from inside each home passed. Therefore, a cable modem transmitting upstream must determine the appropriate settings. Furthermore, the modem has no knowledge of the cable plant and is therefore unaware of how strong a signal to send upstream to the CMTS. To determine how strong a signal is needed to reach the CMTS, the cable modem begins a process known as power ranging. The cable modem sends initial transmissions using a default SID (SID 0) on the upstream channel (described in the UCD message) at a time interval defined in the Manufacturing Automation Protocol (MAP) message as an initial insertion interval. The modem begins at low power and gradually increases transmission power with each subsequent message. After the signal power becomes strong enough for the CMTS to identify it as a modem, the CMTS notifies the cable modem (again using SID 0) that it has been heard and that the two devices will negotiate cable modem transmit power levels until they are optimized.

During the time in which a cable modem is communicating bi-directionally with the CMTS, the two devices remain engaged in a feedback loop to maintain an optimal cable modem transmit power level. Because the signal attenuation in cable plants can vary based on time of day, weather conditions, and other factors, it can occur that a given cable modem's transmit power is adjusted several times a day. To improve control-messaging efficiency, each cable modem is given a reserved maintenance timeslot for regular communication upstream to the CMTS. These timeslots are called periodic maintenance intervals.

Although the DOCSIS standard specifies a wide range of possible digital signal levels for transmission and receipt by cable devices (detailed in Table 13-5), in deployed networks it has been found that higher signal levels are directly related to superior signal quality. This is because of the relative signal strength of ambient noise to the carrier. When digital signal levels are near that of noise present on the cable plant, distortion and interference is prevalent. With higher digital signal levels the ratio of carrier to noise is often more favorable, which results in better transmission and receipt.

Table 13-5   *Transmit and Receive Signal Levels*

Digital Signal Levels	DOCSIS Specifications
From cable modem (upstream Tx power)	+8 to +58 dBmV (QPSK) +8 to +55 dBmV (16 QAM)
Input amplitude at CMTS (upstream)	160 ksym/sec is −16 to +14 dBmV 320 ksym/sec is −13 to +17 dBmV 640 ksym/sec is −10 to +20 dBmV 1280 ksym/sec is −7 to +23 dBmV 2560 ksym/sec is −4 to +26 dBmV
Downstream amplitude as received at the cable modem	−15 to +15 dBmV
Signal relative to adjacent video signal	−6 dB to −10 dB

The cable modem and the CMTS, after power ranging is complete, are mutually aware. One way in which the CMTS tracks the attached cable modems is through keepalive messages (periodic maintenance), which are transmitted at least once every 30 seconds to each cable modem. These messages help the cable devices determine when an attempt to reinitialize should occur. One aspect of the CMTS tracking each cable modem is that the CMTS can send control messages to the cable modem that cause the cable modem to change to another upstream channel, another downstream channel, or both. In situations where some frequencies are preferred from some modems and not others, this aspect of the DOCSIS specification gives the network administrator the power to choose which frequencies are to be used by specific devices and even to change those frequencies dynamically.

Dynamic Host Configuration Protocol (DHCP) Request/Response

After power ranging is complete, the modem, now capable of Layer 1 and Layer 2 communication, establishes Layer 3 (IP) connectivity. IP connectivity is accomplished with the aid of DHCP. DHCP is widely used in IP-based systems to supply dynamic IP addresses and other network configuration information to IP-enabled devices. DOCSIS networks use standard DHCP systems (as defined in RFC 2131) to configure cable modems with IP addressing and other network information.

When the cable modem begins the DHCP process, a DHCP request is sent from the cable modem through the CMTS to a DHCP provisioning server. The DHCP server then replies to the cable modem with an IP address, a subnet mask, a gateway address, a trivial file transfer protocol (TFTP) server address, a DOCSIS configuration file name, time offset, time of day (TOD) server address, and other DHCP and DOCSIS parameters. DHCP supports many parameters and, depending on the deployment, many more options can be transmitted to the cable modem (additional extensions to DHCP are included in RFC 2132). After the DHCP information is received by the cable modem, the cable modem has all the information it requires to establish IP connectivity.

TOD

The cable modem next uses its IP connectivity to request TOD from a TOD server specified in the DHCP response. The TOD format is defined as an open standard in RFC 868. Although not an absolute functional requirement for modem connectivity, TOD information is a required part of the DOCSIS specification and it allows a cable network administrator to troubleshoot a modem by using accurate timestamps. TOD information and timing offset received from the DHCP server can customize timestamps to the appropriate time zone. DOCSIS 1.0 initially mandated that a modem required TOD information or it would not function. Later, the requirement was relaxed to the requirement that each modem should attempt to obtain TOD information, but modems could register without TOD if necessary. As a result, some DOCSIS 1.0 modems fail to register if TOD information is not provided in the DHCP reply. Others can fail if there is no TOD server or if there is a failure in communication with the TOD server.

TFTP

From the TFTP server (defined in RFC 783) an initializing cable modem requests a file. TFTP is a simple protocol that transfers files with a minimum of overhead. The name of the file requested by the cable modem is that specified in the DHCP response that was received by the cable modem earlier in the initialization process. The file, a binary DOCSIS cable modem configuration file (detailed later in this chapter in the section "Binary DOCSIS Configuration Files"), contains numerous operational parameters for the cable modem including security, CoS, and other parameters. The configuration file parameters are then communicated to the CMTS, and the two devices agree upon operational parameters. In this way the CMTS can audit and confirm the validity of the cable modem's provisioned parameters. Often an operator uses the DOCSIS Management Information Bases (MIBs) and encodes Simple Network Management Protocol (SNMP) settings in the DOCSIS configuration file to further control the cable modem.

Registration Request

After the cable modem has received the binary DOCSIS configuration file, it sends a registration request message to the CMTS. The CMTS responds with a registration response message including an assigned SID for the cable modem. The two devices then communicate and negotiate operational parameters by using the normal upstream grant/ request mechanism. The registration request and response process can fail if the CMTS and cable modem fail to agree upon operation parameters such as QoS settings or if the cable modem fails to authenticate itself if configured to do so.

Baseline Privacy Initialization

After it is registered, if configured to do so, the cable modem starts baseline privacy. Baseline privacy and baseline privacy initialization are described later in this chapter in the section "Security and Baseline Privacy."

Online (Maintenance) State

After it is registered, the cable modem is completely online and begins to maintain a station link to the CMTS using keepalive messages that are sent from the CMTS at least once every 30 seconds. The CMTS can use maintenance messages to change the cable modem's upstream transmit frequency and other parameters if necessary. At this time final operational parameters such as baseline privacy (a security mechanism) are negotiated. The cable modem begins to send and receive IP traffic after this final state is achieved.

Binary DOCSIS Configuration Files

Most operational parameters that are transmitted to a cable modem as it initializes are contained in a binary configuration file in a type-length-value (TLV) format as defined in the DOCSIS specification. The DOCSIS 1.0 specification and DOCSIS 1.1 specification each define a configuration file format and parameters that are contained in the file. As a rule, the information contained in the DOCSIS 1.1 configuration file is a superset of that contained in the 1.0 configuration file. Although DOCSIS 1.1 modems are capable of receiving and understanding DOCSIS 1.0 configuration files (the specification was designed for backwards compatibility), most DOCSIS 1.0 modems have difficulties and often fail when supplied with DOCSIS 1.1 configuration files.

Deployments of cable modems typically consist of a few types of modem and a few categories of user. As a result, DOCSIS configuration files are usually created manually for each modem type/user category combination. Because a single file can be distributed to many cable modems during initialization through TFTP, this method works effectively in most environments. Because most deployed cable modem networks are based on DOCSIS 1.0 and deliver basic data-only service, this approach is the most common among MSOs. Free binary DOCSIS configuration file editors are available online from several sources.

In some environments configuration files need to be generated for each modem or for a large set of modem types. Occurring in cable IP networks where services such as VoIP are deployed, individual modem provisioning leads to the necessity for hundreds or thousands of configuration files—an approach that does not scale well for large subscriber bases. As a result, provisioning systems have been developed that can dynamically generate and distribute configuration files as they are requested by cable modems. Advanced provisioning systems such as these combine the functionality of a DHCP and TFTP server together to identify initializing cable modems (usually by MAC address), compare them to a database of customer profiles, and then create a configuration file that matches the customer profile. Often user self-provisioning and enhanced billing features are included.

DOCSIS 1.0 Configuration File

The DOCSIS 1.0 configuration file specifies the operational parameters for a DOCSIS 1.0 cable modem in the following list. Because of the limit of a single SID per cable modem, the operational parameters included define a set of parameters that are applied to all traffic traversing the cable modem.

The list of available parameters configured in a DOCSIS 1.0 configuration file includes the following:

- **Radio frequency**—Defines downstream frequency and upstream channel ID. In the case of the cable modem initializing on the wrong downstream or upstream channel, the configuration file forces the re-registration of the cable modem on the specified channels.

- **Network access**—Cable modems might need to be managed remotely while disallowing subscriber access to network services. The network access flag can allow a modem to register and block the transmission of subscriber traffic, and it allows a network administrator to connect to and configure the modem as necessary. Using this portion of the configuration file is the only recommended method of controlling network access and is the most efficient method to disable a non-paying subscriber.

- **CoS**—Specifies a CoS ID for the cable modem's associated SID. Specifies maximum downstream rate, maximum upstream rate, upstream channel priority, guaranteed minimum upstream rate, and maximum upstream transmit burst for that cable modem. Some primitive DOCSIS 1.0 CMTS units do not support these parameters and only provide best-effort service for all modems. The best DOCSIS CMTS units can enforce these parameters even if the cable modem does not cooperate (or self-police) its upstream bandwidth requests.

- **Baseline privacy**—Defines the baseline privacy (security) settings for the SID associated with the cable modem. Enables baseline privacy. Configures authorize wait timeout, reauthorize wait timeout, authorization grace timeout, operational wait timeout, rekey wait timeout, TEK grace time, and authorize reject wait timeout. Frequent key exchanges can improve overall data security but also increase resource use (CPU load) on both the cable modem and the CMTS. Information on baseline privacy is detailed in the "Security and Baseline Privacy" section later in this chapter.

- **SNMP**—Sets the SNMP manager IP address and SNMP write-access. Because cable modems can be closely managed through SNMP these settings are vital. The configuration file also allows for the setting of any SNMP MIB object through configuration file options. DOCSIS contains a large body of SNMP MIBs that are standardized for both the cable modem and the CMTS. Often vendors provide additional SNMP MIBs to enable the management of advanced features.

- **CPE**—Cable operators can define the number of allowed devices at the customer premises by using this command. Depending on the modem vendor, a single cable modem can be defined to support from 0 to 255 computers or other devices at the customer premises. The configuration file can also define the MAC address or addresses of allowed hosts. Some DOCSIS equipment uses the value 0 or 255 to indicate unlimited CPEs, and others use these values to indicate that no CPEs are allowed.

- **Software upgrade**—Cable modems might need software upgrades after deployment. This configuration file option includes a TFTP server IP address and the filename for an upgraded software image. When modems reinitialize they automatically upgrade, reload, and reregister if the specified filename doesn't match their current filename. Software upgrades are obviously specific to the modem make and model, although this field can be used for all cable modems. Use of this field typically requires a unique configuration file for each type of modem on the cable network to avoid modems uploading invalid or unmatched software versions.

- **Telephone return**—For modems without a cable-based return path, the configuration file can contain a set of telephone modem parameters for upstream connection.

- **Vendor**—Vendor ID, vendor-specific information. Used for modem vendor-specific features such as Cisco DOCSIS 1.0+ features, including VoIP support, a Cisco IOS filename, the number of phone lines, IP Precedence masks, and so on.

- **Miscellaneous**—Other parameters include vendor-specific options, security transform sets, modem authentication parameters, and IP Precedence for the corresponding SID.

DOCSIS 1.1 Configuration File

The DOCSIS 1.1 configuration file format is somewhat more complex than that for a DOCSIS 1.0 cable modem. This is because a DOCSIS 1.1 configuration file must include a set of operational parameters for multiple service flows. Information required for the classification, marking, and rate management of each service flow must be included in the file. The following list includes only those parameters that differ materially from DOCSIS 1.0. A DOCSIS 1.1 configuration file is not complete unless it contains a configuration for both an upstream and a downstream service flow. It is generally incompatible with DOCSIS 1.1 modems if it simultaneously contains DOCSIS 1.0 rate limit parameters.

The list of available parameters configured in a DOCSIS 1.1 configuration file includes the following:

- **CPE**—The 1.1 configuration file can include a list of CPE MAC addresses to filter if necessary.

- **Upstream packet classification**—As traffic is transmitted upstream in DOCSIS 1.1 it is classified into service flows. The upstream packet classification portion of the 1.1 configuration file contains the traffic characteristics by which service flows are differentiated. Traffic can be sorted into service flows based upon the following packet characteristics: IP type of service (ToS) values, ToS mask, IP protocol, IP source address, IP source mask, IP destination address, IP destination mask, IP source port start and port end (allowing for a range of ports), destination port start and port end (allowing for a range of ports), destination MAC address, source MAC address, Ethernet/DSA/MAC type, user priority (IEEE 802.1P), virtual LAN identification (VLAN ID) (IEEE 802.1Q), and any one of many vendor-specific parameters. Each classifier (set of characteristics) is assigned a unique classifier reference number, an associated service flow reference number, a rule priority (when packets are classified, they are compared against classifiers with higher priority first), activation state (on or off), and dynamic service change ability.

- **Downstream packet classification**—DOCSIS 1.1 allows for the same parameters used in the upstream to be set for downstream transmission. Packets transmitted downstream are likewise classified based on the following: IP ToS value, ToS mask, IP protocol, IP source address, IP source mask, IP destination address, IP destination mask, IP source port start and port end, destination port start and port end, destination MAC address, source MAC address, Ethernet/DSA/MAC type, user priority (IEEE 802.1P), VLAN ID (IEEE 802.1Q), and any one of many vendor-specific parameters. Each classifier is assigned a classifier reference number, a service flow reference, a rule priority, activation state, and dynamic service change ability. In general, the CMTS becomes responsible for enforcing and controlling the settings in the downstream packet classification when data traffic is forwarded to the cable modem.

- **Upstream service flow**—After it is classified, traffic upstream is assigned a set of QoS and other parameters for transmission. These parameters include the following: traffic priority (roughly equivalent to ToS bit but used only on the DOCSIS network), maximum sustained traffic rate, maximum traffic burst, minimum reserved traffic rate, assumed minimum reserved rate packet size, timeout for active QoS parameters, timeout for admitted QoS parameters, maximum concatenated burst, service flow scheduling type, request per transmission policy, nominal polling interval, tolerated poll jitter, unsolicited grant size, nominal grant interval, tolerated grant jitter, grants per interval, and vendor-specific settings. Associated with each service flow is a unique flow reference number, a service class name, a QoS parameter set type, and a ToS bit overwrite value. Service class names reference QoS parameters that can be saved as named profiles on the CMTS instead of being specified in the configuration file. The ToS bit overwrite value is important when a service flow requires QoS parameters to be set end-to-end across the MSO's network. By using the ToS bit overwrite value the system administrator causes packets to be given a set ToS bit value when they exit the DOCSIS network.

- **Downstream service flow**—After it is classified, downstream service flows are assigned the same set of values as upstream service flows. However, grant-specific and upstream specific parameters such as tolerated grant jitter, grants per interval, and so on are not specified. Downstream maximum and minimum rates and downstream latency are configurable in DOCSIS 1.1, and only limited downstream parameters are available through DOCSIS 1.0.

- **Payload header suppression**—In certain circumstances, the transmitted headers on a service flow are identical between packets. Payload header suppression (PHS) allows traffic to be transmitted without headers, thus increasing throughput efficiency. PHS parameters can be specified per service flow and can include multiple parameters including vendor-specific PHS parameters.

Example 13-3 shows DOCSIS 1.1 configuration file parameters in simple text. The network access control field is shown with access enabled and is identical to what would be configured with DOCSIS 1.0. Both upstream and downstream flows are defined with upstream classifiers based on port number, IP source address, and IP destination address specified. When encoded in an actual DOCSIS 1.1 file the configuration parameters are formatted as binary TLV groupings.

Example 13-3 *Sample DOCSIS 1.1 Configuration File*

```
03 (Net Access Ctrl) = 1

22 (US Classifier Encoding)

   S01 (Classifier Reference)= 1
   S03 (Flow Reference)     = 5
   S05 (Rule Priority)      = 5
   S09 (IP Packet Classification)
    T07 (Source Port Start)  = 1000
    T08 (Source Port End)    = 1000
    T09 (Dest port Start)    = 1400
    T10 (Dest port Start)    = 1400

23 (US Classifier Encoding)
   S01 (Classifier Reference)= 2
   S03 (Flow Reference)     = 6
   S05 (Rule Priority)      = 5
   S09 (IP Packet Classification)
     T02 (IP Protocol) = 17
     T03 (IP src)  = 9.0.0.0
     T04 (IP src mask) = 255.0.0.0
     T05 (IP dest) = 10.20.112.0
     T06 (IP dest mask) =  255.255.255.0
24 (Upstream Service Flow Encodings)
   S01 (Service Flow Reference) = 1
```

Example 13-3 *Sample DOCSIS 1.1 Configuration File (Continued)*

```
    S06 (QoS Parameter Set Type) = 7
    S07 (Traffic Priority) = 4

25 (Downstream Service Flow Encodings)
    S01 (Service Flow Reference) = 2
    S06 (QoS Parameter Set Type) = 7
    S07 (Traffic Priority) = 1

24 (Upstream Service Flow Encodings)
    S01 (Service Flow Reference) = 5
    S06 (QoS Parameter Set Type) = 7
    S07 (Traffic Priority) = 4
    S08 (Max Traffic Rate) = 300000
    S09 (Max Traffic Burst)= 2500

25 (Upstream Service Flow Encodings)
    S01 (Service Flow Reference) = 6
    S06 (QoS Parameter Set Type) = 7
    S07 (Traffic Priority) = 4
    S08 (Max Sustained Traffic Rate) = 2500000
    S09 (Max Traffic Burst) = 2500
```

Upstream Admission Control

Admission control is an example of a CMTS vendor-specific option, which adds capabilities to a DOCSIS 1.0 or 1.1 network. With admission control the cable modems receive additional information in their configuration files in vendor-specific TLV fields. Cable modems are unaware of the meaning of these TLVs but the CMTS makes use of them to provide added benefits, control, and capabilities to the system.

In a scenario where several upstream channels are in use and many cable modems are connected with throughput guarantees provisioned through the DOCSIS configuration file, it is possible that all cable modems might connect to a single upstream channel that does not have the capacity to meet all bandwidth guarantees. Although not a part of the DOCSIS specification, some vendors have implemented upstream admission control features to limit the overuse of upstream bandwidth and to help load-share modems across multiple upstream channels.

Upstream admission control monitors the aggregate amount of guaranteed upstream bandwidth expected by connected cable modem devices. The parameter is set relative to upstream channel width and is typically expressed as an over-subscription percentage. After the sum of traffic guaranteed to connected modems exceeds the set parameter, cable modems are denied registration and forced to connect to some other upstream channel. If no upstream bandwidth is available on any upstream channel, modems are denied registration completely. Upstream admission control and guaranteed bandwidth together are effective means to ensure that no single customer will ever be prevented from accessing the network, and it also allows the cable service provider to guarantee that no single upstream channel can become so congested that service levels reach unacceptable levels.

Security and Baseline Privacy

Because of the broadcast nature of the cable IP network, security concerns exist regarding information privacy. It is possible that a malicious entity could gain access to a subscriber's data by listening to transmissions destined for one subscriber's modem from a nearby house or other location where the same DOCSIS signals are available from the CMTS. To improve information security on the cable IP network the DOCSIS 1.0 specification includes a specification for BPI.

Baseline privacy describes an encryption process to be performed in hardware on DOCSIS cable devices. Fifty-six-bit Data Encryption Standard (DES) encryption is specified for DOCSIS cable modems, with a provision for 40-bit DES encryption permitting export to countries outside the U.S. (as defined by U.S. legislation). Although export constraints on encryption have been somewhat relaxed, 40-bit DES encryption remains a part of the standard. DES encryption is a widely used encryption algorithm that is also used for IP tunneling and other technologies, and 56-bit DES is considered moderately secure as long as key exchange occurs frequently. The "Baseline Privacy Initialization" section supplies specifics of key exchange.

Configuring BPI on cable modems is simple. Baseline privacy needs to be enabled in the DOCSIS configuration file and on the CMTS. If used in the default configuration, this involves the simple inclusion of a single line to the DOCSIS configuration file. After it is configured, a modem initializes, registers, and begins to transmit encrypted traffic. Only packet payloads are encrypted; headers are transmitted in the clear. Because baseline privacy encryption and decryption occurs in hardware, enabling it does not impact device performance or throughput. Technically, BPI is always enabled, except that the keys consist of zero values (no encryption occurs) and key exchange is bypassed. Only the key management and exchange features are handled in software on the cable modem and CMTS, and the key lifetime is large relative to the CPU loading that is encountered on most cable modems and CMTS equipment. It is suggested that baseline privacy with active encryption be enabled in every network unless a compelling reason against it is found. DOCSIS 1.1 specifies that full BPI be enabled by default.

Baseline Privacy Initialization

After a cable modem has initialized and come online, BPI negotiation begins. To initiate negotiation the cable modem confirms with the CMTS that both are configured to support baseline privacy. The cable modem then sends the CMTS a public key and begins the key exchange process.

The cable modem sends the CMTS a public key. After it is received, the CMTS confirms that the sending cable modem's MAC address belongs to a modem authorized to receive keys and then uses the public key to encrypt a second key, called the key encryption key (KEK). The CMTS then transmits the encrypted KEK to the cable modem. The cable modem uses the public key to decrypt the KEK key and learns the KEK value. The cable modem then requests a traffic encryption key (TEK) from the CMTS. The CMTS encrypts the TEK using the KEK and transmits it to the cable modem. The cable modem decrypts the TEK using the KEK value and learns the TEK.

After both the CMTS and the cable modem have agreed upon the TEK value, encrypted traffic can be sent between the two. The cable modem and the CMTS use the TEK to encrypt and decrypt traffic for the lifetime of the TEK. Because it is relatively simple to break a 56-bit traffic encryption key, these keys expire quickly. Although the default expiration time is 12 hours, the TEK can be set to expire in as quickly as 30 minutes or as long as 7 days. Shorter expiration values are more secure but add moderately more overhead to the BPI process. New TEK values are requested and supplied between the cable modem and the CMTS by using the known KEK value.

KEKs also expire over time and must be renewed. A KEK can be set to expire every 1 to 70 days. The default KEK expiration time is 7 days. Faster expiration again adds moderately more overhead to the BPI process.

Setting the key lifetimes to the absolute minimum settings can result in communication failures as the key grace times are either not set correctly or are set too close to key lifetime values. In practice the default key lifetimes work most reliably, although they work well when set to at least twice the minimum lifetime value.

Pre-Provisioned Certificates and BPI+

Rather than use authentication methods such as passwords or digital signatures, regular BPI as originally specified in DOCSIS 1.0 checks the MAC address of the cable modem to see whether it is qualified to receive a key for the appropriate services. This results in a security vulnerability in systems that employ this form of baseline privacy. A malicious entity can clone a device with an authorized MAC address and steal service or compromise information security. BPI+, an enhanced version of BPI implemented in DOCSIS 1.1, remedies this shortcoming with the addition of pre-provisioned digital signatures. The digital signature, provisioned on each DOCSIS 1.1 cable modem at the time of manufacture, grants a unique identification to each modem and prevents device cloning.

Other Security Concerns and Features

Device cloning is the most frequently used method of gaining unauthorized access to network services in cable IP networks. By mimicking a valid modem's MAC address, IP address, or configuration file a malicious individual can transmit and receive traffic without being billed for the service. To prevent device cloning, several features have been developed by CMTS vendors.

MAC address cloning can be detected and flagged by the CMTS, and network access for all devices with that address can simply be denied. In general, when a cloned device is denied service, the individual responsible for the cloned device attempts a different method for obtaining service. Therefore, network policies that deny a specific MAC address can frequently be removed after a short period of time.

Cloning in DOCSIS 1.1 is prevented by the use of pre-provisioned digital signatures that uniquely identify each cable modem that is using a method other than a MAC address. Because the pre-provisioned certificate includes information based on the device's MAC address, a modem's MAC address and certificate can be paired together. The CMTS can use the digital signature to determine if the traffic traversing the cable IP network comes from a valid digital signature and can drop traffic from invalid devices. The digital certificates are not sent outside the modem, instead a mathematical algorithm exchanges information between the CMTS, cable modem, and digital certificate database server. In this manner individual DOCSIS 1.1 modems are verified to be legitimate.

IP address cloning can be mitigated by the use of specialized features within the DHCP protocol and advanced CMTSs. The use of DHCP option 82 allows a CMTS to match DHCP leases to the MAC address that requested the lease. The CMTS can determine if the IP address and MAC address are consistent with the provided lease. In the case of an unauthorized device that is using a valid IP address, the MAC and IP address pair are identified as invalid and traffic is dropped.

In some cases it might be possible for a malicious entity to use a customized, unauthorized binary DOCSIS configuration file to provision an attached cable modem. Either forged or stolen configuration files can be used. The goal might be to gain access to superior throughput or other QoS parameters and to receive unbilled service. In the case of stolen configuration files, the issue is particularly difficult to resolve because known valid configuration files can easily be used undetected. However, mechanisms exist to combat this type of device cloning. A CMTS authentication feature known as a shared-secret provisions a secret authentication string through the configuration file. If a cable-shared secret is specified on a cable interface, and a cable modem on that interface tries to come online using a DOCSIS configuration file that uses the wrong CMTS authentication string, the cable modem is not allowed to proceed to the online state and a message is logged on the CMTS.

When the binary configuration file is generated using the CTMS authentication feature, the CMTS authentication string is not explicitly stored in the DOCSIS configuration file but is only used as a part of generating the file's checksum. Thus, the CMTS authentication string does not appear if a DOCSIS configuration file is viewed using a binary configuration file editor or any other tool. This means that malicious entities cannot use an obtained copy of the DOCSIS configuration file to discover the CMTS authentication string. It also means that if a DOCSIS configuration file is being modified, special care must be taken to ensure that the CMTS authentication string is reinserted into the DOCSIS configuration file every time it is re-saved; otherwise, the checksum does not take into account the right CMTS authentication string and modems are rejected.

The CMTS CPE Database

Most CMTS products maintain a dynamically populated internal database of connected CPE IP and MAC addresses. The CPE database also contains details on the corresponding cable modems that these CPE devices belong to. In the case of advanced CMTSs, the cable CPE database can identify and troubleshoot security issues such as IP address cloning. The output in Example 13-4 shows an example of a statically configured host displaying unauthorized use of a valid IP address (CMTS is a Cisco uBR7246vxr). Using this feature can identify the MAC address of the cable modem behind which an unauthorized host resides and the modem can be taken offline by a system administrator pending resolution of the issue.

Example 13-4   *Displaying the CMTS CPE Database for a Single Downstream Channel*

```
CMTS# show interface cable 3/0 modem 0
SID   Priv bits  Type     State     IP address     method   MAC address
1     00         host     unknown   192.168.1.77   static   000C.422c.54d0
1     00         modem    up        10.1.1.30      dhcp     0001.9659.4447
2     00         host     unknown   192.168.1.90   dhcp     00a1.52c9.75ad
2     00         modem    up        10.1.1.44      dhcp     0090.9607.3831
```

Fiber Node Combining

Typical CMTS configurations include DOCSIS MAC domains with one downstream transmission source (a single downstream channel on the CMTS) and multiple upstream transmission sources (one or more upstream channels each with multiple cable modems). In most cases a CMTS controls multiple DOCSIS MAC domains on several DOCSIS modem cards. Each DOCSIS MAC domain consists of a downstream transmit port and one or more upstream receive ports. Because each downstream port and upstream port has a finite throughput capacity, a cable operator must decide how to physically connect CMTS ports to the HFC to adequately supply DOCSIS connectivity to subscribers. Physical connections are usually made through high-grade coaxial cable by attaching the CMTS to the headend fiber receivers and transmitters. The process of determining which fiber nodes to associate with which DOCSIS ports is called combining. Three types of combining are commonly used: sparse, dense, and extreme-dense.

NOTE   Those familiar with multicast routing should note that these terms are in no way related to those used for multicast.

As shown in Figure 13-8, sparse combining is a scheme that assumes that a small number of cable modem subscribers exist on each of several fiber nodes. These sparse subscribers must be aggregated together to share a single upstream receive port on the CMTS. Physically, multiple fiber receive ports are coupled together and attached to a single upstream receive port on the CMTS. The CMTS downstream transmit path is split so that each fiber node is attached to the CMTS through a transmit and receive port pair.

Figure 13-8 *Sparse Combining*

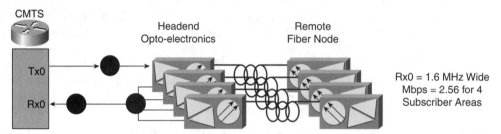

As shown in Figure 13-9, dense combining is a scheme that assumes that many cable modem subscribers are connected to each of several fiber nodes. In this case the subscriber upstream traffic is estimated to be so great that several upstream CMTS receive ports are required to supply the necessary throughput. Dense combining is the combining of several fiber node receive ports into a single path that is then distributed among multiple upstream receive ports on the CMTS in a many-to-many combining scheme. This method shares available upstream throughput for many receive ports among many fiber nodes. The disadvantage of this method is that noise or interference from any one location affects subscribers on all upstream ports and can disrupt service for the entire DOCSIS MAC domain.

Figure 13-9 *Dense Combining*

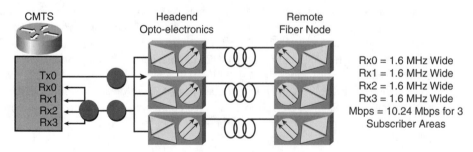

As shown in Figure 13-10, extreme-dense combining is the combining of a single fiber node into multiple upstream receive ports on the CMTS. This combining scheme assumes that the individual fiber node in question is connected to enough subscribers to saturate multiple upstream receive ports with traffic.

Figure 13-10 *Extreme-Dense Combining*

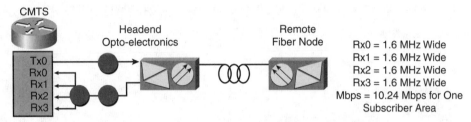

Combining schemes are vital to achieve the appropriate capacity planning on the cable IP network. When designing combining schemes it is key to assign a total available throughput equal to that of the anticipated overall network load for the attached subscribers. It is not uncommon for a cable operator to install a new CMTS chassis with a single receive port on each CMTS modem card that is physically disconnected from the combining scheme so that it can be used later in the case where additional upstream bandwidth becomes necessary on one of the attached nodes.

Combining schemes also take into account noise funneling when combining upstream signals. In some cases it might be best to not combine fiber nodes to keep upstream ingress noise to acceptable levels.

Cable IP Network Topologies

Because of the increasing popularity of cable modems as a high-speed access medium, cable IP networks are increasingly saturated by large amounts of subscriber traffic. Another effect of cable modem popularity is subscriber demand for constant high quality uninterrupted service—extremely high service availability. New IP-based services such as VoIP over cable drive even greater need for high availability, excellent QoS, and service integrity.

Three major designs of cable IP networks exist today. These designs are characterized by the way in which multiple CMTS devices are aggregated together and connected to the MSO's high-speed core network infrastructure. The three primary ways in which CMTSs are aggregated are through Ethernet, optical connections (typically OC12 or OC48), and resilient optical rings (DPT/RPR). It is the goal of each of these network designs to meet the stringent network requirements of cable IP networks while meeting the business goals of the cable operator.

Figure 13-11 shows a reference network architecture that includes Ethernet, SONET/
Optical, and DPT/RPR aggregation mechanisms. These aggregation media are connected
to a core high-speed optical network that can include a DWDM optical ring. The cable
operator network is in turn connected to IP networks (the Internet), the public switched
telephone network (PSTN), and both digital and analog video distribution networks.

Figure 13-11 *Cable IP Network Architectures*

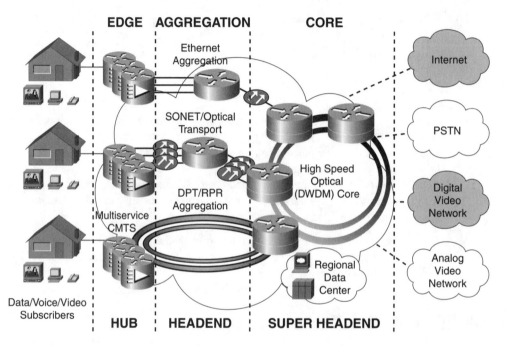

Ethernet Aggregation Architectures

Several MSOs use an aggregated Ethernet approach to connect multiple CMTS devices,
typically to a high performance switch. This is accomplished usually by either a set of
multiple 100BT load sharing Fast Ethernet connections or through one or more Gigabit
Ethernet connections. This simple approach to aggregating CMTSs, a switched Layer 2
approach, is popular because it is easy to understand and configure. Often the Ethernet
aggregation approach is inexpensive, too. However, Ethernet media distance limitations
and poor fault recovery characteristics can sometimes limit the effectiveness of this design.
Additionally, because large networks eventually require the use of routing protocols, the
large aggregation point switches in this design need connectivity to high-speed routers. In
emerging cases where an individual CMTS might support tens-of-thousands of cable

modem subscribers, routing requirements for the CMTS itself are extensive and the aggregation point likely uses routing (Layer 3 capable) platforms.

In the DOCSIS environment it has become evident that the CMTS must be a sophisticated access router that is capable of performing advanced IP-layer filtering and control. A network, which does not contain these features, is subject to traffic flooding (broadcast, multicast, or even unicast), denial of service (DoS) attacks, and virus outbreaks, which can eventually render the network useless

OCx Aggregation Architectures

OCx aggregation, the connection of CMTSs to a high performance optical switch/router through OC3, OC12, or OC48 Packet-over-SONET (PoS) or Asynchronous Transfer Mode (ATM) connections, is a network topology that is similar to Ethernet aggregation. It is simple, easy to understand, and supplies the necessary throughput required for large-scale cable modem deployments. OCx technologies do offer long distance capabilities, unlike Ethernet, and can support connections to distant hub sites and CMTSs. Similar to Ethernet aggregation, however, OCx aggregation does not offer failure tolerance. OC3, OC12, and OC48 aggregation require the presence of a Layer 3 device (router) to perform routing functions.

DPT/RPR Architectures

DPT is a Cisco proprietary optical technology that operates at OC3, OC12, OC48, and ultimately OC192 speeds over potentially long distances. By using spatial reuse protocol (SRP) and a ring topology, each DPT node can source packets onto the optical ring concurrently (unlike, for example, Fiber Distributed Data Interface [FDDI]), which maximizes ring bandwidth. Because of its ring topology, DPT incorporates failure resilience, the ability to aggregate many CMTSs onto a single optical ring, and high throughput rates into a single architecture. Because of these compelling features, MSOs typically use DPT aggregation architectures to enable high cable modem service integrity. As services such as VoIP become more prevalent in cable IP networks, DPT and related technologies will become vital to the integrity of such services.

RPR, a standards-based technology related to DPT, is commonly viewed among cable providers as the heir to DPT architectures for their cable IP networks. However, the IEEE 802.17 (RPR) Working Group has not yet finalized the RPR specification. Cisco has submitted SRP to the Working Group for consideration as the basis for the RPR industry standard. If SRP is included as part of the 802.17 standard, DPT and RPR will likely become near-synonymous terms.

High-Speed Optical (DWDM) Core

The value of high-speed optical core networks is immediately apparent when viewing the fiber that distributes video between headends in the cable service operator's network. To best use existing optical fiber, technologies such as DWDM transport data between core routers in the MSO's network.

The Future of Cable IP Networks

Several years ago the cable industry began to convert its networks to a digital infrastructure. Although television sets and set-top boxes often required an analog signal, broadcast video was distributed between headends and hubs in digital format by using a digitally modulated carrier. This increased the ability of the MSO to transmit broadcast video signals long distances between hubs with minimal loss and overall reduced operating expense. Digital televisions and set-top boxes became common at subscriber sites and much television content is now distributed to the subscriber in digital format.

Cable modems, too, have become commonplace. As part of the widespread adoption of broadband access technologies, cable modems have enjoyed a high degree of popularity among subscribers. As the growth of high-speed access media accelerates, DOCSIS-based cable modem deployments will continue to be successful.

At the time of this writing the rollout of added services such as VoIP, telecommuting services, and tiered data rates is increasing. Most large MSOs are anticipating the wide-scale deployment of VoIP in the near term. Trials are ongoing in numerous cities. Telecommuter services are offered in many locations, too. However, challenges remain for the MSOs to streamline service offerings, develop effective management and provisioning systems, scale their networks, implement appropriate QoS, and build supporting business models. It appears that added services on the cable IP network will be a common part of broadband access in the future.

The next challenge for MSOs will be to further consolidate their networks to a single infrastructure. Specifically, some MSOs plan to eventually convert their digital video distribution network to an IP-based distribution mechanism. This convergence will allow the MSO to manage and maintain a single multiservice network with data, voice, and video traffic and to supply all the necessary network features to support these interactive and non-interactive services. Challenges for this approach include the need to continue to distribute television channels to subscribers in analog or traditional digital (MPEG) format, the need for strong and flexible QoS for interactive traffic, and the extremely large IP throughput requirements imposed by several hundred high quality digital video channels. Despite the challenges, it seems probable that network convergence will eventually occur for MSO data, voice, and video networks.

Summary

Cable modem networks exist on a medium on which noise, network design, and operational excellence are a requirement. The DOCSIS and Euro-DOCSIS standards dictate the manner in which cable modems and cable modem termination systems interact to transmit IP packets. Modulation on the DOCSIS network employs QAM. Because QAM is sensitive to signal interference and attenuation, modulation types are chosen carefully based on cable plant quality.

Cable modems require three types of servers to operate: TOD, DHCP, and TFTP. These servers supply configuration information to the cable modem, which includes a binary DOCSIS cable modem configuration file that gives the cable operator configuration control over attached cable modems and flexibility in service provisioning. Because DOCSIS-based cable IP networks are a shared medium, it is important for the cable operator to configure the QoS, security, and management of the cable network carefully.

Cable IP networks offer the unique opportunity to supply data, voice, and video services to subscribers through the CATV network already deployed. Second line voice is being deployed to customers at the time of this writing and recent industry pundits have indicated that the transport of broadcast quality VoIP will be a reality in the near future.

Resources

- Adams, Michael. *OpenCable Architecture*. Cisco Press. December 3, 1999
- DOCSIS 1.0 specification SP-RFI-I05-991105 — www.cablemodem.com
- DOCSIS 1.1 specification SP-RFIv1.1-IO3-991105 — www.cablemodem.com
- DOCSIS 2.0 specification SP-RFIv2.0-IO1-011231 — www.cablemodem.com
- DOCSIS 1.1 BPI+ specification BPI+_IO7-010829 — www.cablemodem.com
- Oggerino, Chris. *High Availability Network Fundamentals*. Cisco Press. May 9, 2001
- RFC 868, Time Protocol
- RFC 2131, Dynamic Host Configuration Protocol
- RFC 2132, DHCP Options and BOOTP Vendor Extensions

Review Questions

Give the best answer or answers to the following questions. The answers to these questions can be found in Appendix A, "Answers to Review Questions."

1   What sort of framing is used in DOCSIS-based cable IP networks? What other devices in the cable network use the same framing?

_____

_____

2   What types of modulation transmit data upstream and downstream? Why is one type of modulation preferable to another?

_____

_____

3   What are the requirements for cable plant quality? Why are they important? What factors lead to poor plant quality?

_____

_____

4   Which provisioning servers are required by the DOCSIS specification? What value do they provide?

_____

_____

5   What is the difference between DOCSIS and Euro-DOCSIS?

_____

_____

_____

6 Which features of DOCSIS 1.1 improve upstream signaling efficiency?

_____

_____

_____

7 What are the differences between DOCSIS 1.0 and DOCSIS 1.1?

_____

_____

_____

8 How many cable modems can be connected to a single DOCSIS MAC domain? How many are desirable?

_____

_____

_____

This chapter covers the following topics:

- **Synchronous review**—The synchronous review section details the differences between asynchronous and synchronous communication, and why synchronous communication is needed in optical-based network structures.

- **Optical hardware**—The optical hardware section offers a description of some of the common equipment that is found in optical networks and how it is used.

- **Comparison of synchronous optical networks (SONETs) and synchronous digital hierarchies (SDHs)**—The comparison of the SONET and SDH hierarchies defines the main components of each hierarchy and details how they correspond and differ from each other.

- **Operations, administration, management, and provisioning(OAM&P)**—The OAM&P portion of this chapter overviews the overall ideas behind the management and maintenance functionality built into the optical network.

- **Wave division multiplexing (WDM) and dense wavelength division multiplexing (DWDM)**—The WDM and DWDM section provides an operational overview of how they operate, how they differ from each other, and how they are used in today's optical networks.

- **SONET/SDH applications**—The applications section describes some of the more common deployment methods for optical networks, whether using SONET or SDH.

CHAPTER 14

SONET and SDH

Possibly the most important development in recent telecommunication history has been the creation of SONET and the SDH specifications. The ability to transmit billions of bits per second along with enhanced management capacity, gives SONET and SDH an edge over most other telecommunication formats. Strictly speaking, SONET and SDH are physical layer standards that deal with what is the equivalent of the Open System Interconnection (OSI) model's physical layer. Both the North American (SONET) and international (SDH) formats also have many different reports, white papers, and standards that combine to form the complete technology.

This chapter focuses on the physical transmission attributes of the SONET and SDH networks, and on some of the features and applications that they can be used for.

Synchronous Review

SONET and SDH depend on timing to be as near to perfect as possible to operate properly. The timing required in an optical transmission network is different from that of traditional time-division multiplexing (TDM) environments. SONET and SDH use a hierarchical synchronous timing structure instead of a plesiochronous model, as is found in T and E carrier technology.

Different T1s or E1s that come from different carriers can have slight variations in timing that require bit stuffing to overcome during multiplexing. Remember that at the digital service 2 (DS2) and DS3 levels, bit stuffing must occur (asynchronous multiplexing) to remove the timing variations and to ensure the integrity of the circuit. SONET and SDH do not need to facilitate the stuffing of bits for multiplexing because their timing structure is more robust. Some overhead bit stuffing occurs in the creation of the initial signal (discussed later), but the signals themselves are combined without further modification.

Because no bit stuffing is used, this technology is also referred to as a byte-interleaved multiplexing technology rather than the bit-interleaved multiplexing found in asynchronous and plesiochronous networks. As a result, SONET and SDH can allow direct access to lower level digital signals without the need to demultiplex the signal. Byte-interleaved multiplexing is discussed later in this chapter.

So what exactly does synchronous timing mean? Several aspects of this timing method pertain to SONET and SDH. First, synchronous networks can trace the network timing back to a single source. This does not mean that only one timing source exists for the entire network, but that timing is distributed down through the network elements from the most accurate to the least accurate timing source. It is important to understand that the optical networks use a set of clocks for timing, known as Stratum clocks. The available clocks are as follows:

- **Stratum 1**—The Primary Reference Source (PRS) on a network. The Stratum 1 clocks have an extremely precise timing mechanism, similar to an atomic clock system (cesium) or global positioning system (GPS). You typically only see a maximum of two of these in a network (deployed as a redundant pair).

- **Stratum 2**—The first distribution tier for timing sources on a network. Typically assigned as a transit node clock (TNC) to a tandem switch (Class 4).

- **Stratum 3/3E**—A secondary distribution tier. These timing sources can also be a switch, but are typically an end-office switch (Class 5), Digital Access and Crossconnect System (DACS), or an add/drop multiplexer (ADM).

- **Stratum 4/4E**—An end-unit timing source. These devices typically encompass channel banks, and are not intended to distribute timing any further into the service provider network.

In North America the recommended timing mechanism is known as the SONET Minimum Clock (SMC). This specifies that the timing source on a SONET network should fall about halfway between the Stratum 4E and Stratum 3 timing sources. The traditional Stratum 4 clocks cannot provide adequate timing for the SONET network. A lot of equipment in SONET or SDH networks already adheres to Stratum 3 timing standards.

The traditional deployment of atomic timing throughout the SONET or SDH network was difficult and expensive. The single timing source was distributed throughout the network by using a series of T1 or E1 circuits. Figure 14-1 shows the timing hierarchy as it is found in the service provider's network as associated with the Stratum timing levels. The facilities required to deploy this created the need for an improvement.

Over the past few years the expansion of the use of GPS has allowed for service providers to cut down on the number of physical circuits required to deploy network timing. Because it uses a satellite link, GPS deployment is typically less expensive and less involved. The problem with GPS timing distribution is that densely populated business areas typically experience a lot of interference. These problems can range from radio station interference to the physical interference of taller buildings that surround the location.

Figure 14-1   *Synchronous Timing Distribution*

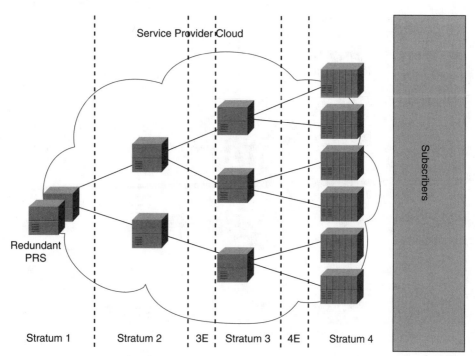

Building Integrated Timing Supply (BITS)

BITS is a North American term that describes a building-centric timing system. Also referred to as a Synchronization Supply Unit (SSU), the BITS system efficiently manages the number of timing interfaces within a structure. Without something such as BITS/SSU in place, you can feasibly have many different timing sources within the same building because of the number of synchronous links that the building might contain. BITS operates by providing the only ingress and egress external timing connections to the building (typically deployed over a T1 or E1), and then distributing timing internally to all circuits that require it. Figure 14-2 shows the distribution of a BITS timing circuit into a building through either a GPS link or a link to an atomic clock.

Figure 14-2   *Basic BITS Timing Distribution*

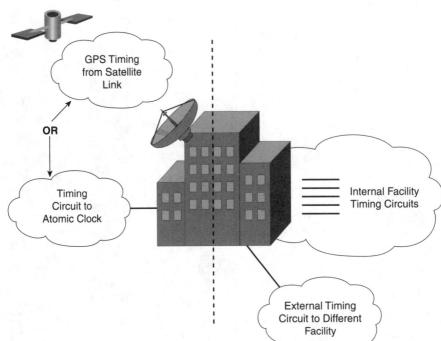

BITS systems can also provide external timing links to structures within the same campus, such as a building adjacent to yours that also belongs to your company. Most of these circuits are deployed as T1 or E1 facilities and many vendors provide these interfaces by using coaxial cable connections. Typically, BITS deployment also includes a redundant timing source that is internal to the building in case a timing source is lost. This provides the required equipment uptime, and the redundant supply is taken from the same BITS source.

Optical Hardware

This section discusses some of the common equipment associated with optical networks. Equipment found on optical networks is typically separated into three different types: path terminating, line terminating, and section terminating. Refer to Table 14-1 for a list of the equipment to be discussed.

Table 14-1   *Optical Network Equipment Types*

Equipment Type	Acronym
Path Terminating Equipment	**PTE**
Terminal Multiplexer	TM
Digital Access and Crossconnect System	DACS or DCS
Line Terminating Equipment	**LTE**
Add/Drop Multiplexer	ADM
Matched Node	MN
Section Terminating Equipment	**STE**
Optical Repeater	N/A
Other Equipment	
Optical Routers	N/A
Fiber Optic Cabling	N/A

PTE

Path terminating equipment consists of end-user devices that directly interact with other digital signal types, such as multiplexers or crossconnect systems. These devices typically do not get deployed into the core of the optical infrastructure.

TM

A TM is a basic multiplexer that is used in optical networks to multiplex many TDM-based and lower level SONET/SDH circuits into a SONET or SDH data stream. These devices are then multiplexed into a larger SONET or SDH network by using an ADM. Figure 14-3 shows a portion of an optical network that funnels circuits from TMs into larger pipes of bandwidth used by ADMs.

Figure 14-3 *TM Multiplexing TDM and Optical Circuits*

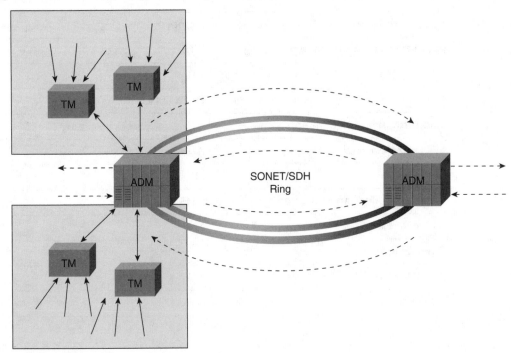

DACS or DCS

A DACS is found in most service provider networks. It is not necessarily specific to SONET or SDH networks (in fact it deals with TDM-based circuits exclusively). This device is important because DACSs are typically deployed in feeder networks that are multiplexed into optical networks by ADMs. The main function of a DACS is to act as a sort of poor man's switch. The device can terminate many DS1 and DS3 signals, and is capable of interconnecting any two DS0s, group of DS0s (DS0 groups or fractional DS1s), DS1s, or DS3s. Think of a legacy switchboard in which an operator has to sit and connect both ends of a phone call. The DACS performs the same function for the TDM network. Figure 14-4 shows a DACS system interconnecting a series of TDM-based circuits either to reroute or groom traffic to a specific location.

Figure 14-4   *DACS Interconnecting DS0s and DS1s*

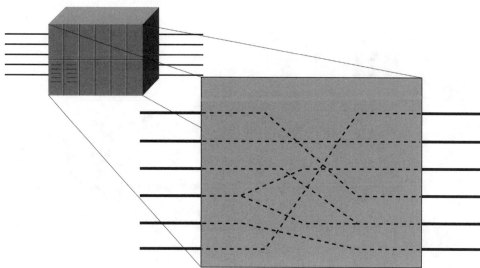

LTE

LTE provides access into the SONET or SDH core to PTE devices. The ADM is the main device that is used in this capacity.

ADM

Optical networks use the ADM to reroute and pass on traffic. The ADM can crossconnect and groom traffic at the DS1 or DS3 levels without the need to completely demultiplex the signal. The basic application of the ADM is to aggregate traffic onto a higher bandwidth link, but also to allow for the add or drop of specific circuit sizes as the rest of the bandwidth is passed through the unit. Remember that if you want to use a specific DS1 from a DS3 circuit you have to demultiplex that DS3 circuit to access the required DS1. An ADM can allow this access by pulling the required circuit directly from the signal stream. Figure 14-5 shows an optical network segment, which focuses on the ADMs that are present in the optical ring.

Figure 14-5 *Basic ADM Operation in a SONET/SDH Ring*

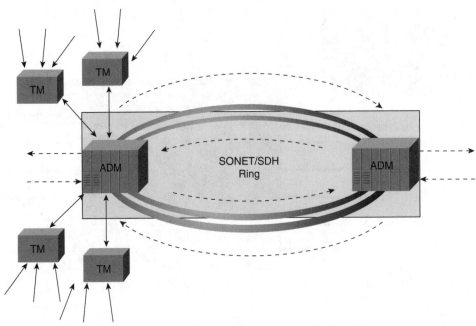

The problem with the ADM is that it multiplexes the DS1 and DS3 signals directly onto a high bandwidth optical link regardless of how much traffic is actually on the circuit. You might wonder why this is a problem. If only 20 percent of a DS3 is used, the circuit is mapped into a higher level Optical Carrier (OC) signal and the remaining bandwidth cannot be used for anything other than the DS3 circuit that was mapped onto it. This creates an inefficient network if this occurs too often.

MNs

MNs are devices that interconnect SONET or SDH rings. They provide a redundant path between rings and reroute traffic in the event of a ring failure. MNs can also be ADMs that are acting in a redundant capacity between rings, but this type of deployment can be expensive. Figure 14-6 shows two optical rings interconnected through a pair of MNs, both with and without repeaters.

Figure 14-6   *Ring Interconnection Using Matched Nodes*

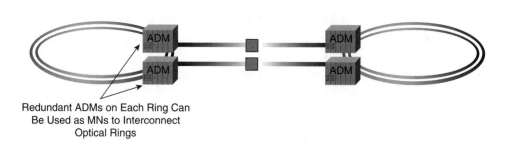

STE is primarily an optical repeater, and it can be considered either an LTE or STE. In the event that signal regeneration is needed, an optical repeater regenerates the signal. Its function is similar to that of a digital repeater in copper circuits in that it extends the signal distance. You will also see references to optical repeaters as regenerators.

Other Equipment

The last few pieces of equipment found in optical networks do not necessarily fall into any of the listed categories but are certainly worth mentioning.

Optical Routers

Optical routers are quickly becoming more popular in a fiber-based network. They are exactly what they sound like, routers with optical interfaces. Many uses exist for them, and as the data and voice networks continue to converge with the next generation of IP networks you will see them deployed more often. Directly related to Cisco products, there are both low- and high-end platforms. One of the lower end platforms is the Optical Service Router (OSR) 7600 series. These routers are intended to integrate the de facto IP standard into the optical networking space by combining the Catalyst 6500 and the Cisco 7500 router. Intended for point of presence (POP) applications, the OSR7600 provides the key bandwidth and IP priority schemes required for today's service providers. This router enables service providers optical capacity combined with routing efficiency at the edge of the network.

Moving onto a larger box, there are the Cisco ONS15000 series optical devices, which are intended for use in what has become known as the metro-optical service space. These optical routers combine SONET and SDH support of DWDM technology with a highly scalable chassis design to provide the most flexibility for service providers in the metro-optical arena.

NOTE   DWDM is discussed later in this chapter in the "WDM and DWDM" section.

Metro-optical devices are large ADMs with added features and functionality that are used on what has been classically referred to as a metropolitan-area network (MAN). Traditionally these networks provided services to enterprise customers, and the TDM infrastructure was adequate for a short period of time. As the number of businesses coming online exploded, it became increasingly difficult to provide such services over a standard T or E carrier-based network. For this reason, many service providers began to deploy fiber backbones in the MAN to keep up with the demand for service and bandwidth. The services provided include multi-service network integration, E-businesses, storage area networking (SAN), and disaster recovery applications.

Fiber-Optic Cabling

SONET and SDH networks are both based on fiber-optic transport. Fiber optics is used for transport because it can transmit high bandwidth rates over long distances. Instead of being limited to a couple thousand feet before regeneration, as is the case with copper wiring, fiber-optic cabling can transport information from 10 to 80 kilometers over single mode fiber cables.

Fiber-optic cabling is all but immune to line problems such as electromagnetic interference (EMI) because light is used and not electricity. In secured environments, fiber-optic transport is preferred because it is difficult to tap and it is simple to detect if a tap is present. Also, there is no signal resonance as with copper wiring, so signal hijacking becomes exponentially more difficult.

Fiber-optic cabling is also lighter than copper cabling because it can transmit more information over the same cable length. So instead of having to deploy pair after pair of copper wiring, you can use a single fiber cable. One of the main disadvantages for fiber optics has been the cost of deployment. Fiber-optic cabling and equipment has generally been more expensive than basic copper twisted pair and its associated facilities.

Two main types of fiber-optic cabling are on the market today—single mode and multimode fiber. Single mode fiber cabling and multimode fiber cabling are designed for different applications. Single mode fiber cables are generally deployed when long distance optical transport is required, and they generally use lasers for light transport. Multimode fiber cables are typically deployed in short-haul fiber applications, and they typically use light emitting diodes (LEDs) for light transport. The basic difference between the two types of cabling, other than cable core diameter, is that single mode fiber cables transport a single light stream or mode of light. Multimode cables transport multiple modes of light. Figure 14-7 shows the light path propagation difference between single mode and multimode fiber-optic cable.

Figure 14-7   *Single Mode and Multimode Fiber Cabling*

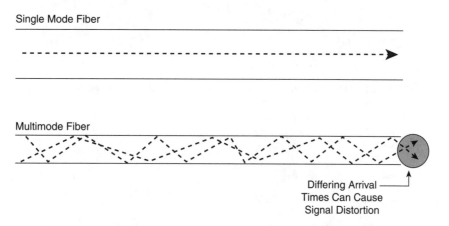

Multimode cabling has traditionally been less expensive to deploy than single mode cabling because the cabling is less expensive to manufacture. The requirements for transport of multiple light modes aren't as stringent as long-haul transport over a single fiber. Some multimode equipment is also less expensive, but that depends on the vendor of the optical equipment. Multimode cabling transports multiple modes of light by placing different modes at angles within the cable. The separate modes are reflected down the cable at differing angles to keep them apart, but this can create signal problems. The main problem facing multimode cables is what is referred to as multimode distortion or modal dispersion. The basic premise of this issue is that there are multiple modes of light within the cable traveling at different angles in the cable core. Because these modes propagate down the cable at different angles, they can be received at the other end of the cable at slightly different times. The differing arrival times distort the signal and tend to be worse with longer cables. If the distortion becomes great enough the signal can be unintelligible at the receiving end.

The fibers in fiber-optic cabling are usually composed of high-grade glass or plastics, and must be devoid of any nicks to the core throughout the length of the cable and at each end. Optical connectors are sensitive and abrasions to the core can cause serious signal problems.

Fiber cables can have one of about ten different connectors ranging from Asynchronous Transfer Mode (ATM) to Fiber Distributed Data Interface (FDDI) applications, but the two most common are the SC and ST cable connectors. Figure 14-8 shows several of the common connectors associated with fiber-optic cabling. You can connect two different types of connectors together with the use of a coupler. The coupler acts as the intermediary interface between cables. Both SC and ST cable connectors can be used on Cisco equipment, but SC connectors are most common.

Figure 14-8   *SC and ST Connectors*

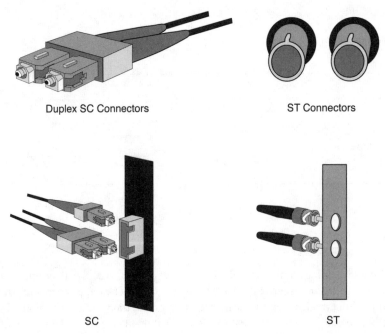

Duplex SC Connectors   ST Connectors

SC   ST

SC connectors come in two flavors: a single connector and a duplex connector. The duplex connector combines Tx and Rx onto the same plug. The ST connectors closely resemble a mini-coaxial connection, which is identified by its ring lock mechanism.

As fiber-optic cabling is deployed, you might hear about dark fiber. Dark fiber is merely fibers in a fiber-optic trunk that aren't currently being used. Most service providers deploy more fiber-optic cabling than required to provide some level of capacity planning for the network. As soon as they need more cable they can start using the already deployed cable.

From the subscriber's vantage point, dark fiber is cable that the service provider assigns to the customer but does not attach to any equipment. In this instance, it is the responsibility of the customer to attach the fiber to the proper equipment.

Comparison of SONET and SDH Hierarchies

SONET and SDH have emerged simultaneously as optical network standards that are used throughout the world. Several basic differences exist between the hierarchies, but they do not cause incompatibility. On the contrary, the international community has strived for compatibility between the North American SONET hierarchy and its own SDH hierarchy. Before you look at the optical hierarchies, it is important that you understand the differences in multiplexing between synchronous and asynchronous/plesiochronous networks.

Byte-Interleaved Multiplexing

SONET and SDH are based on byte-interleaved multiplexing technology. Asynchronous multiplexing, with T3 and E3 technology, uses a bit interleaved multiplexing technology. Because the interleaving takes place at the bit level, individual DS1 signals from the T3 or E3 circuits cannot be accessed individually without a complete demultiplexing of the signal. Byte-interleaved multiplexing takes a slightly different approach to multiplexing.

By interleaving at the byte level (every 8 bits), each signal that is multiplexed into the signal stream remains a separate entity and can therefore be accessed individually. Figure 14-9 shows the differences between bit- and byte-interleaved multiplexing. This feature provides for network flexibility and end-to-end network management.

Concatenation

Although most SONET and SDH links are channelized, a provision exists that allows for unchannelized transmission of information. Concatenated or unchannelized SONET and SDH links form a single large synchronous payload envelope (SPE), and do not specify any lower level digital signals. Even though the circuit is concatenated, the same section, line, and path overhead is used.

SONET identifies concatenated signals by using a c marker at the end of the signal. For example, a concatenated OC-3 is identified as OC-3c. SDH also identifies the difference between channelized and unchannelized with the same c designation.

Figure 14-9   *Bit Versus Byte-Interleaved Multiplexing*

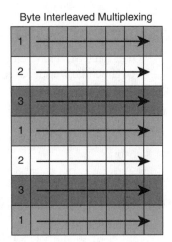

SONET

SONET is the optical network designation for North America. It is based loosely on synchronous technology called Synchronous Transmission (SYNTRAN). As you might recall from Chapter 7, "T3 and E3 Technology," SYNTRAN was designed to provide services at the DS3 level but it used synchronous transport. One of the main objectives of the SONET/SDH movement has been to provide a set of standards that allows different vendors to communicate with each other.

The basic transport structure of the SONET network is the Synchronous Transport Signal (STS). The lowest level in the SONET hierarchy is STS-1, which has a bandwidth rate of 51.84 Mbps (6480 bits per frame * 8000 frames per second). STS-1 was designed to transport digital signal level 3 (DS-3) and lower DS signals. The lower DS rates are transported by using what are called Virtual Tributaries (VTs). VTs are discussed in detail later in this chapter.

At 51.84 Mbps, the STS-1 can easily handle the DS-3 signal rate at 44.736 Mbps. The main reason for the drastic difference in the bandwidth rate is the inclusion of the overhead bytes for management and signal identification for the SONET network.

The STS is considered to be the electrical signal for transport, and the OC identifies the physical transport characteristics. The OC designation directly relates to the STS designation, so STS-1 = OC-1. OC is intended to represent the transport of a STS signal over fiber-optic facilities.

NOTE   American National Standards Institute (ANSI) separates the electrical and physical transport characteristics with STS and OC, but SDH from the International Telecommunication Union (ITU) does not make this distinc-tion. SDH only uses the Synchronous Transport Module (STM) designation for both aspects of transport.

STS signals are synchronously multiplexed in multiples of the base STS-1 signal. In other words, an STS-3 or OC-3 is 3 multiplexed STS-1 signals in the same data stream. STS-48 is 48 iterations of the STS-1 signal, and the equation continues from there all the way up to STS-768. STS-768 or OC-768 is the latest development in the SONET industry, offering a huge 40 Gbps of bandwidth. OC-768 was developed for the new DWDM applications that service providers are beginning to deploy. In some documentation you might see references to OC-24 or OC-96. These designations are not incorrect, but they are no longer in use and are therefore not included in this chapter. Refer to Table 14-2 for a complete listing of the ANSI SONET hierarchy rates.

Table 14-2   *SONET Digital Hierarchy*

STS Designation	OC Designation	Bandwidth
STS-1	OC-1	51.84 Mbps
STS-3	OC-3	155.52 Mbps
STS-12	OC-12	622.08 Mbps
STS-48	OC-48	2488.32 Mbps
STS-192	OC-192	9953.28 Mbps
STS-768	OC-768	39813.12 Mbps

STS-1 Frame Structure

As with every other technology discussed in this book, SONET has its own frame structure. Because it is the most basic frame structure used in the SONET network, the STS-1 frame is discussed in detail. The STS-1 frame consists of 90 columns * 9 rows of 8-bit byte blocks for a total of 810 bytes or 6480 bits. Figure 14-10 shows the basic structure of an STS-1 frame.

Figure 14-10 *STS-1 Basic Frame Structure*

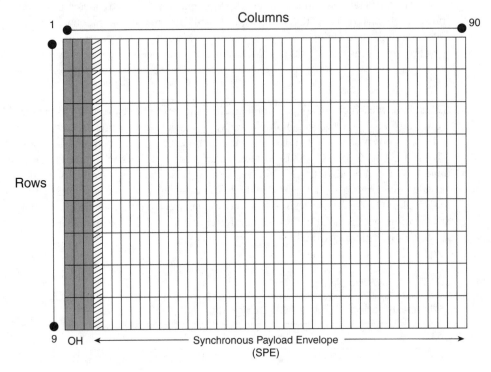

Transport Overhead

Path Overhead

The first three columns are reserved for the line and section overhead and the last 87 columns are reserved for the SPE. The SPE is the portion of the frame that actually carries the lower level digital signals. For example, if a full T3 is used in the SPE, the nominal bandwidth rate for the T3 is 44.736 Mbps. 4.8 Mbps of stuffed information is added to that rate to bring the T3 signal rate to a total bandwidth of 49.54 Mbps. When the path overhead is added to the SPE (570 kbps), you get a total bandwidth of 50.11 Mbps.

The total rate of the SPE is 50.11 Mbps regardless of the digital signal that is being transported. To the SPE rate, 1.728 Mbps of bandwidth is added for the line and section overhead. This gives you the final rate of 51.84 Mbps. Table 14-3 lists all the current SONET rates, with the associated payload and overhead amounts. Remember that because every SONET level above STS-1 is a multiple of STS-1, the overhead rates are in turn a multiple of 1.728 Mbps.

Table 14-3   *SONET Overhead and Payload Rates*

STS Designation	Bandwidth	Overhead	Payload
STS-1	51.84 Mbps	1.73 Mbps	50.11 Mbps
STS-3	155.52 Mbps	5.18 Mbps	150.34 Mbps
STS-12	622.08 Mbps	20.74 Mbps	601.34 Mbps
STS-48	2488.32 Mbps	82.94 Mbps	2405.38 Mbps
STS-192	9953.28 Mbps	331.78 Mbps	9621.50 Mbps
STS-768	39813.12 Mbps	1327.10 Mbps	38486.02 Mbps

STS-1 Frame Overhead

The Frame is broken down into four distinct layers as it pertains to SONET overhead. Admittedly, they are all related to the physical layer to some degree, but each section deals with different aspects of the SONET transmission system:

- **Path**—Responsible for the reliable transport of services that are provided to the PTE (TM, DACS). These services include the mapping of TDM-based circuits into STS-1 frames.

- **Line**—Responsible for the reliable transport of the SPE that is located at the path layer, and for synchronization and multiplexing services. This layer provides overhead that points to the SPE within the frame, specifically when mapping multiple STS-1 signals into a multiplex. Also provided are error monitoring, data communications, orderwire, and protection signaling for line protection.

- **Section**—Responsible for the framing and reliable transport of the SONET frames through the network, and is used with the physical layer to form the base transport medium. This section handles the scrambling of the data stream to provide user security and randomization to avoid mimicking provider network functions. It is also responsible for data communication to provide OAM&P support, error monitoring, and orderwire.

- **Physical**—Responsible for the physical transmission of the bits across the network, and no overhead is associated with this layer.

Figure 14-11 shows the SONET layers and the equipment associated with each layer.

Figure 14-11 *Overhead Layers and Associated Equipment*

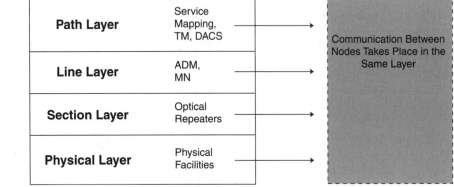

Communication Within
the Same Node Takes Place
on the Vertical Plane

The section and line overhead portions make up a large part of the STS-1 frame. The first portion of overhead that is read during transmission is the section overhead. The overhead is used by any of the STE in the SONET network. Section overhead is split into nine separate bytes, as shown in Figure 14-12.

The following list describes the bits in the section overhead, and what function each bit is used for:

- **A1/A2**—A1 and A2 bytes form the frame alignment signal. The two bytes joined together provide a 16-bit word of 1111011000101000.

- **J0/Z0**—The J0/Z0 byte provides two different functions, which depend on the STS-1 that is viewed. J0 is allocated for a section trace on the first STS-1 in a multiplex. The section trace is designed to identify the origin of the primary STS-1 in the multiplex. In a nutshell, it allows the other terminating end to verify that it is still communicating with the proper node in the SONET network. Every other STS-1 in the multiplex uses this byte as a Z0 byte, which is allocated for future growth.

- **B1**—B1 byte provides a bit interleaved parity 8 (BIP8) code for error checking. This byte is found in the first STS-1 in a multiplex, and it checks the integrity of the previous STS-X frame. The calculations are based on the previous frame after it has been scrambled, but the BIP8 information is added to the current frame prior to its scrambling.

- **E1**—The E1 byte is used for what is called orderwire. Orderwire provides a voice communication channel between specific STE such as optical repeaters and remote terminals. This byte is only defined on the first STS-1 in a multiplex.

Figure 14-12 *Section Overhead*

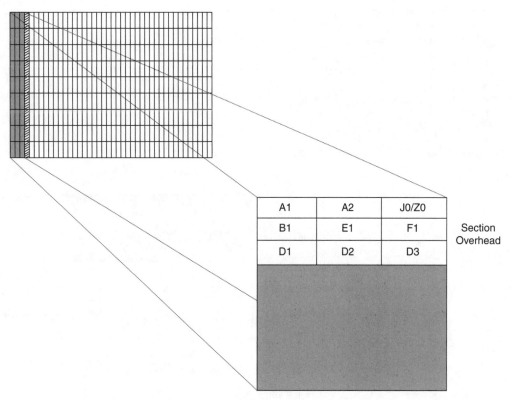

A1	A2	J0/Z0
B1	E1	F1
D1	D2	D3

Section
Overhead

- **F1**—The F1 byte has been reserved for user purposes. The F1 byte is to be transmitted between STE and is only defined on the first STS-1 of a multiplex. This byte has not been explicitly defined because it is to be used by service providers as needed. This byte is typically used as a proprietary communication channel between equipment.

- **D1, D2, D3**—The D bytes are also known as section data communication channels. These bytes represent the main transmission avenue for OAM&P messages through the SONET network. Combined, they provide a data communication channel of 192 kbps and they provide the necessary communication between STE for those functions. The D bytes are also only found on the first STS-1 of a multiplex.

The line overhead provides many of the same functions as the section overhead and it adds pointers to the SPE in the frame, functionality for automatic protection switching (APS), and a more robust communication channel. The line overhead consists of a total of 18 bytes, as shown in Figure 14-13.

Figure 14-13 *Line Overhead*

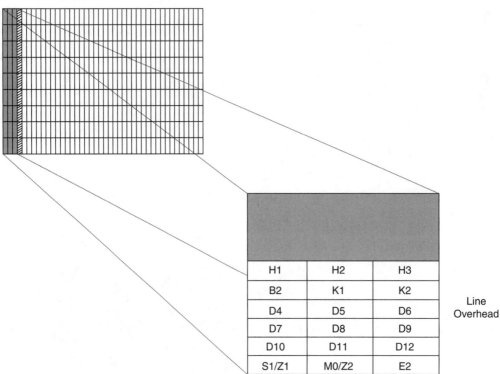

The following list describes the bits in the line overhead, and the function of each bit:

- **H1, H2**—The H1 and H2 bytes are used as the SPE pointer. They are designed to identify or point to the starting octet of the SPE within the STS-1 frame. As pointers, they also account for subtle location differences that can happen between frames because of network problems (frequency justification). The H1 and H2 bytes are used in all STS-1s in a multiplex. In the event that the link is concatenated, the H1 and H2 bytes specify this function. Combined, they form a value equal to 1001XX1111111111 for concatentation.

- **H3**—The H3 is used completely for frequency justification in the STS-1 frame. Found in all STS-1s in a multiplex, this byte can perform positive or negative justification dependent on whether the sending frame is too small or too large respectively.

- **B2**—The B2 byte provides a BIP8 code for error checking. This byte is found in the first STS-1 in a multiplex, and it checks the integrity of the previous STS-*X* frame. The calculations are based on the previous frame after it has been scrambled, but the BIP8 information is added to the current frame prior to its scrambling.

- **K1, K2**—K bytes are used for APS. The purpose of these bytes is to provide a communication path between devices at the line level for APS failover operations. Both commands and conditions are reported through this link. When fiber networks are protected, they are typically running in a dual mode whereby the secondary fiber link can take up SONET or SDH communication in the event of a failure. The secondary fiber link is usually deployed in a counter-rotating direction to the primary.

- **D4-D12**—The D bytes are also known as section data communication channels. These bytes represent the main transmission avenue for OAM&P messages through the SONET network. Combined, they provide a data communication channel of 576 kbps and they provide the necessary communication between STE for those functions. The D bytes are also only found on the first STS-1 of a multiplex.

- **S1**—The S1 byte is used for network synchronization, but only half of the eight bits are used. Bits 5 to 8 are used for the synchronization, and bits 1 to 4 are not currently allocated for any purpose. This byte is only specified on the primary STS-1 of a multiplex. The values assigned to the S1 byte are listed in Table 14-4.

Table 14-4   *Synchronization Status Messages*

Value	Definition
0000	Synchronized Traceability Unknown
0001	Stratum 1 Traceable
0111	Stratum 2 Traceable
1010	Stratum 3 Traceable
1100	± 20 ppm Clock
1110	Reserved for Network
1111	Not Used

- **Z1**—The Z1 byte is reserved as a growth byte and is currently not implemented.

- **M0**—The M0 byte is used for the remote error indication (REI) function in the STS-1 line overhead, and is also referred to as a far-end block error (FEBE). In the event that the BIP-8 algorithm detects an error, this byte carries the notification. As with the S1 byte, only bits 5 to 8 are used. The first four bits are reserved for future use. This byte is used for STS-1 signals only. If the signal rate is above STS-1 (STS-3 and above), the byte used for this function is identified as a M1 byte.

- **Z2**—The Z2 byte is reserved as a growth byte, and is currently not implemented.

- **E2**—The E2 byte is used for an orderwire function at the line level. It is intended to provide a communication path between LTE equipment and its use is optional.

The last type of overhead to be discussed is the path overhead. The path overhead is part of the 87 columns that are assigned to the payload. This overhead is for the operational transport of the SPE through the network, and it remains with the SPE until it is delivered to its final destination. Figure 14-14 shows the location of the path overhead in the STS-1 frame. The most basic form of this overhead is used when transporting a STS-1 signal, but in the event of an upper level STS-1 signal, path overhead is still all that is required.

The following list describes the bits in the path overhead, and the function of each bit:

- **J1**—J1 is allocated for a path trace on the first STS-1 in a multiplex. The path trace is designed to identify the origin of the primary STS-1 in the multiplex. In a nutshell, it allows the remote end to verify that it is still communicating with the proper node in the SONET network.

- **B3**—B3 byte provides a BIP8 code for error checking. This byte is found in the first STS-1 in a multiplex and it checks the integrity of the previous STS-X frame. The calculations are based on the previous frame after it has been scrambled, but the BIP8 information is added to the current frame prior to its scrambling.

- **C2**—The C2 byte is used as a path signal label. The path signal label identifies the contents and structure of the SPE in the STS frame. The C2 byte also identifies defects in any of the payloads that are multiplexed in the STS signal stream. This function is referred to as payload defect indication (PDI-P). This byte has 256 possible designations or values, all of which are denoted in hexadecimal. The first nine of the values describe the content, followed by the associated error messages. Table 14-5 shows payload types and associated error messages.

Figure 14-14   *Path Overhead*

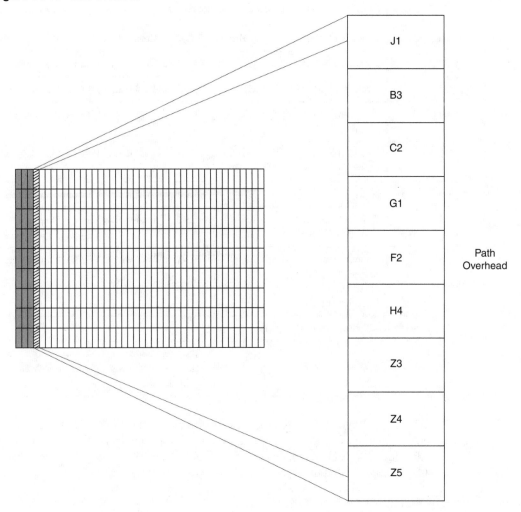

Table 14-5   *Payload Types and Associated Error Messages*

Hex Value	Payload Type	Hex Value	Payload Error
00	Unequipped	E1	STS-1 payload with 1 VTx payload defect
01	Equipped	E2	STS-1 payload with 2 VTx payload defects

continues

Table 14-5 *Payload Types and Associated Error Messages (Continued)*

Hex Value	Payload Type	Hex Value	Payload Error
02	Floating VT Mode	E3	STS-1 payload with 3 VTx payload defects
03	Locked VT Mode	E4	STS-1 payload with 4 VTx payload defects
04	Asynchronous Mapping for DS3	E5	STS-1 payload with 5 VTx payload defects
12	Asynchronous Mapping for DS4	E6	STS-1 payload with 6 VTx payload defects
13	ATM	E7	STS-1 payload with 7 VTx payload defects
14	Distributed Queue Dual Bus (DQDB)	E8	STS-1 payload with 8 VTx payload defects
15	Asynchronous Mapping for Fiber Distributed Data Interface (FDDI)	E9	STS-1 payload with 9 VTx payload defects
Continues to 28 defects (value FC)			
		FC	STS-1 payload with 28 VTx payload defects, or a STS signal with a non-VT payload defect

- **G1**—The G1 byte is allocated for performance monitoring of the SONET path at either end of the connection. The byte is broken down into two main categories that allow for both REI and remote defect indication (RDI-P) reporting. Refer to Figure 14-15 for an illustration of the bit placements.

Figure 14-15 *G1 Byte Path Performance Monitoring*

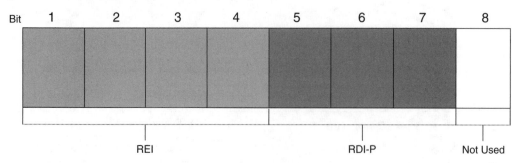

The bit patterns for the REI section specify how many errors have been detected in the path. The values follow standard binary equivalents, and any unused binary values indicate that no errors were detected. For example, 0001 means that one error was detected, and 0101 means that five errors were detected. An all 0s value or any value that is greater than 8 means that no errors were detected.

- **F2**—F2 is a communication path between PTE.
- **H4**—The H4 byte is a multiframe indicator. In the cases that VTs are used, the H4 byte identifies that multiple streams exist within the payload.

Remember that the STS-1 frame was designed to carry a DS3 signal. This is not to say that DS3 signals are always available or even always necessary. Several other TDM-based circuits can be transported over SONET and SDH links such as DS1, DS2, and E1 carrier circuits. In the event that multiple lower level circuits are mapped into the STS frame, they are split into virtual portions of the STS payload that are called tributaries.

You can think of the tributaries as logical portions of the STS payload that are segmented for the necessary amount of bandwidth. Similar to the physical/logical relationships that ISDN PRI uses, SONET maps each DS1 or DS2 (SONET can also map international E1 circuits) into a specific location within the payload and creates a set of pointers so that all VTs can be located at any time.

SONET specifies four separate types of VTs:

- VT1.5—Designed to carry a DS1 signal
- VT2—Designed to carry an E1 signal
- VT3—Designed to carry a DS1C signal
- VT6—Designed to carry a DS2 signal

When VTs are required, the STS SPE is split into seven different segments that are called Virtual Tributary Groups (VTGs). VTGs are subsections of the SPE that actually contain the VTs, and they are not optional. After VT transmission is specified, the VTGs are created, which limits the SPE to VT transport only. In other words, if VTs are used that is all the STS SPE can be used for.

- **Z3-Z5**—Reserved for future use as growth bytes. In some cases, the Z5 byte is used as a tandem connection maintenance (TCM) and path data channel (N1 byte). In this case, bits 1 to 4 are used for the incoming error count (IEC), and bits 5 to 8 are used as the actual communication channel.

SDH

The ITU specifications for SDH are similar to those used in SONET because the idea was to provide an optical network that could be used throughout the world. As you will see in the next few sections, some things are different, such as the terminology and circuit sizes. However, many of the header operations are the same to provide the same type of management and error reporting that is present in the SONET infrastructure.

Similar to SONET, SDH is split up into a hierarchy of multiplexed synchronous signals. Right from the start, the biggest difference between the two hierarchies is the fact that SDH STMs start at a rate of 155.52 Mbps. In other words, instead of having a 55-Mbps signal, the first available speed is at 155 Mbps, which is equivalent to the STS-3 signal in SONET networks. That being said, ITU G.707 does identify a STM-0 signal level equivalent to the STS-1 of SONET, it is just not used as a separate entity. Refer to Table 14-6 for a complete listing of the SDH hierarchy.

Table 14-6 *SDH Hierarchy*

STM Designation	Bandwidth	SONET Equivalent
STM-0	51.84 Mbps	STS-1
STM-1	155.52 Mbps	STS-3
STM-4	622.08 Mbps	STS-12
STM-16	2448.32 Mbps	STS-48
STM-64	9953.28 Mbps	STS-192
STM-256	39813.12 Mbps	STS-768

Remember that with SONET, the STS-1 signal is the base rate for communication. SDH bases all network rates off of STM-1 (155 Mbps). This means that all higher-level SDH rates are exact multiples of STM-1. For example, an STM-16 signal is 16×155.52 Mbps (2448.32 Mbps).

The terminology associated with SDH might confuse those who are accustomed to SONET, but most underlying functions are the same. The VTs that are associated with the SONET network are referred to as *virtual containers* (VCs) in the SDH network. A VC is defined as a logical unit that contains both the payload and the path overhead (POH) associated with a connection. Before discussing the different VCs available, it should be pointed out that the SDH network defines different sections than SONET. Remember SONET uses section, line, and path overhead. SDH differs in that it uses regenerator sections and multiplexer sections in conjunction with low and high order VCs. Figure 14-16 shows an example of the multiplexer and regenerator sections that are used in between nodes in a SDH network hierarchy.

A regenerator is actually the same thing as an optical repeater, and the terms are interchangeable.

The VCs are split into two different categories: low and high order VCs. A low order VC is a signal that is equivalent to the TDM-based circuit that it transports and a high order VC represents the actual STM signal that is being transported. Refer to Table 14-7 for a listing of the most common VCs used in the SDH network.

Figure 14-16   *SDH Network Sections*

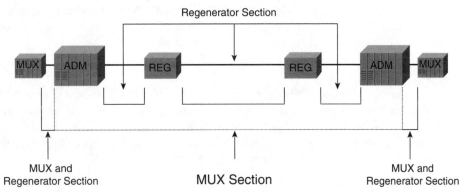

Table 14-7   *High and Low Order VCs, and Their Values*

VC Designation	Bandwidth	Overhead	Payload
Low Order VCs			
VC-11	1.66 Mbps	0.06 Mbps	1.60 Mbps
VC-12	2.24 Mbps	0.06 Mbps	2.18 Mbps
VC-2	6.85 Mbps	0.07 Mbps	6.78 Mbps
High Order VCs			
VC-3	48.96 Mbps	0.58 Mbps	48.38 Mbps
VC-4	150.34 Mbps	0.58 Mbps	149.76 Mbps
VC-4-4c	601.34 Mbps	2.3 Mbps	599.04 Mbps
VC-4-16c	2405.38 Mbps	9.22 Mbps	2396.16 Mbps
VC-4-64c	9621.50 Mbps	36.86 Mbps	9584.64 Mbps
VC-4-256c	38486.02 Mbps	147.46 Mbps	38338.56 Mbps

NOTE   High order VC overhead is based on a multiplier of 0.58 Mbps. For example, the overhead associated with an STM-256 signal is 256×0.58 Mbps (147.46 Mbps).

The easiest way to read the VC identifiers is to remember how they are broken down. The first portion is the VC identifier, the second portion is the STM signal that is being used. For example, VC-4-64c means that there is a VC-4 in a STM-64c (concatenated) signal.

SDH Frame Structure

For the most part, the SDH frame structure is the same as what is used with SONET. The main difference is that it is composed of 270 columns and it has 9 columns of overhead. Figure 14-17 shows a high level overview of an SDH frame. You might think that this doesn't correspond at all with SONET, but remember that SDH begins at what is equivalent to STS-3. In which case, this frame structure matches up nicely.

Figure 14-17 *SDH Frame Structure*

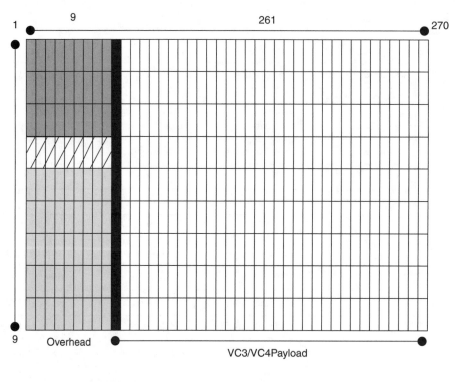

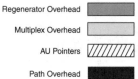

The overhead portions of each frame and their job roles differ little from what was already discussed in the SONET section of the chapter. The major difference is how the bytes are displayed. Figure 14-18 shows the regenerator, multiplex, and AU pointer overhead bits as they are located in the SDH frame.

Figure 14-18   *SDH Overhead Byte Layout*

Regenerator Overhead	A1	A1	A1	A2	A2	A2	C1		
	B1			E1			F1		
	D1			D2			D3		
AU Pointers	H1	H1	H1	H2	H2	H2	H3	H3	H3
Multiplex Overhead	B2	B2	B2	K1			K2		
	D4			D5			D6		
	D7			D8			D9		
	D10			D11			D12		
	S1/Z1				M0/Z2	E2			

AU-3 Pointer Format = H1,H1,H1,H2,H2,H2,H3,H3,H3
AU-4 Pointer Format = H1,Y,Y,H2,1,1,H3,H3,H3
Y = 1001SS11
1 = 11111111

The Same Path Overhead that Is Found in SONET Is Used in SDH

Referring to Figure 14-18, some of the byte usage differences are listed below:

- The J0 byte is used in the same manner, but with a 16-byte trace message.

- The H1, H2, and H3 bytes are referred to as the AU pointer bytes. These bytes locate and align the payload of multiple VCs within the payload. There are two types of AU—AU-3, and AU-4. Their formats are described in Figure 14-18. Bits 5 and 6, which are referred to as the SS bits, are set as 10. The SS bits form a flag that is only used with SDH network equipment.

- The S1 byte is used just as it is with SONET, but it has more coding values.

- A STM-1 signal does not specify the use of a Z0 byte as it does with SONET.

- The N1 byte is called the network operator byte (NOB), but is used for the same TCM functions as in SONET.

- J1, in the path overhead, path trace transports an Access Point Identifier (API). The API identifies the source of the signal and the numerical output begins with a country code.

OAM&P

As stated earlier in the chapter, using synchronous network technology has several benefits. Not only is there more bandwidth available to the service providers by using optical fibers, but SONET and SDH have both been designed with extensive maintenance and error control features. Typically, these features are referred to as OAM&P.

OAM&P allows the service provider to detect, collect, and correct network error conditions. Outside of the North American network theater it is typically referred to as OAM, but the purpose is still the same. Recall that the frames for both SONET and SDH provide a lot of bandwidth for error detection and communication channels between equipment. This facilitates the ability to manage the network from a central location. Refer to Table 14-3 and 14-7 for the overhead assignments in each STS or STM level. A good portion of that overhead is used for the OAM&P functions.

WDM and DWDM

Optical fibers have improved considerably in recent years. The high-grade glass and plastics that are used allow for the transmission of high amounts of bandwidth. The problem with this is that if you are only deploying a STS-1 or a STM-1, you are feasibly wasting facilities (particularly in a long-haul application). WDM was created to help cut down on the number of facilities that need to be deployed.

WDM allows you to take multiple STS or STM signals and transport them over the same optical fiber by transmitting them on different wavelengths. Similar to the concepts that are used with traditional TDM multiplexers, WDM devices multiplex multiple streams of light. As you might imagine, this not only allows for better efficiency of the optical infrastructure, but it also allows for an immense amount of bandwidth that is currently not possible over a single optical link. At this point, the definition is not about multiplexing several different VCs or VTs into a signal stream, but to multiplex several different STS-48s or STS-192s.

Typically, WDM is defined as having the ability to multiplex between 2 and 15 signal streams into a single physical facility. Multiplexes of 16 or more light streams are referred to as DWDM. So if WDM can give you an immense amount of bandwidth, the newer DWDM systems can give your systems enough bandwidth to be staggering. Just think about combining 16 STS-192 signals together (I'll give you a hint: it's in the neighborhood of 159,252.48 Mbps). DWDM is still an evolving technology at this point and faster systems are being developed at a constant rate.

One of the biggest benefits of these systems, in the eyes of a service provider, is the ability to provide an almost limitless amount of bandwidth to their subscribers. Remember that the metro-optical area needs to provide large amounts of bandwidth to many different customers and applications. DWDM is a vehicle for providing that bandwidth.

SONET/SDH Applications

Optical networks can be deployed in several different ways. For the purpose of this chapter, the two most basic configurations are discussed. First and foremost, optical networks can be deployed in a point-to-point application. Figure 14-19 shows the different icons that identify protected or unprotected fiber-optic cabling. That same figure contains two icons — protected and unprotected fiber.

Figure 14-19 *Optical Point-to-Point Configuration*

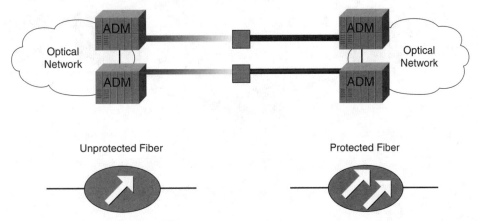

When you hear someone talk about protected versus unprotected fiber, they are talking about whether the fiber connection is redundant or not. Basically, unprotected fiber is a single fiber that when lost, causes a network outage. For this reason, the likelihood of you finding an unprotected fiber in a production network is not good at all. Protected fibers are fibers that if lost, can be rerouted through the network over a set of redundant fibers. The redundant fibers are typically dormant until used by the network. The function of failing over to a good fiber is known as automatic protection switching (APS). Point-to-point connections are best used in long-haul transport of optical signals.

The most typical deployment of fiber-optic networks in a local area is that of optical rings. A ring is exactly as it sounds, a ring of SONET or SDH devices connected into a fiber network so that the topology forms a closed loop. Figure 14-20 shows multiple access points into a basic optical ring configuration. Most devices in a SONET/SDH ring have interfaces to other network segments, thereby allowing communication between ring and non-ring nodes. Each unit has two ports connected in and out of the SONET/SDH ring. These two ports are typically referred to as East and West, but they just represent the ingress and egress locations in each optical device.

Figure 14-20 *Optical Ring Configuration*

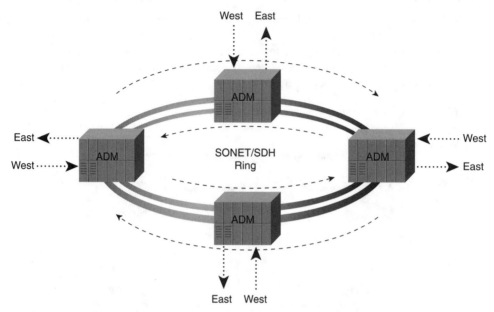

Rings are typically deployed over at least two pairs of fibers and can be deployed with more depending on the level of redundancy that is required. The redundant fibers are deployed as counter-rotating rings with the active ring typically rotating clockwise. This redundancy feature is also known as a *self-healing ring*.

Self-healing, ring-based network topologies can be deployed in one of two main ways:

- Line protection switched
- Path protection switched

Line Protection Switched

The bidirectional line-switched ring (BLSR) is the topology used in line protection switching. A BLSR is characterized as a ring in which traffic is transmitted bidirectionally during normal operation and is also known as a *duplex transmission system*. A BLSR normally operates on two fibers, but uses both for bidirectional transmission. Figure 14-21 shows the operational flow path for a basic deployed BLSR.

Figure 14-21 *BLSR Operation*

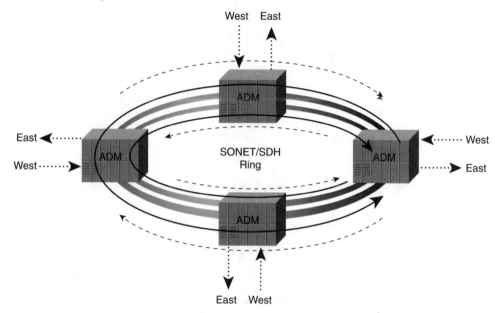

Because neither of the two fibers are allocated as the protection fiber, half of the bandwidth signal is reserved for a failover process. In other words, some of the channels are statically mapped as protection and in the event of a failover, take over operation. For this reason, you typically see about a 50 percent reduction in network bandwidth. This issue is avoided if four fibers are used for the BLSR. If four fibers are used, two are active and two are in a protection mode.

Path Protection Switched

A dual-fed unidirectional path switched ring (UPSR), or path protection switching can also be used. The UPSR uses a path layer indicator to facilitate the failover process. Two fibers typically run in the ring, and traffic flows on each in the opposite direction (dual-fed). The basic operation premise of this topology is that traffic flows in opposite directions around the network on the working and protection fibers at the same time. The same information reaches RTP, but from different nodes. Figure 14-22 shows the operational flow path for a basic deployed UPSR.

Figure 14-22 *UPSR Operation*

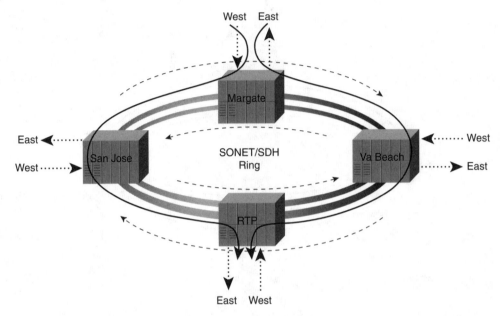

The UPSR format is also known as a 1:1 protection or 1:1 redundancy. During normal operation, two separate copies of the same information exist and either one can be selected as the received information at the destination node. In the event that a failure occurs, the path is switched from the Margate node to the alternate path and the traffic is not hindered at RTP. Figure 14-23 shows the traffic rerouting that occurs when a failure takes place on a UPSR.

If a failover does occur (path switch) the UPSR no longer operates in a ring topology, but rather becomes a bidirectional linear model between nodes. A failover can be caused by optical fiber failure, equipment problems, or high bit error rates (BERs). The bandwidth of the UPSR is shared between all devices in the ring. During the detection of a failover event, an alarm signal is generated at the path level (even if the failure is a line problem). Upon receipt of the alarm indication signal (AIS), the receiving node automatically selects the alternate path as the active path and continues to operate.

Figure 14-23 *UPSR Failure Operation*

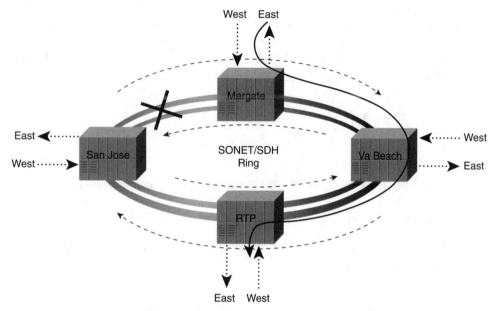

Summary

Synchronous technology has emerged to become the most prolific telecommunication technology on the market today. The initial drafts of SONET were based on a technology called SYNTRAN, which basically transmits DS3 signals in a synchronous format. The timing in the synchronous network distinguishes it from all other mediums because of its accuracy. The definition of synchronous means that all timing can be traced back to a single time source.

Most timing in synchronous networks is derived from atomic (cesium) clocks or satellite links to maintain a high efficiency on network synchronization. The basic timing sources are based on Stratum levels that are designated 1 to 4. The most accurate of the Stratum clocks is the Stratum 1, which can go for 70+ days without a clock slip. Stratum 4 is the least accurate and is not deployed in SONET and SDH networks because of its inability to provide adequate timing. The minimum clocking source recommended for SONET networks is between a Stratum 4E and Stratum 3.

Service providers typically deploy BITS timing systems within their facilities to maintain a single timing source. The BITS system allows for one timing source input for a building, and then provides timing to all other sources in the building infrastructure.

SONET is the North American designation for the optical network. There are two references, one logical and one physical. The logical designation for SONET links is a STS signal and the physical is an OC signal. The primary signal is the STS-1 and it has a bandwidth rate of 51.84 Mbps. Every higher order signal is a direct multiplication of the STS-1 signal. For example, an OC-768 is 768 iterations of the STS-1 signal. In turn, each STS-1 transports a single DS3 or multiple lower-level digital signals in paths called VTs.

SDH is based on many of the same principles as SONET, but the terminology is different. The SDH hierarchy is based on a STM instead of a STS. One of the major differences is that SDH begins at a bandwidth rate of 155 Mbps (STM-1), which is equivalent to an STS-3 in the SONET network. An STM-0 signal does exist (STS-1 equivalent), but it is not deployed as a discrete entity within the network.

One of the benefits of SONET and SDH is that signals can be accessed without demultiplexing the signal. This is possible because SONET and SDH are based on what is called byte-interleaved technology. Asynchronous multiplexing (DS3 muxing), interleaves at the bit level and thus must be demultiplexed before you can access any of the lower level signals. SONET and SDH can provide direct access to signals, while adding and dropping more signals into the stream.

SONET and SDH can be deployed in channelized or unchannelized modes, or as a single pipe of bandwidth. This type of circuit is referred to as a concatenated signal and allows for access to the full bandwidth without any underlying VTs.

Optical network can be deployed in point-to-point configurations or in rings. For the most part, point-to-point deployments are reserved for long-haul transport of the synchronous signals, and rings are deployed in localized areas that require access for several different nodes.

Review Questions

Give the best answer to the following questions. The answers to these questions can be found in Appendix A, "Answers to Review Questions."

1 What is the function of an add/drop multiplexer?

_____

_____

_____

2 What is one basic difference between a BLSR and a UPSR?

_____

_____

_____

3 What is the purpose of the H1 and H2 bytes in the line overhead of a SONET/SDH frame?

_____

_____

_____

4 Why do SONET and SDH use byte-interleaved multiplexing?

_____

_____

_____

5 What is the purpose of the A bytes in the section overhead portion of the frame?

_____

_____

_____

6 For what is DWDM used?

_____

_____

_____

7 How would you interpret VC-4-16c?

_____

_____

_____

Answers to Review Questions

This appendix contains the answers for each chapter's "Review Questions" section. There is also an explanation included with each answer. The answers and explanations in this appendix represent the best possible answers to the questions, but note that alternative answers might be possible too.

Answers to Chapter 1 Review Questions

1. What is the main difference between analog and digital signal streams?

    a. Digital signal streams are immune to line problems such as crosstalk and attenuation.

    b. Digital communication is a continuous signal stream that contains a varying range of frequencies and amplitudes.

    c. Analog signal streams are composed of discrete values that can be transmitted as 1s or 0s.

    d. Analog signals are considered continuous signal streams and digital signals are discrete signals, which are commonly transmitted as 1s or 0s.

Answer: d.

Analog signals are considered continuous signal streams and digital signals are discrete signals, which are commonly transmitted as 1s or 0s.

a. Incorrect. Both digital and analog signal streams are sensitive to attenuation, crosstalk, and noise. These byproducts are associated with the given medium, and not necessarily the signal type itself.

b. Incorrect. Digital signal streams are composed of discrete signal states that are transmitted through the network.

c. Incorrect. Analog signal streams are continuous and they mimic sinusoidal waves.

2. Define the term frequency as it relates to an analog signal.

Answer: Frequency is the number of cycles that an analog waveform goes through in a second. Frequency is commonly measured in Hz, kHz, or MHz.

3. Given Figure A-1, what equipment (denoted by **X**) would you use to alleviate the attenuated analog signal?

Figure 1-12 *Analog Signal Regeneration*

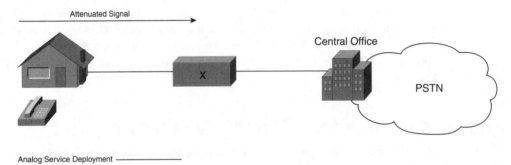

a. Subscriber Line Carrier

b. Network Interface Device

c. Amplifier

d. Modulator-demodulator

e. Digital repeater

Answer: c.

When you use an analog circuit, an amplifier is needed to amplify the signal. Remember that the line noise is also amplified.

a. Incorrect. An SLC deploys copper pairs to multiple subscribers by using one or more high-bandwidth links as communication to the CO.

b. Incorrect. An NID separates the telco's portion of the circuit from the subscriber's portion.

d. Incorrect. A modem commonly communicates with the Internet. Its function is to convert the unipolar digital signal from the computer into an analog signal for transmission through the network.

e. Incorrect. A repeater regenerates an attenuated digital signal. Instead of amplifying the signal, it is completely stripped down, regenerated, and retransmitted.

4. Which of the following items causes crosstalk on a circuit?

   a. Wires in a pair of wires that are untwisted too far from the connector head

   b. Nicks in wire cladding of adjacent wires

   c. Loose connections on either end of a suspected cable

   d. All of the above

Answer: d.

It's important to remember that many things that cause crosstalk have to do with the integrity of the cable and its connectors. Remember that crosstalk is a type of noise that gets worse with frequency, but lessens with distance.

5. At which locations within the local loop can you find a device that is GR-303-CORE compliant?

   a. NID

   b. IDLC

   c. CO

   d. ISDN

Answer: b. and c.

Because the GR-303-CORE standards describe the standards on communication between IDLCs and the CO's switch, both ends must have equipment that is compliant to the specifications.

a. Incorrect. The NID is an interface between the service provider and the subscriber.

d. Incorrect. Although ISDN is a service that can be provided through GR-303-compliant SLCs, it is not a specific device that is placed on the network.

Answers to Chapter 2 Review Questions

1. What is the main difference between CAS and CCS Signaling?

   a. CAS is logically in-band but physically out-of-band.

   b. CCS isn't intrusive to the data, and it is considered in-band.

   c. CAS is considered in-band signaling, and it is intrusive to the data.

   d. There is no difference between them.

Answer: c.

CAS signaling is in-band signaling, which is intrusive to the data. CCS is out-of-band signaling, but it can be physically in-band and logically out-of-band.

a. Incorrect. You wouldn't be logically in-band if you were physically out-of-band.

b. Incorrect. CCS isn't intrusive to the data, but it is not considered in-band signaling.

d. Incorrect. If this were true, this chapter would be a whole lot easier.

2. What are the three main SS7 network nodes that were discussed in this chapter?

Answer: SSP, STP, and SCP.

3. Which geographic region does the U.S. fall under in the ITU point code structure?

   a. 1

   b. 4

   c. 5

   d. 3

   e. None of the above. ANSI point codes are used.

Answer: d.

The United States falls under the SANC range of 3-020 to 3-059.

a. Incorrect. 1 is a reserved number that is not used.

b. Incorrect. 4 is the geographic designation of the Middle East and Asia.

c. Incorrect. 5 is the geographic designation of South Asia, Australia, and New Zealand.

e. Incorrect. Although the United States does have its own standard for point codes, ITU point codes are used when international communication is required.

4. What is the purpose of a C-link?

   a. It connects a SSP to a SSP.

   b. It connects mated pairs of STPs.

   c. It connects devices in different levels of the hierarchy.

   d. It connects a SSP to something similar to a STP.

Answer: b.

Cross links connect the two STPs in a mated pair. This link allows STPs to have a link between them in case of a failover procedure.

a. Incorrect. This is the definition of a F-Link.

c. Incorrect. This is the definition of a D-Link.

d. Incorrect. This is the definition of an A-Link.

5. Which of the following timers have to do with congestion?

    a. T2

    b. T6

    c. T3

    d. T5

    e. T4

Answers: b. and d.

T5 is the congestion timer, which is started when SIBs begin transmission, and T6 is the remote congestion guard timer. With T6, the remote signaling point sets this timer when it starts receiving the LSSUs with SIB set.

a. Incorrect. This timer is the initial alignment timer used in the alignment process.

c. Incorrect. T3 is the timer in the alignment process in which the decision is made on what kind of proving is done.

e. Incorrect. T4 is the proving timer.

6. Which layer in the SS7 stack do point codes operate at?

    a. MTP1

    b. MTP4

    c. MTP2

    d. MTP3

Answer: d.

MTP3 along with SCCP is roughly equivalent to the OSI model's network layer (L3).

a. Incorrect. MTP1 is responsible for the electrical and mechanical aspects of the signaling link.

b. Incorrect. There is no MTP4 per say. After MTP3, everything else is considered upper layer.

c. Incorrect. MTP2 is responsible for the reliable delivery of MTP3 messages, roughly equivalent to the data-link layer of the OSI model (L2).

7. What does the following icon stand for?

   a. SSP and STP

   b. STP

   c. SRF

   d. SSP

   e. NAP

Answer: a.

This image illustrates the SSP with integrated STP functionality.

b. through e. Incorrect. None of these elements are referred to with this icon.

8. What is the recommended percentage of traffic that you should configure a signaling link to carry?

Answer: 40 percent. The reason for this is so that if the signaling link's traffic is rerouted, the link taking over for it only has an 80 percent load.

9. Identify the device that the following definition is discussing: This device functions much the same as a SCP, but it is directly connected to a SSP over a high-speed link. They can provide faster communication with SSPs, but the actual messaging remains the same as is used with SSP to SCP communication.

   a. NAP

   b. AD

   c. IP

   d. STP

Answer: b.

This is the definition of an Adjunct (AD).

a. Incorrect. NAPs provide CCF and CCAF functions within the IN infrastructure. NAPs do not have any direct access to SCPs, but do have the ability to identify calls that are destined for services. In such cases, the NAP must route the call to a SSP with SCP access.

c. Incorrect. The IP contains the SRF. This device is responsible for DTMF digit collection, voice recognition, and Interactive Voice Response (IVR) services.

d. Incorrect. The STP is used as a type of packet switch to route calls throughout the SS7 network.

10. What is one thing you should check if your alignment is failing at the T4 proving timer?

Answer: Check to make sure that your point codes match what the telco has allocated for you and the SLC that you should be using.

Answers to Chapter 3 Review Questions

1. Which of the following are examples of the difference between analog and digital communication (choose two)?

   a. The term frequency only applies to digital communication.

   b. The term bit rate only applies to digital communication.

   c. The quality of an analog signal is generally better than that of a digital signal.

   d. The quality of a digital signal is generally better than that of an analog signal.

   e. Circuits, and sending and receiving equipment, are identical in analog and digital technologies.

Answer: b. and d.

The word bit is a contraction of binary digit (0 or 1), that means digital technology is afoot. It is generally regarded that digital transmission and storage of information is of higher quality than the analog alternative.

2. Which of the following is *not* a stage in the analog-to-digital conversion process?

   a. Sampling

   b. Encoding

   c. Filtering

    d. Pulse conversion

    e. Quantizing

Answer: d.

Pulse conversion does not exist in this case and is not a stage in analog-to-digital conversion.

3. What is the earliest stage in the conversion process at which the signal technically can be considered digital?

    a. Sampling

    b. Quantizing

    c. Filtering

    d. Encoding

    e. Pulse conversion

Answer: b.

Remember, pulse conversion is not an accurate term. The quantized signal might only be made up of 256 discrete values, and although this is not appropriate for transmission or storage, it is the first step toward producing the bit stream that is.

4. Which of the following ITU-T recommendations covers PCM in general?

    a. G.711

    b. G.721

    c. G.726

    d. G.729

Answer: a.

ITU-T Recommendation G.711 specifies the four phases for the conversion of an analog source signal into a digital bit stream (PCM).

5. Which of the following advanced processes adapts the quantizing scale to more closely match the wider or narrower variation between adjacent pulses?

    a. PCM

    b. DPCM

    c. ADPCM

    d. DM

    e. CVSD

    f. SB-ADPCM

Answer: c.

ADPCM is adaptive, which means that the quantizing scale changes, based on the variation (differential) between subsequent sample amplitudes.

Answers to Chapter 4 Review Questions

  1. How many wires do you use on a DDS circuit?

    a. 2

    b. 4

    c. 6

    d. 8

Answer: b.

A DDS circuit uses two pairs of wires for a total of 4.

a. Incorrect. DDS circuits use two pairs of wires, not two wires. In some proprietary SW56 applications it is possible to run over a single pair, but it isn't common.

c. and d. Incorrect. These values are too large for DDS circuits.

  2. Which pins does a DDS circuit use?

    a. 4, 5

    b. 2, 3

    c. 1, 2, 7, 8

    d. 5, 6, 7, 8

Answer: c.

DDS uses pins 1, 2, 7, and 8 for communication.

a. Incorrect. Some technologies such as ISDN use pins 4 and 5, but not DDS.

b. and d. Incorrect. Both of these pin assignments are incorrect. You can use pins 2 and 3 for analog service on a RJ-11 plug, but you do not use 5, 6, 7, and 8 for a specific connector.

3. What is the function of an OCU-DP?

    a. To terminate the DDS circuit and protect the customer's equipment from power surges

    b. To multiplex 24 DS0s into a DS-1 signal

    c. To convert the unipolar signal of a computer into a bipolar balanced signal

    d. To provide the four-wire DDS interface to the customer

Answer: d.

The purpose of the OCU-DP is to provide a four-wire DDS circuit to the customer's premise. It resides in a T1 channel bank, and is multiplexed into a DS-1 signal.

a. Incorrect. This is the definition of a CSU.

b. Incorrect. This the definition of a T1 channel bank or T1 multiplexer. Both of those devices refer to the same function and many times they are the same unit.

c. Incorrect. This is the definition of a DSU.

4. Which line coding do you use on a DDS circuit?

    a. CMI

    b. B3ZS

    c. B8ZS

    d. HDB3

    e. AMI

Answer: e.

You use AMI on DDS circuits.

a. Incorrect. Coded Mark Inversion (CMI) line coding is found on Japanese J1 circuits.

b. Incorrect. B3ZS is found on T3 circuits.

c. Incorrect. B8ZS is found on T1 circuits.

d. Incorrect. HDB3 is found on E1 circuits.

5. What is the function of a multi-junction unit (MJU)?

Answer: An MJU provides a point-to-multipoint DDS service to customers. It resides in the CO along with the OCU-DP. It does not provide a way of deterring one device from using all the bandwidth, as that must be handled by the customer's equipment.

6. Which of the following is not a possible DDS loop rate?

    a. 2.4 kbps

    b. 57.6 kbps

    c. 19.2 kbps

    d. 9.6 kbps

    e. 4.8 kbps

Answer: b.

All the listed loop rates are valid except for 57.6 kbps. 57.6 kbps is actually an asynchronous rate, and DDS is a synchronous network.

7. How is an idle code coded on a 19.2-kbps DDS circuit?

    a. BBBX0V

    b. X0XXBB

    c. 00XXBB

    d. B0BB0V

Answer: a.

This coding represents the transmission of an idle code on a 19.2-kbps DDS circuit.

b. through d. Incorrect. None of these codes are valid on a 19.2-kbps DDS circuit.

8. Which of the following is the maximum loop rate of a DDS circuit, including overhead?

    a. 56 kbps

    b. 64 kbps

    c. 72 kbps

    d. 96 kbps

Answer: c.

The maximum loop rate of a DDS circuit with overhead is 72 kbps. Even though you only use up to 64 kbps, the DDS circuit loop rate has at least 8 kbps overhead.

a. Incorrect. This is a valid loop rate for a DDS circuit.

b. Incorrect. This is a valid loop rate for a DDS circuit.

d. Incorrect. This loop rate is more than the maximum DDS bandwidth rate.

9.   What is the main difference between a DDS circuit with a secondary channel and a DDS circuit without a secondary channel (other than the channel itself)?

Answer: DDS circuits with a secondary channel are framed circuits. It is important to point out that 64-kbps DDS rates are framed even though they do not use the secondary channel.

10.   What is the main benefit of SW56 technology over DDS?

Answer: Switched 56 technology saves the customer money because they are only billed for the usage of the circuit (while a call is active) on top of a small monthly fee.

Answers to Chapter 5 Review Questions

1.   How many DS-0s make up a T1 circuit?

   a.   16

   b.   24

   c.   32

   d.   30

Answer: b.

There are 24 DS-0s in a T1 circuit. The other numbers relate to E1 technology, where there are 32 channels in the E1 circuit, of which 30 are always for user data. Channel 16 in an E1 circuit can be used for signaling.

2.   What is the difference between AMI and B8ZS?

Answer: Although both are line-coding schemes, AMI limits bandwidth per channel to 56 kbps, and B8ZS allows clear-channel, 64-kbps transmission.

3.   What is another term for the alarm indication signal?

   a.   Red alarm

    b. Yellow alarm

    c. Blue alarm

    d. CFA

Answer: c.

AIS is also referred to as keep-alive. CFA refers to red and yellow alarms, which are not the same as the AIS.

  4. How many bits are in a frame, including the F-bit?

    a. 191

    b. 192

    c. 193

    d. 194

Answer: c.

There are 192 bits without the F-bit. 193 includes the F-bit, and 191 and 194 are not possible answers.

  5. How many frames are in a D4 superframe? How many in an extended superframe?

    a. 1,#2

    b. 12,#12

    c. 12,#1

    d. 192,#384

    e. 12,#24

Answer: e.

The D4 superframe is made up of 12 standard T1 frames, and the ESF groups 24 such frames into an extended superframe. The number 192 represents the number of bits in a single frame.

  6. What are the FDL bits used for in ESF formatting?

Answer: The FDL bits provide 4 kbps of non-user bandwidth, for use in communicating between devices, for sending loop codes, and for yellow alarm signaling.

7. What are the CRC-6 bits used for in ESF formatting?

Answer: The CRC-6 bits are used as a checksum between the transmitting device and the receiving device, which allows error detection beyond the capability of the D4 format.

8. In the D4 superframe, what are the two types of F-bits and their uses?

Answer: They are the terminal framing and signaling framing bits. The terminal framing bits detect alignment and the superframe boundary. The signaling framing bits identify where RBS-frames 6 and 12 are located within the superframe.

9. What condition is declared when two out of four consecutive F-bits are found to be in error?

    a. OOF

    b. LOS

    c. BERT

    d. SES

Answer: a.

An OOF condition is declared when two out of any four consecutive F-bits are in error.

b. Incorrect. LOS is declared after 10 seconds of SES.

c. Incorrect. BERT is the test performed to count bit errors.

d. Incorrect. An SES indicates that 320 errors are counted in the space of one second, which could theoretically involve F-bits.

10. What does a node that is in red alarm or that is receiving the keep-alive signal attempt to do?

Answer: It attempts to send out a signal that is intended to place the other end of the circuit in yellow alarm. If the entire circuit is down, this is fruitless.

Answers to Chapter 6 Review Questions

1. How many DS0s are included in an E1 circuit?

    a. 16

    b. 24

    c. 32

    d. 30

Answer: c.

Remember that there are 32 DS0s. 30 or 31 are for bearer traffic, and the other one or two are reserved for signaling and framing. 31 is not listed as a choice, but it is also correct.

a. Incorrect. There are 16 frames in a multiframe.

b. Incorrect. There are 24 DS0s in a T1 circuit.

d. Incorrect. There are 30 or 31 useable DS0s in an E1 circuit, but not 32 because the first timeslot can never be reclaimed for bearer traffic.

  2. What similar function do B8ZS and HDB3 serve?

Answer: They both insert a unique bipolar violation into the signaling stream in the case of a string of 0s. This is to prevent a loss of synchronization due to a lack of line voltage.

  3. What is the function of the third bit in odd frames of NO-CRC-4 framing?

Answer: To provide transport for alarm detection.

  4. How does a J1 circuit differ from a T1 circuit?

Answer: Several ways. 1. There is no option for SF-type framing. You must use ESF-type framing because it allows for a CRC check, if necessary. 2. J1 circuits use CMI for line coding.

  5. If you use a Multifrequency signaling type, such as R2, and a digit is collected with a single tone instead of two; what happens?

Answer: Two tones are required. If it detects only one tone, the receiving end flags it as an error and requests the retransmission of that digit.

  6. Name two signaling formats that allow you to reclaim TS16 for bearer traffic.

Answer: QSIG, ISDN, SS7, or a proprietary signaling format.

  7. How does CMI alleviate the 1s density issues that are commonly associated with AMI line coding?

Answer: CMI is not susceptible to the 1s density issues such as AMI because even binary 0s have a voltage value. Because 0s have a value during the coding process, the receiving equipment is not capable of losing PLL.

  8. What is the maximum cable distance allowed without a digital regenerator on an E1 circuit?

Answer: 4800 ft.

Answers to Chapter 7 Review Questions

1. How many T1s are found in an unchannelized T3?

Answer: There are no T1s in an unchannelized circuit. This is a trick question. Remember that you must have a channelized circuit to split off any of the smaller circuits.

2. True or False. T3 circuits are generally considered to be synchronous, similar to T1s.

Answer: False. The T3 circuits employ an asynchronous multiplexing scheme, and although T1 circuits are synchronous, their relationship to each other is asynchronous.

3. How many 0s must be transmitted in succession before HDB3 transmits a bipolar violation?

    a. 4

    b. 1

    c. 3

    d. 5

Answer: a. Remember that HDB3 (used on E3 circuits) transmits a unique bipolar violation in the event that four consecutive 0s are detected.

b. Incorrect. If this were the case, your circuit would be one big BPV. c. Incorrect. This is the number of 0s that B3ZS needs before transmitting a BPV. d. Incorrect. This is not correct.

4. How many E1 circuits are multiplexed into an E2? E3?

Answer: 4 E1s in an E2, and 16 in an E3. Remember, with the exception of the DS0s, the multiplexing is always in a value of 4.

5. What was the technology SYNTRAN the basis for?

Answer: SYNTRAN was the basis for what is now SONET/SDH.

6. What is the function of a P-bit in a DS3 frame?

Answer: The P-bits function as a way for monitoring the performance of the circuit. The continuous transmission of DS3 frames allots the P-bits for a parity check on the previous frame. In other words, the value that is stated in the current frame is the parity information from the last frame. The values are the same on both bits, either 0 or 1.

7. What is the approximate cable length limit (in feet) of the coaxial cable used for T3 connections?

Answer: 450.

8. How many bits are in an E3 frame?

Answer: 1536 for a structured E3, 4296 for unstructured.

Answers to Chapter 8 Review Questions

1. At which layer of the ISDN stack does Q.931 operate?

Answer: Layer 3, and it is roughly equivalent to the Network Layer of the OSI model.

2. What type of device is commonly found between the S and T interfaces?

Answer: An NT2.

3. How does ISDN BRI service provide both transmit and receive on a single pair of wires?

Answer: Echo cancellation.

4. On a Cisco router, what command would give you the following output: 0x8090A2? What does it mean?

Answer: debug isdn q931. It is the type of call capability that is transmitted through the bearer capability IE. In hex, this means that the call is G.711 μ-law Speech.

5. If your local CO does not have the required facilities to provide you with ISDN service, what might have to be done?

Answer: The service provider might have to FX your circuit through a CO that does have the proper facilities available. If a FX is not possible, you might not be able to get ISDN service.

6. If you are not sure that your BRI service has been connected, what can you do as a quick test to verify connectivity?

Answer: Plug an analog phone into the ISDN jack, and listen for a clicking noise.

7. Which of the following messages is not used during the ISDN call setup phase?

    a. Connect

    b. Ringing

    c. Setup

    d. Call Proceeding

Answer: b.

Ringing is not a message type associated with ISDN setup procedures. The proper message in this case is Alerting.

8. If a call needs to traverse the SS7 network, which message type would the Connect message likely be converted into?

    a. IAM

    b. ACM

    c. RLC

    d. ANM

    e. REL

Answer: d. The ANM, or Answer Message, is equivalent to the purpose of the Connect message. This acknowledges that the call has been connected from end-to-end and that the voice path is now available.

9. How many pairs of wires does an ISDN PRI circuit use?

Answer: Two. Remember that PRI is merely ISDN deployed over T1 or E1 facilities. Therefore, the physical layer attributes of those technologies should be observed.

10. Which of the following messages is sent first during a Q.921 negotiation between ISDN devices?

    a. UA

    b. SAPI

    c. RRp

    d. Setup

    e. SABME

Answer: e.

A SABME instructs the remote end to reset the circuit to a default level to begin Layer-2 negotiations. The SABME must be replied to with an UA.

a. Incorrect. This message is sent in response to the SABME.

c. Incorrect. This is the Receiver Ready poll sent to verify that connection integrity still exists.

d. Incorrect. A Setup message is used by Q.931 to start a call through the ISDN network.

Answers to Chapter 9 Review Questions

1. On what technology is Frame Relay largely based?

Answer: ISDN.

The specifications and operation of Frame Relay are similar to that of ISDN, and are based off of protocols such as LAPD.

2. Which of the following companies was not a part of the original Gang of Four?

   a. Cisco Systems

   b. Digital Equipment Corporation

   c. Nortel Networks

   d. IBM

   e. Stratacom

Answer: d.

IBM was not a member of the original Gang of Four.

3. What is the CIR used for on Frame Relay circuits?

Answer: The CIR identifies the amount of bandwidth that the service provider can guarantee that your circuit receives at all times. The CIR is a large part of the service provider service level agreement (SLA).

4. What type of circuit is Frame Relay?

Answer: This is somewhat of a trick question. Frame Relay is a Layer-2 specification that works on several different types of circuits. It is not defined as a circuit type itself, but as a set of protocols that can operate on DDS, FE1/E1, and FT1/T1. The industry uses the term virtual circuit to refer to the fact that Frame Relay does not specify the physical circuit in use.

5. What is the main difference between a PVC and a SVC?

Answer: A PVC is a logical channel that is configured throughout the network, and is not available on a call-by-call basis, similar to SVCs. SVCs can switch calls through the network in several different directions and the FR switch makes the decision during the connection setup sequence.

6. What are the three bits in the Frame Relay header that manage congestion control?

Answer: FECN, BECN, and DE.

7. What do you use LMI for and what are the three standards in use today?

Answer: You use LMI for PVC status monitoring, usually across the UNI, between the initial access device (which is DTE) and the ingress Frame Relay switch. The three protocols are LMI, Annex A, and Annex D, which are based on specifications FRF 1.1, ITU-T Q.933 Annex A, and ANSI T1.617 Annex D, respectively.

8. What do you call the numerical value that identifies the virtual circuit between two devices? What is the term that refers to this number, which means it only makes sense between two devices?

Answer: The numerical value is the DLCI and it is said to be locally significant.

9. What is the purpose of Inverse ARP?

Answer: Inverse ARP requests the protocol address (such as, IP) for a device at the other end of the virtual circuit, for which the local DLCI is already known.

10. What does the Frame Relay Forum call its documents that are similar to standards?

Answer: They are referred to as Implementation Agreements (IAs).

Answers to Chapter 10 Review Questions

1. What is the difference between UNI and NNI?

Answer: A UNI interface connects an ATM endpoint to an ATM switch, but an NNI interface connects two ATM switches together.

2. Why are there more available VPIs in an NNI header?

Answer: There is no GFC in the header of NNI, which leaves four more bits for the VPI field.

3. What do you call a cell that is destined for one connection but because of an error has been delivered to a different connection?

Answer: A misinserted cell.

4. For what technology was ATM originally designed to be the transport system?

   a. Broadband ISDN

   b. Frame relay

   c. SONET

   d. T3

Answer: a.
ATM was designed for B-ISDN, but it has begun to evolve on its own.

b. Incorrect. Frame Relay is another Layer-2 technology that can be deployed over many different physical interfaces. ATM and Frame Relay have many similarities, but two main differences are that ATM is generally found on higher bandwidth links and ATM has a fixed cell size.

c. and d. Incorrect. Both of these technologies are physical-layer and act as a connection medium for technologies such as ATM, not the other way around.

5. How large is an ATM cell?

   a. 53 bytes

   b. 24 bits

   c. 53 octets

   d. 48 octets

Answer: a. and c. Both bytes and octets refer to a size of 8 bits. Technically both are correct.

b. Incorrect. This is an arbitrary number, but is most commonly found associated with technologies such as IP or SS7.

d. Incorrect. This is the size of the ATM payload without the header. 48-octet payload + 5-octet header = 53-octet cell.

6. Which of the following ranges of VCI cannot be used for standard addressing when the VPI is 0?

   a. 0 – 32

   b. 32 – 63

   c. 0 – 31

   d. 5 – 36

   e. 20 – 35

Answer: c.
0 - 31 are reserved VCI values, and cannot be used. a., b., d., e. Incorrect. These value ranges are not completely reserved.

7. What is the function of the SAR sublayer?

Answer: SAR accepts SDUs from the CS and segments them into 48-octet SAR PDUs that are handed to the ATM layer, where a five-octet head is added and a cell produced. The opposite procedure also occurs.

8. What would be the best AAL type to handle compressed video-conferencing traffic?

    a. AAL0

    b. AAL1

    c. AAL2

    d. AAL3/4

    e. AAL5

Answer: c.
AAL2 employs mechanisms that allow it to send partially filled payloads, accommodating the timing requirement of the source, along with its variable traffic rate, and to pass along the compression algorithm that is being used by the source.

9. What is the difference between traffic shaping and traffic policing?

Answer: They are both methods of controlling network access by monitoring how much information is being sent to the network by the connection, both also possibly resulting in the tagging of cells with a CLP=1 status, but traffic shaping is performed by the subscriber equipment, and policing is performed by network elements. Policing is also known as UPC.

10. What are the two uses of the HEC field on the ATM cell header?

Answer: The HEC allows the detection of cell-boundary delineation and single-bit error correction or multiple-bit error detection.

Answers to Chapter 11 Review Questions

1. What were some of the major motivating factors for the development of SMDS?

Answer: The RBOCs were looking for a data driven, connectionless service offering. B-ISDN standardization was moving at a snails pace. Further, the rapid deployment of client/server applications and networks were driving an increasing need for high-speed LAN-to-LAN connectivity.

2. What are some common Layer-3 protocols that are supported over SMDS?

Answer: All protocols that use LLC can be carried over SMDS.

3. At what layer of the SMDS protocol stack does addressing occur? Segmentation and reassembly?

Answer: Addressing occurs at Layer 3. Segmentation and reassembly occur at Layer 2.

4. What are the five SMDS access classes? Why does E3 technology only support four?

Answer: The five SMDS access-classes are as follows:

Access class 1—4 Mbps

Access class 2—10 Mbps

Access class 3—16 Mbps

Access class 4—25 Mbps

Access class 5—34 Mbps

E3 has a maximum bitrate of 34 Mbps. Because the access-class dictates L3 PDU bandwidth, and accounting for SAR and PLCP overhead, the maximum L3 PDU bitrate over E3 is ~ 25 Mbps.

5. For what is the BETag used?

Answer: To prevent two SIP L3 PDUs from becoming merged if both the last L2_PDU of one L3_PDU and the first L2_PDU of the next L3_PDU are lost.

6. What is a message ID? What purpose does it serve?

Answer: Message IDs identify the L2 PDUs (cells) that comprise an L3 PDU. Message IDs are used in SMDS routing to create a temporary state in the SMDS Switching System for the direction of L2 PDUs toward their destination. Because only the first L2 PDU has the L3 destination address, a switch creates a temporary switch entry based on the MID of the BOM L2 PDU that contains the destination address. It then forwards all L2 PDUs with the same MID toward the destination, until either: the EOM is received and forwarded, or, the MID page timer expires.

7. Why are SMDS L3_PDUs so large?

Answer: To accommodate the existing LAN MTUs of the time. FDDI and Token Ring have large MTUs (4400+ bytes). Token Ring MTUs on 16 Mbps rings can exceed this value.

8. What is the purpose of DXI?

Answer: DXI is used as a carrier protocol for SIP L3 PDUs either between a router and an SMDSU, or a router and an SMDS switch. DXI is similar to HDLC, with the addition of a heartbeat polling mechanism.

9. What are some common problems encountered on SMDS interfaces? How can you tell if the problem is DXI related or circuit related?

Answer: Some problems include: improperly provisioned circuit, mismatched CRC values, mismatched access-classes, bad hardware and software, a dirty line, an overextended DS3 cable, and so on.

On a Cisco router, DXI problems are generally identified by lost heartbeat polls and high CRC errors.

Answers to Chapter 12 Review Questions

1. 1.What are the encoding methods used for DSL?

Answer: Quadrature Amplitude Modulation (QAM), Carrierless Amplitude and Phase Modulation (CAP), and Discrete Multi-Tone Modulation (DMT).

2. What are the three items that characterize analog carrier signals?

Answer: Amplitude, frequency, and phase.

3. What frequency range does voice use in POTS?

Answer: 0–4 kHz.

4. Into how many subchannels does DMT divide the bandwidth?

Answer: 256.

5. What is a bridged tap?

Answer: A bridged tap is an unterminated telephone loop.

6. What is a loading coil and why are they used?

Answer: A loading coil is an inductor that is placed parallel to the telephone loop to extend the distance of a voice circuit.

7. What is a POTS splitter?

Answer: A POTS splitter is a low-pass filter that blocks out the DSL signal but allows the voice signal to pass.

8. What is NEXT?

Answer: Near-end crosstalk occurs when adjacent signals induce energy and error into the primary signal.

9. What are the five methods of transport encapsulation for DSL?

Answer: RFC 1483 bridging, RFC 1483 bridging with RBE, RFC 1483 routing, PPPoA, and PPPoE.

10. What is an NSP?

Answer: A network service provider (NSP) is part of the DSL architecture that provides services to the customer over the DSL network.

Answers to Chapter 13 Review Questions

1. What sort of framing is used in DOCSIS-based cable IP networks? What other devices in the cable network use the same framing?

Answer: DOCSIS networks use MPEG-2 framing to transmit IP packets. MPEG-2 also transmits digital video signals, digital audio, and other data. More information on MPEG-2 is at mpeg.telecomitalialab.com.

2. What types of modulation transmit data upstream and downstream? Why is one type of modulation preferable to another?

Answer: DOCSIS 1.0 and 1.1 use QPSK and 16 QAM to transmit data upstream. 64 QAM and 256 QAM are used in the downstream. Lower modulation profiles provide greater resilience to noise and interference but offer lower throughput.

3. What are the requirements for cable plant quality? Why are they important? What factors lead to poor plant quality?

Answer: Specific requirements are detailed in Table 13-2. When a cable plant does not meet these requirements service quality is impacted, often severely. Factors that lead to poor plant quality can include bad connectors, faulty amplifiers, corroded cabling, fiber node clipping, and many others described in the section Common Plant Issues.

4. Which provisioning servers are required by the DOCSIS specification? What value do they provide?

Answer: DHCP, TOD, and TFTP servers allow cable modems to receive network configuration information, time information, and DOCSIS parameters. Without these servers and the information they supply modems cannot register and come online.

5. What is the difference between DOCSIS and Euro-DOCSIS?

Answer: The primary difference is the supported channel width. DOCSIS supports a 6-MHz wide channel and Euro-DOCSIS supports an 8-MHz wide channel.

6. Which features of DOCSIS 1.1 improve upstream signaling efficiency?

Answer: DOCSIS 1.1 offers concatenation, fragmentation, UGS, UGS-AD, PHS, and other upstream signaling efficiencies.

7. What are the differences between DOCSIS 1.0 and DOCSIS 1.1?

Answer: DOCSIS 1.0 provides for the configuration of a single class of service per cable modem. DOCSIS 1.1 defines a set of SFIDs, each of which can be assigned its own class of service. There are several other differences, too, defined in the text.

8. How many cable modems can be connected to a single DOCSIS MAC domain? How many are desirable?

Answer: The maximum theoretical number supported is over 8100. However, in deployment scenarios somewhere between 200 and 600 modems per upstream is usually desirable. It is vital to understand throughput limitations, customer usage patterns, and other factors before this question can be answered satisfactorily.

Answers to Chapter 14 Review Questions

1. What is the function of an add/drop multiplexer?

Answer: The ADM can crossconnect and groom traffic at the DS1 or DS3 levels without the need to completely demultiplex the signal.

2. What is one basic difference between a BLSR and a UPSR?

Answer: A BLSR uses both fibers for bidirectional transport, and thus must reserve half of the bandwidth for failover applications. A UPSR uses one fiber for active transport, and one for protection.

3. What is the purpose of the H1 and H2 bytes in the line overhead of a SONET/SDH frame?

Answer: These two bytes are used together to form the SPE pointer in the header. H3 is used for positive or negative justification of the SPE that is floating within the frame.

4. Why do SONET and SDH use byte-interleaved multiplexing?

Answer: Byte-interleaved multiplexing allows for the access of lower level signals within a multiplex without the need to demultiplex the entire signal.

5. What is the purpose of the A bytes in the section overhead portion of the frame?

Answer: The A1 and A2 bytes form the frame alignment signal for the STS frame.

6. For what is DWDM used?

Answer: DWDM is a way of multiplexing multiple wavelengths of light streams over the same fiber to provide more efficient use of the facilities. DWDM is generally characterized as being able to multiplex at least 16 different wavelengths at the same time. Anything less is usually denoted as just WDM.

7. How would you interpret VC-4-16c?

Answer: The virtual container is a high order container (VC-4), and it is being transported over a concatenated STM-16.

Signaling Area Network Code (SANC) Designations

The table in this appendix shows SANC country designations

SANC	Country
2-000	Liechtenstein (Principality of)
2-001	Italy
2-002	Netherlands (Kingdom of the)
2-003	Italy
2-004	Greece
2-005	Greece
2-006	Netherlands (Kingdom of the)
2-007	Netherlands (Kingdom of the)
2-008	Netherlands (Kingdom of the)
2-009	Netherlands (Kingdom of the)
2-010	Netherlands (Kingdom of the)
2-011	Netherlands (Kingdom of the)
2-012	Belgium
2-013	Belgium
2-014	Belgium
2-015	Belgium
2-016	France
2-017	France
2-018	France

SANC	Country
2-019	France
2-020	France
2-021	France
2-022	France
2-023	France
2-024	Monaco (Principality of)
2-025	Austria
2-026	Austria
2-027	Spain
2-028	Spain
2-029	Spain
2-030	Spain
2-031	Spain
2-032	Hungary (Republic of)
2-033	Germany (Federal Republic of)
2-034	Germany (Federal Republic of)
2-035	Germany (Federal Republic of)
2-036	Germany (Federal Republic of)
2-037	Germany (Federal Republic of)
2-038	Germany (Federal Republic of)
2-039	Germany (Federal Republic of)
2-040	Yugoslavia (Federal Republic of)
2-041	Italy
2-042	Italy
2-043	Italy

SANC	Country
2-044	Italy
2-045	Italy
2-046	Italy
2-047	Italy
2-048	Italy
2-049	Italy
2-050	Italy
2-051	Italy
2-052	Romania
2-053	Switzerland (Confederation of)
2-054	Switzerland (Confederation of)
2-055	Switzerland (Confederation of)
2-056	Switzerland (Confederation of)
2-057	Switzerland (Confederation of)
2-058	Switzerland (Confederation of)
2-059	Switzerland (Confederation of)
2-060	Czech Republic
2-061	Switzerland (Confederation of)
2-062	Switzerland (Confederation of)
2-063	Switzerland (Confederation of)
2-064	Austria
2-065	Austria
2-066	Austria
2-067	Austria
2-068	United Kingdom of Great Britain and Northern Ireland

SANC	Country
2-069	United Kingdom of Great Britain and Northern Ireland
2-070	United Kingdom of Great Britain and Northern Ireland
2-071	United Kingdom of Great Britain and Northern Ireland
2-072	United Kingdom of Great Britain and Northern Ireland
2-073	United Kingdom of Great Britain and Northern Ireland
2-074	United Kingdom of Great Britain and Northern Ireland
2-075	United Kingdom of Great Britain and Northern Ireland
2-076	Denmark
2-077	Denmark
2-078	Denmark
2-079	Denmark
2-080	Sweden
2-081	Sweden
2-082	Sweden
2-083	Sweden
2-084	Norway
2-085	Norway
2-086	Norway
2-087	Norway
2-088	Finland
2-089	Finland
2-090	Finland
2-091	Finland
2-092	Estonia (Republic of)
2-093	Italy

SANC	Country
2-094	Italy
2-095	Italy
2-096	Latvia (Republic of)
2-097	Belgium
2-098	Belgium
2-099	Belgium
2-100	Russian Federation
2-101	Russian Federation
2-102	Russian Federation
2-103	Russian Federation
2-104	Russian Federation
2-105	Russian Federation
2-106	Russian Federation
2-107	Russian Federation
2-108	Russian Federation
2-109	Russian Federation
2-110	Russian Federation
2-111	Russian Federation
2-112	Russian Federation
2-113	Russian Federation
2-114	Russian Federation
2-115	Russian Federation
2-116	Russian Federation
2-117	Russian Federation
2-118	Russian Federation

SANC	Country
2-119	Russian Federation
2-120	Poland (Republic of)
2-121	Germany (Federal Republic of)
2-122	Germany (Federal Republic of)
2-123	Germany (Federal Republic of)
2-124	Germany (Federal Republic of)
2-125	Germany (Federal Republic of)
2-126	Germany (Federal Republic of)
2-127	Germany (Federal Republic of)
2-128	Germany (Federal Republic of)
2-129	Germany (Federal Republic of)
2-130	Germany (Federal Republic of)
2-131	Germany (Federal Republic of)
2-132	Gibraltar
2-133	Austria
2-134	Poland (Republic of)
2-135	Luxembourg
2-136	Portugal
2-137	Portugal
2-138	Portugal
2-139	Portugal
2-140	Luxembourg
2-141	Luxembourg
2-142	Netherlands (Kingdom of the)
2-144	Ireland

SANC	Country
2-145	Ireland
2-146	Ireland
2-147	United Kingdom of Great Britain and Northern Ireland
2-148	Iceland
2-149	France
2-150	France
2-151	France
2-152	Albania (Republic of)
2-153	United Kingdom of Great Britain and Northern Ireland
2-154	United Kingdom of Great Britain and Northern Ireland
2-155	United Kingdom of Great Britain and Northern Ireland
2-156	Malta
2-157	Italy
2-158	Italy
2-159	Italy
2-160	Cyprus (Republic of)
2-161	United Kingdom of Great Britain and Northern Ireland
2-162	United Kingdom of Great Britain and Northern Ireland
2-163	United Kingdom of Great Britain and Northern Ireland
2-164	United Kingdom of Great Britain and Northern Ireland
2-165	United Kingdom of Great Britain and Northern Ireland
2-166	United Kingdom of Great Britain and Northern Ireland
2-167	United Kingdom of Great Britain and Northern Ireland
2-168	Bulgaria (Republic of)
2-169	United Kingdom of Great Britain and Northern Ireland

SANC	Country
2-170	United Kingdom of Great Britain and Northern Ireland
2-171	Turkey
2-172	Turkey
2-173	Turkey
2-174	United Kingdom of Great Britain and Northern Ireland
2-175	United Kingdom of Great Britain and Northern Ireland
2-176	United Kingdom of Great Britain and Northern Ireland
2-177	United Kingdom of Great Britain and Northern Ireland
2-178	United Kingdom of Great Britain and Northern Ireland
2-179	United Kingdom of Great Britain and Northern Ireland
2-180	Croatia (Republic of)
2-181	Italy
2-182	Slovenia (Republic of)
2-183	Italy
2-184	San Marino (Republic of)
2-185	United Kingdom of Great Britain and Northern Ireland
2-186	United Kingdom of Great Britain and Northern Ireland
2-187	United Kingdom of Great Britain and Northern Ireland
2-188	United Kingdom of Great Britain and Northern Ireland
2-189	United Kingdom of Great Britain and Northern Ireland
2-190	United Kingdom of Great Britain and Northern Ireland
2-191	United Kingdom of Great Britain and Northern Ireland
2-192	Sweden
2-193	Sweden
2-194	Sweden

SANC	Country
2-195	Sweden
2-196	Andorra (Principality of)
2-197	Andorra (Principality of)
2-198	Netherlands (Kingdom of the)
2-200	Armenia (Republic of)
2-201	France
2-202	France
2-203	France
2-204	Belarus (Republic of)
2-205	Sweden
2-207	Italy
2-208	Georgia
2-209	United Kingdom of Great Britain and Northern Ireland
2-210	United Kingdom of Great Britain and Northern Ireland
2-214	Ukraine
2-217	Denmark
2-218	Bosnia and Herzegovina
2-219	Bosnia and Herzegovina
2-220	The Former Yugoslav Republic of Macedonia
2-221	France
2-224	Moldova (Republic of)
2-228	Czech Republic
2-229	Czech Republic
2-230	Czech Republic
2-231	Czech Republic

SANC	Country
2-232	Slovak Republic
2-233	Slovak Republic
2-234	Slovak Republic
2-235	Slovak Republic
2-236	Lithuania (Republic of)
2-237	Spain
2-238	Spain
2-239	Spain
2-240	Spain
2-241	Spain
2-242	Germany (Federal Republic of)
2-243	Germany (Federal Republic of)
2-244	Germany (Federal Republic of)
2-245	Germany (Federal Republic of)
2-246	Germany (Federal Republic of)
2-247	Germany (Federal Republic of)
2-248	Germany (Federal Republic of)
2-249	Germany (Federal Republic of)
2-250	Germany (Federal Republic of)
2-251	Germany (Federal Republic of)
2-252	Germany (Federal Republic of)
2-253	Netherlands (Kingdom of the)
2-254	Finland
2-255	Finland
3-004	Canada

SANC	Country
3-005	Canada
3-006	Canada
3-007	Canada
3-008	Canada
3-009	Canada
3-010	Canada
3-011	Canada
3-012	Canada
3-016	Saint Pierre and Miquelon (Collectivité territoriale de la République française)
3-018	Greenland (Denmark)
3-020	United States of America
3-021	United States of America
3-022	United States of America
3-023	United States of America
3-024	United States of America
3-025	United States of America
3-026	United States of America
3-027	United States of America
3-028	United States of America
3-029	United States of America
3-030	United States of America
3-031	United States of America
3-032	United States of America
3-033	United States of America

SANC	Country
3-034	United States of America
3-035	United States of America
3-036	United States of America
3-037	United States of America
3-038	United States of America
3-039	United States of America
3-040	United States of America
3-041	United States of America
3-042	United States of America
3-043	United States of America
3-044	United States of America
3-045	United States of America
3-046	United States of America
3-047	United States of America
3-048	United States of America
3-049	United States of America
3-050	United States of America
3-051	United States of America
3-052	United States of America
3-053	United States of America
3-054	United States of America
3-055	United States of America
3-056	United States of America
3-057	United States of America
3-058	United States of America

SANC	Country
3-059	United States of America
3-060	Puerto Rico
3-064	United States Virgin Islands
3-068	Mexico
3-069	Mexico
3-070	Mexico
3-071	Mexico
3-072	Mexico
3-073	Mexico
3-074	Mexico
3-075	Mexico
3-076	Jamaica
3-084	Barbados
3-088	Antigua and Barbuda
3-092	Cayman Islands
3-096	British Virgin Islands
3-100	Bermuda
3-104	Grenada
3-108	Montserrat
3-112	Saint Kitts and Nevis
3-116	Saint Lucia
3-120	Saint Vincent and the Grenadines
3-124	Netherlands Antilles
3-128	Bahamas (Commonwealth of the)
3-132	Dominica (Commonwealth of)

SANC	Country
3-136	Cuba
3-140	Dominican Republic
3-144	Haiti (Republic of)
3-148	Trinidad and Tobago
3-152	Turks and Caicos Islands
3-156	Guadeloupe (French Department of)
3-160	Martinique (French Department of)
3-164	Aruba
3-168	Anguilla
3-172	Mexico
3-173	Mexico
3-174	Mexico
3-179	Faroe Islands
3-180	United States of America
3-181	United States of America
3-182	United States of America
3-183	United States of America
3-184	United States of America
3-185	United States of America
3-186	United States of America
3-187	United States of America
3-188	United States of America
3-189	United States of America
3-190	United States of America
3-191	United States of America

SANC	Country
3-192	United States of America
3-193	United States of America
3-194	United States of America
3-195	United States of America
3-196	United States of America
3-197	United States of America
4-008	India (Republic of)
4-009	India (Republic of)
4-020	Pakistan (Islamic Republic of)
4-024	Afghanistan (Islamic State of)
4-026	Sri Lanka (Democratic Socialist Republic of)
4-028	Myanmar (Union of)
4-030	Lebanon
4-032	Jordan (Hashemite Kingdom of)
4-033	Jordan (Hashemite Kingdom of)
4-034	Syrian Arab Republic
4-036	Iraq (Republic of)
4-038	Kuwait (State of)
4-040	Saudi Arabia (Kingdom of)
4-042	Yemen (Republic of)
4-044	Oman (Sultanate of)
4-046	Yemen (Republic of)
4-048	United Arab Emirates
4-050	Israel (State of)
4-051	Israel (State of)

SANC	Country
4-052	Bahrain (State of)
4-054	Qatar (State of)
4-056	Mongolia
4-058	Nepal
4-060	United Arab Emirates
4-062	United Arab Emirates
4-064	Iran (Islamic Republic of)
4-070	Azerbaijani Republic
4-072	Bhutan (Kingdom of)
4-074	Kazakhstan (Republic of)
4-078	Kyrgyz Republic
4-079	Kyrgyz Republic
4-080	Japan
4-081	Japan
4-082	Japan
4-083	Japan
4-085	Japan
4-100	Korea (Republic of)
4-101	Korea (Republic of)
4-104	Viet Nam (Socialist Republic of)
4-105	Hong Kong, China
4-106	Hong Kong, China
4-107	Hong Kong, China
4-108	Hong Kong, China
4-109	Hong Kong, China

SANC	Country
4-110	Macao, China
4-112	Cambodia (Kingdom of)
4-114	Lao People's Democratic Republic
4-120	China (People's Republic of)
4-121	China (People's Republic of)
4-122	China (People's Republic of)
4-123	China (People's Republic of)
4-124	China (People's Republic of)
4-125	China (People's Republic of)
4-126	China (People's Republic of)
4-135	Democratic People's Republic of Korea
4-140	Bangladesh (People's Republic of)
4-144	Maldives (Republic of)
4-145	Korea (Republic of)
4-146	Korea (Republic of)
4-147	Korea (Republic of)
4-148	Korea (Republic of)
4-149	Korea (Republic of)
4-150	Korea (Republic of)
4-151	Korea (Republic of)
4-152	Korea (Republic of)
4-153	Korea (Republic of)
4-154	Korea (Republic of)
4-157	Tajikistan (Republic of)
4-160	Turkmenistan

SANC	Country
4-164	Uzbekistan (Republic of)
4-170	Taiwan, China
4-171	Taiwan, China
4-172	Taiwan, China
4-173	Taiwan, China
4-174	Taiwan, China
4-175	Reserved
4-177	Hong Kong, China
5-004	Malaysia
5-005	Malaysia
5-006	Malaysia
5-007	Malaysia
5-008	Malaysia
5-010	Australia
5-011	Australia
5-012	Australia
5-013	Australia
5-014	Australia
5-015	Australia
5-016	Australia
5-017	Australia
5-018	Australia
5-019	Australia
5-020	Indonesia (Republic of)
5-021	Indonesia (Republic of)

SANC	Country
5-022	Indonesia (Republic of)
5-030	Philippines (Republic of the)
5-031	Philippines (Republic of the)
5-032	Philippines (Republic of the)
5-033	Philippines (Republic of the)
5-034	Philippines (Republic of the)
5-035	Philippines (Republic of the)
5-036	Philippines (Republic of the)
5-040	Thailand
5-041	Thailand
5-042	Thailand
5-050	Singapore (Republic of)
5-051	Singapore (Republic of)
5-052	Singapore (Republic of)
5-053	Singapore (Republic of)
5-054	Singapore (Republic of)
5-055	Singapore (Republic of)
5-056	Brunei Darussalam
5-060	New Zealand
5-063	New Zealand
5-065	New Zealand
5-067	New Zealand
5-070	Guam
5-072	Nauru (Republic of)
5-074	Papua New Guinea

SANC	Country
5-078	Tonga (Kingdom of)
5-080	Solomon Islands
5-082	Vanuatu (Republic of)
5-084	Fiji (Republic of)
5-086	Wallis and Futuna (Territoire français d'outre-mer)
5-088	American Samoa
5-090	Niue
5-092	New Caledonia (Territoire français d'outre-mer)
5-094	French Polynesia (Territoire français d'outre-mer)
5-096	Cook Islands
5-098	Samoa (Independent State of)
5-100	Kiribati (Republic of)
5-102	Tuvalu
5-105	Marshall Islands (Republic of the)
5-107	Micronesia (Federated States of)
5-110	Palau (Republic of)
5-113	Northern Mariana Islands (Commonwealth of the)
5-115	Australia
5-116	Australia
6-004	Egypt (Arab Republic of)
6-006	Algeria (People's Democratic Republic of)
6-008	Morocco (Kingdom of)
6-010	Tunisia
6-012	Libya (Socialist People's Libyan Arab Jamahiriya)
6-014	Gambia (Republic of the)

SANC	Country
6-016	Senegal (Republic of)
6-018	Mauritania (Islamic Republic of)
6-020	Mali (Republic of)
6-022	Guinea (Republic of)
6-024	Côte d'Ivoire (Republic of)
6-026	Burkina Faso
6-028	Niger (Republic of the)
6-030	Togolese Republic
6-032	Benin (Republic of)
6-034	Mauritius (Republic of)
6-036	Liberia (Republic of)
6-038	Sierra Leone
6-040	Ghana
6-042	Nigeria (Federal Republic of)
6-044	Chad (Republic of)
6-046	Central African Republic
6-048	Cameroon (Republic of)
6-050	Cape Verde (Republic of)
6-052	Sao Tome and Principe (Democratic Republic of)
6-054	Equatorial Guinea (Republic of)
6-056	Gabonese Republic
6-058	Congo (Republic of the)
6-060	Democratic Republic of the Congo
6-062	Angola (Republic of)
6-064	Guinea-Bissau (Republic of)

SANC	Country
6-066	Seychelles (Republic of)
6-068	Sudan (Republic of the)
6-070	Rwandese Republic
6-072	Ethiopia (Federal Democratic Republic of)
6-074	Somali Democratic Republic
6-076	Djibouti (Republic of)
6-078	Kenya (Republic of)
6-080	Tanzania (United Republic of)
6-082	Uganda (Republic of)
6-084	Burundi (Republic of)
6-086	Mozambique (Republic of)
6-090	Zambia (Republic of)
6-092	Madagascar (Republic of)
6-094	Reunion (French Department of)
6-096	Zimbabwe (Republic of)
6-098	Namibia (Republic of)
6-100	Malawi
6-102	Lesotho (Kingdom of)
6-104	Botswana (Republic of)
6-106	Swaziland (Kingdom of)
6-108	Comoros (Islamic Federal Republic of the)
6-110	South Africa (Republic of)
6-114	Eritrea
6-116	Ascension
7-004	Belize

SANC	Country
7-008	Guatemala (Republic of)
7-009	Guatemala (Republic of)
7-012	El Salvador (Republic of)
7-013	El Salvador (Republic of)
7-016	Honduras (Republic of)
7-020	Nicaragua
7-024	Costa Rica
7-028	Panama (Republic of)
7-032	Peru
7-033	Peru
7-034	Peru
7-035	Peru
7-036	Peru
7-043	Argentine Republic
7-044	Argentine Republic
7-045	Argentine Republic
7-046	Argentine Republic
7-047	Argentine Republic
7-048	Brazil (Federative Republic of)
7-049	Brazil (Federative Republic of)
7-050	Brazil (Federative Republic of)
7-060	Chile
7-061	Chile
7-062	Chile
7-064	Colombia (Republic of)

SANC	Country
7-065	Colombia (Republic of)
7-068	Venezuela (Bolivarian Republic of)
7-069	Venezuela (Bolivarian Republic of)
7-072	Bolivia (Republic of)
7-076	Guyana
7-080	Ecuador
7-084	French Guiana (French Department of)
7-088	Paraguay (Republic of)
7-092	Suriname (Republic of)
7-096	Uruguay (Eastern Republic of)

Bibliography

For your reference and further study, this appendix contains a list of the resources that the authors used to write this book.

af-bici-0013.003, "BISDN Inter Carrier Interface (B-ICI) Specification Version 2.0 (Integrated)," 1995

af-cs-0167.000, "Guaranteed Frame Rate (GFR) Signaling Specification (PNNI, AINI, and UNI), Version 1.0," 2001

af-sig-0061.000, "ATM User-Network Interface (UNI) Signalling Specification Version 4.0," 1996

af-tm-0056.000, "Traffic Management Specification Version 4.0," 1996

af-tm-0121.000, "Traffic Management Specification Version 4.1," 1999

af-uni-0010.002, "ATM User-Network Interface Specification Version 3.1," 1994

ANSI T1.110-1999, "Signaling System No.7, General Information," 1999

ANSI T1.111-2001, "Signaling System No.7, Message Transfer Part," 2001

ANSI T1.112-2001, "Signaling System No.7, Signaling Connection Control Part Functional Description," 2001

ANSI T1.113-2000, "Signaling System No.7, ISDN User Part," 2000

ANSI T1.113b-2001, "Signaling System No.7, ISDN User Part," 2001

ANSI T1.114-2000, "Signaling System No.7, Transaction Capability Application Part (TCAP)," 2000

ANSI T1.410-1992, "Carrier to Customer Metallic Interface—Digital Data at 64 kbit/s and Subrates," 1992

Bellcore Technical Advisory TA-TSY-000722, Issue 1, "Metropolitan Area Network Generic Framework System Requirements in Support of Switched Multi-megabit Data Service," 1989

Bellcore Technical Reference TR-TSV-000772, Issue 1, "Generic Requirements in Support of SMDS," 1991

Black, Uyless and Sharleen Waters, *SONET and T1: Architectures for Digital Transport Networks*, Prentice Hall PTR, 1997

CRIHAN ATM Course, Version 2.3 – 2.5, "Traffic Management and Control A/D Conversion References," 2000

ESIG-TS-002, "SMDS Subscriber Network Interface Level 1 Specification, Edition 1.0," 1993

ETS 300 347-1, "ETSI," 1994

The Frame Relay Forum, "The Basic Guide to Frame Relay Networking," 1998

Gast, Matthew S., *T1: A Survival Guide*, O'Reilly and Associates, Inc., 2001

GR-303-CORE Issue #4, Telcordia, 2000

Hioki, Warren, *Telecommunications*, Fourth Edition, Prentice Hall, 2001

Horak, Ray, *Communications Systems and Networks*, Second Edition, M&T Books, 2000

IEEE 802.6, "DQDB"

ITU-T I.233, "Frame Mode Bearer Services," 1992

ITU-T I.363.1, "B-ISDN ATM Adaptation Layer Specification: Type 1 AAL"

ITU-T I.363.2, "B-ISDN ATM Adaptation Layer Specification: Type 2 AAL"

ITU-T I.363.3, "B-ISDN ATM Adaptation Layer Specification: Type 3/4 AAL"

ITU-T I.363.5, "B-ISDN ATM Adaptation Layer Specification: Type 5 AAL"

ITU-T I.371, "Traffic Control and Congestion Control in B-ISDN," 2000

ITU-T I.610, "B-ISDN Operation and Maintenance Principles and Functions," 1999

ITU-T Recommendation Q.700, "Introduction to CCITT Signalling System No. 7," 1993

ITU-T Recommendation Q.701, "Functional Description of the Message Transfer Part (MTP) of Signalling System No. 7," 1993

ITU-T Recommendation Q.702, "Signalling System No. 7—Signalling Data Link," 1988

ITU-T Recommendation Q.703, "Signalling Link," 1996

ITU-T Recommendation Q.704, "Signalling Network Functions and Messages," 1996

ITU-T Recommendation Q.705, "Signalling System No. 7—Signalling Network Structure," 1993

ITU-T Recommendation Q.711, "Functional Description of the Signalling Connection Control Part," 1996

ITU-T Recommendation Q.721, "Signalling System No. 7—Functional Description of the Signalling System No. 7 Telephone User Part (TUP)," 1988

ITU-T Recommendation Q.724, "Specifications of Signalling System No. 7—Telephone User Part," 1988

ITU-T Recommendation Q.761, "Signalling System No.7—ISDN User Part Functional Description," 1999

ITU-T Recommendation Q.762, "Signalling System No.7—ISDN User Part General Functions of Messages and Signals," 1999

ITU-T Recommendation Q.764, "Signalling System No. 7—ISDN User Part Signalling Procedures," 1999

ITU-T Recommendation Q.922, "ISDN Data Link Layer Specification for Frame Mode Bearer Services," 1992

ITU-T Recommendation Q.933, "Integrated Services Digital Network (ISDN) Digital Subscriber Signaling System No. 1 (DSS 1)—Signaling Specifications for Frame Mode Switched and Permanent Virtual Connection Control and Status Monitoring," 1995

ITU-T Recommendation Q.1210, "Q.1210-Series Intelligent Network Recommendation Structure," 1995

ITU-T Recommendation Q.1211, "Introduction to Intelligent Network Capability Set 1," 1993

ITU-T Recommendation Q.1213, "Global Functional Plane for Intelligent Network CS-1," 1995

ITU-T Recommendation Q.1214, "Distributed Functional Plane for Intelligent Network CS-1," 1995

ITU-T Recommendation Q.1215, "Physical Plane for Intelligent Network CS-1," 1995

ITU-T Recommendation Q.1218, "Interface Recommendation for Intelligent Network CS-1," 1995

ITU-T Recommendation Q.1220, "Q.1220-Series Intelligent Network Capability Set 2 Recommendation Structure," 1997

ITU-T Recommendation Q.1221, "Introduction to Intelligent Network Capability Set 2," 1997

ITU-T Recommendation Q.1222, "Service Plane for Intelligent Network Capability Set 2," 1997

ITU-T Recommendation Q.1223, "Global Functional Plane for Intelligent Network Capability Set 2," 1997

ITU-T Recommendation Q.1224, "Distributed Functional Plane for Intelligent Network Capability Set 2," 1997

ITU-T Recommendation Q.1225, "Physical Plane for Intelligent Network Capability Set 2," 1997

ITU-T Recommendation Q.1228, "Interface Recommendation for Intelligent Network Capability Set 2," 1997

ITU-T Recommendation Q.1231, "Introduction to Intelligent Network Capability Set 3," 1999

ITU-T Recommendation Q.1236, "Intelligent Network Capability Set 3—Management Information Model Requirements and Methodology," 1999

ITU-T Recommendation Q.1290, "Glossary of Terms Used in the Definition of Intelligent Networks," 1998

Klessig, Robert W. and Kaj Tesin, *SMDS: Wide-Area Data Networking with Switched Multi-Megabit Data Service*, Prentice Hall, 1995

Newton, Harry, *Newton's Telecom Dictionary*, 18th Updated and Expanded Edition, CMP Books, 2002

C

D

E

M

O

P

Q

T

Train with authorized Cisco Learning Partners.

Discover all that's possible on the Internet.

One of the biggest challenges facing networking professionals is how to stay current with today's ever-changing technologies in the global Internet economy. Nobody understands this better than Cisco Learning Partners, the only companies that deliver training developed by Cisco Systems.

Just go to **www.cisco.com/go/training_ad**. You'll find more than 120 Cisco Learning Partners in over 90 countries worldwide.* Only Cisco Learning Partners have instructors that are certified by Cisco to provide recommended training on Cisco networks and to prepare you for certifications.

To get ahead in this world, you first have to be able to keep up. Insist on training that is developed and authorized by Cisco, as indicated by the Cisco Learning Partner or Cisco Learning Solutions Partner logo.

Visit **www.cisco.com/go/training_ad** today.

CISCO SYSTEMS

EMPOWERING THE
INTERNET GENERATION℠

Cisco Press

Learning is serious business.

Invest wisely.

Cisco Interactive Mentor

CIM Voice Internetworking: VoIP Quality of Service

Cisco Systems, Inc.

1-58720-050-3 • Availabe Now

With *CIM Voice Internetworking: VoIP Quality of Service*, you acquire the skills needed to implement and fine tune QoS for Voice over IP routing on Cisco routers. From an overview of QoS concepts to detailed examination of Cisco IOS(r) Software QoS and VoIP routing commands, you will learn how to solve call quality problems caused by delay and inefficient packet compression in Voice over IP networks. Mastering techniques and methods developed by Cisco Technical Assistance Center engineers, you will enable and troubleshoot link efficiency mechanisms and QoS queuing components on multilink PPP and Frame Relay networks.

CIM Voice Internetworking: Basic Voice over IP

Cisco Systems, Inc.

1-58720-023-6 • Availabe Now

With *CIM Voice Internetworking: Basic Voice over IP*, you can master the telephony and voice internetworking knowledge you need to enhance the versatility and value of your communications infrastructure. Offering self-paced instruction and practice, this robust learning tool gives you a quick and cost-effective way to acquire Cisco knowledge and expertise. From an overview of traditional telephony and voice transmission concepts to the basics of routing voice and fax packets over a data network, you'll learn how to configure typical software features of a VoIP network and perform operational application tasks with interactive voice response (IVR). Using techniques developed by Cisco Technical Assistance Center engineers, you'll practice configuring and troubleshooting both analog and digital voice calls over IP networks. An excellent preparation tool for the Cisco Certified Network Professionals (CCNP) Voice Access Specialization and Cisco Certified Internetwork Expert (CCIE) exam.

Cisco AVVID IP Telephony Solutions

Cisco IP Telephony
David Lovell
1-58705-050-1 • **Availabe Now**

Cisco IP Telephony is based on the successful CIPT training class taught by the author and other Cisco-certified training partners. This book provides networking professionals with the fundamentals to implement a Cisco AVVID IP Telephony solution that can be run over a data network, therefore reducing costs associated with running separate data and telephone networks. *Cisco IP Telephony* focuses on using Cisco CallManager and other IP telephony components connected in LANs and WANs. This book provides you with a foundation for working with Cisco IP Telephony products, specifically Cisco CallManager. If your task is to install, configure, support, and maintain a CIPT network, this is the book for you.

Cisco CallManager Fundamentals: A Cisco AVVID Solution
Anne Smith, John Alexander, Chris Pearce, and Delon Whetton
1-58705-008-0 • **Availabe Now**

Cisco CallManager Fundamentals provides examples and reference information about CallManager, the call processing component of the Cisco AVVID (Architecture for Voice, Video, and Integrated Data) IP Telephony solution. *Cisco CallManager Fundamentals* uses examples and architectural descriptions to explain how CallManager processes calls. This book details the inner workings of CallManager so that those responsible for designing and maintaining a Voice over IP (VoIP) solution from Cisco Systems can understand the role each component plays and how they interrelate. You will learn detailed information about hardware and software components, call routing, media processing, system management and monitoring, and call detail records. The authors, all members of the CallManager group at Cisco Systems, also provide a list of features and Cisco solutions that integrate with CallManager. This book is the perfect resource to supplement your understanding of CallManager.

CCIE Professional Development

Cisco OSPF Command and Configuration Handbook
William R. Parkhurst Ph.D., CCIE

1-58705-071-4 • **Availabe Now**

Cisco OSPF Command and Configuration Handbook is a clear, concise, and complete source of documentation for all Cisco IOS Software OSPF commands. The way you use this book will depend on your objectives. If you are preparing for the CCIE written and lab exams, then this book can be used as a laboratory guide to learn the purpose and proper use of every OSPF command. If you are a network designer, then this book can be used as a ready reference for any OSPF command.

Cisco BGP-4 Command and Configuration Handbook
William R. Parkhurst, Ph.D, CCIE

1-58705-017-X • **Availabe Now**

Cisco BGP-4 Command and Configuration Handbook is an exhaustive practical reference to the commands contained within BGP-4. For each command/subcommand, author Bill Parkhurst explains the intended use or function and how to properly configure it. Then he presents scenarios to demonstrate every facet of the command and its use, along with appropriate show and debug commands. Through the discussion of functionality and the scenario-based configuration examples, *Cisco BGP-4 Command and Configuration Handbook* will help you gain a thorough understanding of the practical side of BGP-4.

Voice Technology

Voice over IP Fundamentals
Jonathan Davidson
1-57870-168-6 • **Availabe Now**

Voice over IP (VoIP), which integrates voice and data transmission, is quickly becoming an important factor in network communications. It promises lower operational costs, greater flexibility, and a variety of enhanced applications. *Voice over IP Fundamentals* provides a thorough introduction to this new technology to help experts in both the data and telephone industries plan for the new networks.

Cisco Voice over Frame Relay, ATM, and IP
Steve McQuerry and Kelly McGrew
1-57870-227-5 • **Availabe Now**

Cisco Voice over Frame Relay, ATM, and IP is a direct complement to the Cisco authorized training course of the same name. Based on the content of the CVoice course, this book provides an intermediate-level treatment of Cisco voice technologies. The overall objective of the book is to teach engineers how to design, integrate, and configure voice over Frame Relay, ATM, and IP of enterprise or managed network services using various Cisco 2600, 3600, 3810, and 5300 multiservice access devices.

Deploying Cisco Voice over IP Solutions
Jonathan Davidson
1-58705-030-7 • **Availabe Now**

Deploying Cisco Voice over IP Solutions provides networking professionals the knowledge, advice, and insight necessary to design and deploy Voice over IP (VoIP) networks that meet customers' needs for scalability, services, and security. Beginning with an introduction to the important preliminary design elements that need to be considered before implementing VoIP, Deploying Cisco Voice over IP Solutions also demonstrates the basic tasks involved in designing an effective service provider-based VoIP network. It concludes with design and implementation guidelines for some of the more popular and widely requested VoIP services, such as prepaid services, fax services, and Virtual Private Networks (VPNs).

Integrating Voice and Data Networks
Scott Keagy
1-57870-196-1 • **Availabe Now**

The integration of voice and data networks is creating a fundamental change in the telecommunications and data industries. This change means better phone service, lower prices, new features, less maintenance, and more choices, leading to a complete convergence of the data networking and telecommunications industries into a single community. With all of this growth and change, network engineers and managers need specific information on how to integrate and configure packetized voice networks. *Integrating Voice and Data Networks* is designed as your one-stop shop for learning how to integrate traditional voice technology into existing Cisco data networks.

☐ **YES!** I'm requesting a **free** subscription to *Packet*™ magazine.

☐ No. I'm not interested at this time.

☐ Mr.
☐ Ms.

First Name (Please Print) _____ Last Name _____

Title/Position (Required) _____

Company (Required) _____

Address _____

City _____ State/Province _____

Zip/Postal Code _____ Country _____

Telephone (Include country and area codes) _____ Fax _____

E-mail _____

Signature (Required) _____ Date _____

☐ I would like to receive additional information on Cisco's services and products by e-mail.

1. Do you or your company:
   A ☐ Use Cisco products   C ☐ Both
   B ☐ Resell Cisco products   D ☐ Neither

2. Your organization's relationship to Cisco Systems:
   A ☐ Customer/End User   E ☐ Integrator   J ☐ Consultant
   B ☐ Prospective Customer   F ☐ Non-Authorized Reseller K ☐ Other (specify):
   C ☐ Cisco Reseller   G ☐ Cisco Training Partner
   D ☐ Cisco Distributor   I ☐ Cisco OEM   _____

3. How many people does your entire company employ?
   A ☐ More than 10,000   D ☐ 500 to 999   G ☐ Fewer than 100
   B ☐ 5,000 to 9,999   E ☐ 250 to 499
   c ☐ 1,000 to 4,999   f ☐ 100 to 249

4. Is your company a Service Provider?
   A ☐ Yes   B ☐ No

5. Your involvement in network equipment purchases:
   A ☐ Recommend   B ☐ Approve   C ☐ Neither

6. Your personal involvement in networking:
   A ☐ Entire enterprise at all sites   F ☐ Public network
   B ☐ Departments or network segments at more than one site D ☐ No involvement
   C ☐ Single department or network segment   E ☐ Other (specify):
                                                           _____

7. Your Industry:
   A ☐ Aerospace   G ☐ Education (K–12)   K ☐ Health Care
   B ☐ Agriculture/Mining/Construction   U ☐ Education (College/Univ.) L ☐ Telecommunications
   C ☐ Banking/Finance   H ☐ Government—Federal   M ☐ Utilities/Transportation
   D ☐ Chemical/Pharmaceutical   I ☐ Government—State   N ☐ Other (specify):
   E ☐ Consultant   J ☐ Government—Local   _____
   F ☐ Computer/Systems/Electronics

CPRESS

PACKET

Packet magazine serves as the premier publication linking customers to Cisco Systems, Inc. Delivering complete coverage of cutting-edge networking trends and innovations, *Packet* is a magazine for technical, hands-on users. It delivers industry-specific information for enterprise, service provider, and small and midsized business market segments. A toolchest for planners and decision makers, *Packet* contains a vast array of practical information, boasting sample configurations, real-life customer examples, and tips on getting the most from your Cisco Systems' investments. Simply put, *Packet* magazine is straight talk straight from the worldwide leader in networking for the Internet, Cisco Systems, Inc.

We hope you'll take advantage of this useful resource. I look forward to hearing from you!

Cecelia Glover
Packet Circulation Manager
packet@external.cisco.com
www.cisco.com/go/packet

For the latest on Cisco Press resources and Certification and Training guides, or for information on publishing opportunities, **visit www.ciscopress.com.**

Voice Technology

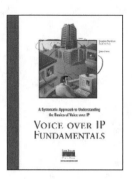

Voice over IP Fundamentals
Jonathan Davidson
1-57870-168-6 • **Availabe Now**

Voice over IP (VoIP), which integrates voice and data transmission, is quickly becoming an important factor in network communications. It promises lower operational costs, greater flexibility, and a variety of enhanced applications. *Voice over IP Fundamentals* provides a thorough introduction to this new technology to help experts in both the data and telephone industries plan for the new networks.

Cisco Voice over Frame Relay, ATM, and IP
Steve McQuerry and Kelly McGrew
1-57870-227-5 • **Availabe Now**

Cisco Voice over Frame Relay, ATM, and IP is a direct complement to the Cisco authorized training course of the same name. Based on the content of the CVoice course, this book provides an intermediate-level treatment of Cisco voice technologies. The overall objective of the book is to teach engineers how to design, integrate, and configure voice over Frame Relay, ATM, and IP of enterprise or managed network services using various Cisco 2600, 3600, 3810, and 5300 multiservice access devices.

Deploying Cisco Voice over IP Solutions

Jonathan Davidson

1-58705-030-7 • **Availabe Now**

Deploying Cisco Voice over IP Solutions provides networking professionals the knowledge, advice, and insight necessary to design and deploy Voice over IP (VoIP) networks that meet customers' needs for scalability, services, and security. Beginning with an introduction to the important preliminary design elements that need to be considered before implementing VoIP, Deploying Cisco Voice over IP Solutions also demonstrates the basic tasks involved in designing an effective service provider-based VoIP network. It concludes with design and implementation guidelines for some of the more popular and widely requested VoIP services, such as prepaid services, fax services, and Virtual Private Networks (VPNs).

Integrating Voice and Data Networks

Scott Keagy

1-57870-196-1 • **Availabe Now**

The integration of voice and data networks is creating a fundamental change in the telecommunications and data industries. This change means better phone service, lower prices, new features, less maintenance, and more choices, leading to a complete convergence of the data networking and telecommunications industries into a single community. With all of this growth and change, network engineers and managers need specific information on how to integrate and configure packetized voice networks. *Integrating Voice and Data Networks* is designed as your one-stop shop for learning how to integrate traditional voice technology into existing Cisco data networks.

CCIE Professional Development

Cisco OSPF Command and Configuration Handbook
William R. Parkhurst Ph.D., CCIE

1-58705-071-4 • **Availabe Now**

Cisco OSPF Command and Configuration Handbook is a clear, concise, and complete source of documentation for all Cisco IOS Software OSPF commands. The way you use this book will depend on your objectives. If you are preparing for the CCIE written and lab exams, then this book can be used as a laboratory guide to learn the purpose and proper use of every OSPF command. If you are a network designer, then this book can be used as a ready reference for any OSPF command.

Cisco BGP-4 Command and Configuration Handbook
William R. Parkhurst, Ph.D, CCIE

1-58705-017-X • **Availabe Now**

Cisco BGP-4 Command and Configuration Handbook is an exhaustive practical reference to the commands contained within BGP-4. For each command/subcommand, author Bill Parkhurst explains the intended use or function and how to properly configure it. Then he presents scenarios to demonstrate every facet of the command and its use, along with appropriate show and debug commands. Through the discussion of functionality and the scenario-based configuration examples, *Cisco BGP-4 Command and Configuration Handbook* will help you gain a thorough understanding of the practical side of BGP-4.